Footprint Ecuador & Galápagos

Robert & Daisy Kunstaetter
5th edition

Whilst this planet has gone cycling on according to the fixed law of gravity, from so simple a beginning endless forms most beautiful and most wonderful have been, and are being, evolved.

Charles Darwin, *The Origin of the Species*

Ecuador & Galápagos Highlights

1 Otavalo
Home of the largest and most colourful craft market in South America

2 Quito
World Heritage treasure trove of colonial art and architecture

3 Mindo
Birdwatchers' and nature-lovers' paradise

4 Parque Nacional Cotopaxi
Where the perfect snow-capped cone of one of the world's highest volcanoes towers above herds of wild horses and llamas

5 Quilotoa Circuit
Visit an emerald-green crater lake amid traditional native villages and markets

6 Baños
Popular highland resort combining adventure and relaxation

7 Tungurahua
Watch an active volcano

8 Parque Nacional Sangay
Trekking and climbing paradise, with three major glaciated summits

9 Devil's Nose
Ride one of the Andes' most spectacular railways

10 Ingapirca
Ecuador's best known Inca archaeological site

See colour maps at back of book

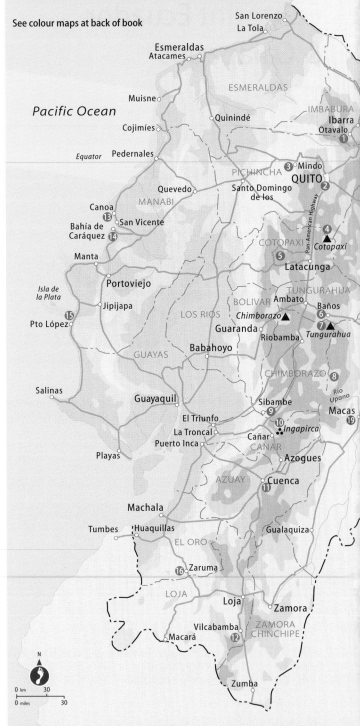

⓫ Cuenca
Congenial colonial city and Ecuador's cultural heartland

⓬ Vilcabamba
Fabled fountain of youth at the rainbow's end, an exceptionally scenic and tranquil resort

⓭ Canoa
Gorgeous ocean, magnificent broad beach and a laid-back village with good facilities

⓮ Bahía de Caraquez
Ecuador's 'eco-city' resort and base for many worthwhile excursions

⓯ Parque Nacional Machalilla Whale watching in season and great visits to Isla de la Plata and Los Frailes beach year-round

⓰ Zaruma
Colonial gold mining town amid scenic uplands, an off-the-beaten-track gem

⓱ Coca
Gateway to the jungle lodges of the lower Río Napo

⓲ Tena
White-water rafting and kayaking centre with ethno-tourism opportunities

⓳ Macas
Gateway to the untouristed southern Oriente

⓴ Galápagos
One of the world's foremost wildlife sanctuaries

Market forces
Otavaleños are Ecuador's shrewdest operators and most successful indigenous group.

A foot in the door

The phrase 'small is beautiful' could have been coined specifically with Ecuador in mind. By South American standards it is tiny (only half the size of France) and dwarfed by its neighbours Colombia and Peru. But it is this relative compactness that is one of its main attractions. Here, you can watch dawn break over the jungle canopy, have lunch high in the Andean mountains, then watch the sun slip into the Pacific Ocean – all in the same day.

Ecuador also boasts extraordinary biological diversity; a fact that did not escape the attention of 18th- and 19th-century scientists and explorers, who came, saw and compiled large volumes extolling its many virtues. The first to put Ecuador on the map was French savant, Charles-Marie de la Condamine, who determined the precise location of the equatorial line here and so helped to give the country its name. The early 19th-century explorer, Alexander Von Humboldt, was impressed by the snow-covered peaks running down the country's spine, dubbing it the 'Avenue of the Volcanoes'. And it was a young Englishman called Charles Darwin, who, in 1835, first brought the world's attention to the Galápagos Islands – Ecuador's premier attraction and the greatest wildlife show on Earth.

Today, visitors to Ecuador can still write home about smoking volcanoes, weird and wonderful creatures, impenetrable jungles and exotic peoples. Two centuries of 'progress' have not diminished the keen sense of adventure that this country inspires. It's all wonderfully unpredictable – just like the country's weather, economy and politics. To the chagrin of the World Bank but the delight of visitors, Ecuador remains a land where everything is possible.

6

1 An artisan in Cuenca weaves together one of Ecuador's most famous exports, the Panama hat. ▸▸ See page 272.

2 The classic Inca site of Ingapirca, the most famous in Ecuador, is strategically placed on the Royal Highway that ran from Cusco to Quito. ▸▸ See page 275.

3 Riding the rails from Riobamba over the Devil's Nose to Alausí is an exhilarating way to see Ecuador's central highlands. ▸▸ See page 245.

4 Tena is a centre for jungle ethno-tourism and a good base for exploring the magnificent cloud forest of the eastern Andes. ▸▸ See page 387.

5 You can spot humpback whales cavorting in the Pacific Ocean off Puerto López. ▸▸ See page 340.

6 Fish and seafood are plentiful along Ecuador's coast. ▸▸ See page 61.

7 Quito's cathedral dominates the colonial city. Its interior demonstrates a Moorish influence. ▸▸ See page 101.

8 Glass beads are among the dazzling array of textiles and crafts on sale at Otavalo's market stalls. ▸▸ See page 170.

9 The magnificent San Rafael waterfall in Oriente is the highest waterfall in Ecuador. ▸▸ See page 385.

10 Although it's not the highest active volcano in the world, Volcán Cotopaxi (5,897 m) is undoubtedly one of the most beautiful, and it's easily reached from Quito. ▸▸ See page 203.

11 Carnaval in Guaranda is one of the best festivals in the country, with music, parades, masks and dancing. ▸▸ See page 228.

12 The Old City of Quito is a UNESCO World Heritage site, with pastel-coloured colonial houses lining steep and narrow streets. ▸▸ See page 101.

A lofty capital

The capital city, Quito, is the perfect base from which to explore the country. Although it stands a mere 23 km south of the Equator, Quito's mountain setting at 2,850m above sea level means it enjoys a pleasant, spring-like climate all year round. You don't have to be an architecture buff to appreciate its elegant and beautifully preserved colonial heart. In sharp contrast is its modern alter ego, boasting sleek contemporary buildings with shiny glass and concrete towers.

Under the volcanoes

South of the capital runs the country's main traffic artery, bordered on both sides by snow-covered volcanoes. Living in the shadow of these volcanoes – many of which are still active – are the indigenous peoples of the highlands, going about their business in much the same way as they did before the Spanish arrived; still wearing traditional dress and conversing in Quichua as did the Incas. Not content with admiring the volcanoes from a distance, adventure-hungry visitors are climbing them in search of the biggest natural high this little country has to offer.

Feeling beached?

On the western side of the Andes lies Ecuador's coast, so different in atmosphere from the highlands that you could be in another country. If your idea of a good time is to lie on a beach all day soaking up the rays and partying into the small hours of the morning, then Ecuador's more popular beach resorts are for you. Those who prefer daylight activity can swim, surf, snorkel, scuba dive, visit nature reserves, or watch humpback whales getting it together in the warm waters off shore.

Crafty culture

From precolonial times, Ecuadorean native artisans have excelled at their craft. Everywhere you turn some particularly seductive piece of *artesanía* is on offer. This word loosely translates as handicrafts, but that doesn't really do them justice. The indigenous peoples make no distinction between decorative arts and functional crafts, so *artesanías* are valued as much for their practical use as for their beauty. The shopper can choose from a dizzying array of textiles, ceramics and carvings, not forgetting Ecuador's most famous handicraft, the Panama hat.

Jungle adventure

No visit to Ecuador would be complete without venturing into its steamy jungles. Only a few hours away from Quito by bus, the eastern slopes of the Andes give way to a vast green carpet stretching into the horizon. Parrots and macaws on the wing and troops of screeching monkeys provide the noisy score for capybara (sheep-sized rodents), caiman, armadillos, tapirs, peccaries and, if you are really lucky, jaguars.

Galápagos Wildlife

The Galápagos Islands

The reason many people come to Ecuador is to visit a group of 19 islands lying almost 1,000 km due west. The Galápagos Islands came to the world's attention following a visit by a young Charles Darwin, whose short stay in the archipelago proved to be revolutionary for science and the study of evolution. The islands, which get their name from the giant tortoises that live there, are home to numerous endemic species of birds and reptiles. Now, this wildlife paradise has become a national park dedicated to the conservation of its many unique species. Everyone returns from this showcase of evolution with a sense of wonder and a feeling of privilege.

Reptiles

The reptiles found on the Galápagos are represented by five families: iguana, lava lizards, geckos, snakes and, of course, the giant tortoise. Of the 27 species of reptiles on the islands, 17 are endemic.

Giant tortoise (*Geochelone elephantopus*)

The Galápagos and the Seychelles are the only two island groups in the world which are inhabited by giant tortoises. The name Galápagos derives from the subspecies saddleback tortoise (*galápago* means saddle). Fourteen subspecies of tortoise have been discovered on the islands, although now only 11 survive, including Lonesome George, a subspecies all by himself. No one knows the maximum age of these huge reptiles, but the oldest inhabitant of the Darwin Research Station may be as old as 170 – old enough to have met Darwin himself.

Perhaps this longevity is due to their living a peaceful life, free from the stresses of modern living. Basically, all they do is eat, sleep and mate. This latter activity takes place during the wet season from January to March. Later, between February and May, the females

head down to the coast to search for a suitable nesting area. The female digs a nest about 30 cm deep, lays between three and 16 eggs then covers them with a protective layer of urine and excrement. Three to eight months later, the eggs hatch, usually between mid-January and March.

In the past, the tortoise population on the islands was estimated at 250,000, but during the 17th and 18th centuries thousands were taken aboard whaling ships. Their ability to survive long periods without food and water made them the ideal source of fresh meat on long voyages. Black rats, feral dogs and pigs, introduced to the islands, affected the population by feeding on their eggs and young, until in 1980 only 15,000 remained. The Darwin Research Station is now rearing young in captivity for re-introduction to the wild, giving visitors the opportunity to see them close up. There are also *galapagos* in captivity on San Cristóbal and Isabela, and you can see them in the wild at the reserve on Santa Cruz.

Marine turtle (*Chelonia mydas*)

Of the eight species of marine turtle in the world only one is found on the islands – the Pacific green turtle. Mating turtles are a common sight in December and January, especially in the Caleta Tortuga Negra, at the northern tip of Santa Cruz. Egg laying usually takes place between January and June, when the female comes ashore to dig a hole and lay 80-120 eggs under cover of darkness. The white sand beach on Floreana is a popular spot. After about two months the hatchlings make the hazardous trip across the beach towards the sea, also after dark, in order to avoid the predatory crabs, herons, frigates and lava gulls on the lookout for a midnight feast.

Marine iguana (*Amblyrynchus cristatus*)

This prehistoric-looking endemic species is the only sea-going lizard in the world and is, in fact, from another era. It could be as much as nine million years old, making it even older than the islands themselves. Marine iguanas are found along the coasts and gather in huge herds on the lava rocks. They vary greatly in size, from 60 cm for the smallest variety (Isla Genovesa) up to 1 m for the largest (Isla Isabela). Their black skin acts as camouflage and allows the iguana to absorb heat from the fierce equatorial sun, although those on Española have red and green colouration. The marine iguana's flat tail is ideal for swimming but, although they can dive to depths of 20 m and stay underwater for up to an hour at a time, they prefer to feed on the seaweed on exposed rocks at low tide.

1 *Thousands of tiny green turtle hatchlings leave the safety of their sandy burrows in the middle of the night to trek to their natural home, the sea.*

2 *The strange colouring of the lava lizard, seemingly bathed in fire, finds a perfect camouflage among the volcanic rocks.*

3 *Male great frigatebirds inflate giant red heart-shaped balloons in an elaborate courtship display to attract females.*

4 *One of the biggest problems for the Galápagos penguin is keeping cool in the equatorial heat.*

5 *The scalloped hammerhead shark is just one of the many amazing creatures at risk from the proposed increase in fishing in the Galápagos area.*

6 *The giant tortoise is the largest living tortoise in the world and can grow up to 6 ft in length.*

Land iguana (*Conolphus pallidus* or *subscristatus*)

There are officially two species of land iguana found on the islands: *conolphus subcristatus* is yellow-orange coloured and inhabits Santa Cruz, Plaza, Isabela and Fernandina islands, while the other, *conolphus pallidus*, is whitish to chocolate brown and found only on Santa Fé. The latter is the biggest land iguana, with the male weighing 6-7 kg and measuring over 1 m in length. Their numbers have been greatly reduced over the years, as the young often fall prey to rats and feral animals; the chances of survival for a young land iguana in the wild is less than 10%. Although less gregarious since the outlawing of feeding by visitors, the land iguana remains a friendly little chap and can be seen at close quarters. It now feeds mainly on the fruits and yellow flowers of the prickly pear cactus.

Birds

Sea birds were probably the first animals to colonize the archipelago. Half of the resident population of birds is endemic to the Galápagos, but only five of the 19 species of sea birds found on the Galápagos are unique to the islands. They are: the Galápagos penguin, the flightless cormorant, the lava gull, the swallowtail gull and the waved albatross. The endemism rate of land birds is much higher, owing to the fact that they are less often migratory. There are 29 species of land birds in the Galápagos, 22 of which are endemic.

Galápagos penguin (*Spheniscus mendiculus*)

This is the most northerly of the world's penguin species and breeds on Islas Fernandina and Isabela, where the Humboldt Current cools the sea. The penguin population is small (under 1,000 in 2000) and fluctuates in response to the El Niño cycle. They may appear distinctly ungraceful on land, hopping clumsily from rock to rock, but underwater they are fast and agile swimmers and can be seen breaking the surface, like dolphins. The best time to see them in the water is between 0500 and 0700.

Flightless cormorant (*Nannopetrum harrisi*)

This is one of the rarest birds in the world, with an estimated population of 800 pairs. It is found only on Isla Fernandino and the west coast of Isla Isabela, where the nutrient-rich Cromwell Current brings a plentiful supply of fish from the central Pacific. Despite losing the ability to fly, partly due to the lack of predators, the cormorant still insists on spreading its wings to dry in the wind, proving that old habits die hard.

Waved albatross (*Dimeda irrorata*)

The largest bird in the Galápagos, with a wing span of 2½ m, is a cousin of the petrels and the puffins. It is not only endemic to the archipelago but also to Isla Española, for this is the only place in the world where it breeds. Outside the April to December breeding season, the albatross spends its time gliding majestically across the Pacific Ocean, sometimes as far as Japan. It returns after six months to begin the spectacular courtship display, a cross between an exotic dance and fencing duel, which is repeated over and over again. Not surprisingly perhaps, given the effort put into this ritual, albatrosses stay faithful to their mate for life.

Frigatebird

Both the **great frigatebird**, *fregata minor*, and **magnificent frigatebird**, *fregata magnificens*, are found on the Galápagos. These 'vultures of the sea' have a wingspan as big as that of the albatross and spend much of their time aloft, gliding in circles with their distinctive long forked tail and angled wings. Having lost the waterproofing of its black plumage, the frigate never lands on the sea; instead it pursues other birds – in particular boobies – and harasses them for food, or catches small fish on the surface of the water with its hooked beak. During the courtship display, the male of both species inflates a huge red sac under its throat, like a heart-shaped scarlet balloon, and flutters its spread wings. This seduces and attracts the female to the nest, which the male has already prepared for the purpose of mating. This amazing ritual can be seen in March and April on San Cristóbal and Genovesa, or throughout the year on North Seymour.

Unlike the great frigatebird, the magnificent frigatebird is an 'inshore feeder' and feeds near the islands. It is very similar in appearance, but the male has a purple sheen on its plumage and the female has a black triangle on the white patch on her throat.

Boobies

These are very common in the islands. Three species are found in the Galápagos: the blue-footed, red-footed and masked booby. The name is thought to derive from their extreme tameness, which led to many being killed for sport in earlier times.

The most common booby is the **blue-footed booby**, *sula nebouxii*. This is the only booby to lay more than one egg at a time (three is not unusual) though if food is insufficient the stronger firstborn will kick its siblings out of the nest. Unlike its red-footed relative, the blue-footed booby fishes inshore, dropping on its prey like an arrow from the sky. They are known best for their comical and complicated courtship 'dance'.

The **red-footed booby**, *sula sula*, is the only Galápagos booby to nest in trees, thanks to the fact that its feet are adapted to gripping branches. It is light brown in colour, although there is also a less common white variety. The largest colony of red-footed boobies is found on Isla Genovesa.

The **masked booby**, *sula dactylactra* (pictured page 9), is the heaviest of the three boobies and has a white plumage with a distinctive black mask on the eyes. Like its blue-footed cousin, the white or masked booby nests directly on the ground and surrounds its nest with waste. It chooses to fish between the other two boobies, thus providing an excellent illustration of the idea of the 'ecological niche'.

Mammals

The number of native mammals in the archipelago is limited to two species of bats, a few species of rats and, of course, sea lions and seals. This is explained by the fact that the islands were never connected to the mainland. Since the arrival of man, however, goats, dogs, donkeys, horses and the black rat have been added to the list and now threaten the fragile ecological balance of the islands.

Sea lion (*Zalophus californianus*)

As the scientific name suggests, the Galápagos sea lion is related to the Californian species, although it is smaller. They are common throughout the archipelago, gathering in large colonies on beaches or on the rocks. The male, which is distinguished from the female by its huge size and domed forehead, is very territorial, especially at the beginning of the May to January mating season. He patrols a territory of 40 to 100 sq m with a group of up to 30 females, chasing off intruders and also keeping an eye on the young, which may wander too far from the safety of the beach. Those males that are too tired or too old to hold a territory gather in 'bachelor clubs'.

The friendly and inquisitive females provide one of the main tourist attractions, especially when cavorting with swimmers. One of the sea lion's favourite games is surfing the big waves and another popular sport is 'water polo', using a marine iguana instead of a ball. Sea lion colonies are found on South Plaza, Santa Fé, Rábida, James Bay (Isla Santiago), Española, San Cristóbal and Isabela.

1 Darwin wasn't impressed by the land iguana, commenting that "they are ugly animals... they have a singularly stupid appearance".

2 White reef sharks are among the most common of the shark species found around the Galápagos.

3 It is easy to spot the large brown pelican gliding and fishing around the islands of the archipelago.

4 Whales are most commonly sighted in the ocean to the west of Isabela and Fernandina.

5 Look out for the blue-footed booby's complicated courtship ritual of posing, whistling and dancing.

6 Bull sea lions are intensely territorial but the females and pups are disarmingly curious and playful.

Fur seal (*Arctocephalus galapaoensis*)

Fur seals and sea lions both belong to the Otaridae or eared seal family. The fur seal's dense, luxuriant pelt attracted great interest and the creature was hunted almost to extinction at the beginning of the 20th century by whalers and other skin hunters. Fortunately, these *lobos de dos pelos* (double-fur sea wolves), as they are known locally, survived and can be seen most easily in Puerto Egas on Santiago island, usually hiding from the sun under rocks or lava cracks. The fur seal is distinguished from the sea lion by its smaller size, its pointed nose, big round sad moist eyes, larger front flippers and more prominent ears.

Marine life

The Galápagos are washed by three currents: the cold Humboldt and Cromwell currents, and the warm El Niño. This provides the islands with a rich, diverse and unique underwater fauna. The number of species of fish has been estimated at 306, of which 17% are endemic, although recent research suggests this number could exceed 400. Among the huge number of fish found in the islands' waters, there are 18 species of morays, five species of rays (stingrays, golden ray, marbled ray, spotted eagle ray and manta rays) and about 12 species of sharks. The most common sharks are the white-tip reef shark, the black-tip reef shark, two species of hammerheads, the Galápagos shark, the grey reef shark, the tiger shark, the hornshark and the whale shark.

Among the marine mammals, at least 16 species of whales and seven species of dolphins have been identified. The most common dolphins are the bottle-nosed dolphin, *tursiops truncatus*, and the common dolphin. Whales include the sperm whale, humpback whale, pilot whale, the orca and the false killer whale, sei whale, minke whale, Bryde's whale, Cuvier's beaked whale and the blue whale. These whales can be seen around all the islands, but most easily to the west of Isabela and Fernandina. The waters are also rich in sea stars, sea urchins, sea cucumbers and crustaceans, including the ubiquitous and distinctive sally lightfoot crab.

From afar, it's easy to visualize the Galápagos landscape as the peaks and troughs of hidden undersea volcanoes.

Contents

18

Essentials

☃ Footprint features

Planning your trip

Where to go

One of Ecuador's great attractions is its relative compactness. Travelling around is easy and, unlike its larger neighbours, much of what you want to see is only a few hours by road from the capital, Quito. The following are but a few of the most popular routes and you are heartily encouraged to strike out beyond the *gringo* trail to discover your own.

Quito (1 week)
This is the point of arrival for most visitors to Ecuador. Quito is actually two distinct cities: the Old City, which has experienced a revival in recent years and contains all the beautiful colonial churches and historic buildings, and the New City, with a million-and-one hotels, restaurants, bars and cafés. Quito boasts a wide range of excellent museums and it is the language course capital of South America. Just about any type of holiday or activity can be arranged here. Two to three days are needed to get a feel for the city itself, and you could easily spend a week or more enjoying excursions around Quito. These include the excellent nature reserves by Mindo and the wonderful thermal baths of Papallacta.

Craft towns and markets (3 or 4 days)
In colonial times, the Spanish organized indigenous slave labour into *obrajes* or workshops, each of which specialized in a particular craft. The artisans' skills were passed down from generation to generation and their legacy is a series of craft towns, each with its own speciality. In **Calderón**, just north of Quito, figurines are made of bread dough. Continue north to **Otavalo**, to take in the largest craft market in South America, best on Saturday but good throughout the week. Excursions from Otavalo include Cuicocha crater lake, with a nice day-hike around the rim, as well as many towns and villages where crafts are produced and sold. Leather is worked in **Cotacachi**, wood is carved in **San Antonio de Ibarra**, textiles are woven around **Peguche**, and beautiful tablecloths are embroidered in **Zuleta**. Carry on north to Ibarra for a different sort of local craft, delicious *helados de paila* (fruit sorbets).

Avenue of the Volcanoes (1 or 2 weeks)
This term was coined by 18th-century German explorer Alexander von Humboldt to describe the chain of snow-capped volcanic peaks which crown the Central Highlands of Ecuador. Two of these, **Cotopaxi** and **Iliniza Norte**, are popular climbs for fit amateurs accompanied by a qualified guide. Head south along the Pan-American highway from Quito to Latacunga, visiting Ilinizas and Cotopaxi National Parks along the way. A worthwhile side-trip west from Latacunga takes in the **Quilotoa Circuit**, including a turquoise crater lake and surrounding native villages. Continue south to **Baños** for spectacular volcano watching when Tungurahua is feeling active, plus thermal baths, great hiking, biking and horseback riding. Head south to **Riobamba** in the shadow of Chimborazo, Ecuador's highest summit. Five massive volcanic peaks can be seen from Loma de Quito park in Riobamba. The city is also the start of the spectacular railway ride over the Devil's Nose.

Galápagos Islands (1 week)
Located 1,000 km due west of the coast of Ecuador, these volcanic islands were for millions of years cut off from the rest of the planet. The few animals and plants which arrived on their shores, evolved along unique lines. The results are among the most

weird and wonderful creatures on earth. Perhaps the most fortuitous arrival of all was a young man named **Charles Darwin**, who turned up in 1835 onboard HMS *Beagle*. He spent only five weeks in Galápagos but the experience was so powerful as to inspire his theory of evolution. Visiting Galápagos remains one of those once-in-a-lifetime experiences. It does not come cheap but is well worth saving for. Most visitors take a cruise among the islands and there are 80 vessels to choose from, carrying between eight and 110 passengers each. You live aboard and sail from island to island, landing at visitor sites, each designed to exhibit a specific set of flora and fauna.

El Oriente: the Ecuadorean Amazon (5 to 10 days)

East of the Andes lies the vast Amazon basin, the greatest rainforest on earth. Ecuador's slice of the Amazon, called *El Oriente* (the east), has even greater biodiversity than Galápagos, with up to 14 species of primates and 550 species of birds observed at a single site! There are several excellent and expensive jungle lodges offering four or five-day packages from Quito. More economical tours can also be booked through agencies in Quito, Baños, Tena, Puyo and Macas. Although independent travel in the jungle itself is not advisable, the following circuit along its periphery provides a taste of the area. From Quito head south to Baños and carry on east by bus to Puyo, an exciting ride through the spectacular gorge of the Pastaza river. Head north from Puyo to Tena, a centre for jungle ethno-tourism and white-water rafting. Nearby is tiny Puerto Misahuallí, on the highest navigable reaches of the Río Napo. From Tena carry on north to Baeza, from where you can make a side-trip to the thundering San Rafael waterfall, Ecuador's highest.

Essentials Planning your trip

South to Peru (2 to 3 weeks)

Cross-border tourism is creating exciting new opportunities in southern Ecuador and northern Peru. *El Austro*, the Southern Highlands, have seen greater Inca influence than other parts of Ecuador and they are home to some the country's finest archaeology. Cuenca, a UNESCO world heritage site, has an immense blue-domed cathedral and an excellent archaeology museum at Pumapungo. It is also a good base for trekking in Cajas National Park. Visit Ingapirca, Ecuador's best-developed Inca site, located north of Cuenca. Continue south from Cuenca through Loja to Vilcabamba. This is a fabled fountain of youth, where people were reported to live over 100 years. Situated alongside Podocarpus National Park, Vilcabamba offers excellent day-hikes as well as longer treks on foot or horseback. In two days travel from Vilcabamba you can reach Chachapoyas, the heart of one of Peru's most exciting archaeological areas. From Chachapoyas you can continue south to further explore Peru.

Beaches and whale watching (1 or 2 weeks)

With so much else going for it, Ecuador is seldom considered a beach destination. Yet the Pacific coast offers white sand, good surf, interesting national parks and terrific seafood. Guayaquil is a logical access point to the area and you can enjoy a stroll along the big city's riverside promenade called *Malecón 2000*. Follow the coast north to Puerto López and Machalilla National Park, stopping along the way to see the excellent archaeology museum in Salango. Puerto López is a centre for watching humpback whales which migrate to the coast of Ecuador between June and September. Carry on northward past the bustling port city of Manta, to the 'eco-city' of Bahía de Caráquez and the little village of Canoa. Here is one of the finest beaches in all of Ecuador, with great places to stay and eat. Even further to the north, the palm-lined beaches around Atacames are known as much for their party atmosphere as for their natural beauty. Further still, in the north of the province of Esmeraldas, are Afro-Ecuadorean villages among mangroves and the last vestiges of unique Pacific rainforest.

When to go

Climate

Ecuador's climate is so varied and variable that any time of the year is good for a visit. In the highlands, temperatures vary more in the course of a day, and with altitude, than they do with the seasons (which mainly reflect changes in rainfall). Every valley seems to have its own micro-climate but precipitation patterns generally depend on

whether a particular area is closer to the eastern or western slopes of the Andes. To the west, June through September are dry and October through May are wet (but there is sometimes a short dry spell in December or January). To the east, October through February are dry and March through September are wet. There is also variation in annual rainfall from north to south, with the southern highlands being drier.

Along the Pacific coast, rainfall likewise drops almost linearly from north to south, so that it can rain throughout the year in northern Esmeraldas and seldom at all near the Peruvian border. The coast can also be enjoyed year-round, although it may be a bit cool from June through September, when mornings are often grey and misty. January through May is the hottest and rainiest time of the year.

In the Oriente, as in the rest of the Amazon basin, heavy rain can fall at any time, but it is usually wettest from March through September. The Galápagos are hot from January through April, when heavy but brief showers are likely. From May through December is the cooler misty season. As if all this was not sufficiently confusing, the climate in Galápagos and throughout Ecuador is also affected by the irregular 5-10 year cycle of the *El Niño* phenomenon (see page).

Tourist seasons

Ecuador's high international tourist season is from June to early September, which is the busiest time for Quito hotels, Galápagos, trekking and climbing. There is a shorter tourist season between December and January, when Galápagos tours may also be booked well in advance. Most Ecuadoreans take long weekends around Carnival, Holy Week, and over New Year; school holidays in the highlands are from July to September, on the coast January to March. While a few resort areas (especially beaches) may become busy at these times, and prices rise accordingly, Ecuador is not overcrowded at any time of the year.

Tour operators → *See page 58 for special interest tour operators*

UK and Ireland
For further information on specialist travel firms, contact the **Latin American Travel Association** at P.O Box 1338, Long Ashton, Bristol, UK, BS41 9YA, T020-87152913, www.lata.org.
Condor Journeys and Adventures, 2 Ferry Bank, Colintraive, Argyll PA22 3AR, T01700-841318, www.condorjourneys-adventures.com, www.galapagos-holidays.com Ecuador and Galápagos specialist tour operator; tailor made and activity holidays.
Cox & Kings Travel, Gordon House, 10 Greencoat Pl, London SW1P 1PH, T020-7873 5000, www.coxandkings.co.uk

Discovery Initiatives, The Travel House, 51 Castle St, Cirencester, Glos GL7 1QD, T01285-643333, www.discoveryinitiatives. com Tailor-made trips to Ecuador and the Galápagos.

Exodus Travels, Grange Mills, Weir Rd, London SW12 0NE, T0870-2405550, www.exodustravels.co.uk Experienced in adventure travel, including cultural tours and trekking and biking holidays.

Explore, 1 Frederick St, Aldershot, Hants GU11 1LQ, T0870-3334002, www.explore.co.uk Highly respected operator with offices in Eire, Australia, New Zealand, USA and Canada, running 2-5 week tours in more than 90 countries worldwide, including Ecuador.

Galápagos Adventure Tours, 79 Maltings Place, 169 Tower Bridge Rd, London SE1 3LJ, T020-74071478, www.selectlatinamerica .co.uk Run by David Horwell who has an

abundant knowledge of the Galápagos. Escorted tours to the islands as well as the Andes and rainforest.

Galápagos Classic Cruises, 6 Keyes Rd, London NW2 3XA, T020-8933 0613, www.galapagoscruises.co.uk An experienced company providing specialist and adventure tours for individuals and groups.

Geodyssey, 116 Tollington Park, London, N4 3RB, T020-7281 7788, www.geodyssey.co.uk Indepth travel service for Ecuador and the Galápagos, with specialist itineraries and tailormade tours available.

Journey Latin America, 12-13 Heathfield Terr, Chiswick, London W4 4JE, T020-8747 8315, and 12 St Anne's Sq, 2nd floor, Manchester M2 7HW, T0161-8321441, www.journeylatinamerica.co.uk The world's leading tailor-made specialist for Latin America, running escorted tours throughout the region, they also offer a wide range of flight options.

Last Frontiers, Fleet Marston Farm, Aylesbury, Buckinghamshire HP18 0QT, T01296-653000, www.lastfrontiers.com South American specialists offering tailor-made itineraries to Ecuador including the Galápagos, plus specialist themed tours.

Select Latin America (incorporating Galapagos Adventure Tours), 79 Maltings Pl, 169 Tower Bridge Rd, London SE1 3LJ, T020-7407 1478, www.selectlatinamerica.com Quality tailor-made holidays and small group tours.

South American Experience, 47 Causton St, Pimlico, London SW1P 4AT, T020-7976 5511, www.southamerican experience.co.uk Flights, accommodation and tailor-made trips.

Sunvil Latin America, Sunvil House, Upper Sq, Old Isleworth, Middlesex, TW7 7BJ, T020-8758 4774, www.sunvil.co.uk Fly-drive and small group holidays for adventurous travellers.

Trips Worldwide, 14 Frederick Pl, Clifton, Bristol BS8 1AS, T0117-3114400, www.trips worldwide.co.uk Broad range of travel options and tours across Latin America.

Tucan Travel, 316 Uxbridge Rd, London, W3 9QP, T020-8896 1600, www.tucantravel.com Offers adventure tours and overland expeditions.

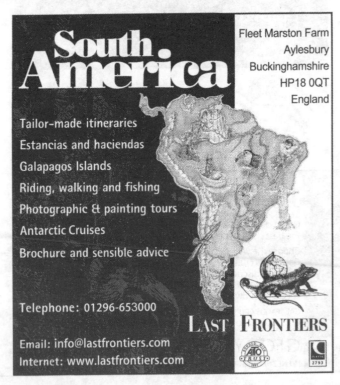

North America

eXito Latin American Travel Specialists, 712 Bancroft Rd #455, Walnut Creek, CA 94598, USA, T1800-6554053 toll free, www.exitotravel.com Latin American experts.

Ladatco Tours, 2200 South Dixie Highway, Suite 704, Coconut Grove, FL 33133, T1800-3276162, www.ladatco.com South American specialists, operate explorer tours.

Myths and Mountains, 976 Tee Ct, Incline Village, Nevada 89451, USA, T1800-670 6984, www.mythsandmountains.com Cultural and natural tours of Galápagos and Ecuador.

Tambo Tours, 20919 Coral Bridge La, Suite 225-A, Spring, TX, 77388, USA, T1-888-2-GO-PERU, T001-281 5289448, www.2goperu.com Long established adventure and tour specialist with offices in Peru and USA. Customised trips to the Amazon and archaeological sites of Peru and Ecuador. Daily departures for groups and individuals.

Tropical Nature Travel, mail: PO Box 5276, Gainsville, FL 32627-5276, USA, T1-877-827 8350, www.tropicalnaturetravel.com

Eco-tour operator offering wildlife, culture and nature tours of Ecuador and Galápagos.

Australia and New Zealand

Contours Travel, Level 6, 310 King St, Melbourne, Vic 3000, T3-9670 6900, www.contourstravel.com.au Specializes in Latin American destinations.

South America

Domiruth Travel Service, Jr. Rio de Janeiro 216-218, Miraflores, Lima, Peru, T1-6106000, www.domiruth.com.pe Peruvian tour operator offering a variety of packages and bus tours.

Grayline Ecuador, Santa Maria E4-125 y Fco Pizarro, 5th floor, Quito, T1-800 GRAY LINE, reservations@graylineecuador.com Local experts with day tours from and around Quito.

Zenith Travel, Juan Leon Mera y Roca, 2nd floor, Quito, T02-2529993, www.zenith ecuador.com Specializes in tours to the Galápagos Islands, Ecuador and Peru. Owner Marcos Endara speaks English and French.

Essentials Planning your trip

Finding out more

Tourist information

Tourist information and promotion is handled at the national level by the **Ministerio de Turismo** ① *Eloy Alfaro N32-300 y Carlos Tobar, Quito, T02-2507559, www.vivecuador.com* The Ministerio also has regional offices in the larger provincial capitals and almost every municipality also has its own tourist office; details are given in the respective towns and cities. Outside Ecuador, tourist information can sometimes be obtained from Ecuadorean embassies and consulates (see box on page 36).

South American Explorers (SAE) ① *USA head office: 126 Indian Creek Rd, Ithaca, NY 14850, T607-2770488, www.saexplorers.org; Jorge Washington 311 y Leonidas Plaza, Quito, T/F02-2225228, quitoclub@saexplorers.org Mon-Fri 0930-1700, Sat 0900-1200. There are also SAE clubhouses in Lima and Cusco, Peru*, is a USA based non-profit organization, which provides its members with a wide range of travel information about Ecuador and South America. It offers a resource centre, a library and a quarterly journal as well as selling guidebooks and maps. SAE can hold mail for its members. SAE services are only available to members of the club. Annual membership costs US$50 single, US$80 for a couple. A visit to an SAE clubhouse is recommended before you sign up, to see if this organization suits your needs.

Useful websites

Daily newspapers

The most frequently updated sites are on-line editions of Ecuador's major daily newspapers, all in Spanish.

www.elcomercio.com *El Comercio* (Quito).
www.elmercurio.com.ec *El Mercurio* (Cuenca).
www.eluniverso.com *El Universo* (Guayaquil).
www.hoy.com.ec *El Hoy* (Quito).

Government sites

There are many Ecuadorean government sites with administrative, economic and statistical information. The following are merely a selection of the most relevant.
www.ecuador.org A good bilingual introduction, provided by the Ecuadorean embassy in Washington.
www.igepn.edu.ec For advisories of volcanic activity from the National Geophysics Institute.
www.vivecuador.com Maintained by the Ministerio de Turismo.

Tour and general information

English and multilingual commercial tourist sites for Ecuador abound. They are all cut from a similar mould, displaying varying amounts of background information alongside advertising, and they may not list establishments who do not advertise with them. Such sites include:

www.ecuadordiscover.com
www.ecuadorexplorer.com
www.ecuadortoursonline.com
www.ecuador-travel-guide.org
www.ecuaworld.com
www.thebestofecuador.com

Some offer online booking for hotels, tours and other services. Bookings in Ecuador can also be made through international sites such as **www.hostelworld.com**
www.ecuadorhandbook.com Multilingual site about Ecuador for this book, maintained by the authors.
www.trekkinginecuador.com Also by the authors, for hikers and trekkers.

Galápagos websites
www.darwinfoundation.org
Multilingual background and scientific information about Galápagos from the Charles Darwin Foundation.

Language

The official languages of Ecuador are **Spanish** and **Quichua**. English and a few other European languages may be spoken in some establishments catering to tourists in Quito and the most popular tourist destinations. Away from these places, knowledge of Spanish is essential. You can begin your travels in Ecuador with a period of language study. Language training opportunities abound; see Language schools listed in the directory text of Quito, Cuenca, Otavalo, Baños, Manta, Canoa and Vilcabamba. With even a modest knowledge of Spanish you will be able to befriend Ecuadoreans, to interchange ideas and insights with them. Without any language skills, you will feel like someone trying to peep through the keyhole at Ecuador.

Those who are planning to work or have extensive contact with highland Indian groups, would do well to learn some **Quichua** beforehand. In any case, you'll have already come across more Quichua than you realize, through lyrics of the traditional Andean 'flute and panpipes' music, through thousands of placenames (like *Ingapirca*, *Inka wall*), and through such classic names of the Andean environment as the *condor*, *puma* and – of course – the *llama*. For additional details see box page 30. To find a course and books try the **Abya-Yala centre** in the Museo Amazónico in Quito (page 110) or the **Casa Indígena** in Riobamba. Also see www.quechua.org.uk

Information on language schools and travel is available from the following: **AmeriSpan** ① *117 South 17th St, Suite 1401, Philadelphia, PA 19103 USA, T1-800-8796640 (USA and Canada), T215-7511100 (worldwide), www.amerispan.com*; and **Spanish Abroad** ① *5112 N 40th St, Suite 203, Phoenix, AZ 85018 USA. T1-888-7227623 (USA and Canada), T0800-0287706 (UK), T602-7786791 (worldwide), www.spanishabroad.com* **Latin American Language Services** ① *96 Cotterill Rd, Surbiton, Surrey, KT6 7UK, T020-8286 1817, F8241 3483, www.lals.co.uk* UK tour operator specializing in Spanish language courses.

Disabled travellers

As with most Latin American countries, facilities for the disabled traveller are sadly lacking in Ecuador. Wheelchair ramps are a rare luxury in most of the country, but they are present in the resort town of Baños, see page 230. Getting a wheelchair into a bathroom or toilet is well nigh impossible, except for some of the more upmarket hotels (for example **Swissôtel** in Quito and the more modest **El Edén** in Baños). Pavements are often in a poor state of repair. Disabled Ecuadoreans obviously have

Essentials Planning your trip

Quichua

Quichua is the main indigenous language in Ecuador, spoken by around a fifth of the population. The same goes for Peru and Bolivia (where it's called Quechua), making it the most widely spoken surviving native language of the entire New World.

Quechua is most famous as the 'official' language of the Inca Empire, and the people who built Machu Picchu ('Old Peak'). Yet contrary to popular belief, Quechua does not come *originally* from Cuzco or the Incas. While its precise origins remain somewhat mysterious, it certainly started out as a single language, some 1500 years ago or more, and most likely somewhere in the central Peruvian Andes, from where it gradually spread both north and south over many centuries, long *before* the Inca Empire.

As Quechua expanded over this vast area it drifted apart into a number of regional forms, and has thus long ceased to be a single monolithic language (hence the pronunciations of *Quichua* vs. *Quechua* for a start). So Quichua-speakers from Ecuador now have a fair bit of difficulty communicating with those from Cuzco or Bolivia, and none of them can understand someone from Ancash in central Peru. The differences are of a similar order to those between Portuguese, Spanish, Catalan and Italian (which also all diverged from one original language, Latin). So it simply makes no sense to think of any one region like Cuzco as home to the 'original' or 'correct' Quechua.

How and when Quichua reached what is now Ecuador is still unclear. It is not certain that it was brought by the Incas, and may already have arrived somewhat earlier as a trading language spreading north from Peru. As such it was not the original native language of any one 'Quichua' tribe in Ecuador. On the contrary, it was taken over by a large number of diverse mountain and jungle peoples, whose native languages it eventually replaced. Even within Ecuador itself, there are plenty of distinct regional accents of Quichua.

Quichua is a key channel of continuity with the captivating pre-European past and indigenous identity of the Andes. What that also means, though, is that Quechua has long had a distinctly underprivileged status vis-à-vis the dominant Spanish; it continues to decline and its long-term future looks bleak. Of late, however, at least some Quichua-speaking communities in Ecuador have had success in asserting themselves and recovering a sense of identity, unity and pride in their culture and origins, and to a lesser extent also in their language. The Otavalo traders are one example (see p168). And Quichua is at last being fitfully introduced in primary education, and starting to be written.

Yet the centuries of stigma from the Spanish-speaking élite have far from worn off entirely, and some people can still easily be made to feel embarrassed to be Quichua-speakers. Foreign visitors in particular should be tactful and sensitive to this. The best way is to take an interest in the language, making sure to get the message across that your interest is because you value it. After all, Quichua is just as authentic, if not more alive and human, than all the other heritage of the native Americas.

Better still, take the plunge and learn some Quichua for yourself. You'll be rewarded with truly privileged access to the indigenous people of Ecuador, and an astonishing eye-opener into just how different a language and its way of seeing the world can be. See p29 for courses.

By Paul Heggarty
(www.quechua.org.uk).

to cope with these problems and mainly rely on the help of others to move around; fortunately most bystanders are very helpful. Quito's trolley system has wheelchair access in principle, but it is too crowded to make this practical.

Some travel companies are beginning to specialize in exciting holidays, tailor-made for individuals depending on their level of disability. For those with access to the internet, a Global Access – Disabled Travel Network Site is www.geocities.com/Paris/1502. It is dedicated to providing information for 'disabled adventurers' and includes a number of reviews and tips from members of the public. You might want to read *Nothing Ventured* edited by Alison Walsh (Harper Collins), which gives personal accounts of worldwide journeys by disabled travellers, plus advice and listings.

Gay and lesbian travellers

The 1998 constitution prohibits discrimination on the basis of sexual orientation and attitudes have gradually become more liberal in Quito and Guayaquil. Outside these two largest cities, however, values are still intensely conservative and there remains a general bias, even hostility, against gay people. As in most Latin countries, effeminate behaviour in men is condemned, and the derogatory term *maricón* is commonly used to describe such a person, irrespective of their sexual orientation. Same-sex couples travelling in Ecuador should aim to avoid public displays of affection.

In Quito, a place to meet or obtain information is the **Matrioshka bar** ① *in La Mariscal neighbourhood of Quito, Pinto 376 y Juan León Mera, T02-2552668*. **Zenith Travel** ① *JL Mera 453 y Roca, Quito, T02-2529993, www.zenithecuador.com*, has a department that caters exclusively for gay and lesbian travellers, English and French spoken.

Senior travellers

Mainland Ecuador has long been a popular destination for the young and adventurous, while older travellers have traditionally focused their visits on Galápagos, Quito and perhaps Otavalo. There is, however, no good reason for more mature travellers to shun the less-beaten path. Those in good health should face no special difficulties travelling independently, but it is very important to know and respect your own limits and to give yourself sufficient time to acclimatize to altitude in the highlands. If you require a special diet or medications, these must be brought from home, as they may not be available locally. Seniors' discounts in Ecuador, even more so than those for students (see above), tend to be restricted to Ecuadorean citizens, but bear in mind that a local retiree may have to make ends meet on a miserly pension. Some discounts for foreign seniors may be available at museums and on inter-city buses but not flights. You are far more likely to benefit from the strong traditional respect for the elderly in Ecuadorean society. At the same time, you will be sure to notice that the country's demographic profile is the inverse of that in most parts of the developed world. People under 25 years of age are the majority here, so it should be no surprise that older gringo travellers tend to stand out – except in Vilcabamba which is famous for its longevity!

For general information about active, adventurous travel for those 50 or better, see *Travel Unlimited: Uncommon Adventures for the Mature Traveler*, by Alison Gardner (Avalon Travel Publishing, 2000), and www.travelwithachallenge.com See also Insurance, p38, for suggestions on senior-friendly insurers.

Student travellers

Foreign students visiting Ecuador may be eligible for some discounts, including 15% off high-season flights to Galápagos, while other concessions are restricted to those who are Ecuadorean citizens. This is in a way unfair, but you should keep in mind that, no matter how tight your budget, you probably have far more resources at your disposal than the average Ecuadorean student. By all means, shop around and bargain for the best student deal you can find, but also remember to be fair, especially when dealing with individuals or small family-run operations.

Tourist establishments in Ecuador which offer discounts to foreign students generally honour the **International Student Identity Card** (**ISIC**), but only if the card was issued in your home country. For your nearest ISIC office, consult www.isic.org. Student cards must carry a photograph if they are to be any use for discounts.

Travelling with children

Bus travel People contemplating overland travel in Ecuador with children should remember that a lot of time can be spent waiting for and riding buses. You should take reading material with you as it is difficult to find and expensive. Also look for the locally available comic strip *Condorito*, which is quite popular and a good way for older children to learn a bit of Spanish.

Fares On all long-distance buses you pay for each seat, and there are no half-fares. For shorter trips it is cheaper, if less comfortable, to seat small children on your knee. Sometimes there are spare seats which children can occupy after tickets have been collected. In city buses, small children generally do not pay a fare, but are not entitled to a seat when paying customers are standing. On domestic flights in Ecuador, children below age two pay 10% of the adult fare, between ages two and 12 they pay 50%. Make sure that children accompanying you are fully covered by your travel insurance policy.

Food This can be a problem if the children are not adaptable. It is easier to take food with you on longer trips than to rely on meal stops where the food may not be to taste. Avocados are safe, readily available, easy to eat and nutritious; they can be fed to babies as young as six months and most older children like them. Best stick to simple things like bread, however, bananas and tangerines, while you are actually on the road. Biscuits, packaged junk food and bottled drinks abound. A small immersion heater and jug for making hot drinks is invaluable, but remember that electric current is 110v in Ecuador. In restaurants, you can normally buy a *media porción* (half portion), or divide one full-size helping between two children.

Travel with children can bring you into closer contact with local families and, generally, presents no special problems – in fact the path may even be smoother for family groups. Officials are sometimes more amenable where children are concerned and they are pleased if your child knows a little Spanish. For more detailed advice, see *Adventuring with Children*, by Nan Jeffrey (Avalon House, 1995).

Women travellers

Generally women travellers should find visiting Ecuador an enjoyable experience. Gender stereotyping is gradually diminishing, however machismo is alive and well here. You should be prepared for this and try not to overreact. When you set out, err on the side of caution until your instincts have adjusted to the customs of a new culture.

It is easier for men to take the friendliness of locals at face value; women may be subject to unwanted attention. Minimize this by not wearing suggestive clothing and do not flirt. By wearing a wedding ring, carrying a photograph of your 'husband' and 'children', and saying that your 'husband' is close at hand, you may dissuade an aspiring suitor. If politeness fails, do not feel bad about showing offence and departing. When accepting a social invitation, make sure that someone knows the address and the time you left. Ask if you can bring a friend (even if you do not intend to do so). Above all, use common sense: a lone woman going off to try *ayahuasca* in a remote jungle village with a male guide is obviously asking for trouble.

If, as a single woman, you can befriend an Ecuadorean woman, you will learn much more about the country as well as finding out how best to deal with suggestive comments, whistles and hisses that might come your way. Travelling with another *gringa* may not exempt you from this attention, but at least should give you moral support.

Note that tampons may be hard to find in smaller towns; sanitary napkins are available everywhere. The largest selection of such products is found in the major cities, where you can stock up if necessary.

Living and working in Ecuador ▸▸ *see also volunteering, p83*

Starting in the early 1990s, and especially in recent years, Ecuador has attracted increasing numbers of foreign residents. They have swelled the ranks of the country's traditional expatriates (diplomats, NGO volunteers and multinational employees), with retirees of all ages, as well as those seeking a new and interesting start.

Ecuadoreans have traditionally welcomed outsiders warmly, although a certain cultural barrier was always noticeable, especially in the highlands and even more so in indigenous communities. Growing numbers of successful foreign-owned businesses, however, particularly when heavily concentrated in small towns like Otavalo, Baños or Vilcabamba, have generated their share of envy and anti-gringo sentiment among some segments of the local population.

Ecuador as a whole remains a pleasant and thoroughly interesting place for a foreigner to make his or her home. It is not, however, without its important risks and challenges. Come and enjoy an extended visit and get to know the country well before making major life choices.

Visas for longer stays

There are many options for foreigners who wish to stay in Ecuador longer than six months a year, but if you enter as a tourist then you cannot change your status while inside the country. The two classes of visas for longer stays are immigrant visas (categories 10-I to 10-VI) and non-immigrant visas (categories 12-I to 12-X). Immigrant visas are available for retirees with a guaranteed income (such as a pension or annuity), investors, professionals permanently employed in Ecuador, and spouses or other close relatives of Ecuadorean citizens or immigrants. They are granted by the **Dirección Nacional de Extranjería** ① *10 de Agosto y Murgeón, Edificio Autorepuestos del Interior, 4th floor, Quito, T02-2231022, Mon-Fri 0800-1300*. Non-immigrant visas are available for students, temporary employees, missionaries, volunteers, those involved in cultural exchange programmes, as well as their spouses and children. They are granted by the Cancillería in Quito, **Dirección General de Asuntos Migratorios** ① *10 de Agosto 18-55 y San Gregorio, Edificio Solís, 2nd floor, T02-2227025, dgasumig@mmrree.gov.ec, Mon-Tue and Thr-Fri 0930-1230*. Outside the country, applications for all visas must be filed with Ecuador's diplomatic representatives (see box on page 36). Allow several months for the application process.

After arriving in Ecuador, both immigrant and non-immigrant visa holders (not tourists) must register first with the Dirección Nacional de Extranjería in Quito and then with the immigration police office in the province where they will live, in order to obtain their *censo* (foreign resident census card), which must be renewed annually. Those with immigrant visas must additionally obtain a *cédula* (national identity card) from the **Registro Civil**. Foreign men up to age 55 with immigrant visas must also obtain a *cédula militar* from the armed forces. Immigrant visa holders many not leave Ecuador for more than 90 days a year, during the first two years of their visas, nor for more than 18 consecutive months at any time; these restrictions do not apply to non-immigrant visas. All visas must periodically be renewed by the same government agencies which grant them. A request for a change of visa category must be filed at least 30 days prior to the expiration of your current visa.

All immigration procedures are complex and time-consuming, and the regulations frequently change. Many expatriates choose to retain the services of a specialized lawyer; this is not always required. Be sure to get a personal recommendation, however, before hiring such an immigration attorney, as some are unscrupulous and will severely overcharge as well as creating more problems than they resolve.

Leaving Ecuador

Foreign residents face varying requirements, including a *salida* (exit permit) issued by the immigration police and valid for one year; as well as the *censo*, *cédula*, and *cédula militar* mentioned above. Foreign minors (other than tourists) travelling alone, or accompanied by only one parent, require authorization from the **Tribunal de Menores** before they are allowed to leave Ecuador.

Before you travel

Getting in

Passports and visas

All visitors to Ecuador must have a passport valid for at least six months and, in principle, an onward or return ticket. The latter is seldom asked for, but can be grounds for refusal of entry in some cases. Only citizens of the following countries require a consular visa to visit Ecuador as tourists: Afghanistan, Algeria, Bangladesh, China, Costa Rica, Cuba, Honduras, India, Iraq, Jordan, South Korea, Lebanon, Libya, Nigeria, Pakistan, Palestinian Authority, Sri Lanka, Sudan, Syria, Tunisia, Vietnam and Yemen. Persons of the Sikh faith may require a visa regardless of nationality and are advised to check with an Ecuadorean diplomatic representative (see Embassies box) before travelling. Upon entry all visitors are required to complete a brief international embarkation/ disembarkation card, which is stamped along with your passport. Keep this card in your passport, losing it can cause problems when leaving the country or at a spot check.

▸ Always carry your passport in Ecuador, failure to do so can result in arrest and deportation.

Spot checks

You are required by Ecuadorean law to carry your passport at all times. An ordinary photocopy of your passport is not an officially acceptable substitute and you may not be permitted to return to your hotel to fetch the original document. Some travellers nevertheless prefer to carry a photocopy and leave their passport in safekeeping at their hotel. A photocopy certified by your embassy is more likely to be acceptable, but it's a judgement call, entirely at the discretion of the individual police officer.

Ecuadorean embassies

For additional countries, addresses, opening hours, and updates see www.mmrree.gov.ec

Australia, 6 Pindari Crescent, O'Malley, ACT 2606, T2-6286 4021, embecu@bigpond.net.au

Austria, Goldschmiedgasse 10/2/24, A-1010 Vienna, T1-5353208, mecaustria@chello.at

Belgium, Av Louise 363, 9th Floor, 1050 Brussels, T2-6443050, amb.equateur@skynet.be

Canada, 50 O'Connor St No 316, Ottawa, ON K1P 6L2, T613-5638206, www.consecuador-quebec.org

France, 34 Ave de Messine, 75008 Paris, T1-45611021, embajadaenfrancia@ambassade-equateur.fr

Germany, Kaiser-Friedrich Strasse 90, 1 OG, 10585 Berlin, T30-2386217, www.botschaft-ecuador.org

Israel, 4 Rehov Weizmann (Asia House), 4th floor, Tel Aviv 64239, T3-6958764, mecuaisr@netvision.net.il

Italy, Vía Antonio Bertolini No. 8 (Paroli), 00197 Roma, T06-45439007, mecuroma@ecuador.it

Japan, No 38 Kowa Building, Room 806, 4-12-24 Nishi-Azabu, Minato-Ku, Tokyo 1060031, T3-34992800, www.ecuador-embassy.or.jp

Netherlands, Koninginnengracht 84, 2514 AJ The Hague, T70-3463753, F70-8658910

New Zealand, Level 9, 2 Saint Martins Lane, Auckland, T9-3030590, langlinks@aix.co.nz

Spain, Calle Velásquez No.114-2° derecha, Madrid, T91-5625436, embajada@mecuador.es

Sweden, Engelbrektsgatan 13, SE-114 32 Stockholm, T8-6796043, www.embajada-ecuador.se

Switzerland, Kramgasse 54, 3011 Bern, T31-3511755, www.eda.admin.ch

UK, Flat 3B, 3 Hans Cres, Knightsbridge, London, SW1X 0LS, T020-7584 1367, http://ecuador.embassy homepage.com

USA, 2535 15th Street NW, Washington DC 20009, T202-234 7200, www.ecuador.org

Spot checks for passports are most often carried out near border areas and at police checkpoints on highways throughout the country, as well as in bars, discos and resorts popular with foreigners. Be cautious, however, when approached by someone claiming to be an immigration officer on the street. They should be in uniform, if not seek assistance from several bystanders, and insist on walking to the nearest police station before you hand over any documents. Do not get in a taxi or other vehicle with such an individual. A legitimate immigration officer should not ask to see your money.

As long as your documents are in order, serious hassles with the immigration authorities in Ecuador are fortunately very rare. Remember, however, that tourists are not permitted to work under any circumstances. Foreigners have also on occasion been detained and deported for involvement in political or other 'sensitive' activities, including environmental activism – see Prohibitions, page 45. If you should encounter serious difficulties with the immigration police, then these may be reported to your embassy or consulate. Some embassies also recommend that you register with them details of your passport and accommodation in case of emergency.

Length of visit

Tourists are entitled to visit Ecuador for up to 90 days during any 12-month period. This may, in some cases, be extended to a maximum of 180 days at the discretion of the **Policía Nacional de Migración** (national immigration police). Those travelling by land from Peru or Colombia are usually granted 30 days on arrival, but their stay can be extended. When arriving at Quito or Guayaquil airport you may be asked how long you plan to stay in the country. When in doubt, request 90 days.

Extensions

Extensions for stays up to 90 days may be requested at any *jefatura provincial* (provincial headquarters) of the **Policía Nacional de Migración**. Most are located in provincial capitals, addresses are given under each town. Smaller offices are not always staffed or familiar with all procedures; Quito, Guayaquil and Cuenca are your best bet. In Quito you must go to the **Jefatura Provincial de Migración de** Pichincha ① *Isla Seymour 44-174 y Río Coca, T02-2247510*, not the Dirección Nacional de Migración on Av Amazonas. Requests for extensions beyond 90 days on the other hand, can only be made in Quito at the **Dirección Nacional de Migración** ① *Amazonas 171 y República, T02-2454122*. All immigration offices are normally open Monday-Friday 0800-1230 and 1500-1830. If you are lucky, obtaining an extension can take less than an hour, but always leave yourself a few days slack as there may be delays. At present only a nominal fee/fine of US$0.40 is charged for extensions, but this is subject to change. All the above regulations change frequently, if you are unsure about current requirements, then enquire well before your time expires. Polite conduct and a neat appearance are important when dealing with the immigration authorities.

Customs and security checks

On arrival

Customs inspection is carried out at airports after you clear immigration. When travelling by land, customs authorities may also set up checkpoints along the country's highways. Tourists seldom encounter any difficulties but if you are planning to bring any particularly voluminous, unusual, or valuable items to Ecuador (for example professional video equipment or a boat) then you should enquire beforehand with an Ecuadorean diplomatic representative (see box on page 36) and obtain any necessary permits, or be prepared to pay the prevailing customs duties. Reasonable amounts of climbing gear and a laptop computer are generally not a problem. For details on bringing a vehicle into Ecuador see under Car, page 54. Never bring any firearms.

Shipping goods to Ecuador

Except for documents, customs duties must be paid on all goods shipped to Ecuador. Enforcement is strict, duties are high and procedures are slow and complicated. You are therefore advised to bring anything you think you will need with you when you travel, rather than having it sent to you once you are in the country.

On departure

Your airline baggage may be inspected by security personnel and will *always* be sniffed by dogs searching for drugs. Never transport anything you have not packed yourself, you will be held responsible for the contents. In addition, some passengers may be selected by Interpol agents at the airport (the officers may be uniformed or plain-clothed) to undergo compulsory x-ray examination to make sure they have not ingested packets of drugs. You may be asked to pay for the examination. Although legal, this is an unpleasant intimidating experience which fortunately affects only a very few travellers. Always politely ask for officers' identification and write down their names. Report any irregularities at once to your diplomatic representative in Ecuador or authorities in your home country.

No export duties are charged on souvenirs you take home from Ecuador, but there are various items for which you require special permits. These include specimens of wild plants and animals, original archaeological artefacts, certain works of art and any objects considered part of the country's national heritage. When in doubt, ensure that you enquire well in advance.

What to take

Everybody has their own list, below are a few things which are particularly useful for travelling in Ecuador. Try to think light and compact. All but the most specialized products are available in Quito and Guayaquil, while many basic commodities are readily purchased throughout the country.

A **moneybelt** or **pouch** is absolutely indispensable. Be sure to bring an adequate supply of any **medications** you take on a regular basis, plus two weeks spare, as these may not be available in Ecuador. Sturdy comfortable **footwear** is a must for travels anywhere. **Sun protection** is very important in all regions of the country and for visitors of all complexions. This should include a sun hat, high quality sun glasses and sun screen for both skin and lips. Take **insect repellent** if you plan to visit the coast or jungle. Also recommended are **flip-flops** or thongs for use on the beach, at hot springs and in hotel showers, where they protect against both athlete's foot and electric shock when instant-heating shower heads are used. If you use **contact lenses**, be sure also to bring a pair of glasses. A small lightweight **towel** is an asset, as is a short length of travel **clothesline**. A compact **torch** (flashlight), **alarm** watch and **pocket knife** may all be useful. Always carry some **toilet paper**, as this is seldom found in public washrooms unless it is sold at the entrance. See Health, page 86, for a medical checklist.

A good general principle is to take half the clothes and twice the money you think you will need.

Insurance

Always take out travel insurance before you set off and read the small print carefully. Check that the policy covers the activities you intend or may end up doing. Also check exactly what your medical cover includes, i.e. ambulance, helicopter rescue or emergency flights back home. Also check the payment protocol. You may have to cough up first (literally) before the insurance company reimburses you. It is always best to dig out all the receipts for expensive personal effects like jewellery or cameras. Take photos of these items and note down all serial numbers.

Travel insurance is a must for all visitors to Ecuador.

You are advised to shop around. **STA Travel** and other reputable student travel organizations offer good-value policies. Young travellers from North America can try the **International Student Insurance Service** (ISIS), which is available through **STA Travel** ① *T1-800-7770112, www.sta-travel.com* Other recommended travel insurance companies in North America include: **Travel Guard** ① *T1-800-8261300, www.noelgroup.com* **Access America** ① *T1-800-2848300;* **Travel Insurance Services** ① *T1-800-9371387;* and **Travel Assistance International** ① *T1-800-8212828.* Older travellers should note that some companies will not cover people over 65 years old, or may charge higher premiums. The best policies for older travellers (UK) are offered by **Age Concern** ① *T01883-346964* and **Saga** ① *www.saga.co.uk*

Money

Currency

For almost a century before dollarization, Ecuador's currency was the sucre. Today, sucre notes and coins have no value except as souvenirs. Since 2000, the US dollar is the only official currency of Ecuador. Only US dollar bills circulate. US coins are used alongside the equivalent size and value Ecuadorean coins. Ecuadorean coins have no value outside the country. Some merchants are reluctant to accept bills larger than $20, both because counterfeit notes are a problem and because change may be scarce. Travellers should carefully check any bills they receive as change.

Exchange

There are a variety of different ways for visitors to bring their funds to Ecuador. You are strongly advised to combine two or more of these, so as not to be stuck if there are problems with any one alternative. Although Euros are slowly gaining acceptance, it is best not to bring any currencies other than US dollars to Ecuador, neither as cash nor travellers' cheques; they are difficult to exchange and generally fetch a poor rate. Pounds are very difficult to exchange.

ATMs

ATMs are very common throughout Ecuador, and many are linked to international systems such as Plus or Cirrus. Visitors with the appropriately encoded cards can therefore obtain cash from these machines. Not all ATMs accept all cards, however, so you will have to look around. In general, credit cards work better than debit cards, but there are many exceptions and quirks. Smaller towns may have a single ATM which accepts only one type of card, or no ATM at all. The details of which cards work are constantly changing. Always check with your home bank before travelling regarding charges and conditions which apply to international ATM transactions. Also bear in mind that these electronic systems are not always reliable in Ecuador, and cash-point scams abound.

Do not rely exclusively on ATMs in Ecuador, always bring some US$ cash, travellers' cheques, or both.

Travellers' cheques

US dollar travellers' cheques can be exchanged for cash in Ecuador, but usually only in Quito, Guayaquil, Cuenca, and the larger provincial capitals. **American Express** is the most widely accepted brand, and have offices in Quito and Guayaquil (see respective city listings); others may be difficult to exchange. Amex sell travellers' cheques against an Amex card (or a cardholder's personal cheque) and replace them if lost or stolen, but they do not give cash for travellers' cheques, nor travellers' cheques for cash. A police report is required if they are stolen. **Banco de Guayaquil** and **Produbanco** have branches in several cities, charge 1% commision and provide efficient service. **Banco del Pacífico** is more restrictive and expensive, but is the only bank with branches in Galápagos. Most other banks do not change travellers' cheques at all. There may be long queues and paperwork at all banks. Travellers' cheques may only be exchanged during limited hours, most reliably Monday-Friday until 1300. A passport is required and, less frequently, the original purchase receipt for the travellers' cheques. *Casas de cambio* (exchange houses) may also change travellers' cheques, but there are not many of these establishments left after dollarization.

Credit cards

The most commonly accepted credit cards in Ecuador include **Visa, MasterCard, Diners,** and to a lesser extent **American Express**. Many smaller hotels, restaurants, tour agencies and shops may display credit card symbols but not honour the cards 'just at the moment', or they may apply a surcharge (at least 10%) for credit card customers. Luxury or first-class establishments will usually have no difficulty honouring most credit cards. MasterCard holders can obtain cash advances at the company's offices in Quito, Guayaquil, Cuenca and Ambato. Advances on Visa, may be obtained from Banco de Guayaquil and Banco del Pichincha, the latter has the longest queues.

Money transfers

Bank transfers, wires, telexes or cables to Ecuador are not recommended because of potentially long delays, high taxes and service charges. **Western Union** has offices throughout Ecuador and can reliably transfer funds into or out of the country in a matter of minutes, but high taxes and charges also apply. The most efficient and economical alternative is to purchase travellers' cheques on an Amex card or with a personal cheque, as described above. Note that money orders are not accepted anywhere in Ecuador.

Cost of living/travelling

Despite its US dollar economy, Ecuador remains well within the reach of budget travellers. A basic hotel room costs as little as US$5 per person, a simple meal US$1.50, and transportation costs are especially low. A basic daily travel budget is currently US$15-20 per person, based on two people travelling together. For US$50 a day, you can have a good deal of comfort and even a little elegance, while US$100 is getting up into the luxury range. For hotel and restaurant price ranges, see inside the front cover and boxes on pages 59 and 62.

Getting there

Air

International flights into Ecuador arrive either at **Quito** (UIO) or **Guayaquil** (GYE). There are frequent flights between Quito and Guayaquil, as well as ample bus services. International airfares from North America and Europe to Ecuador vary with low and high season. The latter is generally July to September and December. International flights to Ecuador from other South or Central American countries, however, usually have one price year-round.

From Europe

KLM and **Iberia** offer the only direct flights from Europe to Ecuador, originating in Amsterdam and Madrid respectively. **Lufthansa** and **Air France** fly from Frankfurt and Paris, respectively, to Bogotá, where passengers are transferred to local carriers for the flight to Ecuador. **Continental Airlines** flies to Ecuador from many European cities via Newark or Houston. **American Airlines** does likewise via Miami. There are two new airlines flying from Europe to both Quito and Guayaquil, offering better rates than many other airlines at this time: **Air Europa,** flying three times a week from Madrid, and **Air Madrid,** flying twice a week from Madrid.

From North America

Miami's heavily congested international airport is by far the most important air transport hub linking Ecuador with all of North America. **American Airlines** has at least one flight daily from Miami to each of Quito and Guayaquil; on some days there are two flights. **Lan Chile/Lan Ecuador** also flies from Miami to Quito and Guayaquil, as well as New York City (JFK). Competitive fares from Miami to Quito or Guayaquil may be offered by **Copa Airlines** and **TACA**, through their respective hubs in Panama City and San José, Costa Rica. **Continental Airlines** flies to Quito and Guayaquil from less congested Houston and Newark, with some flights routed through Panama City.

From Australia and New Zealand

There are three options: 1) To Los Angeles (USA) with **Qantas**, **Air New Zealand** or **United**, continuing to Quito via Houston with **Continental**; 2) To Papetete (Tahiti) with **Qantas** or **Air New Zealand**, continuing to Quito via Easter Island and Santiago (Chile) with **Lan Chile**; 3) To Buenos Aires (Argentina) from Auckland with **Aerolineas Argentinas**, continuing to Quito with **Lan Chile** or another South American carrier. These are all expensive long-haul routes. The 'Circle Pacific' fares offered by some airline alliances, such as **One World** or **Star Alliance**, may be convenient alternatives and worth investigating.

From Latin American cities

There are direct flights to Quito and/or Guayaquil from Santiago, Lima, Bogotá, Caracas, Panama City, and San José (Costa Rica). Easy connections can be made with other South American cities. **Copa Airlines** and **TACA** (see above) offer convenient connections between Ecuador and various destinations in Central America, Mexico and the Caribbean.

Road and river

There are regular connections by bus to Quito and Guayaquil from Peru and Colombia (note public safety concerns in the latter), as well as South American countries farther afield, but no vehicle road connecting Central and South America. The most commonly used overland routes are via the Tulcán-Ipiales border crossing in the north, and the Huaquillas-Aguas Verdes border in the south, although Loja-Macará-La Tina-Piura is an excellent alternative route to Peru.

There are also several smaller border crossings to Peru. The most frequented of these is Zumba-Namballe, on the way from Vilcabamba to Chachapoyas. You can

Discount flight agents

Australia and New Zealand
Flight Centre, 82 Elizabeth St, Sydney, T133 133, www.flightcentre. com.au; 205 Queen St, Auckland, T0800-243544. Also branches in other towns and cities.
STA Travel, T1300-360960, www.statravel.com.au; www.statravel.co.nz. Branches in major towns and university campuses across Australia and New Zealand.
Travel.com.au, 76-80 Clarence St, Sydney, T02-92496000 www.travel.com.au.

UK and Ireland
STA Travel, T0870-1600599, www.statravel.co.uk. Branches in major cities and many university campuses. Specialists in low-cost student/youth flights and tours, also student IDs and insurance.
Trailfinders, 194 Kensington High St, London W8 7RG, T0845-0585858, www.trailfinders.com. London, Oxford, Belfast, Glasgow, Dublin and other major UK cities.

North America
Air Brokers International, 323 Geary St, Suite 411, San Francisco, CA94102, T01-800-883 3273, www.airbrokers.com Consolidator and specialist on RTW and Circle Pacific tickets.
Discount Airfares Worldwide On-Line, www.etn.nl/discount.htm A hub of consolidator and discount agent links.
STA Travel, 5900 Wilshire Blvd, Suite 2110, Los Angeles, CA 90036, T1-800-7814040, www.statravel.com Also branches in New York, San Francisco, Boston, Miami, Chicago, Seattle and Washington DC.
Travel CUTS, 187 College St, Toronto, ON, M5T 1P7, T1-800-592 2887 (US), T1866-2469762 (Canada), www.travelcuts.com Specialist in student discount fares, IDs and other travel services. Branches in other Canadian and US cities.

also cross on foot from Lalamor, and by vehicle from Jimbura, both remote villages in the province of Loja. For details of river travel to and from Peru, see Coca (page 400).

For details on immigration procedures at these borders, see under the relevant sections of respective towns. Note that it is usually much cheaper to buy bus tickets as far as the nearest border town, cross on foot or by taxi, and then purchase tickets locally in the country you have just entered. If entering Ecuador by car, details of customs procedures are given on page 54.

Touching down

Airport information

For most visitors, the point of arrival will be **Mariscal Sucre** airport in Quito. For details of Guayaquil's **Simón Bolívar** airport see page 308.

Public transport

Taxi The safest and easiest way to travel between town and the airport is to take a taxi. The airport taxi cooperative has booths at international and national arrivals.

They have set rates to different zones, you pay right there and hand the ticket to the driver. The fare from the airport to the New City is about US$5; to the Old City US$6 (more at night). Alternatively, several van companies also have booths at international arrivals, these are good value for groups of six or more. Individuals who buy a ticket for a van may have to wait until they get enough passengers.

Bus This is **not recommended** unless you have virtually no luggage or are desperately low on funds. Buses and trolley alike are too crowded for you to enter with even a small backpack and the chances of having something vanish en route are very high. If you really have no other choice, the bus stop is one block from the terminal to the west (towards Pichincha), in front of **Centro Comercial Aeropuerto**. For the New City take a southbound bus marked 'Carcelén-Congreso' or 'Pinar Alto-Hotel Quito', these run along Av Amazonas and later C Juan León Mera, fare US$0.25. For the Old City and parts of the New City, take a green *alimentador* (feeder bus line) from the same location as above. This goes to the northern terminus of the trolley, which runs north-south throughout Quito; combined fare US$0.25. There is no bus or trolley service late at night when most flights from North America arrive. For details see Flying into Quito at night, page 97.

Airport facilities

Quito airport was refurbished in 2003; it is still a bit cramped but functional. There are often long queues for international departures and airlines recommend you arrive three hours before your flight. The airport is divided into four sections: international arrivals, international departures, national arrivals and national departures. You must show your passport and flight ticket (electronic tickets are accepted) to enter the airline check in area of international departures. There is a telephone office plus a few debit card-operated public phones; buy the debit cards at one of the airport shops. There is a post office outside, between international departures and national arrivals. Upstairs at international departures is a bar-restaurant which serves meals and snacks, as well as a couple of fast food places; all are pricey. There are expensive souvenir shops in international departures and luxury duty-free in the international departure lounge, after you clear immigration. All the main car rental companies are located just outside international arrivals. For details of their offices in Quito, see page 139.

Beware of self-styled porters: men or boys who will try to grab your luggage as you leave the terminal and offer to find you a cab in the hope of receiving a tip or stealing your bags. Legitimate porters wear ID tags and there is no shortage of taxis right at hand. Watch your gear at all times.

Departure tax

A 12% tax is charged on international air tickets for flights originating in Ecuador, regardless of where bought, as well as on domestic tickets. A departure tax of US$25 is payable in cash by all passengers leaving on international flights (except those who stay less than 24 hours in the country). Pay the departure tax when checking in with your airline, or at a booth in the international departures area. You will not be allowed to board without proof of payment.

Local customs and laws

Clothing

Most Ecuadoreans, if they can afford it, devote great care to their clothes and appearance. It is appreciated if visitors do likewise. How you dress is mostly how people will judge you. This is particularly important when dealing with officials. In general, clothing is less formal in the lowlands, both on the coast and in Oriente, where men and women do wear shorts. In the highlands, people are far more

❗ Touching down

Business hours Banks: Mon-Fri 0900-1600. **Government offices**:
Mon-Fri variable hours but most close for lunch. **Other offices**:
0900-1230, 1430-1800. **Shops**: 0900-1900, close at midday in smaller
towns, open until 2100 on the coast.

Electricity 110 volts AC, 60 cycles, US-type flat-pin plugs

Emergency phone 911 in Quito and Cuenca, 101 elsewhere

IDD +593

Languages Spanish and Quichua

Official time GMT-5, -6 in Galápagos.

VAT (IVA) 12%

Weights and measures Metric, some English measures for hardware,
some Spanish measures for produce.

conservative; wearing shorts is considered acceptable for sports and on hiking trails, but not at a church or cemetery. Do not go bare-chested in populated areas in the highlands. Nude bathing is unacceptable anywhere in Ecuador.

You should pack spring clothing for Quito (mornings and evenings are cold), but in Guayaquil tropical or light-weight clothes are needed. Women should pack one medium to long length skirt and men might want to consider bringing a smart sweater or jacket. Suits and dresses are compulsory for business people.

Conduct

Remember that politeness – even a little ceremoniousness – is expected and appreciated in Ecuador. In this connection professional or business cards are very useful. Men should always remove any headgear and say "con permiso" when entering offices, and be prepared to shake hands often; always say "Buenos días" (until midday), "Buenas tardes" (in the afternoon) or "Buenas noches" (after dark) and wait for a reply before proceeding further. Remember that the traveller from abroad has enjoyed greater advantages in life than most Ecuadorean minor officials, and should be friendly and courteous in consequence. Never be impatient and do not criticize situations in public: the officials may know more English than you think and they can certainly interpret gestures and facial expressions. In commercial transactions (buying a meal, taxis, goods in a shop etc) politeness should be accompanied by firmness; always ask the price first.

Politeness should also be extended to street vendors; saying "No, gracias" with a smile is far better than an arrogant dismissal. Whether you give money to beggars is a personal matter, but your decision should be influenced by whether a person is begging out of need or trying to cash in on the *gringo* trail. In the former case, local people giving may provide an indication. Giving money or candies to children is a separate issue, upon which most agree: don't do it. Instead of giving to beggars, consider donating your time or money to a community development project or NGO working in Ecuador; see Volunteer programmes, page 83.

Time-keeping

Ecuadoreans, like most Latin Americans, have a fairly relaxed attitude towards time. They will think nothing of arriving an hour or so late on social occasions. If you expect to meet someone at an exact time, you can tell them that you want to meet at such and such an hour "en punto".

Tipping

In most of the better restaurants a 10% service charge is included in the bill, but you can give a modest extra tip if the service is especially good. The most basic restaurants do not include a tip in the bill, and tips are not expected. Taxi drivers are usually not tipped, but you can always round up the fare for particularly good service. Tipping for all other services is entirely discretionary, how much depends on the quality of service given.

Prohibitions

Illegal drugs are the most common way for foreigners to get into serious trouble. Possession is punishable by up to 16 years' imprisonment; see Drugs under Safety, page 46. Never carry **firearms**, their possession could also land you in serious difficulties.

Almost all foreigners serving long sentences in Ecuador's squalid jails are there for possession of illegal drugs.

Ecuador is an open democratic society, but the conspicuous involvement of foreigners in local **politics** or other sensitive matters is seldom appreciated. The authorities do not hesitate to arrest and swiftly deport those who are considered to have overstepped their bounds, such as foreign environmentalists protesting the construction of an oil pipeline. If you feel strongly about Ecuadorean matters and would like to bring your opinion to bear on them, then you will have far more success by proceeding discretely through local contacts, or by lobbying international organizations from your home country.

Responsible tourism

The travel trade is growing rapidly and impacts of this supposedly 'smokeless' industry are becoming increasingly apparent. Ecuador is no exception, and may be especially vulnerable to adverse effects because of the country's small size and the high volume of tourism concentrated in certain areas. Sometimes these impacts may seem remote and unrelated to an individual trip or holiday (for example air travel is clearly implicated in global warming and damage to the ozone layer), but individual choice and awareness can make a difference in many instances (see box), and collectively, travellers are having a significant effect in shaping a more responsible and sustainable industry.

Of course travel can also have beneficial impacts and this is something to which every traveller can contribute – many national parks such as Cotopaxi are in part funded by receipts from visitors. Similarly, travellers can promote patronage and protection of important archaeological sites and heritage through their interest and contributions via entrance fees. They can also support small-scale enterprises by staying in locally run hotels and hostels, eating in local restaurants and by purchasing local goods, supplies and crafts. Such opportunities for patronizing local businesses and trades abound in Ecuador.

During the past decade there has been a phenomenal growth in tourism that promotes and supports the conservation of natural environments and is also fair and equitable to local communities. This 'ecotourism' segment is probably the fastest growing sector of the travel industry in all of South America and especially in Ecuador. Perhaps the best known Ecuadorean example of such development on a large scale is the **Kapawi lodge** in southern Oriente (see under Macas, page 403). The more grassroots projects include: **Ricancie** on the upper Río Napo near Tena (see page 388), **Runa Tupari** around Cotacachi (see page 172), **Sani lodge** and **Añangu** on the lower Río Napo below Coca (see page 402) and **Yachana lodge** which is accessed from Misahuallí (see page 391). There are also many others; contact **Ecuador Verde**, T09-9720890, www.ecuadorverde.com

⁞ How big is your footprint?

→ Where possible choose a destination, tour operator or hotel with a proven ethical and environmental commitment, and if in doubt ask.

→ Spend money on locally produced (rather than imported) goods and services and use common sense when bargaining – your few dollars saved may be a week's salary to others.

→ Use water and electricity carefully – travellers may receive preferential supply while the needs of local communities are overlooked.

→ Don't give money or sweets to children – it encourages begging – instead give to a recognized project, charity or school.

→ Learn about local etiquette and culture – consider local norms and behaviour – and dress appropriately for local cultures and situations.

→ Protect wildlife and other natural resources – don't buy souvenirs or goods made from wildlife unless they are clearly sustainably produced and are not protected under CITES legislation.

→ Always ask before taking photographs or videos of people.

→ Consider staying in local, rather than foreign owned, accommodation – the economic benefits for host communities are far greater – and there are far greater opportunities to learn about local culture.

Ecotourism organizations

The following have begun to develop and/or promote ecotourism projects, raise awareness and destinations and their websites are an excellent source of information and details for sites and initiatives throughout South America.

Conservation International, T1-202-9121000, www.conservation.org

The Eco-Tourism Society, T202-3479203, www.ecotourism.org

Planeta, www.planeta.com

Tourism Concern, T020-7753 3330, www.tourismconcern.org.uk

Green Globe, T0207-9308333, www.greenglobe21.com

The Centre for Environmentally Sustainable Tourism (CERT), www.c-e-r-t.org

Eco projects

These offer opportunities to participate directly in scientific research and development projects throughout the region.

Earthwatch, T1-800-7760188 (US & Canada), T01865-318838 (UK), www.earthwatch.org Also in Australia and Japan.

Discovery International, T020-7229 9881, www.discoveryinitiatives.com

Safety

Safe and hassle-free travels are the rule in Ecuador but cannot be taken for granted, they require a conscious effort on the part of every visitor. Routine precautions are generally sufficient to ensure a wonderful visit but the consequences of carelessness can be very severe. Please be careful and have a great time; Ecuadoreans are far more likely to go out of their way to help you, not hurt you. See page 33 for information on women travelling alone.

⁞ *Safety in a nutshell: 1) travel only by daylight; 2) hide your valuables; 3) keep away from drugs.*

Protecting money and valuables

Make photocopies of important documents and give them to your family, embassy or travelling companion, this will speed up replacement if documents are lost or stolen and will still allow you to have some ID while getting replacements. Keep all documents (including your passport, airline tickets and credit cards) secure and hide your main cash supply in several different places. If one stash is lost or stolen, you will still have the others to fall back on. The following means of concealing cash and documents have all been recommended: extra pockets sewn inside shirts and trousers; pockets closed with a zip or safety pin; moneybelts (best worn below the waist and never within sight); neck or leg pouches; and elastic support bandages for keeping money and travellers' cheques above the elbow or below the knee. Never carry valuables in an ordinary pocket, purse or day-pack. Cargo pockets on shorts or trousers are especially prone to being picked or slashed. You should keep cameras in bags or briefcases and generally out of sight. Do not wear expensive wrist watches or any jewellery. Even prescription eyeglasses can be a target if they have expensive-looking frames; take a spare set or your prescription just in case. If you wear a shoulder-bag in a market, carry it in front of you. Backpacks should be lockable but are nonetheless vulnerable to slashers: in crowded places wear your day-pack on your chest with both straps looped over your shoulders. Whenever visiting an area which is particularly unsafe (see below) take the bare minimum of belongings with you.

Hotel security
The cheapest hotels are usually found near markets and bus stations but these are also the least safe areas of most Ecuadorean towns. Look for something a little better if you can afford it, and if you must stay in a suspect area, always return to your hotel before dark. It is best, if you can trust your hotel, to leave any valuables you don't need in their safe-deposit box. But always keep an inventory of what you have deposited. If you don't trust the hotel, change hotels to one you feel safe in. If there is only one choice for places to stay, lock everything in your pack and secure that in your room; a light bicycle chain or cable and a small padlock will provide at least a psychological deterrent for would-be thieves. Even in an apparently safe hotel, do not leave valuable objects strewn about your room.

Urban street crime
Pickpockets, bag snatchers and slashers are always a hazard for tourists, especially in crowded areas such as markets or the downtown cores of major cities. Keep alert and avoid swarms of people. Crowded city buses and the Quito trolley are another magnet for thieves. Criminal gangs, at times well armed, also operate in the larger cities of Ecuador, especially in poor neighbourhoods and at night. You should likewise avoid deserted areas, such as parks or plazas after hours. If someone follows you when you're in the street, slip into a nearby shop or hail a cab. If you are the victim of an armed assault, never resist or hold back your valuables; they can always be replaced but your health or life cannot. Always purchase travel insurance before visiting Ecuador.

The old scam of smearing tourists with mustard, ketchup, shaving cream and almost anything else, in order to distract and rob them, is alive and well in Ecuador. An apparently well meaning bystander usually helps clean you up, while their accomplice expertly cleans you out. If you are smeared, move along quickly to a secure location or hail a cab. Furthermore, don't bend over to pick up money or other items in the street.

Highway robbery
Banditry on the roads of Ecuador is a very serious problem and occurs mostly at night. Travel only by daylight. There is plenty of daytime service going everywhere, and you never have to take a night bus. Never accept food or cigarettes offered by fellow passengers, they may be drugged and this is a common way of robbing travellers.

⠸ The gringo trail

There exists in Ecuador a well defined route for many travellers. It runs roughly from north to south through Otavalo, for its market; Quito, from which a climbing excursion may be taken; Baños, from which a jungle excursion may be taken; Riobamba, for the train ride; Cuenca, to visit Ingapirca; and Vilcabamba, for a well-deserved rest. This 'gringo trail' offers the best opportunities for socializing with other travellers, finding facilities and services geared specifically to foreign tastes and of course seeing a few of the tourist highlights of the country. It also offers a sometimes false sense of security, since thieves know their chances are greatest where tourists congregate.

There is, however, more – so much more – to be experienced in Ecuador. The country remains a treasure trove of spectacular places and unforgettable experiences, all waiting to be discovered and responsibly explored beyond the gringo trail. You are heartily encouraged to venture further afield and do some real exploring on your own, to get to know Ecuadoreans as well as fellow tourists and to take home a more sincere impression of the country.

Be especially careful arriving at or leaving from bus stations. They are obvious places to catch people (tourists or not) carrying a lot of important belongings. Do not set your bag down without putting your foot on it, or to just even double check your tickets or look at your watch; it will grow legs and walk away. Day-packs are easy to grab and run with, and are generally filled with your most important belongings. Take taxis to and from bus stations in major cities (look on it as an inexpensive insurance policy).

Dangerous areas

The countryside and small towns are generally the safest areas of Ecuador, and fortunately account for the largest and most interesting parts of the country. The Galápagos Islands are also particularly safe. The big cities – Quito, Guayaquil and Cuenca – call for the greatest care. The coast is slightly more prone to violence than the highlands, but hard drinking at fiestas can bring out the worst in people anywhere. The northern border with Colombia, including the provinces of Esmeraldas, Carchi, and especially Sucumbíos, call for special precautions. Armed conflict and the drug trade in Colombia has affected all northern border areas, and Colombian insurgents are a growing presence in parts of this region. Do not travel to or near the northern border without first carefully enquiring about the current public safety situation.

Drugs

Although drugs are readily available, anyone found carrying even the smallest amount may be automatically considered a trafficker. If arrested on any charge the wait for trial in prison can take several years. Your foreign passport will not shield you in this situation, indeed you may be dealt with more harshly because of it. Honest officials may wish to make an example of you, while corrupt ones will try to squeeze you or your family for as much money as they can. If you are unconvinced, then visit an Ecuadorean prison to see for yourself. Your embassy or consulate can give you the names of citizens of your country serving sentences who would appreciate a visitor.

Some people come to Ecuador specifically to consume or buy drugs, and the gringo drug scene shifts from place to place every couple of years. Quito nightlife is always prone to drug problems and Montañita, on the Pacific coast, is currently a hot spot. The authorities carry out sporadic raids in these places, and nobody is spared. Although drug planting by police is rare in Ecuador, the greatest risk is where drugs

Police

A special tourist police (uniformed and identified by arm-bands) operates in old town Quito, Panecillo, La Mariscal, Mitad del Mundo, Otavalo, Cotopaxi National Park and a few other locations; they may be approached for advice and assistance. Police on bicycles patrol some of Quito's parks. Almost all police officers are helpful and friendly to tourists.

‡ *Emergency police phone numbers: 911 in Quito and Cuenca, 101 elsewhere.*

Unfortunately institutional corruption, including police corruption, is an important problem in Ecuador. Tourists are seldom affected but should be sensitive to the situation. If you are asked for a bribe (the polite euphemism is 'algo para la colita', a little something for a soft drink), then it is best to play innocent; be patient and the official will usually relent. This will also discourage harassment of other gringos. Never offer to bribe a police officer: you don't know the rules, so don't try to play the game.

Con tricks involving real or fake police officers are uncommon in Ecuador. You should nonetheless be wary of 'plainclothes policemen', politely ask to see their identification and if in doubt insist on going to the nearest police station before handing over anything.

Getting around

Air

TAME ① *www.tame.com.ec*, is the main internal airline. It offers return flights from Quito to Cuenca, Esmeraldas, Galápagos (Baltra and San Cristóbal, for details see page 422), Guayaquil, Lago Agrio, Loja, Macas, Manta, Tulcán and Cali (Colombia); also from Guayaquil to Cuenca, Loja, Machala and Galápagos.

Smaller local airlines include **Aerogal** ① *www.aerogal.com.ec*, serving Quito, Cuenca, Galápagos and Guayaquil; and **Icaro** ① *T1-800-883567, www.icaro.com.ec*, which flies from Quito to Coca, Cuenca, Esmeraldas, Guayaquil and Manta. A few military fights serve isolated communities in Oriente, but these are generally not open to foreigners. Air taxis and charters can be organized to any airstrip in the country; to the jungle best from Quito or Shell, to the coast best from Guayaquil.

Ecuador is a small country and internal airfares are generally less than US$70 one way for all destinations except Galápagos, although they may rise if there is an increase in fuel prices. Flying times are typically under one hour. Foreigners must pay more than Ecuadoreans for flights to Galápagos and the Oriente. Routes and frequencies change often and up-to-date information may not be available outside Ecuador, so always enquire locally.

Seats are not assigned on internal flights, including to the Galápagos. Passengers may have to disembark at intermediate stops and check in again, even though they have booked all the way to the final destination of the plane. Airline offices are given under each relevant town or city.

Road

The road network is extensive and getting around by public transport is easy. The Panamericana runs down the length of the Andes connecting all the major towns and cities. A curiosity is that almost any large paved road may be referred to by locals as 'La Pana'. The state of Ecuador's roads is constantly changing due to the cyclical forces of nature and the lack of ongoing maintenance. Rainy seasons in general, and the *El Niño* climatic phenomenon in particular, can cause heavy damage in both the highlands and coast. When the roads reach an intolerable state, a reconstruction campaign is focused on the most heavily affected areas, but usually only the surface is repaired. These roads are then excellent for a while, until the cycle of deterioration begins all over again. At the close of this edition (early 2005) many coastal roads were excellent while those in the highlands were generally good. Some of the most important roads have been given in concession to private firms, who are responsible for their maintenance and collect tolls.

❧ Throughout Ecuador, intercity travel by car or bus is safest during the daytime.

Several important roads, mostly paved, link the highlands and the Pacific coast. These include from north to south: Ibarra to San Lorenzo, Quito to Esmeraldas via Calacalí and La Independencia, Quito to Guayaquil via Alóag and Santo Domingo de los Colorados (the busiest highway in Ecuador), Latacunga to Quevedo via La Maná (beautiful and partly paved), Ambato to Babahoyo via Guaranda, Riobamba to Guayaquil via Pallatanga and Bucay, Cuenca to Guayaquil via Zhud and La Troncal, Cuenca to Guayaquil via Molleturo, Cuenca to Machala via Girón and Pasaje, and Loja to Machala or Huaquillas.

Santo Domingo de los Colorados is the hub of most roads on the coast of Ecuador. From Guayaquil, the coastal route south to Peru is a major artery. From Guayaquil north, there are coastal roads all the way to Mataje on the Colombian border.

On the eastern side of the Andes, the roads in Oriente are mostly unpaved and may be impassable due to landslides during the rainy season. The **Carretera Perimetral de la Selva** (jungle perimeter road, a seldom-used term) runs from Lago Agrio in the north to Zamora in the south, via Baeza, Tena, Puyo and Macas. Sporadic improvements and paving took place since 2004, but many sections remain in very poor condition. Roads connect Coca to both Lago Agrio and Baeza. There are road links from the highlands to the jungle by the following routes, also from north to south: Quito to Baeza via Papallacta (upper half is paved), Ambato to Puyo via Baños (fully paved), Cuenca to Oriente via three different routes (all unpaved and rough but beautiful), and Loja to Zamora (fully paved). Those driving in the Oriente should be reasonably self sufficient. In the province of Sucumbíos you should also pay special attention to safety.

Bus

Buses in Ecuador are cheap, frequent and go everywhere, making them an ideal way to get around. The current rule of thumb for prices is approximately US$1 per hour. The bus timetable on page 52 shows travelling times and prices for most major

Essentials Getting around

❗ Bus travel tips

Bus travel in Ecuador can be lots of fun and a great way to get to know the country and its people. A few simple precautions will help ensure a safe trip. As with public safety in general, don't be scared - just careful.

Travel only by daylight. The risks are highest after dark, both for traffic accidents and for hold-ups. While the incidence of the latter is relatively low when you consider the number of buses on the road, highway banditry is a serious problem in Ecuador and its consequences can be severe. Buses are usually held up by heavily armed gangs, never resist or hold back your valuables. Shootings and rapes have occurred during hold-ups and foreign women may be at higher risk. Under the circumstances, travelling overnight in to save on accommodation is a poor strategy, besides you miss the views and arrive too tired to enjoy the next day's touring.

Some of the better bus lines take precautions against hold-ups like not stopping to pick up passengers between towns. Police checkpoints are also set up along major roads in an attempt to deter bandits. You will be asked for ID at such checkpoints so have your passport at hand, you and your belongings may also be searched.

Politely refuse any food, drink, sweets or cigarettes offered by strangers on a bus. These may be drugged as a way of robbing you. Two tourists travelling together in adjacent seats are at less risk.

Always carry money and valuable documents in your money belt with you on the bus, but also have some spare cash at hand. Keep a separate stash of cash and travellers' cheques in with your luggage. Never use the overhead rack for your belongings. If you want to hold your seat at a stop, leave a newspaper or other insignificant item on it, not your bag.

Luggage can be checked-in with the larger bus companies and will be stowed in a locked compartment. On smaller buses it usually rides on the roof, in which case you should make sure it is covered with a tarpaulin to protect against dust and rain. In all cases it is your own responsibility to keep an eye on your gear, never leave it unattended at bus stations. Many travellers place their luggage in a *costal* (potato or flour sack) for bus rides, this helps keep it clean and makes it a bit less conspicuous.

Only the most modern buses have toilets on board; neither these nor the sanitary facilities at rest stops are likely to be spotlessly clean. Avoid the very back of the bus if you can, as you will be right next to the toilet and the ride can be particularly dusty and bumpy. Take warm clothing when travelling in the highlands.

It is possible to buy food and drinks on the roadside, but keep an eye out for hygiene and make sure you have small change on hand. Bus drivers usually know the best places for meal stops and some roadside *comedores* can be quite good. On a longer journey, take snacks and a small bottle of mineral water just in case.

destinations. Frequencies range from every 15 minutes to several a day. Details of local services are given in the transport section of each city or town. Some companies have comfortable air conditioned units for use on their longer routes. Fares for these are higher and some companies have set up their own stations, away from the main bus terminals, exclusively for these better buses. Most buses, though, leave from the central bus terminal (*terminal terrestre*) in each town. These buses are sometimes crowded and tall people may find the lack of leg room uncomfortable. For more information see box, page 51.

Bus timetable

Figures in red italic indicate direct services; all others require connections, usually in Quito, Guayaquil, Cuenca, Santo Domingo or Ambato. Times are for travelling only, excluding meal stops and connections.

	Ambato	Bahia	Baños	Coca	Cuenca	Esmeraldas	Guaranda	Guayaquil	Huaquillas	Ibarra	Lago Agrio
Ambato	–	9 hrs $8	1 hr $0.80	12 hrs $12	7 hrs $7	8 hrs $8	2 hrs $2	6 hrs $6	11 hrs $12.50	5 hrs $5	14 hrs $10
Bahia	9 hrs $8	–	9 hrs $10.50	16 hrs $17	9½ hrs $13	8 hrs $8	10 hrs $9	6 hrs $5	11 hrs $11.50	11 hrs $9.50	19 hrs $14.50
Baños	1 hr $0.80	9 hrs $10.50	–	11 hrs $11	8 hrs $8	7 hrs $9	3 hrs $2.75	7 hrs $6.50	11 hrs $13.50	6 hrs $6	15 hrs $11
Coca	12 hrs $12	16 hrs $17	11 hrs $11	–	18 hrs $21	14 hrs $17	13 hrs $14	16 hrs $18	20 hrs $20	11 hrs $12.50	2 hrs $3
Cuenca	7 hrs $7	9½ hrs $13	8 hrs $8	18 hrs $21	–	12 hrs $12	7½ hrs $8	3½ hrs $8	6 hrs $6	12 hrs $13.50	21 hrs $18.50
Esmeraldas	8 hrs $8	8 hrs $8	7 hrs $9	14 hrs $17	12 hrs $12	–	10 hrs $10	8 hrs $8.50	15 hrs $17	8½ hrs $9.50	17 hrs $14.50
Guaranda	2 hrs $2	10 hrs $9	3 hrs $2.75	13 hrs $14	7½ hrs $8	10 hrs $10	–	4 hrs $4	9 hrs $9.50	7 hrs $7	16 hrs $12
Guayaquil	6 hrs $6	6 hrs $5	7 hrs $6.50	16 hrs $18	3½ hrs $8	8 hrs $8.50	4 hrs $4	–	5 hrs $5.50	11 hrs $11	19 hrs $16.50
Huaquillas	11 hrs $12.50	11 hrs $11.50	11 hrs $13.50	20 hrs $20	6 hrs $6	15 hrs $17	9 hrs $9.50	5 hrs $5.50	–	15 hrs $12.50	23 hrs $17.50
Ibarra	5 hrs $5	11 hrs $9.50	6 hrs $6	11 hrs $12.50	12 hrs $13.50	8½ hrs $9.50	7 hrs $7	11 hrs $11	15 hrs $12.50	–	14 hrs $10
Lago Agrio	14 hrs $10	19 hrs $14.50	15 hrs $11	2 hrs $3	21 hrs $18.50	17 hrs $14.50	16 hrs $12	19 hrs $16.50	23 hrs $17.50	14 hrs $10	–
Latacunga	1 hr $1	10 hrs $9	2 hrs $2	10 hrs $12	9 hrs $9.50	8 hrs $9	3 hrs $3	6 hrs $6.50	11 hrs $12	4½ hrs $4.25	13 hrs $9.50
Loja	11 hrs $11	14 hrs $14.50	12 hrs $12	22 hrs $23	4½ hrs $7.50	13 hrs $19	12 hrs $13	8 hrs $10	6 hrs $5	16 hrs $16	21 hrs $21.50
Macas	6½ hrs $7	17 hrs $17	7 hrs $6	8½ hrs $9	10 hrs $9	15 hrs $9	8½ hrs $9	13 hrs $13	16 hrs $15	12 hrs $12	10 hrs $10.50
Machala	9 hrs $8	9 hrs $10	10 hrs $9	20 hrs $21	4 hrs $4.50	14 hrs $16	7 hrs $9	3 hrs $5	1½ hrs $1.75	13 hrs $12.50	21 hrs $17.50
Manta	9 hrs $10	3 hrs $2.90	10 hrs $13.50	17 hrs $20	10 hrs $12	10 hrs $8	7 hrs $8	3 hrs $4	8 hrs $8.50	11 hrs $12.50	20 hrs $10
Otavalo	4½ hrs $4.50	10 hrs $9	5½ hrs $5.50	10 hrs $12	12 hrs $13	8 hrs $9	7 hrs $6.50	10 hrs $11	14 hrs $12	45 mins $0.50	13 hrs $9.50
Pto López	10 hrs $11	5 hrs $5	11 hrs $13.50	19 hrs $20	7½ hrs $8	12 hrs $17	8 hrs $9	4 hrs $4.80	9 hrs $9.50	14 hrs $12.50	22 hrs $17.50
Puyo	3 hrs $3	14 hrs $12	1½ hrs $2	10 hrs $10	10 hrs $10	11 hrs $11	5 hrs $5	9 hrs $8.50	18 hrs $15	8 hrs $7.50	7½ hrs $8
Quito	2½ hrs $2.50	8 hrs $7	3½ hrs $3.40	8 hrs $10	10 hrs $11	6 hrs $7	5 hrs $4.50	8 hrs $9	12 hrs $10	2½ hrs $2.50	11 hrs $7.50
Riobamba	1 hr $1.25	11 hrs $9.50	2 hrs $2	12 hrs $13.50	6 hrs $6	9 hrs $9.50	2 hrs $2	5 hrs $4.50	10 hrs $12	6 hrs $6.50	15 hrs $11.50
Sto Domingo	4 hrs $3	5 hrs $5	4 hrs $3.75	13 hrs $12	8½ hrs $9	3 hrs $3.50	6 hrs $5	5 hrs $6	7 hrs $6	5½ hrs $5	14 hrs $10
Tena	6 hrs $5	13 hrs $13.50	5 hrs $4.20	6 hrs $7	12 hrs $17.50	11 hrs $13	8 hrs $7	11 hrs $11	17 hrs $16.50	7½ hrs $9	9 hrs $11
Tulcán	7½ hrs $6.50	13 hrs $11	8½ hrs $7.50	13 hrs $14	15 hrs $15	11 hrs $11	10 hrs $8.50	11 hrs $13	18 hrs $18	2½ hrs $2	7 hrs $7

Essentials Getting around

Prices are for regular, not *executivo* or other special services. All prices and times are subject to change.

Latacunga	Loja	Macas	Machala	Manta	Otavalo	Pto López	Puyo	Quito	Riobamba	Sto Domingo	Tena	Tulcán
1 hr $1	11 hrs $11	6½ hrs $7	9 hrs $8	9 hrs $10	4½ hrs $4.50	10 hrs $11	3 hrs $3	2½ hrs $2.50	1 hr $1.25	4 hrs $3	6 hrs $5	7½ hrs $6.50
10 hrs $9	14 hrs $15	17 hrs $17	9 hrs $10	3 hrs $2.90	10 hrs $9	5 hrs $5	14 hrs $12	8 hrs $7	11 hrs $9.50	5 hrs $5	13 hrs $13.50	13 hrs $11
2 hrs $2	12 hrs $12	7 hrs $6	10 hrs $9	10 hrs $13.50	5½ hrs $5.50	11 hrs $13.50	1½ hrs $2	3½ hrs $3.40	2 hrs $2	4 hrs $3.75	5 hrs $4.20	8½ hrs $7.50
10 hrs $12	22 hrs $23	8½ hrs $9	20 hrs $21	17 hrs $20	10 hrs $12	19 hrs $20	10 hrs $10	8 hrs $10	12 hrs $13.50	13 hrs $12	6 hrs $7	13 hrs $14
9 hrs $9.50	4½ hrs $7.50	10 hrs $9	4 hrs $4.50	10 hrs $12	12 hrs $13	7½ hrs $8	10 hrs $10	10 hrs $11	6 hrs $6	8½ hrs $9	12 hrs $17.50	15 hrs $15
8 hrs $9	13 hrs $19	15 hrs $15	14 hrs $16	10 hrs $8	8 hrs $9	12 hrs $17	11 hrs $11	6 hrs $7	9 hrs $9.50	3 hrs $3.50	11 hrs $13	11 hrs $11
3 hrs $3	12 hrs $13	8½ hrs $9	7 hrs $9	7 hrs $8	7 hrs $6.50	8 hrs $9	5 hrs $5	5 hrs $4.50	2 hrs $2	6 hrs $5	8 hrs $7	10 hrs $8.50
6 hrs $6.50	8 hrs $10	13 hrs $13	3 hrs $5	3 hrs $4	10 hrs $11	4 hrs $4.80	9 hrs $8.50	8 hrs $9	5 hrs $4.50	5 hrs $6	11 hrs $11	11 hrs $13
11 hrs $12	6 hrs $5	16 hrs $15	1½ hrs $1.75	8 hrs $8.50	14 hrs $12	9 hrs $9.50	18 hrs $15	12 hrs $10	10 hrs $12	7 hrs $6	17 hrs $16.50	18 hrs $18
4½ hrs $4.25	16 hrs $16	12 hrs $12	13 hrs $12.50	11 hrs $12.50	45 min $0.50	14 hrs $12.50	8 hrs $7.50	2½ hrs $2.50	6 hrs $6.50	5½ hrs $5	7½ hrs $9	2½ hrs $2
13 hrs $9.50	22 hrs $21.50	10 hrs $10.50	21 hrs $17.50	20 hrs $17.50	13 hrs $9.50	22 hrs $17.50	7½ hrs $8	11 hrs $7.50	15 hrs $11.50	14 hrs $10	9 hrs $11	7 hrs $7
–	12 hrs $12	7½ hrs $8	9 hrs $9	9 hrs $12	4 hrs $3.75	10 hrs $12	4 hrs $4	2 hrs $1.75	2 hrs $2.25	5 hrs $4	7 hrs $6	7 hrs $6
12 hrs $12	–	15 hrs $16.50	6 hrs $6	11 hrs $14	16 hrs $16	12 hrs $15	14 hrs $14	14 hrs $14	10 hrs $12	10 hrs $13	16 hrs $16	19 hrs $18
7½ hrs $8	15 hrs $16.50	–	14 hrs $13.50	18 hrs $20	11 hrs $12	20 hrs $20	4½ hrs $5	9 hrs $10	7½ hrs $8.50	11 hrs $10	4½ hrs $4.75	14 hrs $14
9 hrs $9	6 hrs $6	14 hrs $13.50	–	6 hrs $9	12 hrs $12	7 hrs $10	16 hrs $11	10 hrs $10	8 hrs $9.50	6 hrs $5.50	15 hrs $13	14 hrs $14
9 hrs $12	11 hrs $14	18 hrs $20	6 hrs $9	–	11 hrs $12	2 hrs $2.75	15 hrs $15	8½ hrs $10	8 hrs $8.50	6 hrs $5.50	14 hrs $16.50	14 hrs $14
4 hrs $3.75	16 hrs $16	11 hrs $12	12 hrs $12	11 hrs $12	–	13 hrs $12	8 hrs $7	2 hrs $2	6 hrs $6	5 hrs $4.50	7 hrs $8.50	3 hrs $3
10 hrs $12	12 hrs $15	20 hrs $20	7 hrs $10	2 hrs $2.75	13 hrs $12	–	17 hrs $15	11 hrs $10	9 hrs $9.50	9 hrs $12.50	16 hrs $16.50	15 hrs $14
4 hrs $4	14 hrs $14	4½ hrs $5	16 hrs $11	15 hrs $15	8 hrs $7	17 hrs $15	–	6 hrs $5	4 hrs $3.75	7 hrs $6	3 hrs $2.50	11 hrs $9
2 hrs $1.75	14 hrs $14	9 hrs $10	10 hrs $10	8½ hrs $10	2 hrs $2	11 hrs $10	6 hrs $5	–	4 hrs $3.75	3 hrs $2.50	5 hrs $6.25	5 hrs $4
2 hrs $2.25	10 hrs $12	7½ hrs $8.50	8 hrs $9.50	8 hrs $8.50	6 hrs $6	9 hrs $9.50	4 hrs $3.75	4 hrs $3.75	–	5 hrs $4.25	6 hrs $7	9 hrs $8
5 hrs $4	10 hrs $13	11 hrs $10	6 hrs $5.50	6 hrs $5.50	6 hrs $4.50	9 hrs $12.50	7 hrs $6	3 hrs $2.50	5 hrs $4.25	–	8 hrs $8	8 hrs $6.50
7 hrs $6	16 hrs $16	4½ hrs $4.75	15 hrs $13	14 hrs $16.50	7 hrs $8.50	16 hrs $16.50	3 hrs $2.50	5 hrs $6.25	6 hrs $7	8 hrs $8	–	10 hrs $10.50
7 hrs $6	19 hrs $18	14 hrs $14	14 hrs $14	14 hrs $14	3 hrs $3	15 hrs $14	11 hrs $9	5 hrs $4	9 hrs $8	8 hrs $6.5	10 hrs $10.50	–

Driving in Ecuador has been described as 'an experience', partly because of unexpected potholes and other obstructions and the lack of road signs, partly because of local drivers' tendency to use the middle of the road. Beware the bus drivers, who often drive very fast and rather recklessly (passengers also please note).

There are only two grades of gasoline sold in Ecuador, 'Extra' (82 octane, currently US$1.48 per US gallon) and 'Super' (92 Octane, currently US$1.98 per US gallon). Both are unleaded. Extra is available everywhere, while super may not be available in more remote areas. Diesel fuel (currently US$1.03 per US gallon) is notoriously dirty and available everywhere.

The road maps published by **Ediguías** are the most useful, see maps, page 58.

To rent, buy or bring? The big choice for would-be foreign motorists, is whether to rent a vehicle, buy one in Ecuador, or bring their own from home. Each option has its own advantages and drawbacks. Rentals are of course the most convenient for short term visitors, but they are quite expensive and the insurance deductibles are sky-high. If you will stay for a few months or longer, it can make sense to purchase a local car and sell it before you leave. Vehicles are relatively expensive in Ecuador but there are many used ones on the market and they tend to maintain their value. There will be paperwork involved with transfer of ownership, registration, insurance, etc, but this is not an insurmountable obstacle. Bringing your own vehicle from home makes sense if you are travelling through Ecuador as part of a longer journey, and offers the advantage of driving something you know and trust. It is not a good idea, however, to bring a car from abroad if you wish to stay only in Ecuador for an extended period, as the import procedures are prohibitively complex, time-consuming and expensive.

Security Try never to leave the car unattended except in a locked garage or guarded parking space. Remove all belongings and leave the empty glove compartment open when the car is unattended. Also lock the clutch or accelerator to the steering wheel with a heavy, obvious chain or lock. Street children will generally protect your car in exchange for a tip. Be sure to note down key numbers and carry spares of the most important ones (but don't keep all spares inside the vehicle).

Documents There are police checks on many roads in Ecuador and you will be detained if you are unable to present your documents. Always carry your passport and driving licence. An international drivers licence is not, strictly speaking, required in Ecuador but it may nonetheless be helpful. You also need the registration document (title) in the name of the driver, or, in the case of a car registered in someone else's name, a notarized letter of authorization. The original invoice from when the car was purchased may also be required in order to ascertain its value. All documents must be originals accompanied by a Spanish translation, preferably certified by an Ecuadorean embassy or consulate.

The rules for bringing a foreign car into Ecuador are complex, change frequently and are inconsistently applied. Customs officials at points of entry seem to have absolute discretionary powers. It is therefore a game of chance: you could breeze through on a smile and a nod, or spend weeks and hundreds of dollars pursuing fruitless paperwork. Our most recent reports suggest the following.

In principle, a carnet de passage en douane is an indispensable requirement for bringing a car into Ecuador and the maximum allowable stay is 30 days. The carnet (sometimes locally called a *tríptico*) is an international customs document – a sort of passport for your car – issued by the automobile club of your home country (AAA, CAA, RAC, AA, etc) or the country where the vehicle is registered. The requirements for obtaining a carnet vary from country to country but usually involve leaving a deposit equal to the value of the vehicle; enquire well before you travel. If you do not have a carnet, then regulations state that you can only cross Ecuador with your car from north to south, or vice versa, in a maximum of three days. You must be accompanied throughout this period by a customs officer and will be required to pay for their meals and accommodation.

In practice, some motorists travelling overland from both Colombia and Peru without a carnet are nonetheless granted entry to Ecuador. In some cases details of the vehicle are stamped into the owners passports. Up to 90 days' stay may be granted and you may be able to leave through different borders than where you entered, but you may also be denied entry without a carnet. At the same time, other travellers have faced long delays and great expense in the port of Guayaquil even with a carnet for their vehicle. The ports of Manta and Esmeraldas are recommended alternatives.

Shipping Prices vary but they are seldom cheap. Vehicles are generally shipped in a container, which reduces the risk of theft and damage. Sending a 20-ft container from Guayaquil to Panama, for example, costs US$1,000. There are, in addition, many miscellaneous fees and charges which can easily add up to several hundred dollars. Shipping a vehicle through Guayaquil is hazardous due to theft; you will be charged by customs for every day the car is left there and will need assistance from an agent. Shop around and try to get a personal recommendation, as customs agents' services vary greatly in price and quality, some are listed in the Guayaquil chapter. Spare cash may be needed to expedite paperwork. Manta and Esmeraldas are smaller, more relaxed and efficient alternative ports, but receive fewer ships so you may be faced with a longer wait. If bringing in a motorcycle by air it can take over a week to get it out of customs. You need a customs agent, who can be found around the main customs building near Quito airport; try to fix the price in advance. Best to accompany the agent all the time. For details of required documents, see above.

Car hire

Various international and local car hire companies are clustered around the airports of Quito, Guayaquil and Cuenca. It may be difficult to rent a vehicle in smaller cities, however, where there are usually only a few rental cars available and these are often in use. Even in Quito, rental cars may be scarce during high season (June to September, and December to January); it is best to reserve in advance for these times. The names and addresses of agencies are given in the main text.

In order to rent a car in Ecuador you must be at least 21 years old and have an international credit card. Surcharges may apply to clients between age 21 and 25. You may pay cash, which is sometimes cheaper and may allow you to bargain, but they want a credit card for security. You may be asked to sign two blank credit card vouchers, one for the rental fee itself and the other as a security deposit, and authorization for a charge of as much as US$3,500 may be requested against your credit card account. These arrangements are all above board and the uncashed vouchers will be returned to you when you return the vehicle. Always make certain that you understand the rental agreement before signing the contract, and be especially careful when dealing with smaller agencies. Also, check the car's condition, not forgetting things like wheel nuts, and make sure it has good ground clearance. Always garage the car securely at night.

Rates vary depending on the rental company and vehicle, but a small car suitable for city driving hired from a reputable agency currently costs about US$350 per week including unlimited mileage, all taxes and insurance. A four-wheel-drive can be double.

Car hire insurance Some car hire firms do not have adequate insurance policies and you will have to pay heavily in the event of an accident. Check exactly what the hirer's insurance policy covers. Most policies include a deductible, which you will have to cover out-of-pocket. This deductible also varies with the agency and vehicle, up to to US$3,500 or more. Beware of being billed for scratches which were on the vehicle before you hired it.

Defensive driving

Defensive driving is especially important in Ecuador. It is best to try and settle minor fender-benders amicably without notifying the police. In case of a serious accident it is common for both the drivers and vehicles to be detained. The ensuing judicial process can be long and complicated and, as a foreigner, you will be at a considerable disadvantage. For this reason, and because you are on unfamiliar turf, you should drive defensively at all times. Always be on the lookout for pedestrians, especially near elevated crosswalks which are seldom used. The recklessness of the locals should make you more, not less, careful. If you do not feel comfortable driving in Ecuador but would like the independence of your own vehicle, cars with drivers can be hired from many tour agencies.

Cycling

Given ample time and reasonable energy, the bicycle is one of the best modes of transport for exploring Ecuador with. It can be ridden, carried by almost every form of transport from an aeroplane to a jungle canoe, and can even be lifted across one's shoulders over short distances. Cyclists can be the envy of travellers using more orthodox transport, since they can travel at their own pace, explore more remote regions and meet people who are not normally in contact with tourists.

Tips Strong and waterproof front and back panniers are a must. When packed these are likely to be heavy and should be carried on the strongest racks available. Poor quality racks have ruined many a journey for they take incredible strain on unpaved roads. Everything should be packed in plastic bags to give extra protection against dust and rain.

Wind, not hills, is the enemy of the cyclist. Try to make the best use of the times of day when there is little; mornings tend to be best but there is no steadfast rule. The air in Ecuador's highlands can be very dry. Take care to avoid dehydration, by drinking regularly. In hot, dry areas with limited supplies of water, be sure to carry an ample supply. For food, carry a few staples (sugar, salt, dried milk, porridge oats, raisins, dried soups etc) and supplement these with local foods, of which there is no shortage.

Security Thieves are attracted to towns and cities, so when sight-seeing, try to leave your bicycle with someone such as a café owner or shopkeeper. Country people tend to be more honest and are usually friendly and very inquisitive. However, don't take unnecessary risks; always see that your bicycle is secure (most hotels will allow bikes to be kept in rooms).

Dogs can be vicious. If you see them approaching, then you should stop, dismount, and walk a few paces with the bike between you and the dogs. Once you are merely another pedestrian, they will usually relent. Otherwise, bend over to pick up a few stones, or just pretend if there are no stones nearby. Most dogs simply make a lot of noise without attacking. If you are bitten, however, then you must see a doctor because rabies is present in Ecuador.

Traffic on main roads can be a nightmare; it is usually far more rewarding to keep to the smaller roads or to paths if they exist. When riding in big cities like Quito, Ecuadorean cyclists recommend behaving like a car and occupying the entire lane; this is safer and drivers usually respect you. Use hand signals to indicate when turning or switching lanes. Most cyclists agree that the main danger comes from other traffic. A rearview mirror has been frequently recommended to forewarn you of vehicles which are too close behind. You also need to watch out for oncoming, overtaking vehicles, unstable loads on trucks, protruding loads etc. Make yourself conspicuous by wearing bright clothing and a helmet.

Repairs Most towns have a bicycle shop of some description, but it is best to do your own repairs and adjustments whenever possible. Big city bike shops may also have boxes/cartons in which to send bicycles home.

The **Expedition Advisory Centre**, administered by the **Royal Geographical Society** ① *1 Kensington Gore, London SW7 2AR, T020-7591 3030, www.rgs.org/eac*, has a useful monograph entitled *Bicycle Expeditions*, by Paul Vickers, which can be downloaded free from their website. In the UK there is also the **Cyclist's Touring Club (CTC)** ① *Cotterell House, 69 Meadrow, Godalming, Surrey GU7 3HS, T01483-417217, www.ctc.org.uk*, for touring and technical information. In addition to the **Ediguías** road maps recommended for cars (see page 58), a series of very practical *hojas de ruta* are available from the **IGM** in Quito. They include detailed road maps and elevation profiles for routes between the major towns.

Hitchhiking

Public transport in Ecuador is so abundant that there is no need to hitchhike along the major highways. On small out-of-the-way country roads, however, giving passers-by a ride is common practice and safe for drivers and passengers alike, especially in the back of a pick-up or larger truck. A small fee is usually charged, best ask in advance. In truly remote areas there may not be enough traffic to make hitching worthwhile.

For obvious reasons, a lone female should not hitch by herself. Besides, you are more likely to get a lift if you are with a partner, be they male or female. The best combination is a male and female together.

Motorcycling

People are generally very amicable to motorcyclists and you can make many friends by returning friendship to those who show an interest in you. Simple motorcycles are a common means of transport, often carrying an entire family, while fancy dirt bikes have become popular in recent years with some wealthy young Ecuadoreans.

Clothes and equipment A tough waterproof jacket, comfortable strong boots, gloves and a helmet with which you can use glass goggles which will not scratch and wear out like a plastic visor. The best quality tent and camping gear that you can afford and a petrol stove which runs on bike fuel is helpful. Also see Camping, page 60.

Security Never leave a fully laden bike on its own. An Abus D or chain will keep the bike safe. Never leave the bike outside a hotel at night. Most hotels allow you to bring the bike inside.

Dogs They are ubiquitous in Ecuadorean towns and the countryside, they love to chase bikes, and they have been known to bite riders. See precautions for cyclists.

Documents Passport, driving licence and registration (title) documents are all necessary. The rules for bringing a motorcycle into Ecuador are, in principle, the same as those for a car (see above) but may sometimes be applied more leniently.

Repairs Get the book for international dealer coverage from your manufacturer, but don't rely on it. They frequently have few or no parts for modern, large machinery, but Ecuadorean mechanics are skilled at making do.

Taxis

Taxis are a convenient, safe and cheap option for tourists in the cities and towns. In Quito, all taxis must use meters by law; for details of taxi services in the capital see page 139. Meters are not used in other cities, where a flat rate is charged within the town centre, generally US$1 at the present time (US$2 in Guayaquil). Ask around to get the going rate. All legally registered taxis have the number of their cooperative and the individual operator's number prominently painted on the the vehicle. Note these and the licence plate number if you feel you have been seriously overcharged or mistreated. You may then complain to the transit police or tourist office, but be reasonable as the amounts involved are usually small and most taxi drivers are honest and helpful.

Rail

Sadly, the spectacular Ecuadorean railway system has all but ceased operations. In 2005 only tourist rides were being offered, the most popular one goes over the Devil's Nose from Riobamba to Sibambe and back. From Quito, the only service is a weekend excursion to the El Boliche station near Cotopaxi National Park. Trains also run 45 km out of Ibarra to Tulquizán and back.

Maps and city guides

The **Instituto Geográfico Militar** in Quito (see page 100) produces a series of good topographic maps covering most of the country at the following scales: 1:250,000, 1:100,000, 1:50,000 and 1:25,000; US$2 per sheet. The latter two scales are most useful for climbing and trekking. Maps of the seacoast and border areas are classified (*reservado*) and cannot be purchased without a military permit, but this is usually easy to obtain. For further details see Maps in the Quito chapter, page 100. A recommended series of road maps and city guides by Nelson Gómez, published by **Ediguías** in Quito, includes handy pocket maps/guides of Quito, Guayaquil, Cuenca, Otavalo and Galápagos (the latter two in English). These are available in bookshops throughout the country, but most reliably in the capital.

Sleeping

There are over 1200 hotels in Ecuador, with something to suit every taste and budget. The greatest selection and most upscale establishments are found in the largest cities and more popular resorts. In less-visited places the choice of better-class hotels may be limited, but friendly and functional family-run lodgings can be had almost everywhere.

There is no regulated terminology for categories of accommodation in Ecuador, but you should be aware of the generally accepted meanings for the following. *Hotel* is the generic term, much as it is in English. *Hospedaje* means accommodation, of any kind. *Pensión* and *residencial* usually refer to more modest and economical establishments. An *hostal* or *posada* (inn) may be an elegant expensive place, while *hosterías* or *haciendas* usually offer upmarket rural lodgings. A *motel* is not a 'motor hotel' as it is in North America, rather it is a place where couples go for a few hours of privacy. At New Year, Easter and Carnival accommodation can sometimes be hard to find and prices are likely to rise. It is advisable to book in advance at these times and during school holidays and local festivals.

Hotel owners may try to let their less attractive rooms first, but they are not insulted if you ask for a bigger room, better beds or a quieter area. In cities, remember that rooms away from the street will usually be less noisy. The difference is often marked. Likewise, if you feel a place is overpriced then do not hesitate to bargain politely. Always take a look at the rooms and facilities before you check in, there are usually several nearby hotels to choose from and a few minutes spent selecting among them can make the difference between a pleasant stay and miserable one.

In cheaper places, do not merely ask about hot water (or any water for that matter); open the tap and see for yourself. Tall travellers (above 180 cm) should note that many cheaper hotels, especially in the highlands, are built with the modest stature of local residents in mind. Make sure you fit in the bed and remember to duck for doorways.

Air conditioning is only of interest in the lowlands of the coast and Oriente. If you want an air-conditioned room expect to pay around 30% extra, otherwise look for a

Hotel prices and facilities

Prices are for two people sharing a double room, including taxes and service charges.

LL (US$150 and over) and **L** (US$100-149) These hotels are usually only found in Quito, Guayaquil, Cuenca and the main tourist centres. They should offer pool, gym or spa, all business facilities, meeting rooms, banquet halls, several elegant restaurants, bars and often a small casino. Most will provide a safe deposit box in each room. Another option in this price range – sometimes cheaper – is a hacienda (country estate), a number of which have opened their doors to tourists. For details see page 74.

AL (US$66-99), **A** (US$46-65) and **B** (US$31-45) The better value hotels in these categories provide a good deal more than standard facilities and comfort. Most will include breakfast and many offer 'extras' such as cable TV, minibar, and tea and coffee making facilities. They may also provide their own airport transfers. Service is generally very good and most accept credit cards.

C (US$21-30) Hotels in this category range from very good to functional. You can expect your own bathroom, plenty of hot water, a towel, soap and toilet paper, TV, communal sitting area and a reasonably sized, comfortable room.

D (US$12-20, the most common category at present) and **E** (US$7-11) In this category, expect cleanliness, sometimes a private bathroom, hot water in the highlands, maybe a small TV, a fan in tropical areas, but no other frills.

F (US$4-6) and **G** (US$3 and under, an endangered species) A room in these price ranges usually consists of little more than a bed and four walls, with little room. The bathroom is shared and soap, towels, toilet paper or a toilet seat are seldom supplied. In colder regions they may not have enough blankets, so take your own or a sleeping bag. In the lowlands insects are common in cheap hotels, use the mosquito net (or bring your own), and ignore the cockroaches – they are harmless.

Essentials Sleeping

place with a good fan or sea breeze, and mosquito net. Conversely, hot water is only necessary in the highlands, where almost all places have it. A cool shower feels refreshing in the steamy climate of the coast and jungle, where only expensive tourist lodgings would think of heating water. The electric showers frequently used in cheaper hotels should be treated with respect. If you do not know how to use them, then ask someone to show you, and always wear rubber sandals or thongs.

Most better hotels have their own restaurants serving all meals. Few budget places have this facility, though some may serve a simple breakfast. Better hotels will often have their own secure parking but even more modest ones can usually recommend a nearby safe public car park. Most places have sufficient room to safely park a bicycle or motorcycle.

Some hotels charge per person or per bed, while others have a set rate per room regardless of the number of occupants. If travelling alone, it is usually cheaper to share with others in a room with three or four beds.

Due to increasingly strict tax enforcement even some cheaper hotels now charge 12% *IVA* (VAT or sales tax), but enquire beforehand if this is included in their price. At the higher end of the scale 22% (12% tax + 10% service) is usually added to the bill.

The cheapest (and often nastiest) hotels can be found around markets and bus stations. If you're just passing through and need a bed for the night, they may be OK. In small towns, better accommodation may be found around the main plaza.

When booking a hotel from an airport or bus station by phone, always talk to the hotel yourself; do not let anyone do it for you. You may be told the hotel of your choice is full and be directed to one which pays a higher commission. Likewise, make sure that taxi drivers take you to the hotel you want, rather the one they think is best.

Many cheap hotels (as well as simple restaurants and bars) have inadequate water supplies. Almost without exception used toilet paper should not be flushed, but placed in the receptacle provided. This is also the case in most Ecuadorean homes and may apply even in quite expensive hotels; when in doubt ask. Tampons and sanitary napkins should likewise be disposed of in the rubbish bin. Failing to observe this custom will block the drain, a considerable health risk.

Camping

Camping in protected natural areas can be one of the most satisfying experiences during a visit to Ecuador – see Trekking, page 81, for details. Organized campsites, car or trailer camping on the other hand are virtually unheard of. Because of the abundance of cheap hotels you should never have to camp in Ecuador, except for cyclists who may be stuck between towns. In this case the best strategy is to ask permission to camp on someone's private land, preferably within sight of their home for safety. It is not safe to pitch your tent at random near villages and even less so on beaches. Those travelling with their own trailer or campervan can also ask permission to park overnight on private property, in a guarded car park or at a 24-hour petrol station (although this may be noisy). It is unsafe to sleep in your vehicle on the street or roadside.

Homestays

Homestays are a good idea, especially popular with travellers attending Spanish schools in Quito. The schools can make these arrangements as part of your programme. You can live with a local family for weeks or months, which is a good way to practise your Spanish and learn about the local culture. Do not be shy to change families, however, if you feel uncomfortable with the one you have been assigned. Look for people who are genuinely interested in sharing (as you should also be), rather than merely providing room and board. Try a new place for a week or so, before signing up for an extended period.

Eating

Food

Ecuadoreans take their meals pretty seriously, not only for nutrition but also as a social experience. In all but the largest cities, most families still gather around the lunch table at home to eat and discuss the day's events. Sharing food is also a very important part of traditional celebrations and hospitality. A poor family, who generally must get by on a very basic diet, might prepare a feast for a baptism, wedding or high school graduation.

In many Ecuadorean homes, breakfast (*desayuno*) is fresh fruit juice, coffee, bread, margarine, and perhaps a little jam or white cheese. On the coast, a *ceviche* may be enjoyed with a cold drink at mid-morning. Lunch (*almuerzo*) is by far the most important meal of the day. It may begin with a small appetizer, such as an *empañada*, followed by soup – compulsory and often the most filling course. Then comes a large serving of white rice, accompanied by modest quantities of meat, chicken or fish and some cooked vegetables or salad. Dessert, if served at all, might be a small portion of fruit or sweets. Lunch is also accompanied by fruit juice or a soft drink. Supper (*merienda* or *cena*) is either a smaller repetition of lunch or a warm drink with bread, cheese, perhaps cold cuts, *humitas* or *quimbolitos*. A recommended cookbook is *Comidas del Ecuador* by Michelle Fried, available in Quito bookshops.

Typical dishes
The details of the above vary extensively with each region based on custom and traditionally available ingredients. The following are some typical dishes worth trying:

In the highlands *Locro de papas* is a potato and cheese soup. *Mote* (white hominy) is a staple in the region around Cuenca, but used in a variety of dishes throughout the Sierra. *Caldo de patas* is cow heel soup with *mote*. *Llapingachos* (fried potato and cheese patties) and *empanadas de morocho* (a ground corn shell filled with meat) are popular side dishes and snacks. *Morocho*, on the other hand, is a thick drink or porridge made from the same white corn, milk, sugar and cinnamon. *Sancocho de yuca* is a meat and vegetable soup with manioc root. The more adventurous may want to try the delicious roast *cuy* (guinea pig), most typical of highland dishes. Also good is *fritada* (fried pork) and *hornado* (roast pork). Vegetarians can partake of such typically Andean specialities as *chochos* (lupins) and *quinua* (quinoa, a grain related to millet). *Humitas* are made of tender ground corn steamed in corn leaves, and similar are *quimbolitos*, which are prepared with white corn flour and steamed in achira leaves. *Humitas* and *quimbolitos* come in both sweet and savoury varieties.

On the coast Seafood is excellent and popular everywhere. *Ceviche* is marinated fish or seafood which is usually served with popcorn, *tostado* (roasted maize) or *chifles* (plantain chips). Only *ceviche de pescado* (fish) and *ceviche de concha* (clams), which are marinated raw, potentially pose a health hazard. The other varieties of *ceviche* such as *camarón* (shrimp/prawn), and *langostino* (jumbo shrimp/king prawn) all of which are cooked before being marinated, are generally safe delicacies, though you should always check the cleanliness of the establishment. *Langosta* (lobster) is an increasingly endangered species but continues to be illegally fished; so please be conscientious. Other coastal dishes include *empanadas de verde* which are fried snacks: a ground plantain shell filled with cheese, meat or shrimp. *Sopa de bola de verde* is plantain dumpling soup. *Encocadas* are dishes prepared with coconut milk and fish or seafood, which are very

⁞ Restaurant price categories

All of the following prices are based on a complete meal for one person including a non-alcoholic drink, tax and service (a total of 22% in upmarket places). Very cheap places offer only a 2 or 3 course set meal.

⫙⫙⫙⫙	more than US$12
⫙⫙⫙	US$6-12
⫙⫙	US$3-6
⫙	less that US$3

popular in the province of Esmeraldas. *Cocadas* are sweets made with coconut. *Viche* is fish or seafood soup made with ground peanuts, and the ubiquitous *patacones* are thick fried plantain slices served as a side dish.

In the Oriente Most dishes are prepared with *yuca* (manioc or cassava root) and a wide variety of river fish. *Ayampacos* are spiced meat, chicken or palm hearts wrapped in bijao leaves and roasted over the coals.

Special foods *Fanesca* is a fish soup with beans, many grains, ground peanuts and more, sold during Easter Week throughout the country. *Colada morada* (a thick dark purple fruit drink) and *guaguas de pan* (bread dolls) are made around the time of Finados, the Day of the Dead, at the beginning of November. Special *tamales* and sweet and sticky *pristiños* are Christmas specialities.

Ecuadorean food is not particularly spicy. However, in most homes and restaurants, the meal is accompanied by a small bowl of *ají* (hot pepper sauce) which may vary greatly in potency. Those unfamiliar with this condiment are advised to exercise caution at first. *Colada* is a generic name which can refer to cream soups or sweet beverages. In addition to the prepared foods mentioned above, Ecuador offers a large variety of delicious temperate and tropical fruits, some of which are unique to South America (see box page 63).

Drink

The usual soft drinks, known as *colas*, are widely available. Much better and more interesting is the bewildering array of fresh-made tropical fruit juices, see box. On the downside, this is not coffee paradise. Instant coffee or liquid concentrate is common, so ask for *café pasado* if you want real filtered coffee. Bottled water (*agua mineral*) is available everywhere, with and without gas.

As for alcohol, the main beers include Pilsener, Brahama, Clausen and Club, all of which are reasonable. Some Quito bars have good microbrews and also offer a wide selection of foreign beers. Good quality Argentine and Chilean wines are available in the larger cities and generally cheaper than European or US ones. *Aguardiente* (literally 'fire-water') is potent unmatured rum, also known as *paico* and *trago de caña*, or just *trago*. *Chicha*, a native beverage fermented from special corn in the highlands (*chicha de jora*), and from *yuca* (manioc root) or *chonta* (palm fruit) in Oriente, is not for those with a delicate stomach.

Eating out

The simplest and most common eateries found throughout Ecuador are little family run *comedores* or *salones* serving only set meals: *almuerzos* and *meriendas* of the

⦂ Fruit salad

Treat your palate to some of Ecuador's exquisite and exotic fruits. They are great on their own, as *ensalada de frutas*, or make delicious juices (*jugos*), smoothies (*batidos*) and ice creams (*helados*). Always make sure these are prepared with purified water and pasteurized milk.
Babaco, mountain papaya. Makes great juice.
Chirimoya, custard apple. A very special treat, soft when ripe but check for tiny holes in the skin which usually mean worms inside.
Granadilla, golden passion fruit. Slurp it straight from the shell.
Guanábana, soursop. Makes excellent juice and ice cream.
Guava, ice cream bean. Large pod with sweet white pulp around hard black seeds. Not to be confused with guayaba, below.
Guayaba, guava. Good plain or in syrup, also makes nice jam and juice.
Mango, the season is short: Dec and Jan. Try the little *mangos de chupar*, for sucking rather than slicing.

Maracuyá, yellow passion fruit. Makes a very refreshing juice and ice cream.
Mora, raspberry or blackberry. Not all that exotic but makes an excellent and popular juice and ice cream.
Naranjilla, very popular juice, often cooked with a dash of oatmeal to make it less tart.
Orito, baby banana. Thumb-size banana, thin skinned and very sweet.
Papaya, great plain or as juice.
Piña, pineapple. Great plain or juice.
Taxo, banana passion fruit. Peel open the thin skin and slurp the fruit without chewing the seeds.
Tomate de Arbol, tamarillo or tree tomato. Popular as juice but also good plain or in syrup.
Tuna, prickly pear. Sweet and tasty but never pick them yourself. Tiny blond spines hurt your hands and mouth unless they are carefully removed first.
Zapote or sapote. Fleshy and sweet, get some dental floss for the fibres that get stuck between your teeth.

type described above. These currently cost US$1.50-3 and are easiest to find at midday. As long as the establishment is clean, you are unlikely to go wrong at one of these places, but you are unlikely to discover a hidden gastronomic treasure either. Make sure that juices are prepared with boiled or bottled water. One step up, and available in provincial capitals, are restaurants which serve both set meals (perhaps an *almuerzo ejecutivo* for lunch) and à la carte (at night). They may feature Ecuadorean or international food, more swanky surroundings, and can be very good for around US$3-6. Outside main cities and resorts, the above are seldom supplemented by more than *chifas* (Chinese restaurants, some quite good, others terrible) and Italian or pizza places which can be very nice; both generally in our cheap to mid-range price categories. Vegetarians must be adaptable in small towns, but can count on the good will and ingenuity of local cooks.

In Quito, Guayaquil, Cuenca and the more popular tourist resorts, the sky is the limit for variety, quality, elegance and price of restaurant dining. You can find anything from gourmet French cuisine to sushi or tapas, very upscale Ecuadorean *comida típica*, good vegetarian, plush cafés and neon-on-plastic North American burger chains. 'Fusion' is currently trendy, combining Ecuadorean ingredients with innovative recipes to create dishes like ostrich in mango sauce (not widely available). Splurge if you can, to make the most of dining out in a few the better places, which are still economical by international standards. Another class of restaurant, which has flourished specifically in areas frequented by foreigners, serves undifferentiated tourist fare: a little Mexican, a little vegetarian, a little of everything but nothing in particular. Their cheap to mid-range prices and familiar-looking menus may attract some tourists, but you can usually do better elsewhere. On the periphery of cities are many *paradores*, places where Ecuadorean families go on weekends to enjoy typical dishes or grilled meat. These can provide good quality and value in our mid-range category.

At the lowest end of the price range, every market in Ecuador has a section set aside for prepared foods. You always take a chance eating in a market, but if a place is clean then you might still find a tasty nourishing meal for under US$1.50. Food vendors in the street, however, who have no way to properly wash their hands or utensils, should be avoided. You will not save money by getting sick.

Bakeries, of which there are many, and a few very good ice-cream parlours round out the Ecuadorean eating scene.

Festivals and events

Festivals are an intrinsic part of Ecuadorean life. In pre-Hispanic times they were organized around the solar cycle and agricultural calendar. After the conquest, the church integrated the indigenous festivals with their own feast days and so today's festivals are a mix of Roman Catholicism and indigenous traditions. Every community in every part of the country celebrates their own particular festival in honour of their patron saint and there are many more that are celebrated in common up and down the country, particularly in the Sierra.

Appropriate behaviour

Outsiders are usually welcome at all but the most intimate and spiritual of celebrations and, as a gringo, you might even be a guest of honour. Ecuadoreans can be very sensitive, however, and you should make every effort not to offend (for example by not taking a ceremony seriously or by refusing food, drink or an invitation to dance). At the same time, you should keep in mind that most fiestas are accompanied by heavy drinking and the resulting disinhibition is seldom pleasant. It is best to enjoy the usually solemn beginning of most celebrations as well as the liveliness which follows, but politely depart before things get totally out of control.

Festivals

Feb-Mar Carnaval is held during the week before Lent and ends on Ash Wed. While the Ecuadorean version can't rival that of Brazil for fame or colour, Ecuador has its own carnival speciality: throwing balloons filled with water or, less frequently, bags of flour and any other missile guaranteed to cause a mess. Water pistols are sold on every street corner at this time of year and even the odd bucket gets put to use. It can take visitors aback at first, but if you can keep your composure or – better yet, join in the mayhem – it can all be good fun. For the more sensitive tourist, there is the option of heading to Ambato, 1 hr south of Quito, where water-throwing is banned and flour is replaced by flowers at the city's **Fiesta de las Frutas y las Flores.**

Mar-Apr Semana Santa (Holy Week) is held the week before Easter and begins on **Palm Sunday** (*Domingo de Ramos*). This is celebrated throughout the country, but is especially dramatic in Quito, with a spectacularly solemn procession through the streets on **Good Friday**; also in Riobamba on Tue.

A particularly important part of Holy Week is the tradition of eating *fanesca* with family and friends. *Fanesca* is a soup made with salt fish and many different grains, and a good example of the syncretism of Catholic and earlier beliefs. In this case the Catholic component is the lack of meat, which was not consumed during Lent, while the many grains came from native traditions to celebrate the beginning of the harvest at this time of year. The original native version might have been made with *cuy*.

May-Jun Corpus Cristi is a feast held on Thu after Trinity Sun, usually in mid-Jun. This is a major event in the Central Highlands, especially in the provinces of Cotopaxi and Tungurahua, but also in Chimborazo province and in Saraguro and Loja. In Salasaca (Tungurahua) the festival is celebrated with music, dance and elaborate costumes, while in Pujilí (Cotopaxi) groups of masked *danzantes* make their way through the streets and the valiant climb *palos encebados*, 10 m-high greased poles, in order to obtain prizes including live sheep.

21 Jun Inti Raymi, the solstice, has enjoyed something of a revival in recent years. Ceremonies are held at archaeological sites such as Ingapirca and Cochasquí, as well as in native communities like Otavalo and Cotacachi. Inti Raymi often blends with **San Juan Bautista** on 24 Jun, the main festival of the Otavalo valley. For an entire week, the local men dress up in a variety of costumes and dance constantly, moving from house to house. At one point, they head to the chapel of San Juan and start throwing rocks at each other, so keep your distance. This ritual spilling of blood is apparently a sacrifice to *Pachamama*, or Mother Earth.

29 Jun San Pedro y San Pablo is another major fiesta in Imbabura province. (Saints Peter and Paul). On the night before, bonfires are lit in the streets and young women who want to have children are supposed to jump over the fires. This festival is particularly important in Cotacachi and Cayambe, and is also celebrated in southern Chimborazo, in Alausí and Achupallas.

16 Jul Virgen del Carmen, with the biggest celebrations going on in Cuenca and in Chambo, just outside Riobamba.

24 Sep Mama Negra is a big festival in Latacunga, where a man dressed as 'the black mother', dances through the streets.

2 Nov Día de los Difuntos or **Finados** (Day of the Dead), is an important holiday nationwide. This tradition has been practised since time immemorial. In the Incaic calendar,

Nov was the 8th month and represented *Ayamarca*, or land of the dead. The celebration is another example of religious adaptation in which the ancient beliefs of native cultures are mixed with the rites of the Catholic Church. *Colada morada*, a sweet drink made from various fruits and purple corn is prepared, as are *guaguas de pan* (bread dolls). In a few places, native families may build a special altar in their homes or take their departed relatives' favourite food and drink to the cemetery. Most Ecuadoreans commemorate *Día de los Difuntos* in more prosaic fashion, by placing flowers at the graveside of their deceased relatives.

Dec Navidad (Christmas) is an intimate family celebration, starting with *Misa del Gallo* (midnight mass) followed by a festive meal. *Pases del Niño* (processions of the [Christ] child), take place through the country on various dates around Christmas time. Families who possess a statue of the baby Jesus carry them in procession to the local church, where they are blessed during a special Mass. The most famous *Pase del Niño* is in Cuenca on the morning of 24 Dec. Other notable celebrations take place in Saraguro, in Loja province, in Pujilí and Tanicuchí in Cotopaxi province and throughout the province of Cañar.

31 Dec Año Viejo (New Year's Eve) has a typically Ecuadorean aspect in the life-size effigies or puppets which are constructed and displayed throughout the country on 31 Dec. These puppets, called *años viejos*, usually depict politicians or other prominent local, national or international personalities and important events of the year gone by. Children dressed in black are the old year's widows, and beg for alms: candy or coins. Just before midnight the *años viejo's* will is read, full of satire, and at the stroke of midnight the effigies are doused with gasoline and burned, wiping out the old year and all that it had brought with it. In addition to sawdust, the *años viejos* usually contain a few firecrackers making for an exciting finale; best keep your distance.

Public holidays

The following are national public holidays. Other local holidays are listed under the corresponding cities and towns. **1 January,** New Year's Day; Carnival, **Monday and**

⁞ A market for every day of the week

Monday: Ambato.
Tuesday: Latacunga.
Wednesday: Pujilí.
Thursday: Guamote and Saquisilí.
Friday: Salarón, near Riobamba.

Saturday: Latacunga,
Otavalo, Riobamba, and
Zumbahaua.
Sunday: Cajabamba, near
Riobamba.

Tuesday before Lent; **Easter, Holy Thursday; Good Friday; Holy Saturday; 1 May** Labour Day; **24 May**, Battle of Pichincha, Independence Day; **10 August**, 1st attempt at independence; **2 November** Day of the Dead; **25 December** Christmas Day.

Shopping

Almost everyone who visits Ecuador will end up buying a souvenir of some sort from the vast array of arts and crafts (*artesanías*) on offer. The most colourful places to shop for souvenirs, and pretty much anything else in Ecuador, are the street markets which can be found absolutely everywhere. The country also has its share of shiny, modern shopping centres, especially in Guayaquil and the capital, but remember that the high overheads are reflected in the prices.

Otavalo's massive market is the best-known place for buying wall hangings and sweaters. Another market, at **Saquisilí**, south of Quito, is renowned for shawls, blankets and embroidered garments. Fewer handicrafts can be found on the coast, but this is where you can buy an authentic Panama hat at a fraction of the cost in Europe. The best, called *superfinos*, are reputed to be made in the little town of Montecristi, but the villages around Cuenca claim to produce superior models. **Cuenca** is a good place to buy Panama hats, and other types of hat can be bought throughout the Andes. Ecuador also produces fine silver jewellery, ceramics and brightly painted carvings, usually made from balsa wood. Particularly good buys are the many beautiful items fashioned from *tagua*, or vegetable ivory. By purchasing these you are promoting valuable conservation of the rainforests where the *tagua* palm grows.

All manner of *artesanías* can be bought in **Quito**, either on the street or in any of the shops. There's not actually much difference in the price. The advantage of buying your souvenirs in a shop is that they'll usually package your gifts well enough to prevent damage on the flight home. Craft cooperatives are also a good place to shop, since there is a better chance that a fair share of the price will go to the artisan. For more details of handicrafts and where to find them, see Arts and crafts (page 466). For local markets and shops see Shopping under the relevant town, city or village.

Bargaining

Stall holders in markets expect you to bargain, so don't disappoint them. Many tourists enjoy the satisfaction of beating down the seller's original price and finding a real 'bargain', but don't take it too far. Always remain good natured, even if things are not going your way (remember that you're on vacation and they're working). And don't make a fool of yourself by arguing for hours over a few cents. The item you're bargaining for may have taken weeks to make and you're probably carrying more cash in your wallet than the market seller earns in a month.

Sport and activities

Birdwatching

The lowlands are rich in cotingas, manakins, toucans, antbirds and spectacular birds of prey, while the cloud forests are noted for their abundance of hummingbirds, tanagers, mountain toucans and cock-of-the-rock. As a result of this wonderful avian diversity, a network of birding lodges has sprung up and ecotourism has never been easier.

Here we list the best lodges and roads for birding according to their biological region; both the sites and the regions are more fully described in the main text. For further information about Ecuador's wonderful biodiversity, see Flora and fauna, page 475. Within each region described below, the sites are listed from north to south. See Books, page 481, for further reading.

Western lowlands and lower foothills
Bilsa (400-700 m), a virgin site in Esmeraldas province, contains even the rarest foothill birds (such as Banded Ground-cuckoo and Long-Wattled Umbrellabird), though access can be an ordeal in the wet season. This site has 305 known species.

Tinalandia (700-900 m), near Alluriquín on the Alóag-Santo Domingo road, is a great introduction to the world of tropical birds. There are lots of colourful species (more than 360 have been seen here) and they are easier to observe here than at most other places, but some of the larger species have been lost from this area. The lodge itself is very accessible and comfortable.

Río Palenque (200 m) between Santo Domingo and Quevedo is one of the last islands of western lowland forest. It is a very rich birding area, with 370 species. It has begun to lose some species because of its isolation from other forests.

Parque Nacional Machalilla (0-850 m), on the coast near Puerto López, has lightly disturbed dry forest and cloud forest, with many dry-forest specialities. The higher areas are slightly difficult to access. There are 115 known species here.

Ecuasal ponds (0 m), on the Santa Elena peninsula which hold a variety of seabirds and shorebirds; famous for their Chilean Flamingos and other migratory species.

Cerro Blanco (250-300 m), just outside Guayaquil, is one of the best remaining examples of dry forest. There have been breeding Great Green Macaws on occasion, and even Jaguars have been spotted. It has 190 known species of birds.

Manta Real (300-1,200 m) is a cloud forest transition area on the Guayaquil-Cuenca road, with some very rare birds endemic to southwestern Ecuador and adjacent Peru. There are 120 species known from the area.

Manglares-Churute (50-650 m), just southeast of Guayaquil, contains a dry-to moist forest and a mangrove forest. The bird list includes only 65 species but the area is poorly studied.

The petrified forest of **Puyango** (300-400 m) has live trees as well, and typical dry forest birds. It has 130 known species.

Western Andes
Páramo del Angel (2,500-4,500 m) south of Tulcán is a spectacular grassland dotted with tall tree-like herbs called frailejones; 160 bird species are known from here.

Cerro Golondrinas (2,000-4,000 m) is near the Páramo del Angel, and there are highly recommended guided treks available through both.

● *Ecuador is one of the richest places in the world for birds, and some of the planet's most*
● *beautiful species can be found here.*

Intag Cloud Forest Reserve (1,800-2,800 m), **Junín Community Reserve** (1500-2200 m), **Alto Chocó** and **Siempre Verde** are all cloud forests near the Reserva Ecológica Cotacachi-Cayapas, with a full set of cloud forest birds. Access is via Otavalo.

Los Cedros Reserve (1,000-2,700 m) near the Cotacachi-Cayapas Ecological Reserve has excellent forest over an interesting range of elevations. Populations of many bird species are higher here than in more accessible places.

Yanacocha (3,300-4,000 m) is a surprisingly well-preserved high elevation forest on the west side of the Pichincha volcano. Access is from Quito.

The **Nono-Mindo road** (1,500-3,400 m) is a famous birding route starting from Quito and passes through a wide variety of forest types. It is somewhat disturbed in its higher sections but quite good in its lower half, where there are now several excellent lodges.

Tandayapa Lodge (1,700 m) on the Nono-Mindo road is well done, easily accessible and comfortable. Serious birders seeking rarities will benefit from the knowledgeable guides who can show practically any species they are asked to find. There are 318 species that have been seen here.

Bellavista (1,800-2,300 m) on the Nono-Mindo road is a perfectly situated lodge with colourful easy-to-see birds, and plenty of rarities for hardcore birders.

El Pahuma (1,600-2,600 m) is an easy day trip from Quito (about an hour) on the Calacalí-Esmeraldas road, with lots of birds and even an occasional Spectacled Bear. A visitor centre with lodging is under construction, along with a botanical garden. A preliminary survey found about 130 species of birds here.

Maquipucuna (1,200-2,800 m) just off the Calacalí-Esmeraldas road has extensive good forest, and cabins for guests. There are about 300 species here.

Mindo (1,300-2,400), the most ecotourism-conscious town in Ecuador (see page 153) has many good lodges. Even the road into town (easily reached from Quito in two hours) is excellent for good views of beautiful birds like quetzals and tanagers. More than 400 species occur in the whole area.

The **Chiriboga road** (900-3,200 m) from the south of Quito to near Santo Domingo is good for birds in its middle and lower sections, but it can be very muddy; a four-wheel-drive vehicle is recommended.

Otonga (800-2,300 m) is a private reserve rising into the mountains south of the Aloag-Santo Domingo road. The bird life here is known for not being shy, especially the Dark-backed Wood-Quails.

Chilla, **Guanazán**, **Manú** and **Selva Alegre** (2,800-3,000 m), on the road from Saraguro to the coast, have remnant forests and good birds.

Piñas Forest/Buenaventura (800-1,000 m) 24 km north of the road from Loja to the coast is a Jocotoco Foundation bird reserve, particularly important because there are few remaining tracts in the area. Piñas has over 310 bird species and many rare ones are present.

Guachanamá Ridge (2,000-2,800 m) between Celica and Alamor in extreme southwest Ecuador contains many rare southwestern endemic birds.

Sozoranga-Nueva Fátima road (1,300-2,600 m) near the Peruvian border in Loja has remnants of a wide variety of mid-elevation forests, and has many southwest endemics. There are 190 known species in the area.

Inter-Andean forests and páramos

Guandera (3,100-3,800 m), near the Colombian border, has beautiful temperate forest with Espeletia *páramo* and many rare birds.

Pasochoa (2,700-4,200 m) provides a very easy cloud forest to visit just south of Quito. Not virgin, but lots of birds (about 120 species).

Parque Nacional Cotopaxi (3,700-6,000 m), 1½ hours south of Quito, is a spectacular setting in which to find birds of the high arid *páramo*. There is also a birdy lake and marsh, Limpiopungo. About 90 species are known from the park.

Parque Nacional Cajas (3,000-4,500 m) has extensive *páramo* and high elevation forest, accessible from Cuenca. It has 125 known species, including Condor and the Violet-tailed Metaltail, a hummingbird endemic to this area.

The **Oña-Saraguro-Santiago road** (2,000-2,600 m) between Cuenca and Loja has great roadside birding in high-elevation forest remnants. About 145 species have been seen here.

Eastern Andes

Papallacta (3,000-4,400 m), 1½ hours east of Quito, has a dramatic cold wet landscape of grassland and high elevation forest. Condors are regular here, along with many other highland birds.

Guango (2,700 m) is a new lodge with good birding in temperate forest below Papallacta. 95 high-elevation species have been found here so far.

Baeza (1,900-2,400 m), about two hours east of Quito, has forest remnants near town which can be surprisingly birdy. The road to the antenna above town is especially rich.

San Isidro (2,000 m), half an hour from Baeza just off the Baeza-Tena road, is a comfortable lodge with bird-rich forests all around, and wonderful hospitality. The bird list exceeds 260 species.

SierrAzul (2,200-2,400 m), 12 km beyond San Isidro, protects a slightly higher elevation; good birds and some endangered mammals. About 140 bird species seen.

Guacamayos Ridge (1,700-2,300 m) on the Baeza-Tena road has excellent roadside forest rich in bird life.

San Rafael Falls (1,400 m) on the Baeza-Lago Agrio road is a good place to see Cocks-of-the-Rock and other subtropical birds. Access is an easy walk once you reach the site. Over 200 bird species have been found there, and the true total is higher.

The **Loreto road** (300-1,400 m) connecting the Baeza-Tena road to Coca makes a fabulous subtropical transect with many very rare birds. More than 300 species have been found there.

The **Baños** area (1,500-5,000 m) has good forests at a wide range of elevations, though much of it can only be reached after serious hiking.

The **Gualaceo-Limón road** (1,400-3,350 m) northeast of Cuenca has perhaps the best roadside birding on the east slope, in a spectacular natural setting. It is not well studied, but already the bird list exceeds 200 species. A complete list will probably exceed 300 species.

Parque Nacional Podocarpus (950-3,700 m) near Loja is one of the most diverse protected areas in the world. There are several easy access points at different elevations. The park is very rich in birds, including many rarities and some newly discovered species; there could be up to 800 species in the park!

The **Loja-Zamora road** (1,000-2,850 m): some segments of the old road (parallel to the current one) are very good for birds. A total of 375 species have been found along the new and old roads.

Tapichalaca Reserve (1800-3100 m) south of Loja between Yangana and Valladolid protects the cloud forest home of the newly discovered Jocotoco Antpitta. A fine lodge has been built here by the Jocotoco Foundation.

Oriente jungle

Cuyabeno lodges (200-300 m) in the northern Oriente are located in seasonally flooded forests not found elsewhere, and lots of wildlife. These lodges have well over 400 species of birds.

Rio Napo area lodges (200-300 m) in the north and central Oriente provide a wide spectrum of facilities and prices, in forest ranging from moderately disturbed to absolutely pristine. Some of these lodges are among the most bird-rich single-elevation sites in the world, with lists exceeding 550 species.

Archidona/Tena/Misahuallí area lodges (300-600 m) in west-central Oriente are much easier and cheaper to reach than other sites, and the lodges are especially comfortable. The forest in this area is somewhat disturbed, however, so larger birds and mammals are scarce or absent. Gareno Lodge, farther from Tena but still accessible by vehicle, has virgin forest and a full set of wildlife including occasional nesting Harpy Eagles.

Pastaza area lodges (200-300 m) in the southern Oriente have a slightly different set of birds than the other areas, and a different cultural environment.

Galápagos

Only the inhabited islands may be visited without taking an organized and guided tour. To visit the uninhabited ones independently, you have to obtain scientific permission, which is difficult. Many, if not most, Galápagos tours are now sold on-line. English or multilingual sites specializing in tours to the Islands include www.galapagosislands.com and www.galapagosdiscover.com   There are a great many others, see also the Galápagos chapter, page 18.

Guided tours

There is great pleasure in coming to grips with tropical birds on your own, but a good professional bird guide can show you many more species than you will find by yourself. The quality of guides varies greatly; if you choose to take a guided tour, make sure you get a guide who knows bird calls well, since this is the way most tropical birds are found. There are excellent professional bird tour companies in Europe and the US; in addition, there are some Ecuadorean companies which specialize in bird tours. Price is usually a good indicator of quality.

Birdwatching and wildlife tours

Quito
Andean Birding, contact Jonas Nielson, T02-2244426, www.andeanbirding.com
BirdEcuador, contact Irene Bustamante, Carrion N21-01 entre L Mera y Reina Victoria, T02-2547403, F2228902, birdecua@hoy.net
Neblina Forest, contact Mercedes Rivadeneira, Centro Comercial La Galeria, local #65, Los Shyris y Gaspar de Villarroel, T02-2140015, USA toll-free T1-800-5382149, www.neblinaforest.com

In the UK
Naturetrek, Cheriton Mill, Cheriton, Alresford, Hants SO24 0NG, T01962-733051, F736426, www.naturetrek.co.uk Birdwatching tours throughout the continent; also botany, natural history tours, treks and cruises.

North America
Wildland Adventures, 3516 NE 155 St, Seattle, WA 98155, USA, T800-3454453, www.wildland.com   Specializes in cultural and natural history tours to the Galápagos, Andes and Amazon.

Conservation issues

Natural habitat is quickly being destroyed in Ecuador, and many birds are threatened with extinction. Responsible ecotourism is one way to fight this trend; by visiting the lodges listed above you are making it economically feasible for the owners to protect their land instead of farming or logging it. Another way you can help protect important Ecuadorean forest tracts is by donating to foundations that buy land for nature reserves. **The Jocotoco Foundation** specializes in buying up critical bird habitat in Ecuador; it is a small, lean foundation directed by the world's top experts on South American birds (for example Robert Ridgely, author of *Birds of South America*, and Neils Krabbe, co-author of *Birds of the High Andes*). Their work deserves support. For more information see www.jocotoco.com

Climbing

Ecuador's mountains are one of its greatest attractions and there are 10 summits over 5,000 m high, of which nine have glaciers, with routes ranging from easy snow-plods to hard and technical routes. From Quito, using public transport, you can arrive at the base of seven of the country's big 10 mountains the same day and summit the next day – after you have acclimatized.

Acclimatization means letting your body adapt to the high altitude. No one should attempt to climb over 5,000 m until they have spent at least a week at the height of Quito (2,800 m) or equivalent. Many of the sub-5,000 m mountains are enjoyable walk-ups and a number of the big 10 are suitable for beginners, while others are only suitable for experienced mountaineers. See also Books, page 481.

Outrageously easy access makes Ecuador a fantastic place to get some high altitude climbing experience.

Note Deglaciation is rapidly altering the face of Ecuador's mountains. Neither the descriptions provided in this book, nor those in specialized climbing guides, can be assumed to remain correct. Conditions and routes are constantly changing. Even experienced mountaineers should not attempt to climb in Ecuador without consulting their local colleagues about conditions. Beginners should never attempt a glaciated summit without a competent local guide.

The big ten

If you've never climbed and want to suck some air at high altitude, **Cotopaxi** (5,897 m) is your best bet. While not, as often stated, the highest active volcano in the world, Cotopaxi is undoubtedly one of the most beautiful mountains in the world and the view down into the crater from the rim is unforgettable. Access is easy: you drive to 4,600 m in three hours from Quito, and the normal route is suitable for complete beginners climbing with a competent guide. Starting in Quito, you spend one night at the hut, climb the next morning and are back in town that afternoon. On the down side, Cotopaxi is the most climbed mountain in the Andes, the hut is often crowded and so is the normal route. See also page 203.

The lowest of the big 10, **Tungurahua**, at 5,016 m, has been dangerous and off-limits to climbers since 1999 due to volcanic activity. See Baños, page 230.

Ecuador's highest peak, the giant **Chimborazo**, at 6,310 m, was long considered the highest mountain on Earth. It is, if you measure its height from the centre of the planet. Stand on the summit and thanks to the equatorial bulge you are closer to the stars than at any other point on the Earth's surface. However, the climb is long – 1,300 m of ascent from the hut – and cold. Due to ash fall from Tungurahua and the effects of the tropical sun, there are at times impassable *penitentes* – conical ice formations – near the summit. See also page 246. Opposite Chimborazo is **Carihuairazo** (5,020 m), which is technically more interesting than its neighbour.

Other mountains regularly climbed include **Cayambe** (5,789 m), the only place on the planet where the latitude is 0° and so is the temperature. It's a technically easy climb but dangerous, because of the large number of crevasses and the fact that its eastern location means that cloud rolls in most days from the jungle, reducing visibility to another zero. See also page 163.

Access to **Antisana** (5,705 m) is also easy. You can now drive to base camp in three hours from Quito, but you must obtain permission beforehand from a local landowner. The normal route is technically easy but, as with Cayambe, it is dangerous due to the large number of crevasses.

Iliniza Norte (5,116 m) is the only one of the big 10 that does not have a glacier. It is a rock scramble but parts of the route are exposed, unstable and dangerous. You need a rope and the experience to use it or hire a guide. Opposite is **Iliniza Sur** (5,263 m), beautiful but technically challenging and only for experienced climbers. See page 203.

Essentials Sport & activities

The least climbed of the big 10 are **El Altar** (5,319 m) and **Sangay** (5,323 m). El Altar is a spectacularly beautiful blown-out volcano with an emerald-green crater lake and nine separate peaks, all of them technically difficult (see page 249). Sangay is the world's most continuously active volcano. The route is long – five to seven days – and technically easy, but extremely dangerous due to the likelihood of being hit by lumps of rock being ejected from the volcano. See page 249.

The normal routes (and huts) on Cotopaxi, Chimborazo and Iliniza Norte can be crowded. Outside these three you are likely to have the mountains to yourself, and if you climb any route other than the normal route on these three you will also keep away from the crowds.

Other mountains

Apart from the big 10 there are many other mountains worth climbing in Ecuador, whether you are acclimatizing for the bigger peaks, don't like the ice and snow or just want to try something different. Around Otavalo are three mountains: Ecuador's 11th highest peak **Cotacachi** (4,939 m) which is made of loose and dangerous rock, **Imbabura** (4,630 m), a walk-up best started from the La Esperanza to the north, and **Fuya Fuya** (4,263 m), the highest point of the massive Mojanda volcano. (See page 173, and note public safety problems in this area.)

Above Quito are the **Pichinchas**: **Guagua** (4,794 m) and **Rucu** (4,790 m). Guagua is a good acclimatization climb. Unfortunately, Rucu should not be climbed due to continuous problems with armed hold-ups. See page 148.

In the Cotopaxi national park are the triple peaked **Rumiñahui** (4,722 m) and **Sincholagua** (4,901 m). For Rumiñahui Norte and Sincholagua, a rope and helmet are essential to reach the summits. Rumiñahui Central is the easiest scramble, starting from Limpiopungo, while Rumiñahui Sur is climbed from the northwest via Machachi and Pansaleo (see page 204). Opposite, on the other side of the central valley, is **Corazón** (4,791 m), which is a long but easy walk-up and gives fantastic views of Cotopaxi and the Ilinizas.

Two of the most esoteric peaks in Ecuador are **Sara Urcu** (4,676 m) and **Cerro Hermoso** (4,571 m). Sara Urcu is south of Cayambe. Whymper climbed it in 1880 but the climb was not repeated until 1955. It has Ecuador's lowest and easternmost glacier. You thrash about in the wet and vegetation for several days while your ice axe and crampons rust, before getting to the glacier and putting them on. It is very easy to get extremely lost in this area. A map and compass and the ability to use them are essential. A GPS is recommended. Map reading is also a requirement for Cerro Hermoso, the highest point of the mysterious Llanganates range, where dense vegetation and complicated topography allegedly help conceal 750 tons of Inca gold collected for Atahualpa's ransom and stashed after his murder. The peak is a walk-up, once you've found it. Access is easier from the north but it is still a five-day plus expedition and only for the fit, acclimatized and experienced.

> ⦂ *Climbing to Cruz Loma, Las Antenas and Rucu Pichincha is not recommended because of public safety problems.*

To the east, in the jungle, are two active volcanoes **Reventador** (3,562 m) and **Sumaco** (3,900 m), whose position was not determined until 1921. These two can be climbed if you like hot and sweaty conditions and have your machete-user's licence to hack your way through the vegetation to get to base of the volcanoes. Note however that Reventador has erupted several times since 2002 and was not safe to climb at the close of this edition (Spring 2005). See also page 385.

When to climb

There are two climbing seasons in Ecuador: June to August and December to February. Allegedly, the eastern cordillera is drier December-February and the western cordillera June-August (though it is often windy in August) and Cotopaxi has more clear days than any other peak. It is best to avoid the wetter seasons March-May and year and it is worth remembering that Cotopaxi has been climbed on every day of the year and that Whymper's grand tour in 1880, when he made seven first ascents, was December to July. Bad weather is just predominant for the mountains on the eastern side of the eastern cordillera (for example El Altar, Sangay, Llanganates, Sara Urcu). Being on the equator, days and nights are 12 hours long. As a result, climbs are attempted all year round all over the country.

More important than the time of year is the time of day. You should aim to reach the summit of any of the snow-capped peaks at 0700 so that descent is completed well before midday. As the equatorial sun warms the snow it attains the consistency of sugar which makes it hard going and also dangerous, and avalanches are far more likely. On top of this, any rock held in place by ice will start its gravity-induced downward journey once the sun has melted the cementing ice.

Nights and early mornings are generally clear. However, cloud normally comes in by midday if not earlier, often reducing visibility to zero. This is another reason to climb at night but if the route is not tracked out by previous parties it is worth marking the way with flags; white footsteps in white snow in a white-out are difficult to follow. The weather tends to be better at full moon and the equatorial moon is so strong that you do not need your headtorch if climbing by moonlight, from full moon down to half moon.

Sunburn and altitude

Ultraviolet light at high altitude on or near the equator is very, very strong. Without proper eye protection it is possible to get snowblindness after as little as 15 minutes above 5,000 m. It does not matter if it is sunny or cloudy; in fact more UV light is reflected on cloudy days. Snowblindness is not normally apparent until the night after the damage has been done. The pain has been described as like to having acid or boiling water poured into your eyes. The next day, the victim often cannot see and will have to be led down the mountain. Snowblindness can produce permanent eye injury and victims are more susceptible in the future. Wear sunglasses that give 100% protection against UV light. Ski goggles with 100% UV protection lenses are useful for cloudy days, bad weather, and as spares in case you break or lose your glacier glasses. Sunburn is serious at high altitude and will happen on overcast days. In good weather the heat is incredible: you want to strip off but if you will get the worst sunburn of your life. The power of the equatorial sun reflecting off snow will burn the skin under the chin, up the nostrils and behind the ears, so remember to apply protection to all these areas. Use weatherproof sun block with a rating of factor 25 or higher.

Rescue

Mountain rescue facilities in Ecuador are rudimentary and poorly organized, so be as self-sufficient as possible. There is no helicopter rescue and little cooperation from the army, police or government. If you will be climbing extensively in Ecuador, it is a good idea to register with your embassy or consulate and advise them of any insurance you may have to cover the costs of rescue or repatriation by air ambulance. The first place the authorities usually contact in the event of an emergency involving a foreign climber is the embassy of their home country. Cellular phones can be used from some mountains. In an emergency try contacting **Safari Tours** ① *in Quito, T02-2552505, open 7 days a week*, or **Compañía de Guías de Montaña** ① *in Quito, T02-2504773*.

Equipment

Anything you might lose, break or forget is usually available from one of the Quito climbing and outdoor shops, but sometimes none of them will have what you want. Gear from the US tends to be cheaper in Ecuador than in Europe but European gear tends to be very expensive. A number of shops hire gear as do agencies, but always check the condition of rented equipment very carefully before you take it out.

Most provide the basic services: electric light; running water; and cooking facilities. They usually have a warden throughout the main climbing season. Nightly tariffs are usually US$10-20.

Diving and snorkelling

The coast of Ecuador is a paradise for divers, combining both cool and warm water dive destinations in one of the most biologically diverse marine environments on earth. The Galápagos Islands are undoubtedly the most popular destination, but diving in lesser-known waters such as those off the central coast of Ecuador has been gaining popularity in recent years. The secluded coves of **Isla de la Plata**, 45 km off the coast of Machalilla National Park, contain an abundance of multicoloured tropical fish which make diving and snorkelling a great experience. Colonies of sea lions can be seen, as well as migrating humpback whales, from late June to September, and many species of marine birds.

The **Galápagos Islands** are well known for their distinctive marine environments and offer more than 20 dive sites including opportunities for night diving. Each island contains its own unique environment and many are home to underwater life forms endemic to this part of the world. For a detailed description of Galápagos dive sites and marine life, see page 448.

Diving is becoming more popular with tourists since the cost of doing a PADI course in Ecuador is relatively low. There are several agencies in Quito which feature diving and full instruction on their programmes. Equipment can be hired, but it is advisable to check everything thoroughly. The larger bookshops also stock diving books and identification guides for fish and other marine life. Among the agencies specializing in diving are **Quasar Nautica** and **Tropic Ecological Adventures** (see starting page 134 for their addresses). See also the Galápagos chapter, page 18, for diving agencies in Puerto Ayora.

Haciendas

The great haciendas of Ecuador were founded shortly after the Spanish Conquest, either as Jesuit *obrajes* (slave workshops) or land grants to the conquistadors. When the Jesuits fell from favour and were expelled from South America, these huge land holdings passed to important families close to the Spanish royalty; notables such as the Marquez de Solanda and Marquez de Maenza, to name just two. They were enormous properties covering entire watersheds; most of the owners never even laid eyes on all their land. The earliest visitors to Ecuador, people like La Condamine and Humbolt, were guests at these haciendas.

The Hacienda system lasted until agrarian reform in the 1960s. The much reduced land holdings which remained in the hands of wealthy families, frequently surrounding beautiful historic homes, were then gradually converted to receive paying guests. **Chorlaví**, near Ibarra; **Cusín**, by Lago San Pablo; **La Ciénega**, near Lasso; **Rumipamba de las Rosas**, near Salcedo; **Andaluza**, outside Riobamba; and **Uzhupud**, between Gualaceo and Paute; were among the first to take in tourists. They have since become successful upscale *hosterías* and are listed under the corresponding geographic locations in the text. They are no longer working haciendas but are nonetheless pleasant and comfortable places to stay.

Encouraged by the success of these first tourist haciendas, a few more opened to the public in the 1990s: **Pinsaquí**, north of Otavalo; **Guachalá**, near Cayambe; and **Yanahurco**, near Cotopaxi National Park. They offer accommodation attached to working farms, and feature activities like horse riding and cattle roundups. Recently, some of the most historic haciendas have also opened their doors to a few discerning and well-heeled guests. These are truly ancestral homes and a gateway to the country's past, to a time when *hacendados* (wealthy landowners) ruled supreme in their own little fiefdoms. Their descendants remain among Ecuador's economic and social élite and, even today, they and their servants welcome outsiders with the slightest hint of aloof condescension. Prices are usually in our L range and up. See www.hacienda-ecuador.com and the websites given below.

Haciendas

Hacienda Chillo-Jijón, Jacinto Jijón, the owner, entertains guests personally at meals and helps to arrange many different types of excursions. Prices are all-inclusive, right down to the after-dinner brandy. It is located in Sangolquí, close enough to Quito to make a day or evening visit to a concert or the museums worthwhile. See www.hacienda-ecuador.com

Hacienda Leito, offers spectacular views of the Tungurahua volcano, which is currently belching smoke and ash. The Jesuit buildings were demolished by an earthquake in 1949, and reconstruction was carried out directly on the original foundations. It was remodeled in 1999, opening huge windows and making 20 comfortable rooms. It is located on the old road from Patate to Baños.

Hacienda Zuleta, was the favourite home of Galo Plaza, twice president of Ecuador. The hacienda has pre-Inca pyramids on the grounds, and produces fine cheese and other dairy products. The adjacent village of Zuleta is famous for its colourful hand embroidery. It is found on a secondary road between Cayambe and Ibarra, www.zuleta.com

La Carriona, began as a Jesuit work farm and, when the Jesuits left, it passed to the ownership of the Marqueza de Solanda. The original adobe walls were 2 m thick and the buildings surround a traditional stone patio. The gardens feature many mature trees, and organic vegetables are grown for guests and family alike. It is located in the Valle de los Chillos outside Quito, www.lacarriona.com

La Compañía, near Cayambe, is today a successful rose farm, exporting thousands of flowers daily to Russia and the USA. The current *hacienda* house was built in 1919 and still has the beautiful original wallpaper, as well as immense bouquets of roses.

San Agustin de Callo, was built on Inca foundations and has 2 complete Inca rooms within the main buildings. Mignon Plaza, granddaughter of former president Leonidas Plaza, encouraged archaeologists to excavate the foundations and placed lighting and window panes to display what was uncovered. Evening meals are served by candlelight in the principal Inca room. It is located near Parque Nacional Cotopaxi, see www.incahacienda.com

Two other haciendas are open for meals and visits but do not offer accommodation:

Hualilahua de Jijón, near Machachi, offers breakfast and lunch with the family and a day of horse riding or other farm activities.

La Herrería, in Valle de los Chillos, www.hacienda-ecuador.com, once the home of President Camilo Ponce, and now a fabulous museum.

Horse riding

The horse was only introduced to South America during the Spanish conquest but it has become an important part of rural life throughout Ecuador. Horse riding, whether for a brief excursion or a multi-day trek, is an excellent way to get to know the countryside, its people and local equestrian traditions. Horse rentals are available in many popular resort areas including Otavalo, Baños and Vilcabamba (see the corresponding sections in the travelling text). Visits to haciendas throughout the country also usually offer the possibility of horse riding.

Tour operators

Green Horse Ranch, outside Quito, contact Astrid Müller, T02-2374847, www.horseranch.de
Ride Andes, an high-end international outfit, contact Sally Vergette, www.rideandes.com

Shungu Huasi, outside Cayambe, T02-2792094, www.plentagos.com
Various agencies in Otavalo, Baños, and especially Vilcabamba also offer good horse riding tours. For details see under Sports and activities for the corresponding cities.

Hot springs

Ecuador is located on the 'Ring of Fire' and has many volcanoes: active, dormant and non-active (dead). Hot springs are associated with all three, although they are mostly found with the older volcanoes where sufficient time has elapsed since the last eruptions for water systems to become established. Here is a selection of Ecuador's best springs:

Locations and directions

Aguas Hediondas, about 1½ hrs west of Tulcán, see p195.
Baños, the hot springs of Baños (Tungurahua)are the best known in Ecuador. There are 4 separate bathing complexes here, and the town of Baños is overflowing with *residencias*, *pensiones*, guest houses, restaurants and activities. See p230.
Baños, there is another Baños, near Cuenca, which has the hottest commercial springs in the country. It is only 10 mins by city bus from the city, see p265.
Baños San Vicente, these springs are close to Salinas and Libertad on the coast. They are famed for the curative properties of the warm mud lake which people slide into before baking themselves dry. See p321.
Chachimbiro, accessed from Ibarra, p186.

Nangulví, can be reached from Otavalo, for further information see p167.
Oyacachi, there is public transport from Cayambe to Canguahua hourly; beyond there, only infrequently, but rental trucks are available. Alternatively, hire a horse or walk about 25 km. Several families in the village will provide floors to sleep on, or you can ask to sleep in one of the churches or in the school.
Papallacta, these hot springs, the best developed site in the country, can be visited in a day trip from Quito, as can the more modest ones at **El Tingo** and **La Merced**. See p147 for details about Papallacta.
El Placer, access to this spring takes a couple of days' trekking, but it's well worth the effort. It is located in Sangay National Park by the headwaters of the Río Palora. Access is from the village of Alao, reached from Riobamba. A detailed route description is given in *Trekking in Ecuador* (p482).

Mountain biking

More and more people come to Ecuador to ride through the spectacular mountain scenery or along the coastal roads. The upper Amazon basin also offers a rough but relatively traffic-free route from north to south. In general, for biking as for hiking, the farther from the main gringo trail, the safer you are. See Quito mountain biking, page 133, for agencies offering bike tours and bike shops. See also Cycling, page 56.

What many people don't take into account is the frequently extreme conditions in which they find themselves biking. Dehydration can be a very real issue when cycling at high altitudes or in the hot tropical lowlands. Bottled water is available at many small stores in villages, but along some of the more spectacular routes they are few and far between. A water pump or other sterilizing systems should always be carried. Sunscreen is essential at high altitudes even on cloudy days. Wrap around sunglasses help to restrict the amount of dust which gets into the eyes.

Quito also produces a series of very practical (though dated) *hojas de ruta* which include elevation profiles. You should in addition seek a little local knowledge, since maps are not updated frequently and new roads are often not indicated, nor are landslides which may make certain routes impassable. Maps do not always distinguish between cobbled and good *lastre* (gravel) graded surfaces.

Routes

Departing from Quito in northerly and southerly directions it is difficult to avoid the busy paved Panamericana for about the first 30 km. For those going **south** the Machachi area makes a good destination for a first day. To the **north** a lot of traffic can be avoided by biking to **Mitad del Mundo**, an easy first day, and then taking the old road with its dramatic scenery via **San José de Minas** to travel to the **Otavalo** area. Those who wish to stay on the paved road should consider **Guayllabamba** (easy) or **Cayambe** (via Otón, with lovely views but harder) a first day destination.

The road **east from Baños to Puyo** toward the jungle is very popular and beautiful, and there are ample opportunities to rent bikes here. A paved vehicle road from Baños to Puyo, including several tunnels, was completed in 2004. This has left the very scenic old road which snakes over the cliffsides for the exclusive use of bikers.

Trying to cover too great a distance, especially at the beginning of a trip, is a common mistake; 40-50 km a day is a respectable distance to cover at altitudes above 2,500 m. Beyond 50 km from Quito the traffic decreases and more alternative roads become available. In many areas the Panamericana is paralleled by older cobbled or dirt roads, with very little traffic.

General advice

A good bike lock is essential equipment, the best will be long enough to pass through both wheels and the frame. Most bus lines will carry bicycles on the roof racks for little or no extra charge. It is advisable to supervise the loading and assure that the derailer is not jammed up against luggage which might damage it. If you can, take some cardboard to protect the bike while it rides the bus. If you take a long journey with major altitude changes let a little air out of the tyres especially when going from lower to higher altitudes. Bikes may be taken on commercial flights in place of a suitcase, always check that there will be space. Routes to the jungle have more luggage restrictions, as do those to the Galápagos.

Paragliding and hang-gliding

These are pretty special activities amid the high mountains, and its devotees can sometimes be seen in the rays of the afternoon sun drifting off Pichincha toward Quito. The sports are also practised at several other highland locations as well as at Crucita and Canoa on the Pacific coast. In **Quito**, **Escuela Pichincha de Vuelo Libre** ① *Carlos Endara Oe3-60 y Amazonas, T02-2256592 (office hours) T09-9478349 (mob), parapent@uio.satnet.net,* is a good point of contact. The school offers complete courses as well as tandem flights for novices. Speak to Enrique Castro here, he can also advise about other sites and contacts in **Ibarra**, **Ambato**, **Riobamba** and **Cuenca**. In **Crucita**, Luis Tobar at **Hostal Voladores** ① *T05-2340200, hvoladores@hotmail.com,* offers tandem flights, rentals and four to six-day paragliding courses.

Essentials Sport & activities

Rafting and kayaking

Ecuador is a whitewater paradise. Warm waters, tropical rainforest and dozens of accessible rivers concentrated in such a small area have made the country a 'hotspot' for rafters and kayakers the world over. So much so that the Quijos river was chosen by the International Rafting Federation as the site of the 2005 World Rafting Championships. And with regional rainy seasons occurring at different times throughout the year the action never stops – there's always a river to run.

Rafting is an activity open to almost anyone with a sense of adventure. Worldwide the sport continues to grow, as is the case in Ecuador, with the majority of participants first-timers. No previous rafting experience is needed to join a trip if each boat has an experienced guide at the helm. Trips can run from one to six days.

Rafting trips are offered by operators in Quito, Tena and Baños with guides, equipment, transport and food provided. Although not new, the rafting industry has until recently remained relatively undeveloped. Standards vary so it is really important to ask a few questions before booking a trip. The most important things to look for are experienced guides and top notch equipment. Without exception, the reputable companies are run by foreign or foreign-trained Ecuadorean guides. Many guides now have a license issued by the Ministry of Tourism but be warned that as there are no controls in place this does not guarantee that safety standards are always met. Ask about the guides' rafting, river rescue and first aid training, about the rafting and personal safety equipment, if they carry first aid, raft repair and river rescue kits, if they utilize safety kayakers and have on-river emergency communications. Although there are some inherent dangers in river running, these are the factors that make a rafting trip relatively safe.

Kayakers find the biggest problem is choosing which of the dozens of enticing rivers to run in the time they have available. The following river descriptions include the most popular runs. However as new rivers are being 'opened' every year the list is by no means exhaustive. For information on river conditions, the ins and outs of travelling with kayaks, rental of kayaking equipment and guiding services, contact Yacu Amu Rafting/Ríos Ecuador. 'Learn to' courses may be offered that give newcomers the chance to find out what they've been missing. There's no better place to learn this exciting sport than on Ecuador's warm tropical rivers.

Grades

The majority of Ecuador's whitewater rivers share a number of characteristics. Plunging off the Andes the upper sections are very steep creeks offering, if they're runnable at all, serious technical grade V, suitable for expert kayakers only. As the creeks join on the lower slopes they form rivers navigable by both raft and kayak (ie less steep, more volume). Some of these rivers offer up to 100 km of continuous grade III-IV whitewater, before flattening out to rush towards the Pacific Ocean on one side of the ranges or deep into the Amazon Basin on the other.

Water quality

Since some of Ecuador's rivers are severely polluted, always ask about water quality before signing up for a trip. Water quality may vary significantly depending on such factors as proximity of towns, local agricultural practices, last rainfall, river volume, and the relative proportions of surface and ground water. It's a complex equation but as a general rule the rivers running straight off the eastern and western slopes of the Andes are less subject to pollution than the highland rivers which drain some of the most densely populated regions of the country before their descent into the jungle or to the Pacific.

Pacific Coast rivers

Owing to their proximity to Quito, the **Blanco river** and its tributaries are the most frequently run in Ecuador. There is almost 200 km of raftable whitewater in the Blanco valley, with the **Toachi/Blanco** combination and the **Upper Blanco** being the most popular day trips. The former starts as a technical grade III-IV run, including the infamous rapids of the **El Sapo canyon**, before joining the Blanco where big waves abound year round. The latter is probably the world's longest day trip – 47 km of non-stop grade III-IV rapids in a little over four hours on the river (February-June only). Trips are also offered on the **Caoni** (grade II-III) and **Mulate** (III) rivers.

In addition to those already mentioned, kayakers have a number of other possibilities to choose from depending on the time of year and their skills and experience. The **Mindo** (III-IV), **Saloya** (IV-V), **Pachejal** (III-IV), **Upper Caoni** (IV), **Pilatón** (IV-V), **Damas** (IV-V) and **Upper Toachi** (IV-V) are all options.

Río Quijos

The waters of the Quijos river and its tributaries are a whitewater playground. Within a 30 km radius of the town of El Chaco you'll find everything from steep, technical grade V creek runs to big volume, roller coaster grade III and IV. The **Quijos** (IV-V) has quickly earned the reputation of a classic for rafting and kayaking, boasting challenging world-class whitewater and spectacular canyon scenery. Other popular kayaking runs can be found on the **Papallacta** (V), **Cosanga** (III-IV) and **Oyacachi** (IV-V) tributaries. Day tripping is the norm on the upper runs, although further downstream a two-day trip is possible, starting near the town of El Reventador. At the end of the upper section the collected waters of the Quijos catchment plunge dramatically over **San Rafael Falls**, which at 145 m is the highest waterfall in Ecuador. Access to the Quijos valley is generally easy as it forms the main corridor from Quito down into the jungle along a paved road. The most popular put-ins and take-outs are accessible by road, some have parking and latrines. An exception is putting in for the run from El Reventador which requires a 40-minute scramble down muddy slopes from the main road.

The best time to dip your paddle depends on how hard you want to push yourself. The rainy season on the eastern slopes generally runs from March to September so at this time you can expect high flows and truly continuous whitewater (for expert kayakers only). The rest of the year, the dry season, is when the commercial rafting and kayaking operators run trips. During these months there's still plenty of action and water and air temperatures are more comfortable.

Oriente

In the jungle surrounding Tena, the **Napo river** and its tributaries offer a tremendous amount of whitewater in a small area. It's very easy to spend a week based here and paddle a different river every day. The grade III **Upper Napo** or **Jatunyacu**, the most popular rafting trip, is runnable year round, while the gem of this region, the **Lower Misahuallí** (IV), is rafted during the drier months from October to March. This river passes through pristine jungle in a remote canyon, the highlight being the heart-stopping portage around **Casanova Falls**. For the experienced rafter, the **Upper Misahualli** offers a continuous, technical grade IV descent requiring agility and teamwork from April to September.

Additional kayaking options include various sections of the **Misahualli**, **Jondachi**, **Anzu** and **Hollín** rivers. Difficulty is very much water-level-dependent but most are grade IV or V when they have sufficient water to paddle.

Río Pastaza

This is generally not run on the lower reaches although a canyon between Shell and the Puyo-Macas road bridge contains some good grade IV rapids at high levels. The most popular trip out of Baños is a 1½-hour run on the grade II-III **Patate river**, a

Essentials Sport & activities

highland tributary of the **Pastaza**. It should be noted that the upper reaches of the Patate drain the city of Ambato to which are added the denim-blue waters of **Pelileo**, jean capital of Ecuador. Another tributary, the **Topo** (grade V), has been reported by some expert kayakers to be the best steep creek run in the country.

Río Upano

Best known for the **Namangosa Gorge** in which dozens of waterfalls plummet up to 100 m through primary rainforest into the river. To date this spectacle has been witnessed by few river runners. While the gorge is undoubtedly the highlight, what makes a journey down the **Upano** special is witnessing the changing character of an Amazonian river. Trickling from a string of mountain lakes the Upano quickly gathers force, carving a path southward through the province of **Morona Santiago**. As it rushes past **Macas** it is shallow and braided. Picking a route from the myriad channels is a real challenge; make the wrong choice and an unscheduled portage will result.

The pace steadily increases until the river plunges into the magnificent Namangosa Gorge. Some falls cascade down staggered cliffs while others freefall into the jungle below. This 'Lost World' atmosphere is made even more daunting by the seething rapids below. The rapids are big class IV with lots of funny water including raft-flipping boils and kayak(er)-swallowing eddylines. Once out of the gorge, the river broadens and deepens to become a calm but powerful giant on its way to meet the mighty **Amazon**.

Five and six day rafting trips start near Macas. A few kayakers have attempted the upper reaches of the river and returned with stories to be filed under E for epic. The run from Macas to the end of the gorge is about 120 km and takes four to five days. Some choose to continue another day or so further downstream to the village of Santiago Mayatico which is the final possible take-out. From here it's only a few miles as the toucan flies to the border with Peru.

Recommended months are October to February and this is when commercial trips are offered. During the rest of the year the river can flood unexpectedly. In fact during April and May, when the river peaks, the gorge fills so much that a local Shuar indian once travelled upstream to Macas in a motorized canoe.

Tour operators

Quito

All agencies in Quito offer 1 and 2 day trips on the Toachi and Blanco rivers.

Eco-Adventur, Pasaje Cordova N23-26 y Wilson, Quito, T02-2520647, F2223720, www.cuadoradventure.ec

Explorandes, Presidente Wilson 537 y Diego de Almagro, Quito, T02-2222699, F2556938, www.explorandes.com

ROW Expediciones, Pablo Arturo Suarez 191 y Eloy Alfaro, Quito, T02-2239224, F2544794, www.rowexpediciones.com 6-day trips on the Upano Nov-Feb, guides from Idaho, USA.

Yacu Amu Rafting, Foch 746 y J L Mera, Quito, T02-2904054, F2904055, www.yacuamu.com 1-3 day trips on the Quijos combined with a stay at Papallacta Hot Springs Resort. Also 5-6 day trips on the Upano Oct-Feb, customized itineraries, kayaking information, equipment rental, 4-day kayak school with qualified instructors, guiding service and all-inclusive packages for those who want to leave the organizing to someone else. Highly recommended because they are professional and have the highest quality equipment.

Tena

Ríos Ecuador, Malecón between the footbridges, Tena, T06-2886346, F2886727, www.riosecuador.com Year-round rafting trips on the Upper Napo, Anzu and Misahualli rivers. Also kayaking trips, 4-day kayaking school, rental and information. Good guides and high safety standards. Works with Yacu Amu Rafting in Quito.

Baños

Agencies here offer year-round trips on the Patate and Pastaza river.

Geotours, Ambato y Thomas Halflants, T03-2741344, geotours@hotmail.com

Surfing

Ecuador has a few select surfing spots which are becoming increasingly popular. On the mainland, from north to south, are: **Mompiche** (Esmeraldas), south of Muisne; **San Mateo** (Manabí), south of Manta; **Montañita** (Guayas), between Olón and Manglaralto; and **Playas** near Guayaquil. In Galápagos, there is good surfing at **Playa Punta Carola** outside Puerto Baquerizo Moreno on San Cristóbal Island. Waves are generally best from December to March, except at Playas where the surfing season is usually from June to September.

Trekking

Ecuador's varied landscape, diverse ecological environments, and friendly villagers within a compact area, make travelling by foot a refreshing break from crowded buses. Although the most commonly travelled routes are in the Sierra, there are also a few excellent trekking opportunities on the Coast and in the Oriente. Likewise you can descend from the windswept *páramo* through Andean Slope cloud forest to tropical rain forest and observe most of the ecosystems of Ecuador during a single excursion.

Many hikes pass through protected areas which are managed by the **Ministerio del Ambiente**. Approximately 15% of continental Ecuador lies within national parks, ecological reserves and recreation areas, and most of these are threatened by development pressures. The only mainland parks that are minimally staffed and have any infrastructure are **Cotopaxi**, **Cajas**, **Podocarpus** and **Machalilla**. Excellent trekking opportunities are to be found, however, in the countryside throughout Ecuador, whether or not the land is part of a park or reserve. The official entrance fees for parks and conservation units range from US$5 to US$20 for foreigners. They vary from park to park, see National Parks, page 478, for a complete list. In any event, the less-visited parks and less-used park entrances will have no one around to collect the fee.

It is still the ruggedness and lack of access that protects most of these areas from environmental impact and makes them so appealing to wilderness travellers. There are not nearly as many well-marked trails as you would find in national parks in developed countries. In some places ancient routes have been used for thousands of years by *campesinos* and are relatively easy to follow. In other areas you may be bush-whacking through the forest with a machete. A basic knowledge of how to ask for directions in Spanish and map and compass skills are perhaps the most important elements to a successful trek. It is also possible to hire experienced guides (US$50-100 per day) from the major cities or less. Topographic maps should be purchased at the IGM in Quito (see page 100). The 1:50,000 scale maps are most useful, of which there is coverage of most of the country. For more remote locations bring a handheld GPS, but remember that it is no substitute for comprehensive navigation and map-reading skills.

Guiding

Quito companies which offer guiding include: **Angermeyer's**, **Compañía de Guias de Montaña**, **Pamir**, **Safari**, **Sierra Nevada** and **Surtrek**. Complete contact information is found under Quito activities and tours, page 132. Guides and gear can also be hired at agencies in Otavalo, Latacunga, Baños, Riobamba, Cuenca, Loja and Vilcabamba.

Equipment

It is best to bring trekking equipment from home, but if you are travelling light most gear can be purchased or hired at outfitters in Quito. Check rented gear very carefully. For a complete list of Quito shops which sell or rent gear, see page 129; as well as the towns listed above.

All drinking water must be boiled or treated. Iodine tablets are easy and reliable but may be difficult to locate in Quito. Common stove fuels which may be found in Ecuador include white gas (this may be difficult, try Kywi hardware stores in Quito), kerosene (most hardware stores), and gas canisters (outfitters listed above). All gasoline in Ecuador is unleaded and may be burnt by some stoves.

The standard hiking shoe for Ecuador is the rubber boot, which is worn by most *campesinos* while working in the countryside. Travellers may balk at using footwear that only costs US$5 and can be purchased in any town, but they keep feet warm and dry through muddy terrain, unlike conventional leather or goretex hiking boots. As long as the trail is not rocky they are also very comfortable. Note, however, that very large sizes may be hard to find.

Hazards

Altitude sickness (locally called *soroche*) can be a problem for recent arrivals, and dehydration can affect anyone. It is important to drink lots of water and not push yourself too hard when you have just arrived. Trekkers in Ecuador must be as self-sufficient as possible. If an accident occurs self-evacuation may be your only option, see rescue under Climbing, page 73.

Note Some of the more popular hikes in the country such as Laguna Cuicocha and Lagunas de Mojanda have experienced armed robberies. The basic rule of thumb is that the farther off the gringo track, the safer you are. It is important to always enquire locally about the safety of a particular trek.

Different terrains

Hiking in **the Sierra** is mostly across high elevation *páramo*, through agricultural lands, and past indigenous communities living in traditional ways. There are

outstanding views of glaciated peaks in the north and pre-Columbian ruins in the south. On **the coast** there are only a few areas developed for hiking ranging from dry forest to coastal rain forest. **The Oriente** is mostly virgin tropical rain forest and offers excellent hiking even outside the protected areas. The forest canopy shades out the brushy vegetation, making cross-country travel relatively easy. Since there are no vantage points to get a bearing it is also easy to get lost, and a GPS does not work in a dense forest. Local guides are therefore required because of this difficulty in navigation and because you will be walking on land owned by indigenous tribes. **The Andean Slopes** are steep and often covered by virtually impenetrable cloud forests and it rains a lot. Many ancient trading routes head down the river valleys. Some of these trails are still used; others may be overgrown and difficult to follow but offer the reward of intact ecosystems. You may be travelling across land that is either owned outright by indigenous people or jointly managed with the **Ministerio de Ambiente**. It is important to be respectful of the people and request permission to pass through or camp. Sometimes a fee may be charged by locals but it is usually minimal.

Climate

Although each region has its own wet and dry seasons, the climate is inherently unpredictable and, as a trekker, you must be prepared for all conditions at any time of the year. See pages 22 and 72 for further details.

Further information

A useful web site is **www.trekkinginecuador.com** See also Books, page 482.

Volunteer programmes

'Voluntourism' is popular in Ecuador, attracting many visitors, from students to retirees. It is a good way to become more intimately acquainted with the country (blemishes and all) and, at the same time, to try and lend a hand to its people. If you are seriously interested in volunteering, you should research both local and international organizations well before you leave home. Try to choose a position which matches your individual skills. Think carefully about the kind of work that you would find most satisfying, and also be realistic about how much you might be able to achieve. The shorter your stay, the more limited should be your expectations in all regards. You must speak at least basic Spanish, and preferably a good deal more, in order to work effectively in a local community setting. Also remember that you are volunteering in order to get to know and help the 'real Ecuador' and that conditions can sometimes be pretty harsh. In almost all cases you will have to pay your own airfare, and also contribute toward your room and board. There are a number of different areas where voluntary work is possible, of which we list a few below.

Projects

Bospas Farm, along the road from Ibarra to San Lorenzo, contact Piet Sabbe, T06-2648692, bospasforest@gardener.com, www.ecuativer.com/bospas, is a centre for permaculture and reforestation. It offers flexible internship/volunteer opportunities and farmstays.

Los Cedros Research Station, in the Intag area, Quito T02-2231768, www.reservalos cedros.org , is a cloud forest reserve protecting many bird and orchid species. Volunteer programmes require a minimum one month commitment.

Corporación Ornitológica del Ecuador (CECIA), Quito, Joaquín Tinajero E3-05 y Jorge Drom, T02-2271800, www.cecia.org, works with bird conservation in the Quito area and other locations in Ecuador. Volunteer opportunuies are sporadic and vary according to current projects and needs.

Fundación Arcoiris, Segundo Cueva Celi 03-15 y Clodoveo Carrión, Loja,

T07-2572926, www.arcoiris.org.ec, works with a variety of nature conservation and sustainable community development projects in the far south of the country.

Fundación Jatun Sacha, Pasaje Eugenio de Santillán N34-248 y Maurián, Quito, T02-2432246, www.jatunsacha.org, has many different sites at which volunteers can work, all in exceptional natural areas. Note that this is a large organization. Volunteer programmes are just one small part of what they do and volunteers must be prepared to work independently.

Fundación Maquipuicuna, Baquerizo Moreno E9-153 y Tamayo, Quito, T02-2507200, www.maqui.org, supports the conservation of biodiversity and sustainable use of natural resources. They need help with reforestation, trail building, environmental education and organic gardening at their reserve northwest of Quito.

Fundación Natura, Av República 481 y Almagro, Quito, T02-2503385, www.fnatura.Org, is a large Ecuadorean NGO that promotes environmental awareness and education. They require volunteers at their Pasochoa reserve south of Quito, and other areas.

Rainforest Concern, Contact Fiona Pérez in Quito, T02-2457143; or Peter Bennett, 27 Lansdowne Cres, London W11 2NS, T020-7229 2093, www.rainforest concern.org, a British charity, works with various environmental projects in Ecuador, including reforestation in Santa Lucía cloud forest as well as buying and protecting rainforest in Oriente.

Río Muchacho Organic Farm, contact Nicola Mears or Darío Proaño in Bahía de Caráquez, Bolívar 902 y Arenas, T05-2691107, www.riomuchacho.com, in the coastal province of Manabí, is a small organization which works with local education, community development and sustainable agriculture. They offer a variety of flexible volunteer experiences.

Jungle guiding

The best way to learn about the rainforest is to become a guide at one of the lodges. Qualified field biologists with good interpersonal skills are always in demand, especially if they know birds well. The job can be difficult but will leave a lasting imprint on your life. Check with any of the lodges in the Oriente chapter. You should enquire carefully about terms in advance.

Yachting

Several hundred private yachts call on the Galápagos Islands every year, generally en route from Panama to the Marquesas Islands and Tahiti. Details for yachters visiting Galápagos are given on pages 422 and 424.

Although fewer independent sailors have traditionally called on the Pacific coast ports of mainland Ecuador, there are ample opportunities to do so. Yacht clubs are found in **Salinas, La Libertad** (Puerto Lucía) and **Punta Blanca** (all in Guayas), **Bahía de Caráquez** (Manabí) and **Casa Blanca** (Esmeraldas). Arrangements for secure berthing can sometimes also be made in smaller commercial ports like **Esmeraldas** and **Manta**. If your vessel requires repairs, maintenance, or you just want some time to go travelling ashore, then the mainland offers more facilities and lower prices than Galápagos.

Health

It should be no surprise that the health care in the region is varied: there are some decent private and government clinics/hospitals, which more often than not follow the more aggressive American style of medicine (where you will be referred straight to a specialist), but as with all medical care, first impressions count. If a facility is grubby and staff wear grey coats instead of white ones, then be wary of the general standard of medicine and hygiene. The best medical facilities and physicians who speak languages other than Spanish are located in Quito, Guayaquil and Cuenca. It is worth contacting your embassy or consulate on arrival and asking where the recommended (ie those used by diplomats) clinics are. Providing embassies with information on your whereabouts can also be useful if a friend/relative gets ill at home and there is a desperate search for you around the globe. You can also ask them about locally recommended do's and don'ts. If you do get ill, and you have the opportunity, you should ask your medical insurer whether they are satisfied that the medical centre or hospital that you have been referred to is of a suitable standard.

Before discussing the disease-related health risks involved in travel within Ecuador, remember to try to avoid **road accidents**. You can reduce the likelihood of accidents by not travelling at night, avoiding overcrowded buses, not drinking and driving, wearing a seatbelt in cars and a helmet on motorbikes (even if most Ecuadoreans do not).

Disease risk

The greater disease risk in Ecuador is caused by the greater volume of disease carriers in the shape of mosquitoes and sandflies. The key viral disease in the lowlands is **Dengue fever**, which is transmitted by a mosquito that bites during the day. The disease is like a very nasty form of the 'flu with two-three days of illness, followed by a short period of recovery, then a second attack of illness. Westerners very rarely get the worst haemorrhagic form of the disease. Bacterial diseases include **tuberculosis** (TB) and some causes of the more common traveller's **diarrhoea**. The parasitic diseases are many but the two key ones are **malaria** and South American trypanosomiasis (known as **Chagas Disease**). The latter kills fit, young South American footballers but in Ecuador is uncommon outside remote rural areas of the province of Manabí.

Before you go

Ideally, you should see your GP or travel clinic at least six weeks before your departure for general advice on travel risks, malaria and vaccinations. Make sure you have travel insurance, get a dental check (especially if you are going to be away for more than a month), know your own blood group and if you suffer a long-term condition such as diabetes or epilepsy make sure someone knows or that you have a Medic Alert bracelet/necklace with this information on it.

Vaccinations

Diphtheria Recommended. **Hepatitis A** Recommended as the disease can be caught easily from food/water. **Polio** Recommended if nil in last 10 years. **Tetanus** Recommended if nil in last 10 years (but five doses is enough for life). **Typhoid** Recommended if nil in last three years. **Yellow Fever** It is best and easiest to get vaccinated. There is no significant risk, however, outside the Oriente jungle. Yellow fever certificate required for those over one year old entering from an infected area. **Rabies** Recommended if travelling to jungle and/or remote areas. **Malaria** precautions are essential in most areas below 1500 m all year round, see below.

Health organizations and websites

Foreign and Commonwealth Office (FCO), www.fco.gov.uk This is a key travel advice site, with useful information on the country, people, climate and lists the UK embassies/consulates. It has links to the Department of Health travel advice site, listed below. **Department of Health Travel Advice**, www.doh.gov.uk/traveladvice This excellent site is also available as a free booklet, the T6, from Post Offices. It lists the vaccine advice requirements for each country. **Medic Alert** (UK), www.medicalert.co.uk This foundation produces bracelets and necklaces for those with existing medical problems. Once you have ordered your bracelet/necklace you write your key medical details on paper inside it, so that if you collapse, people can identify the cause.

Blood Care Foundation, www.bloodcare.org.uk The Blood Care Foundation is a Kent-based charity "dedicated to the provision of screened blood and resuscitation fluids in countries where these are not readily available." They dispatch non-infected blood to your hospital/clinic. The blood is flown in from various centres around the world.

Health Protection Agency, www.hpa.org.uk Up-to-date malaria advice guidelines. It gives specific advice about the right drugs for each location. It also has useful information for those who are pregnant, suffering from epilepsy or planning to travel with children.

Centers for Disease Control and Prevention (USA), www.cdc.gov This site from the US Government gives excellent advice on travel health, has useful disease maps and details of disease outbreaks.

World Health Organisation, www.who.int The WHO site has links to the WHO Blue Book on travel advice. The book lists the diseases in different regions of the world, describes vaccination schedules and identifies areas of malarial risk.

Tropical Medicine Bureau, www.tmb.ie This Irish-based site has a good collection of general travel health information and disease risks.

Fit for Travel, www.fitfortravel.scot.nhs.uk This site from Scotland provides a quick A-Z of vaccine and travel health advice requirements for each country.

British Travel Health Association, www.btha.org This is the official site of an organization of travel health professionals.

NetDoctor, www.netdoctor.co.uk This general health advice site has a useful section on travel and has an 'ask the expert', interactive chat forum.

Books and leaflets

Dawood, Dr R, (ed)*Traveller's Health*, (OUP, 2002) The car-manual for your off-the-beaten track trip.

Lankester, Dr T, *Good Health, Good Travel* (Hodder and Stoughton, 1995). Covers all aspects of staying healthy abroad, for the longer term traveller.

Warrell, D and Anderson, S (eds), *The Royal Geographic Society Expedition Medicine* (Expedition Advisory Centre, 2nd ed, 2002). Expert-written reference guide to avoiding accidents and illness.

Young Pelton, R et al, *The World's Most Dangerous Places* (Harper Collins, 5th ed, 2003). Descriptions of the world's most dangerous places, first-hand accounts and advice on how to stay safe.

The Travellers Guide to Health (T6) can be obtained by calling the Health Literature Line on T0800-555777.

What to take

Anti-malarials Important to take for all areas under 1500 m all year round. There is no risk in Quito or the Galápagos Islands. Specialist advice is required as to which type to take. General principles are that all except Malarone should be continued for four weeks after leaving the malarial area. Malarone needs to be continued for only seven days afterwards (if a tablet is missed or vomited seek specialist advice). The start times for the anti-malarials vary in that if you have never taken Lariam (Mefloquine) before it is advised to start it at least two to three weeks before the entry to a malarial zone (this is to help identify serious side-effects early). Chloroquine and Paludrine are often started a week before the trip to establish a pattern but Doxycycline and Malarone can be started only one to two days before entry to the malarial area.

Ciproxin (Ciprofloaxcin) A useful antibiotic for some forms of travellers' diarrhoea (see below).

Immodium A great standby for those diarrhoeas that occur at awkward times (ie before a long coach/train journey or on a trek). It helps stop the flow of diarrhoea.

MedicAlert These simple bracelets, or an equivalent, should be carried or worn by anyone with a significant medical condition.

Mosquito repellents Remember that DEET (Di-ethyltoluamide) is the gold standard. Apply the repellent every four to six hours but more often if you are sweating heavily. If a non-DEET product is used check who tested it. Validated products (tested at the London School of Hygiene and Tropical Medicine) include

Mosiguard, Non-DEET Jungle formula and non-DEET Autan. If you want to use citronella remember that it must be applied very frequently (ie hourly) to be effective. If you are a popular target for insect bites or develop lumps quite soon after being bitten, carry an Aspivenin kit. This syringe suction device draws out some of the allergic materials and provides quick relief.

Pain killers Paracetomol or a similar painkiller can have multiple uses for symptoms but remember that more than eight paracetomol a day can lead to liver failure.

Pepto-Bismol Used a lot by Americans for diarrhoea. It certainly relieves symptoms but like Immodium it is not a cure for underlying disease. Be aware that it turns the stool black as well as making it more solid.

Sun block The Australians have a great campaign, which has reduced skin cancer. It is called Slip, Slap, Slop. Slip on a shirt, Slap on a hat, Slop on sun screen.

For longer trips involving jungle treks taking a clean needle pack, clean dental pack and water filtration devices are common-sense measures.

An A-Z of health risks

Altitude sickness

Symptoms: This can creep up on you as just a mild headache with nausea or lethargy. The more serious disease is caused by fluid collecting in the brain in the enclosed space of the skull and can lead to coma and death. There is also a lung disease version with breathlessness and fluid infiltration of the lungs.

Cures: The best cure is to descend as soon as possible.

Prevention: Get acclimatized. Ascend to the heights slowly. Flying into Quito from sea level is likely to leave you affected by altitude sickness for the first few days, so give yourself a chance to acclimatize before heading off on trips and treks.

Chagas disease

Symptoms: The disease occurs in remote rural areas of the province of Manabí, inland from the seacoast. It affects locals more than travellers, but travellers can be exposed by sleeping in mud-constructed huts where the bug that carries the parasite bites and defaecates on an exposed part of skin. You may notice nothing at all or a local swelling, with fever, tiredness and enlargement of lymph glands, spleen and liver. The seriousness of the parasite infection is caused by the long-term effects which include gross enlargement of the heart and/or guts.

Cures: Early treatment is required with toxic drugs.

Prevention: Sleep under a permethrin treated bed net and use insect repellents.

Dengue fever

Symptoms: This disease can be contracted throughout the coast and jungle of Ecuador. In travellers this can cause a severe 'flu-like illness which includes symptoms of fever, lethargy, enlarged lymph glands and muscle pains. It starts suddenly, lasts for two to three days, seems to get better for two to three days and then kicks in again for another two to three days. It is usually all over in an unpleasant week. The local children are prone to the much nastier haemorrhagic form of the disease, which causes them to bleed from internal organs, mucous membranes and often leads to their death.

Cures: The traveller's version of the disease is self limiting and forces rest and recuperation on the sufferer.

Prevention: The mosquitoes that carry the Dengue virus bite during the day unlike the malaria mosquitoes. Which sadly means that repellent application and covered limbs are a 24-hour issue. Check your accommodation for flower pots and shallow pools of water since these are where the dengue-carrying mosquitoes breed.

Diarrhoea and intestinal upset

Symptoms: Diarrhoea can refer either to loose stools or an increased frequency; both of these can be a nuisance. It should be short lasting but persistence beyond two weeks, with blood or pain, require specialist medical attention.

Cures: Ciproxin (Ciprofloaxcin) is a useful antibiotic for bacterial traveller's diarrhoea. It can be obtained by private prescription in the UK which is expensive, or bought over the counter in Ecuadorean pharmacies. You need to take one 500mg tablet when the diarrhoea starts and if you do not feel better in 24 hours, the diarrhoea is likely to have a non-bacterial cause and may be viral (in which case there is little you can do apart from keep yourself rehydrated and wait for it to settle on its own). The key treatment with all diarrhoeas is rehydration. Try to keep hydrated by taking the right mixture of salt and water. This is available as Oral Rehydration Salts (ORS) in ready-made sachets or can be made up by adding a teaspoon of sugar and a half teaspoon of salt to a litre of clean water. Immodium and Pepto- Bismol provide symptomatic relief.

Prevention: The standard advice is to be careful with water and ice for drinking. If you have any doubts then boil it or filter and treat it. There are many filter/treatment devices now available on the market. Food can also transmit disease. Be wary of salads, re-heated foods or food that has been left out in the sun having been previously cooked. There is a simple adage that says wash it, peel it, boil it or forget it. Also be wary of unpasteurized dairy products, these can transmit a range of diseases from brucellosis (fevers and constipation), to listeria (meningitis) and tubercolosis of the gut (obstruction, constipation, fevers and weight loss).

Hepatitis

Symptoms: Hepatitis means inflammation of the liver. Viral causes of the disease can be acquired in Ecuador. The most obvious symptom is a yellowing of your skin or the whites of your eyes. Prior to this all that you may notice is itching and tiredness.

Cures: Early on, depending on the type of hepatitis, a vaccine or immunoglobulin may reduce the duration of the illness.

Prevention: Pre-travel hepatitis A vaccine is the best bet. Hepatitis B (for which there is also a vaccine) is spread through blood and unprotected sexual intercourse, both of these can be avoided. Unfortunately there is no vaccine for hepatitis C or the increasing alphabetical list of other Hepatitis viruses.

Leishmaniasis

Symptoms: A skin form of this disease occurs in rural Esmeraldas and Manabí, as well as the Oriente jungle. If infected, you may notice a raised lump, which leads to a purplish discoloration on white skin and a possible ulcer. The parasite is transmitted by the bite of a sandfly. Sandflies do not fly very far and the greatest risk is at ground level, so if you can avoid sleeping on the jungle floor, do so. There is another rarer form which is caused by a sub-species of the parasite, this affects the musocal tissues such as lips and nose. Treatment and mode of transmission are the same.

Cures: Several weeks treatment is required under specialist supervision. The drugs themselves are toxic but if not taken in sufficient amounts, recurrence is more likely.

Prevention: Sleep above ground, under a permethrin-treated net, use insect repellent and get a specialist opinion on any unusual skin lesions as soon as you can.

Malaria and insect bite prevention

Malaria risk is about 50% of the deadly *P. falciparum* type. Malaria exists at altitudes less than 1,500 m all year round. The highest risk is found throughout Oriente and in rural areas of the coast, especially during the rainy season. The risk of malaria is negligible if you visit only Quito, the highlands and Galápagos.

The choice of malaria drug depends on where you will travel, which type of malaria you may be exposed to, and your medical/psychological history. Always check with your doctor or travel clinic for the most up-to-date advice.

Symptoms: Malaria is a very serious disease. It can start as something just resembling an attack of flu. You may feel tired, lethargic, headachy; or experience the more characteristic high fever and severe shaking chills. It is easy to ignore vague symptoms which may actually be malaria. If in doubt whilst abroad and on return home, get tested as soon as possible.

Cures: Treatment is with drugs, which may be either oral or into a vein depending on the seriousness of the infection. Remember ABCD: Awareness (of whether the disease is present in the area you are travelling in), Bite avoidance, Chemoprophylaxis and Diagnosis.

Prevention: This is best summarized by the B and C of the ABCD: bite avoidance and chemoprophylaxis. Wear clothes that cover arms and legs and use effective insect repellents in areas with known risks of insect-spread disease. Use a mosquito net dipped in permethrin as both a physical and chemical barrier at night in the same areas. Guard against the contraction of malaria with the correct anti-malarials (see above). Some would prefer to take test kits for malaria with them and have standby treatment available. However, the field tests of the blood kits have had poor results: when you have malaria you are usually too ill to be able to do the tests correctly enough to make the right diagnosis. Standby treatment (treatment that you carry and take yourself for malaria) should still ideally be supervised by a doctor since the drugs themselves can be toxic if taken incorrectly. The Royal Homeopathic Hospital in the UK does not advocate homeopathic options for either malaria prevention or treatment of malaria.

Liver fluke

This fluke occurs in remote rural areas of Ecuador. A fluke is a sort of flattened worm.

Symptoms: The liver fluke may cause jaundice, gall stone symptoms, right-sided abdominal pain, various liver test abnormalities and changes in the white cell pattern of the blood.

Cure: There is a drug but liver fluke infestation is difficult to treat.

Prevention: Be careful with unwashed vegetables.

Sexual health

The range of visible and invisible diseases is awesome. Unprotected sex can spread HIV, Hepatitis B and C, Gonorrhea (green discharge), chlamydia (nothing to see but may cause painful urination and later female infertility), painful recurrent herpes, syphilis and warts, just to name a few. You can cut down the risk by using condoms or avoiding sex altogether. If you do stray, consider getting a sexual health check on your return home.

Sun protection

Symptoms: White Britons are notorious for becoming red in hot countries because they like to stay out longer than everyone else and do not use adequate sun protection. This can lead to sunburn, which is painful and followed by flaking of skin. Aloe vera gel is a good pain reliever for sunburn. Long-term sun damage leads to a loss of elasticity of skin and the development of pre-cancerous lesions. Many years later a mild or a very malignant form of cancer may develop. The milder basal cell carcinoma, if detected early, can be treated by cutting it out or freezing it. The much nastier malignant melanoma may have already spread to bone and brain at the time that it is first noticed.

Prevention: Sun screen. Follow the Australians with their Slip, Slap, Slop campaign. SPF stands for Sun Protection Factor. It is measured by determining how long a given person takes to 'burn' with and without the sunscreen product on. So, if it takes 10 times longer to burn with the sunscreen product applied, then that product has an SPF of 10. If it only takes twice as long then the SPF is 2. The higher the SPF the greater the protection. However, do not just use higher factors just to stay out in the sun longer. 'Flash frying' (desperate bursts of excessive exposure), as it is called, is known to increase the risks of skin cancer.

Underwater health
Symptoms: If you go diving make sure that you are fit do so. **The British Scuba Association (BSAC)** ① *Telford's Quay, South Pier Rd, Ellesmere Port, Cheshire CH65 4FL, UK, T0151 3-506200, F506215, www.bsac.com,* can put you in touch with doctors who do medical examinations. Protect your feet from cuts, beach dog parasites (larva migrans) and sea urchins. The latter are almost impossible to remove but can be dissolved with lime or vinegar. Keep an eye out for secondary infection.
Cures: Antibiotics for secondary infections. Serious diving injuries may need time in a decompression chamber.
Prevention: Check that the dive company know what they are doing, have appropriate certification from **BSAC** or **Professional Association of Diving Instructors** (PADI) ① *Unit 7, St Philips Central, Albert Rd, St Philips, Bristol BS2 0TD, T0117-3007234, www.padi.com*, and that the equipment is well maintained.

Keeping in touch

Internet

The internet is exceptionally accessible in Ecuador and has replaced postal and telephone services for most travellers. There are so many internet places in the larger cities and towns that you will be tripping over them. They are frequented not only by tourists, but also by many locals, and are sometimes crowded, smoky and noisy. Mind your belongings while you navigate, lest they do likewise.

Some form of internet access may be found almost everywhere in Ecuador, except for the most remote locations in the Oriente. Both the cost and speed of access vary, with the best service available in Quito, Guayaquil and Cuenca. Hourly rates currently average US$1-2.

Net to Phone
Almost every place that offers internet will also have Net to Phone, and there are a few that offer only this service. Net to Phone rates are typically under US$0.25 per minute to North America and Europe, about half the price of calling by ordinary telephone. Audio quality varies, however, and background noise can be a problem in busy cybercafés.

Post and couriers

Despite a face-lift in 2004 accompanied by a substantial price increase, it remains to be seen whether the Ecuadorean post office has really improved. During the previous five years it was unreliable for both sending and receiving mail. Even now, urgent or valuable documents should never be entrusted to it. We have received reports of parcels, letters and especially postcards which never arrived, and *correo certificado* (registered mail) may be even more prone to problems than ordinary

airmail. Those items which did arrive, were at times delayed for several months.
National and international courier service is available as an alternative, for further details see below.

Opening hours for post offices vary from town to town and from branch to branch. In Quito they are generally Monday-Friday 0800-1800 and Saturday 0800-1200. Postal branches in small towns may not be familiar with all rates and procedures. Your chances are better at the main branches in provincial capitals or, better yet, in Quito: at Colón corner Almagro in La Mariscal district, at the main sorting centre on Japón near Naciones Unidas (behind the CCI shopping centre), or at Ulloa y Ramírez Dávalos (Monday-Friday 0730-1600) for very large parcels.

Many beautiful postcards are sold in Ecuador. The most efficient and economical way for them to reach their destination is to mail them from home or deliver them personally.

Letters and postcards Minimum airmail rates for up to 20 g are currently US$1.25 to the Americas, US$2 to Europe, and US$2.25 to the rest of the world; registered mail US$1 extra.

Parcels Up to 30 kg, maximum dimensions permitted are 70 x 30 x 30 cm. Current minimum rates by air parcel post for up to 2 kg: to the Americas US$26.40, to Europe US$43.30, to the rest of the world US$50. There is no surface (sea) mail from Ecuador, but SAL/APR (surface air-lifted) service may be available as a slower and more economical alternative to airmail.

Couriers

Courier companies are the only safe alternative for sending or receiving valuable time-sensitive mail in Ecuador. For international service, **DHL** has offices throughout the country; convenient locations in Quito include Colón 1333 y Foch and República 433 y Almagro, T02-2485100. For courier service within Ecuador, **Servientrega** has offices throughout the country, reliable one to two day service is available to all areas, US$3-4 for up to 2 kg. There are many other courier companies operating in Ecuador, but quality of service and reliability vary greatly.

Telephone

Ecuador's telephone system is currently operated by three regional state companies, whose names you should look for on telephone offices: **Andinatel** in the northern highlands and northern Oriente; **Pacifictel** on the coast, in the southern highlands and southern Oriente; and **ETAPA** in Cuenca. There are also three private companies, **Alegro**, **Movistar** and **Porta**, which provide cellular phone service. The latter two also have debit card operated public cell phones, and **Movistar** also operates *centros de llamada* (see below). Public cell phones are more economical than regular phones for calling other cellular numbers in Ecuador.

The service provided by all of the above is generally adequate, best in the larger cities, worst in small towns and villages. Most public cellular phones have their numbers posted and allow you to receive calls. Debit cards for public cell phones may be purchased at kiosks and many small shops; they are specific to one company (ie you cannot use Porta cards in Movistar phones nor vice versa).

Overall, the best places to make local, national or international calls are one of the very many *centros de llamada* (**calling centres**) located throughout cities and towns. There are so many of these establishments that we cannot list them in our maps or text, look and ask around and you will usually find one close at hand. You are assigned a cabin, dial your own calls, and pay on the way out.

Essentials Keeping in touch

⁞ Dialling codes

09 mobile numbers

Main cities
02 Quito
04 Guayaquil
07 Cuenca

Provinces
02 Pichincha
03 Bolívar, Chimborazo, Cotopaxi, Pastaza, Tungurahua
04 Guayas
05 Galápagos, Manabí, Los Ríos
06 Carchi, Esmeraldas, Imbabura, Napo, Orellana, Sucumbíos, Zamora Chinchipe
07 Azuay, Cañar, El Oro, Loja, Morona Santiago

Emergency and useful phone numbers
101 Police
102 Fire

131 Red Cross
911 All emergencies (Quito and Cuenca only)
100 Directory information
105 National operator
116/117 International operator

To make direct international calls from Ecuador dial **00** followed by the country code, the area code (dropping any initial zeroes) and the local number.

The country code for Ecuador is **+593.** Collect calls from Ecuador to the USA may be made by dialling **T1800-999119**. The access numbers for other countries change frequently and may not work from all locations, enquire with your long distance carrier before leaving home. **Note** All telephone numbers in Ecuador have 7 digits.

Rates fluctuate considerably. Examples of current calling centre rates are: US$0.38 per minute to the USA, US$0.46 per minute to the UK or Australia. Hefty surcharges may be applied to calls made from hotels, ask for their rates in advance.

Since 2002 Ecuador gradually converted from 6- to 7-digit phone numbers, which are now universally used throughout the country. Many people nonetheless still think in terms of 6-digit numbers. When asked for a phone number, they may give only the last 6 digits and assume you will add a '2' at the beginning. Note however that there are now also numbers starting with digits other than '2'. When in doubt, ask for the complete 7-digit number.

Some foreign cell phones (GSM 850) roam in Ecuador but calls made in this way are very expensive, US$2-5 per minute. Prepaid SIM chip plans are not available unless you purchase an Ecuadorean cell phone, which will of course give you a local number and is much cheaper than the above. Internet access via GPRS is available, but can be difficult to configure. For details see www.movistar.com.ec and www.porta.net

Media

The main national newspapers are given along with their website on page 28. They all offer reasonably accurate reporting without any strong political bias. Ecuadorean television tends to be more sensationalist than the print media, and radio is best reserved for music. Foreign newspapers and magazines are only available in some luxury hotels and a few speciality shops in Quito and Guayaquil. International satellite television is becoming increasingly common.

❉ Footprint features

Introduction

Few cities have a setting to match that of Quito, the second highest capital in Latin America. It sits on a narrow valley running north to south, at the foot of the volcano Pichincha (4,794 m). Quito is a city of many faces. The Old City, a UNESCO World Heritage site, is the colonial centre, where pastel-coloured houses and ornate churches line a warren of steep and narrow streets. Following a revitalization programme in recent years, the Centro Colonial is once again the heart of the city. North of the Old City is Modern Quito – or New City – an altogether different place. Its broad avenues are lined with fine private residences, parks, embassies and villas. Here you'll find Quito's main tourist and business area: banks, tour agencies, airlines, language schools, smart shops and restaurants, bars and cafés, and a huge variety of hotels in the district known as La Mariscal, and further north as far as Avenida Naciones Unidas. Quito's working class neighbourhoods stretch to the south of the Old City, while suburban sprawl fills the valleys to the east. In the far north and south are relatively small industrial zones.

★ Don't miss...

1 **The Old City** Stroll through the streets or ride a horse-drawn carriage to explore Quito in style, page 101.

2 **Taking in the views** Admire the city and the surrounding snow-capped peaks from the top of El Panecillo, page 105, or the Basílica, page 105.

3 **Museo Nacional del Banco Central** Gain a comprehensive introduction to Ecuadorean culture at the Casa de la Cultura, page 107.

4 **Mitad del Mundo** Indulge your inner tourist at the equator, page 144.

5 **Papallacta** Pamper yourself in the thermal baths, page 147.

6 **Mindo** Get back to nature among the lush cloud forest, rivers and waterfalls, page 153.

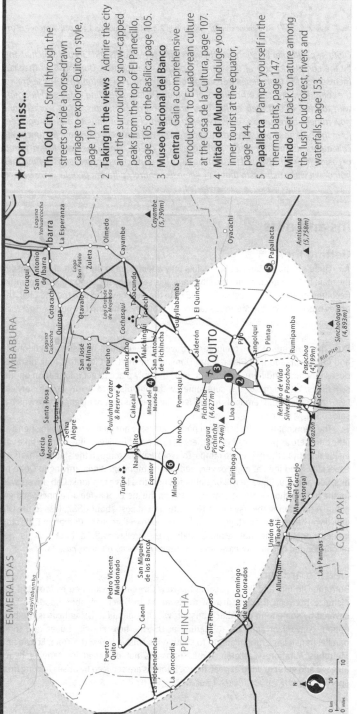

Quito → *Phone code 02 Colour map 2, grid C4 Population 1,460,000 Altitude 2,850 m*

Quito's spectacular location and the wonderful revival of its Old City are matched only by the complex charm of the capital's people, the "Chullas Quiteños" as they call themselves; the term defies translation but is akin to 'real Quitonians'. These are not the colourfully dressed inhabitants of highland villages, tending crops and haggling with tourists to sell their crafts. They are young professionals, office workers and government bureaucrats, conservatively attired and courteous to a fault, and they form the backbone of a very urban society. You will see them going out for lunch with colleagues during the week, making even a cheap almuerzo seem like a formal occasion. You will also find them in the city's bars and clubs on weekends, letting their hair down with such gusto that they seem like entirely different people. ⟩⟩ For Sleeping, Eating and all other listings, see pages 114-144.

Ins and outs

Getting there

Air Quito's airport, Mariscal Sucre, lies only about 5 km to the north of La Mariscal, the main hotel district, within the city limits. It is served by the airport taxi cooperative (recommended as the safest option, US$5 to the New City, US$6 to the Old City), the trolley bus (*El Trole*), the Metrobus (articulated bus system) and city buses. ⟩⟩ *For details of transport to and from the airport, see Touching down, page 42.*

Bus The main bus station for inter-city travel is the Terminal Terrestre at Maldonado and Cumandá, south of Plaza Santo Domingo, in the Old City. Most long-distance buses start and end here, and this is really the only place to get information on bus schedules, although several companies with long-distance luxury coach services also have offices and terminals in the New City. There is a 24-hr luggage store which is safe, US$1.75 per day.

The Terminal Terrestre is neither particularly safe nor pleasant, so try to spend as little time here as possible. If going there by taxi, pay the driver a little extra to take you inside directly to the departure ramps, to avoid walking through the station. This is an especially good idea at night or very early in the morning. When arriving in Quito by bus, you and your luggage will be unloaded next to a large taxi rank. Cab drivers wait for the buses; choose one, either agree to use the meter or agree on a price, and get going. A ride during the day to the New City should cost about US$4, less to the Old City. If you have almost no luggage and know Quito well, then the Cumandá Trole stop is right outside the bus station. Riding the trolley with a backpack is not recommended because of crowding and theft. ⟩⟩ *See also Transport, page 137*

Getting around

Both the Old City and La Mariscal in the New City can be explored by foot, but the distance between them and from these areas to other neighbourhoods is best covered by some form of public transport which is plentiful. Using taxis is the best option, convenient and cheap (starting at US$1). There are city buses and three parallel transit lines running north to south on exclusive lanes: the **Trole**, **Ecovía** and **Metrobus Miraflores-Carcelén**. Public transit is not designed for carrying heavy luggage and gets crowded at peak hours. Suburbs are serviced by buses leaving from specific stops. ⟩⟩ *See also Transport, page 137.*

⁝ Flying into Quito at night

Quito airport is open from 0400 to 0130. Most flights from North America arrive between 1900 and midnight. If a flight to Quito is delayed much after midnight, then it is usually diverted to land in Guayaquil. Most airport services are closed at night, the telephone calling centre is at International Departures, open 0500-2300. There is nowhere to wait until dawn and it can get quite cold outside.

The hotels near the airport are poor, so you are better off going into the city. Select a couple of places near one another so you can have a choice. The hotel booking service at International Arrivals can help you enquire if they have room and the current price. Take a taxi to check them out, there is no bus service after about 2000 and

walking is out of the question.

Try to team up with at least one other traveller and get a taxi voucher in the arrivals area. Ask to be taken to your hotel of first choice. One person can remain with the luggage in the cab while the other checks out the hotel; if it is unsuitable, have the cab take you to the next place on your list. If you are in a group of six or more, the van services from the airport can be a good deal.

In the words of an old saying, "All dogs look black at night". Remember that it is always intimidating to arrive in an unfamiliar place after dark. Spend a bit more for safe and comfortable accommodation for your first night in Quito. After a good sleep, you will quickly get your bearings the next morning.

Road The city's main arteries run north-south and traffic congestion along them is a serious problem. Note that there is a ring road around Quito, and a bypass to the south via the Autopista del Valle de Los Chillos and the Carretera de Amaguaña.

Orientation

Quito is a long, narrow city, stretching from north to south for almost 40 km, and east to west only between 3 and 5 km. The best way to get orientated is to look for **Pichincha**, the mountain which lies to the west of the city. The **El Panecillo** hill is a landmark at the south end of the Old City.

The areas of most interest to visitors are the revitalized **colonial city**, with its many churches, historical monuments, museums and some hotels and restaurants, best accessed by trolley; **La Mariscal** or **Mariscal Sucre** district, east from Av 10 de Agosto to Av 12 de Octubre, and north from Av Patria to Av Orellana, where you find many hotels, restaurants, bars, discos, travel agencies and some banks; and the environs of **Parque La Carolina**, north of La Mariscal as far as Av Naciones Unidas and from Av 10 de Agosto east to and Av Eloy Alfaro, where the newer hotels, restaurants, main banking district, airline offices and a number of shopping malls are located.

Street numbers For a number of years the municipal authorities in Quito have been implementing a new street numbering system. The north-south axis is C Rocafuerte. All streets north of this street are lettered **N** and numbered in sequence, and likewise streets running south, which are lettered **S**. The east-west axis is Av 10 de Agosto, C Guayaquil and C Maldonado; streets running east are lettered **E** and numbered in sequence, and those running west are lettered **Oe** (*oeste*). Street numbers are followed by a dash, then the individual building number, indicating the distance in metres from the corner – eg E5-127, or N12-43. By early 2005 the north and centre of the city had been renumbered, however many Quiteños do not use the new numbers and both numbering systems are in operation. The addresses listed below use both systems.

Quito orientation

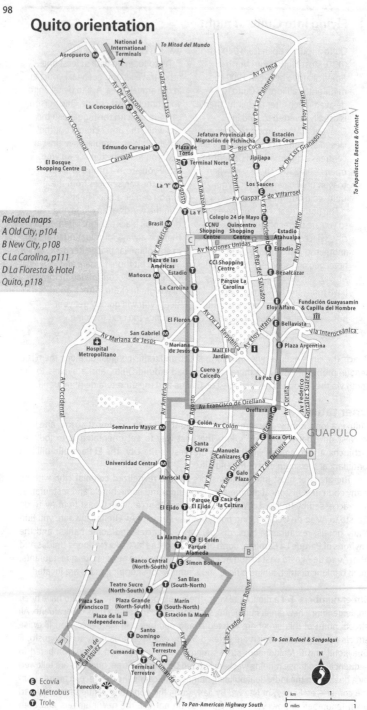

Related maps
A Old City, p104
B New City, p108
C La Carolina, p111
D La Floresta & Hotel
Quito, p118

To Mitad del Mundo

National &
International
Terminals

Aeropuerto

Av Galo Plaza Lasso

Av El Inca

Av De Las Palmeras

La Concepción

Av De La Prensa

Av De Los Granados

Av Eloy Alfaro

Edmundo Carvajal

Carvajal

Av Occidental

El Bosque
Shopping Centre

Jefatura Provincial de
Migración de Pichincha

Estación
Río Coca

Plaza
de Toros

Río Coca

Terminal Norte

Jipijapa

Av De Los Shyris

Av Amazonas

La 'Y'

Av 10 de Agosto

Los Sauces

Av Gaspar de Villarroel

La Y

Brasil

Colegio 24 de Mayo

CCNU
Shopping
Centre

Quincentro
Shopping
Centre

Estadio
Atahualpa

Av De Diciembre

C

Av Naciones Unidas

Estadio

Plaza de las
Américas

CCI Shopping
Centre

Av Rep del Salvador

Mañosca

Av América

Estadio

Parque La
Carolina

Benalcázar

La Carolina

Eloy Alfaro

Fundación Guayasamín
& Capilla del Hombre

El Florón

Av De La República

Av Eloy Alfaro

Bellavista

Vía Interoceánica

San Gabriel

Av Mariana de Jesús

Mariana
de Jesús

Plaza Argentina

Hospital
Metropolitano

Mall El
Jardín

Cuero y
Caicedo

La Paz

Av Federico
González Suárez

Av América

Av Francisco de Orellana

Av Coruña

GUAPULO

Seminario Mayor

Colón

Av Colón

Orellana

Av 6 de Diciembre

Baca Ortiz

Av 12 de Octubre

D

Santa
Clara

Manuela
Cañizares

Universidad Central

Av 10 de Agosto

Av Amazonas

Galo
Plaza

Mariscal

Parque
El Ejido

Casa de
la Cultura

El Ejido

La Alameda

El Belén

Parque
Alameda

B

Banco Central
(North-South)

Simón Bolívar

Teatro Sucre
(North-South)

San Blas
(South-North)

Plaza San
Francisco

Plaza Grande
(North-South)

Marín
(South-North)

Plaza de la
Independencia

Estación la Marín

Santo
Domingo

Av Pichincha

Av Libertador Simón Bolívar

To San Rafael & Sangolquí

A

Av Bahía de Caráquez

Cumandá

Terminal
Terrestre

Terminal
Terrestre

Av Cumandá

Panecillo

To Pan-American Highway South

To Papallacta, Baeza & Oriente

E Ecovía
M Metrobus
T Trole

N

0 km   1
0 miles   1

Efforts by the authorities have resulted in improved public safety in the city. However, beware that theft and violent crime are still hazards. Both the Old City, away from a two block core around the Plaza de la Independencia, and the New City, including La Mariscal, are dangerous after 2200 and pickpockets are active at all hours. Take the necessary precautions: watch your belongings at all times, avoid crowds, use taxis at night and whenever you carry valuables. Be careful on crowded buses and on the Trole. Even more caution is required around the Terminal Terrestre and La Marín. Bag slashing can be a problem at bus terminals. City parks should be avoided at night and caution is recommended at quiet times, when it is best to stay along the periphery. In the Old City avoid going west of C Imbabura. The **Policía de Turismo** has its headquarters at Reina Victoria y Roca, T02-2543983, they have information booths in several locations in La Mariscal and one at El Panecillo. Members of the **Policía Metropolitana**, who patrol the Old City on foot, speak some English and are very helpful.

Visiting **Panecillo** has long been considered a risky business, but neighbourhood brigades are patrolling the area and have improved public safety; they charge visitors US$0.25 per person or US$1 per vehicle. However, taking a taxi up is a lot safer than walking. Do not carry valuables and seek local advice before going on foot.

Guagua Pichincha is an active volcano located 14 km west of Quito. The crater is a 800-m-deep breached caldera open to the west (ie facing away from Quito). Eruptions during 1999 made for some unforgettable photos but caused only minor inconvenience to the city, in the form of light ash fall. There has been no visible volcanic activity since then to the close of this edition. ▶▶ *See also Safety, page 46*

Climate
Quito is within 25 km of the equator, but it stands high enough to make its climate much like that of spring in England; the days pleasantly warm and the nights cool. Because of the height, visitors may initially feel some discomfort and should slow their pace for the first day or so. The mean temperature is 13°C; rainfall, 1,473 mm. The rainy season is October-May, with a lull in December, and the heaviest rainfall in April, though heavy storms in July are not unknown. Rain usually falls in the afternoon. The day length (sunrise to sunset) is almost constant throughout the year. Quito suffers from air and noise pollution, principally due to traffic congestion. These are worst at rush hours and especially severe during the Christmas shopping season. During school holidays, July-September, the air is considerably better.

Tourist information
The **Corporación Metropolitana de Turismo** ① *Toll free T1-800-767767, www.quito.com.ec*, has information offices with English-speaking personnel, some brochures and maps, and an excellent website. Offices are in various locations: International arrivals at the **airport** ① *T02-3300163, daily 0600-0000*; in the **Old City** ① *Edificio El Cadisán, García Moreno N12-01 y Mejía, T02-2572566, Mon-Sat 0900-1800, Sun 1000-1600*, also has a souvenir shop; in the **New City** ① *Parque Gabriela Mistral, Cordero y Reina Victoria, T02-2551566, Mon-Fri 0900-1700*, and at the **Museo del Banco Central** ① *Av Patria y 6 de Diciembre, T02-2221116, Mon-Fri 0900-1700, Sat-Sun 1000-1600*.

The **Empresa de Desarrollo del Centro Histórico** ① *Pasaje Arzobispal at Plaza de la Independencia, ground floor, T02-258-6591, daily 0900-0000*, in the Old City runs walking tours and has an information office and kiosk where maps are sold, some English and French spoken. Kiosk at Chile y Venezuela opposite Plaza de la Independencia, schedule varies according to events happening in the city. The **Policía Nacional de Turismo** ① *T02-2543983, Mon-Sat 1100-2100*, has several information kiosks in La Mariscal and one in El Panecillo, brochures, some English spoken. The

Ministerio de Turismo ① *Eloy Alfaro N32-300, between República and Los Shyris, ground floor, T02-2507559/560, www.vivecuador.com, Mon-Fri 0830-1700*, has an information counter with brochures for all of Ecuador, English spoken.

South American Explorers (SAE) ① *Jorge Washington 311 y Leonidas Plaza, Quito, T/F02-2225228, quitoclub@saexplorers.org Mon-Fri 0930-1700, Sat 0900-1200*, is a US-based non-profit organization, which provides its members with a wide range of travel information about Ecuador and South America. See also page 28.

Maps Instituto Geográfico Militar ① *Senierges y Telmo Paz y Miño, on top of the hill to the east of Parque El Ejido. From Av 12 de Octubre, opposite the Casa de la Cultura, take Jiménez (a small street) up the hill. After crossing Av Colombia continue uphill on Paz y Miño behind the Military Hospital and then turn right to the guarded main entrance. You have to deposit your passport or identification card. T02-2229075, www.igm.gov.ec* Beautiful views from the grounds. Map and aerial photo indexes are all laid out for inspection. The map sales room (helpful staff) is open Mon-Thu 0800-1600, Fri 0800-1300. Map and geographic reference libraries are located next to the sales room. ▸▸ *For more information on maps and guide books, see page 58.*

Guided tours The **Empresa de Desarrollo del Centro Histórico** offers **Paseos Culturales**, guided walking tours along two circuits in the colonial city ① *Plaza de la Independencia, Chile y García Moreno, ground floor of the Palacio Arzobispal, T02-2586591, Tue-Sun 0900-1100 and 1400-1430, 2½-3 hours, US$10, Children and seniors US$5, includes museum entrance fees. Night tours require a minimum of 8 persons, 1900-2000, walking tour US$5, bus tours US$12 per person, advance booking required.* These include visits with English-speaking guides, who are part of the Metropolitan Police, to museums, plazas, churches, convents and historical buildings. They also have two night tours, one walking through different plazas and a bus tour to El Panecillo and La Cima de la Libertad lookouts.

For those who would rather ride in style, **Coches de la Colonia** ① *Plaza de la Independencia, C Chile outside the Palacio Arzobispal, T02-2950392, reservations recommended on weekends; Sun-Thu 1600-2200, Fri-Sun 1600-0000, US$4, children and seniors US$2, carriage for 4 US$12, carriage for 9 US$24*, will take you on a 20-minute tour of the colonial heart on a horse-drawn carriage with an English speaking guide.

History

Archaeological studies suggest that the valley of Quito and the surrounding areas have been occupied for some 10,000 years. The remains of ancient Palaeoindian peoples, nomadic hunters who used obsidian to make stone tools, have been found at various sites around town. During the subsequent Formative era, pre-Ecuadorian peoples began to settle in villages, till fields and make ceramics. One of the best-known Formative sites of highland Ecuador is located in northwest Quito, in Cotocollao.

Quito is named after the **Quitus**, a tribe which inhabited the region in pre-Inca times. By the beginning of the 16th century, the northern highlands of Ecuador were conquered by the Incas and Quito became the capital of the northern half of the empire under the rule of Huayna Capac and later his son Atahualpa. As the Spanish conquest approached, Rumiñahui, Atahualpa's general, razed the city, to prevent it from falling into the invaders' hands.

The colonial city of Quito was founded by Sebastián de Benalcázar, Pizarro's lieutenant, on December 6, 1534. It was built at the foot of Panecillo on the ruins of the ancient city, using the rubble as construction material and today you can still find examples of Inca stonework in the façades and floors of some colonial buildings such as the Cathedral and the church of San Francisco. Following the conquest, Quito became the seat of government of the **Real Audencia de Quito**, the crown colony, which governed current day Ecuador as well as parts of southern Colombia and northern Peru.

The city changed gradually over time. The Government Palace, for example, was built in the 17th century as the seat of government of the Real Audiencia, yet changes were introduced at the end of the colonial period and the beginning of the republican period in the 19th century.

The 20th century saw the expansion of the city both to the north and south, first with the development of residential neighbourhoods and later with a transfer of the commercial and banking heart north of the colonial centre. In 1978, Quito was declared a UNESCO World Heritage site. In the 1980s and 1990s the number of high-rise buildings increased, the suburban valleys of Los Chillos and Tumbaco to the east of town were incorporated into a new **Distrito Metropolitano**, and a number of new poor neighbourhoods sprawled in the far north and south. The city continues to grow, and at the start of the millennium Quito stretched almost 40 km from north to south. The new century has also brought the revitalization of the colonial centre.

Sights

Old City

Plazas and monuments

The Centro Histórico, Quito's colonial district is a pleasant place to stroll and admire the architecture, monuments and art. At night, the illuminated plazas and churches are very beautiful. The core of the Old City is quite safe with frequent patrols by the Metropolitan Police. On Sundays the area is closed to vehicles (0900-1600) and fills with pedestrians, locals as well as tourists.

'Cadisán' is a new term in Old Quito. The restored colonial home of Capitán Diego de Sandoval, it houses the tourist information office, municipal parking and a smart restaurant.

The heart of the colonial city is **Plaza de la Independencia** or **Plaza Grande**, dominated by the **Cathedral** ① *Mon-Sat 1000-1600, Sun 1000-1400. US$1.50*, built 1550-62, with grey stone porticos and green tile cupolas. The portal and tower were only completed in the 20th century. On its outer walls are plaques listing the names of the founding fathers of Quito. Inside, in a small chapel tucked away in a corner, are the tombs of the independence hero, General Antonio José de Sucre, and other historical personalities. Also a famous *Descent from the Cross* by the Indian painter Caspicara. There are many other 17th and 18th century paintings and some fine examples of the works of the Quito School of Art (see Painting and sculpture, page 470). The interior decoration, especially the roof, shows Moorish influence. A former refectory with paintings of all of Quito's archbishops and a display of robes used by priests in the 17th century are shown in a small museum.

A good way to learn about the colonial city is to take a walking tour, p 100.

Beside the Cathedral, around the corner, is **El Sagrario** ① *Mon-Sat 0800-1800, Sun 0800-1330, free*, originally built in the 17th century as the Cathedral's main chapel and is very beautiful. It has some impressive baroque columns, its inner doors are gold-plated and built in the Churrigueresque style.

Facing the Cathedral is the **Palacio Arzobispal**, the Archbishop's palace. Part of the building, the Pasaje Arzobispal, now houses shops and restaurants around stone

24 hours in Quito

If you only do one thing in Quito then make sure it is a tour of the Old City. Here you can admire the stunning colonial architecture as you wander up and down a maze of steep cobbled streets. The Empresa de Desarrollo del Centro Histórico offers very good tours with English-speaking guides.

If you would rather do it on your own, start in **Plaza de la Independencia**, the heart of the colonial city, then follow C García Moreno to **Iglesia La Compañía**, the most ornate of Quito's churches, up C Sucre to **Plaza de San Francisco**, dominated by its impressive church and monastery. Then head down C Bolívar to **Plaza de Santo Domingo**, where there's another fine colonial church to see.

For a wonderful view of the city and encircling volcanoes and mountains, take a taxi up to the top of **El Panecillo**, which is instantly recognizable by the statue of the Virgen de Quito on top.

By now you'll no doubt be feeling peckish so back at **Plaza de la Independencia**, sample some traditional Ecuadorean cuisine at one of the restaurants at the Palacio Arzobispal. At **Hasta la vuelta Señor**,

you can learn about Padre Almeida, one of Quito's legendary characters. If you prefer more upscale surroundings, on the same street are **La Cueva del Oso** and the very exclusive **Mea Culpa**.

After lunch, you might want to indulge in a little culture, so take the Ecovía to the **Casa de la Cultura** in Parque El Ejido, where you can bone up on archaeology, indigenous costumes, musical instruments and modern art, as well as many temporary exhibits.

Need a breather? Take a break to leisurely read your guidebook and enjoy a coffee at **Café Trovero**, in La Mariscal, before catching up on your emails in one of the area's myriad cybercafés.

Modern Quito is your oyster for international dining, but if the yen is for more typically Ecuadorean fare, try the simple **Mama Clorinda**, or the nouvelle cuisine of **El Galpón**.

Then it's time to sample Quito's nightlife. **Turtle's Head Bar** and **Ghoz** are perennial gringo faves, but if you want to experience a night of hot and sweaty salsa, head for **Seseribó**, where you can wiggle your hips with the best of them.

courtyards. Next to it, in the northwest corner, is the former **Hotel Majestic**, with an eclectic façade, including baroque columns. Built in 1930, it was the first building in the old city with more than two storeys; it is being refurbished back into a hotel. On the east side of the Plaza is the modern concrete **Palacio Municipal** which fits in surprisingly well.

Plaza de San Francisco (or Bolívar) is west of Plaza de la Independencia. On the northwest side of this plaza is the great church and monastery of the patron saint of Quito, San Francisco (see below). This was the site of the market in pre-Inca times and and of Hayna Capac's palace during the Inca occupation.

Plaza de Santo Domingo (or Sucre), to the southeast of Plaza de la Independencia, has the church and monastery of Santo Domingo and the Chapel of the Rosary. In the centre of the plaza is a statue to Sucre, pointing to the slopes of Pichincha where he won the decisive battle for the independence of Ecuador. On the south side of the plaza is the **Arco de la Capilla del Rosario**, one of the city's colonial arches. Going through it you enter **La Mama Cuchara** (the 'great big spoon'), a dead-end street which conserves its colonial flavour.

To the northeast of Plaza de la Independencia, is the **Plaza del Teatro** with the neoclassical 19th century **Teatro Sucre** ⓘ *C Guayaquil y Manabí, To2-2280982*. This beautiful, small theatre remained closed for several years until renovations were completed at the end of 2003, giving Quito back its main cultural centre.A second theatre in the Old City is **Teatro Bolívar** ⓘ *Espejo y Flores, To2-2582486*, built in 1933 and restored in 1997, but badly damaged by fire in 1999. A foundation is trying to obtain the funds for its rehabilitation.

Other squares include: **Plazoleta Benalcázar**, which has a statue of the founder of Quito; **Plazoleta González Suárez**, which has a statue of the former bishop and historian; **La Marín** or Plazoleta Marín, focal point of urban transport (best avoided); **Plaza de la Recoleta** to the south of the centre, and **Plaza de San Blas** to the north of the centre by the eponymous church.

Calle Morales, the main street of **La Ronda** district, is one of the oldest streets in the city, worth seeing for its narrow cobbled way and wrought-iron balconies. It is better known as Calle La Ronda and is now part of a red light district; beware of pickpockets and do not visit at night.

Churches → *For details of the Cathedral, see Plazas and monuments above.*

San Francisco,ⓘ *Mon-Fri 0800-1200, 1500-1800, Sat-Sun 0900-1200*, built in 1553, is Quito's first and largest colonial church. It is here that the famous Quito School of Art was founded. The two towers were felled by an earthquake in 1868 and rebuilt. A modest statue of the founder, Fray Jodoco Ricke, the Flemish Franciscan who sowed the first wheat in Ecuador, stands at the foot of the stairs to the church portal. Worth seeing are the fine wood carvings in the choir, a magnificent high altar of gold and an exquisite carved ceiling. The church is rich in art treasures, the best known of which is *La Virgen de Quito* by Legarda, which depicts the Virgin Mary with silver wings. The statue atop Panecillo is based on this painting. There are also some

> **⦂** *There are 86 churches in Quito; if you don't have that much time, the star attractions are La Compañía, San Francisco and Santo Domingo.*

paintings in the aisles by Miguel de Santiago, the colonial *mestizo* painter. His paintings of the life of Saint Francis decorate the monastery of San Francisco close by, where the collection of painting and sculpture by artists of the Quito School of Art was renovated in 1994. (See museums below) Adjoining San Francisco is the **Cantuña Chapel** ⓘ *Mon-Fri 0800-1200 and 1500-1800, Sat-Sun 0900-1700*, which has impressive sculptures.

Completed around 1620, the church and monastery of **Santo Domingo** ⓘ *Daily 0700-1300, 1700-1900*, has a carved Moorish ceiling over its large central nave and rich wood carvings. In the main altar is an impressive silver throne, *el trono de la Virgen*, weighing several hundred pounds. To the right of the main altar is the remarkable **Capilla del Rosario**, built on top of the arch of the same name. Santo Domingo housed the Colegio Mayor de San Fernando, where Latin and philosophy were taught in colonial times. Nowadays it houses a fine religious art museum (see below).

The fine Jesuit church of **La Compañía** ⓘ *Calle García Moreno, one block south of Plaza de la Independencia, Mon-Fri 1000-1700, Sat 1000-1600, Sun 1200-1600, US$2*, has the most ornate and richly sculptured façade and interior. Several of its most precious treasures, including a painting of the Virgen Dolorosa framed in emeralds and gold, are kept in the vaults of the Banco Central and appear only at special festivals. Replicas of the impressive paintings of hell and the final judgement by Miguel de Santiago can be seen at the entrance. Extensive restoration was completed in 2002.

La Merced ⓘ *Mon-Sat 0630-1200, 1230-1800*, not far away to the north, was built at the beginning of the 17th century, in baroque and moorish style, to commemorate Pichincha's eruptions which threatened to destroy the city. General Sucre and his troops prayed here for the wellbeing of the nation, following the decisive battle which gave Ecuador its independence in 1822. In the adjacent monastery of La Merced is Quito's oldest clock, built in 1817 in London. Fine cloisters are entered through a door to the left of the altar. La Merced church contains many splendidly elaborate styles, the main altar has wood carvings by Legarda; note the statue of Neptune on the main patio fountain.

Many of the heroes of Ecuador's struggle for independence are buried in the monastery of **San Agustín** ① *Flores y Chile, Mon-Sat 0700-1200, 1300-1800.* The church has beautiful cloisters on three sides, where the first act of independence

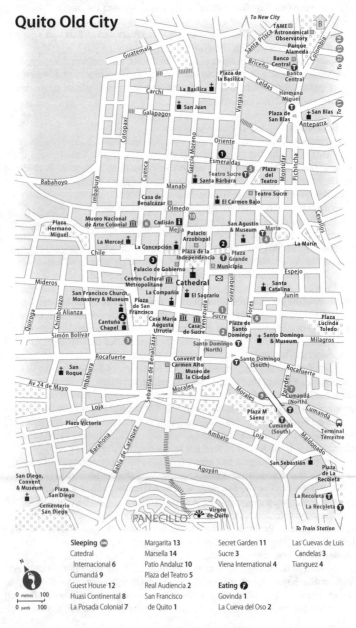

from Spain was signed on 10 August 1809; it is now a national shrine. The church was extensively renovated due to earthquake damage, the wood-carved columns and gilded altars are among the few remains of the original 16th-century construction. The monastery was once the home of the Universidad de San Fulgencio, Quito's first university, founded in the 16th century, and has a large collection of paintings by Miguel de Santiago and an attractive fountain made from a single block of stone.

The large **Basílica del Voto Nacional** ① *Plaza de la Basílica, Venezuela y Carchi T02-2286084, 0900-1700, US$2, gift shop.* has many gargoyles depicting Ecuadorean fauna from the mainland and Galápagos, stained glass windows with native orchids and fine, bas-relief bronze doors. Underneath is a large cemetery. Construction started in 1926 and took 72 years; some final details remain unfinished due to lack of funding. It is possible to go up to the towers, where there is also a cafeteria. The views of the city are magnificent. Recommended.

City lookouts

Quito's setting, in a valley surrounded by mountains, affords many views of the city itself and the encircling cones of volcanoes. A rounded hill called **El Panecillo** (the little breadloaf) ① *0900-1800 daily. US$1 per vehicle or US$0.25 per person if walking, for the neighbourhood safety brigade. Entry to the interior of the monument is US$2. There are craft sales at the base and Pim's Restaurant is along the road, before you reach the monument,* lies to the south of the Plaza de San Francisco. Gazing benignly over the Old City from the top of Panecillo is the impressive statue of the Virgen de Quito, a replica of the painting by Legarda found in the San Francisco Church. There are excellent views from the observation platform up the statue.

> ‡ All high-lying areas of the city are natural lookouts.

Note It is not safe to walk up the Panecillo by the series of steps and paths which begin on García Moreno (where it meets Ambato). See Public safety in Essentials, page 46. You should take a taxi up and down, which costs US$3 from the Old City, including a short wait at the top to admire the spectacular view.

The towers of the **Basílica** (see Churches above) are great for viewing the city. If you want to go all the way to the top have your hands free for the upper ladders and walkways, this part is not for those with fear of heights. The **Cima de la Libertad** (see Museums page 114) also provides good views of the city. To the east of the colonial city is **Parque Itchimbía**, a natural lookout over the city with walking and cycle trails and a cultural centre housed in a 19th-century metal structure imported from Europe, once one of the city's markets. Another place with commanding views over the city is **Cruz Loma** on the flanks of Pichincha (3996 m). In 2004, construction started on a *teleférico* (cable car) and tourist complex with lookout, restaurants and other amenities. Further information is available from www.centrohistoricodequito.com (Spanish only).

Museums → *Check museum opening times in advance.*

Quito prides itself on its art and the city's galleries, churches and museums boast many fine examples. ►► *See also Fine art and sculpture, page 470.*

Housed in the restored 16th-century Hospital San Juan de Dios, a beautiful building, is the **Museo de la Ciudad** ① *García Moreno 572 y Rocafuerte, T02-2283882. Tue-Sun 0930-1730, US$2, students US$1.50, English, French, German or Italian guide service $6 per group.* It takes you through Quito's history from pre-Hispanic times to the 19th century. One floor has an interesting mosaic made of wooden parquet with a city map.

Museo Nacional de Arte Colonial ① *Cuenca y Mejía, T02-2282297, undergoing restoration in 2005,* features a small collection of Ecuadorean sculpture and painting, housed in the 17th-century mansion of Marqués de Villacís, which also has an attractive patio and fountain.

Museo del Convento de San Francisco ① *Plaza de San Francisco, T02-2281124, Mon-Sat 0900-1800, Sun 0900-1200, US$2*, has a fine collection of religious art; there are pieces by many renowned local and European artists. The architecture of the convent is also of interest.

In the restored monastery of **San Diego** (by the cemetery of the same name, just west of Panecillo) is the **Museo de San Diego** ① *Calicuchima 117 y Farfán, entrance to the right of the church, T02-2952516, 0930-1300, 1430-1730 daily, US$2*. Guided tours (Spanish only, 40 minutes) take you around four patios where colonial architecture, sculpture and painting are shown. Of special interest are the gilded pulpit by Juan Bautista Menacho and the Last Supper painting in the refectory, in which a *cuy* and *humitas* have taken the place of the paschal lamb.

Museo de San Agustín ① *Chile y Guayaquil, T02-2580263, Mon-Sat 0900-1200 and Mon-Fri 1500-1730, US$2*, has an interesting exhibition of religious art and restoration work.There is a similar collection in the **Museo Dominicano Fray Pedro Bedón** ① *Plaza de Santo Domingo, T02-2282695. Mon-Fri 0830-1200, 1330-1700. US$2*, named after the friar and painter who created the first brotherhood of Indian painters. Bedón's work and that of other renowned colonial artists is displayed.

An impressive colonial building which belonged to the Jesuits, later housing the royal Cuartel Real de Lima and most recently the municipal library, was restored and reopened in 2000 as the **Centro Cultural Metropolitano**. It houses several temporary exhibits (*free*) and the **Museo de Cera** ① *Espejo y García Moreno, T02-2584363. Tue-Sun 0900-1700, US$1.50*, depicting the execution of the revolutionaries of 1809. The museum, housed in the original cell, is well worth a visit, but is not for the claustrophobic.

Museo Histórico Casa de Sucre ① *Venezuela 573 y Sucre, T02-2952860, Tue-Thu 0900-1600, Fri-Sat 0900-1300, US$1*, is the beautiful, restored house of Sucre, with a museum about life in the 19th century and Sucre's role in Ecuador's independence.

The **Casa de Benalcázar**, built in the 18th century on land that belonged to Sebastián de Benalcázar, the Spanish founder of Quito, now houses the **Instituto Ecuatoriano de Cultura Hispánica** ① *Olmedo y Benalcázar, T02-2288102, Mon-Fri 0900-1200, 1400-1600, free*. The house with a courtyard and some religious statues and paintings is open to the public. Its façade was part of the Quito house of inquisition.

Museo Manuela Sáenz ① *Junín y Montúfar, T02-2958321, Mon-Fri 0830-1300, 1400-1730, US$0.80*, is a tribute to a legendary *Quiteña* who played an important role in the struggle for independence. Some of her personal belongings as well as works of art and weapons are on display.

Casa Museo María Augusta Urrutia ① *García Moreno 760 y Sucre, T02-2580107, Tue-Sun 0930-1800, evenings for restaurant, US$2.50*, the home of a *Quiteña* who devoted her life (1901-1987) to charity, shows the lifestyle of 20th-century aristocracy, with furniture of the colonial and republican period. Also has a restaurant.

Museo Camilo Egas ① *Venezuela 1302 y Esmeraldas, T02-2572012, Tue-Fri 0900-1700, Sat-Sun 1000-1600, US$1, Sun free*, housed in a restored 18th-century home, exhibits the work of the Ecuadorean artist Camilo Egas (1889-1962). It is interesting to see the evolution of style over time, the life of the Ecuadorean Indian in the 1920s and life in New York during the depression. There are also temporary exhibits and children's workshops.

Museo Archivo de Arquitectura ① *Junín 610 y Jiménez, T02-2583938, Mon 0900-1630, Tue-Fri 0900-1830, Sat 1000-1830, US$0.50*, housed in a lovely restored building, has sketches of different buildings in the city and rotating exhibits with scale models.

New City

Parks and monuments

Just north of the colonial city is **Parque la Alameda** ① *To2-2570765, display of old instruments, Mon-Fri 0900-1200, 1430-1730, US$0.50, ring the bell. Also open from 1900 on clear nights for groups of 5 or more and when there are special astral events, US$1,* with an impressive equestrian monument to Simón Bolívar at its southern tip, various lakes and, at the northwest corner, *el churo,* a spiral lookout tower with a good view. In the centre of the park is the oldest astronomical observatory in South America.

❗ *Quito's parks are not safe at night, see Orientation and safety, p97.*

In **Parque El Ejido**, on the south side of Avenida Patria, there are exhibitions of paintings on the weekend, when the park fills with local families. Opposite El Ejido along Av 6 de Diciembre are the **Casa de la Cultura** complex and the small **Parque El Arbolito**, chosen by the indigenous movement as the place to gather before protests.

Further north is the larger **Parque La Carolina**, another popular place for weekend outings among Quiteños. Located north of Avenida Eloy Alfaro and south of Avenida Naciones Unidas and between Avenida Amazonas and Avenida de Los Shyris, it is a place to enjoy ball games, aerobics, boating and cycling. Within the park are the Museo de Ciencias Naturales and the Vivarium. The **Parque Metropolitano**, east of Estadio Atahualpa, is reputed to be the largest urban park in South America and is good for walking, running or biking through the forest. There are some picnic areas with grills. Take Batán-Colmena bus from C Reina Victoria in la Mariscal or C Venezuela in the Old City (every 30 minutes, if marked Bellavista it takes you near the southern entrance, otherwise it goes to the main entrance on C Guanguiltahua). Alternatively take the Ecovía along 6 de Diciembre to the stadium (Naciones Unidas stop) and walk 30 minutes uphill or a bus along Eloy Alfaro to Plaza Costa Rica from where it is a 20-minute walk to the park.

In La Mariscal, at the intersection of Reina Victoria and Foch, is **Plaza del Quinde** (hummingbird) a small plaza with a fountain and sculptures where concerts are held on Thursday nights (starting 1800-1900).

Casa de la Cultura

Opposite Parque El Ejido, at the junction of 6 de Diciembre and Avenida Patria, there is a large complex housing the **Casa de la Cultura** and the museum of the Banco Central del Ecuador (entrance on Patria). Of the many fine museums in Quito, perhaps the most comprehensive is the **Museo Nacional del Banco Central del** Ecuador ① *To2-2223259, Tue-Fri 0900-1700, Sat, Sun and holidays 1000-1600. US$1.50, US$0.50 for students with ISIC or university student card, children US$0.25.* It has three floors, with five different sections. The Sala de Arqueología is particularly impressive. It consists of a series of halls with exhibits and illustrated panels with explanations in English as well as Spanish. It covers successive cultures from 12000 BC to AD 1534 with excellent

❗ *The Museo del Banco Central at the Casa de la Cultura is the place to go if you only have time for one museum.*

diagrams and extensive collections of beautiful pre-Columbian ceramics. The Sala de Oro has a good collection of pre-Hispanic gold objects. The remaining three sections house art collections. The Sala de Arte Colonial is rich in paintings and sculptures especially of religious themes. The Sala de Arte Republicano houses works of the early years of the Republic. The Sala de Arte Contemporáneo presents contemporary art. There are also temporary exhibits, videos on Ecuadorean culture, a bookshop and a cafetería which serves good coffee. For guided tours in English, French or German call ahead and make an appointment. Highly recommended.

Casa de la Cultura Ecuatoriana ① *To2-2223392 (ext 320), Mon-Fri 0900-1700, Sat 1000-1400, US$3,* hosts many temporary exhibits and cultural events. In addition, the following permanent collections are presented in museums belonging to the Casa de la Cultura: **Museo de Arte Moderno**, paintings and sculpture since 1830; **Museo de Traje Indígena**, a collection of traditional dress and adornments of indigenous groups; **Museo de Instrumentos Musicales**, an impressive collection of musical instruments, said to be the second in importance in the world.

Quito New City

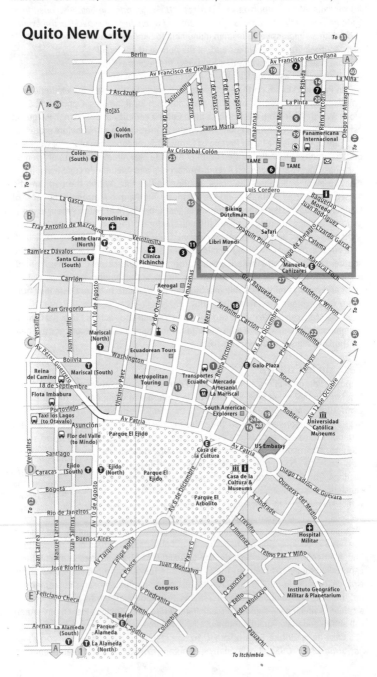

Other museums

The **Museo Jijón y Caamaño** ⓘ *12 de Octubre y Roca, T02-2565627 (ext 1242), Mon-Fri 0800-1600, US$0.60,* housed in the library building of the Universidad Católica, has a well-displayed private collection of archaeological objects, historical documents and paintings by renowned Ecuadorian artists.

Mariscal detail

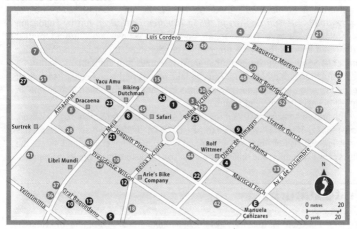

Sleeping 😴
Adventure **51** *detail map*
Alcalá **49** *detail map*
Alston Inn **37** *detail map*
Amaranta **24** *D3*
Amazonas Inn **8** *detail map*
Ambassador **23** *B2*
Antinea **52** *detail map*
Bask **5** *detail map*
Café Cultura **1** *C2*
Casa de Guápulo **38** *C3*
Casa Helbling **2** *C3*
Casa Paxee **14** *B1*
Casa Sol **33** *detail map*
Chalet Suisse **3** *detail map*
Cayman **50** *detail map*
Crossroads **45** *detail map*
El Cafecito **4** *detail map*
El Ciprés **34** *C3*
El Taxo **7** *detail map*
Embassy **27** *C3*
Fuente de Piedra II **36**
 detail map
Gan Eden **42** *detail map*
Hostal de la Rábida **9** *A3*
Hostal del Hoja **25** *B1*
Hostelling
 International **10** *detail map*
Hothello **11** *C2*
Jardín del Sol **46** *??*
Kinara **12** *D1*
La Pradera **31** *A3*

L'Auberge Inn **13** *E2*
Loro Verde **47** *detail map*
Los Alpes **19** *D3*
Mansión del Angel **29**
 detail map
Nuestra Casa **26** *A1*
Picket **43** *detail map*
Plaza Internacional
 & la Cartuja **16** *D3*
Posada de la Abuela **39** *A3*
Posada del Arupo **48**
 detail map
Posada del Maple **17**
 detail map
Queen's Hostel **18** *detail map*
Reina Isabel **41** *detail map*
Rincón Escandinavo **32**
 detail map
Río Amazonas **20** *detail map*
Sebastián **21** *detail map*
Sierra Madre **22** *C3*
Sierra Nevada **35** *B2*
Titisee **44** *detail map*
Vieja Cuba **40** *A3*
Villa Nancy **15** *C3*
Villantigua **28** *D3*
Windsor **6** *C2*

Eating 🍴
Adam's Rib **1** *detail map*
Café Colibrí **27** *detail map*
Café Trovero **21** *detail map*

Chandani Tandoori **6** *B3*
Chez Alain **10** *detail map*
Crêpes & Waffles **2** *A3*
El Arabe **18** *C2*
El Hornero **3** *B2*
El Maple **4** *detail map*
Grain de Café **5** *detail map*
Ile de France **7** *A3*
Le Arcate **13** *detail map*
Magic Bean **8** *detail map*
Mama Clorinda **25** *detail map*
Mango Tree Café **23** *detail map*
Mongo's & Sushi **24**
 detail map
Paléo **26** *detail map*
Porto Pia **22** *detail map*
Shorton Grill **9** *detail map*
Terraza del Tártaro **11** *B2*
Tex Mex **12** *detail map*

Bars & clubs 🍸
Bogarín **30** *detail map*
Ghoz **14** *A3*
la Boca de Lobo **29**
 detail map
No Bar **15** *detail map*
Papillon **16** *A3*
Patatu's **28** *detail map*
Reina Victoria Pub **17** *C2*
Turtle's Head **19** *A3*
Varadero & La
 Bodeguita de Cuba **20** *A3*

0 metres 50
0 yards 50

The **Museo Weilbauer** ⓘ *12 de Octubre y Carrión, T02-2565627 (ext 1369), Mon-Fri 0800-1600, free*, also at the university, has an important archaeological collection from many cultures, in all regions of Ecuador, a photo collection from Oriente and a library.

Museo de Ciencias Naturales ⓘ *Rumipamba 341 y Los Shyris, T02-2449824, Mon-Fri 0830-1130, 1345-1630, Sat 1000-1400, US$2, students US$1*, at the east end of Parque La Carolina, has a collection of stuffed Ecuadorian fauna and flora.

Museo del Colegio Mejía ⓘ *Ante y Venezuela, T02-2583412, Mon-Fri 0800-1200, 1400-1800, US$1*, has natural science and ethnographic exhibits.

Vivarium ⓘ *Rumipamba 3008 y Amazonas, at Parque La Carolina, T02-2230988, Tue-Sun 0930-1730, US$2 (children half price)*, run by **Fundación Herpetológica Gustavo Orces**, is an organization whose aims are to protect endangered species through a programme of education. They have an impressive number of South American and other snakes, reptiles and amphibians, and run a successful breeding programme. You can take photos of the boa constrictors. Staff are friendly and there are good explanations in Spanish (information is available on request in English, French and German).

The **Museo Amazónico** ⓘ *Centro Cultural Abya Yala, 12 de Octubre 1430 y Wilson, T02-2506247, Mon-Fri 0830-1230, 1400-1700, US$2, children and seniors US$1*, has interesting displays of Amazonian flora and fauna and tribal culture and shows the effects of oil exploration and drilling. There is also a bookstore (most books in Spanish).

Quito suburbs

To the east of Quito lie the valleys of the Machángara, San Pedro, Pita and Huambi rivers. Formerly Quito's market garden, the area is rapidly filling with suburbs and the towns are now part of the city's metropolitan area. With a milder climate the valleys and their thermal pools attract inner city dwellers on weekends.

The beautiful district of **Guápulo**, a colonial town, is perched on the edge of a ravine on the eastern fringe of Quito, overlooking the Río Machángara. It is popular with Quito's bohemian community and a worthwhile place to visit. Of interest are its beautiful church and adjoining museum. To get there, take bus Hospital del Sur-Guápulo from Calle Venezuela by Plaza de la Independencia, Guápulo-Dos Puentes eastbound along Avenida Patria, or walk down the steep stairway which leads off Avenida González Suárez, near the **Hotel Quito**.

The **Santuario de Guápulo** ⓘ *daily 0900-1800*, is a lovely 17th-century church, built by Indian slaves and dedicated to Nuestra Señora de Guápulo. It is well worth seeing for its many paintings, gilded altars, stone carvings and, above all, the marvellously carved pulpit by Juan Bautista Menacho, one of the loveliest in the whole continent.

The **Valle de los Chillos** lies southeast of the centre of Quito. It is accessed via the Autopista General Rumiñahui, which starts at El Tébol, east of the Terminal Terrestre. Sangolquí is the largest city here, it has a pleasant park and a nice church. There is a busy Sunday market (and a smaller one on Thursday) and few tourists. On two traffic circles east of town are lovely tile sculptures by the well known 20th-century artist Gonzalo Endara Crow: an ear of corn, the main crop of the valley, and a hummingbird.

To the north of los Chillos is the extinct volcano Ilaló and north of it the **Valle de Tumbaco.** Here are the suburbs of Cumbayá, Cunuyacu, Tumbaco, Puembo and Pifo, accessed through the Vía Interoceánica, the road leading east from Quito to Papallacta, Baeza and the northern Oriente.

In Quito's northwestern suburb of **Cotocollao** is the archaeological site of the same name, dating back over 3,000 years to the Formative period. Ash found covering this settlement suggests that it might have been abandoned around 2,300

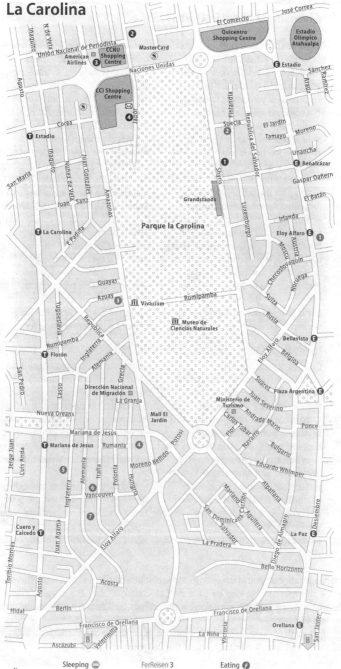

N

Not to scale

Sleeping 🛏	FerReisen **3**	**Eating** 🍴
Akros **1**	Finlandia **2**	La Guarida del Coyote **2**
Apartamentos	Hostal la Carolina **6**	Las Palmeras **4**
Modernos **4**	Sol de Quito **7**	Los Troncos **1**
Chevalier **5**		Pizzerías **3**

☃ Choosing a hotel in Quito

There are over 350 hotels in Quito, of which we list about 100. With so much accommodation being offered, you can find a good place to stay regardless of your tastes or budget, but some travellers are bewildered by the huge selection. To narrow your search, read up on the city, its neighbourhoods and hotels before you arrive.

There are not many good places to stay near the bus station and, at present, none whatsoever by the airport. This is more than compensated for, however, by the abundance of cheap taxis. Think ahead about what type of lodgings and what part of town best suit you, and take a cab to your first choice. Many Quito hotels are easily contacted by phone or email for advance reservations, although this is seldom required, except in July and August. See also Hotel prices and facilities (page 59) and Flying into Quito at night (page 97).

Quito's many hotels may be categorized by a combination of their style, price and location.

International hotel chains and business hotels Quito is well supplied with these, all in the New City. They occupy the highest end of the price range, and often charge foreign guests considerably more than they charge locals. **Swissôtel** stands out in this group for its opulence and excellent service, as does **Hotel Quito** for its lovely views. Most others are cut from a common mould: large modern buildings, elegant and expensive restaurants and bars, small casinos, all services and comforts. They look and feel like big busy hotels anywhere in the world, with little that is distinctively Ecuadorean.

Upscale inns *Quiteño* hospitality excels in this class of select establishments. Scattered throughout the New City, they include elegant little places like **La Cartuja**, **Hostal de La Rábida** and **Villa Nancy** (on Muros). Some are in beautifully refurbished private homes. These gems are expensive, but usually offer a great deal in return: personal service in tasteful, tranquil and very comfortable surroundings.

Apart-Hotels and suites These furnished apartments are a good choice for longer stays and for families. Some also rent by the day. They usually include a living room and fully equipped kitchen, with all utensils. There is a good selection located throughout the New City, with a broad range of prices and facilities. Apartments for rent (mostly unfurnished) are also advertised in **El Comercio** and **El Hoy** as well as their on-line editions (see websites, page).

Old City Hotels here, rather like the Centro Histórico itself, are being revitalized. Some are clustered around the bus terminal, while others are found near the district's many colonial

years ago, after a particularly strong eruption of nearby Volcán Pululahua. There is a small site museum, **Museo de Sitio de Cotocollao** ⓘ *Near the Museo-Biblioteca Aureliano Pólit (see Museums below)*, with ceramics, burials and a scale model of the ancient village.

Just north of Quito along the Panamericana are **Calderón**, where bread figurines are made and **Guayllabamba**, home of the Quito zoo, see page 162.

Museums

Overlooking the city from the northeast is the grandiose **Capilla del Hombre** ⓘ *Mariano Calvache y Lorenzo Chávez, Bellavista, near the Ecuavisa TV station. Easiest to take a taxi here, or take the Batán-Colmena bus, marked Bellavista, T02-2448492, Tue-Sun*

plazas. You can find five-star luxury at **El Patio Andaluz**, some good comfortable places like **Real Audiencia** and **Vienna Internacional**, alongside some of the cheapest and most basic digs in town (where you might have to share the facilities with short-stay couples). Staying here provides an interesting insight into the often overlooked, but very typical, way of life in Quito's historical heart.

Between the Old and New Cities (including the area west of La Mariscal) This is indeed a grey zone, with neither the charm of colonial Quito, nor the vibrant tourist scene of La Mariscal, nor the tranquillity of La Floresta. It is, nonetheless, convenient to all areas and the home to some particularly good-value accommodation, such as **L'Auberge Inn** and **Secret Garden**, both very popular with travellers.

La Mariscal By far the greatest number of lodgings are concentrated here, between Av Patria to the south and Av Orellana to the north, Av 10 de Agosto to the west and Av 12 de Octubre to the east. This is Quito's tourist neighbourhood *par excellence* – the place for those who want to be in the heart of the action. Here you will be surrounded by restaurants, bars, nightlife, tour agencies, craft shops, cybercafés, Spanish schools, and even laundromats. With so much going on, it is not surprising that parts of La Mariscal are noisy, nor that this is where thieves can find the highest concentration of tourists. Hotels in La Mariscal come in all shapes, sizes and prices, and the greatest number of budget places are found here. Shopping around is essential to obtain good value, especially since there is a rapid turnover of establishments. At the same time, the area also has its share of repeatedly recommended favourites, places like **Casa Sol**, **Casa Helbling**, **Posada del Maple** and **Amazonas Inn**.

La Floresta Situated east of La Mariscal, this is an older residential neighbourhood which offers a variety of good accommodation in more relaxed surroundings. Examples include **Ciprés**, **La Casa de Eliza**, and **Casona de Mario**.

La Carolina and Quito suburbs With the rapid growth of the New City, lodgings are also striking out beyond their traditional bounds. In La Carolina (north of La Mariscal) and in a few off-the-beaten-track suburban locations, are interesting options for those who prefer not to be surrounded by other hotels. Parking is also generally less complicated in these out-of-the-way places, especially if you have a large vehicle. In this category, **San Jorge** has the distinction of offering the only rural accommodation within easy reach of Quito. **Casa de Guápulo**, on a steep hillside (not an easy drive), likewise provides unusual and very attractive surroundings.

1000-1700, US$3, students and seniors US$2, US$5 if also visiting the museum, a monument to Latin America conceived by the famous Ecuadorean artist Oswaldo Guayasamín (1919-1999) and completed after his death. The fate of people in this continent is presented through the artist's murals and paintings. An eternal flame represents the ongoing fight for human rights, in the extensive grounds are sculptures (including a Maya stela) and conmemorative plaques.

A few blocks away is the fine **Museo Guayasamín** ① *Bosmediano 543, T02-2446455, Mon-Fri 1000-1700, US$3*. As well as the artist's works there is a Pre-Columbian and colonial collection, which is highly recommended. You can buy works of art and jewellery.

Quito Quito suburbs

In San Rafael, just east of the city is **La Casa de Kingman Museo** ① *Portoviejo y Dávila, 1 block from the San Rafael park in Valle de los Chillos, T02-2861065, www.fundacionkingman.com, Thu-Fri 1000-1600, Sat-Sun 1000-1700, US$3, students US$2, children under 7 free. Take a taxi or a Sangolquí bound bus from La Marín as far as the San Rafael park.* The home of this renowned artist, unchanged from when he lived there, is now open to the public. In addition to a collection of the artist's own work, you can see colonial, republican and 20th-century art.

The **Museo Fray Antonio Rodríguez** ① *Mon-Sat 0900-1800, T02-2565652*, in Guápulo, has three halls with religious art and furniture, from the 16th to the 20th centuries. Guided tours (Spanish only) include a visit to the beautiful Santuario de Guápulo (see Sights above).

Cima de la Libertad ① *Tue-Fri 0830-1630, Sat-Sun 1000-1400, US$1, children and seniors US$0.25. The Tourist Office recommends taking a taxi there as the suburbs are dangerous. You can also take the Trole south to El Recreo and a taxi from there*, is a national monument on the flanks of Pichincha, at the site of the decisive 1822 Battle of Pichincha. It has a large mural by Eduardo Kingman, a history museum and great views.

Museo-Biblioteca Aureliano Pólit ① *José Nogales 220 y Francisco de Arco, Cotocollao stop on the Metrobus, Mon-Fri 0800-1700, US$2*, is in the former Jesuit seminary north of the airport. It has a unique collection of antique maps of Ecuador.
▸▸ For museums at Mitad del Mundo, see Around Quito, page 144.

🛏 Sleeping

For further advice on where to stay, see Choosing a hotel in Quito, p112

Old City *p101, map p104*

L Patio Andaluz, García Moreno N6-52 y Olmedo, T02-2280830, www.hotelpatioandaluz.com. Self-styled 'boutique hotel' in the heart of the colonial city, includes breakfast, exclusive restaurant with Ecuadorean and Spanish cuisine, spa, 5-star comfort and service in a 16th-century house with large arches, balconies and patios. Library and gift shop.

C Real Audiencia, Bolívar Oe3-18 y Guayaquil at Plaza Santo Domingo, T02-2950590, F2580213. Includes breakfast, restaurant/bar on top floor, spacious, well furnished rooms, great views.

C San Francisco de Quito, Sucre 217 y Guayaquil, T02-2287758, F2951241. Converted colonial building, with breakfast, attractive patio but can be noisy at night.

C Viena Internacional, Flores 600 y Chile, T02-2959611, F2954633. Good restaurant, nice rooms, English spoken.

D Catedral Internacional, Mejía 638 y Cuenca, T02-2955438. In an colonial house, good rooms.

D Cumandá, Morales 449 y Maldonado near Terminal Terrestre, T02-2956984, www.hotel-cumanda.com Restaurant, parking, comfortable, excellent service, noisy area but quieter at the back.

D Huasi Continental, Flores N3-08 y Sucre, T02-2957327, F2958441. Refurbished colonial house, 40 rooms, restaurant.

D Plaza del Teatro, Guayaquil 1373 y Esmeraldas, T02-2959462. Restaurant, parking, carpeted rooms, stylish, good service.

E Posada Colonial, Paredes 188 y Rocafuerte, T02-2282859. A simple hostel in a beautiful old building, cheaper with shared bath, hot water, parking, sitting room with TV.

F Sucre, Bolívar 615 and Cuenca, Plaza San Francisco, T02-2954025. Shared bath, hot water, laundry facilities, a bit noisy, has terrace with great views over the Old City, very cheap and basic, often full, also used for short stays.

Between the Old and New Cities

C Kinara, Bogotá 534 y América, T02-2228524, kinara@andinanet.net Includes breakfast, laundry, cooking facilities, library, English/French spoken, free tea and coffee, spotless. Highly recommended.

D Carrión, Carrión 1259 y Versalles, T02-2548256, F2909769. Café and bar, laundry facilities, garden, good value, fills up early.

D Guest House, Julio Castro 379 y Valparaíso, T02-2222564, marcoatm@hoy.net Nicely restored old house, laundry and cooking facilities, nice rooms and views, friendly and helpful, part of Tours Unlimited, new in 2004.

D Hostal del Hoja, Gerónimo Leyton N23-89 y La Gasca, T02-2560832, delhoja@mixmail.com Includes breakfast, shared bath, cooking facilities, dorms, small place, very helpful.

D L'Auberge Inn, Colombia 1138 y Yaguachi, T02-2552912, www.auberge-inn-hostal.com Spacious clean rooms, restaurant, cheaper with shared bath, excellent hot water, cooking facilities, parking, duvets on beds, lovely garden terrace and communal area, pool table, includes use of spa, helpful, good atmosphere, discounts for SAE members. Recommended.

D Nuestra Casa, Las Casas 435 y Versalles, T02-2225470, mlmo@uio.satnet.net Shared bath, laundry and cooking facilities, converted family house, dinner available, camping in garden. Recommended.

D Secret Garden, Antepara E4-60 y Los Ríos, T02-2956704, www.secretgardenquito.com Restored old house, lovely rooftop terrace restaurant serves inexpensive breakfast and dinner (vegetarian available), one room with private bath, cheaper in dorm, nice atmosphere, a popular meeting place for travellers, Ecuadorean-Australian run, opened in 2003. Recommended.

D-E Bambú, Solano 1758 y Colombia, T02-2226738. Family-run hostel, cheaper with shared bath and in dorm, laundry and cooking facilities, garden with hammocks, nice views from terrace, monthly rates US$90-$130, good value.

E Casa Paxee, Romualdo Navarro 326 y La Gasca, T02-2500441. Includes breakfast, private bath, hot water, laundry and cooking facilities, 3 rooms only, discounts available for longer stays.

Quito Sleeping

E Margarita, Los Ríos 1995 y Espinoza, T02-2950441. Private bath, hot water, parking, good beds, sheets changed daily, great value. Highly recommended.

E Marsella, Los Ríos 2035 y Espinoza, T02-2955884. A popular hostel, breakfast available, cheaper with shared bath, hot water, good rooftop terrace with views, top floor rooms best but noisy. Good value.

New City *p107, map p109*

International chains and business hotels

For details of international hotel chains in the city, check the websites: www.hilton.com, www.hojo.com, www.marriotthotels.com, www.mercure.com, www.radisson.com, www.sheraton.com

LL Swissôtel, 12 de Octubre 1820 y Cordero, T02-2566497, http://quito.swissotel.com Superb 5-star accommodation, includes buffet breakfast, Japanese, French and Italian restaurants, also bar, deli and café, state-of-the-art fitness centre, business centre, 3 non-smoking floors and handicapped facilities. Recommended.

L Akros, 6 de Diciembre N34-120 y Checoslovaquia, T02-2468800, www.hotelakros.com Includes welcome cocktail and buffet breakfast, excellent restaurant and bar, internet, spacious rooms.

L-AL Hotel Quito, González Suárez N27-142 y 12 de Octubre, T02-2544600, F2567284. On a hillside overlooking the New City, includes buffet breakfast, good restaurant, pool open to non-residents, internet, lovely views.

AL Sebastián, Almagro N24-416 y Cordero, T02-2222400, hotelsebastian @hotelsebastian.com Restaurant, internet, parking, comfortable and very good.

Upscale inns

L Mansión del Angel, Wilson E5-29 y J L Mera, T02-2557721, F2237819. Nicely refurbished old building, includes breakfast, very elegant, lovely atmosphere.

L-AL Villa Nancy, Muros 146 y 12 de Octubre, T02-2562473, www.villanancy.com In quiet residential area, includes breakfast, small lobby bar, internet, airport transfers, quiet, homely and comfortable, helpful multilingual staff. Recommended.

AL-A Sol de Quito, Alemania N30-170 y Vancouver, T02-2541773, www.soldequito.com Lovely converted home with large sitting room and library decorated with antiques, includes breakfast, restaurant, internet, parking, comfortable rooms, suites have beautiful carved doors. Recommended.

A La Casa Sol, Calama 127 y 6 de Diciembre, T02-2230798, www.lacasasol.com A small quaint inn with courtyard , includes breakfast, 24-hour cafeteria, very helpful, English and French spoken. Highly recommended.

A La Cartuja, Plaza 170 y 18 de Septiembre, T02-2523577, www.hotelacartuja.com In the former British Embassy, includes breakfast, good restaurant but limited menu, beautifully decorated, spacious comfortable rooms, lovely garden, very helpful and hospitable. Highly recommended.

A Los Alpes, Tamayo 233 y Washington, T02-2561110, www.hotellosalpes.com Includes breakfast, excellent restaurant, pleasant and comfortable, popular.

A Santa Bárbara, 12 de Octubre N26-15 y Coruña, T02-2225121, www.hotel-santabarbara.com Beautiful refurbished colonial-style house and gardens, sitting room with fireplace, includes breakfast, restaurant, internet, parking, English, French and Italian spoken.

A Satori, Pedro Ponce Carrasco 262 y Almagro, T/F02-2239575, info@satoriecuador.com Includes breakfast, restaurant, on a quiet side street, good rooms, pleasant and comfortable.

A-B Posada de la Abuela, Santa María 235 y La Rábida, T02-225334, www.posabuela.com Cosy little inn, includes breakfast, parking, some rooms with fireplace, safety deposit box. Lovely refurbished 1920s home with pleasant sitting room in a covered patio.

B Sierra Madre, Veintimilla 464 y Tamayo, T02-2505687, www.hotelsierramadre.com Fully renovated old-style villa, includes breakfast, restaurant, parking, nice sun roof, comfortable.

B Villantigua, Washington E9-48 y Tamayo, T02-2528564, alariv@uio.satnet.net Nice old house furnished with antiques, includes breakfast, some suites with fireplace (more expensive), rooms slightly faded, multilingual staff, quiet.

Apart-hotels and suites

L Colina Suites, La Colina N26-119 y Orellana, T02-2234678, www.lacolinasuites.com Includes buffet breakfast, cafeteria, small spa, internet, includes airport pickup or dropoff, from US$2,000 a month.

AL American Suites, Eloy Alfaro 3333 y Correa, T02-2275120, www.americansuites.com Restaurant, pool and sauna, internet, parking, modern, from US$2,200 a month.

A Amaranta, Leonidas Plaza N20-32 y Washington, T02-2560585. Includes breakfast, good restaurant, parking, comfortable, well-equipped suites, from US$1,600 a month.

A Antinea, Rodríguez 175 y Almagro, T02-2506839, www.hotelantinea.com Includes breakfast, parking, suites and apartments from $800 a month.

C Apartamentos Modernos, Amazonas N31-75 y Mariana de Jesús, T02-2233766 ext 800, modernos@uio.satnet.net Parking, convenient location near El Jardín Mall and Parque La Carolina, English and German spoken, very clean, 1 and 2 bedroom flats from US$500 per month, good value.

La Mariscal *map p108*

L-AL Vieja Cuba, Almagro 1212 y La Niña, T02-2906729, viejacuba@andinanet.net. Nicely refurbished old home, cafeteria and restaurant with Afro-Cuban restaurant, internet, very stylish, great attention to detail.

AL Café Cultura, Robles E6-62 y Reina Victoria, T02-2504078, www.cafecultura.com In old French Embassy, good restaurant with log fire, parking, mixed reports about the rooms and service, reports of thin walls on second floor, lovely garden.

AL Reina Isabel, Amazonas 842 y Veintimilla, T02-2544454, www.hotelreinaisabel.com Business hotel, includes breakfast, restaurant, parking, very nice, modern.

AL Río Amazonas, Cordero E4-375 y Amazonas, T02-2556667, www.hotelrio amazonas.com Business hotel with restaurant, internet, parking, pleasant, full facilities.

A Chalet Suisse, Reina Victoria N24-191 y Calama, T02-2562700, F2563966. Includes breakfast, excellent restaurant, rooms to street are noisy.

A Embassy, Wilson E8-22 y 6 de Diciembre, T02-2563103, www.hembassy.com Price includes breakfast, restaurant, parking, well-furnished rooms, also suites with kitchens (more expensive).

A Hostal de la Rábida, La Rábida 227 y Santa María, T/F02-2221720, www.hotelrabida.com Nice home in La Mariscal, good restaurant, parking, Italian-run, bright, comfortable. Recommended.

A Windsor, Roca 668 y Amazonas, T02-2224033, www.windsorhotel.com.ec Modern high-rise hotel, includes breakfast, cafeteria with outdoor sitting, internet, comfortable rooms, some with jacuzzi, those facing Amazonas are a bit noisy, pickup service, good value.

A-D La Casa Sol, Calama 127 y Av 6 de Diciembre, T02-2230798, www.lacasasol.com Bed and breakfast Andean-style hostal with pleasant rooms set around a courtyard. Hot water and private bathrooms in all rooms, suites available.

B Cayman, Rodríguez E7-29 y Reina Victoria, T02-2567616, www.hotelcaymanquito.com Pleasant hotel, includes breakfast, cafeteria, parking, rooms a bit small, sitting room with fireplace, lovely bright breakfast room, garden, very clean and good.

B Fuente de Piedra II, JL Mera 721 y Baquedano, T02-2900323, www.ecuahotel.com Nicely decorated modern hotel, includes breakfast, some rooms are small, nice sitting area, pleasant and comfortable, 2nd location on Wilson 211 y Tamayo.

B Hothello, Amazonas N20-20 y 18 de Septiembre, T/F02-2565835. Small modern hotel, includes nice breakfast, café, rooms are bright and tastefully decorated, heating, helpful multilingual staff. Recommended.

B Jardín del Sol, Calama 166 y Almagro, T02-2230941, www.hostalecuador.com Includes breakfast, snack bar, internet, parking, modern and nice.

B Plaza Internacional, Plaza 150 y 18 de Septiembre, T02-2524530, hplaza@uio.satnet.net Refurbished late 19th-century home of President Leonidas Plaza, includes breakfast, restaurant, showing its age, but still pleasant and comfortable, multilingual staff, very helpful.

B Portón, San Javier 203 y Orellana, T02-2231712, elporton@rdyec.net Includes breakfast, cafeteria, rooms in rustic style cabins and suites, room service, small, quiet and friendly.

La Floresta & Hotel Quito

B Sierra Nevada, Pinto E4-50 y Cordero,
T02-2528264, www.hotelsierranevada.com
Part of Sierra Nevada Expeditions tour
agency, includes breakfast, cafeteria, parking,
aging but still fine, sitting room with
fireplace, gardens and terraces, climbing
wall, multilingual staff.

B-D The Magic Bean, Foch 681 y J L Mera,
T02-2566181, magic@ecuadorexplorer.com
Includes breakfast, good restaurant, cheaper
in dorm, good beds, American owned.

C Alcalá, Luis Cordero E5-48 y Reina Victoria,
T02-2227396, www.alcalahostal.com
Nice bright hostel, includes breakfast,
sitting area, same owners and facilities as
Posada del Maple.

C Alston Inn, J L Mera N23-41 y Veintimilla,
T02-2229955, alston@uio.satnet.net
Parking, English spoken.

C Posada del Arupo, Juan Rodríguez E7-22
y Reina Victoria, T02-2557543. Includes
breakfast, laundry and cooking facilities,
very clean, English and French spoken.
Recommended.

C Posada del Maple, Rodríguez E8-49 y
Almagro, T02-2544507, www.posadadel
maple.com Popular hostel, includes
breakfast, restaurant, cheaper with shared
bath and in dorm, laundry and cooking
facilities, warm atmosphere, free tea and
coffee. Recommended.

C Rincón Escandinavo, Plaza N24-306
y Baquerizo Moreno, T02-2225965,
hotelres@porta.net Small, well-furnished
modern hotel, restaurant, English spoken.

C Villa Nancy, Carrión E8-158
y 6 de Diciembre, T02-2563084,
www.villa-nancy.com Nice friendly place,
includes breakfast, some rooms with private
bath, cooking facilities, sitting room, airport
pickup, travel information, Swiss-Ecuadorean
run, helpful.

C-D Casa Helbling, Veintimilla E8-166
y 6 de Diciembre, T02-2226013,
www.casahelbling.de Cheaper with shared
bath, laundry and cooking facilities, parking,
helpful, German spoken, family atmosphere,
good information, tours arranged.
Recommended.

C-D Crossroads, Foch E5-23 y JL Mera,
T02-2234735, www.crossroadshostal.com
Good restaurant serves breakfast and snacks,
cheaper with shared bath, excellent hot
showers, choice of videos.

C-D Hostelling International,
Pinto 325 y Reina Victoria, T02-2543995,
www.hostelling-ecuador.org Large hostel
with capacity for 75, cafeteria, cheaper in
dormitory with lockers and shared bath,
coin-operated washing machines, a variety
of simple rooms from double with private
bath to dorms, discounts for IYHF members
and other student cards.

D Adventure, Pinto E2-24 y Amazonas,
T02-2226340, rfcedeno@interactive.net.ec
Cheaper with shared bath, cooking facilities,
simple and clean, terrace, helpful.

D Amazonas Inn, Pinto E4-324 y Amazonas,
T02-2225723, amazonasinn@yahoo.com
Café, carpeted rooms, some are sunny, those
on 1st floor are best, very clean and friendly.
Recommended.

D El Cafecito, Cordero 1124 y Reina Victoria,
T02-2234862, www.cafecito.net Popular
with backpackers, vegetarian restaurant,
shared bath, room called 'tomato' has a nice
balcony, Canadian-owned, relaxed
atmosphere but noisy at night.

D El Taxo, Foch 909 y Cordero, T02-2225593.
Hostel in a large family house, shared bath,
internet, cooking facilities, open fire, good
meeting place, helpful.

D Esmeraldas, 6 Diciembre 1554 y
Veintimilla, T02-2542771. Ample parking,
comfortable, friendly, family run, good value.

D Iguana Lodge, Calama E4-45 y JL Mera,
T02-2569784. Includes breakfast, cheaper
with shared bath, large common room
makes for a very sociable atmosphere,
friendly hosts speak English and French.

D Loro Verde, Rodriguez 241 y Almagro,
T02-2226173. Cafeteria, cooking facilities,
clean and friendly.

D Pickett, Wilson 712 y J L Mera,
T02-2551205. Laundry facilities,
carpeted rooms, popular.

D Queen's Hostel / Hostal De La Reina,
Reina Victoria 836 y Wilson, T02-2551844,
queen@uio.telconet.net Nice small hotel,
popular among travellers and Ecuadoreans,
includes breakfast, cafeteria, laundry and
cooking facilities, sitting room with fireplace.
Recommended.

D Titisee, Foch E7-60 y Reina Victoria,
T02-2529063. Nice place and owner, cheaper
with shared bath, cooking facilities, large
rooms, lounge. Recommended.

E **Bask**, Lizardo García 537 y Reina Victoria, T02-2503456. Cafeteria, private bath, hot water, cooking facilities, free coffee, nice atmosphere.

E **Gan Eden**, Pinto 163 y 6 de Diciembre, T02-2223480, ganeden163@hotmail.com Restaurant serves cheap breakfast and good Israeli food, cheaper with shared bath, hot water, cooking facilities, double rooms or dorm, very helpful.

La Floresta *map p118*

A **Floresta**, Isabel La Católica 1015 y Salazar, T02-2225376, F2250422. Includes breakfast, restaurant, parking, large room, very quiet.

A **La Villa**, Toledo 1455 y Coruña, T02-2222755, nevadatu@uio.satnet.net Includes breakfast, restaurant, carpeted rooms and suites with minibar, European-style building.

A-B **Mi Casa**, Andalucía N24-151 y Francisco Galavis, T/F02-2225383, www.ecuanex.apc.org/mi_casa Upscale inn, includes large breakfast, sauna, comfortable rooms and suites, gardens, small quiet place, family run, multilingual owner.

B-C **Aleida's**, Andalucía 559 y Salazar, T02-2234570, aleidas@ecuanex.net.ec Cheaper with shared bath, internet, 3 types of rooms, decorated with wood, patio.

D **Casona de Mario**, Andalucía 213 y Galicia, T/F02-2230129, lacasona@punto.net.ec Popular friendly hostel, shared bath, laundry facilities, well equipped kitchen, very clean rooms, sitting room, nice big garden, book exchange, helpful owner. Highly recommended.

D **Ciprés**, Lérida 381 y Pontevedra, T02-2549558, turisavn@ecuanex.net.ec Includes breakfast, cheaper in dorm with shared bath, cooking facilities, parking, transport to airport or bus terminal if staying 3 days, very helpful. Recommended.

E **Casa de Eliza**, Isabel La Católica N24-679, T02-2226602, manteca@uio.satnet.net Laundry and cooking facilities, parking, shared rooms and bath, very popular and homely, no smoking.

La Carolina *map p111*

A **Finlandia**, Finlandia 227 y Suecia, T02-2244288, www.hotelfinlandia.com.ec Lovely small hostal in residential area, buffet breakfast, restaurant serves cheap set meals, internet, parking, spacious rooms, sitting room with fireplace, small garden.

A **La Pradera**, San Salvador 222 y Pasaje Martín Carrión, T02-2226833, www.hostallapradera.com Nicely decorated converted home in residential area, includes breakfast, restaurant serves meals at mid-range prices, parking, comfortable rooms, sitting room, nice patio with hammocks, quiet.

B **Hostal La Carolina**, Italia 324 y Vancouver, T02-2542471, hoscarol@uio.satnet.net Converted home in residential area, includes breakfast, restaurant, internet, parking, good comfortable rooms, those in back are quieter, helpful.

C **Chevalier**, Inglaterra N31-173 y Mariana de Jesús, T02-2220917, residencialchevalier@hotmail.com Converted home in quiet residential area, breakfast available, parking, comfortable rooms, sitting room with fireplace, rooftop terrace, good value.

C **FerReisen**, Azuay 147 y Amazonas, T02-2242682, www.ferreisen.de Includes breakfast, internet, ample parking, on a quiet side street, German and English spoken, friendly.

Quito suburbs *p110*

L **Cuevas de Alvaro**, 10 km east of Pifo on the way to Papallacta , T02-2547403, birdecua@hoy.net All rooms are in caves, built right into the rock - an interesting concept! This is a good spot to see condors at certain times of the year. Includes 3 meals, excursions and use of horses. Advance reservations required.

AL **La Carriona**, Km 2½ vía Sangolquí-Amaguaña, T02-2331974, www.lacarriona.com In a beautiful colonial hacienda, includes breakfast, pool and spa, some rooms in the old hacienda house, others in more modern section but in same style, includes horse riding.

A **Hostería Sommergarten**, Chimborazo 248 y Riofrío, Urbanización Santa Rosa, Sangolquí, T02-2330315, www.ecuador-sommerfern.com Comfortable bungalows in nicely kept grounds, price includes breakfast, restaurant, pool and sauna, tours and transport available.

B San Jorge, Km 4 Vía Antigua Cotocollao- Nono, T02-2494002, www.hostsanjorge.com.ec A traditional hacienda on the slopes of Pichincha, includes breakfast, restaurant, pool, sauna and turkish bath, parking, quiet, peaceful, nature reserve, horse riding and birdwatching, all within easy reach of Quito. Recommended.

C Hostería Alemana, Av Manuel Córdoba Galarza 700 m south of Mitad del Mundo (frequent buses to the city), T02-2394243. German-run. Very good restaurant.

D Casa de Guápulo, C Leonidas Plaza (Guápulo), T/F02-2220473. Includes breakfast, restaurant and bar, parking and airport transfer. Peaceful, multilingual staff.

🍴 Eating

Old City *p101, map p104*

♥♥♥♥ El Patio Trattoria, García Moreno 1201 y Mejía, in Cadisán, T02-2288140, Mon 2000-0000, Tue-Sat 1200-0000, Sun 1200-1700. Gourmet Italian cuisine, featuring delicacies such as salmon (a imported treat in Ecuador). Elegant and tastefully decorated, indoor and outdoor seating.

♥♥♥♥ La Cueva del Oso, Chile Oe3-66 y Venezuela, across from the Plaza de la Independencia, T02-2572786, Mon-Sat 1200-0000, Sun 1200-1600. A good place to sample Ecuadorean specialities such as *fritada* or the warming *locro de papas*, in elegant covered courtyard, art deco interior, great atmosphere.

♥♥♥♥ María Augusta Urrutia, García Moreno 760 at the museum, T02-2584173, Thu-Sat 1200-2300, Sun 1200-1700. Ecuadorean and international food based on Sra Urrutia's recipies, served in the elegant surroundings of this aristocratic home.

♥♥♥♥ Mea Culpa, Palacio Arzobispal, Chile y Venezuela, T02-2951190, Mon-Sat 1230-1530, 1900-2300. International and Mediterranean gourmet cuisine, specialities include such ostrich in mango sauce, housed in the 17th century Palacio Arzobispal overlooking Plaza de la Independencia, it combines the elegance of colonial decor with opulent gourmet dining. Reservations recommended, formal attire, dress code strictly enforced.

♥♥♥♥ Rincón de Cantuña, García Moreno N6-52, T02-2280830, daily 0700-2300. A combination of Spanish and Ecuadorean cuisine plus classical international fare, elegant dining in covered, arched patio.

♥♥♥♥ Theatrum, Plaza del Teatro, 2nd floor of Teatro Sucre, T02-2289669, Mon-Fri 1230-1600, 1930-2330, Sat 1930-2330, Sun 1230-1600. Excellent creative gourmet cuisine, try their pork medallions in lavender honey. Exclusive dining in the city's most important theatre.

♥♥♥ Hasta la Vuelta Señor, Pasaje Arzobispal, 3rd floor, T02-2580887, Mon-Sat 1200-2300, Sun 1200-1600. Ecuadorean *comida típica* and snacks, try their *empanadas* (pasties) or a *seco de chivo* (goat stew). A typical Fonda Quiteña perched on an indoor balcony; learn about the legend of Padre Almeida.

♥♥♥ Pim's, Panecillo below the statue of the Virgin, T02-3170878, Mon-Sat 1200-2330, San 1200-1700. International dishes and snacks, magnificent views of Quito.

♥♥♥-♥♥ Las Cuevas de Luis Candelas, Benalcázar 713 y Chile, daily 1100-1830. Spanish and Ecuadorean dishes including *ceviche*. Cheap set lunches, pleasant atmosphere with flamenco music, busy decor and a bathroom that must be seen.

♥ Govinda, Esmeraldas 853 y Venezuela, Mon-Sat 0800-1900. Vegetarian dishes, set meals and à la carte, also breakfast.

Cafés

Café del Fraile, Pasaje Arzobispal, 2nd floor, Mon-Sat 1000-0000, Sun 1200-1930. Snacks and drinks, on a balcony above one of the patios of the Palacio Arzobispal.

Café del Museo, García Moreno 572 at the Museo de la Ciudad, Tue-Sun 0930-1700. Snacks such as *tamales* and *humitas*, soups, coffee, elegant decor.

El Portal, Pasaje Arzobispal, local interior, ground floor, easier to reach from C Venezuela entrance, Mon-Sat 1030-2030, Sun 1030-1800. Snacks, 20 varieties of coffee, drinks, modern decor with paintings.

Tianguez, Plaza de San Francisco under the church portico, daily 0930-1830. Good coffee, snacks, sandwiches, Ecuadorean specialities. Popular with visitors, also craft shop, postcards, run by Fundación Sinchi Sacha.

Dining out in Quito

Quito offers excellent, varied, and increasingly cosmopolitan and upmarket dining. The vast majority of restaurants are in the New City, where almost any type of cuisine can be found. The Old City has a number of very elegant expensive establishments serving international and Ecuadorean specialities. There are also a great many simple little places serving very cheap and adequate set meals, *almuerzos* and *meriendas*, throughout the city. With so much else on offer in Quito there is no room for them in our listings, but have a look around and you are sure to find one close by. There are also a number of reasonable restaurants in the food courts of shopping malls; for their addresses see Shopping below.

Many restaurants throughout the city close on Sunday evenings. Those with stickers indicating acceptance of credit cards do not necessarily do so, ask first. In many of the more expensive restaurants 22% tax and service is added to the bill.

New City *p107, map p109*

Ecuadorean

El Galpón, Colón E10-53, in back of Folklor Olga Fisch, T02-2540209, Tue-Sun 1230-1500, 1830-2100. Very good Ecuadorean cooking featuring traditional dishes with innovative twists like lamb in naranjilla sauce. Decorated with antiques, a pleasant place for relaxed dining.

La Choza, 12 de Octubre N24-551 y Cordero, T02-2230839, Mon-Fri 1200-1600, 1900-2230, Sat-Sun 1200-1630. Traditional cuisine, good music and special decor.

La Querencia, Eloy Alfaro N34-194 y Catalina Aldaz, T02-2446654, Mon-Sat 1000-2300, Sun 1000-1800. Typical Ecuadorean and some international dishes, try their *empanadas de morocho* entrée, good views and atmosphere.

Rincón de La Ronda, Belo Horizonte 406 y Almagro, T02-2540459, daily 1200- 2300. Very good local and international food, huge Sun buffet, Sun night folklore show. Touristy.

Mama Clorinda, Reina Victoria 1144 y Calama, T02-2544362, Sun-Mon 1200-1700, Tue-Sat 1200-2100. A la carte and set meals, filling, good value.

Fast food

There has been a fast food explosion in Quito and you can find many of the better-known US chains here. All the shopping centres have food courts with a variety of fast food outlets including traditional Ecuadorean, Chinese and Italian food in addition to the ubiquitous hamburger, pizza, etc. For pizzerias also see listing below.

French and Swiss

Chalet Suisse, Reina Victoria N24-191 y Calama, T02-2562700, daily 1100-1500, 1900-2300. Good steaks, also some Swiss dishes, good quality and service.

Rincón de Francia, Roca 779 y 9 de Octubre, T02-2554668, www.rinconde francia.com, Mon-Fri 1200-1600, 2000-2300, Sat 1200-1530, 2000-2200. Excellent food, reservations essential, slow service.

Swiss Corner, Los Shyris 2137 y El Telégrafo, T02-2468007, Mon-Sat 0700-2030, Sun 0700-1600. Swiss dishes, also delicatessen and pastry shop, small quaint place.

Raclette, Mall El Jardín, Amazonas y Mariana de Jesús, p3, T02-2980266, Mon-Sat 1130-2200, Sun 1200-1600. Swiss specialities including *raclette* and fondue with a great variety of ingredients, simple, modern decor.

Paléo, Cordero E5-48 y Reina Victoria, T02-2553019, Mon-Sat 1230-1530 1830-2100. Authentic Swiss cooking with specialities such as *rösti* and *raclette*. Also serve a good economical set lunch, pleasant ambience, recommended.

Chez Alain, Baquedano 409 y JL Mera, Mon-Fri 1200-1600, 1830-2200. Choice of good 4-course set meals at lunch and à la carte in the evening, with a pleasant relaxed atmosphere.

German

†††-†† Café Colibrí, Pinto 619 y Cordero, daily 0800-1830. Large choice of breakfasts and German specialities, pleasant garden setting.

Grill

†††† Los Troncos, Los Shyris 1280 y Portugal, T02-2437377, Mon-Sat 1000-2200, Sun 1000-1600. Good Argentine grill, serves beef, chicken, pork, fish, pasta, salads, small and friendly, busy on Sun.

†††† Shorton Grill, Calama E7-73 y Almagro, also at Urrutia N14-233 y Eloy Alfaro, T02-2523645, daily 1200-2300. Meat, seafood and salad, large portions and smart decor.

†††† La Casa de Mi Abuela, JL Mera 1649 y la Niña, T02-2565667, Mon-Sat 1100-1430, 1900-2200, Sun 1100-1430. Very good meat and salads, pleasant atmosphere.

†††† Mongo's, Calama E5-10 y JL Mera, T02-2556159, daily 1200-2200. Mongolian BBQ, select your ingredients and have them cooked on the grill. Price depends on whether you take one plate or all you can eat.

Indian

†† Chandani Tandoori, JL Mera N24-277 y Cordero, Mon-Sat 1100-2200. Simple little place with good authentic Indian cuisine, economical set meals, good variety and value, popular and recommended.

International

All of the luxury class hotels have very good international restaurants (see Sleeping above). **Swissôtel** has several superb restaurants including Japanese, Swiss, grill and a cafeteria with excellent breakfast, lunch and afternoon-tea buffets. The **Hilton Colón** has a 24-hr cafeteria with an excellent lunch buffet, daily except Sat, and an excellent Italian restaurant. In the **Hotel Quito**, the rooftop restaurant has excellent views and serves a buffet breakfast and lunch and à la carte dinner.

†††† La Cocina de Kristy, Whymper 1184 y Orellana, T02-2501210, Tue-Sat 1230-1600, 1800-2300, Sun 1230-1600. Great food, upmarket, great view from the terrace. Recommended.

†††† Terraza del Tártaro, Veintimilla 1106 y Amazonas (no sign), at the top of the building, T02-2527987, Mon-Sat 1200-1600,

1800-2200, Sun 1200-1600. Excellent views, pleasant atmosphere.

††† Crêpes & Waffles, La Rábida 461 y Orellana, T02-2500658, Mon-Thu 1200-2130, Fri-Sat 1200-2330, Sun 1200-2130. Succulent and savoury crêpes and salads as well as delicious desserts.

††† El Zócalo, JL Mera y Calama, T02-2233929, Mon-Sat 1100-0200, Sun 1100-0100. Terrace bar with OK food, varied menu, lively atmosphere, live music on Fri night, a meeting place for young people, slow service.

†† Grain de Café, Baquedano 332 y Reina Victoria, Mon-Sat 0700-2200. Meat or vegetarian set lunches, good cakes and coffee, cocktails, good service.

Italian

†††† Il Grillo, Baquerizo Moreno 533 y Almagro, T02-2225531, Mon-Fri 1200-1500, 1900-2300, Sat 1900-2300. Great pizzas, upmarket, refurbished in 2004.

†††† Il Risotto, Eloy Alfaro N34-447 y Portugal, T02-2246850, Mon-Sat 1200-1500, 1900-2200, Sun 1200-1530. Very popular and very good Italian cooking.

†††† Pavarotti, 12 de Octubre 1955 y Cordero, above Restaurant La Choza, T02-2566668, Tue-Sat 1200-1600,1900-2300, Sun 1200-1600. Creative Italian cuisine and very attentive service.

†††† Porta Pia, Pinto E7-85 y Almagro, T02-2521471, Mon-Fri 1230-1500, 1800-2200, Sun 1230-1530. Tasty authentic Italian cuisine, elegant decor and very attentive service.

††† Capuletto, Eloy Alfaro N32-544 y Los Shyris, T02-2550611, Mon-Sat 0900-0000, Sun 0900-2200. Italian deli serving excellent fresh pasta and desserts, lovely outdoor patio with fountain.

†† Tomato, JL Mera E5-10 y Calama, daily 0800-0100. Good value buffet breakfast, choice of set lunches, very good pizza and pasta, recommended.

Latin American

†††† La Bodeguita de Cuba, Reina Victoria 1721 y la Pinta, T02-2464517, Tue-Sat 1200-1600, 1830-2200, Sun 1130-1600. Good Cuban cooking, music and drinks at Varadero Bar next door.

††† La Guarida del Coyote, Foch y JL Mera, Eloy Alfaro E25-94 y Catalina Aldaz, and

Japón 542 y Naciones Unidas, T02-2553066, Tue-Sun 1200-2300. Excellent Mexican food.
♟♟ Tex Mex, Reina Victoria 847 y Wilson, T02-2527689, Mon-Sat 1300-2200. Lively atmosphere, draught beer.
♟♟ Rincón Ecuatoriano Chileno, 6 de Diciembre N28-30 y Bello Horizonte, daily 1200-1600. Delicious, very good value, busy on weekends.

Middle Eastern
♟♟♟ El Arabe, Reina Victoria 627 y Carrión, T02-2549414, Mon-Sat 1100-0000. Good authentic food.
♟♟ Gan Eden, Pinto 163 y 6 de Diciembre, daily 0800-2200. Israeli meals and snacks, including falafel.

North American
♟♟♟ Adam's Rib, Calama E6-16 y Reina Victoria, T02-2563196, Mon-Fri 1200-2230, Sat closed, Sun 1030-2100. Happy hour 1730-2100. Ribs, steaks, good BBQ, great pecan pie, Sun brunch 1030-1300. A popular meeting place for US expats.
♟♟♟ American Deli, República de El Salvador 1058 y Naciones Unidas, Washington y Amazonas and at several malls, T02-2451252, daily 1300-2100. Sandwiches, hamburgers, desserts.
♟♟♟ Applebee's, Eloy Alfaro y Amazonas, T02-2556737, daily 1800-0100. US chain, good for ribs, live music Thu-Sat 2300-0100.
♟♟♟ Mango Tree Café, Foch 721 y Amazonas, Closed Sun and holidays. Salads, fruit juices, coffee, homemade bread and bagels, nice patio and decor.
♟♟♟ TGI Friday's, Quicentro Shopping, T02-2264636, daily 1200-2200. American franchise, food and drinks.
♟♟♟ The Magic Bean, Foch 681 y JL Mera, T02-2566181, Mon-Sat 1200-1530, 1900-2200, Sun 1200-1530. Specializes in fine coffees and natural foods, more than 20 varieties of pancakes, good salads, large portions, outdoor seating.
♟♟ Bagel Connection, Reina Victoria y Pinto, Mon-Sat 0800-1900, Sun 0830-1300. Breakfast, bagels with a variety of spreads, also take-away service.

Oriental
♟♟♟♟ Sake, Paul Rivet N30-166 y Whymper, T02-2524818, Mon-Sat 1200-1530,

1900-2300, Sun 1230-1600. Sushi bar and other Japanese dishes, very trendy, great food, nicely decorated.
♟♟♟ Happy Panda, Cordero E9-348 e Isabel la Católica, T02-2547322, Tue-Sat 1600-2200. Excellent Hunan specialities.
♟♟♟ Hong Tai, La Niña 234 y Yanez Pinzón, T02-2226150, Tue-Sat 1300-1500, 1900-2300, Sun 1300-1600. Good authentic Chinese.
♟♟♟ Pekín, Whimper 300 y Orellana, T02-2235273, Mon-Sat 1200-1500, 1900-2230, Sun 1200-2030. Excellent Chinese food, very nice atmosphere.
♟♟ Sushi, Calama E5-104 y JL Mera, Mon-Sat 1200-2300, Sun 1200-1600. Sushi bar, pleasant atmosphere with nice balcony, good value happy hour 1700-1900.
♟♟ Yu Su Café, Edificio Torres de Almagro, Almagrro y Colón. Very good sushi bar, clean and pleasant, Korean-run, take-out service.

Pizza
There are many good pizzerias, most with several outlets and a home delivery service (phone numbers given below). Only a few of the most centrally-located ones are listed. Prices are generally mid-range.
Le Arcate, Baquedano 358 y JL Mera, T02-2237659, 1100-1500, 1800-2300, closed Mon. Wood oven pizza, good, excellent banana flambé, same management as **Il Risotto**.
Ch Farina, Carrión, entre JL Mera y Amazonas, T2558139, and Naciones Unidas y Amazonas (open 24 hrs), T02-244 4400. Fast service, good, popular.
El Hornero, Veintimilla y Amazonas, República de El Salvador y Los Shyris and on Gonzalez Suárez, T1-800-500500, 1200-2300. Very good wood oven pizzas, try one with *choclo* (fresh corn). Recommended.

Seafood
Be selective when choosing a seafood restaurant, visitors have become ill after eating at unhygienic establishments.
♟♟♟♟ Avalón, Orellana 155 y 12 de Octubre, T02-2509875, Tue-Sat 1200-1500, 1800-2300, Sun 1200-1700. Excellent seafood and meat dishes, upmarket.
♟♟♟♟ El Cebiche, JL Mera 1236 y Calama, and Amazonas 2428 y Moreno Bellido, T02-2526380, Tue-Sun 1000-1600. Delicious *ceviche*.

La Jaiba, Coruña y San Ignacio, T02-2543887, Mon 1100-1530, Tue-Sat 1100-1600, 1900-2100, Sun 1100-1630. Varied seafood menu, an old favourite in Quito at new premises after 36 years, good service.

Puerto Camarón, 6 de Diciembre y Granaderos, Centro Comercial Olímpico, T02-2265761, Tue-Sat 1000-1500, 1800-2100, Sun 1000-1600. A selection of good quality fish and seafood. Recommended.

La Canoa Manabita, Calama y Reina Victoria, daily 1200-2100. Great seafood and very clean.

Las Palmeras, Japón N36-87 y Naciones Unidas, opposite Parque la Carolina, daily 0800-1800. Very good *comida Esmeraldeña*, try their hearty *viche* soup, outdoor tables, good value.

Spanish

El Mesón de Triana, Isabel La Católica 1015 y Salazar, T02-2502844, Mon-Fri 1200-1500, 1900-2300, Sat 1200-1500. Varied Spanish and international menu, tapas, nice decor with Talavera ceramics.

La Nueva Castilla, La Pinta 435 y Amazonas, T02-2566979, Mon-Sat 1200-1500, 1900-2200. Typical Spanish fare, another old favourite in new premises.

La Paella Valenciana, República y Almagro, Tue-Sat 1200-1500, 1900-2300, Sun 1200-1600. Huge portions, superb fish, seafood and paella, an institution.

Vegetarian

Las Ensaladas/Mi Frutería, Quicentro Shopping, daily 1000-2200. Gorgeous fresh fruit salads and coastal Ecuadorean food.

El Maple, Foch E8-15 y Almagro, daily 0730-2330. Strictly vegetarian, varied menu, good meals and fruit juices, covered patio setting, new premises in 2004. Recommended.

Cafés

Bangalô, Foch 451 y Almagro, Mon-Sat lunchtime and 1600-2000. Excellent cakes, quiches, coffees, great atmosphere, good jazz at weekends.

Books & Coffee, JL Mera 12-27 y Calama, Mon, Tue and Sat 0900-2000, Wed-Fri 0900-2300. Cappuccino, espresso, book exchange, local newspapers, a good place to sit and write.

Café del Suizo, Foch 714 y JL Mera. Nice coffee, snacks like quiche, great chocolate cake, pleasant atmosphere.

Café Trovero, JL Mera y Pinto, Mon-Fri 1230-2200, Sat 1330-2200. Espresso and sandwich bar, pastries, pleasant atmosphere, nicely decorated with plants.

El Cafecito, Luis Cordero 1124 y Reina Victoria, at the hotel, daily 0900 until late. Pancakes, set meal of the day and the best chocolate brownies.

Hothello, Amazonas N20-20 y 18 de Septiembre, at the hotel, daily 0700-2200. Good breakfast, snacks and sandwiches, coffee, Parisian-style café.

Mirador de Guápulo, Rafael León Larrea, behind Hotel Quito, daily 1000-0000. Snacks such as *empanadas*, crêpes, sandwiches, drinks, great views of Guápulo, the Tumbaco valley, and Cayambe, portable heaters for outdoor seating at night.

Mosaico, Manuel Samaniego N8-95 y Antepara, near Parque Itchimbía. Snacks such as *humitas* and *quimbolitos*, drinks, a place to go for the lovely views of the city, slow service.

Bakeries

Quito seems to have a good bakery on every corner. A few of the most outstanding include:

Arenas, Coruña y Orellana, Checa y Larrea and several other locations. Hot bread throughout the day. Try the *pan de cereales* or the *pan alpino*.

La Cosecha, Los Shyris y El Comercio, try their garlic bread.

Cyrano, Portugal y Los Shyris, excellent pumpernickel and whole wheat breads, outstanding pastries.

Also try the hotel bakery at the **Río Amazonas**, **Sal y Pimienta** at the Hilton Colón and **Swissôtel**, whose bakery serves excellent speciality breads and pastries.

Ice-cream parlours

Crêpes and Waffles, on Orellana, see International restaurants above.

Corfú, Portugal y Los Shyris, next to **Cyrano**, excellent and pricey.

Helados de Paila, Los Shyris, opposite and just north of the grandstands. Good sherbet

from local fruits, just like in Ibarra.
Gelateria Uno, 6 de Diciembre, Centro Comercial Olímpico, north of the stadium. Very good Italian ice-cream.

Venezia, at the south end of the same shopping centre. Italian ice-cream, also coffee, snacks and pizza.

❶ Bars and clubs → *To learn more about the nightlife scene, check www.farras.com*

Quito's nightlife is largely concentrated in La Mariscal. A municipal ordinance requires all establishments to close by 0300, however, this is not strictly enforced. Many of the bars turn into informal discos after 2200. Note that the word *nightclub* in Ecuadorean usage can mean brothel.

Bars and clubs are subject to frequent drug raids by police: don't risk it (see Drugs, p). You can also be arrested for not having your passport. A photocopy of the passport and entry stamp may suffice, but it depends on the police officer; see Spot checks, p.

New City *p107, map p109*

Bars
La Boca del Lobo, Calama 284 y Reina Victoria, T02-2234083, Mon-Sat 1700-0000. Café-bar, snacks and meals at mid-range prices, very laid-back, good meeting place, nice atmosphere, trendy young bar.
Bogarín, Reina Victoria N24-217 y Lizardo García, T02-2555057, Tue-Sat 1800-0200. Café-bar, snacks, live music.
Café Toledo 1, Toledo 720 y Lérida and number 2, Francisco Salazar y Tamayo, from 1700. Café-bar, live music every night.
Cats, Lizardo García 537 y Reina Victoria. Informal disco-bar, varied music including rock, no Latin music, popular.
Ghoz Bar, La Niña 425 y Reina Victoria, T02-2239826, from 1800. Swiss-owned, excellent Swiss food, pool, darts, videos, games, music, German book exchange.
Kilkenny Irish Pub, Lizardo García y Reina Victoria. Typical pub secene, '80s music, microbrewery.
Kings Cross Bar, Reina Victoria 1781 y La Niña, T02-2523597. Classic rock, good BBQ, hamburgers, wings. Popular with old hippies. Recommended.
Líquida, Portugal y Eloy Alfaro, T02-2453466, Thu-Sat 2100-0200. Varied music, shows at 2230 and 0030.

Matices Piano Bar, Isabel La Católica y Cordero, T02-2555020, 1630-0200. Excellent food, live piano music, owner is a well-known local pianist and composer, Dr Nelson Maldonado.
Matrioshka, Pinto 376 y JL Mera, T02-2552668, Wed-Sat from 1900, but only gets started around 2200. Gay and lesbian bar.
No Bar, Calama y JL Mera, open till 0200, closed on Sun. Good mix of Latin and Euro dance music on weekdays, always packed at weekends, entry US$4 at weekends, happy hour 1800-2000.
Papillon, Pinzón y Colón, popular with local yuppies.
Patatu's, Wilson y JL Mera, 2030-0200, closed Sun. Good drinks, pool table, happy hour all night Mon, loud music, dancing. A special place for those who want to show off their dancing skills, owner speaks English.
El Pobre Diablo, Isabel La Católica y Galavis, 1 block north of Madrid, T02-2224982, Mon-Sat 1600-0000. Good atmosphere, relaxed and friendly, jazz music, sandwiches, Ecuadorean snacks and some meals, a good place to hang out and chill, popular.
Reina Victoria Pub, Reina Victoria 530 y Roca, T02-2226369, Mon-Sat from 1700. English-style pub, good selection of microbrews and of Scottish and Irish single malt whiskeys, moderately priced bar meals, darts, happy hour 1800-2000, relaxed atmosphere, fireplace, popular meeting point for British and US expats.
La Trastienda, Toledo 708 y Lérida, T02-2524655, Wed-Sat 2000-0300. Varied music, live shows.
The Turtle´s Head Bar, La Niña 626 y JL Mera, T02-2565544, Mon-Sat 1700-0200, Sun 1200-0200. Amazing microbrews, fish and chips, curry, Sun lunch, pool table, darts.
Varadero, Reina Victoria 1721 y La Pinta, T02-2542575, Mon-Fri 1200-0000, Sat 1800-0300. Bar-restaurant, live Cuban music Wed-Sat, meals and snacks, good cocktails, older crowd and couples.

Clubs

Clubs are open Wed/Thu-Sat 2000-0300.
La Bunga, Camilo Destruge y Salazar, La Floresta. Young crowd, music includes ska.
Mayo 68, Lizardo García N10-662 y JL Mera, T02-2908169. Salsoteca, small, mix of ages.
Music Evolution, 6 de Diciembre y Los Shyris, Sector El Inca. Large disco, varied music, young crowd.
Oz, Maldonado y Pujilí, in the south near El Recreo Trole stop. Fine mix of music and people, huge, 5 dance halls, the 'in' place for dancing.

Le Pierrot, Carrión N22-54 y Amazonas. Good variety of live music, very smoky, popular with locals especially on Fri.
Seseribó, Veintimilla y 12 de Octubre, T02-2563598, Thu-Sat 2100-0100. Caribbean music and salsa, a must for salseros, very popular especially Thu and Fri. Recommended.
Vauzá, Tamayo y F Salazar. Varied music. Large bar in the middle of the dance floor, mature crowd.
El Verde, Ponce Carrasco E8-15 y Almagro, T02-2239627. A variety of music, mature crowd, pricey.

⊕ Entertainment

There are always many cultural events taking place in Quito, usually free of charge. See the listings section of *El Comercio* and other papers for details, especially on Fri. Aug is a particularly active month, see festivals below.

Art galleries

Art Forum, JL Mera N23-106.
La Galería, Juan Rodríguez 168 y Almagro, T02-2225807.
Fundación Guayasamín, in Bellavista, see Museums above.
Galería Pomaire, Amazonas 863 y Veintimilla, T02-2540074.
Posada de las Artes Kingman, Almagro 1550 y Pradera, T02-2526335, www.fundacionkingman.com Mon-Fri 0900-1300, 1500-1900.
Viteri, Orellana 473 y Whimper, T02-2561548.

Cinema

Films are listed daily in Section C or D of *El Comercio*, www.elcomercio.com
Casa de la Cultura (see p107) has a film library and often has film festivals or shows foreign language films. Closed for remodelling in early 2005.
Cinemark, at Plaza de las Américas, Av América y República, T02-2260301, www.cinemark.com.ec Multiplex, many screens, restaurants, Thu-Sun US$4, Mon-Tue US$3, Wed US$2.

Metrocines, at Pasaje Amador, an arcade between Venezuela and García Moreno, just south of Plaza de la Independencia, US$2.60.
Multicines, CCI, Amazonas y Naciones Unidas (in the basement), T1-800-352463, www.multicines.com.ec Excellent movies, 8 screens, similar prices to *Cinemark*.
Multicines, El Recreo, at El Recreo Trole stop in the south of the city. Same movies as CCI, 10 screens, cheaper rates than in the north.
Ocho y medio, Valladolid y Guipuzcoa, La Floresta. Cinema and café, good for art films, monthly programme available from **Libri Mundi** and other shops, US$3-4.
Universitario, Av América y Av Pérez Guerrero, Plaza Indoamérica, Universidad Central, US$3.

Dance lessons

One-to-one or group lessons are offered for US$5-6 per hr.
Ritmo Tropical, Amazonas N24-155 y Calama, T02-2227094, ritmotropical5@hotmail.com Salsa, merengue, cumbia, vallenato and folkloric dances, Aracely Beltrán, propietor is a recommended teacher.
Son Latino, Reina Victoria 1225 y García, T02-2234340, specializes in several varieties of salsa, 10-hr programmes cost US$40.
Tropical Dancing School, Foch E4-256 y Amazonas, T02-2224713, salsa, merengue and cumbia.

Folk dance shows

'Jacchigua', the Ecuadorean folk ballet, performs at Teatro Demetrio Aguilera Malta, at Casa de la Cultura, 6 de Diciembre y Patria, Casa de la Cultura stop on the Ecovía, T02-2952025. Wed at 1930. Entertaining, colourful and touristy, reserve ahead, US$25.
Ballet Andino Humanizarte performs at Teatro Humanizarte, Leonidas Plaza N24-226 y Baquerizo Moreno, T02-2226116.
'Miércoles Andinos', Ecuadorean folk ballet every Wed at 1930, US$7. Plays and comedies are also often in their repertoire, restaurant on the premises.

Live music

Classical

Classical music concerts are seasonal, enquire ahead for schedules.
Auditorio de las Cámaras (Chamber of Commerce), Amazonas y República, T02-2260265/6 (ext 231). Occasional concerts.
Orquesta Sinfónica Nacional, concerts at Teatro Politécnico, Queseras del Medio, opposite Coliseo Rumiñahui, La Floresta, T02-2565733. On special occasions they perform at Teatro Sucre or in one of the colonial churches.

Folk

Folk music is popular and the entertainment, as well as the venue, are known as a *peña*. Most *peñas* do not come alive until 2230.
La Casa de la Peña, García Moreno 1713 y Galápagos, by the Basílica, T02-2284179, lacasadelapenia@hotmail.com, Thu-Sun from 2130. Show of Quito legends, Sat at 2200. Popular with locals on Fri and Sat.

Ñucanchi, Av Universitaria Oe5-188 y Armero, T02-2540967, Tue-Sat 2200-0200.
Pacha Camac, Noches de Quito, Washington 530 y JL Mera, T02-2234855, Wed-Sat 2200-0200.

Pop

Tickets are sold in advance.
Coliseo Rumiñahui, Toledo y Queseras del Medio, La Floresta.
Plaza de Toros, Amazonas y Juan de Azcaray, in the north.
Plaza del Quinde, Foch y Reina Victoria, concerts every Thu night starting 1800-1900.

Theatre

Agora, the open-air theatre of the Casa de la Cultura, at 12 de Octubre y Patria, stages many concerts.
Centro Cultural Afro-Ecuatoriano (CCA), Tamayo 985 y Lizardo García, T02-2522318. Sometimes has cultural events and published material, and is a useful contact for those interested in the black community.
Patio de Comedias, 18 de Septiembre, between Amazonas and 9 de Octubre. Plays are also staged here.
Teatro Bolívar, see sights page 103, Espejo 847 y Guayaquil, office Flores 421 y Junín, T02-2582486, www.teatrobolivar.org
Despite restoration work there are still tours, presentations and festivals held here, the proceeds being used for the renovations, see web page for schedule.
Teatro Prometeo, adjoining the Casa de la Cultura Ecuatoriana, 6 de Diciembre y Tarqui.
Teatro Sucre, see p103, at Plaza del Teatro, Manabí between Flores and Guayaquil, T02-2281644, www.teatrosucre.com
Has a listing of events for the year.

❀ Festivals and events

For details of national festivals see p64.
Jan Año Nuevo On New Year's Eve *años viejos* are on display throughout the city. A good spot to see them is on Amazonas, between Patria and Colón.
Feb-Mar Carnaval Water throwing is common at Carnival and in weeks before.
Mar-Apr Semana Santa The solemn Good Friday procession in the Old City is most

impressive, with thousands of devout citizens taking part.
24 May Independencia 24 May is Independence, commemorating the Battle of Pichincha in 1822 with early morning cannonfire and parades; everything closes.
Aug Agosto Arte y Cultura Throughout the month of Aug the municipality organizes

cultural events, dancing and music in different places throughout the city.

1-6 Dec Día de Quito The city's main festival is celebrated throughout the week ending 6 Dec. It commemorates the founding of the city with elaborate parades, bullfights, performances and music in the streets. It is very lively and there is a great deal of drinking. The main events culminate on the evening of 5 Dec, and the 6th is the day to sleep it all off; everything (except a few restaurants) closes.

few restaurants) closes.

25 Dec Navidad Foremost among Christmas celebrations is the *Misa del Gallo*, midnight mass. During the weeks leading to Christmas, Quiteños prepare *nacimientos*, manger scenes, in their homes and at public places where some real works of art can be admired. A large, elaborate manger is set up at El Panecillo. Over Christmas Quito is crowded and the streets are packed with beggars, street vendors and shoppers.

☉ Shopping

Trading hours are generally 0900-1900 on weekdays, although some shops close at midday, as they do in smaller cities. Sat afternoon and Sun most shops are closed. The Old City remains a very important commercial area. Outside the colonial centre, especially to the north, much of the shopping is now done in malls (shopping centres), see listing below.

Books and newspapers

Foreign newspapers are for sale at newstands in luxury hotels and in some shops along Amazonas. **Lufthansa** will supply German newspapers if they have spare copies.

Abya-Yala, 12 de Octubre 14-30 y Wilson, T02-2506247. Good for books about indigenous cultures and anthropology. Also has an excellent library and museum.

Confederate Books, Calama 410 y JL Mera, T02-252 7890, open 1000-1900. Has an excellent selection of second-hand books, including travel guides, mainly in English but German and French are also available.

Libri Mundi, JLMera N23-83 y Veintimilla, T02-2234791, Mon-Sat 0800-1800 and at Quicentro Shopping, open daily. Excellent selection of Spanish, English, French and also some Italian books. Sells a wide selection of guidebooks including several Footprint titles including the *South American Handbook*. Knowledgeable and helpful staff, noticeboard of what's on in Quito. Highly recommended.

Libro Express, Amazonas 816 y Veintimilla, T02-2548113, also at Quicentro Shopping and El Bosque. Has a good stock of maps,

guides and international magazines.

Mr Books, Mall El Jardín, 3rd floor, T02-2980281, open daily. Excellent bookshop, good selection, many in English including Footprint travel guides. Recommended.

Camping, climbing and trekking gear

Los Alpes, Reina Victoria N23-45 y Baquedano, T/F02-2232362. Equipment sale and hire, guides for climbing and trekking.

Altamontaña, Jorge Washington 425 y 6 de Diciembre, T02-2524422. Imported climbing equipment for sale and rent, good advice, experienced climbing and trekking guides.

The Altar, JL Mera 615 y Carrión, T02-2523671. Equipment rental at good prices. Imported and local gear for sale.

Antisana, Centro Comercial El Bosque, ground floor, T02-2451605. Local and imported equipment, no rentals.

Aventura Sport, Quicentro Shopping, top floor, T02-2924373. Tents, good selection of glacier sunglasses, upmarket.

Camping Sports, Colón 942 y Reina Victoria, T02-2521626. Local and imported equipment, no rentals.

Equipos Cotopaxi, 6 de Diciembre 927 y Patria, T02-2500038. Local and imported gear for sale, no rentals. Lockable pack covers, made to measure can be ordered.

The Explorer, Reina Victoria E6-32 y Pinto, T02-2550911. Reasonable prices for renting or buying, very helpful, will buy US or European equipment. Guiding service for climbing, trekking and jungle.

Tatoo, JL Mera 820 y Wilson, T02-2904533. Quality backpacks, boots, tents and outdoor clothing, thermal wear, Gore-Tex outerwear.

Camping fuel can at times be difficult to find. *Bluet Camping Gas* is generally available in the above shops. White gas is sometimes available at **Kywi hardware stores**, at Centro Comercial Olímpico, 6 de Diciembre, 2 blocks north of the stadium (and several other locations). It is better to have a multifuel stove, but some white gas stoves (eg the SVEA Optirnus 123) will also burn unleaded gasoline, available at service stations.

Handicrafts

Typical Ecuadorean *artesanías* include: wood carvings, wooden plates, silver of all types, textiles, ceramics, buttons, toys and other objects fashioned from tagua nuts, hand-painted tiles, naïve paintings on leather, Panama hats, hand-woven rugs and a variety of antiques dating back to colonial times, see p466.

There are many craft shops in La Mariscal and around the plazas in the Old City. At **Parque El Ejido** (Av Patria side), artists sell their crafts and paintings on weekends. Indigenous garments (for natives rather than tourists) can be seen and bought on the north end of the Plaza de Santo Domingo and along the nearest stretch of C Flores. Some of the craft markets and recommended shops are listed below. There are also **souvenir shops** on García Moreno under the portico of the Palacio Presidencial in the colonial city.

General handicrafts
Antigüedades Chordeleg, at Hilton Colón. For goldwork and antiques.
Camari, Marchena 260 y Versalles. Direct sale shop run by an artisan organization.
El Indio, Roca E4-35 y Amazonas, T02-2555227, daily 0900-1900. A craft market with stalls selling a variety of products, also has a coffee shop.
The Ethnic Collection, Amazonas N21-63 y Robles, T02-2500155, www.ethniccollection.com Wide variety of clothing, leather, bags, jewellery, balsa wood and ceramic items from across Ecuador.
Folklore, Colón E10-53 y Caamaño, near Hotel Quito, T02-2541315, the store of the late Olga Fisch. It stocks a most attractive array of handicrafts and rugs, and is distinctly expensive, as accords with the designer's international reputation. Branch stores at Hotel Hilton Colón and Hotel Patio Andaluz.
Fundación Sinchi Sacha, Café Tianguez at Plaza de San Francisco, cooperative selling select ceramics and other arts and crafts from the Oriente. Recommended.
Galería Latina, JL Mera 823 y Veintimilla, T02-2221098. Fine selection of alpaca and other handicrafts from Ecuador, Peru and Bolivia. Occasionally visiting artists demonstrate their crafts.
Hilana, 6 de Diciembre 1921 y Baquerizo Moreno. Beautiful and unique 100% wool blankets in Ecuadorean motifs, excellent quality, purchase by metre possible.
La Bodega, JL Mera 614 y Carrión. Recommended for antiques and handicrafts
Mercado Artesanal La Mariscal, Jorge Washington, between Reina Victoria and JL Mera, daily 1000-1800. This interesting and worthwhile market, which occupies most of a city block, was built by the municipality to house street vendors, here you can find a large selection of crafts.
Museo de Artesanía, 12 de Octubre 1738 y Madrid, Mon-Fri 0900-1900, Sat 0900-1700. Another craft market with many vendors and products.
Productos Andinos, Urbina 111 y Cordero, T02-2224565. An artisans' cooperative selling a great variety of good quality items.
Saucisa, Amazonas 2487 y Pinto, T02-2543487 and a couple other locations in La Mariscal. Very good place to buy Andean music CDs and Andean musical instruments.

Leather goods
Almacenes Chimborazo, Amazonas y Naciones Unidas (next to El Espiral shopping centre) and Flores 319 in the Old City
Aramis, Amazonas 1234.
Su Kartera, Sucre 351 y García Moreno, T02-2512160, also at Veintimilla 1185, between 9 de Octubre and Amazonas. Manufacturers of bags, briefcases, shoes, belts etc.

Panama hats
Marcel Creations, Roca 766, entre Amazonas y 9 de Octubre. Good selection.
Homero Ortega, Isabel La Católica N24-100, T02-25267715. Outlet for one of the hat manufacturers in Cuenca.

Jewellery

Alquimia, Juan Rodríguez 139. High-quality silversmith.

Argentum, JL Mera 614. Reasonably priced.

H Stern's, has stores at the airport, **Hotel Hilton Colón** and **Hotel Quito**.

Hamilton, 12 de Octubre 1942 y Cordero. Fine silver and gold crafts and jewellery, native designs.

Jeritsa, Mall El Jardín, local 234, T02-2980194, good selection of gold and silver.

Jewelry & Design, Mall El Jardín, local 166.

Taller Guayasamín, in Bellavista (see p113). Jewellery with native designs.

Tinta, JL Mera 1020 y Foch, good selection of silver, reasonable prices, good service.

Malls

There are a number of modern, smart looking malls in the New City, all with food courts, open usually Mon-Sat 1000-2000 and Sun 1000-1400.

El Bosque, Av Occidental y Carvajal, in the northwest of the New City.

Centro Comercial Iñaquito, known as CCI, Amazonas y Naciones Unidas.

Mall El Jardín, Amazonas between Mariana de Jesús and República.

Quicentro Shopping, Naciones Unidas between Los Shyris and 6 de Diciembre.

El Recreo, Av Maldonado at the Trole stop, in the south of the city.

Markets

Watch your belongings and pockets at all markets. For fruits and vegetables and to get the overall *mercado* experience, the main markets are:

Mercado Central, Av Pichincha y Olmedo, in the Old City, refurbished in 2004, Teatro Sucre Trole stop southbound or San Blas northbound, Ecovía etación La Marín.

Mercado Santa Clara, Versalles y Ramírez Dávalos, Santa Clara Trole stop.

Mercado Iñaquito, Iñaquito y Villalengua, west of Amazonas, La Y Trole stop.

Mercado Ipiales, on Chile uphill from Imbabura. Stolen goods are sometimes sold here among the clothing and appliances (a particularly unsafe area).

If you're looking for your stolen camera, try Plaza Arenas on Vargas, next to Colegio La Salle, and camera shops which sell used equipment, see Photography below.

Photography

There are many places which develop film along Amazonas and in the malls.

Foto Imágen, Mariana de Jesús E5-11 e Italia, T02-2469762, camera sales and repairs.

Fotomania, 6 de Diciembre N19-23 y Patria, T02-2547512, new and second-hand cameras, also black and white processing.

Ron Jones, Lizardo García E9-104 y Andrés Xaura, 1 block east of 6 de Diciembre, T02-2507622. A highly recommended professional lab for slides and prints, helpful and informative.

Suba Foto, Maldonado 1371 y Rocafuerte in the Old City, sells second-hand cameras.

Sports equipment

El Globo shops, 10 de Agosto y Roca, Amazonas y Gaspar de Villaroel and Venezuela 936, stock snorkelling gear, as do **Importaciones Kao**, Colón y Almagro, at Quicentro Shopping and at El Bosque.

Supermarkets

La Feria, Bolívar 334, between Venezuela and García Moreno. Good wines and spirits, and Swiss, German and Dutch cheeses.

Mi Comisariato supermarket and department store at Quicentro Shopping and García Moreno y Mejía in the Old City.

Santa María with good prices, Av Iñaquito y Pereira and Versalles y Carrión.

Supermaxi at Mall El Jardín, CCI, El Bosque, Centro Comercial Plaza Aeropuerto (Av de la Prensa y Homero Salas), Multicentro shopping complex (6 de Diciembre y La Niña, about 2 blocks north of Colón) and Megamaxi (6 de Diciembre y Julio Moreno), and El Recreo. The largest chain in the city is a very well stocked supermarket and department store with a wide range of local and imported goods, not cheap, Mon-Sat 1000-2000, Sun 1000-1300.

▲▲ Activities and tours

Ball games

The city's parks are filled at weekends with locals playing ball games. Professional football (soccer) is played at Estadio Atahualpa, 6 de Diciembre y Naciones Unidas and at Estadio Casa Blanca, in Carcelén to the north. Schedules vary, check the newspapers.

Basketball and volleyball are played in the Coliseo Julio César Hidalgo on Av Pichincha and Coliseo Rumiñahui on Toledo y Queseras del Medio. Informal 'ecuavolley' is played in all neighbourhood parks.

A local game, *pelota de guante* (glove ball), is played on Sat afternoons and Sun at Estadio Mejía and in Parque El Ejido.

Friendly games of rugby are played when there are enough people, see noticeboard at the Reina Victoria Pub.

Bullfighting

Plaza de Toros Iñaquito, Amazonas y Tomás de Berlanga, during the 1st week of December for *fietas de Quito*. Tickets on sale at 1500 the day before the bullfight, you may have to buy from touts.
The Unión de Toreros, Edificio Casa Paz, Av Amazonas, has information on all bullfights around the country; these take place all year. They do not have details of the parochial *toros de pueblo*, these take place during each village's *fiestas patronales*.

Climbing and trekking

Climbs and trekking tours can be arranged in Quito and several other cities. See Essentials, pp 71 and 81, for more information. The following Quito agencies have all been recommended to us; see Tour operators below for their contact details; all use qualified guides.

Agama Expediciones, is run by experienced climbing guide Eduardo Agama and also own **Albergue Cara Sur** on Cotopaxi, p204.
Campo Base, run by Manuel and Diego Jácome, very experienced climbing guides, they have a mountain lodge 15 km south of Sangolquí, near Sicholagua, good for acclimatization at 3050m, for details see p134.
Compañía de Guías, English, German, French and Italian spoken.
Pamir Travel and Adventures, chief guide Hugo Torres is very experienced and speaks English.
Safari Tours, 2 climbers per guide, trekking tours, has own transport and equipment, large and small groups, several languages spoken, very knowledgeable, well organized and planned. Also runs a high altitude glacier school, with courses of 2-3 days with bilingual guides.
Sierra Nevada, chief guide Freddy Ramírez is fluent in French, English and German, has his own equipment, and takes large groups.
Surtrek, arranges guided climbs of most peaks, also rents and sells equipment, 2 climbers per guide, large and small groups.

Independent guides do not normally provide transport or a full service (ie food, equipment, insurance) and without a permit from the Ministerio del Ambiente, they might be refused entry to the national parks. The following independent guides have been recommended: **Iván Rojas**, T02-2558380, **Benno Schlauri**, T02-2340709.

Climbing clubs
The Quito climbing clubs welcome new members, but they do not provide guiding services. Do not expect to get a free mountaineering trip from them. It is not really worth joining if you are in Ecuador for only a few weeks. There are active climbing clubs at the following institutions: **Colegio San Gabriel**, **Universidad Católica**, **Club Nuevos Horizontes** (Colón 2038 y 10 de Agosto, T02-2552154) and **Club Sadday** (Alonso de Angulo y Galo Molina).

Equipment
Stores that sell climbing and camping equipment (see Shopping above) also rent some items and can be a source of general information. They are often looking for used European/North American equipment; contact them if you wish to sell before leaving.

Cycling

See Sports and special interest travel, p67, for more information on cycling in Ecuador.

Bicycle shops
Bike Stop, 6 de Diciembre 3925 y Checoslovaquia, T02-2255404. Stocks a wide range of bikes.
Bicisport, in Quicentro Shopping, top floor, and 6 de Diciembre 6327 y Tomás de Berlanga, T02-2460894. Stocks imported high-quality bikes and parts.
Bike Tech, 6 de Diciembre N39-59 y El Telégrafo, T02-2263421. A meeting place for long-distance cyclists. Owner Santiago Lara has informal 'meets' almost every weekend, anyone is welcome, no charge, they ride 20 or more routes around Quito. Also a good repair shop and cheap parts. Friendly and glad to advise on routes. Recommended.
Ciclo Vivas, 6 de Diciembre 2810 y Orellana, T02-2566100. Stocks Jamis, Shimano and Wheeler.
Sobre Ruedas, Av 10 de Agosto N52-162, Ciudadela Kennedy, T02-2416781. Repairs, tours, rentals and sales.

Ciclopaseos
Quito has a couple of bike paths, one around the perimeter of Parque La Carolina and a second one in the south, an area with vegetation along Quebrada Ortega in the Quitumbe neighbourhood. The city organizes a *ciclopaseo*, a cycle day on the last Sun of every month. Key avenues are closed to vehicular traffic and thousands of cyclists cross the city in 24 km from north to south. This is very popular, the last ciclopaseo in

2004 had over 30,000 cyclists; there are plans to increase the frequency to every fortnight.

Mountain bike tours
There are specialized agencies offering one-or several day biking tours; a number of other agencies also offer cycling tours or rent bikes.
Aries, Wilson 578 y Reina Victoria, T/F02-2906052, after hours T09-9816603, www.ariesbikecompany.com

1-3 day tours, all equipment provided.
The Biking Dutchman, Foch 714 y JL Mera, T02-2542806, after hours T09-9730267, www.biking-dutchman.com The pioneers of mountain biking in Ecuador, one and several day tours, great fun, good food, very well organized, English, German and Dutch (of course) spoken. Recommended.
Safari (see Tour operators below) biking tours in small groups, free route planning.

Jogging

Hash House Harriers is a club for runners and walkers which meets fortnightly. Enquire at **Reina Victoria Pub**, T02-2226369.

Paragliding

Escuela Pichincha de Vuelo Libre, Carlos Endara Oe3-60 y Amazonas, T02-2256592 (office hrs), T09-9478349 (after hours), parapent@uio.satnet.net Offers complete courses for US$350-500 and tandem flights for US$40-60.

Swimming

There are a number of good, clean, heated public pools in the city. Swimming cap, towel and soap are compulsory for admission. One is in **Miraflores**, at the upper end of Av Universitaria, a 10-min walk from Amazonas. Open Tue-Sun 0900-1600. Another is at **Batán Alto**, on Cochapata, Ecovía to Los Sauces station and walk up Gaspar de Villaroel.
Colegio Benalcázar, 6 de Diciembre y Portugal, Benalcázar stop on the Ecovía. Pool and sauna are also open to the public.

Tour operators

When booking tours, note that national park fees are rarely included. For park fees, see p478. The following companies have all been recommended at some time. Many are clustered in the Mariscal district, where you are encouraged to have a stroll and shop around. Most Quito agencies sell a variety of tours in all regions of Ecuador; they may run some of those tours themselves, while they act as sales agents for others. See also listings above for companies specializing in

climbing/trekking, river rafting or mountain biking and p380, 391, 399 and 402 for jungle lodges. Choosing a responsible tour operator is very important, not only as a way of getting the best experience for your money, but also to limit impact on areas you will visit and ensure benefits for local communities. See Responsible tourism, p45.

Advantage Travel, El Telégafo E10-63 y Juan de Alcántara, T02-2462871, www.advantagecuador.com Run tours to Machalilla and Isla de la Plata. Also operate 4-5 day jungle tours on the *Manatee* floating hotel, on the Río Napo.

Agama Expediciones, Washington 425 y 6 de Diciembre, p 2, T02-2903164, climbing and trekking tours, also have a mountain lodge, see Climbing and trekking above.

Andando Tours, Coruña N26-311 y Orellana, T02-2566010, www.andandotours.com Run the first-class Galápagos vessel *Sagiota* and are agents for the *Beagle* and *Samba*, in the same category.

Biotravel. We have received several complaints about this agency which sells Galápagos tours.

Campo Base, Jacinto de Evia N60-121 (north of the airport), T02-2599737, www.campobaseturismo.com Climbing, trekking and cycling tours, also have a mountain lodge, see Climbing and trekking above and run trekking and climbing tours in the Río Pita area.

Compañía de Guías de Montaña, Jorge Washington 425 y 6 de Dicembre, T/F02-2504773, www.companiadeguias.com Climbing and trekking specialists, but also sell other tours.

Dracaena, Pinto 446 y Amazonas, T02-2546590, dracaena@andinanet.net Runs very good jungle trips in Cuyabeno.

Ecotours Ecuador, Magnolias n-51 y Crisantemos, La Primavera, Cumbaya, T02-2897316, www.ecotoursecuador.com Exclusive booking agent and tour operator for the Napo Wildlife Centre, owned by non-profit conservation group Eco Ecuador.

Ecoventura, Almagro N31-80 y Whymper, T/F02-2231034, www.ecoventura.com Operate first-class Galápagos cruises and sell tours throughout Ecuador.

Ecuador Verde País, Calama E6-19 y Reina Victoria, T02-2220614, www.cabanas jamu.com Run **Jamu Lodge** in Cuyabeno.

Ecuadorian Tours (American Express representative), Av Amazonas 329 y J Washington, several other locations, T02-2560488, www.ecuadoriantours.com Tours in all regions and airline tickets.

Enchanted Expeditions, P.O. Box 17-1200599, De las Alondras y De los Lirios Esq, T02-2569960, www.enchantedexpeditions.com Operate Galápagos cruises in various categories, sell jungle trips to Cuyabeno and highland tours.

Equateur Voyages Passion, in Auberge Inn Hostal, Gran Colombia 1138 y Yahuachi, T02-3227605, www.equateur-voyages.com Full range of adventure tours. Run a 4-5 day jungle tour on the Shiripuno River from Coca. Competitive prices for Galápagos cruises.

Etnotur, Luis Cordero 13-13 y JL Mera, T02-2564565, etnocru@uio.satnet.net English spoken. Operators of the catamaran *Ahmara* in Galápagos.

Galacruises Expeditions, Jorge Washington 748 between Amazonas and 9 de Octubre, T02-2556036, www.galacruises.com Own the *Sea Man* cruiser and *Archipel I, II* catamarans, Galápagos diving and nature cruises.

Galápagos Boat Company, Foch E5-39, T02-2220426, www.safari.com.ec Broker for about 60 boats in the islands, can find the best deals around.

Galasam, Cordero 1354 y Amazonas, T02-2903909, www.galasam.com Has a large fleet of boats in different categories for Galápagos cruises. Full range of tours in highlands, jungle trips to their own lodge on the Rio Aguarico.

Galextur, Portugal 600 y 6 de Diciembre, T02-2269626, ingmar1@attglobal.net Run 4-8 day land-based tours with daily sailings to different islands. Good service.

Green Planet, JL Mera N23-84 y Wilson, T02-2520570, greenpla@interactive.net.ec

Ecologically sensitive jungle tours in Cuyabeno and the Tena area, friendly staff and guides, good food. Recommended.

Kapok Expeditions, Pinto E4-225, T/F02-2556348, www.kapokexpeditions.com Jungle tours to Cuyabeno and Yasuní, trekking, Machalilla, hacienda tours.

Kempery Tours, Ramirez Dávalos 117 y Av.Amazonas, T02-2505599, www.kempery.com Good value tours, 4-14 day jungle trips to Bataburo Lodge in Huaorani territory and operate Galápagos cruises; also sell horse riding and other tours, multilingual service. Recommended.

Klein Tours, Eloy Alfaro N34-151 y Catalina Aldaz, also Shyris N34-280 y Holanda, T02-2267000, www.kleintours.com Galápagos and mainland tours, tailor-made, English, French and German spoken.

Metropolitan Touring, República de El Salvador N36-84, also Amazonas 239 y 18 de Septiembre and several other locations, T02-2988200, www.metropolitan-touring.com A very large organization. Run Galápagos cruises, also arranges climbing, trekking expeditions, as well as city tours of Quito, Machalilla National Park, private rail journeys, jungle camps.

Neotropic Turis, Amazonas N24-03 y Wilson, T02-2521212, www.neotropicturis.com Operates the Cuyabeno Lodge (see Cuyabeno Wildlife reserve, p397), jungle trips and organizes trips in all regions. Recommended.

Pamir Travel and Adventures, JL Mera 721 y Ventimilla, T02-2542605, F2547576. Galápagos cruises, climbing and jungle tours.

Positiv Turismo, Voz Andes N41-81, T02-2440604, www.positivturismo.com Swiss-Austrian-run company offers trips to Galápagos, cultural trips, trekking and special interest tours.

Quasar Naútica and Land Services, Brasil 293 y Granda Centeno, Edificio IACA p 2, T02-2446996, www.quasarnautica.com Highly recommeded 7-10 day naturalist and diving Galápagos cruises on 8-16 berth luxury and power yachts.

Rolf Wittmer, Foch E7-81 y Almagro, T02-2526938, www.rwittmer.com Run 2 first class yachts, *Tip Top II* and *III*.

Safari Tours, Foch E5-39 y JL Mera, T02-2552505, USA/Canada toll free T1-800-4348182, www.safari.com.ec Run by Jean

Brown and Pattie Serrano, both informative and knowledgeable. Excellent adventure travel, personalized itineraries, mountain climbing, cycling, rafting, trekking and cultural tours. They also book Galápagos tours, sell jungle trips and run a high-altitude glacier school. An excellent source of travel information. Open 7 days a week 0900-1900. Highly recommended.

Sangay Touring, Amazonas N24-196 y Cordero, T02-2508922, www.guide2 galapagos.com Run by Martin and Robin Slater, operate a variety of custom designed tours and sell Galápagos trips, efficient service.

Sierra Nevada, Pinto 637 y Cordero, T02-2553658, snevada@accessinter.net Specialized adventure tours (climbing, trekking, whitewater rafting) and jungle expeditions.

Surtrek, Amazonas 897 y Wilson, T02-2561129, F2561132, www.surtrek.com Climbing and trekking expeditions, jungle and Galápagos tours, also flights.

Tours Unlimited, Julio Castro 579 y Valparaíso, T02-2222564, www.tours-unlimited.com Custom-made itineraries in all regions, specializing in trips for honeymooners.

Tropic Ecological Adventures, República E7-320 y Almagro, Edificio Taurus 1-A, T02-2225907, www.tropiceco.com Run by Andy Drumm and Sofía Darquea, naturalist guides with many years experience in Galápagos, work closely with conservation groups, winners of awards for responsible tourism in 1997, 2000. Their ecologically responsible and educational tours are recommended for anyone seriously interested in the environment, part of each fee is given to indigenous communities and ecological projects. Also Galápagos and highland trips.

Zenith Travel, JL Mera 453 y Roca, Edificio Chiriboga, p 2, T02-2529993, www.zenithecuador.com Run a variety of tours in Ecuador and Peru, sell Galápagos tours. English and French spoken.

🚌 Transport

Air

Mariscal Sucre Airport, T02-2944900. Airport facilities and ground transportation to/from the airport are described under Touching down, p42. For information on national flights see Getting around by air, p49.

Airline offices
Domestic Aerogal, Amazonas 7797 opposite the airport, T02-2257202, 1-800-2376425, aerogal@andinanet.net **Atesa**, Guipúzcoa 122 y Gerona, T02- 2303242, seconaca@pi.pro.ec **Icaro**, Amazonas N32-137, opposite El Jardín mall, also at JL Mera y Orellana opposite the Marriott, T02-2450928, T1-800-883567, www.icaro. com.ec **TAME**, Amazonas 13-54 y Colón, Colón y La Rábida and 6 de Diciembre N26-112, T02-2909900 to 909, www.tame.com.ec

  International Air Europa, Colón y Reina Victoria, Edificio Banco de Guayaquil, p6, T02-2567646, www.aireuropa.com
Air France, 12 de Octubre N24-562 y Cordero, World Trade Center, Torre A, #710, T02-2524201 **Air Madrid**, Shyris y Bélgica, T02-2458447, www.airmadrid.com

American Airlines, Amazonas 4545 y Pereira, T02-2260900, www.aa.com **Avianca**, República de El Salvador 780 y Portugal, edif Twin Towers, mezzanine, T02-2264392. Coruña 1311 y San Ignacio, T02-2232015, www.avianca.com.co **Continental Airlines**, 12 de Octubre 1830 y Cordero, World Trade Center, mezzanine, also Naciones Unidas y República de El Salvador, EdificioCity Plaza, ground floor, T02-2557170, www.continental.com **Copa Airlines**, República de El Salvador 361 y Moscú, Edificio Aseguradora del Sur, ground floor, T02-2273082, www.copair.com **Iberia**, Eloy Alfaro 939 y Amazonas, Edificio Finandes, p5, T02-2566009 **KLM**, 12 de Octubre y A Lincoln, edif Torre 1492, #110, T02-2986820 **Lan Chile, Lan Ecuador, Lan Peru**, Pasaje Río Guayas E3-131 y Amazonas, Edificio Rumiñahui, opposite Parque La Carolina, T02-2992300, 1-800-526328, www.lanchile.com **Lufthansa**, 18 de Septiembre 238 y Reina Victoria, T02-2508396, ihulotcl@ecnet.ec **Santa Bárbara**, Portugal 794 y República de El Salvador, T02-2253972 **TACA**, República de El Salvador N35-67 y Portugal, T02-2923170.

Bus

Local

Quito has 3 parallel transport lines running from north to south on exclusive lanes, covering almost the length of the city. The fare is US$0.25. There are plans to integrate these lines into a single transport system in late 2005.

Trole Trole is an integrated system of trolley buses and feeder bus lines (*alimentadores*, painted turquoise), T02-2665016, Mon-Fri 0500-2345, weekends and holidays 0600-2145. It runs along Av 10 de Agosto in the north of the city, C Guayaquil (southbound) and C Flores (northbound) in the Old City, and mainly along Av Pedro Vicente Maldonado in the south. The northern terminus, **Terminal Norte**, is north of 'La Y', the junction of 10 de Agosto, Av América and Av de la Prensa; at El Recreo, on Av Maldonado is an important transfer station, known as **Terminal Sur**, and the southern terminus, **Morán Valverde**, is in Ciudadela Quitumbe in the far south of the city.

Feeder bus lines serve suburbs from the northern and southern terminals and from El Recreo station. Some trolleys run the full length of the line, while others run only a section, the destination is marked in front of the vehicle. There is a special entrance for wheelchairs.

Ecovía Ecovía is a line of articulated-buses running along Av 6 de Diciembre, from **La Marín** near the Old City to the **Estación Río Coca**, at C Río Coca east of 6 de Diciembre, in the north, T02-2430726, Mon-Sat 0500-2130, Sun and holidays 0600-2100. Ecovía feeder buses are dark red.

Metrobus Also runs articulated buses along Avenida América and Av de la Prensa from the neighbourhood of **Miraflores**, at the southern end of the New City, to **Carcelén**, a suburb in the north, Mon-Fri 0600-2200, weekends and holidays 0600-2100.

City buses There are also 3 types of city buses. *Selectivos* are red, take mostly sitting passengers and a limited number standing, and charge US$0.25. *Bus Tipo* are royal blue, take sitting and standing passengers, also US$0.25. There are few *populares* left, these are light blue, cost US$0.18, can get very crowded. Many bus lines go through **La Marín** at the north end of the Old City. Extra caution is advised here: it is a rough area and pickpockets abound; best avoided at night.

Outer suburbs are served by *Interparroquial* buses painted green. Those running east to the valleys of **Cumbayá**, **Tumbaco** and beyond leave from the **Estación Río Coca** (see Ecovía above). Buses southeast to **Valle de los Chillos** leave from **La Marín**. Buses going northwest leave from **San Blas**, those north from **C Larrea** and **Asunción** and those going south from **Villaflora**.

Long distance

The main **Terminal Terrestre** for all national services is in the Old City, at Maldonado y Cumandá. There are company booking offices in the terminal but staff shout destinations of buses leaving and you can hop on board and pay later; but confirm the fare in advance and check if another company is not leaving sooner. For the less frequent routes, or at busy times of the year (long weekends or holidays), consider purchasing your ticket a day in advance. See the bus timetable for prices and travel times, p52.

Bus companies Several companies have private stations, generally in the New City, buses departing from these stations will also make a stop at the Terminal Terrestre before leaving the city: **Flota Imbabura**, Manuel Larrea 1211 y Portoviejo, T02-2236940, for **Cuenca** and **Guayaquil**; **Panamericana Internacional**, Colón 852 y Reina Victoria, T02-2501585, for **Huaquillas**, **Machala**, **Cuenca**, **Loja**, **Guayaquil**, **Manta** and **Esmeraldas**; Reina del Camino, Larrea y 18 de Septiembre, T02-2585697, for **Portoviejo**, **Bahía** and **Manta**; Transportes Ecuador, JL Mera 330 y Jorge Washington, T02-2503642, for **Guayaquil**; Transportes Esmeraldas, Santa María 870 y Amazonas, T02-2505099, for **Esmeraldas**.

International

Ormeño Internacional, from **Perú**, has an office at Los Shyris N34-432 y Portugal, opposite Parque la Carolina, T2460027. They go twice per week to **Lima**, US$70, 36 hrs, **La Paz**, US$150, **Santiago**, US$165, 4 days, and **Buenos Aires**, US$200, 1 week. For these and other South American destinations, it is cheaper to take a bus to the border and change there.

Panamericana Internacional, (see Long Distance above) also run an international service: daily to **Bogotá**, changing buses in Tulcán and Ipiales, US$70, 28 hrs; **Caracas**, US$100; to **Lima**, changing buses in Aguas Verdes and Túmbes, US$70, 38 hrs.

Car hire

The main car hire companies have counters at the airport and city offices. The phone numbers shown without an address are at the airport. For rental prices and procedures, see car hire, p55.

Budget, T02-2459052; Amazonas 1408 y Colón T02-2221814; and at Hilton Colón, T02-2523328, www.budget-ec.com
Ecuacars, T02-2247298; Colón 1280 y Amazonas, T02-2529781. **Expo**, T02-2433127; Av América N21-66 y Bolívia, T02-2228688, T1-800-736822; exporent@interactive.net.ec
Hertz, T02-2254257, www.hertz.com
Localiza, 6 de Diciembre E8-124 y Veintimilla, T02-2270222, T1-800-562254, www.localiza.com.ec **Sicorent**, T02-2432858, sicorent_uio@hotmail.com

To hire 8-14 passenger vans with driver, a couple of companies are at international arrivals at the airport: **Achupallas Tours**, T02-3301493, vanrent@andinanet.net
Trans-Rabbit, T02-2232133.

Vehicle repairs
New car dealers have repair shops specializing in the brands they sell, a list can be found in the yellow pages under *automotores*. For motorbike repairs, look under *motocicletas* and *motos*.
AMIPA, Auxilio Mecánico Inmediato para Automóviles, T02-3318398, T09-9734222. Reliable roadside mechanical assistance for cars and motorbikes in the Quito metropolitan area (including Los Chillos and Tumbaco valleys), service for members and non-members.
Alvarez Barba, 10 de Agosto N51-97, T02-2472568, for BMW, Jeep, Mercedes Benz, Peugeot, Porche, Volvo.
Atlas, Inglaterra 533 y Vancouver, T02-2234341, Land Rover specialists.
Autocom, Eloy Alfaro y de las Anonas, T02-2412461, for Land Rover and Hyundai.
Automobile, Río Coca 500 y Colimes, T02-2442196, for Jeep, Fiat, Chevrolet and

many Japanese brands. There are several other repair shops along the same street.
Dar Car's, 6 de Diciembre 7758, T02-2412221, for many Japanese brands, Jeep and Ford.
Euro Servicio, Los Shyris y Río Coca, T02-2432033, for BMW, Mercedes Benz and Porsche, very busy. Can also get BMW motorcycle parts from Germany in 2 wks.
Juan Molestina, 6 de Diciembre y Bélgica, fuel and travel equipment shop, helpful for motorbike spare parts.
Kosche, Eiffel 138 y Los Shyris, T02-2442204. BMW and Mercedes Benz specialists, but will also do other brands.
The Paint Bull, 10 de Agosto N32-163 y Rumipamba, T02-2551212, for American brands, Toyota and Fiat.
Ponce Yépez, 10 de Agosto 9085, T02-2400222, for VW.
SERR, de las Azucenas y Las Higueras, T02-2257926, for Land Rover.
Slip, de las Azucenas y Eloy Alfaro, for Range Rover.

Taxi

Local
Taxis are a safe, cheap and efficient way to get around the city. Rides cost from US$1 during the day, there is no increase for extra passengers. You can expect to pay about US$1-2 more at night. All taxis must have working meters (*taxímetros*) by law, so make sure the meter is running (drivers sometimes say their meters are out of order). If the meter is not running, politely fix the fare before getting in. All legally registered taxis have large numbers prominently displayed on the side of the vehicle and on a decal on the windshield. They are safer and cheaper than unauthorized taxis. Note the registration and the licence plate numbers if you feel you have been seriously overcharged or mistreated, then complain to the transit police or tourist office. But be reasonable and remember that most taxi drivers are honest and helpful.

At night it is safer to use a radio taxi, there are several companies including: **Taxi Amigo**, T02-2222222/2333333, **City Taxi**, T02-2633333 and **Central de Radio Taxis**, T02-2500600. Some of these radio taxi companies may use unmarked vehicles; when calling ask the dispatcher exactly what car will pick you up.

To hire a taxi by the hour costs from US$7 in the city, US$8 if going out of town.

Long distance

For trips outside Quito, agree taxi tariffs beforehand. Expect to pay US$70-85 a day. Outside the luxury hotels, cooperative taxi drivers have a list of agreed excursion prices and most drivers are knowledgeable. Arrangements can also be made through the radio taxi numbers listed above. For taxi tours with a guide, try Hugo Herrera, T02-2267891/2236492 who speaks good English and is recommended. The van companies listed under Car hire also rent vehicles with driver for touring.

Train

Regular passenger service has been discontinued throughout the country: see Getting around, page 58. For information on the tourist train from Quito to Cotopaxi, see p147.

see Getting around, page 58. For information on the tourist train from Quito to Cotopaxi, see p147.

❶ Directory

For all emergencies in Quito call 911.

Banks

Banks are generally open Mon-Fri 0830-1800 and some also on Sat 0900-1300. Service for cash advances and TC exchange is usually only Mon-Fri until about 1500 (the earlier the better). Expect queues and paperwork at all banks. The procedures and commissions indicated below are subject to frequent change. For the best way to bring your funds into the country, see Money, p39.

The **American Express** representative is Ecuadorean Tours, Amazonas 329 y Jorge Washington, T02-2560488. Replaces lost Amex TCs and sells TCs to Amex card holders, but does not exchange TCs or sell them for cash. Mon-Fri 0830-1700. **Banco del Austro**, Amazonas y Santa María. Cash advances on Visa. Mon-Fri 0830-1700. **Banco de Guayaquil**, Colón y Reina Victoria, 3rd Floor. Amex and Visa TCs, 1% commission. Cirrus, Maestro or Plus ATM with maximum withdrawal of US$100, cash advances on Visa, fast and efficient. **Mastercard headquarters**, Naciones Unidas 825, next door to Banco del Pacífico. Cash advances, efficient service. Mon-Fri 0830-1700. **Banco del Pacífico**, main branch at Naciones Unidas between Los Shyris and Amazonas, also Amazonas y Roca, Mall El Jardín and Centro Comercial El Bosque. Amex TCs in US$ only, maximum US$200 per day, US$5 charge per transaction, also Mastercard and Visa through Cirrus and Maestro ATMs. **Banco del Pichincha**, Amazonas 13-54 y Colón, Venezuela y Espejo,

half block from Plaza de la Independencia and many other branches. Cash through Cirrus ATM only. **Mutualista Pichincha**, 18 de Septiembre y JL Mera, García Moreno 1130 y Chile and other branches. Cash advances on Mastercard 0900-1630. **Produbanco**, Amazonas N35-211 y Japón (opposite CCI), Amazonas y Robles (also open Sat 0900-1300), Benalcazar 852 y Olmedo (cash advances only) and at the airport. Cash and TCs in various currencies, 1-2% commission, good service, cash advance on Mastercard. Mon-Fri 0830-1500.

Casa de cambio Vazcorp, Amazonas N21-147 y Roca, T02-2529212. Charges 1.8% commission for US$ TCs, 2% for TCs in other currencies. Also currency exhange and sells TCs. Mon-Fri 0845-1745, Sat 0900-1300.

Dentists

Drs Sixto y Silvia Altamirano, Amazonas 2689 y República, T02-2244119. Excellent. **Dr Roberto Mena**, Coruña E24-865 e Isabel la Católica, T02-2559923. Speaks English.

Doctors

Most embassies have the telephone numbers of doctors who speak non-Spanish languages. The following are recommended. **Dr Wilson Pancho**, República de El Salvador 112, T02-2463139/2469546. Speaks German. **Dr John Rosenberg**, Med Center Travel Clinic, Foch 476 y Almagro, T022521104, 09-9739734, internal and travel medicine with a full range of vaccines, speaks English and German, very helpful.

Embassies and consulates

All open Mon-Fri unless otherwise noted. **Argentina**, Amazonas N21-147 y Roca, p8, T02-2562292, embarge2@andinanet.net 0900-1600. **Austria**, Gaspar de Villaroel E9-53 y Los Shyris, p3, T02-2443272, 1000-1200. **Belgium**, República de El Salvador 1082 y Naciones Unidas, p10, T02-2276145, Ambelqui@ecnet.ec, Mon-Thu 0900-1200, Mon-Wed 1430-1700. **Bolivia**, Eloy Alfaro 2432 y Fernando Ayarza, T02-2244830, embolivia-quito@ andinanet.net, 0800-1600. **Brazil**, Amazonas 1429 y Colón, Edificio España, p9, T02-2563086, ebrasi@uio.satnet.net, 0900-1800. **Canada**, 6 de Diciembre 2816 y Paul Rivet, Edificio Josueth González p4, T02-2232114, 0900-1200. **Chile**, Juan Pablo Sanz 3617 y Amazonas, Edificio Xerox p4, embchile@andinanet.net, T02-2249406, 0800-1700. **Colombia** (consulate), Atahualpa 955 y República, Edificio Digicom p3, T02-2458012, 0900-1300 1400-1600.

Costa Rica, Rumipamba 692 y República, p2, T02-2254945, embajcr@uio.satnet.net, 0800-1330. **Cuba**, El Mercurio 365 y La Razón, T02-2259183, 0900-1300. **El Salvador**, República de El Salvador 733 y Portugal, embajada@elsalvador.com.ec, 0900-1500. **France** (consulate), Almagro 1550 y La Pradera, p2, T02-2569883, francie@andinanet.net, 0900-1300, 1500-1800. **Germany**, Naciones Unidas E10-44 y República de El Salvador, Edificio City Plaza, T02-2970820, alemania@interactive.net.ec, 0830-1130. **Guatemala**, República de El Salvador 733 y Portugal, Edificio Gabriela 301, T02-2459700, embaguat-ecu@andinanet.net, 0900-1300. **Honduras**, 12 de Octubre 1942 y Cordero, World Trade Center p5, T02-2223985, embhquito@yahoo.com, 0900-1400. **Ireland**, Ulloa 2651 y Rumipamba, T02-2451577, 0900-1300. **Israel**, 12 de Octubre y Salazar, Edificio Plaza 2000, p9, T02-2238055, israemb@interactive.net.ec, 1000-1300. **Italy**, La Isla 111 y H Albornoz, T02-2561077, ambital@ambitalquito.org, 0830-1230. **Japan**, JL Mera N19-36 y Patria, Edificio Corporación Financiera Nacional, p7, T02-2561899, japembecquio.satnet.net, 0930-1200, 1400-1700. **Netherlands**, 12 de Octubre 1942 y Cordero, World Trade Center p1, T02-2229229, 0830-1300,

1400-1730. **Norway**, Pasaje Alfonso Jerves 134 y Orellana, T02-2509514, 0900-1200. **Panama**, Alpallana 505 y Whimper, Edificio ESPRO p6, T02-2508856, panaembaecuador @hotmail.com, 0900-1400. **Paraguay**, 12 de Octubre 1942 y Cordero, Edificio World Trade Center p9, T02-2231990, embapar@uio.telconet.net, 0830-1330. **Peru**, República de El Salvador 495 e Irlanda, Edificio Irlanda, T02-2468410, embpeecu@uio.satnet,net, 0900-1300, 1500-1800. **Spain**, La Pinta 455 y Amazonas, T02-2564373, embespec@uio.satnet.net, 0900-1200. **Sweden**, República de El Salvador N34-399 e Irlanda, T02-2278189. **Switzerland**, Amazonas 3617 y Juan Pablo Sanz, Edificio Xerox p2, T02-2434948, vertretung@qui.rep.aadmin.ch, 0900-1200. **United Kingdom**, Naciones Unidas y República de El Salvador, Edificio Citiplaza p14, T02-2970800, britemq@impsat.net.ec, Mon-Thu 0730-1230, 1300-1600, Fri 0830-1230. **Uruguay**, 6 de Diciembre 2816 y Paul Rivet, Edificio Josueth González p9, T02-2544228, emburug1@emburuguay.int.ec, 0900-1500. **USA**, 12 de Octubre y Patria, T02-2562890, 0800-1230, 1330-1700. **Venezuela**, Los Cabildos 115 e Hidalgo de Pinto, Quito Tenis, T02-2444873, embavenecua@inteeractive.net.ec, 0900-1300, 1400-1630.

Hospitals

The following private hospitals are good but none are cheap, Metropolitano and Pichincha are the most expensive. **Clínica Pasteur**, Eloy Alfaro 552 y 9 de Octubre, T02-2234004. **Clínica Pichincha**, Veintimilla E3-30 y Páez, T02-2562296, ambulance T02-2501565. **Hospital Metropolitano**, Mariana de Jesús y Av Occidental, T02-2261520, ambulance T02-2265020. **Hospital Voz Andes**, Villalengua Oe2-37 y 10 de Agosto, T02-2262142, out-patient department T02-2439343. Run by HCJB Christian missionary organization. **Novaclínica Santa Cecilia**, Veintimilla 1394 y 10 de Agosto, T02-2545390, emergency T02-2545000.

Internet

Quito has very many cyber cafés, particularly in La Mariscal. Rates start at about US$0.60 per hr, but US$1 per hr is more typical. Some

⁞ Language schools in Quito

Quito is one of the most important centres for Spanish language study in all of Latin America, with about 80 schools operating in the city. Many people combine language study with touring and opportunities for cross-cultural exposure, and some schools are well set up to organize this. Homestays with an Ecuadorean family are often part of the experience. There are schools and programmes to suit every taste and budget, far too many to list here. Instead we focus on how to choose a language school, and list just a few of those which have received consistently favourable recommendations on page 143.

If you are short on time then it can be a good idea to make your arrangements from home, either directly with one of the schools or through an agency such as **AmeriSpan Unlimited**, USA and Canada toll-free T1-800-879-6640, www.amerispan.com, who can offer you a wide variety of options. If you have more time and less money, then it may be cheaper to organize your own studies after you arrive. You can try one or two places without committing yourself for an extended period.

Internacional de Español (IE), Selva Alegre Oe6-66 y Ruiz de Castilla, T02-3103338, www.diplomaie.com is an organization which trains Spanish as a second language teachers, publishes textbooks and maintains a list of schools throughout Ecuador. They provide general information, help students select a school and sell course materials.

South American Explorers also provides its members with a list of recommended schools and these may give club members discounts.

Recommended course books are *Español, Español* (a Spanish language text), *Ejercicios, Ejercicios* (a work book), and Grammar (a Spanish grammar text with English explanations), all published by Internacional de Español. Another good text, but difficult to find in Ecuador is *Español, Curso de Perfeccionamiento*, by Juan Felipe García Santos (Universidad de Salamanca, Sep, 1990).

Identify your budget and goals for the course: rigorous grammatical and technical training, fluent conversation skills, getting to know Ecuadoreans or just enough basic Spanish to get you through your trip. Visit a few places to get a feel for what they charge and offer. Prices vary greatly, from US$4 to US$10 per hour, but you do not always get what you pay for. If you book for a longer period, you may get a discount. There is also tremendous variation in teacher qualifications, infrastructure and resource materials. A great deal of emphasis has traditionally been placed on one-to-one teaching, but remember that a well-structured small classroom setting can also be very good.

The quality of homestays likewise varies, the cost including meals running from US$12 to US$25 per day. Try to book just one week at first to see how a place suits you, don't be pressed into signing a long-term contract right at the start. For language courses as well as homestays, deal directly with the people who will provide services to you, and avoid intermediaries.

Finally, remember that Quito is not the only place in Ecuador where you can study Spanish. Although some of the best schools are located in the capital there are also good options in Otavalo, Baños, Cuenca and elsewhere (listed in the corresponding sections of the text).

places get crowded, smoky and very noisy. Remember that internet access is cheapest and fastest in Quito, Guayaquil and Cuenca, more expensive and slower in small towns and more remote areas. Watch your belongings while in the internet cafés, there have been some reports of theft.

Language schools

See also box, p142.
New City Amazonas, Washington 718 y Amazonas, Edificio Rocafuerte, p3, T02-2527509, www.eduamazonas.com Also have a jungle program. **Bipo & Toni's Academia de Español**, Carrión E8-183 y Plaza, T/F02-2556614, www.bipo.net
Academia Latinamericana de Español, Noruega 156 y 6 de Diciembre, T02-2250946, www.latinoschools.com **Colón**, Colón 2088 y Versalles, T02-2562485, www.colonspanish school.com **Equinoccial**, Reina Victoria 1325 y García, T/F02-2564488, www.ecuadorspanish.com Small school. **Galápagos**, Amazonas 1004 y Wilson, p1, T02-2565213, www.galapagos.edu.ec
La Lengua, Colón 1001 y JL Mera, p8, T/F02-2501271, www.la-lengua.com
Latinoamericana, José Queri 2 y Eloy Alfaro, T02-2452824, also at Noruega 156 y 6 de Diciembre, T02-2452824, www.latino school.com **Mitad del Mundo**, Patria 640 y 9 de Octubre, Edificio Patria 1204, T02-2546827, www.mitadmundo.com.ec Repeatedly recommended. **Pichincha**, Carrión N4-37 y 6 de Diciembre, T02-2220478, www.pichincha spanishschool.com **Quito**, Marchena Oe1-30 y 10 de Agosto, T02- 2553647, also at Chiriboga N47-133 y Páez, T02-2462972, www.academiaquito.com.ec **Simón Bolívar**, Plaza 353 y Roca, T/F02-2236688, www.simon-bolivar.com Offer many activities and have travel agency.
Sintaxis, 10 de Agosto 15-55 y 18 de Septiembre, Edificio Andrade, p 5, T02-2520006, www.sintaxis.net Repeatedly recommended. **South American**, Amazonas N26-59 y Santa María, T02-2544715, www.southamerican.edu.ec **Superior**, Darquea Terán 1650 y 10 de Agosto, T02-2223242, www.instituto-superior.net They also have a school in Otavalo (Sucre 1110 y Morales, p2, T06-2922414), in Galápagos (advanced booking required) and can arrange voluntary work. **Universidad Católica**, 12 de Octubre y Roca, contact Carmen Sarzosa, T02-2228781, csarzosa@puceuio.puce.edu.ec

Old City Beraca, García Moreno 858 between Sucre and Espejo, Pasaje Amador, p3, T02-2288092, also in the New City at Amazonas 1114 y Pinto, T02-2958687. **Los Andes**, García Moreno 1245 y Olmedo, p2, T02-2955107, quitocolonial@yupimail.com has schools outside Quito and can arrange volunteer work. **San Francisco**, Sucre 518 y Benalcázar (Plaza San Francisco), p3, T02-2282849, also in the New City at Amazonas 2262 y Ramírez Dávalos, T02-2553476, sanfranciscoss@latinmail.com

Laundry

There are many laundromats around La Mariscal, clustered around the corner of Foch and Reina Victoria, along Pinto and along Wilson. Wash and dry costs about US$0.80 per kg, some deliver pre-paid laundry. Also **Lavandería**, Olmedo 552, in the Old City.

Dry cleaning Martinizing, 1-hr service, 12 de Octubre 1486, Diego de Almagro y La Pradera, and in 6 shopping centres, plus other locations, expensive. **La Química**, Mallorca 335 y Madrid, La Floresta and Olmedo y Cotopaxi in the Old City. **Norte**,

Amazonas 7339, 6 de Diciembre 1840 y Eloy Alfaro, and Pinzón y La Niña.

Pharmacies

Fybeca is a reliable chain of 35 pharmacies throughout the city. Their 24-hr branches are at Amazonas y Tomás de Berlanga near the Plaza de Toros, and at Centro Comercial El Recreo in the south. **Farmacia Colón**, 10 de Agosto 2292 y Cordero, T2226534, also 24 hr. Check the listing of *farmacias de turno* in *El Comercio* on Sat for 24-hr chemists during the following week. Always check expiry dates on any medications and avoid purchasing anything that requires refrigeration in the smaller drug stores.

Post office

See Post, p90, for details of rates, procedures and precautions.

There are 23 postal branches throughout Quito, opening times vary but are generally Mon-Fri 0800-1800, Sat 0800-1200. In principle all branches provide all services, but your best chances are at **Colón y Almagro** in the Mariscal district, and at the **main sorting centre** on Japón near Naciones Unidas, behind the CCI shopping centre. The branch on **Eloy Alfaro** 354 y 9 de Octubre is especially chaotic and unhelpful, best avoided. There is also a branch in the **Old City**, on Espejo, between Guayaquil y Venezuela,

and between the old and new towns at **Ulloa and Ramírez Dávalos**, behind Mercado Santa Clara (Mon-Fri 0730-1600). This is the centre for parcel post; you may be directed here to send large packages.

Poste Restante is available at the post offices at **Espejo** and at **Eloy Alfaro**. All *poste restante* letters are sent to Espejo unless marked 'Correo Central, Eloy Alfaro', but you are advised to check both *postes restantes*, whichever address you use.

For those with an Amex card, letters can be sent care of **American Express**, Casilla 17-01-0265, Quito. **South American Explorers**, see p28, also holds mail for its members.

Useful contacts

Cultural centres Alliance Française at Eloy Alfaro 1900. French courses, films and cultural events. **Casa Humboldt**, Vancouver y Polonia, T02-2548480. German centre, films, talks, exhibitions. **Emergencies** T911 for all types of emergency in Quito. **Immigration offices** See Getting in, Extensions, p37. **Police** T101. Policía de Turismo, Reina Victoria y Roca, T02-2543983. Report robberies at **Dirección de Seguridad Pública**, Cuenca y Mideros, T02-2954604, in the Old City or **Policía Judicial**, Roca 582 y JL Mera, in La Mariscal, T02-2550243.

Around Quito

Despite Quito's bustling big city atmosphere, it is surrounded by pretty and suprisingly tranquil countryside, with many opportunities for day excursions as well as longer trips. A combination of city and interparroquial buses and pick-up taxis will get you to most destinations. Excursions are also offered by Quito tour operators. The monument on the equator, the country's best-known tourist site, is just a few minutes away; there are nature reserves, craft-producing towns, excellent thermal swimming pools, walking and climbing routes, and a scenic train ride. To the west of Quito on the slopes of Pichincha is a region of spectacular natural beauty with many crystal clear rivers and waterfalls, worth taking several days to explore.
▶▶ For Sleeping, Eating and all other listings, see pages 148-150.

Mitad del Mundo and around → *Colour map 2, grid B4*

Some 23 km north of Quito is the **Mitad del Mundo Equatorial Line Monument** at an altitude of 2,483 m, near San Antonio de Pichincha. The location of the equatorial line here was determined by Charles-Marie de la Condamine and his French expedition in 1736, and agrees to within 150 m with modern GPS measurements. A paved road runs from Quito to the Monument.

The monument forms the focal point of the **Ciudad Mitad del Mundo** ① *T02-2394806, Mon-Thu 0900-1800, Fri-Sun 0900-1900 (very crowded on Sun). Entry US$1.50, children US$0.75 includes entry to the pavilions; Museo Etnográfico US$3 (includes guided tour of museum in Spanish or English); parking US$1*, a park and leisure area built as a typical colonial town, with restaurants, gift shops, a post office with philatelic sales, travel agency, pavilions of the nations which participated in the expedition (each has a museum covering a variety of topics), a numismatic collection and so on, all run by the **Consejo Provincial de Pichincha**. There are free live music and dance performances on Sundays and holidays (1300-1800). It is all rather touristy but the monument itself has an interesting **Museo Etnográfico** inside. A lift takes you to the top, then you walk down with the museum laid out all around with exhibits of different indigenous cultures every few steps.

There is a **Planetarium** ① *Tue-Sun 0900-1600, US$1.50, group of 15 minimum*, with 30-minute shows. Worth visiting is the interesting scale model of colonial Quito, about 10 sq m, with artificial day and night, which took seven years to build. The artist also has models of Cuenca and Manhattan (New York, USA); all are very impressive (daily 0900-1700, US$1).

Just north of the complex and a bit difficult to find is the eclectic, entertaining and interesting **Museo Inti-Ñan** ① *200 m north of the complex, look for a small sign and lane to your left, T02-2395122, 0930-1730 daily, US$2, English-, French- and German-speaking guides available.* It shows different experiments relating to the equator and exhibits about native life and sun-worshipping peoples. Recommended.

Pululahua

A few kilometres beyond Mitad del Mundo, off the road to Calacalí, is the **Pululahua crater** ① *Park entry fee US$5, payable at Moraspungo, two basic cabins near the Moraspungo entrance: US$5 per person, take sleeping bag, warm clothing and food.* It is well worth visiting but try to go in the morning, as there is often cloud later. In the crater, with its own warm microclimate, is the hamlet of Pululahua, surrounded by agricultural land and to the west of it, the **Reserva Geobotánica Pululahua**. The crater is open and drops to the west; the climate gets warmer and the vegetation more lush as you descend. There are two access points to the crater, one road leads to the *mirador*, a lookout on the rim, with wonderful views of the agricultural area in the crater floor. From here a rough track leads down into the crater. It's a half hour walk down, and one hour back up. A second much longer road allows you to drive into the crater. For a very scenic but long (15-20 km) walk, go down from the *mirador*, beyond the village of Pululahua turn left and follow the vehicular road back up to the rim and the main highway.

To reach Pululahua, continue on the road past Mitad del Mundo towards Calacalí. After nearly 5 km (one hour's walk) the road bears left and begins to climb steeply. A smaller paved road to the right leads to the *mirador*, 30 minutes walking. To drive to the reserve, continue beyond the turn-off for the *mirador*, 8 km from Mitad del Mundo, take the turn-off to the right past the gas station; it is 2.4 km to the Moraspungo park gate where a very scenic drive into the crater begins. In 8 km you reach the valley floor. From there you can turn right towards the village of Pululahua, or left and continue downhill to the sugar-cane growing area of Nieblí.

Around San Antonio de Pichincha

In the vicinity of the Mitad del Mundo, 3 km from San Antonio de Pichincha, are the ruins of **Rumicucho** ① *US$0.50. Books about this site by Eduardo Almeida.* Built on a magnificent location, with views south to Quito and to the north, it is a sample of one of the most common Inca site types in the northern Andes, the fortress. It was built over pre-existing structures and is believed to have guarded a pass from the north. The site was excavated and partially restored by the Banco Central. Pre-Inca ceramics, weaving implements and ceremonial objects were found here. Unfortunately the site was looted. Today you can only see remains of walls, probably pre-Inca, on five levels of terraces. The site is administered by the local community.

About 8 km from Quito on the road to San Antonio de Pichincha, is the village of **Pomasqui**, near where was a tree in which Jesus Christ appeared to perform various miracles, *El Señor del Arbol*, now enshrined in its own building. In the church nearby are paintings depicting the miracles (mostly involving horrendous road accidents), which are well worth seeing. You may have to find the caretaker to unlock the church.

From San Antonio a dirt road heads north towards **Perucho** from where you can continue to Otavalo. South of Perucho another road turns sharply southeast to the Guayllabamba-Tabacundo road, via **Puéllaro**.

South and east of Quito

Río Pita

To the southeast of Quito in the Valle de los Chillos is the Río Pita. Its ice-cold water, fed by the meltdown of Cotopaxi, runs through a scenic rocky canyon surrounded by remnants of Andean forest. There are several waterfalls in the area. A small trail follows the shore and crosses the river a couple of times, to reach rapids known as **La Chorrera de Molinuco** ① *entry US$1*, within a municipal reserve. The trail is not always clear, local guides can lead you.

The river is reached from the village of **Rumipamba**, 15 km due south of Sangolquí, there are a couple of lodges in the area. The waterfall is two hours' walking from town. Continuing beyond Rumipamba you can approach **Volcán Sincholagua**, which is more than 3,000 m above sea level, but be prepared for cold and wet conditions.

Reserva Ecológica Antisana

① *Park entry US$5. Access requires passing through the private Hacienda Antisana, a permit from the landowner is required (US$10); enquire beforehand in Píntag, Sr José Delgado, T02-2435828.*

The magnificent **Volcán Antisana** (5,758 m) tempts visitors when its veil of mist dissipates and it can be seen in the distance from Quito. It is part of the Reserva Ecológica Antisana which spans the Cordillera Oriental from the highlands east to the jungle. It is a magnificent area for hiking and camping, where condors may be seen. There are no services, so visitors must be self-sufficient, and the area is quite rugged.

Access to the reserve is through **Píntag**, 22 km southeast of Sangolquí. Beyond Pintag the road turns to rough gravel and divides, the right fork goes to the base of Sincholagua (4,898 m), the left fork goes to Laguna La Mica at the base of Antisana. The reserve can also be accessed from Papallacta and from Baeza.

Refugio de Vida Silvestre Pasochoa

① *Run by Fundación Natura, República 481 y Almagro, T02-2503391. US$7, guides are available for groups, it can be touristy at weekends. Shelter US$5 per person, has cooking facilities and hot shower, take sleeping bag, it gets very cold. Camping US$3 per person. There are no shops, take food and water.*

This reserve, formerly known as Bosque Protector Pasochoa, is 45 minutes southeast of Quito by car towards the south end of Valle de Los Chillos. The reserve is situated between 2,700 m and 4,200 m and preserves a remnant of humid Andean forest. It has more than 120 species of birds (unfortunately some of the fauna has been frightened away by the noise of the visitors) and 50 species of trees. This is a good place for a family picnic or an acclimatization hike close to Quito. There are walks of various lengths, between 30 minutes and eight hours.

Papallacta → *Phone code 06 Altitude 3,200 m*

Papallacta is a village 64 km east of Quito, along the Vía Interoceánica, the road between Quito and el Oriente. It is on the eastern slopes of the range, an attractive area where you leave the *páramo* for more humid cloud forests. The region has wonderful thermal baths and offers good walking within the **Reserva Ecológica Cayambe-Coca**. One access point to the reserve is from **La Virgen**, at the pass before descending to the eastern slopes, and there is a ranger's station on the south side of the road. Here is an area of strikingly beautiful páramo dotted with lakes, popular among fishermen. In this area is **Hostería Campucocha**. Past La Virgen is **Laguna Papallacta**, formed by a lava flow. Around the lake are a couple of community-run thermal springs. The **Fundación Ecológica Rumicocha** ① *ferumico@pi.pro.ec, 0800-1200, 1400-1600*, with projects in this region, has a small office on the main street of the village of Papallacta, run by Sra Mariana Liguia, who is friendly. There are leaflets on the Cayambe-Coca reserve.

The **Termas de Papallacta** ① *0700-2100, US$5, children under 12 US$2.50*, are the most attractively developed set of hot springs in Ecuador. The hot water is channelled into three pools large enough for swimming, three smaller shallow pools and two tiny family-size pools. There is also a steam room, hot showers and two cold plunge pools as well as access to the river. The baths are crowded at weekends but usually quiet through the week. The view, on a clear day, of Antisana from the Papallacta road or while enjoying the thermal waters is superb. In addition to the pools there is a spa centre with a therapeutic pool, jacuzzi, massage, very clean and relaxing. The Termas de Papallacta complex includes an extension of land following the Río Papallacta upstream from the baths to forested areas. There are well-maintained trails, entry US$1. Access to the complex is along a secondary road branching off the Via Interoceánica, 1 km west of Papallacta. It is 1 km uphill from the turn-off to the complex.

There are additional pools at the **Hotel Termas de Papallacta** and in the other hotels on the road to the Termas, all for exclusive use of their guests. More springs in this area provide the village of Papallacta with abundant hot water and fill three simple but clean pools at the **Balneario Municipal** ① *Mon-Fri 0700-1700, Sat-Sun 0600-1800, US$2, children and seniors US$1*, below the village towards the river.

Tourist train to Cotopaxi

① *Trains depart from Quito railway station, 2 km south of the Old City, along the continuation of C Maldonado (Chimbacalle trolley stop if northbound, Machángara if southbound, then walk uphill along Maldonado). Sat and Sun 0800, returns 1430. US$4.60 return, children under 12 US$2.30. Tickets must be purchased in advance at Bolívar 443 y García Moreno, T02-2582927 (Mon 1300-1630, Tue-Fri 0800-1600); you need a passport number for all the tickets you purchase and the person's age. Last-minute sales at the station are only for boxcars, same price.*

South of Quito lies the lush agricultural area of **Machachi**, with lovely views of the surrounding peaks, the area can be explored on foot or horse. Beyond is **Parque Nacional Cotopaxi**, a very popular destination (see page 203). Tours are arranged by Quito agencies. A **tourist train** runs from the lovely but run-down railway station in Quito to the Cotopaxi station in **Area Nacional de Recreación El Boliche** ① *entrance fee US$10*, abutting on Parque Nacional Cotopaxi. The ride takes three hours, so it gives you time to walk around and enjoy the views. Dress warmly and take lunch.

Climbing Pichincha

Pichincha has several peaks. Overlooking Quito from the west are two low antenna-topped peaks, **Cruz Loma** to the south and **Las Antenas** to the north. **Rucu Pichincha** (Old Pichincha 4,627 m), sometimes sprinkled with snow, can be seen from some parts of Quito, and can be climbed either via Cruz Loma or Las Antenas. Unfortunately, public safety along all of the above routes is so poor that you are advised not to climb here even in a large group. The highest of Pichincha's summits is that of **Guagua Pichincha** (Baby Pichincha, 4,794 m), at the southern end of the massif; between it and Rucu are a couple of lesser peaks. It is possible to reach Guagua Pichincha's crater rim by road and to climb to the summit from there.

After almost 350 years of dormancy, Guagua Pichincha renewed its volcanic activity in 1999. The level of activity subsequently diminished, but descent into the crater remains dangerous because of the loose rock and poor trail conditions. Descending to the crater floor is not recommended and, in particular, should never be undertaken during the rainy season. The caretakers at the *refugio* (shelter) can give you first-hand up-to-date information concerning conditions. Climbing to the *refugio* and crater rim is currently safe but you should always enquire beforehand, since volcanic activity can change at any time. The **National Geophysics Institute** provides updates in Spanish at www.igepn.edu.ec

To climb Guagua Pichincha, go to **Lloa**, a small, friendly village set in beautiful surroundings. From there a 4x4 track goes almost to the *refugio* at the rim of the crater, just below the summit at 4,800 m. Depending on road conditions you might be able to get a pick-up from Lloa to the *refugio*. If walking you will need all day to make it up to the *refugio*. So set off early. The road to the summit is signposted from the right-hand corner of the main plaza as you face the volcano, and is easy to follow. There are a couple of forks, but head straight for the peak each time. It can take up to eight hours, allowing for a long lunch break and plenty of rests, to reach the **refugio**, which is maintained and manned by the Defensa Civil. It will provide a bed and water for US$5 per person. The warden has his own cooking facilities which he may share with you. It gets very cold at night and there is no heating or blankets. Be sure to keep an eye on your things. Entry to the refugio on a day visit is US$1.

> ❖ *Lloa is also the starting point for a 3-day walk to Mindo. It is a demanding trek and navigation is important. Take care when crossing rivers.*

The walk from the *refugio* to the summit is very short. You can scramble a bit further to the 'real' summit (above the *refugio*) which is tricky but worth it for the views; many other volcanoes can be seen on a clear morning. The descent back to Lloa takes only three hours, but is hard on the legs. There is a restaurant in Lloa, on the main road to Quito, which sells good soup. The last bus for Quito leaves Lloa around 1830, or walk a few hundred metres down the main road until you reach a fork. Wait here for a truck, which may take you to the outskirts of the city for around US$1.

⊖ Sleeping

Río Pita *p146*
AL Los Alisos Lodge, 20 min from Rumipamba, T02-2225825, www.losalisos.com Cabins for up to 6 and rooms, includes 3 meals, walking or horse riding tours in the area. Contact through Via Tierra operator in Quito.
B Campo Base, at La Moca, 2 km before reaching Rumipamba, T02-2599737, www.campobaseturismo.com A 4-bedroom

country lodge at 3,050 m, a good place for acclimatization, trekking and climbing. Includes breakfast and dinner, shared bath, offers tours in the area. Run by Campo Base tour operator in Quito.

Papallacta *p147*
LL Campucocha, at 'La Virgen' pass on the road from Quito, T06-2560171,

www.campucocha.com A very upscale trout-fishing lodge, includes 3 meals and open bar, a wide range of amenities, birdwatching, horse riding as well as indoor activities. Minimum 2 days advance booking required.

AL La Posada Papallacta, opposite Termas, T06-2320322, www.papallacta.com.ec Part of the Termas complex, good expensive restaurant, thermal pools both indoors and set in a lovely garden, nice lounge with fireplace, comfortable rooms heated with thermal water, some rooms have a private jacuzzi. Recommended.

C Antisana, on road to the Termas, T06-2320626. Small place, restaurant, cheaper with shared bath and cold water, some new rooms, others basic but clean.

D Coturpa, next to the public baths in Papallacta town, T06-2320640. Includes breakfast, thermal pool and sauna, functional and good value, new in 2004.

D Hostería La Pampa, on road to the Termas, T06-2320624. With restaurant, thermal pool, looks nice from the outside but rooms are simple.

D La Choza de Don Wilson, intersection of highway and road to Termas, T06-2320627. Good restaurant, very friendly and attentive.

E Rincón El Viajero, in Papallacta town. Restaurant, shared bath, hot water, basic but clean and friendly, good value.

East of Papallacta

L Guango Lodge, in a temperate forest area rich in birds. Reservations needed, T02-2547403, www.ecuadorexplorer.com/sanisidro. Price includes 3 good meals. Grey-breasted mountain toucans are regularly seen here along with other birds.

❼ Eating

Mitad del Mundo and around *p144*
₸₸₸₸ El Cráter, on the rim of the crater of Pululahua, signed access before (east) the road to the *mirador*, T02-2239399, daily 1230-1700. Popular upscale restaurant with excellent views, international and Ecuadorian food.

₸₸₸ Cochabamba, at the complex, T02-2394300. Varied menu, touristy but that's hardly surprising.

₸₸₸ Equinoccio, Av Manuel Córdoba Galarza, just north of the equator complex, T02-2394091, daily 1000-1600. Ecuadorian food, touristy, live music on Sun. Issues 'certificates' for their guests.

Papallacta *p147*
In addition to restaurants at the hotels, above, there are several simple *comedores* in Papallacta village and along the road to the Termas complex. Trout is a local speciality.

▲ Activities and tours

Mitad del Mundo and around *p144*
Calimatours, Manzana de los Correos, Oficina 11, at Mitad del Mundo complex, T02-2394796, calima@andinanet.net Runs tours to Pululahua (US$4 for 1 hr, US$8 for 2 hrs) and Rumicucho (US$7 includes entry fee), offers general information, very helpful, open daily 0900-1800, some English spoken. Recommended.

Another agency with an office at the Mitad del Mundo complex is run by people from the **Pululahua commune**. They also run tours to Pululahua and Rumicucho.

South and east of Quito *p146*
Campo Base (see Tour operators, p134) runs trekking and climbing tours in the **Río Pita** area. The local community of Rumipamba can arrange a guide, T06-2864241. Tours from Quito to **Pasochoa** cost US$40 per person. Quito operators also offer tours to **Guagua Pichincha**, p134.

❸ Transport

Mitad del Mundo and around *p144*
From Quito take a 'Mitad del Mundo' interparroquial bus from the Av del Maestro stop on the Metrobus. By taxi from the New City US$12. An excursion to Mitad del Mundo by taxi, with a 1 hr wait is about US$20, US$30 if it includes a visit to Pululahua. Otherwise, to reach the crater rim at **Pululahua** from Mitad del Mundo, take a Calacalí-bound bus and alight at the turn-off, however these are infrequent. There is no public transport to the reserve but there is plenty of traffic at weekends for hitching a lift. To **Rumicucho**, take a taxi from Mitad del Mundo, about US$10.

Río Pita *p146*

From Quito take a bus from La Marín or from Av 12 de Octubre to **Sangolquí**. From Sangolquí, by the Municipio, **Calsig Express** buses go to **Rumipamba** at 0600, 1300 and 1830, US$0.50, 45 min; pick-up from Sangolquí, US$6. On weekends and holidays there are buses to the entrance of the **Molinuco reserve**, from where the walk to the falls is only 50 min.

Pasochoa *p146*

From Quito buses run from La Marín to **Amaguaña**, US$0.39 – ask the driver to let you off at the 'Ejido de Amaguaña'. From there follow the signs for **Pasochoa**; it's an 8-km walk, with not much traffic for hitching, except at weekends.

By car, take the highway to Los Chillos; at San Rafael (second traffic light) continue straight on towards Sangolquí and on to Amaguaña. About 1½ km past Amaguaña turn left onto a cobblestone road and follow the signs to Pasochoa.

The road from Amaguaña to the reserve is poor, so Quito taxis do not like to go there; you can hire one to Amaguaña (US$20) and take a pick-up from there, US$6 one way. There is a **Movistar** public phone at the information centre; take a debit card so you can request a pick-up on the way out or better arrange ahead, **Cooperativa Pacheco Jr** in Amaguaña, T02-2877047.

Papallacta *p147*

Many buses a day pass Papallacta on their way to and from Lago Agrio, Coca or Tena (drivers sometimes charge full fare). From **Quito**, 2 hrs, US$2. If going to the **Termas**, ask to be let off at the turn-off to the springs before town; it is then a 30-min walk up the hill to the complex. At the turn-off is **Restaurante La Esquina**, which offers transport to the Termas, US$0.50-1 per person depending on the number of people. Travelling back to Quito at night is not recommended.

Climbing Pichincha *p148*

A school bus makes 4-5 trips a day, back and forth between **Lloa** and **Quito**, starting at 0600 in Lloa. The first one leaves Quito around 0700, the last one returns from Lloa about 1830, US$0.40, 30 mins. This bus goes from C Angamarca, at the entrance of the neighbourhood called Mena 2 in southwestern Quito.

To get there, take an *alimentador* bus from El Recreo stop on the Trole, or any Chillogallo bound bus, one goes along 12 de Octubre in the New City. Ask to be let off at El Triángulo, the intersection of Av Mariscal Sucre and the road to Lloa. Walk 1 block west (up) to where the Lloa bus stops. It might also be possible to catch a lift on a truck (dump trucks go to a mine near Lloa on weekdays). A taxi to Lloa costs around US$15.

Western slopes of Pichincha

→ *Phone code 02 Colour map 2, grid B4*

Despite their proximity to the capital, the western slopes of Pichincha and its surroundings are surprisingly wild, with fine opportunities for walking and especially birdwatching. This scenic area has lovely cloud forests and a number of ecotourism reserves. The main tourist town in this area is Mindo. To the west of Mindo is a warm subtropical area of clear rivers and waterfalls, where a growing number of tourist developments are springing up. ▸▸ *For Sleeping, Eating and all other listings, see pages 156-158.*

Ins and outs

There are four roads that drop into the western lowlands from Quito. The northernmost, the **Calacalí–La Independencia road**, starts by the Mitad del Mundo monument, goes through Calacalí, Nanegalito, San Miguel de los Bancos and other towns, before joining the Santo Domingo–Esmeraldas road at La Independencia. This is the simplest of the four roads to drive, since it is paved and traffic is light. Note that markers along the road refer to the distance from the toll booth outside Quito, on the way to Mitad del Mundo.

Parallel to this road is the much rougher **Nono–Mindo road**, famous for its excellent birdwatching. This road begins off Avenida Occidental, Quito's western ring road; you must ask for directions to find it. At the beginning of this road is **Hostería San Jorge**, above Quito (see Quito Sleeping, Suburbs page 120). There are several connections between the paved Calacalí road and the rough Nono-Mindo road, so it is possible to drive on the paved road most of the way even if your destination is one of the lodges on the Nono-Mindo road. There is regular bus service along the Calacalí-La Independencia road, which provides the most direct access to **Mindo** (see page 153). The Nono road is very scenic but it is unpaved and takes longer. The area around these two roads is known as the Noroccidente.

Just south of Quito are two other roads to the western lowlands, the **Chiriboga road** and the main **Alóag–Santo Domingo road**. The Chiriboga road is little used, prone to landslides and complicated to find; go to Quito's southern neighbourhood of Chillogallo and then on to San Juan de Chillogallo. There is irregular bus service on the first half of this road out of Quito; it is often muddy and difficult, especially November to April, when a four-wheel drive is needed. The Alóag–Santo Domingo road is the main connection between Quito and Guayaquil and is served by buses from the Terminal Terrestre in Quito; see Quito to Santo Domingo, page 371, for a description of the route.

Reserves and lodges

Tinalandia, near Santo Domingo, is one of the best places to see many species of birds with minimal effort. For details, see page 372.

Bellavista

ⓘ *T02-2116047 or in Quito T02-2903165, www.bellavistacloudforest.com*
L *Accommodation with private bath, hot shower and full board (good vegetarian food);* **AL** *private room or dormitory with shared bath. Camping also possible, US$5 per person. A biological station on the property is available for researchers,* **E** *per person without meals. Package tours can be arranged including transport from Quito; to get there on your own take a bus to Nanegalito and hire a pick-up truck, US$15-20, or get off at Km 52 taking the dirt road to the left (coming from Quito).*

This dramatic dome-shaped lodge is perched in beautiful cloud forest at Km 62 on the old road to Mindo via Tandayapa. Faster access is recommended along the Calacalí-la Independencia road. Various access options: shortest is via Km 52 just after a bridge 4 km before Nanegalito, also at Km 62 (past Nanegalito) – usually all roads are

Quito Western slopes of Pichincha

accessible to normal vehicles, and all have Bellavista signs. The reserve is part of a mosaic of private protected areas dedicated to conservation of one of the richest accessible areas of west slope cloud forest. Bellavista at 2,200 m is the highest of these, and the easiest place to see the incredible plate-billed Mountain-Toucan. Over 300 species of birds have been seen in the Tandayapa Valley, including large numbers of hummingbirds drawn to the many feeders at the lodge. The area is also rich in orchids and other cloud forest plants. Recommended, best to book in advance.

Guajalito

ⓘ *Reservations are required, To2-2600531 (Quito), vlastimilz@mail.usfq.edu.ec Price is in our B range, meals included. Accessible by bus from Chillogallo.*

Guajalito is a rustic lodge at Km 59 on the Chiriboga road. It is surrounded by a very large forest reserve, with a wide variety of birds. This is a good base for birdwatching along the road and for getting inside the forest, which is normally impossible elsewhere because of steepness or deforestation.

Maquipucuna Reserve

ⓘ *US$5, guide US$10 per day for group of 5. Accommodation in our L range, including 3 meals, options with shared bath and/or without meals are cheaper. Contact Fundacion Maquipucuna in Quito, To2-2507200, www.maqui.org At Nanegalito turn right on a dirt road to Nanegal; keep going until a sign on the right for the reserve (before Nanegal). Pass through the village of Marianitas and it's another 20 mins to the reserve. The road is poor, especially in the Jan-May wet season, 4WD vehicles recommended. By public transport, take a bus to Nanegalito (43 km from Mitad del Mundo) and hire a truck, US$20, or arrange transport with Maquipucuna in Quito, return service from your hotel in Quito US$100 for 4, pick up in Nanegalito, US$20.*

The **Maquipucuna Reserve** has 4,500 ha, surrounded by an additional 14,000 ha of protected forest. It can be reached in two hours from Quito with a private vehicle. The cloud forest at 1,200-2,800 m contains a tremendous diversity of flora and fauna, including over 325 species of birds. Especially noteworthy are the colourful tanager flocks, mountain-toucans, parrots and quetzals. The reserve has trails ranging in length from 15 minutes to all day. There is also a research station and an experimental organic garden. Near Maquipucuna are a couple of community conservation and ecotourism projects, see Santa Lucía and Yunguilla.

Reserva Orquideológica El Pahuma

ⓘ *30 km from Mitad del Mundo, contact Alejandro Trillo, To2-2252053, www.ceiba.org, entry US$3, guide US$3.50 per day. Take any bus for Nanegalito or points west. Accommodation is in simple but nice lodge at the information centre: C in private room with shared bath and cold water, E per person in dorm, meals available. Very rustic accommodation in a cabin, 2 hours' climb from the entrance, no facilities, F per person including entry fee. Camping G per person.*

Reserva Orquideológica El Pahuma, a 600-ha reserve, is less than one hour from Quito on the Calacalí-La Independencia road. The information centre is on the south side of the road. It is an interesting collaboration between a local landowner and the Ceiba Foundation for Tropical Conservation. It features an orchid garden and an orchid propagation programme. Trails start at 1,900 m and go to 2,600 m. Birds such as mountain toucans and tanagers are present, and Spectacled Bears have been seen.

Otonga

ⓘ *Contact the Tapias or Dr Onore in Quito, To2-2567550. Price D includes basic food, bring a sleeping bag and flashlight.*

Otonga is an extensive private reserve near Las Pampas, south of the Alóag-Santo Domingo road. There is a basic shelter about two hours' walk from the end of the side road which branches off the Santo Domingo road at Union de Toachi. Much of the forest is virgin and rich in unusual orchids, gesneriads and birds.

Santa Lucía

ⓘ *Bosque Nublado Santa Lucía, Barrio La Delicia, Nanegal, T02-2157242, www.santa-lucia.org A 3-day visit AL per person full board, take a truck from Nanegalito; from the entrance to Maquipucuna it is a 1-hr walk uphill to the lodge. Day tours combining Pululahua, Yunguilla and Santa Lucía available.*

Santa Lucía is a community-based conservation and ecotourism project. It protects a beautiful 650-ha tract of cloud forest to the east of Maquipucuna Reserve. The area is very rich in birds and other wildlife. They have a lodge for visitors. The British organization **Rainforest Concern** is involved with this reserve and offers volunteer programmes (see page 83).

Tandayapa Lodge

ⓘ *Contact T02-2225180 (Quito), www.tandayapa.com Accommodation in L range, including 3 meals, some rooms have a canopy platform for observation, large common area for socializing, the lodge will arrange transport from Quito.*

The **Tandayapa Lodge** is on the Nono-Mindo road and can be reached in 1½ hours from Quito via the Calacali-La Independencia road; take the signed turn-off to Tandayapa at Km 52, just past **Café Tiepolo**. At the intersection with the Nono-Mindo road turn right. It is longer but more scenic to take the Nono road all the way from Quito. This is a very comfortable lodge at about 1,700 m, with trails going higher. The lodge is owned by dedicated birders who strive to keep track of all rarities on the property; they can reliably show you practically any of 318 species, even such rare birds as the white-faced nunbird or the lyre-tailed nightjar. Recommended for serious birdwatchers.

Yunguilla

ⓘ *Further information from Germán Collaguazo, T09-9580694, www.yunguilla.org*

Yunguilla is a community-run ecotourism project located by the upper elevation border of Maquipucuna Reserve, to the southeast. It is reached by pick-up truck from Calacalí. They have a cabin for visitors (*C* **Tahuallullu**, includes three meals) and guiding service for treks in the forest and down to Maquipucuna (US$10 per person).

Mindo and around → *Phone code 02 Population 1,800 Altitude 1,250 m*

Mindo is a small town surrounded by dairy farms, rivers and lush cloud forest that climbs the western slopes of Pichincha. It is an excellent base for many outdoor activities: walking, horse riding, bathing in waterfalls, tubing (floating down the river in inner tubes), bird and butterfly watching, and more. A total of 350 species of birds have been identified in the Mindo area; it is one of the best places in the country to see the cock-of-the-rock, the golden-headed quetzal and the toucan-barbet. The steep access road into town is particularly good for birdwatching, as is the private 'Yellow House Trail' (**Hacienda San Vicente**, see Sleeping, page 156). There are a couple of **orchid gardens** in Mindo, including **Armonía** ⓘ *2 blocks from the church, by the stadium, at Cabañas Armonía, US1$*, which has a collection of regional orchids displayed on trees.

Ins and outs

The most direct access from Quito to Mindo is along the Calacalí–Independencia road; at Km 79 to the south is the turn-off for **Mindo**, from where it is 8 km down a side road to the town. Mindo can also be reached from Santo Domingo. A very rewarding albeit more demanding approach to Mindo is the three-day walk from the town of Lloa (10 km west of the the southern end of Quito; see page 148). Mindo is a small town; attractions nearby are reached by walking or by pick-up taxi. The tourist information office, in the main park, has information about the attractions and local hotels.

Bosque Protector Mindo-Nambillo

Some 19,200 ha around Mindo, ranging in altitude from 1,400 to 4,780 m (the rim of the crater of Guagua Pichincha), have been set aside as a nature reserve. The reserve features spectacular flora and fauna, beautiful cloud forest and many waterfalls. Access to the reserve proper is restricted to scientists, but there is a buffer zone of private reserves which offers many opportunities for exploring. The area is also rich in insects and a fine sample can be admired at the **Caligo Butterfly Farm** ① *0900-1500 daily, US$3, T02-2440360, caligobutterfly@hotmail.com*, 3 km from town on the road to Mindo Garden, where the stages of metamorphosis are well displayed and explained (English spoken), a great place to photograph butterflies. Recommended.

Several **waterfalls** can be visited, all on private land. Since the owners cut and maintain access trails, they charge an entrance fee. On the Río Nambillo is the **Cascada de Nambillo** ① *US$5, US$3 for students, 4 hrs return*. On a small tributary of the Nambillo are the **Cascadas La Primavera** ① *US$3, camping US$3, 5-6 hrs return*, three scenic falls, nearby are a shelter and a place to camp. The **Cascadas de San Antonio**, where you can go rappelling, are on the Río Saguambi and the **Cascada de Azúcar** is along one of its tributaries. Both are within the La Isla Reserve and can be only visited with a guide (see above). At the tourist information office by the park you can pay the entry fee for the waterfalls and obtain directions on how to reach them or hire a guide.

A very popular activity in the Mindo area is *regattas*, the local name for inner-tubing, floating down a river on a raft made of several inner tubes tied together. The number of tubes that can run together depends on the water level. Several local agencies and hotels offer this activity for US$4-6. It is usually done on the Río Mindo, but experts also run the Río Blanco, where competitions are held during local holidays.

One of the many nice roads for walking starts by the high school near the entrance to town and heads west to an area known as Cunuco. Here is **Finca La Palma** ① *T02-2492940, entry US$1*, a working farm with fish ponds by the Río Mindo. There is an economical restaurant featuring tilapia, a camping area with tents (**E** for camping in their tents, cheaper if you bring your own), horses for rent (US$4 per hour), inner-tubing and swimming in the river.

Environmental groups and private reserves

Several environmental groups working in the Mindo area operate private reserves, most of which abut on the main reserve. Lodges such as **Mindo Garden, El Monte** and **Séptimo Paraíso** also own private reserves. They all run tours on their properties.

Amigos de la Naturaleza de Mindo runs the **Centro de Educación Ambiental** (CEA) ① *US$1, simple lodging E-F per person; package with accommodation, full board and excursion C per person (guide included for a minimum of 3 passengers); camping US$2 per person*. Take food if you wish to prepare your own, there are good kitchen facilities. The centre is located 4 km from town, within a 17-ha buffer zone at the edge of the reserve and has simple lodgings and well-maintained trails. Volunteer programmes can be organized. All arrangements have to be made in advance; contact **Amigos de la Naturaleza de Mindo**, 1½ blocks from the parque central in Mindo, T/F02-2765463.

The environmental group **Acción por la Vida** runs **La Isla** ① *US$2 (includes camping), rappel US$7 (includes entry fee), visits only with local guides, information and booking through César Fiallo, El Bijao, T02-2765470*. This is a 12-ha forest reserve on the Río Saguambi. There is a camping area with cooking facilities and a covered dining area. Several waterfalls are used for rappelling. It is a 40-minute walk to the camping area and about one hour from there to the waterfalls.

Fundación Puntos Verdes is an environmental organization, which works on conservation, reforestation programmes, education, waste management, etc, with communities along the Calacalí–La Independencia road. They operate from **Finca Mindo Lindo**, a 7-ha reserve, 1 km west of the Mindo turn-off, and also run volunteer programmes. For contact information, see Sleeping, page 156.

Nanegalito and north to the Río Guayllabamba → *Phone code 02*

Just off the Calacalí–La Independencia road, 27 km from Calacalí, is the town of **Nanegalito**. A road due north of here goes to Nanegal and is the access to the Maquipucuna and Santa Lucía reserves. To the northwest a road goes to Gualea, Pacto and Sanhuangal on the banks of the Río Guayllabamba. From Gualea another road branches north to Chontal, also on the Río Guayllabamba.

In the village of **Tulipe**, on the road to Gualea and 9 km from the Calacalí–La Independencia road is the **Tulipe archaeological site**, a series of large stone-lined pools and feeder canals which are unique in Ecuador. They were first studied in 1982; the Fondo de Salvamento (Fonsal) from the Municipio de Quito is conducting further studies and restoration but, to date, their origin or probable use has not been determined. The stonework could suggest Inca influence, however the material recovered in excavations is pre-Inca. They could have been ceremonial pools, bathing pools or pools used as mirrors to study the stars. Ask permision to enter from the people who own the property; there's no charge, but you can contribute by buying something from their store.

The lower Río Guayllabamba runs through a lush subtropical area at altitudes around 500 m, where tourism is slowly developing. The towns of **Sanhuangal**, **Chontal** and **Magdalena Bajo** have simple lodgings. In the Río Magdalena area is also the 130-ha Osho Resort and meditation centre (see Sleeping page 157). Chontal is also the access for **Los Cedros Research Station and Reserve**, see page 174.

West of Mindo

San Miguel de los Bancos → *Phone code 02*

Los Bancos, as the locals call it, is a pleasant market town surrounded by farms. It is perched on a ridge top above the Río Blanco and has a nice climate. A dirt and gravel road goes south from town and then splits right to Santo Domingo via Valle Hermoso and left to Alluriquín. Just west of town is **Productos Lácteos Guerrero** (see page 158).

A nice day excursion from Los Bancos is to **Cascada La Sucia**. Take a **Reina de las Mercedes** bus or *ranchera* bound for Alluriquín (get current schedule in town) and get off at the bridge over the Río Blanco, about 15 mins from Los Bancos. Just after crossing the bridge, turn left on a small dirt road and walk past the hamlet of Río Blanco (no services) for 2 km, through pleasant country filled with butterflies and birds. At the end of the road, turn left and descend to ford a small river, a tributary of the Blanco. Just upstream is a lovely cascade which spills into a great swimming hole. Remember to leave enough time to catch a vehicle back to Los Bancos. The last one goes by the bridge at about 1730, but enquire ahead. Otherwise it is a 5-km walk uphill from the bridge to town. Take water and sun protection; it gets quite warm.

Pedro Vicente Maldonado → *Phone code 02*

Pedro Vicente Maldonado is a small supply town in a subtropical cattle-ranching area. A secondary road goes from here northwest to the Río Guayllabamba. The main road bypasses town to the south. About 8 km west of PV Maldonado along the main road, is **Finca San Carlos**. Within the farm is **Laguna Azul** ① *Finca San Carlos, Km 144 (124 on old sign), T02-2765346, US$1, 15-min walk, local children will show you the way and expect a tip*, a lovely pool at the base of a striking 35-m waterfall on the Río Negro.

Accessed from PV Maldonado is **Reserva Río Guaycuyacu** ① *From PV Maldonado take a ranchera to Cielo Verde (0600, 1300 and sometimes 1600, returning 2 hrs later, US$2, 2 hrs); from Quito 1 daily bus to Cielo Verde at 1300, Transportes Minas, Antepara 445 y Pedro Fermín Cevallos, San Blas; from Cielo Verde it is a 30-min hike. Booking essential, write to: Galápagos 565, Quito, guaycuyacu@yahoo.com.* This exotic fruit farm has 400 varieties of fruit and offers birdwatching. Accommodation includes three hearty vegetarian meals a day, for a maximum of eight guests.

Puerto Quito → *Phone code 02 Population about 2,300 Altitude 400 m*

On the shores of the lovely Río Caoni is Puerto Quito, a small town which was once intended to be the capital's port. The main road bypasses the centre of town to the south. Along the Caoni and other rivers in the region are several reserves and resorts. This is a good area for birdwatching, swimming in rivers and natural pools, walking, kayaking, or simply relaxing in pleasant natural surroundings.

The Calacalí road meets the Santo Domingo–Esmeraldas road 28 km southwest of Puerto Quito. Just south of the junction, on the way to Santo Domingo, is the village of **La Independencia** and 5 km further south the town of **La Concordia**, see page 373.

● Sleeping

Mindo and around *p153*

LL Sachatamia, 1 km E of Mindo turn-off on Calacalí–La Independencia road, T02-2765436, www.sachatamia.com A pleasant lodge surrounded by forest, includes 3 meals, small pool, rooms and cabins, walking trails, birdwatching.

L El Monte, 2 km from Mindo on road to CEA, then cross river on cable car near the butterfly farm, best to contact office in town beforehand, T02-2765427, www.ecuadorcloudforest.com Includes 3 meals and some (but not all) excursions, bird watching, tubing, walking, swimming. Horse riding and English-speaking guide extra.

L Mindo Gardens, 3 km from Mindo on road to CEA, T02-2252488. Includes 3 meals, very good food, expensive restaurant open to the public, also snack bar serving pizza, comfortable, tastefully decorated cabins, beautiful setting, good birdwatching.

AL El Carmelo de Mindo, in 32 ha reserve, 1 km west of town, T02-2765449, www.mindo.com.ec Includes 3 meals, restaurant, pool and river bathing, rooms, cabins, and tree-house, camping US$5 pp, excursions, fishing, riding, mid-week discounts.

AL Séptimo Paraíso, 2 km from Calacalí–La Independencia road along Mindo access road, then 500 m right on a small side road, well signed, T09-9934133, www.septimoparaiso.com Includes breakfast, expensive restaurant, pool, ample parking, all wood lodge, comfortable rooms, lovely grounds in a 300-ha reserve with walking trails. Isolated from Mindo town.

A Curiquindi Huasi, 3 km from Mindo on road to Cunuco, T02-2431772, or leave message at Mindo, T02-2765456. Includes breakfast, comfortable cabins for up to 4, nice grounds near Río Mindo.

A Finca Mindo Lindo, 1 km W of the Mindo turn-off along the Calacalí–La Independencia road, T02-2455344, puntos_verdes @hotmail.com Includes breakfast, other meals available, day visits and overnight stays, relaxing, guided tours.

A Hacienda San Vicente, 'Yellow House', 500 m south of the plaza, T02-2765464. Includes excellent breakfast and dinner, family-run, friendly, nice rooms, good trails nearby, good value. Recommended.

B-C El Descanso, 300 m from main street, take first right after bridge, T02-2765383, www.eldescanso.net Includes breakfast, cheaper in loft with shared bath, ample parking, nice house, comfortable and friendly. Recommended.

B-D Jardín de Orquideas, 2 blocks from church, follow signs, T02-2765471. Includes breakfast, pricey restaurant, vegetarian meals available, cheaper with shared bath, nice atmosphere, beautiful gardens.

D Arco Iris, Quito y 9 de Octubre, on main Plaza, T/F02-2765445. Restaurant downstairs, cheaper with shared bath, simple, clean, OK.

D Gypsy, off main Plaza, T02-2765451 for messages. Includes breakfast, good meals on request, shared bath, small basic rooms, friendly and helpful.

D Paulin, on main road at entrance to town, T02-2765379. Snack bar and bakery, electric shower, nice cabin for up to 6, friendly.

D-E El Bijao, Av Quito, near entrance to town, T02-2765470. Good restaurant, cheaper with shared bath, laundry facilities, simple but nice, family run, very friendly, knowledgeable and helpful, good value. Recommended.

D-F Casa de Cecilia, 2 blocks from plaza, T02-2765453, casadececilia@gmx.net Cheap meals available, shared bath, internet, US$2 for use of kitchen, cheaper in dorm with mattresses on floor, pleasant and friendly atmosphere, popular with volunteer groups.

E Flor del Valle, on lane beside church. Shared bath, hot water, good value, basic.

Nanegalito and north to the Río Guayllabamba *p17*

L Urcu Puyujunda, in Las Tolas, on a side road going west just past Tulipe, T02-2546253, www.cloudforestecuador.com Rustic cabins for 6 in a cloud forest area at 1,800 m, includes 3 meals, transport from Quito and guided tours.

There are also a couple of very basic places to stay in Nanegalito: **E Don Fabara**, next to the church, with shared bath and warm water, is the better of the two.

San Miguel de los Bancos *p155*

D La Trainera, on the main street, T02-2770278. Simple little place, restaurant.

D-E Rancho Ilusión, 2 km west of town at Km 97, T09-9589320. In a pleasant country setting, restaurant with German specialities, good value.

Pedro Vicente Maldonado *p155*

LL Arasha, 4 km west of PV Maldonado, Km 141, T02-2765348, www.arasharesort.com Resort and spa with pools, waterfalls (artificial and natural), jacuzzi and hiking trails, world-class chef and kitchen (meals not included in price of accommodation), tours. Elegant and very upmarket. Quito office T02-2253937, F2260992.

C Posada el Horizonte, 1.5 km east of PV Maldonado, T02-2252412. Tastefully

decorated cabins on a working ranch, some with kitchen and fridge, restaurant, pool, horse riding, excursions.

E Sander, E on the main st, T02-2392206. Cheaper with shared bath, cold water.

Puerto Quito *p156*

L Kaony Lodge, near the village of Caoni, 10 km from Puerto Quito, T09-9739262, www.kaonylodge.com Comfortable bamboo and thatch cabins. Pool, price includes 4 meals (lunch to lunch on 2nd day) and excursions. Quito T02-2544892.

AL Shishink, 13 km south of Puerto Quito, turn-off at the village of Puerto Rico, T02-2245128, www.cascadazul.com A resort with thatched cabins. Price includes meals and excursions. There are waterfalls, natural pools, caves and outdoor activities.

A Aldea Salamandra, About 2½ km east of Puerto Quito, then 650 m southeast along a dirt road, T02-2561146 ext 294 (Quito), aldeasalamandra@yahoo.com A 5-ha reserve (the forest in this area has seen better days) with simple bamboo and thatch cabins by the river. Includes all meals and excursions, some cabins with private bath, cold water, mosquito nets, some have balconies with hammocks, one tree house directly over the river, also nice open-air dining area.

A La Isla, 1½ km past Aldea Salamandra, along the same road and on an island between the Caoni and Achiote rivers, T02-2765281. A variety of cabins from simple tree-houses to more comfortable cottages. Includes all meals and excursions, cold water, pool, rafting and kayaking, horse riding, ample grounds.

C Cabañas Don Gaucho, 22 km west of Puerto Quito, T02-2330315, www.ecuador-sommerfern.com Comfortable, well-furnished rooms with balcony. Includes breakfast, restaurant specializing in Argentinian *parrilladas*, fan, nice grounds on the banks of the Río Salazar. Tours to tropical forest, fruit plantations, Colorado Indians.

D Grand Hotel Puerto Quito, along the highway bypass, T09-9706337. Restaurant, pool and sauna, nice views of the river, rafting trips. Good value.

E Bambú, on the main st, T02-2765251. Restaurant, private bath, some rooms with fan, parking.

🍴 Eating

There are several simple *comedores* along the main streets in **Pedro Vicente Maldonado** and **Puerto Quito**.

Mindo and around *p153*

🍴🍴🍴 Armonía, by Hotel Jardín de Orquideas. Vegetarian set lunch and à la carte.

🍴🍴 Bambú, by the main park. Set lunches, pizza and à la carte.

🍴🍴 El Bijao, at the hotel. Very good breakfast and set lunch.

🍴🍴 El Chef, Av Quito. Very good set meals and à la carte, meat specialities.

🍴 Arco Iris, at the park. Set lunches.

San Miguel de los Bancos *p155*

🍴🍴 El Remanso del Valle. Roadside eatery, just west of town.

🍴🍴 Il Grillo, on the main st. Set lunch, à la carte and pizza.

🎉 Festivals and events

Mindo and around *p153*

18 May Fiestas de Mindo are held during the weekend closest to 18 May. Celebrations include sporting events, regattas, masses and partying.

6 Sep Fiestas Patronales are held during the weekend closest to 6 Sep in honour of the Virgen del Cisne.

🛍 Shopping

Mindo and around *p153*

Productos Lácteos Guerrero, on the main park in Mindo, sell very good dairy products and special jams made from regional fruits including the rare and wonderful *arashá*. Another branch is just west of Los Bancos.

🚌 Transport

Nanegalito and north to the Río Guayllabamba *p17*

Nanegalito is served by frequent buses between Quito and Esmeraldas. US$3 from Quito, service from the Terminal Terrestre and from the Trans Esmeraldas terminal, Santa María 870.

To **Tulipe**, Transportes Otavalo, in Quito, from Asunción y Manuel Larrea, 5 daily, at 0630, 1000, 1200, US$1.50, 2 hrs, also *interparroquiales* from Miraflores, by the Universidad Central. Last one returns to Quito at 1530.

To **Chontal**, Transportes Minas, in Quito, from Antepara 445 y Pedro Fermín Cevallos, San Blas, daily at 1100 and 1500, sometimes also at 0600, US$4, 4 hrs.

Mindo and around *p153*

From **Quito**, Cooperativa Flor del Valle (Cayambe), M Larrea N10-44 y Asunción (not from the Terminal Terrestre), T02-2527495. Mon-Fri at 0800 and 1545, Sat-Sun at 0700, 0800, 0900, 1545; US$2.50, 2½ hrs.

To **Quito**, Mon-Fri 0600, 1200, Sat-Sun 1400, 1500, 1600, 1700. The weekend buses fill quickly, buy ahead. If buses to Quito are booked, try taking a Santo Domingo-bound bus as far as the main highway or to San Miguel de los Bancos and transfer there.

To **Santo Domingo**, Cooperativa Kennedy at 0700, 1300 and 1700, US$3.50, 3½ hrs, returning from Mindo at 0720, 1140 and 1400.

San Miguel de los Bancos *p155*

Several companies leave from the Terminal Terrestre in **Quito** for Los Bancos, US$3, 2½ hrs, continuing on to Pedro Vicente Maldonado and Puerto Quito; **Trans Esmeraldas** also go from their own station in the New City, Santa María 870. Once in Las Bancos there are buses to **Mindo**, 3 daily (service from Santo Domingo), US$1, 30 mins; and **Santo Domingo**, frequent along the main road, 2 daily via Valle Hermoso, US$3, 3 hrs. Also to **Alluriquín**, 4 daily on the secondary road. Buses to **Esmeraldas** pass through Los Bancos or take a Santo Domingo-bound bus and transfer at La Independencia.

Pedro Vicente Maldonado *p155*

The town is served by through buses between Quito and Esmeraldas (see San Miguel de los Bancos, above).

Puerto Quito *p156*

The town is served by through buses between Quito and Esmeraldas (see San Miguel de los Bancos, above).

Northern Highlands

❖ Footprint features

Introduction

North from Quito to the border with Colombia is an area of great natural beauty and cultural interest. The landscape is mountainous, with views of Cotacachi, Imbabura, Chiles and glacier-covered Cayambe, interspersed with lakes. This is also a region renowned for its *artesanía*. Countless villages specialize in their own particular craft, be it textiles, hats, woodcarvings, bread figures or leather goods. And, of course, there is Otavalo, with its outstanding market, a must on everyone's itinerary.

The Panamericana, fully paved, runs northeast from Quito to Otavalo (94 km), Ibarra (114 km), and Tulcán (240 km), from where it continues to Ipiales in Colombia. Secondary roads go west from all these cities, and descend to subtropical lowlands. From Ibarra a paved road runs northwest to the Pacific port of San Lorenzo and south of Tulcán a road goes east to Lago Agrio. To the east is the impressive snow-capped cone of Cayambe (5790 m), part of the Reserva Ecológica Cayambe-Coca.

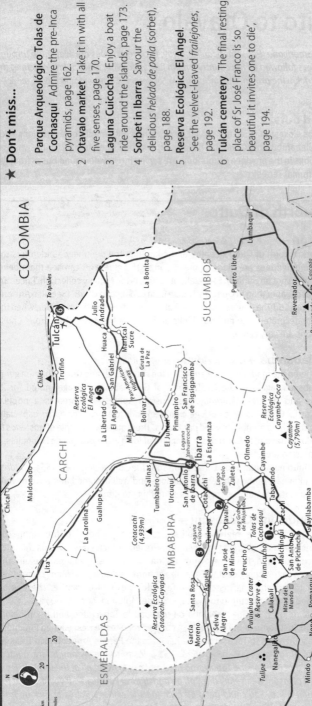

★ Don't miss...

1 **Parque Arqueológico Tolas de Cochasquí** Admire the pre-Inca pyramids, page 162.

2 **Otavalo market** Take it in with all five senses, page 170.

3 **Laguna Cuicocha** Enjoy a boat ride around the islands, page 173.

4 **Sorbet in Ibarra** Savour the delicious *helado de paila* (sorbet), page 188.

5 **Reserva Ecológica El Ángel.** See the velvet-leaved *frailejones*, page 192.

6 **Tulcán cemetery** The final resting place of Sr José Franco is 'so beautiful it invites one to die', page 194.

Quito to Otavalo

The Panamericana (Pan-American Highway, a toll road) goes north of Quito through arid valleys followed by the country's main flower growing area, before reaching the lake district in the province of Imbabura. ▸▸ *For Sleeping, Eating and other listings, see pages 165-167.*

Ins and outs

The towns closest to Quito are served by city buses. Intermediate destinations such as Guayllabamba and Cayambe have their own bus terminals in Quito, whereas destinations in the province of Imbabura are served by Otavalo-bound buses from the Quito Terminal Terrestre.

Just north of Quito

Calderón → *Phone code 02, Colour map 2,grid B5*

Some 32 km north of Quito's centre, and 5 km from the periphery, Calderón is the place where figurines are made of bread dough and glue. You can see them being made, though not on Sunday. Especially attractive is the Nativity collection. Prices are somewhat cheaper than in Quito and range from US$0.50 to US$8. (See also Arts and Crafts, page 468.) The figures can be seen in the cemetery on 1-2 November, when the graves are decorated with flowers, drinks and food for the dead. The Corpus Christi processions are very colourful.

Guayllabamba → *Phone code 02 Colour map 2, grid B5*

After Calderón the road north descends into the spectacular arid Guayllabamba gorge and climbs out again to the fertile oasis of Guayllabamba village, noted for its avocados and delicious *chirimoyas* or custard apples. The area is a popular destination for Quiteños, who flock here on weekends to eat *comida típica*, especially *locro de papas*, in a number of good *paradores*. There are also a couple of *hosterías* to stay in. Along the road to Cayambe, 2 km north of town is the **Bosque de Bromelias**, a small protected area.

The **Quito municipal zoo** ① *T02-2368898, Tue-Sun 0900-1700, US$3, children $1.75*, is 3 km east of the village. It is spacious and well designed and a worthwhile family outing. It gets quite warm so take something to drink.

Tabacundo and Cochasquí → *Phone code 02*

At Guayllabamba, the highway splits into two branches. To the right, the Panamericana runs northeast to Cayambe. The left branch goes towards the town of Tabacundo, in a flower growing region, from where you can rejoin the Pamamericana travelling east to Cayambe or northeast to Cajas. Many buses take the latter route, which is faster and offers nice views of Cayambe. There is an access road from Tabacundo to the Lagunas de Mojanda, see page 172.

About 10 km past Guayllabamba on the road to Tabacundo and 8 km before Tabacundo, just south of the toll booth, a cobbled road to the west (signed Pirámides de Cochasquí) leads to Tocachi and further on to the **Parque Arqueológico Tolas de Cochasquí** ① *T02-2541818, 0830-1630, US$3. Visits to the pyramids are guided. Take a bus that goes on the Tabacundo road and ask to be let off at the turn-off. From there it's a pleasant 8-km walk through an agricultural landscape. If you arrive at the sign around 0800, you could get a lift from the site workers. A taxi or pick-up from Cayambe costs US$10. Two-day horse-riding tours from Cayambe are available (See*

The 839 ha protected area contains 15 truncated clay pyramids, nine with long ramps, built between AD 950 and 1550 by Indians of the Cara or Cayambi-Caranqui nation. The pyramids are covered by earth and grass but a few have been excavated, giving a good idea of their construction. Among the many pre-Inca mounds found in northern Ecuador, these are the most elaborate. The site is considered by many archaeologists to have been the ceremonial centre of a large cultural area extending from Quito to north of Ibarra in the centuries immediately preceding the Inca conquest. There is a site museum with interesting historical explanations in Spanish. At 3100m above sea level, the views from the pyramids, south to Quito, are marvellous.

El Quinche → *Phone code 02   Colour map 2, grid B5*

About 6 km southeast of Guayllabamba, along a road that conects Pifo and the Panamericana, is the small village of El Quinche, where there is a huge sanctuary to **Nuestra Señora del Quinche** in the plaza. It has nice stained-glass windows, a lovely carved wooden entrance, a very large gold altar, and many paintings illustrating miracles; ask the caretaker for the details. The image was the work of the sculptor Diego Robles around 1600 in Oyacachi. It was transferred to El Quinche because the local Indians did not wish to worship the image. Processions on 21 November attract thousands of devotees. There are several restaurants and simple places to stay.

Near El Quinche, on a hill called Pambamarca, with magnificent views to Quito and, on a clear day, even as far as the coastal plain, is the fortress of **Quitoloma**. This is one of the largest pre-Columbian fortresses of the new world, with two concentric walls and ditches, one of numerous fortresses in this area. Some of these may have been originally built by the Cayambe and Caranqui inhabitants, but most were built (or at least rebuilt and reoccupied) by the Incas. These are not public sites, they belong to the communities. To visit them, ask for instructions and permission in nearby villages.

Cayambe and around

→ *Phone code 02   Colour map 2, grid B5   Population 30,450   Altitude 2,850 m*

Cayambe, on the eastern (righthand) branch of the Panamericana, 25 km northeast of Guayllabamba, is dominated by the snow-capped volcano of the same name. The surrounding countryside consists of a few remaining dairy farms and a great many flower plantations. Roses and carnations are grown for export and have turned Cayambe into a boom town. As a result rural property values have soared, the use of agro-chemicals is doing damage, and the inflow of itinerant labourers has led to a deterioration of public safety. The area is noted for its *bizcochos*, which are small shortbread-type biscuits served with *queso de hoja*, tasty string cheese. Market day is Sunday, along Calle Rocafuerte.

On the edge of town are the **Pyramids of Puntiachil** ① *Entrance at Olmedo 702, US$1 includes guided tour in Spanish, there is also a small private museum*, an important but poorly-preserved archaeologic site of the Cayambe culture in the late pre-Inca era. There are several large mounds and a large occupation area. Studies suggest it probably was a political and ceremonial centre.

Reserva Ecológica Cayambe-Coca → *Colour map 2, grid B5*

Cayambe is a good place to access the western side of the **Reserva Ecológica Cayambe-Coca** ① *park entry US$10*, which spans the Cordillera Oriental and extends down to the eastern lowlands. Further north, the Laguna Puruhanta sector of the park can be accessed from Pimampiro via Nueva América, see page 191.

Cayambe Volcano

At 5,790 m, Cayambe is Ecuador's third-highest peak. About 1 km south of the town of Cayambe is an unmarked cobbled road heading east via Juan Montalvo, leading in 26 km to the Ruales-Oleas-Berge refuge at about 4,800 m. The *refugio* costs US$17 per person per night; it can sleep 37 people in bunks, but bring a sleeping bag, as it is very cold. There is a kitchen, fireplace, running water, electric light and a radio for rescue. It is named after three Ecuadorean climbers killed by an avalanche in 1974 while pioneering a new route up from the west.

> **!** *Cayambe, the highest point in the world that lies directly on the equator, is a difficult, technical climb, only for experienced climbers.*

This is now the standard route, using the refuge as a base. The route heads off to the left of a rocky outcrop immediately above the *refugio*. To the right of the outcrop is an excellent area of crevasses, seracs and low rock and ice walls for practising technical skills. The climb is heavily crevassed, especially near the summit, there is an avalanche risk near the summit and southeasterly winds are a problem. It is more difficult and dangerous than either Chimborazo or Cotopaxi. An alternative route is to the northeast summit (5,570 m), which is the most difficult, with the possible need to bivouac.

Laguna San Marcos

To the east of the town of Olmedo (see below) is the scenic Laguna San Marcos, surrounded by cloud forest. It is popular with fishermen and the access to some difficult trekking in remote country. It is 40 minutes by car or three hours on foot from Olmedo. Note that San Marcos is part of a waterworks project and access may be restricted, enquire in Cayambe.

Oyacachi to El Chaco trek

An adventurous trek takes you from the highlands to the Oriente lowlands in three to four days. Starting in the village of Oyacachi at 3,100 m, it follows the Oyacachi river first along the north bank and later on the southern bank, crossing several tributaries along the way (a pulley may be necessary for these crossings). The walk ends at El Chaco, at 1,550 m, on the western shore of the Quijos river and along the Baeza-Lago Agrio road. The season for this walk is November to February; it is impassable during the rainy season.

Cayambe to Otavalo

Two routes can be taken from Cayambe north. To the east is an unpaved road, the very scenic *carretera vieja* or old road, which runs 18 km to Olmedo. There are no hotels or restaurants in Olmedo, but there are a couple of shops and lodging may be available with the local nuns. There is also an Andinatel office, on the plaza. The surrounding countryside is pleasant for strolling. A secondary road goes east from Olmedo to Laguna San Marcos and beyond, within the Reserva Ecológica Cayambe-Coca.

North of Olmedo the cobbled road is not so good (four-wheel drive vehicles are recommended). It is about 9 km from Olmedo to Zuleta, where beautiful embroidery on napkins and tablecloths is done (see page 184). About 15 km beyond Zuleta is La Esperanza, 8 km before Ibarra.

To the west, the main paved road heads north from Cayambe and crosses the *páramo* at the Nudo de Cajas, where it meets the Guayllabamba-Tabacundo road and suddenly descends to the scenic basin of Lago San Pablo and beyond to Otavalo.

● *The equator crosses the Panamericana 8 km south of Cayambe in the Guachalá area. A* ● *concrete globe beside the road marks the spot.*

An alternative route from Quito to Otavalo is via San Antonio de Pichincha (Mitad del Mundo), past the Inca ruins of **Rumicucho** (see page 145), Perucho and San José de Minas. In the valley below Minas, at Cubi, there are warm springs. The road curves through the dry but impressive landscape down to the Río Guayllabamba, then climbs again, passing some picturesque oasis villages. After Minas the road is in very bad condition and a jeep is necessary for the next climb and then descent to join the Otavalo-Selva Alegre road about 15 km west from Otavalo. The journey takes about three hours altogether and is rough, hot and dusty, but the scenery is magnificent. This is a great biking route since there is little traffic. At Perucho, a good secondary road goes southeast to the Guayllabamba-Tabacundo highway.

● Sleeping

Tabacundo and Cochasquí *p162*
AL Hostería San Luis, About 4 km north of Tabacundo by the village of Tupigachi, T02-2360464, F2360103. Part of a large working hacienda, includes breakfast, restaurant serves international and regional cuisine, heated pool and spa, 38 rooms with fireplaces, lovely landscaped grounds, fishing pond, sports fields, horses for rent, nice views of Cayambe.
C Centro Turístico Quilago, Opposite the Cochasquí site, T09-7103867, F2520852. Must make arrangements in advance. Simple cabins, includes breakfast, restaurant, electric shower, local crafts shop, tours of Cochasquí and vicinity, camping US$6 per tent.

Cayambe *p163*
Hotels may be full during the week before Valentine's Day (high season at the flower plantations).
AL Jatun Huasi, Panamericana Norte Km 1½, T02-2363775, F2363832. North American motel-style, rooms with fireplace, includes breakfast, restaurant, indoor pool, parking, frigo-bar.
A-B Hacienda Guachalá, south of Cayambe on the road to Cangahua, T02-2363042, www.guachala.com A colonial hacienda, once a large *encomienda* (slave workshop) producing textiles for Spain. The chapel (1580) is built on top of an Inca structure. Simple rooms (can do with some maintenance) with fireplaces, delicious meals at mid-range prices, spring-fed covered swimming pool, parking, attentive service, good walking, horses, excursions to nearby pre-Inca ruins, small museum with historical photos. Recommended.

C Shungu Huasi, Camino a Granobles s/n, 1 km northwest of town, T02-2792094, www.shunguhuasi.com Comfortable cabins in a 6½-ha ranch, includes breakfast, excellent Italian restaurant, good hot water supply, internet, parking, nice setting, attentive service by owners, offers horse riding. Italian-Canadian-Ecuadorean run. Recommended.
C-D Cabañas de Nápoles, Panamericana Norte Km 1, T02-2360366. Adequate cabins by the highway, good restaurant, laundry facilities, parking.
D Gran Colombia, Panamericana y Calderón, T02-2361238, F2362421. Modern multi-storey building, restaurant, parking, rooms to the street get traffic noise.
E Crystal, 9 de Octubre 215 y Terán, T02-2361460. Simple hostal, cheaper with shared bath, hot water, small rooms.
E Mitad del Mundo, Panamericana a little south of town, T02-2360226. Restaurant, cheaper with shared bath, pool (open weekends), laundry, parking, good value.

● Eating

Just north of Quito *p162*
Guayllabamba .
♦♦♦-♦♦ **El Típico Locro**, Panamericana norte, Km 35 (along the bypass road). Good *comida típica*, *locro de papas* is the speciality; other dishes such as *seco de chivo* are also good.

Cayambe *p163*
There are a number of roadside cafés along the Panamericana serving the local speciality, *bizcochos y queso de hoja* (biscuits and string cheese).

▼▼▼ Casa de Fernando, Panamericana Norte Km 1½. Varied menu, good.
▼▼▼ El Molino, Panamericana Norte, Km 3. Excellent breakfast, lunch and early dinner, French cuisine, cosy atmosphere.
▼▼▼ Shungu Huasi, At the hotel, T02-2792094, daily 1200-2200. Excellent authentic Italian cuisine, in very pleasant surroundings, good service. Recommended.
▼▼ Aroma Cafetería, Bolívar 404 y Ascázubi, open until 2100, Sun until 1800, closed Wed. Large choice of set lunches and à la carte, variety of desserts, very good.
▼▼ El Bucanero, Ascázubi y Alianza. Good seafood, simple and clean.
▼ La Casa Vieja, Ascázubi 908 y Sucre. Good local snacks such as *humitas* and *quimbolitos*, fruit juices, breakfasts, set lunches.

⊛ Festivals and events

Just north of Quito *p162*
Tabacundo and Cochasquí
At Cochasquí festivals take place on the equinoxes and solstices with folk dancing and ceremonies related to the agricultural cycle.

Cayambe *p163*
Mar There is a fiesta in March for the equinox with plenty of local music.
Jun 21-9 Inti Raymi during the summer solstice, 21 June, blends into the San Pedro celebrations around 29 June.

⊙ Shopping

Cayambe *p163*
Akí, Restauración 603 y Junín. Supermarket.

▲▲ Activities and tours

Just north of Quito *p162*
Tabacundo and Cochasqui
Centro Turístico Quilago, opposite the entrance to the ruins, T09-7103867. Guided tours of the ruins, Tue-Sun 0900-1700.

Cayambe *p163*
Shungu Huasi, see Cayambe Sleeping. Runs horse riding and car tours to all attractions in the area. Horse rentals ($10/hr), full-day horse-riding tour (US$55), 2-day horse-riding tours to Cochasquí (US$140), an interesting

ride, crossing lovely scenery and a couple of microclimates), 2-day horse-riding tours to Lagunas de Mojanda (US$160). Prices include guide, 2 nights accommodation and meals.

⊖ Transport

Just north of Quito *p162*
Calderón
From **Quito**, city buses at Santa Prisca, along Avenida América and from La Delicia stop of the Corredor Miraflores-Carcelén (enquire ahead as transport along América was about to change when going to press).

Guayllabamba
From **Quito**, Flota Pichincha, from the service station at América y Colón, or any bus bound for Cayambe or Otavalo (these leave you outside town).

Tabacundo and Cochasquí
From **Quito**, Otavalo-bound buses from the Terminal Terrestre, check that they are taking the Tabacundo road. For **Cochasquí** get off at the toll booth along the Guayllabamba-Tabacundo road and walk or take a pick-up from Cayambe or Tabacundo.
From **Cayambe**, Libertad y Av Natalia Jarrín, to Tabacundo every 5 mins, US$0.17, 20 mins.

El Quinche
From **Quito**, frequent service from Estación Río Coca via Pifo, also service from **Guayllabamba**.

Cayambe *p163*
From **Quito**, direct with Flor del Valle, M Larrea y Asunción, every 10 mins, 0500-1900, US$1, 1½ hrs. Their Cayambe station is at Montalvo y Junín. Some Quito-Otavalo buses stop in Cayambe. They depart every few minutes from the Terminal Terrestre in Quito.
To **Otavalo**, from traffic circle at the corner of Bolívar and Av Natalia Jarrín, every 15 mins, US$0.60, 40 mins.
To **Ibarra**, transfer in Otavalo, frequent service, or via Olmedo and Zuleta at 0700 and 1230 only.

Reserva Ecológica Cayambe-Coca
Cayambe Volcano How close to the refuge

you will be able to get by vehicle depends on the condition of the road at the time and the type of vehicle. Most can go as far as the **Hacienda Piemonte El Hato** (at about 3,500 m) from where it is a 3-4 hr walk, longer if heavily laden or if it is windy, but it is a beautiful walk. Regular pick-ups can often make it to 'la Z', a sharp curve on the road from where it is a 30-min walk to the *refugio*. 4WDs can often make it to the *refugio*. Pick-ups can be hired by the market in Cayambe, corner Junín y Ascázubi, US$30, 1½-2 hrs. It is difficult to get transport back to Cayambe. A milk truck runs from Cayambe's hospital to the hacienda at 0600, returning between 1700-1900.

An alternative route is via **Olmedo**, through **Hacienda La Chimba** to Laguna San Marcos. This gives access to the northeast summit.

Laguna San Marcos
In **Cayambe** take a bus for Olmedo where pick-ups can be hired to go to the lake, US$10, 40 minutes. Pick-ups direct from Cayambe, Junín y Ascázubi, US40, 1¼ hrs.

Oyacachi-El Chaco Trek
Take a truck from Cayambe to **Oyacachi** via Cangahua, a very scenic route. **From El Chaco** there is a bus service to Quito via Baeza or to Lago Agrio in the northern Oriente.

Cayambe to Otavalo *p164*
Buses to **Olmedo**, from Cayambe, corner Restauración y Vivar, every 30 mins, 0630-1830, US$0.40, 45 mins. Continues to Ibarra via Zuleta and La Esperanza.

San José de Minas
From **Quito**, buses leave from Asunción y Larrea and from Antepara y San Blas. Most service goes through Guayllabamba and not the San Antonio de Pichincha route.

❶ Directory

Cayambe *p163*
Banks Banco del Pacífico, Junín y Panamericana, Tcs. **Banco del Pichincha**, Bolívar y Ascázubi, VISA ATM. **Post office** Rocafuerte y Sucre, 2nd floor of Centro Comercial.

Otavalo and surroundings

→ *Phone code 06 Colour map 2, grid B5 Population 31,000 Altitude 2,530 m*
Otavalo is set in beautiful countryside which is well worth exploring. The town itself is nothing to write home about, but visitors don't come here for the architecture. Otavalo is one of South America's most important centres of ethno-tourism and its enormous Saturday market, featuring a dazzling array of textiles and crafts, is second to none. Absolutely not to be missed. It's best to travel on Friday, in order to avoid overcrowded buses on Saturday and to enjoy the nightlife. For those interested in learning more about how local crafts are made, a visit to surrounding villages can be interesting.
▶▶ *For Sleeping, Eating and other listings, see page 175-182.*

Ins and outs → *See Transport, page 181, for further details*

Getting there
The bus station is at Atahualpa and Ordoñez in the northeast of the city and just off the Panamericana. Through buses going further north drop you at the highway which is not recommended; **Transportes Otavalo** and **Los Lagos** are the only long distance companies going into town. Near the terminal is a lifelike monument, showing Otavaleños performing a traditional dance. There are few hotels around the bus terminal, but most are in the centre which is within walking distance (about six blocks), taxis and city buses are also available. There is no longer a train service to Otavalo.

⁝ The Otavaleños

In a country where the term *indio* can still be intended as an insult and a very few highland Indians continue to address whites as *patroncito* (little master), the Otavaleños stand out in stark contrast. They are a proud and prosperous people, who have made their name not only as successful weavers and international businessmen, but also as unsurpassed symbols of cultural fortitude. Today, they make up the economic elite of their town and its surroundings, and provide an example which other highland native groups have begun to follow.

There is considerable debate over the origin of the Otavaleños. In present-day Imbabura, pre-Inca people were Caranquis, or Imbaya, and, in Otavalo, the Cayambi. They were subjugated by the Caras who expanded into the highlands from the Manabí coast. The Caras resisted the Incas for 17 years, but the conquering Incas eventually moved the local population away to replace them with vassals from Peru and Bolivia. One theory is that the Otavaleños are descended from these forced migrants and also Chibcha salt traders from Colombia, while some current-day Otavaleños prefer to stress their local pre-Inca roots.

Otavalo men wear their hair long and plaited under a black trophy hat. They wear white, calf-length trousers and blue ponchos. The women's colourful costumes consist of embroidered blouses, shoulder wraps and a plethora of gold coloured necklace beads. Their ankle-length skirts, known as *anacos*, are fastened with an intricately woven cloth belt or *faja*. Traditional footwear for both genders is the *alpargata*, a sandal whose sole was originally made of coiled hemp rope, but today has been replaced by rubber.

Impeccable cleanliness is another striking aspect of many Otavaleños' attire. Perhaps the most outstanding feature of the Otavaleños, however, is their profound sense of pride and self-assurance. This is aided not only by the group's economic success, but also by achievements in academic and cultural realms. In the words of one local elder: "My grandfather was illiterate, my father completed primary school and I finished high school in Quito. My son is a PhD and has served as a cabinet minister!"

Getting around

The centre is quite small, Calle Sucre the main street has wide sidewalks and is a pleasant place to walk. You can walk between the craft market at Plaza de Ponchos and the produce market at Plaza 24 de Mayo. The livestock market is more of a hike. City buses go to nearby villages such as Peguche and those around Lago San Pablo.

Information

The **Oficina Municipal de Turismo** ① *Bolívar 8-38 y Calderón, T06-2921313, sdt@andinanet.net Mon-Sat 0800-1230, 1400-1730*, has local and regional information. The website of the Municipio de Otavalo, **www.otavalo.gov.ec,** has general information including list of hotels, Spanish only.

The **IGM** produces a detailed tourist map of the province of Imbabura. There is also a handy pocket map from **Ediguias,** with good maps of the province and city maps of Otavalo and Ibarra.

Sights

While most visitors come to Otavalo to meet its native people and buy their crafts, you cannot escape the influence of the modern world here, a product of the city's very success in trade and tourism. The streets are lined not only with small kiosks selling homespun wares, but also with wholesale warehouses and international freight forwarders, as well as numerous hotels, cafés and restaurants catering to decidedly foreign tastes.

> ⚑ *Otavalo is a generally safe town but beware of pickpockets, especially in crowded markets.*

In the Plaza Bolívar is a statue of **Rumiñahui**, Atahualpa's general. There was outrage among indigenous residents over suggestions that the monument be replaced with a statue of Bolívar himself, symptomatic of the ongoing rivalry between native Otavaleños and their *mestizo* neighbours.

Otavalo has a number of museums as well as the famous market. **Instituto Otavaleño de Antropología** ① *Av de los Sarances y Pendoneros, 1 block west of the Panamericana, To6-2920321, Mon-Thu 0830-1200, 1430-1800, Fri 0830-1200,*

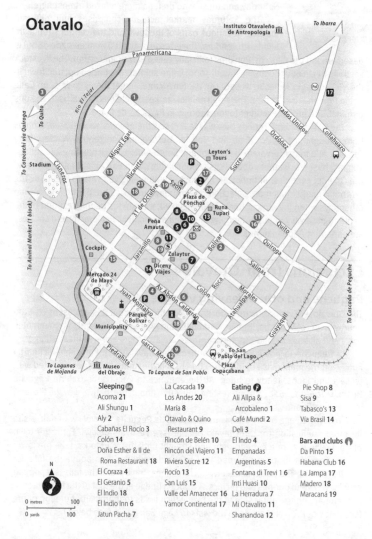

Otavalo

Sleeping		La Cascada 19	Eating	Pie Shop 8
Acoma 21		Los Andes 20	Ali Allpa &	Sisa 9
Ali Shungu 1		María 8	Arcobaleno 1	Tabasco's 13
Aly 2		Otavalo & Quino	Café Mundi 2	Vía Brasil 14
Cabañas El Rocío 3		Restaurant 9	Deli 3	
Colón 14		Rincón de Belén 10	El Indo 4	**Bars and clubs**
Doña Esther & Il de		Rincón del Viajero 11	Empanadas	Da Pinto 15
Roma Restaurant 18		Riviera Sucre 12	Argentinas 5	Habana Club 16
El Coraza 4		Rocío 13	Fontana di Trevi 1 6	La Jampa 17
El Geranio 5		San Luis 9	Inti Huasi 10	Madero 18
El Indio 18		Valle del Amanecer 16	La Herradura 7	Maracaná 19
El Indio Inn 6		Yamor Continental 17	Mi Otavalito 11	
Jatun Pacha 7			Shanandoa 12	

N

0 metres 100
0 yards 100

1430-1700, free, at the Universidad de Otavalo, has a library, a faded archaeological museum with artefacts from the northern highlands, a collection of musical instruments, as well as an ethnographic display of regional costumes and traditional activities.

Museo Arqueológico César Vásquez Fuller with an excellent collection from all over Ecuador was sold to the Municipio. It will be relocated, enquire locally.

Museo de Tejidos El Obraje ① *Sucre 608 y Olmedo, T06-2920261, Mon-Sat 0800-1200, 1400-1700, US$2,* a small private museum run by Luis Maldonado Sr, shows the process of traditional Otavalo weaving from shearing to final products. Traditional weaving lessons are available. There is another weaving museum in Peguche, see below.

Markets

On Saturday, the main market day, Otavalo can be experienced in all its glory. However, the crafts market is on throughout the week for people who cannot go on Saturday and those who prefer a more relaxed atmosphere.

⁝ *Polite bargaining is appropriate in the market and in the shops.*

The **Saturday market** actually comprises four different markets in various parts of the town and the central streets are filled with vendors. The *artesanías* (crafts) market (0700-1800) is based around the Plaza de Ponchos (officially called Plaza Centenario). The livestock sections begin at 0500 and last until 1000. Large animals are traded outside town in the Viejo Colegio Agrícola, west of the Panamericana. To get there, go west on Calle Colón from the town centre. The small animal market is held on Atahualpa by the bus terminal. The produce market (0700-1400) is in Plaza 24 de Mayo.

The Otavaleños sell goods they weave and sew themselves, as well as *artesanías* from throughout Ecuador, Peru and Bolivia. *Mestizo* and indigenous vendors from Otavalo, and from elsewhere in Ecuador and South America, sell paintings, jewellery, shigras, baskets, leather goods, hats, woodcarvings from San Antonio de Ibarra and the Oriente, ceramics, antiques and almost anything else you care to mention. The *artesanía* market has more selection on Saturday but prices are a little higher than other days when the atmosphere is more relaxed. Indigenous people respond better to photography if you buy something first, then ask politely. Reciprocity and courtesy are important Andean norms.

Excursions from Otavalo

Peguche and other weaving villages → *Phone code 06*

The Otavalo weavers come from dozens of communities, but it is easiest to visit the nearby towns of Peguche, Ilumán, Carabuela and Agato which are only 15-30 minutes away and all have a good bus service. There are also tours going to these villages.

In **Peguche** (a few kilometres northeast of Otavalo), the Cotacachi-Pichamba family, off the main plaza behind the church, sells beautiful tapestries, finished with tassels and loops, ready to hang. At the entrance to Peguche is **Galería Peguche Huasi** ① *T06-2922620,* an interesting museum about the native way of life and weaving tradition.

Near the village of Peguche is the **Cascada de Peguche**, a lovely waterfall, a site for ritual purification for the Otavalo people (see Festivals below). From the town plaza, facing the church, head right and straight until the road forks, take the lower fork to the right (but not the road that heads downhill). Climb above the falls for excellent views. The patch of eucalyptus forest near the base of the falls is a popular spot for weekend outings and picnics. A wooden bridge at the foot of the falls leads to a steep path on the other side of the river which leads to Ibarra. From the top of the falls (left side) you can continue the walk to Lago San Pablo (see below).

In **Ilumán** (east of the Panamericana, north of the turn-off for Cotacachi), the Conterón-de la Torre family of **Artesanías Inti Chumbi**, on the northeast corner of the plaza, gives backstrap loom weaving demonstrations and sells crafts. There are also many felt hatmakers in town who will make hats to order.

In **Agato** (northeast of Otavalo), the Andrango-Chiza family of **Tahuantinsuyo Weaving Workshop** gives weaving demonstrations and sells textiles.

In **Carabuela** (west of the Panamericana, just south of the road to Cotacachi) many homes sell crafts including wool sweaters. **Carlos de la Torre**, a backstrap weaver, can be found above the Evangelist Church.

Lago San Pablo → *Phone code 06   Colour map 2, grid B5*

To the southeast of Otavalo, at the foot of Cerro Imbabura and just off the Panamericana is the scenic Lago San Pablo, the largest natural lake in the country. A secondary road circumnavigates the lake. Along it are several native villages and a number of upmarket *hosterías* (inns). San Pablo is a popular weekend destination for wealthier Ecuadoreans looking for water sports, good food, or just a place to get away.

There is a network of old roads and trails between Otavalo and the Lago San Pablo area, none of which takes more than an hour or two to explore. It is worth walking either to or back from the lake for the views. The walk there via **El Lechero** (a lookout by a large tree, considered sacred among indigenous people) is recommended, though you will be pestered by children begging. For safety, best go in a group. The trail starts at the south end of Calle Morales in Otavalo. The walk back via

Around Otavalo

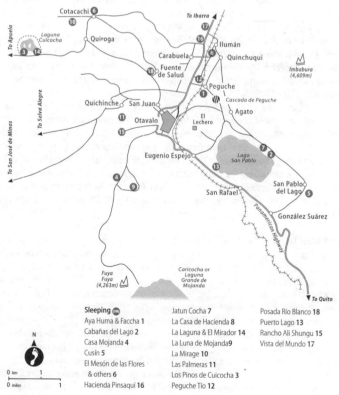

Sleeping
Aya Huma & Faccha **1**
Cabañas del Lago **2**
Casa Mojanda **4**
Cusín **5**
El Mesón de las Flores
   & others **6**
Hacienda Pinsaquí **16**

Jatun Cocha **7**
La Casa de Hacienda **8**
La Laguna & El Mirador **14**
La Luna de Mojanda **9**
La Mirage **10**
Las Palmeras **11**
Los Pinos de Cuicocha **3**
Peguche Tío **12**

Posada Río Blanco **18**
Puerto Lago **13**
Rancho Ali Shungu **15**
Vista del Mundo **17**

the outlet stream from the lake, staying on the right-hand side of the gorge, takes two to three hours, and is also recommended, or you can flag down a passing bus. Alternatively, take a bus to San Pablo, then walk back towards the lake. The views of Imbabura are wonderful. To explore the lake itself, boats can be hired at **Cabañas del Lago, Jatun Cocha** or **Puerto Lago** (see Sleeping below).

From **San Pablo del Lago** it is possible to climb **Cerro Imbabura**, a dormant volcano, at 4,630 m and almost always under cloud – allow at least six hours to reach the summit and four hours for the descent. Navigation is tricky. An alternative access, preferred by many, is from La Esperanza, south of Ibarra (see page 184). Easier, and no less impressive, is the nearby **Cerro Huarmi Imbabura**, 3,845 m.

On a hill called Curiloma, near the community of Pucará Alto, between Otavalo and Lago San Pablo is **Parque Cóndor** ① *To2-2406502, condor@accessinter.net, Tue-Sun 0930-1700, US$3, children US$1.50, 30 min walking from the Cascada de Peguche or 45 min walking from Otavalo, can also be accessed from the Panamericana, there are a couple of buses daily from Otavalo to Pucará Alto*, a 17-ha reserve created to rescue and rehabilitate birds of prey, including condors. Environmental education for the community is one of the park's goals. Some 15 species of birds can be seen, they also have free flying demonstrations.

Lagunas de Mojanda

Southwest of Otavalo are the impressive Lagunas de Mojanda, accessed by cobbled roads from Otavalo or Tabacundo or by a path from Cochasquí. Note however that there have been several reports of armed hold-ups of campers by Mojanda and those travelling the nearby roads, some visitors have been hurt. Independent travel is therefore not recommended here; Otavalo agencies offer tours to the lakes. The authorities are taking measures to improve safety.

Caricocha (or Laguna Grande de Mojanda), a crater lake is the largest of the Mojanda lakes. It is 18 km away from and 1,200 m higher than Otavalo. About 25 minutes' walk above Caricocha is **Laguna Huarmicocha** and a further 25 minutes is **Laguna Yanacocha**. The views on the descent are excellent. There are no services by the lakes. Take a warm jacket, food and drinks, a tent and warm sleeping bags if camping.

From Caricocha a trail continues south about 5 km before dividing: the left-hand path leads to **Tocachi**, the right-hand to **Cochasquí** (see page 162). Both are about 20 km from Laguna Grande and offer beautiful views of Quito and Cotopaxi (cloud permitting). You can climb **Fuya Fuya** (4,263 m) and **Yanaurco** (4,259 m), but the mountain huts on the shore of Caricocha and on the path to Fuya Fuya are derelict. For an alternative circuit, take a Quito bus as far as Tabacundo, hitch or hire a truck to Lagunas (difficult at weekends), then walk back to Otavalo by the old Inca trail, on the right after 2-3 km. A taxi or camioneta from Otavalo is US$8 one way, arrange your return trip in advance but don't pay ahead.

Cotacachi → *Phone code 06 Population 7,376 Altitude 2,440*

West of the Panamericana between Otavalo and Ibarra is Cotacachi, a progressive town where leather goods are made and sold. It can also be accessed along a cobbled road directly from Otavalo via Quiroga. The **Oficina Municipal de Turismo** ① *Casa de las Culturas, Bolívar y 9 de Octubre, p 2, To6-2915140, www.cotacachi.gov.ec Mon-Fri 0900-1300, 1500-1900, Sat-Sun 0900-1700*, has ocal and regional map and information and is very helpful.

The **Casa de las Culturas** ① *Bolívar y 9 de Octubre*, a beautifully refurbished building, combines 19th century architecture with modern styles. It is a monument to peace in which wide open spaces are joined by ramps, representing the lack of barriers between the various ethnic and cultural groups which make up the Cantón Cotacachi: Indians, highland and lowland Mestizos and Blacks. The building is decorated with a few original Guayasamín paintings and ancient ceramics. It houses a library, internet café, the tourist information office, and temporary exhibits. Musical and artistic presentations are also held here.

The **Museo de las Culturas** ① *García Moreno 13-41 y Bolívar, T06-29915945, Mon-Fri 0900-1200, 1400-1700, Sat 1400-1700, Sun 1000-1300, US$1*, off the main plaza is housed in a nicely refurbished old building with a patio and fountain. It has good displays of Ecuadorean history including maps for different periods, regional crafts (ceramics, basketry, textiles, sissal, silver and leather), regional festivals and traditions, and musical instruments. Some English explanations.

To promote rural and ethno-cultural tourism, the municipality has set up the **Runa Tupari** ① *T06-2925985, nativetravel@runatupari.com*, or 'meet the natives' programme. A series of country inns in nearby villages, including **La Calera** south of town, **Tunibamba** to the north, **Chilcapamba** and **Morochos** to the west. Visitors experience life with a native family by taking part in daily activities. The comfortable inns have space for three, fireplace, bathroom and hot shower. US$20 per person including breakfast and dinner and transport from Otavalo. Arrange with **Runa Tupari** or other operators in Otavalo, see page 181.

Reserva Ecológica Cotacachi-Cayapas

To the west of the town of Cotacachi is the scenic **Cotacachi-Cayapas reserve** ① *Park entry US$5, payable only if going beyond Cuicocha. Day visit to Laguna Cuicocha US$1; visitors' centre at Cuicocha US$1*, which extends from Laguna Cuicocha and the Cotacachi volcano to the tropical lowlands on the Río Cayapas in Esmeraldas. One highland area of the reserve can be easily accessed along a paved road, 15 km from Cotacachi via Quiroga. The Piñán Lakes region further north is accessed from Urcuquí, northwest of Ibarra, see page 186.

> *The full US$5 park fee is payable for people climbing Cotacachi.*

The lovely crater lake of **Laguna Cuicocha** sits at the foot of Cotacachi Volcano at an altitude of 3,070 m, and is a popular place for a Sunday outing. The visitors' centre has good natural history and cultural displays (entry US$1). The lake's two islands are closed to the public for biological studies. There is a pier and an *hostería* on the east shore of the lake. Motor boat rides around the islands cost US$1.50 per person for a minimum of eight people.

> *There have been armed robberies of people walking around the lake. Do not take valuables. Do not eat the berries which grow near the lake, as some are poisonous.*

There is a well-marked, 8-km path around the lake, which takes four to five hours and provides spectacular views of the Cotacachi, Imbabura and, occasionally, glacier-covered Cayambe peaks. The best views are to be had in the early morning, when condors can sometimes be seen. There is a lookout at 3 km, two hours from the start. It's best to do the route in an anticlockwise direction and take water and a waterproof jacket. The trail ends at the **Hostería Los Pinos de Cuicocha** (meals available from where you have to walk on the road 4 km back to the park entrance. At **El Mirador** you can also get a meal and transport back to Quiroga, Cotacachi or Otavalo.

The three-hour walk back from the lake to Cotacachi is beautiful. After 1 km on the road from the park entrance, turn left (at the first bend) on to the unpaved road. You can also walk to Otavalo, following the paved road to Quiroga and the secondary road from there.

To the north of Laguna Cuicocha and also within the reserve is the ragged peak of **Cotacachi Volcano** (4,944 m). This beautiful mountain, often sprinkled with snow, is best admired from the pier side of Cuicocha. The road at the entrance to the park continues from Cuicocha to some antennas on the eastern flank of the mountain; this side is often shrouded in mist. To climb it, it's best approached from the ridge to the west. It is a demanding climb and at the top there is dangerous loose rock. Detailed maps of the region can be bought from the IGM in Quito. Climbing tours to Cotacachi are available through **El Mirador** and Otavalo agencies.

Intag region → *Phone code 06 Colour map 2, grid B4*

To the northwest of Otavalo lies the lush subtropical region of Intag, after the river of the same name. One access to this area is along the road that follows the southern edge of Cuicocha, crosses the western range and gradually descends to the southwest. Another access is off the road which goes from Otavalo to Selva Alegre. Several reserves were created in the area to protect its rich cloud forests.

The hamlet of **Santa Rosa**, 35 km from Cuicocha, is at the heart of several reserves. There is a women's cooperative, their nice *cabuya* (sissal) wares are sold in town. In the **Intag Cloud Forest Reserve**, one hour's walk from Santa Rosa, is a friendly lodge ① *The lodge only accepts groups of 6 or more and specializes in university groups. Prices depend on group size, about US$45 per person per day. Reservations by mail or fax: Casilla 18, Otavalo, F06-2923392 or through Safari Tours in Quito,* with good vegetarian food. The reserve contains primary cloud forest at 1,800-2,800 m, and there is a trail to Los Cedros (see below). The owners are very involved in community environmental work, see www.decoin.org

Just east of Santa Rosa, a poor road turns north. This is the access to **Reserva Alto Chocó** ① *Run by Fundación Zoobreviven, Marco Pavón, Quito T02-2235366,* 30 minutes' walk from the turn-off. Accommodation is in simple rooms, **F** per person, no meals. There are some trails through forest to waterfalls, a reforestation project is underway and they welcome volunteers.

Apuela is a small town 46 km from Cuicocha. **Defensa y Conservación Ecológica de Intag (Decoin)** ① *Thu-Sun, T06-2648593, www.decoin.org,* an NGO working on conservation through community projects, has an office uphill from the plaza. Beyond Apuela, 5 km south, are the thermal baths of **Nangulví** ① *US$0.32.* As with most developed springs in the country they tend to be busy at weekends. There are four hot pools here and one large cold one for plunging. The area is relaxed and pleasant for walking, with a waterfall one hour away. Between Apuela and Nangulví, a side road goes to **Peñaherrera**, down which is the **Tolas de Gualimán arcaheological site**, several mounds with ramps, from the Caranqui culture. The main road continues southwest beyond Nangulví, one hour's driving to **García Moreno**.

Beyond García Moreno is the **Junín Cloud Forest Reserve**, a 800-ha forest at 1,500-2,000 m. The local community is trying ecotourism as an alternative to forest destruction and has built **A** accommodation. From García Moreno, the lodge can be reached by a 1½-hour truck ride or four-hour hike depending on road conditions (worst January-April). When hiking in, mules carry your luggage. There are good walking possibilities, including a trail to Los Cedros (see below). The scenery is lovely, with forest and waterfalls. In the 1990s this community succesfully fought a foreign mining company which tried to obtain rights to mine for gold in their reserve. The threat is once again present, with a different company trying to get in. They can use all the help they can get, in support of their ecotourism project. Further information can be obtained from www.decoin.org

On the southwest boundary of Reserva Cotacachi-Cayapas is **Los Cedros Research Station** ① *Nice A facilities, including all meals. Volunteer programme US$250 per month, minimum stay 1 month. Reservations necessary, in Quito contact: T02-2231768, www.reservaloscedros.org,* 6,400 ha of pristine cloud forest famous for the number of new orchid species discovered there. Bird life is abundant, and large species are more common and less shy than in many other places. Access

● Sleeping

Otavalo *p167, map p169*
Hotels may be full on Fri nights, before
the market, when prices go up.
A Ali Shungu, Quito y Miguel Egas,
T06-2920750, www.alishungu.com
Nicely decorated hotel with lovely
garden, comfortable rooms, good
restaurant with live music on weekends,
parking, no smoking, safe deposit
boxes, can arrange transport from
Quito, credit cards only accepted over
the internet using Paypal, surcharge
for credit cards and TCs, US run.
Recommended.
B Coraza, Calderón y Sucre, T/F06-2921225,
www.ecuahotel.com Modern hotel,
includes breakfast, good restaurant, quiet
and comfortable. Recommended.
B El Indio Inn, Bolívar 904 y Calderón,
T06-2922922, hindioinn@andinanet.net
Atractive hotel, includes breakfast,
restaurant, parking, carpeted rooms and
suites, spotlessly clean, refurbished in 2004.
B Hotel Otavalo, Roca 504 y J Montalvo,
T06-2923712, www.hotelotavalo.com.ec
Refurbished colonial house, good breakfast
included, pricey restaurant, large rooms,
patio, good service, helpful.
B Yamor Continental, Av Paz Ponce de
León y Jacinto Collahuazo, near bus terminal,
T06-2920451, F2920982. Faded premises but
pleasant setting surrounded by gardens,
restaurant, pool, parking.
B-D Acoma, Salinas 07-57 y 31 de Octubre,
T06-2926570. A lovely modern hotel built in
colonial style, includes breakfast, cafeteria,
cheaper with shared bath, parking,
comfortable rooms, some with balcony, one
room with bathtub, one suite with
kitchenette in A range, good value.
C Doña Esther, Montalvo 4-44 y Bolívar,
T06-2920739, www.otavalohotel.com Nicely
restored colonial house, good pizzeria
downstairs, simple rooms with nice wooden
floors, colourful decor.
C-D Riviera Sucre, García Moreno 380 y
Roca, T06-2920241, www.rivierasucre.com
Good breakfasts, cafeteria, cheaper with
shared bath, laundry facilities, book

exchange, nice garden, friendly, good
meeting place.
D Aly, Salinas y Bolívar, T06-2926397.
Modern multi-storey hotel, restaurant,
cheaper with shared bath.
D Cabañas El Rocío, Barrio San Juan
W of Panamericana, near stadium ,
T06-2920584. Parking, enquire at
Residencial Rocío. Helpful owners,
attractive, gardens, views.
D El Indio, Sucre 1214 y Salinas, near Plaza
de Ponchos, T06-2920060. In multi-storey
building, restaurant, cheaper with shared
bath, friendly and helpful service.
D Jatun Pacha, 31 de Octubre 19 entre
Quito y Panamericana, T06-2922223,
F2922871. Includes breakfast, nice, modern,
cheaper in dorm, discount for IYHF card
holders, bicycle rentals.
D Rincón de Belén, Roca 8-20 y J Montalvo,
T/F06-2921860. Modern hotel, grill
downstairs, functional rooms.
D Rincón del Viajero, Roca 11-07 y
Quiroga, T06-2921741,
rincondelviajero@hotmail.com Very
pleasant hostel and meeting place. Includes
a choice of nice breakfasts, cheaper with
shared bath, laundry facilities, parking,
rooftop hammocks, sitting room with
fireplace, US-Ecuadorean run, friendly.
Recommended.
D Valle del Amanecer, Roca y Quiroga,
T06-2920990, F2920286. Small rooms
around a courtyard, includes breakfast,
popular, mountain bike hire.
D-E Los Andes, Sucre y Quiroga by Plaza de
Ponchos, T06-2921057. Modern building,
cafeteria, cheaper with shared bath, simple
small rooms but good value.
E La Cascada, Sucre 506 y Colón,
T06-2920165. Cheaper with shared bath, hot
water, basic.
E María, Jaramillo y Colón, T/F06-2920672.
Modern multi-storey building, cafeteria,
private bath, hot water, bright rooms. Good
value, recommended.
E Rocío, Morales y Egas, T06-2920584.
Cheaper with shared bath, hot showers,
helpful, popular, good value.

E San Luis, Abdón Calderón 6-02 y 31 de Octubre, T06-2920614. Cheaper with shared bath, basic, family run.

E-F Colón, Colón 7-13 y Ricaurte, T06-2926037. Simple residencial, cheaper with shared bath, hot water, clean, good value.

E-F El Geranio, Ricaurte y Colón, T06-2920185, hgeranio@hotmail.com Breakfast available, cheaper with shared bath, hot water, laundry and cooking facilities, quiet, family run, helpful, popular, also runs economical trips. Good value, recommended.

Outskirts of Otavalo

LL Casa Mojanda, Vía Mojanda Km 3.5, PO Box 160, T06-2922986, www.casa mojanda.com Adobe cabins in beautiful setting. Includes breakfast and dinner prepared with ingredients from their own organic garden. Traditional hot tub with great views, quiet, good library, horse riding. Highly recommended.

L Hacienda Pinsaquí, Panamericana Norte Km 5, 300 m north of the turn-off for Cotacachi, T06-2946116, www.haciendapinsaqui.com Converted hacienda with 23 suites, includes breakfast, restaurant with lovely dining room, lounge with fireplace, beautiful antiques, colonial ambience, gardens, horse riding.

L Rancho Ali Shungu, 5 km west of Otavalo by the village of Yambiro, T06-2920750, www.ranchoalishungu.com Country inn on a 16-ha private reserve. Four comfortable guest houses with capacity for 6, each with living room and kitchenette. Includes full-course breakfast and dinner, vegetarian available, contact Hotel Ali Shungu in Otavalo, 2 night min stay in high season.

L Vista del Mundo, Panamericana at Pinsaquí toll, halfway between Otavalo and Ibarra, T06-2946333, www.thegoldenspa.com Luxury hotel, spa (treatments are extra), and convention centre, built around the theme of world peace. Breakfast, dinner and use of heated pool, elegant expensive restaurant serves good food. Unusual and interesting.

A Las Palmeras, outside Quichinche, 15 mins by bus from Otavalo, T06-2922607, www.laspalmerasinn.com Includes breakfast, restaurant, cheaper with shared bath, parking, rural setting, nice grounds, English-owned, friendly.

B La Casa de Hacienda, entrance at Panamericana Norte Km 3, then 300 m east, T06-2923105, www.casadehacienda.com Tasteful cabins with fireplace, includes breakfast, restaurant serves Ecuadorean and international food, parking, advance reservations required for horse riding.

D La Luna de Mojanda, On a side road going south off the Mojanda road at Km 4, T09-9737415, lalunaecuador@yahoo.co.uk Pleasant country hostel in nice surroundings, restaurant, cheaper in dorm, parking, some rooms with fireplace and private bath, others shared, terrace with hammocks, camping possible, taxi from Otavalo US$3 or take Punyaro city bus, excursions arranged, popular. Recommended.

E Posada Río Blanco, on the road to Quiroga, near the Fuente de la Salud baths, T09-9839692, ruthy_71@yahoo.com Pleasant hostel in rural setting, breakfast and meals available, private bath, hot water, parking, small rooms with single bed or bunks, take a Cotacachi bound bus which goes via Quiroga, horse riding and excursions with advance arrangements.

Excursions from Otavalo *p170*
Peguche and other weaving villages

C Aya Huma, on the railway line in Peguche, T06-2922663, www.ayahuma.com In a country setting between the unused rail tracks and the river. Restaurant, cheaper in annexe with cooking facilities, quiet, pleasant atmosphere, live music Sat night, Dutch-run, popular. Highly recommended.
C Peguche Tío, near centre of the village of Peguche, T/F06-2922619, peguchetio@mail.com Rural hotel decorated with some works of art, restaurant, internet, interesting collection of ceramics and old artefacts, sports fields, caters for groups.

Lago San Pablo

L Cusín, by the village of San Pablo del Lago to the southeast of the lake, T06-2918013, www.haciendacusin.com A converted 17th century hacienda with lovely coutyard and garden, includes breakfast, fine expensive restaurant, 25 rooms with fireplaces, sports facilities, pool, library, book in advance, British-run, English and German spoken.
AL Puerto Lago, Just off the Panamericana, on the west side of the lake, T06-2920920, www.puertolago.net Modern *hostería* in a lovely setting on the lakeshore, good expensive restaurant overlooking the lake, rooms and suites with fireplaces, very hospitable, a good place to watch the sunset, includes the use of row-boats, pedalos and kayaks, other water sports extra.
A Cabañas del Lago, on northeast shore of the lake, T06-2918001. Nice cabins on the lakeshore, restaurant overlooking the lake, rooms decorated with rustic furniture, some have fireplaces, lovely garden, boats and pedalos, other water sports such as knee boards and water skiing on weekends only (extra), room prices higher Fri and Sat.
A Jatun Cocha, On the east side of the lake, past the village of San Pablo del Lago, T/F06-2918191, www.ranfturismo.com Hacienda-style lodge, includes breakfast, restaurant serves set meals at mid-range prices and à la carte in the expensive range,

pool and sauna, parking, tastefully decorated rooms with fireplaces, water sports include kayaks and windsurfing, bicycles, horses.

Cotacachi

LL La Mirage, 500 m west of town, T06-2915237, www.mirage.com.ec Luxurious converted hacienda, includes breakfast and dinner, lovely expensive restaurant, pool and gym, elegant suites and common areas, beautiful gardens, antiques, conference facilities and spa.
B Mesón de las Flores, García Moreno 1376 y Sucre, T06-2916009, F2915828. Refurbished colonial house in the heart of town, includes breakfast, restaurant in lovely patio (mid-range to expensive), carpeted rooms, live music at lunch Sat-Sun. Recommended.
B Rancho Santa Fe, 1 km west of town, T06-2916338. Resort complex with sport fields and pool, includes breakfast, restaurant with local specialities and international dishes, mid-range prices, parking, carpeted rooms with small sitting room, sports fields including tennis courts, suited to families.
B Runa Tupari, Inns in native communities, see Cotacachi Sights, T06-2925985, nativetravel@runatupari.com Cottages for 3 with fireplace, price includes breakfast, dinner and transport from Otavalo, built with tourist needs in mind.
C Sumac Huasi, Montalvo 11-09 y Moncayo, T06-2915873, sumac_h@imbanet.net Modern pleasant hotel, includes breakfast, well-furnished large rooms, and a nice rooftop terrace.
D Munaylla, 10 de Agosto y Sucre, T06-2916169. Modern multi-storey building, comfortable rooms, friendly, good value.
D Plaza Bolívar, Bolívar 12-26 y 10 de Agosto, 3rd floor, T06-2915755, marcelmun@yahoo.es Refurbished older building, indoor parking, small rooms, family run, friendly, owner Marcelo is very knowledgeable about the area.
E Bachita, Sucre 16-82 y Peñaherrera, T06-2915063. Simple little place, cheaper with shared bath and cold water, quiet and friendly.

D Cabañas Río Grande, in Nangulví, next to the baths, T06-2920171. Comfortable log cabins for 4 (price per cabin), restaurant.

D Gualimán, Along the road to Peñaherrera, near the archaeological site. Cabins overlooking the Nangulví area.

E Cabañas Monterrey, in Pilambiro Bajo, north of Nangulví. Simple cabins.

E Fanicita, in Apuela, on the plaza, T06-2648552. Basic, shared bath, electric shower.

E Pradera Tropical, in Apuela, near the school (no sign, ask), T06-2648557. Rustic cabins for 3, shared bath, cold water, friendly.

❷ Eating

Otavalo *p167, map p169*

₮₮₮ Ali Shungu, Quito y Miguel Egas, at the hotel, daily 0700-2100. Serves all meals, good food, wide choice including vegetarian, ample dining room decorated with native motifs. Recommended.

₮₮₮ Il de Roma, J Montalvo 4-44 at Hotel Doña Esther. Good pizza and pasta, warm atmosphere.

₮₮₮ Quino, Roca 740 y Juan Montalvo, T06-2924994, daily 1100-2300. Traditional coastal cooking and some meat dishes, pleasant seating around a patio.

₮₮₮ Tabasco's, Sucre y Salinas, Plaza de Ponchos, T06-2922475. Standard Mexican fare, overpriced and not that special. Some outdoor tables, lovely views from terrace.

₮₮₮ Via Brasil, Sucre y Abdón Calderón, 2nd floor, T06-2924827, Wed-Sun 1200-2200. Brazilian *rodizio* with a variety of meat choices and nice salad bar, *feijoada*, *caipirinha*, nicely decorated, authentic, Brazilian-Ecuadorean run.

₮₮₮-₮₮ Arcobalena, Salinas 507 y Sucre, 0730-1030, 1200-1400, 1500-2200. Extensive selection of pasta including home-made gnocchi, risotto, pizza, desserts. Also serves breakfast and set lunches, one section is more elegant while the 2nd one is more relaxed, pleasant atmosphere, new in 2005.

₮₮₮-₮₮ Fontana di Trevi, Sucre 12-05 y Salinas, 2nd floor, 1130-2200. Good pizza and pasta, nice juices, overlooking Calle Sucre, friendly service.

₮₮₮-₮₮ SISA, Abdón Calderón 4-09 y Sucre, daily 0700-2200. Cultural centre, restaurant on second floor serve excellent set meals and à la carte, coffee shop with capuccino, slow service, also bookstore, weekly international films, live music Fri-Sun.

₮₮ Ali Allpa, Salinas 509 at Plaza de Ponchos. Good value set meals and à la carte, trout, vegetarian, meat, recommended.

₮₮ Aly Micuy, Salinas y Bolívar, at the hotel, Mon-Sat 0730-2130, Sun 1200-1700. International and local dishes à la carte.

₮₮ Café Mundi, Quiroga 608 y Jaramillo, Plaza de Ponchos, daily 0700-2200. Varied menu including vegetarian, nice atmosphere.

₮₮ El Indio, Sucre y Salinas. Good fried chicken and steaks, local speciality *fritada* (fried pork).

₮₮ Mi Otavalito, Sucre y Morales. Good for set lunch and international food à la carte.

₮ La Herradura, Bolivar 10-05. Good set meal (1200-1430) and à la carte, outdoor tables.

Cafés

Deli, Quiroga y Bolívar, Fri and Sat only. Small place serving Mexican snacks such as tacos, also pizza.

Empanadas Argentinas, Morales 502 y Sucre. Very good savoury and sweet *empanadas*.

Shanandoa Pie Shop, Salinas y Jaramillo. Pies, milk shakes and ice-cream, recommended for breakfast, popular and friendly meeting place, book exchange, daily movies at 1700 and 1900.

Cotacachi *p172*

A local speciality is *carne colorada* (spiced pork, although restaurants catering to tourists may also prepare it using beef).

₮₮₮ Asadero La Tola, Rocafuerte 018 y 9 de Octubre, T06-2915509. Grill in an old courtyard.

₮₮₮ El Leñador, Sucre 1012 y Montalvo, T06-2915083. Varied menu.

₮₮₮-₮₮ La Marqueza, 10 de Agosto y Bolívar, daily 0730-2130. Slightly upscale restaurant, 4 course set lunches and à la carte.

₮₮ El Viejo Molino, 10 de Agosto 10-65 y Moncayo. Nice set meals and à la carte, good value and quality.

🌓 Bars and clubs

Otavalo *p167, map p169*
Peñas are bars which present live folk music (more details on p128), most open Fri and Sat from 2000, entrance US$2.
Fauno Bar, Morales y Sucre, T09-7078124, Tue-Sun 1400-0200. Drinks, snacks, live music.
Habana Club, Quito y 31 de Octubre, T06-2920493. Lively disco, live music some weekends, drinks, cover US$2.
Madero Peña Bar, Morales 10-60 y Ricaurte, T06-2920033. Live folk music, drinks, also dancing.
Maracaná, Salinas 6-12 y Jaramillo, T06-2920941. Disco, varied music, happy hour, live music some weekends, young crowd.
Peña Amauta, Morales 5-11 y Jaramillo, T06-2922475. Good local bands, varied music, friendly and welcoming, popular with foreigners.
Peña Da Pinto, Colón 4-10 y Bolívar, T09-4188438, www.dapinto.com Colourfully decorated, live Latin music on weekends, drinks and snacks.
Peña la Jampa, Jaramillo y Quiroga, T06-2922988, Fri-Sat 1930-0300. Andean and dancing music, popular with Ecuadoreans and foreigners.
During festivals, there are nightlife tours on a *chiva* (open-sided bus with a musical group on board), it stops at the Plaza de Ponchos and ends its route at the **Habana Club**.

❄ Festivals and events

Indigenous celebrations overlap with Catholic holidays, prolonging festivities for a week or more. The celebrations take place throughout the Otavalo region and are not restricted to the city. If you wish to visit fiestas in the local villages, ask the musicians in the tourist restaurants, they may invite you; outsiders are not always welcome. The music is good and there is a lot of drinking, but transport back to Otavalo is hard to find.

Otavalo *p167, map p169*
21-29 Jun Los San Juanes **Inti Raymi** celebrations of the summer solstice (21 Jun) are combined with the **Fiesta de San Juan** (24 Jun) and the **Fiesta de San Pedro**

y **San Pablo** (29 Jun). Action takes place in and around Otavalo. The celebration begins with a ritual bath in the Peguche waterfall (a personal spiritual activity, best carried out without visitors and certainly without cameras). There are bullfights in the plaza and regattas on Lago San Pablo, 4 km away (see Around Otavalo below for transport). In Otavalo, indigenous families have costume parties, that at times spill over onto the streets. In the San Juan neighbourhood, near the Yanayacu baths, there is a week-long celebration.
Sep Yamor The **Fiesta del Yamor** and **Colla Raimi** (fall equinox or festival of the moon) are held during the first 2 weeks of Sep. This is the largest festivity in the province of Imbabura, it takes place in several cities and is mainly a mestizo celebration.Events include music, dancing, bullfighting, fireworks and sporting events, including swimming and reed boat races across Lago San Pablo.
Oct Fundación Mojandas Arriba is an annual 2-day hike from Quito over Mojanda to reach Otavalo for the 31 Oct foundation celebrations commemorating the day Simon Bolívar elevated Otavalo to the status of a city. It is walked by hundreds each year and follows the old trails with an overnight stop at Malchinguí.

Excursions from Otavalo *p170*
Peguche and other weaving villages
Feb-Mar Pawkar Raimi is a festival held in Peguche during Carnival with much music, food and drinking. It is also a time when many locals who live abroad return for the festivities.

Cotacachi *p172*
Mar-Apr Semana Santa celebrations include well attended *Viernes Santo* (Good Friday) processions at midday and in the evening.
21-28 Jun San Juan or Inti Raymi festivities of the sun and corn harvest take place during the summer solstice. Some of the characters in the parades include the *huarmi tucushca* (a man dressed as a woman), *el capitán* representing the boss, and *el soldado*, a dancer.
25 Jul Santa Ana festivities in honour of the town's patron saint are held around 25 July.

Celebrations include the Danza de Los Yumbos or dance of the mountain people.
Sep Jora The celebration of the equinox takes place during the 3rd week of Sep with sports events, concerts, dances, parades and a *chicha de jora* contest.
2 Nov Día de los Difuntos Deceased relatives are remembered. Among the indigenous people, altars are prepared in the home where symbols of energy – food, a stone, a cross and the statue of the virgin – are placed. At the cemetery, there are rituals with offerings and special characters such as *Angel Calpi*, someone dressed as the messenger between the living and the dead. There is also the custom of sharing with the needy.

O Shopping

Otavalo *p167, map p169*
Otavalo can seem like a giant souvenir shop at times. As well as the market, there are countless shops selling sweaters, tapestries and other souvenirs.

Books
The Book Market, Jaramillo 6-28 y Salinas, is highly recommended for buying, selling or exchanging books in English, French, German and other languages at cheap prices. Guidebooks, maps, postcards, CDs and cassettes.
SISA, see Eating above, has a good bookshop.

Food
Salinerito, Bolívar 10-08, for good cheese and cold cuts.

Handicrafts
Galería de Arte Quipus, Sucre y Morales, paintings with native motifs.
Galería Inti Ñan, Salinas 509 y Sucre, Plaza de Ponchos, also has a nice selection of paintings with native themes.
Hilana, Sucre esquina Morales, sells wool blankets.
Palos de Lluvia, Morales 506 y Sucre, rain sticks and other crafts.
Tagua Muyu, Sucre 10-11 y Colón, *tagua* (vegetable ivory) carvings.

Cotacachi *p172*
Cotacachi is an important centre for the leather industry. A wide variety of hand and machine crafted items can be purchased here. There are nice jackets, purses, belts, wallets, etc. Popular among visitors are the collapsible leather duffle bags which grow to fit all your souvenirs. Credit cards are widely accepted but there is a surcharge.

▲ Activities and tours

Otavalo *p167, map p169*
Ball games
Near the market, on Quiroga y Sucre, a ball game is played in the afternoons called *pelota de mano*. It is similar to the game in Ibarra (described on page 189) except that the ball is about the size of a table-tennis ball, made of leather, and hit with the hands, not a bat.

Climbing and trekking
Otavalo operators offer climbing and trekking tours in the region, including Cotacachi and Imbabura volcanos and Piñán Lakes to the northwest of Ibarra. **Suni tours** has been recommended.

Cycling
Some tour operators rent bikes and offer cycling tours (downhill cycling with vehicle for the uphill portions) for US$35-40 a day trip, see below. Mountain bike hire from:
Eco Hobby, Quiroga y Bolívar esquina, T06-2921558.
Jatun Pacha (see Sleeping above), US$4 per hr, includes helmet.
Taller Ciclo Primaxi, García Moreno y Atahualpa 2-49 and at the entrance to Peguche, good bikes, US$1 per hr. Recommended.
Valle del Amanecer (see Sleeping above), US$8 per day.

Horse riding
Several operators (see below) offer riding tours, **Suni Tours** has been recommended.

Swimming
Fuente de Salud, about 4 km north of Otavalo on the road to Quiroga. Cold ferrous baths, said to be very curative, but opening hours are very irregular.

Neptuno, at Morales and Guayaquil, has a
popular pool.
Yanayacu, on the Panamericana, has
3 swimming pools, volleyball courts and
is full of locals on Sun.

Tour operators
All agencies offer similar tours and prices.
One-day tours with English-speaking
guides to artisans' homes and villages,
which usually provide opportunities to
buy handicrafts cheaper than in the market,
cost US$20 per person. Day trips to
Cuicocha or **Mojanda**, US$20-30.
  Horse riding tours around Otavalo:
5 hrs to Tangali thermal springs or El Lechero
lookout US$20; full day to Cuicocha crater
lake US$30-35. Other destinations are the
Intag subtropical region, Nangulví and
Chachimbiro thermal baths. There is
variation in the duration of the tours,
find out before signing up.
Chachimbiro Tours, Colón 412 y Sucre,
T06-2923633, chachimbiro@andinanet.net
Trips to the *Complejo de Ecoturismo
Chachimbiro* 1 hr northwest of Otavalo
(thermal baths, spa, see p186).
Diceny Viajes, Sucre 10-11 y Colón,
T06-2921217, zulayviajes@hotmail.com
Run by Zulay Sarabino, an indigenous
Otavaleña, English and French spoken,
native guides knowledgeable about the area
and culture, climbing trips to Cotacachi
volcano, favourable reports. Recommended.
Leyton's Tours, Quito y Jaramillo,
T06-2922388, leytontour@yahoo.com
Horseback and bicycle tours.
Runa Tupari, Sucre y Quiroga,
Plaza de Ponchos T/F06-2925985,
nativetravel@runatupari.com Trips to
community inns in the Cotacachi area,
US$20 per person per day, half board,
includes transport (see Cotacachi below),
also the usual tours at higher-than-average
prices, English and French spoken.
Suni Tours, no store-front at this time,
contact owner Iván Suárez through Hostal
Valle del Amanecer or T06-2923383,
suarezivan@hotmail.com,
www.geocities.com/sunitour Interesting
itineraries, trekking and horse riding tours,
climbing, cycling, trips to Intag, Piñán,
Cayambe, Oyacachi, rafting on the Río Intag.
English spoken, guides carry radios.

Recommended. In early 2005 this agency
was in the process of expanding and will
operate with a new name later in the year.
Zulaytur, Sucre y Colón, p2, T06-2921176,
F2922969. Run by Rodrigo Mora. English
spoken, information, map of town, slide
show, horse riding, interesting day trip to
local artisan communities. Their tours,
especially the latter, have been repeatedly
recommended.

⊙ Transport

For main inter-city routes see the bus
timetable, p52.

Otavalo *p167, map p169*
From **Quito**, Terminal Terrestre, take a
Cooperativa Otavalo or **Cooperativa Los
Lagos** bus, as they are the only ones which go
into Otavalo; other companies bound for
Ibarra or Tulcán will drop you off on the
highway, which is far from the centre and not
safe after dark. From the Terminal in Quito,
buses go along the Av Occidental and later Av
de la Prensa in Cotocollao, where you can also
get on. Every 10 mins, US$2, 2 hrs.
  Taxi A fast and efficient alternative is
shared taxis with **Supertaxis Los Lagos** (in
Quito at Asunción 3-82, T02-2565992; in
Otavalo at Roca 8-04, T06-2923203) who will
pick you up at your hotel (in the New City
only); hourly Mon-Fri 0700-1900, Sat
0700-1600, Sun 0800-1800, 2 hrs, US$7.50
per person, buy ticket at their office the day
before travelling. A regular taxi costs US$50
one way, US$80 return with 3 hrs wait.
  To **Cayambe**, every 15 mins, US$0.60, 40
mins. To **Quiroga**, every 20 mins, US$0.18,
15 mins.
  Parking Do not leave your car
unattended on the street, especially on
Saturday. There are public car parks at
Juan Montalvo y Sucre, by Parque Bolívar,
and on Quito between 31 de Octubre and
Jarmillo.

Excursions from Otavalo *p170*
Peguche and other weaving villages
From **Otavalo**, take a city bus along Av
Atahualpa, these stop outside the bus
terminal and Plaza Copacabana (Atahualpa y
Montalvo), every 15 mins, US$0.18. You can
also take a taxi or go with a tour.

From **Otavalo** terminal, buses to San Pablo del Lago leave every 30 mins, more often on Sat, US$0.18. A taxi costs US$4.

Cotacachi

The bus terminal is at 10 de Agosto y Salinas by the market. To **Otavalo**, every 10 mins, service alternates between the Panamericana and Quiroga roads, US$0.20, 20 mins. To **Quiroga**, every 20 mins, US$0.18, 10 mins. To **Ibarra**, every 15 mins, US$0.45, 45 mins. To **Quito**, transfer in Otavalo.

Laguna Cuicocha

Pick-ups From **Otavalo** US$10. From **Cotacachi** market, US$4 one way, US$8 return with short wait. From **Quiroga** US$4. Return service from the lake available from Cabañas El Mirador, same rates.

Intag region

From **Otavalo** Daily **Transportes Otavalo** to **García Moreno** at 0800, 1000 and 1400, return at 0800, 1000 and 1300; **Trans 6 de Julio** to **Barcelona** (turn-off past Nangulví) at 1200 and to **Peñaherrera** at 1500.

To: **Apuela** US$1.94, 2½ hrs, **Nangulví** US$2.25, 3 hrs, **García Moreno**, US$2.80, 4 hrs.

❶ Directory

Otavalo *p167, map p169*
Banks Banco del Pacífico, Bolívar 614 y García Moreno. **Banco del Pichincha**, Bolívar y Piedrahita. **Casa de Cambio**, Sucre 11-05 y Colón. TCs 3% commission, also currency exchange, poor rates. **Vaz Corp**, Jaramillo y Saona, Plaza de Ponchos, T06-2922926, Tue-Sat 0900-1700. TCs 1.80-2% commission, also change Euros and Colombian Pesos, reasonable rates. **Internet** Many in town especially along C Sucre, US$1 per hr.
Language schools Fundación Jacinto Jijón y Caamaño, Bolívar 8-04 y Montalvo, p 2, T06-2920725. Spanish and Quichua lessons. **Instituto Superior de Español**, Sucre 11-10 y Morales, p 2, T06-2992414, www.instituto-superior.net (see also p143). **Mundo Andino Internacional**, Salinas 509, p 3, at Plaza de Ponchos T/F06-2925478, mundoandinoinn@hotmail.com Dancing and cooking classes at no extra cost.
Laundry Colón, Colón y Jaramillo, US$0.90 per kg or US$2.50 per machine. **New Laundry**, Roca y Quiroga, at Hostal Valle del Amanecer. US$1.20 per kg. **Tecno Clean**, C Olmedo 32. Dry cleaning. **Post office** Sucre y Salinas esquina at Plaza de Ponchos, p 1, entrance on Sucre.

Cotacachi *p172*
Banks Banco del Pichincha, Imbabura y Rocafuerte, ATM. **Internet** US$1 per hr. Casa de las Culturas is always full.

Ibarra and surroundings

→ *Phone code 06 Colour map 2, grid B5 Population 108,600 Altitude 2,225*
Once a pleasant colonial town (founded in 1606), Ibarra is the main commercial centre of the northern highlands, with an increasingly big city feel. It has many good hotels and restaurants. Prices are lower than Otavalo and there are fewer tourists. The city has an interesting ethnic mix, with blacks from the Chota valley and Esmeraldas alongside Otavaleños and other highland Indians, mestizos and Colombian immigrants. Nearby are craft towns producing beautiful wood carvings and embroidered tablecloths. To the north lies the dry, warm Chota valley and to the northwest a lovely subtropical region descending to the coast. ▶▶ *For Sleeping, Eating and all other listings, see pages 186-190.*

Ins and outs

Getting there Since 2004, Ibarra has a new bus terminal on Av Teodoro Gómez y Av Eugenio Espejo, to the southwest of the centre, T06-2644676. At the terminal there are small shops, two food courts and a telephone office. All inter-city transport runs from here. Some regional destinations are served by buses which leave from other locations or by city buses. City buses go from the terminal to the centre or you can walk in 15 minutes.

Getting around The city centre, where most hotels, restaurants and attractions are located, is compact, with the Santo Domingo church a few blocks north from the centre. City buses and taxis are plentiful to reach other neighbourhoods.

Information The **Ministerio de Turismo** ① *García Moreno 376 y Rocafuerte, T06-2958547, www.imbabura.gov.ec, Mon-Fri 0830-1300, 1400-1700*, is very helpful and provides plentiful free city maps and leaflets. Staff speak English. **Cámara Provincial de Turismo de Imbabura** ① *Oviedo y Bolívar, of 102, T/F06-2642531, www.imbaburaturismo.com, Mon-Fri 0800-1300, 1500-1800*. Regional information, very helpful, Spanish only. **Dirección Municipal de Turismo** ① *Av Eugenio Espejo y Av Teodoro Gómez, opposite the Terminal Terrestre, T06-2608489, Mon-Fri 0800-1630*. Spanish only.

Ibarra

The city has two fine parks with flowering trees. On **Parque Pedro Moncayo** stand the **Cathedral**, with paintings of the Quito School of Art, the Municipio and the Gobernación. One block away, at Flores y Olmedo, is the smaller **Parque de la Merced**, named after its church with gilded altar, also known as Parque 9 de

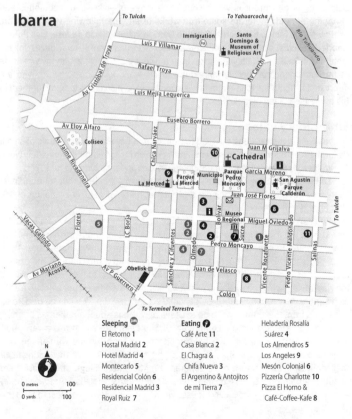

Ibarra

Sleeping
El Retorno 1
Hostal Madrid 2
Hotel Madrid 4
Montecarlo 5
Residencial Colón 6
Residencial Madrid 3
Royal Ruiz 7

Eating
Café Arte 11
Casa Blanca 2
El Chagra &
  Chifa Nueva 3
El Argentino & Antojitos
  de mi Tierra 7

Heladería Rosalía
  Suárez 4
Los Almendros 5
Los Angeles 9
Mesón Colonial 6
Pizzería Charlotte 10
Pizza El Horno &
  Café-Coffee-Kafe 8

Octubre. There are also a couple smaller plazoletas, including **Plazoleta Francisco Calderón**, on Sucre y Pedro Moncayo, with some restaurants and outdoor seating.

Some interesting paintings are to be seen in the church of **Santo Domingo** and its museum of religious art. On the premises is also a small **zoo** ① *at the north end of Simón Bolívar, 0800-1800 daily, US$0.60*. At the small Parque Abdón Calderón is the **San Agustín** church. On Sucre, at the end of Avenida A Pérez Guerrero, is the **Basílica de La Dolorosa**, damaged by an earthquake in May 1987, but reopened in December 1992. A walk down Pérez Guerrero leads to the bustling, large, covered **Mercado Amazonas** on Sánchez y Cifuentes, by the railway station, open daily, busiest at the weekend.

Museo Regional Sierra Norte ① *Sucre 7-21 y Oviedo, T06-2952777, Mon-Sat, 0830-1330, 1430-1630, US$0.50*, run by the **Banco Central del Ecuador**, has four sections: Man's arrival to Ecuador, an archaeology section with interesting displays about the pre-Inca cultures of the northern highlands, the Inca period and a gold display. Explanations in Spanish and English. There is also a hall for temporary art exhibits, a library and a bookshop.

Around Ibarra

San Antonio de Ibarra → *Phone code 06*

About 10 minutes south of Ibarra, just off the Panamericana between Otavalo and Ibarra, is San Antonio de Ibarra, a village well known for its wood carvings. The trade is so successful that the main street is lined with galleries and boutiques, and bargaining is difficult. It is worth seeing the range of styles and techniques and shopping around, there are some true works of art. The following workshops are worth visiting: **Moreo Santacruz, Osvaldo Garrido** in the **Palacio de Arte, Luís Potosí, Gabriel Cevallos**, and **Juan Padilla**. The latter who has won several prizes for his creations, is in Barrio Bellavista, 2 km from the centre of the village, on the west side of the Panamericana; he has an exhibit of his work, welcomes visitors who are interested in sculpting to join him in his workshop and also offers lodging for them in his home (see Sleeping below).

Embroidery villages → *Phone code 06*

To the south of Ibarra, along the road to Olmedo and Cayambe, are a couple of small, mainly indigenous villages. This scenic area is known for its beautiful embroidery work. The women wear very elegant embroidered blouses and matching pleated skirts.

La Esperanza, 8 km from Ibarra, is a pretty village set in beautiful surroundings. There are a couple of simple lodgings and eateries here. Ask in town for makers of fine clothes and embroidery.

You can climb **Cubilche** volcano in three hours from La Esperanza for beautiful views. From the top you can walk down to Lago San Pablo, another three hours. You can also climb **Imbabura** volcano more easily than from San Pablo del Lago. Allow 10-12 hours for the round trip, take a good map, food and warm clothing. The easiest route is to head right from **Hotel Casa Aída**, take the first road to the right and walk all the way up, following the tracks up past a water tank. It's a difficult but enjoyable walk with superb views; watch out for some loose scree at the top. You can go back to La Esperanza from the summit or go on to Otavalo, which is about another 3-4 hours.

Near La Esperanza is the community of **San Clemente** which has a very good grass-roots tourism project. They have good lodging opportunities with indigenous families. Your stay there implies becoming part of the family and participating in all their daily activities. South of La Esperanza is the small village of **Zuleta**, where beautiful embroidery is done on napkins and tablecloths. There is a Sunday market, a good place to admire the lovely blouses worn by the local women. Near town is the elegant **Hacienda Zuleta** of the former president Galo Plaza, which offers exclusive accommodation (see Sleeping below). Advance arrangements are required: book through Quito agencies or www.zuleta.com From Zuleta the road continues to Olmedo and Cayambe.

Laguna Yahuarcocha → *Phone code 06*
ⓘ *Entry to Yahuarcocha for vehicles US$0.30, boat rental US$1, frequent buses from the market area in Ibarra.*

Laguna Yahuarcocha is a popular weekend recreation spot for Ibarreños who go to paddle on the lake, ride a bike, eat *tilapia*, or party at one of the clubs. The beauty of the lake has been disfigured by the building of two motor-racing circuits around its shores. The smaller one is closed to vehicles and used by cyclists. The lake is gradually drying up with *totora* reeds encroaching on its margins. They are woven into *esteras* (mats) and sold in huge rolls at the roadside. Reed boats can sometimes be seen. The lively weekend atmosphere at the lake hides its more sombre past. Yahuarcocha means 'blood lake', and was the site of a decisive battle which the Incas won over the native Caranquis, a nation which resisted the Inca conquest for a long time.

It is possible to walk the 4 km to Yahuarcocha in about 1½ hours. Follow Calle 27 to the end of town, cross the river and walk to the right at the first junction. At the end of this road, behind two low buildings on the left, there is a small path going steeply uphill. There are beautiful views of Ibarra and then, from the top of the hill, over the lake surrounded by mountains and the village of the same name.

Ibarra to the coast → *Phone code 06*
For many decades, Ibarra's link to the coast was a spectacular train ride joining the city with the Pacific community of San Lorenzo. Rail service to the coast was discontinued, but the beautiful subtropical area can still be visited either taking a shorter train ride or along an equally scenic road.

Train ride from Ibarra ⓘ *The autoferro runs when there are enough passengers at the station 30 mins before departure (15 people going one way or fewer return). Mon-Fri at 0700, returning at 1400, Sat, Sun and holidays at 0800, returning at 1600. US$3.80 one way. Tickets must be purchased 30 mins before departure. Reservations are recommended for weekend travel, T06-2950390. The train station is near the obelisk, T06-2955050, open daily 0700-1200 and 1400-1800. The autoferro can also be hired for the day for US$190. If there are heavy rains service may be interrupted, check ahead if it is running.* Along the start of the spectacular route to San Lorenzo, a motorized rail-car (*autoferro*) runs 45 km out of Ibarra, about two hours to Primer Paso, just past Tulquizán. It is an interesting excursion through nice scenery. The *autoferro* stays for a few hours before returning, so you can spend some time exploring the surroundings, a transition zone between the highlands and coast. **Hostería Tulquizán** is across the river, see below. To continue to the subtropical zone (30 minutes to Guallupe) or return to Ibarra by bus, get off at Tulquizán, where the road crosses the tracks. Train enthusiasts may wish to visit the railway yards beyond the station in Ibarra, with several old locomotives.

Road to the coast A very scenic fully-paved road takes you from Ibarra to the ocean in as little as four hours. Completed in 2002, this is the northernmost route connecting the highlands with the Pacific. Although it is has opened new opportunities for communities along the way, there is also increased logging and accelerated destruction of the remaining forests in Ecuador's unique Chocó bioregion.

The road starts from the Panamericana, 24 km north of Ibarra. It goes by the town of **Salinas**, then drops northwest following the valley of the Río Mira to the subtropical lowlands. About 15 minutes beyond Salinas is **Tulquizán**; here is **Hostería Tulquizán**, a resort by the river (closed for renovations in early 2005, see Sleeping). Lower down, 43 km from the Salinas turn-off, are the villages of **Guallupe**, **El Limonal**, and **San Juan de Lachas**, separated by a stream and the Río Mira. The former two villages are part of the **Parroquia La Carolina**, and you may hear this name as well, or see it in a map. Here are **Bospas Farm**, an organic fruit farm offering lodging, treks, horse riding tours and volunteer opportunities and two *hosterías* with swimming pools, popular on weekends (see Sleeping for details). At San Juan de Lachas, the locals produce ceramic masks and figurines which are sold outside the church.

From Guallupe, the main road continues parallel to the Río Mira. In 28 km, it reaches **Lita** (altitude 512 m), a town near the old railway line, with good swimming in the river. It is 66 km from Lita to **Calderón**, where this road meets the coastal highway coming from Esmeraldas. About 7 km beyond is **San Lorenzo** (see page 342).

Northwest of Ibarra → *Phone code 06*

Along a secondary road to the northwest of Ibarra is the pretty town of **Urcuquí** with a basic hotel and a park. On Sunday the locals play unusual ball games. Urcuquí is the starting point for walking to the **Piñán lakes**, a beautiful, remote, high *páramo* region, part of the Reserva Ecológica Cotacachi-Cayapas. The local community of Piñán has a tourism programme and native guides and muleteers. Otavalo agencies offer trekking tours to Piñán.

Beyond Urcuquí, about two hours' drive from Ibarra, 8 km from the village of Tumbabiro, along a side road is the **Complejo de Turismo Ecológico** Chachimbiro ① *entry to the recreational pools US$2, to the medicinal pools and spa US$3. Tours are available from Chachimbiro Tours in Otavalo (see page 180), run by* **Fundación Cordillera**. The complex is part of a project to encourage sustainable development and environmental education in the region. **Proyecto Chachimbiro** has made many improvements including trails, organic gardens and a therapeutic centre. Within the complex are clean, hot, mineral swimming pools; there is one exceedingly hot pool for therapy and several of mixed water for soaking and playing. Weekends can be quite crowded. There are also cabins (see Sleeping, below) and restaurants.

● Sleeping

Ibarra *p182, map p183*

A Ajaví, Av Mariano Acosta 16-38 y Circunvalación, along main rd into town from south, T06-2955221, h-ajavi@imbanet.net Slightly upscale hotel, comfortable rooms, good restaurant serves regional and international cuisine, mid-range to expensive, pool, parking, gets tour groups for Sat lunch.

B El Prado, in Barrio El Olivo, off the Pan-American at Km 1½, T/F06-2959570. Fancy *hostería* set in fruit orchards, includes breakfast, restaurant, pool and spa, parking, ample carpeted rooms, sport fields, taxi from town US$1.

C Montecarlo, Av Jaime Rivadeneira 5-61 y Oviedo, T06-2958266, F2958182. Nice hotel just outside the centre, by the obelisk, includes breakfast, restaurant, heated pool open weekends only, parking, comfortable.

C Royal Ruiz, Olmedo 9-40 y P Moncayo, T06-2641999, h.royalruiz@andinanet.net Modern hotel, includes breakfast, restaurant, solar heated water, parking, comfortable carpeted rooms.

D El Retorno, Pasaje Pedro Moncayo 4-32 entre Sucre y Rocafuerte, T06-2957722. Ample rooms, restaurant, cheaper with shared bath, nice views from terrace. Good value, recommended.

D Hostal Madrid, Olmedo 8-69 y Moncayo, T06-2644918, rubenmoncayo@hotmail.com Modern hotel, parking, comfortable rooms. Recommended.

D Hotel Madrid, Moncayo 7-41 y Olmedo, T06-2959017, F2950796. Multi-storey building, comfortable rooms.

D Ibarra, Obispo Mosquera 6-158 y Sánchez y Cifuentes, near market, T06-2955091. Simple but adequate hotel, restaurant serves breakfast and very cheap lunch, parking.

E Residencial Madrid, Olmedo 8-57 y Oviedo, T06-2951760. Private bath, hot water, simple.

Outskirts south of Ibarra
Along the Pan-American Highway south towards Otavalo are several *hosterías* (country inns), some in converted haciendas.
A Hostería Chorlaví, Panamericana Sur Km 4, T06-2932222, chorlavi@andinanet.net A converted old hacienda with comfortable rooms, includes breakfast, very good expensive restaurant with excellent *parillada*, set meals and à la carte, pool, parking, popular, busy on weekends, folk music and crafts on Sun.
B Hostería Natabuela, Panamericana Sur Km 8, T06-2932032, sproano@andinanet.net A country inn, restaurant, covered pool, sauna, parking, comfortable rooms.
B Hostería Rancho Carolina, Panamerica Sur Km 4, next to Chorlaví, T06-2932444, F2932215. Hacienda-style inn, includes breakfast, restaurant, small pool, parking, a bit faded, friendly service.

Around Ibarra *p184*
San Antonio de Ibarra
D Casa de Hilario, Barrio Bellavista, 2 km south of the village of San Antonio and on the opposite side of the Panamericana (500 m along the road which starts where stone sculptures are made), T06-2932059. The home of Juan Padilla, a sculptor. He welcomes people who are interested in learning more about his art. Breakfast available, shared bath, 3 rooms in the family home. He can provide transport from San Antonio or take a bus from the Ibarra terminal terrestre, taxi US$3.

Embroidery villages
LL Hacienda Zuleta, Near the village of Zuleta, T06-2262577, www.zuleta.com See p75.
C Pukyu Pamba, In San Clemente, 30 mins south of Ibarra. Part of a community-run programme, housing in nice inns, price includes 3 good, tasty meals.
D Casa Aída, in La Esperanza village. Simple comfortable rooms, breakfast US$2.50, large restaurant, clean, room 7 has nice views, friendly, Aída speaks some English.

E Café María, in La Esperanza, next to Casa Aída. Basic rooms, will heat water, laundry and cooking facilities, friendly and helpful.

Laguna Yahuarcocha
All the hotels listed are around the lake.
B Rancho Totoral, T06-2955544. Spacious rooms, restaurant with excellent cooking serves many local dishes at mid-range to expensive prices, golf course, beautiful, tranquil during the week.
C Imperio del Sol, T06-2959794. Includes breakfast, mid-range restaurant, carpeted rooms and suites with views of the lake.
C Parador El Conquistador, T06-2953985. Large restaurant, meals at mid-range prices, comfortable carpeted rooms, disco Thu-Sat.

Ibarra to the Coast
D Bospas Farm, in El Limonal, about 800 m uphill from the main square, T06-2648692, www.ecuativer.com/bospas An organic fruit farm in a lovely setting. Three private rooms with a terrace and an attic dorm for 8 (cheaper), splendid views of the valley, includes breakfast, good inexpensive meals available, camping by the river, treks and horse riding trips on a choice of trails offered, salsa lessons, volunteer opportunities (minimum 1 month), Belgian-Ecuadorean run. Recommended.
D Hostería El Limonal, in El Limonal, by the square, T06-2648688. A popular place for a family outing with simple accommodation, restaurant, cold water, 3 pools, can get noisy on weekends, friendly and helpful.
D Hostería Martyzú, in El Limonal, on the highway at the entrance to town, T06-2648693. Restaurant, shared bath, cold water, pool, can get noisy on weekends.
F Residencial, in Lita, uphill from the unused train station. A basic residencial, shared bath, cold water, clean; sometimes there are water shortages in town.

Northwest of Ibarra
C-D Complejo Chachimbiro, at the thermal baths complex, also has an office in Otavalo (see Tour operators, p180), T06-2648133, chachimbiro@andinanet.net Cabins with private bath and jacuzzi, also cheaper cabins with shared bath, 2 restaurants, part of a recreational and spa complex.

❷ Eating

Ibarra *p182, map p183*

Local specialities include locally made walnut nougat (*nogadas*) and bottled blackberry syrup concentrate (*arrope de mora*); quality varies, ask to try a sample before you buy. The best selection of these, plus others such as guava jam, are to be found in the line of kiosks opposite the Basílica de la Merced. *Helados de paila* made in large copper basins (*pailas*), are available in many *heladerías* throughout the town.

There are many restaurants on Olmedo between Flores and Oviedo. The expensive restaurants at **Chorlaví** and **Ajaví** are recommended, but can be crowded with tour buses on Sat and Sun lunchtime.

Café Floralp, Av Teodoro Gómez 7-49 y Atahualpa. A variety of crêpes, fondue, good breakfast, bread, yoghurt, cold cuts, excellent coffee, good selection of Chilean wines, the 'in place' to meet and eat, Swiss-owned. Warmly recommended.

El Argentino, Sucre y P Moncayo, at Plazoleta Francisco Calderón, Tue-Sun. Good mixed grill and salads, a small pleasant restaurant, outdoor seating when the weather permits.

Gourmet de Luc, Olmedo 9-48, at Hotel Royal Ruiz. Slightly upscale restaurant, serves economical set lunches and à la carte.

Los Almendros, Velasco 5-59 y Sucre. Good set lunches and à la carte.

Mesón Colonial, Rocafuerte 5-53, at Parque Abdón Calderón, closed Sun. In a colonial house, extensive à la carte menu, good food and service.

Pizza El Horno, Rocafuerte 6-38 y Flores, Sat night, closed Mon. Good pizzas and Italian dishes, live music.

Casa Blanca, Bolívar 7-83, closed Sun. Excellent, family run, located in colonial house with seating around a central patio with fountain, delicious food.

Chifa Nueva, Olmedo 7-20. Reasonable Chinese food, large portions.

El Chagra, Olmedo 7-44. *Platos típicos*, good trout, recommended.

Pizzería Charlotte, Bolívar 4-07 y Grijalva, daily 1100-2300. Pizza and Italian dishes, in residential neighbourhood west of the centre, popular with locals.

Los Angeles, Sánchez y Cifuentes 7-35 next to the Iglesia de la Merced. Good set lunches.

Cafés

Antojitos de Mi Tierra, Sucre y P Moncayo, at Plazoleta Francisco Calderón, daily in the afternoon. Cafeteria with outdoor seating, serves local drinks and snacks such as *humitas*, *quimbolitos* and *tamales*.

Café Arte, Salinas 5-43 y Oviedo, daily 1700 until late. Café-bar serving drinks, Mexican snacks, sandwiches and some à la carte dishes.

Café Pushkin, Olmedo 7-75, opens 0730. A simple but traditional café for breakfast and afternoon tea, good bread.

Café-Coffee-Kafe, Rocafuerte 6-48 y Flores. Cafeteria serves drinks and snacks.

Ice cream parlours

There are several excellent *heladerías* serving *helados de paila*, home-made fruit sherbets, including:

Heladería Rosalía Suárez, Oviedo y Olmedo, an Ibarra tradition since 1896, very good, try the *mora* (raspberry) or *guanábana* (soursop) flavours. Highly recommended.

La Bermejita, at Olmedo 7-15.

There are several others at the corner of Olmedo y Flores, Parque La Merced.

Around Ibarra *p184*
Laguna Yahuarcocha

The hotels around the lake have restaurants. On weekends there are food stalls near the village of Yahuarcocha serving *tilapia*.

❶ Bars and clubs

Ibarra *p182, map p183*

At the corner of Bolívar and Oviedo are some cafés, bars and clubs, a popular place to hang out for local youth, especially Fri and Sat night.

Bar Buda, Sucre y Pedro Moncayo, at Plazoleta Francisco Calderón. Outdoor seating, a good place to meet a friend for a drink in the afternoon.

El Encuentro, Olmedo 9-59. Piano bar, interesting drinks, very popular, pleasant atmosphere, unusual decor.

El Zarape, on Circunvalación. *Peña* and Mexican restaurant.

Sambuca, Oviedo y Olmedo. Discotheque, young crowd.
Studio 54 at Laguna Yaguarcocha. Club.

❂ Festivals and events

Ibarra *p182, map p183*
28 Apr El Retorno celebrates the return of the people of Ibarra to their city after 4 years absence following the 1868 earthquake. There are music festivals, bullfights, parades and sporting events.
16 Jul Virgen del Carmen Many devout people celebrate this festival in honour of the Virgen del Carmen.
Sep Fiesta de los Lagos is held over the last weekend of Sep, Thu-Sun, to commemorate the foundation of Ibarra. It begins with *El Pregón*, a parade of floats through the city.

❂ Shopping

Ibarra *p182, map p183*
Supermarkets
Akí, Bolívar y Colón.
Supermaxi, south of the centre on Eugenio Espejo.
Supermercado El Rosado, Olmedo 9-46.

▲ Activities and tours

Ibarra *p182, map p183*
Paddle ball A unique form of paddle ball is played on Sat and Sun near the railway station and other parts of town; ask around for details. The players have huge spiked paddles for striking the 1 kg ball. On weekdays they play a similar game with a lighter ball.
    Paragliding is practised near Ibarra; enquire with Escuela de Vuelo Pichincha in Quito for local contacts, see p134.
    Swimming Balneario Primavera, Sánchez y Cifuentes 3-33.
    Tennis Ibarra Tennis Club, at Ciudad Jardín, T06-2950914.
    Turkish bath Heated pool, Turkish bath, also offers aerobics classes and remedial massage, for membership T06-2957425.

Tour operators
Intipungo, Rocafuerte 6-08 y Flores, T06-2957766, intiibr@interactive.net.ec Regional tours.

Metropolitan Touring, Flores 5-76 y Sucre, see Quito operators, p134.
Nevitur, Bolívar 7-35 y Oviedo, T06-2958701, F2640040. Excellent guides, vans for trips throughout the country.

❂ Transport

For main inter-city routes see the bus timetable, p52.

Ibarra *p182, map p183*
Bus **Quito**, frequent service by bus. Shared taxis with **Supertaxis Los Lagos** (in Quito at Asunción 3-81, T06-2565992; in Ibarra at Flores 924 y Sánchez Cifuentes, **(Parque La Merced**, T06-2955150) who will pick you up at your hotel (in the New City only), hourly Mon-Fri 0700-1900, Sat 0700-1600, Sun 0800-1800, 2½ hrs, US$7.50 per person, buy ticket at their office the day before travelling.
    Cotacachi, every 15 mins, US$0.45, 45 mins, some continue to **Quiroga**.
    Ambato, CITA goes via El Quinche and bypasses Quito, 5 daily, US$5, 5 hrs.
    Train Regular passenger service from Ibarra has been discontinued. For information on the tourist train see Train ride from Ibarra, p185 .

Around Ibarra *p182*
San Antonio de Ibarra
City buses from outside the Mercado Amazonas, US$0.18, taxi US$2.50.

Embroidery villages
Buses for **La Esperanza**, **Zuleta**, **Olmedo** and **Cayambe** leave from Parque Germán Grijalva in Ibarra (east of the Terminal Terrestre, follow C Sánchez y Cifuentes, south from the centre). To **La Esperanza**, every 30 mins, US$0.25, 30 mins.
    Not all buses continue to **Zuleta** and beyond, only 2 daily go as far as **Cayambe** along this route. For faster service to **Cayambe** take a Quito-bound bus from the terminal, check that it goes via Cayambe not Tabacundo.
    A taxi from Ibarra to **La Esperanza** is US$4-5.

Laguna Yahuarcocha
City buses run from Ibarra.

Several companies leave from the Terminal Terrestre in Ibarra. Some go all the way to **San Lorenzo**, US$4, 3 hrs; others only as far as **Lita**, US$3.50, 2 hrs. From San Lorenzo there is a service south along the coast to **Esmeraldas**.

Northwest of Ibarra

Urcuquí, Cooperativa Urcuquí from the Terminal Terrestre in Ibarra, every 20 mins, US$0.50, 30 mins.

Chachimbiro, Cooperativa Urcuquí from the Terminal Terrestre in Ibarra, at 0730 and 1200, returning at 1230 and 1500, US$1.25, 1½ hrs.

● Directory

Ibarra p182, map p183
Banks Banco del Pacífico, Olmedo y P Moncayo. Banco del Austro, Colón 7-51.

Banco del Pichincha, Bolívar y Mosquera.
Hospital Clínica Médica del Norte, Oviedo 8-24, T2955099. Open 24 hrs. **Internet** Several in the centre, prices around US$1 per hr. **Language schools** Centro Ecuatoriano Canadiense de Idiomas (CECI), Pérez Guerrero 6-12 y Bolívar, T2951911, US$3.50 per hr. CIMA, Obelisco Casa No 2, p 2. **Post office** Flores opposite Parque Pedro Moncayo, p 2. **Useful addresses** Immigration, Olmedo y LF Villamar, T06-2951712.

Around Ibarra p184
Language schools In La Esperanza, at the local high school, Sr Orlando Lanchimba Guzmán has been recommended for Spanish lessons. He can only teach 1 hr per day so you need plenty of time. While there, you can also teach English in the school.

North to Colombia

To the north of Ibarra is a land of striking contrasts. Deep eroded canyons and warm subtropical valleys stand side by side with wind-swept páramos and potato fields. The highlight of this area is Reserva Ecológica El Angel, home of the largest stand of frailejones (large velvety leaved plants) in Ecuador. The main city in the region is Tulcán, about 5 km south of the Colombian border. ▸▸ *For Sleeping, Eating and other listings, see pages 196-198.*

Ins and outs → See Transport, page 197, for further details

Getting there

North of Ibarra, the Panamericana goes past Laguna Yahuarcocha and the turn-off to San Lorenzo before descending to the hot dry Chota valley. About 30 km north of Ibarra, at Mascarilla, is a police checkpoint (have your documents at hand), after which the highway divides.

One branch follows an older route northeast through Mira and El Angel to Tulcán on the Colombian border. This road is paved and in good condition as far as El Angel, but deteriorates rapidly thereafter. The El Angel-Tulcán section is unpaved and in very poor condition but the scenery is beautiful. It is often impassable beyond Laguna El Voladero. The second branch, the modern toll Panamericana, is in excellent shape but with many heavy lorries, runs east through the Chota valley to Juncal, before turning north to reach Tulcán via Bolívar and San Gabriel. A good paved road runs between Bolívar and El Angel, connecting the two branches. A second lateral road, between San Gabriel and El Angel, requires a four-wheel drive vehicle and is often impassable during the rainy season.

From Julio Andrade, south of Tulcán, a secondary road goes east to La Bonita, Lumbaquí and Lago Agrio in the jungle. From Tulcán another secondary road goes west to Tufiño, Maldonado and Chical. Both these routes run near the Colombian border.

In Tulcán, the airport is north along the road to the border. There are flights from Quito and Cali (Colombia). The Terminal Terrestre is 1½ km from the centre. There is frequent service from Quito and points in between. From the border there are minivans, shared taxis and taxis.

Information

Unidad Municipal de Turismo, Tulcán, at the entrance to the cemetery T2985760. Helpful, Some English, Mon-Fri 0800-1300, 1500-1800. A second municipal information office is due to open by mid 2005 at Rumichaca, the old stone bridge across the border. The **Ministerio de Turismo** has an information office at the border, open Mon-Fri 0830-1700.

Safety Tulcán and the traditionally tranquil border province of Carchi have seen an increase in tension due to drug trafficking and the *guerrilla* conflict in neighbouring Colombia. Do not travel outside town (except along the Panamericana) without enquiring in advance about current conditions. It is also prudent not to wander about late at night. The area around the bus terminal in Tulcán is unsafe.

Valle del Chota and Pimampiro

→ *Phone code 06 Colour map 2, grid B5*

The lush, sugarcane growing valley of the Río Chota lies at an altitude of 1700 m, to the north of Ibarra. It is an important centre of the Afro-Ecuadorean culture, with 38 communities in the valleys of the Chota and Mira rivers. The region has many tourist complexes, popular with vacationing Colombians and Ecuadoreans who come down from the highlands for the warmer temperatures and *sabor tropical*.

Ceramic masks and figurines are made in the villages of **Mascarilla**, where the road divides, and in **Carpuela**, further east. The crafts are sold in community shops right along the Panamericana. A couple kilometres east of Mascarilla is the **Honka Monka museum of Afro-Ecuadorean culture.** Off the Panamericana near Carpuela is the larger village of **Ambuquí** around which the resorts are located (see Sleeping, page 196). Just beyond is **El Juncal**, the turn-off east to Pimampiro, after which the highway turns north to cross the Río Chota into the province of Carchi and begins its steep climb out of the valley.

The quiet town of **Pimampiro**, the centre of a bean-producing area, lies 8 km off the Panamericana along a paved road. The surrounding countryside offers excellent walking. There is a Sunday market. South of Pimampiro is the town of **Mariano Acosta**, beyond which is **Nueva América** ⓘ *several days advance notice are required for all services from Nueva América, call the Unidad de Medio Ambiente, Municipio de Pimampiro, T06-2937117 (ext 16)*, a small community at 3,400 m which has developed a tourism project. They have a house for visitors (US$6 per person, take a warm sleeping bag), can provide meals, and guides. The scenery along the route to town is very nice and views of Cayambe once you get there are magnificent. Near town is the 502-ha Bosque Nueva América, a cloud forest reserve with trails. The community also runs a medicinal plants project.

Nueva América is along one of the access routes to **Laguna Puruhanta**, a magnificent lake surrounded by forest, popular with fishermen. It is part of **Reserva Ecológica Cayambe-Coca** (see also page 163). The walk to the lake along the Río Pisque is very nice but quite demanding; weather conditions can be harsh and the trail muddy, there are a couple of river crossings on single log bridges. Allow three or more days for the excursion and take a tent, sleeping bag, warm waterproof clothing, food, stove and fuel. Further information on this walk can be found in www.trekkinginecuador.com In Nueva América you can hire a guide and pack animals, although the latter can only go part of the way.

El Angel and around → *Phone code 06 Colour map 2, grid B5*

The westernmost of the two routes going north towards Tulcán climbs steeply from Mascarilla, 16 km to the town of **Mira** (population 2,900). Some of the finest quality woollens come from this part of the country and are sold for export in Otavalo. Locally you can find them up the hill opposite the bus stop.

Beyond Mira, 18 km to the northeast, is **El Angel** (population 4,400, altitude 3,000 m), a sleepy highland town that comes to life during its Monday market. It is the birthplace of José Franco, designer of the famous topiary in the Tulcán cemetery, and the main plaza retains a few trees that were originally sculpted by him. The shops in town are well stocked.

About 3 km south of El Angel, along the road to Mira, is the turn-off for the thermal baths of **La Calera**. From here a steep but good cobbled road descends for 6½ km into a lovely valley to the baths themselves, with good views along the way. There are two pools with warm water in pleasant surroundings, admission US$0.50. The baths are deserted during the week, when only the smaller pool is filled. There is no public transport; hire a taxi from El Angel, US$4 one way. The baths are crowded with locals on weekends and holidays, when transport costs US$0.50 per person. With a sleeping bag it is possible to stay the night in the main building, but take food.

To the northwest of El Angel, beyond the **Reserva Ecológica El Angel** (see below) lies the valley of the Río Morán, a lovely cloud forest region descending towards the coast. Here is the **Cotinga Lodge**, a good place for birdwatching (contact through **Hostería El Angel**, see page 196). Beyond the Morán valley, in the forested hills towards the Mira valley, is the **Cerro Golondrinas Cloudforest** ① *further information from La Casa de Eliza in Quito, T02-2226602*, which can also be accessed along a road starting in Guallupe, off the main road from Ibarra to the coast.

Reserva Ecológica El Angel → *Colour map 2, grid B5*
① *The Ministerio del Ambiente's park office is at the Municipio, T/F06-2977597. Information and pamphlets are available. Park entry fee US$10.*
El Angel is the main access point for this reserve, created in 1992 to protect 15,715 ha of *páramo* ranging in altitude from 3,400 to 4,768 m. The reserve contains the southernmost large stands of the velvet-leaved *frailejón* plant, *Espeletia hartwegiana*, also found in the Andes of Colombia and Venezuela. Also here are the spiny *achupallas* with giant compound flowers, related to the *Puya Raymondi* of Peru and Bolivia. The wildlife includes *curiquingues* (birds of prey), deer, foxes, and a few condors. There are several small lakes in the reserve. It can be muddy during the rainy season; the best time to visit is May to August. The north side of the reserve can also be accessed, going west from Tufiño, along the Tulcán-Chical road. Here are the Lagunas Verdes and Volcán Chiles sectors. These areas are near the Colombian border and are not safe.

The closest place to admire the interesting *frailejón* plants is **El Voladero**, following the poor, direct road between El Angel and Tulcán for 16 km. Here is a ranger station from where a self-guided trail climbs over a low ridge (30 minutes' walk) to two crystal clear lakes. Camping is possible, but you must be self-sufficient and take great care not to damage the fragile *páramo* surroundings. Pick-ups/taxis can be hired in the main plaza of El Angel for a day trip to El Voladero; US$15 return with short wait.

The centre of the park is reached along a longer and equally poor road. It starts in the town of **La Libertad**, 3½ km north of El Angel, from where it climbs gradually to reach the high *páramo* and, in one hour, the **El Salado** ranger station. Another hour ahead is **Cerro Socabones**, from where you can trek or take pack animals to the village of **Morán** (local guide Hugo Quintanchala can take you further through the valley). Many paths criss-cross the *páramo* and it is easy to get lost. Transport from El Angel to Cerro Socabones, US$25 return. A helpful driver is Sr Calderón, T06-2977274.

San Gabriel and around → *Phone code 06   Colour map 2, grid B5-B6*

To the north of the Valle del Chota the Panamericana climbs to an agricultural area rich in potatoes and cattle ranching. Seventeen kilometres north of El Juncal is **Bolívar** (population 4,400), a neat little town with houses and the interior of its church painted in lively pastel colours, a well kept plaza and a Friday market.

About 5 km north of Bolívar is the turn-off east for the town of La Paz, from which a steep but good cobbled road descends for 5 km to the **Gruta de La Paz**. Views along the road are breathtaking, including two spectacular waterfalls. The place is also called *Rumichaca* (Quichua for stone bridge) after the massive natural bridge which forms the *gruta* (grotto) – not to be confused with the Rumichaca on the Colombian border. The entire area is a religious shrine, receiving large numbers of pilgrims during Holy Week, Christmas, and especially around 8 July, feast day of the Virgen de La Paz. In addition to the chapel in the grotto itself, there is a large basilica, a Franciscan convent, a guest house for pilgrims, a restaurant and shops selling religious articles. These are open on weekends and pilgrimage days only; there are very few visitors at other times. It is possible to camp for free opposite the convent. The river which emerges from the grotto is rather polluted, and the sewer smell detracts from its otherwise great natural beauty. A second, signposted access road to La Paz goes from the Panamericana, 3 km south of San Gabriel.

There are clean **thermal baths** ① *Wed-Sun (crowded at weekends), US$0.50, showers US$0.25*, (showers and one pool) just below the grotto. Look for the caretaker if the gate to the pool is locked. Several scenic trails through the valley start from behind the hotel.

About 10 km north of La Paz is **San Gabriel** (population 12,600), an important commercial centre. The spectacular 60-m high **Paluz** waterfall is 4 km north of town, beyond another smaller waterfall. Follow Calle Bolívar out of the main plaza and turn right after the bridge. It's well worth the walk. There is a rather chilly 'thermal' bath along the way.

About 20 km east of San Gabriel along a secondary road is the tiny community of **Mariscal Sucre**, also known as Colonia Huaqueña, which has no tourist facilities but is very hospitable. It can be reached by taxi from San Gabriel in one hour; sometimes shared four-wheel drive vehicles also go there, which are a cheaper option. This is the gateway to the **Guandera Reserve and Biological Station**, part of the Jatun Sacha Foundation's system of reserves. It includes over 1,000 ha of *frailejón páramo* and twisted mossy temperate forest. There are rare birds like the chestnut-bellied Cotinga and crescent-faced Antpitta and many orchids. There is a C guest house 30 minutes' walk from Mariscal Sucre. It is very cold at night so bring warm clothes. Reservations and further information about visits and volunteer programmes from Jatun Sacha Foundation in Quito (see Volunteer programmes, page 83).

Fifteen kilometres north of San Gabriel are the villages of Huaca and Julio Andrade, from where the roads to **El Carmelo** and **La Bonita** start. The former is a back way for contraband into Colombia, the latter is in a nice subtropical area, on the new road into Sucumbíos province, which connects with the Baeza-Lago Agrio road at Lumbaquí; very scenic. This road parallels the border, enquire about public safety before going on these roads (see Dangerous areas, page 48).

Tulcán and around

→ *Phone code 06   Colour map 2, grid A6   Population 47,100   Altitude 2,960 m*

The El Angel road and the Panamericana join at Las Juntas, 2 km south of Tulcán, a commercial centre and capital of the province of Carchi. It is always chilly. To the east of the city is a bypass road going directly to the Colombian border. There is a great deal of informal trade here with Colombia, and a textile and dry goods fair takes place on Thursday and Sunday.

Tulcán is a long city. You can walk between the Plaza de la Independencia and Parque Ayora, and from the latter to the cemetery, but the bus terminal is best reached by taxi or city bus. Inter-city buses depart from the Terminal Terrestre, while regional service goes from different points in town.

Ins and outs

Unidad Municipal de Turismo ① *at the entrance to the cemetery, T06-2985760. Helpful, some English, Mon-Fri 0800-1300, 1500-1800.* A second municipal information office is due to open by mid 2005 at Rumichaca, the old stone bridge across the border. **Ministerio de Turismo** ① *information office at the border, open Mon-Fri 0830-1700.*

Safety Tulcán and the traditionally tranquil border province of Carchi have seen an increase in tension due to drug trafficking and the *guerrilla* conflict in neighbouring Colombia. Do not travel outside town (except along the Panamericana) without enquiring in advance about current conditions. It is also prudent not to wander about late at night. The area around the bus terminal in Tulcán is unsafe.

Sights

The centre stretches along Calle Sucre which goes by the main square, **Parque La Independencia**, and along Calle Bolívar, one block west. The bus terminal is some distance to the south, and transport to the border leaves from **Parque Ayora**, five blocks north of the main square. Parque Ayora has an amazing cantilevered statue of Abdón Calderón and his horse leaping into mid-air.

Two blocks away is the **cemetery**, where the art of topiary is taken to incredible, beautiful extremes. Cypress bushes are trimmed into archways and fantastic figures of animals, angels,

Tulcán

0 metres 100
0 yards 100

Sleeping 🛏
Colombia 1
Florida 2
Lumar 4
Machado 5
Lucero Princess 6
Sáenz Internacional 7
Sara Espíndola 8
Torres de Oro 9

Eating 🍴
Antojitos Express 1
Café Tulcán 2
Chifa Pak Choy 8
El Patio 3
Los Leños 6
Mama Rosita 7
Tequila 4
Wimpy 5

geometric shapes and so on, in *haut* and *bas* relief. Note the figures based on the stone carvings at San Agustín in Colombia, to the left just past the main entrance. To see the various stages of this art form, go to the back of the cemetery where young bushes are being pruned. The artistry, started in 1936, is that of the late Sr José Franco, now buried among the splendour he created. His epitaph reads: 'In Tulcán, a cemetery so beautiful that it invites one to die!' The tradition is carried on by his sons. At the entrance to the cemetery are a crafts exhibition hall and information centre.

West of Tulcán → *Phone code 06*

To the west of Tulcán, along the Colombian border, lies a scenic area of rivers and waterfalls, followed by *páramos* with geothermal activity at the foot of Volcán Chiles and further on tropical lowlands. This is also the access to the northern section of Reserva Ecológica El Angel. It is a rough secondary road with military checkpoints. **Tufiño**, just on the border is 18 km from Tulcán; **Maldonado**, already in a subtropical area descending to the coast, is 57 km further west and **Chical**, at the end of the road, is 12 km beyond.

> ❗ *Warning Travel along the Tulcán-Maldonado road is not recommended due to its proximity to the Colombian border.*

By far the best hot springs of the region are **Aguas Hediondas** (stinking waters), a complex of indoor and outdoor pools fed by a stream of boiling sulphurous mineral water in an impressive valley. The baths are deserted on weekdays. Camping is possible but bring all gear and food. From the baths there is a path that goes towards Volcán Chiles, condors can sometimes be seen hovering above the high cliffs surrounding the valley. To reach Aguas Hediondas follow the winding road 3 km west of Tufiño, to where a rusting white sign marks the turn-off to the right. From here it is 8 km through strange scenery to the magnificent natural hot river.

> ❗ *Warning The area around the source is walled off because of extremely dangerous sulphur fumes (deaths have occured in the past), never attempt to enter.*

Past the turn-off for Aguas Hediondas the road climbs to the *páramo* on the southern slopes of **Volcán Chiles**, its summit is the border with Colombia. The volcano can be climbed in about six hours, but this border area is unsafe. To the south, also within the Reserva Ecológica El Angel, are the Lagunas Verdes (see page 192). The road then begins its long descent to Maldonado and Chical; see safety warnings above.

Border with Colombia

The border crossing to Colombia is at **Rumichaca** (stone bridge in Quichua), just north of Tulcán. A concrete bridge spans the Río Carchi and border facilities are at either side of it. Just west of the modern bridge is the original *rumichaca*, a natural stone bridge. The old building which sits on the bridge is being refurbished and will house a museum, a tourist information office and other facilities.

> ❗ *Money changers on both sides of the border will exchange cash Pesos for US$.*

The border is open 24 hours for pedestrians, but vehicles can only cross 0600-2200. On the Ecuadorean side, immigration and customs (for car papers) are in the same building. There is also an **Andinatel** office for phone calls, a **tourist information office** ⓘ *Mon-Fri 0830-1700*, with maps and general information and a snack bar. It's a short walk across the bridge from the Ecuadorean side to the Colombian side. **Note** You are not allowed to cross to Ipiales for the day without having your passport stamped. Both Ecuadorean exit stamp and Colombian entry stamp are required.

On the Colombian side there is an organized complex. Here are the **DAS** (immigration), customs, **INTRA** (Dept of Transportation, car papers stamped here) and **ICA** (Department of Agriculture). There is the **Ecuadorean Consulate** ⓘ *Mon-Fri 0830-1200, 1430-1800*, a Telecom office for phone calls, a restaurant and clean bathrooms.

About 2 km from Rumichaca is the Colombian town of **Ipiales**, 'the city of the three volcanoes'. It has an Indian market every Friday morning. There is a good selection of hotels and frequent transport links by air and road to other cities in Colombia. About 7 km east of Ipiales is the famous Sanctuary and pilgrimage centre of **Las Lajas,** on a bridge over the Río Guáitara, which is definitely worth a visit for its architecture and setting. For more details see *Footprint Colombia* or the *South American Handbook.*

● Sleeping

Valle del Chota and Pimampiro *p191*
L-A Hostería Oasis, Panamericana Norte, Km 39, T/F06-2941200, roasis@uio.satnet.net A resort with cabins for up to 5 and mini-cabins for 2 (standard and suites). Includes 3 meals, tour and use of all recreational facilities, facilities include 3 large pools (one is a wave pool).
B Hostería Aruba, Panamericana Norte, Km 39, T06-2941146. Modern cabins, restaurant, small pool, parking, waterslide, playground, several snack bars, disco, good.
B Hostería El Kibutz, Panamericana Norte, Km 37, T06-2942340. Comfortable cabins for up to 5 with fridge, pool, parking, smaller and more relaxed than some of the other *hosterías*.
E Residencial, in Pimampiro, on C Flores, has no sign, ask for the Hurtado family. A basic, friendly family-run hostel, poor water supply.

El Angel and around *p192*
C Hostería El Angel, at the entrance to El Angel, T/F06-2977584, www.ecuador-sommerfer.com A pleasant inn which caters to groups, includes breakfast, meals available on request, parking, reservations required, contact Quito T/F02-2221480. Offers trips into reserve.
E Los Faroles, José Grijalva 5-96 on the plaza, T06-2977144. Simple rooms in family home, restaurant downstairs, shared bath, hot water.
F Residencial Mira, in Mira, 1 block from the park, behind Municipio, T06-2280228. Basic, clean residencial, good beds, shared bath.

San Gabriel and around *p193*
D Casa de los Abonos, Mejía y Los Andes, above the agricultural supply shop , T06-2291832. Modern, clean, best in town. Includes breakfast.

F-G Residencial Ideal, Montúfar 08-26, T06-2290265. Cheaper with shared bath, electric shower, basic.

Tulcán and around *p193, map p194*
There are many hotels along C Sucre.
B Sara Espíndola, Sucre y Ayacucho, on plaza, T06-2985925, F2986209. Includes breakfast, nice restaurant, parking, comfortable rooms, helpful staff, best in town.
C Machado, Bolívar y Ayacucho, T06-2984221, F2980099. Includes breakfast, parking, comfortable.
D Lumar, Sucre y Rocafuerte, T06-2980402. Modern, clean and comfortable.
D Torres de Oro, Sucre y Rocafuerte, T06-2980296. Includes breakfast, restaurant, parking, modern, clean and nice.
E Los Alpes, JR Arellano next to bus station, T06-2982235. Restaurant, private bath, hot water, adequate, good value.
E Sáenz Internacional, Sucre y Rocafuerte, T06-2981916. Private bath, hot water, very nice and modern. Good value, recommended.
E-F Florida, Sucre y 10 de Agosto, T06-2983849. Cheaper with shared bath, hot water, modern section at back, good value.
F Colombia, Colón 52-017 y Ayacucho, T06-2982761. Shared bath, hot water, parking, clean and simple.

● Eating

Valle del Chota and Pimampiro *p191*
Many of the resorts in the area welcome non-guests to their restaurants and offer day-passes for the use of the facilities.
† **El Forastero**, In Pimampiro, Flores y Olmedo, esquina. Good set meals.

El Angel and around *p192*
†† **Asadero Los Faroles**, Downstairs from the hotel. Roast chicken and trout, plus

set meals. There are several other chicken places in El Angel. There are very few restaurants in Mira.

Tulcán and around *p193, map p194*
There are several *chifas* and many cheap chicken places in town.
🍴 Hotel Sara Espíndola, At the hotel. Set meals and à la carte, fanciest option in town.
🍴 Antojitos Express, Olmedo y Ayacucho, next door to Hotel Sara Espíndola. Set meals.
🍴 Café Tulcán, Sucre 52-029 y Ayacucho. Good coffee, desserts, snacks and juices.
🍴 El Patio, Bolívar 50-050 y 10 de Agosto. Colombian specialities.
🍴 Los Leños, Olmedo y Ayacucho. Set meals and à la carte.
🍴 Mama Rosita, Sucre entre Boyacá y Atahualpa. Ecuadorian *comida típica*.
🍴 Tequila, Sucre entre Junín y Boyacá. Varied à la carte menu.
🍴 Chifa Pak Choy, Sucre y Pichincha. Chinese.

⊙ Shopping

Tulcán and around *p193, map p194*
Handicrafts
At the entrance to the cemetery there is a crafts exhibition hall and shop.

⊙ Transport

For main inter-city routes see the bus timetable, p52.

Valle del Chota and Pimampiro *p191*
From **Ibarra**, Cooperativa Oriental departs the Terminal Terrestre, every 20 mins, goes through the Valle del Chota to **Pimampiro**, US$1, 1¼ hrs; to **Ambuquí** US$0.80, 45 mins. Tulcán-bound buses also go through the Valle del Chota.

For **Nueva América**, there are buses and pick-ups from Pimampiro to Mariano Acosta, US$0.50, 1½ hrs. In Mariano Acosta you can hire a pick-up to Nueva América, US$6-8, 45 mins, or walk 2½ hrs uphill, ask for the path out of Mariano Acosta. You can also hire a pick-up from Pimampiro to Nueva América.

El Angel and around *p192*
From **Ibarra** Terminal Terrestre to **Mira**, every 30 mins, US$0.90, 1 hr; to **El Angel**, hourly, US$1.30, 1½ hrs. From El Angel to **Mira**, every 30 mins, US$.50, 20 mins. From El Angel to **Tulcán**, US$1.30, 1½ hrs. From El Angel to **Quito**, US$4, 4 hrs.

San Gabriel and around *p193*
From San Gabriel to **Tulcán**, vans and jeeps US$0.60, shared taxis US$0.80, 30 mins, all from the main plaza. To **Ibarra**, buses, US$1.65, 2 hrs. To **Quito**, buses, US$3.50, 3½ hrs. For **La Paz**, public transport from Tulcán and San Gabriel on weekends only; you must hire a taxi at other times.

Tulcán and around *p193, map p194*
Air
TAME, Sucre y Ayacucho, T06-2980675, flies Mon, Wed and Fri to **Quito**, US$36, and to **Cali**, Colombia, US$78, comfirm schedules and prices in advance. The airport is on the road to Rumichaca, the Colombian border, taxi to the airport US$1.50.

Bus
The *Terminal Terrestre* is 1½ km uphill, south of the centre. It's best to take a taxi US$1 from Parque Ayora. There is frequent service to **Quito** and all destinations along the way and also to **Guayaquil**.
To **Huaquillas**, on the Peruvian border, with **Panamericana Internacional**, 1 luxury coach a day, US$20, 17-18 hrs; with **Trans Gacela** US$18. To **Lago Agrio**, 2 daily.

West of Tulcán
Buses going west from Tulcán leave from opposite the Colegio Nacional Tulcán on Calle Sierra. **Tufiño** every 2 hrs, US$0.80, 45 mins; last bus back at 1700.
Maldonado and **Chical** at noon, returning early the next morning, US$4, 5 hrs. Note safety warnings for this area.

Border with Colombia *p195*
Tulcán to **Rumichaca**, minivans and shared taxis leave when full from Parque Ayora near the cemetery, 15 mins, US$0.80. A taxi from anywhere in Tulcán to the border costs

Northern Highlands North to Colombia *Listings*

🔵 *For an explanation of the Sleeping and Eating price codes used in this guide, see the*
⚫ *inside front cover. Other relevant information is provided in Essentials, pages 58-64.*

US$4. A taxi from the bus terminal to Parque Ayora, US$1, there are also city buses from the terminal to Parque Ayora, but these may be too crowded for luggage. **Note** These vehicles will take you across the international bridge to the Colombian complex. Be sure to walk back to the Ecuadorean side to get your passport stamped.

Rumichaca to **Ipiales**, colectivos from the border take you to C14, Cra 11, US$0.40. Taxi Rumichaca to the centre US$2.50. Taxi Rumichaca to Ipiales airport US$6.50.

● Directory

Tulcán *p193, map p194*
Banks Banco del Austro, Bolívar y Ayacucho. **Banco del Pichincha**, at Plaza de la Independencia. Few places accept credit cards. There is nowhere in Tulcán to change TCs. Street changers at Parque La Independencia deal in Colombian Pesos. **Internet** Many in town, US$1. **Post office** Bolívar 53-27. **Useful addresses** **Colombian Consulate**, Bolívar 368 y Junín, T06-2987302, visas require up to 20 days, Mon-Fri 0800-1300, 1430-1530.

Central Highlands

⁝ Footprint features

Introduction

South of Quito is some of the loveliest mountain scenery in Ecuador. This part of the country was named the 'Avenue of the Volcanoes' by the German explorer, Alexander Von Humboldt, and it is easy to see why. An impressive roll call of towering peaks lines the route south: Cotopaxi, the Ilinizas, Carihuayrazo and Chimborazo, to name but a few. This area obviously attracts its fair share of trekkers and climbers, while the less active tourist can browse through the many colourful Indian markets and colonial towns that nestle among the high volcanic cones.

After you've explored the mountains to your heart's delight, rest up and pamper yourself at Baños, named and famed for its thermal baths. Its spa is popular with tourists and Ecuadoreans alike, situated on the main road from the Central Highlands to the Oriente jungle. It is also the base for activities ranging from mountain biking to café lounging, and Ecuador's special attraction: volcano watching.

⚡ Don't miss...

1 **Cotopaxi** Climb one of the world's highest active volcanoes, page 203.

2 **Quilotoa Circuit** Hike from inn to inn along this popular walking route, page 210.

3 **Mariane** Visit this Baños eatery to savour its authentic Provençal cuisine, page 237.

4 **The Devil's Nose** Take the train along the popular high-altitude route from Riobamba to Sibambe, page 245.

5 **Parque Nacional Sangay** Do some serious trekking among volcanic peaks and magnificent scenery, page 248.

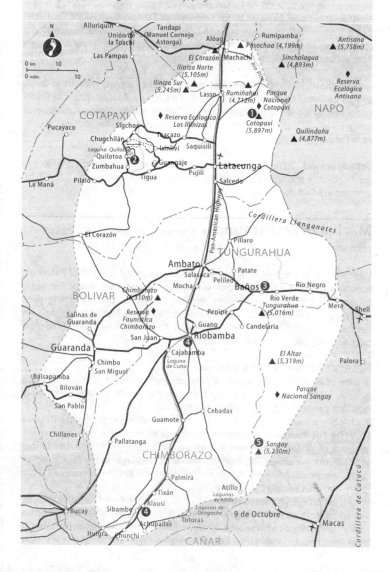

Central Highlands

Quito to Latacunga

South of Quito is a rich cattle ranching area, the home of the chagra, *Ecuador's cowboy. Several haciendas offer lodging for visitors who are interested in experiencing farm life. It is a very scenic area dotted with volcanic peaks, well suited to walking and horse riding. Those aiming higher can experience the thrill of climbing one of the peaks of Ilinizas or the perfect cone of Cotopaxi.* ➤➤ *For Sleeping, Eating and other listings, see page 205-207.*

Ins and outs

The Panamericana climbs gradually out of the Quito basin. At Tambillo, a road emerges from the Valle de los Chillos and joins the main highway. At Alóag, a road heads west to Santo Domingo de los Colorados and the northern Pacific Lowlands; this is the country's main link between coast and mountains. The Panamericana continues south through the Machachi valley from where it climbs along the western flank of Cotopaxi before descending to Latacunga.

Getting there Machachi is served by buses from the Terminal Terrestre in Quito, as well as from El Recreo to the south of the Old City. Tour operators in Quito, Latacunga, Baños and Riobamba do tours to Parque Nacioanl Cotopaxi and Reserva Ecológica Los Ilinizas. You can also hire a pick-up truck from Machachi or Lasso to go to the parks.

Getting around There is frequent transport between towns, however it is difficult to get transport to return from the parks or to go from one to another, so it has to be arranged in advance.

Machachi and around → *Phone code 02 Colour map 4, grid A6 Population 12,500 Altitude 2,900 m*

Machachi lies in a cattle-raising valley nestled between the summits of Pasochoa, Rumiñahui and Corazón, with good views from its pleasant *parque central*. The area is famous for its mineral water springs and icy cold, crystal clear **swimming pool**. ① *0800-1530 daily.* The water, 'Agua Güitig' or 'Tesalia', is bottled in a plant 4 km from the town and sold throughout the country. Free, self-guided tours of the plant can be taken 0800-1200 (take identification).

Reserva Ecológica Los Ilinizas

① *Entry US$5. Refugio, the shelter, is fully equipped with beds for 12 and cooking facilities, take a mat and sleeping bag because it fills quickly, US$8 per person per night (the caretaker locks the shelter when he is out).*

Machachi is a good starting point for a visit to the northern section of the **Reserva Ecológica Los Ilinizas**, a 150,000-ha nature reserve created in 1996 to preserve remnants of western slope forest and *páramo*. It includes El Corazón, Los Ilinizas and Quilotoa volcanoes. The area is suitable for trekking and the twin peaks of Iliniza are popular among climbers. The southern section is reached from Latacunga, see Quilotoa Circuit (page 210).

Access is through a turn-off west of the Panamericana, 6 km south of Machachi, from where it is 7 km to the village of El Chaupi. A dirt road continues from here to 'La Virgen' (statue) about 9 km beyond. Nearby are some woods where you can camp. It takes three hours to walk with a full pack from 'La Virgen' to the *refugio*, a shelter below the saddle between the two peaks, at 4,750 m. Depending on road conditions, a 4WD vehicle may be able to go beyond 'La Virgen'. To walk from El Chaupi to the *refugio* takes 7-8 hours.

Climbing Los Ilinizas → *Colour map 4, grid A6*

Iliniza Norte (5,105 m), although not a technical climb, should not be underestimated, a few exposed rocky sections require utmost caution. Some climbers suggest using a rope and a helmet is recommended if other parties are there because of falling rock. Allow two to four hours for the ascent from the refuge, and take a compass as it's easy to mistake the descent. Iliniza Sur (5,245 m) is a four-hour ice climb. There are some steep, technical sections on this route, especially a 50-65° 400-m ice slope, and full climbing gear and experience are absolutely necessary. Note that because of deglaciation the climb is increasingly difficult. Also see Climbing, page 71.

Parque Nacional Cotopaxi

The beautiful snow-capped cone of **Volcán Cotopaxi** (5,897 m) is at the heart of this lovely national park and is one of the prime tourist destinations in the country. If you only climb one of Ecuador's many volcanoes, then this should be the one. Many agencies run tours here. A good map of the park, *Mapa Ecoturístico del Volcán Cotopaxi*, is published by the IGM, see page 58. Note that Cotopaxi is an active volcano; its activity is monitored by the **National Geophysics Institute**, see www.igepn.edu.ec

Ins and outs

There are four access points to Parque Nacional Cotopaxi. The **main** access is 25 km south of Machachi and 6 km north of Lasso, along the Panamericana, and is marked by a Parque Nacional Cotopaxi sign. Turn east off the Panamericana at the sign; nearly 1 km beyond, turn left at a T-junction and a few hundred metres later turn sharp right. Beyond this the road is either signed or you take the El Boliche route. This is the main entrance and it is quicker and easier to follow than the El Boliche route. It leads first to the park gate, then climbs to a small museum and on to the plateau and lake of Limpio Pungo. Past Limpio Pungo the road deteriorates and a branch right climbs steeply to a car park at 4,600 m, from where a trail continues to the mountain shelter at 4,800 m. Walking from the Panamericana to the refuge takes an entire day or more.

The **El Boliche** access, 16 km south of Machachi along the Panamericana, starts at a sign for the Clirsen satellite tracking station, which is not open to the public. This route goes past Clirsen and the old Cotopaxi railway station, then via **Area Nacional de Recreación El Boliche**. There is a shared entry fee for El Boliche and Cotopaxi; you should only pay once, but enquire beforehand on site. Follow the route for over 30 km along a signposted dirt road to reach the museum and Limpio Pungo plateau.

The **Pedregal** access is from the north. Cyclists should consider this approach, rather than the main access, because the latter route is too soft to climb on a bike. From Machachi it is 13 km on a cobbled road, then 2 km of sand to Santa Ana del Pedregal. A further 5 km of sand leads to the northern park entrance, then it is 15 km to the car park for the *refugio*. The last 7 km are steep and soft. The descent cycling takes 1½ hrs, as opposed to 7 hrs going up. Quito operators run bicycling tours here.

The **Ticatilín** access approaches Cotopaxi from the south. From the Panamericana, 1 km north of Lasso, at a spot known as Aglomerados Cotopaxi (the northern access to Sangolquí) a road goes to the village of San Ramón and on to the community of Ticatilín where a contribution is expected for them to open the chain at the access point (US$1-2 per vehicle depending on the number of occupants). If coming from the south, San Ramón is accessed from Mulaló. It leads to a less impacted *páramo* and the private Albergue Cotopaxi Cara Sur. Walking four hours from here you reach Campo Alto, a tent camp used by climbers.

Attractions and park services

ⓘ *Visitors must register at the main gate, entry US$10, gates 0700-1500, although you can stay until 1800.*

The park administration and a small museum are located 10 km from the park gates, just before the plateau of Laguna Limpio Pungo. The **Museo Mariscal Sucre** ⓘ *0800-1200 and 1300-1700*, has a 3D model of the park, interesting displays about Cotopaxi's volcanic activity and stuffed animals. By the museum is a restaurant serving Ecuadorean food, open weekends and holidays.

The **Limpio Pungo** plateau (3,850 m) with a shallow lake sits between Cotopaxi and **Volcán Rumiñahui** (4,712 m) to the northwest. It is a lovely spot from which to observe Cotopaxi and a place to learn about the *páramo* flora and fauna. The hills at the base of Rumiñahui are excellent for birdwatching and it is possible to see several species peculiar to the *páramo*. On the plains watch out for herds of wild horses, and the odd mountain lion or wild bull. This is a very nice area for walking. Just north of Cotopaxi are the peaks of **Sincholagua** (4,893 m) and **Pasochoa** (4,225 m). To the southeast is the beautiful and elusive **Quilindaña** (4,890 m). There are two very run-down *cabañas* and some campsites (US$2 per tent, no facilities), at La Rinconada and Cóndor Huayco, both between the museum and Laguna Limpio Pungo; camping is not permitted around the lake itself. It is very cold, water needs to be purified, and food should be protected from foxes.

On the southwestern flank of Cotopaxi, known as **Cara Sur,** is the private **Albergue Cotopaxi Cara Sur** at 4,000 m (see Sleeping) and four hours walking from it, at 4,800 m, **Campo Alto**, a tent camp run by the same people (F per person). This area offers good walking in the *páramo*, condors are sometimes seen, and you can climb **Morurco** (4,881 m) to the base of the rock (the summit is too unstable and not recommended).

From Limpio Pungo one road branches off to climb the north flank of Cotopaxi to a parking area at 4,600 m. The road can be covered in snow at times. From here a sandy trail continues to climb to the **Refugio José Ribas** (mountain shelter) at 4,800 m. It is 30 mins to an hour on foot, beware of altitude sickness, go slowly. Entry to the refuge costs US$1, or US$16.80 to stay overnight. The refuge has a kitchen, water, and 30 bunks with mattresses. Bring a good sleeping bag and mat, as well as a padlock for your excess luggage when you climb; or use the lockable luggage deposit, US$2.50. In high season the shelter gets very crowded.

From the turn-off for the shelter, a narrow dirt road continues north and shortly splits. One branch goes to the northern park entrance and on to El Pedregal, the second turns east along the *páramo*, making an incomplete clockwise circuit around Volcán Cotopaxi. Parts of the road are washed out and it crosses rock-strewn lahars, so a 4WD vehicle is recommended. Beautiful views and the undeveloped **El Salitre** archaeological site can be found in this area. The Inca fortress at El Salitre apparently guarded a pass from the eastern slopes of the Andes, which can be seen south of the site.

To the southeast of the park lies an area of rugged *páramos* and mountains dropping down to the jungle. This region has several large haciendas which form the **Fundación Páramo**, a private reserve. See Hacienda Yanahurco in Sleeping below.

Climbing Cotopaxi and Rumiñahui

Because of the altitude and weather conditions, Cotopaxi is a serious climb, equipment and experience are required. Take a guide if you're inexperienced on ice and snow. Agencies in Quito and throughout the Central Highlands offer Cotopaxi climbing trips.

The best season is December to April. There are strong winds and clouds from August to December but the ascent is still possible for experienced mountaineers. The route is more difficult to find on Cotopaxi than on Chimborazo and the snow and ice section is more heavily crevassed and is also steeper, but the climbing time is less. Also see Climbing, page 71.

A full moon is both a practical and magical experience.

Check out snow conditions with the guardian of the refuge before climbing. The ascent from the refuge along the traditional route on the north face takes 5-8 hours. It's best to start climbing at 0100 as the snow deteriorates in the sun. Climb the sandy slope above the hut and head up rightwards on to the glacier. The route then goes roughly to the right of Yanasacha (a bare black rock cliff) and on to the summit. Allow 2-4 hours for the descent.

To climb the southwestern flank of **Cotopaxi**, the access is from Ticatilín. To reach the summit of Cotopaxi in one day, you need to stay at **Campo Alto**, a tent camp at 4,780 m (F per person). The route is reported easier and safer than the north face, but a little longer. The last hour goes along the rim of the crater with impressive views.

Rumiñahui can be climbed from the park road, starting at Laguna Limpio Pungo from where it takes about 1-1½ hours to the mountain base. The climb itself is straightforward and not technical. There is no difficulty, though it is quite a scramble on the rockier parts and it can be very slippery and muddy in places after rain. There are three summits: **Cima Máxima** is the highest, at 4,722 m; **Cima Sur** and **Cima Central** are the others. The quickest route to Cima Máxima is via the central summit, as the climb is easier and not as steep. Note that the rock at the summits is unstable. There are excellent views of Cotopaxi and the Ilinizas. From the base to the summits takes about 3-4 hours. Allow around 3-3½ hours for the descent to Limpio Pungo. This is a good acclimatization climb. Take cold and wet weather gear. Even outside the winter months there can be showers of sleet and hailstones.

Lasso → *Phone code 03 Colour map 4, grid A6 Altitude 3,000 m*

The old railway tracks and the Panamericana cross one another at Lasso, a small town with a milk-bottling plant, 33 km south of Alóag. In the surrounding countryside are several *hosterías*, converted country estates offering accommodation and meals. Along the Panamericana are *paradores* or roadside restaurants.

North of Lasso and south of the main entrance to Parque Nacional Cotopaxi, to the east of the Panamericana is a rounded hill known as Cerro Callo or Cerro San Agustín, a volcanic outcrop, once thought to be a prehistoric burial site. At its base are two nearly complete Inca buildings and the remains of several others incorporated into **Hacienda San Agustín de Callo** (see Sleeping, below).

● Sleeping

Machachi and around *p202*
LL Hacienda La Alegría,
www.haciendalaalegria.com A working farm outside Machachi with horses and cattle, nice views, can organize excursions. Price includes all meals (very good food), horse riding, pick-up and drop-off in Quito.
C La Estación de Machachi, 3 km W of the Panamericana, by railway station outside the village of Aloasí, T02-2309246 or Quito T02-2447052. Parking, lovely old home, fireplaces, hiking access to Volcán Corazón,

advance reservations required.
C-D Papa Gayo, in Hacienda Bolívia, 500 m W of the Panamericana, T02-2310002, h_eran@yahoo.com Chilly old farmhouse, nice communal area with fireplace and library. Restaurant, cheaper with shared bath, parking, homely atmosphere and friendly owner who arranges excursions, popular.
D Chiguac, Los Caras y Colón, 4 blocks from the main park, T02-2310396, germanimor@punto.net.ec Small family-run hostel, clean comfortable rooms, includes

breakfast, restaurant, shared bath.
E Estancia Real, Luis Cordero y Panzaleo, 3 blocks E of park, T02-2315760. Private bath, hot water, parking, OK.

El Chaupi
B Hacienda San José del Chaupi, 3 km SW of El Chaupi, T09-9713986. Includes breakfast, meals available on request, parking, converted farm house and cabins, horse riding, call in advance.
E Posada El Chaupi, in front of bus stop, T02-2860830. Meals with family on request, shared bath, electric shower, run by the Salazar family, basic and very friendly.

Parque Nacional Cotopaxi *p203*
LL Hacienda El Tambo, to the north of Quilindaña in the southeastern side of the park. Contact information as for **Hacienda El Porvenir** below. Rustic hacienda inn (with shared bath) by the Río Tambo, where an Inca inn or tambo once stood. Price includes all meals, transport from Quito, activities such as horse riding or cycling, and guiding. Advance reservations required.
LL Hacienda San Agustín de Callo, entrance from the Panamericana just north of the main park access, marked by a painted stone, it is 10-min ride from the highway, T02-2719160, www.incahacienda.com An exclusive inn, encompassing suites with fireplaces in room and bath, bathtub. Breakfast and dinner included, horse rides and bicycles. For day visitors, there is a very expensive restaurant serving meals in 1 of the more complete Inca rooms, or pay US$7 just to enter.
L Hacienda Yanahurco, due east of Cotopaxi, part of the Fundación Páramo, T02-2241593 (Quito), www.ecuador-yanahurco.com Ranch-style rooms with fireplace or heater, includes meals, 2-4 day programmes, all-inclusive.
AL-A Hacienda El Porvenir, between El Pedregal and the northern access to the park, T09-9727934, www.tierradelvolcan.com Lodge in a working hacienda at the foot of Rumiñahui. Includes breakfast. Horses and mountain bikes for hire. Camping **F** per person.

Package including full board, transport from Quito available.
A-C Cuello de Luna, 2 km northwest of the park's main access on a dirt road, T09-9700330, www.cuellodeluna.com Comfortable rooms with fireplaces, includes breakfast, meals available, parking, cheaper in dorm (a very low loft). Transport to Cotopaxi, can arrange for horse riding and mountain biking.
B Tambopaxi, at the northern end of the park, along the El Pedregal access (1 hr drive from Machachi) or 4 km north of the turn-off for the climbing shelter, T02-2220242 (Quito), www.tambopaxi.com Mountain shelter at 3,750 m. 3 double rooms and several dorms, duvet blankets, good restaurant, shared bath with hot shower.
D Albergue Cotopaxi Cara Sur, at the southwestern end of the park, the end of the Ticatilín access road, T02-2903164 (Agama Expediciones, Quito), www.cotopaxi-carasur.com Mountain shelter at 4,000 m. 3 cabins with total capacity of 40, meals available with advance notice, outhouses, hot shower, use of kitchen, bunk beds and blankets, transport from Quito and climbing tours available. Campo Alto tent camp 4 hrs walk up from the shelter, horses to take gear to camp US$12.

Lasso *p205*
AL-A Hostería La Ciénega, 2 km south of Lasso, west of the Panamericana, T02-2719052, www.geocities.com/haciendaec/ A historical hacienda reached via an avenue of massive old eucalyptus trees. Rooms with heater or fireplace, good expensive restaurant, there are nice gardens and a private chapel. It belongs to the Lasso family (whose land once spread from Quito to Ambato), but is administered by others.
A-B Hostería San Mateo, 4 km south of Lasso on the west side of the Panamericana, T/F02-2719471, www.hosteriasanmateo.com Small *hostería*, part of the adjoining working hacienda. Bright rooms, pricey restaurant with set meals and à la carte, horse riding included, friendly service.
B Posada del Rey, facing La Ciénega, T02-2719319. A family place with sports

● *For an explanation of the Sleeping and Eating price codes used in this guide, see the*
● *inside front cover. Other relevant information is provided in Essentials, pages 58-64.*

fields and games. Carpeted rooms, includes breakfast, mid-range restaurant with choice of 3 set meals and à la carte, covered pool, a bit characterless and overpriced.

B-C Pachosalag, at the north end of town along the Panamericana, T02-2719194. Hotel by the roadside, includes breakfast, economical restaurant, ample parking, fireplace in common area, a bit overpriced.

D Cabañas los Volcanes, at the south end of Lasso, T02-2719524. Small hostel by the side of the road, shared bath, nice rooms, transport to the mountains.

🍴 Eating

Machachi and around *p202*
₮₮₮₮-₮₮₮ Café de la Vaca, 4 km south of Machachi on the Panamericana, Wed-Sun. Fresh produce from the farm, very good lunches and dinners.

₮₮₮ El Chagra, Take the road that passes in front of the church, on the right-hand side and it's about 5 km further on. Good Ecuadorean food.

₮₮ Kibi's Burguer, Colón y Mejía, 1 block from the park. Snacks, fruit salads, popular with locals.

₮ El Mesón del Valle, Near the Parque Central. Good food, helpful owner.

Lasso *p205*
₮₮ Parador Chalupas, opposite La Avelina. Also a popular cafetería, busy on weekends.

₮₮ Parador La Avelina, on the Panamericana, 5 km south of Lasso. Cafetería known for its cheese and icecream, a traditional stop for Ecuadoreans travelling this route.

₮ Express, by the railway station. Serves simple, hardy Ecuadorean meals. There are several others.

🎉 Festivals and events

Machachi and around *p202*
Jul El Chagra Annual highland rodeo is held during the 3rd week of July.

🚌 Transport

Machachi and around *p202*
Bus stop for **Quito** is at Av Amazonas 1 block south of the park – **Especiales** go to the

Terminal Terrestre, US$0.55, 1 hr; **Populares** to El Recreo, 2-3 blocks north of the Trole station of the same name, US$0.75, 1 hr. Buses for **Latacunga**, from the obelisk at the Panamericana, US$0.55, 1 hr.

Reserva Ecológica Los Ilinizas
From **Machachi** to **El Chaupi**, every 30 min from Av Amazonas opposite the market, 0600-1930, US$0.30, 30 min. Horses can be hired at **Hacienda San José** or ask around the village. Pick-up from Machachi to 'La Virgen', US$25.

Parque Nacional Cotopaxi *p203*
Main park entrance and Refugio Ribas
From **Quito** take a Latacunga-bound bus and get off at the main access point. Do not take an express bus as you can't get off before Latacunga. At the turn-off to the park there are usually vehicles from Cooperativa Zona Verde which go up to the park. US$20 to the car park before the refuge for up to 5 passengers.

From **Machachi**, pick-ups go via the cobbled road to El Pedregal on to the Limpio Pungo and the *refugio* car park, US$35.

From **Lasso**, pick-up US$25 one-way to the *refugio* car park, 1½ hrs, US$40 return with 1 hr wait.

From **Latacunga**, transport can be arranged, enquire with Hotels **Estambul** or **Tilipulo**.

On weekends it may be possible to **hitchhike** from the main access. If you are on a tight schedule, arrange for transport for the return. Otherwise, you may be able get a cheaper ride down in a pick-up which has just dropped off another party.

Cara Sur
From **Quito**, Agama Expediciones in Quito offers transport to the **Albergue Cara Sur**, US$60 per vehicle up to 5 passengers. Alternatively take a Latacunga-bound bus and get off at Aglomerados Cotopaxi and take a pick-up from there.

From **Aglomerados Cotopaxi**, US$15 per vehicle for up to 5 passengers.

Latacunga and the Quilotoa Circuit → *Phone code 03   Colour map 4, grid A6*

Latacunga, an authentic highland city, is the gateway to the popular Quilotoa Circuit, a loop through several colourful villages in the Cotopaxi countryside. The scenery is grand and varied, ranging from the immense Río Toachi Canyon, through patchwork fields and high páramo to cloud forest. The emerald crater lake of Quilotoa, in particular, is not to be missed. ➤ *For Sleeping, Eating and other listings, see pages 213-219.*

Ins and outs

Latacunga is 91 km south of Quito along the Panamericana. From Latacunga a scenic road goes west to La Maná and Quevedo on the coastal plain, see page 374. The loop known as the Quilotoa Circuit is made by going along this road as far as Zumbahua and then taking secondary roads to the north as far as Sigchos and then back east to the Panamericana and Latacunga. Quevedo can also be reached by turning off the main road through Angamarca and El Corazón, a spectacular ride. The town of Salcedo is 10 km south of Latacunga along the Panamericana.

Getting there Latacunga is well served by buses along the Panamericana from the north and south as well as from Quevedo. The smaller communities along the Quilotoa circuit have at least one daily bus from Latacunga. Buses returning from the communities to Latacunga often leave very early, before dawn.

Getting around Getting from one town to another along the Quilotoa circuit can at times be difficult, as the bus routes go from Latacunga to each individual town. To get from one town to another it may be necessary to transfer buses, and the schedules can be inconvenient. It is all do-able and worthwhile however, just allow enough time. Alternative ways to explore the Quilotoa Circuit are cycling and walking. The area lends itself to trekking or cycling from town to town.

Latacunga → *Phone code 03   Colour map 4, grid A6   Population 52,000   Altitude 2,800 m*

The capital of Cotopaxi Province, Latacunga, was built largely from the local light grey pumice and the colonial character of the town has been well preserved. Cotopaxi is 29 km away and dominates the city. Many other mountains can also be seen on a clear day and the wind sweeping off them is cold. The architecture, scenery and climate are well complemented by the local people, making Latacunga a thoroughly authentic highland town.

Ins and outs
Getting there   The Panamericana goes by the western side of town, the Terminal Terrestre is just along it. A few simple hotels and restaurants are dotted along the highway, with better quality and more selection in the centre. This area is separated from the centre of town by the Río Cutuchi, spanned by a couple of bridges.

Getting around The Terminal is a 10-minute walk from the centre. The centre is compact and it is quite pleasant to walk around it.

regional information, Spanish only. **Oficina de Turismo** ① *Terminal Terrestre, 2nd floor, Mon-Fri 0900-1200, 1330-1800, Sat 0900-1600, Sun 0900-1400,* staffed by high school students from the tourism programme at Colegio Luis Fernando Ruiz, local and some regional information, friendly.

Sights

The central park, **Parque Vicente León**, is a colourful and beautifully maintained garden with tall palm trees. It is locked at night. There are several other gardens in the town including **Parque San Francisco** and **Lago Flores**, also known as La Laguna.

Casa de los Marqueses de Miraflores ① *Sánchez de Orellana y Abel Echeverría, T03-2801410, Mon-Fri 0800-1200, 1400-1800, free,* is housed in a restored colonial mansion with a lovely inner courtyard and gardens. Some of the rooms have been converted into a modest museum and it includes exhibits about the Mama Negra celebrations (see Festivals below), colonial art, archaeology, numismatics and a library. The house itself is worth a visit.

Casa de la Cultura ① *Antonia Vela 3-49 y Padre Salcedo, T03-813247, Tue-Fri 0800-1200, 1400-1800, Sat 0800-1500, US$1,* was built in 1993 around the remains of a Jesuit monastery and incorporates the old Monserrat watermill. The finely designed modern building contains an excellent museum with pre-Columbian ceramics, weavings, costumes and models of festival masks. There is also an art gallery, library and theatre. Week-long festivals with exhibits, concerts and so on, are held here around 1 April (Fiesta de la Provincia), 9 August (Día de la Cultura) and 11 November (Fiesta de Latacunga).

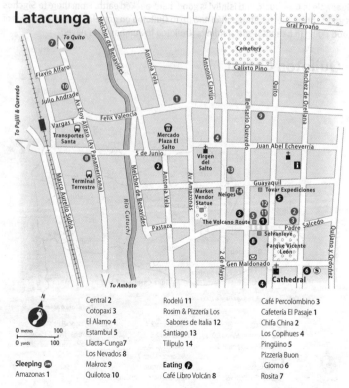

Latacunga

Sleeping ◎		Central 2	Rodelú 11	Café Percolombino 3
Amazonas 1		Cotopaxi 3	Rosim & Pizzería Los	Cafetería El Pasaje 1
		El Alamo 4	Sabores de Italia 12	Chifa China 2
		Estambul 5	Santiago 13	Los Copihues 4
		Llacta-Cunga 7	Tilipulo 14	Pingüino 5
		Los Nevados 8		Pizzería Buon
		Makroz 9	**Eating** ◐	Giorno 6
		Quilotoa 10	Café Libro Volcán 8	Rosita 7

Central Highlands Latacunga & the Quilotoa Circuit

The Quilotoa Circuit → *Phone code 03*

This is a popular route with visitors, yet preserves an authentic feel in the many small villages and vast expanses of open countryside. You could easily spend a few days or more hiking, horse riding, cycling, visiting indigenous markets or just relaxing.

A recommended round trip is from Latacunga to Pujilí, Tigua, Zumbahua, Quilotoa, Guayama (if walking), Chugchilán, Sigchos, Isinliví, Toacazo, Saquisilí, and back to Latacunga, which can be done in two to three days by bus. Some enjoy riding on the roof for the views and thrills, but hang on tight and wrap up well. The whole loop covers around 200 km and can be covered in a car or by taxi in 7-8 hours of non-stop driving, but it is a long, hard trip. A better idea is to break it up into two to three days or more. Accommodation is available in all the villages listed.

❧ *Be prepared for cold temperatures, many places along the loop are above 3,000 m.*

Despite this area's previously excellent public safety record, in 2003 two tourists were killed while hiking, in what appears to have been a bungled robbery attempt. Those responsible were apprehended and there have not been any incidents since. Note that this is a poor region, watch your belongings and beware of minor rip-offs.

Cycling around Quilotoa

This is a great route for biking and only a few sections of the loop are cobbled or rough. The best access is from Lasso or Latacunga. Between **Toacazo** and **Sigchos** on the newer northern route there's quite a lot of cobble. Taking the older southern route via Isinliví avoids most of it, but there's a rough 4 km stretch coming down from Güingopana (the stunning views almost compensate). The route north from near **Guangaje** to **Guantualó** and **Isinliví** is good, hard-packed earth. From there to **Sigchos** is good gravel, then to **Chugchilán** and up to **Quilotoa** on gravel. It makes four days of good riding in beautiful surroundings. Quilotoa to Zumbahua is paved.

Quilotoa Circuit

Sleeping 🛏
Black Sheep Inn, Mama Hilda's
   & Hostal Cloud Forest **3**
Chucurito **4**
La Posada, Residenciales
   Sigchos & Turismo **5**

Llullu Llama **2**
Pachamama **6**
Quilotoa, Richard
   & Condor Matzi **7**
Quinta Colorada **1**
Rancho Müller & San Carlos **9**

Residencial Pujill **10**
Samana Huasi & Hacienda
Posada Tigua **8**

N
Not to scale

From **Saquisilí** there are a series of little lanes which take you up to Yanaurco Alto and then either over Güingopana to Isinliví or south to Cruz Blanco near Guangaje. There's no accommodation here, but with a sleeping bag you can sleep overnight in the local school.

From **Zumbahua** an interesting route goes south. Take the main road towards Quevedo, turn south at Apagua on the pass and then climb to the pass above Angamarca. There is one dip on the road at a tiny village, then it is a major descent to Angamarca. You will find a small and very basic *pensión* on the plaza, or ask at the church. Below Angamarca, 3 km downhill, is the village of **Shuyo**, with a small shop with rooms used by bus drivers; if you arrive early there is usually space.

The road continues to **El Corazón**. From here you can freewheel down to **Moraspungo** and **Quevedo**, or continue through the mountains to **Facundo Vela** and up to Radio Loma and into Salinas (of cheese fame, see page 224). This latter route has a long tough uphill section from Facundo Vela, and sleeping bags are needed to sleep in village schools or the church.

Trekking around Quilotoa

There are ample opportunities for walking in the Quilotoa circuit area. There are good day walks from all of the towns along the route and what makes the area special is the number of hostels even in some very small places. An interesting 'hostel-hopping' trek is described in *Trekking in Ecuador* (see page 482 for further details).

The **Quilotoa crater lake** is reached in a few hours walking from Tigua, Zumbahua, Chugchilán and Isinliví (a full day is required from the latter). You can walk right round the Quilotoa crater rim in 6-7 hours, but parts of the path are very slippery and dangerous. Enquire locally beforehand and take a stick to fend off dogs on the road. Also be prepared for sudden changes in the weather. You can also walk to Chugchilán (11 km, 5-6 hours) following the crater rim clockwise then descending to the hamlet of **Guayama**, where there are a couple shops with basic supplies and a hostel, and continuing across the canyon of the Río Sigüi. From Guayama you can also continue to Isinliví. It is a 8 to 10 hour walk from Quilotoa to Isinliví.

The route

Latacunga to Zumbahua

Along the paved road west from Latacunga to Quevedo (see page 374), 15 km from the city, is **Pujilí**, which has a beautiful church. There is some local ceramic work, a good market on Sunday, and a smaller one on Wednesday. The town has excellent Corpus Christi celebrations.

From Pujilí the road climbs steeply to cross the western cordillera. Beyond the pass, it descends through high rolling country with some lovely views. Ten kilometres from Pujilí is the **Tigua area** where the local people produce interesting crafts, such as primitivist paintings on leather (a form of art that started here and has spread to other parts of Cotopaxi), hand-carved wooden masks and baskets. The best artists are the Toaquiza family. In the village of Tigua-Chimbacucho, by the side of the road, is a community-run hotel and an art gallery where local work can be admired and bought. You may meet some of the artists here. Visits to artisan's workshops are possible with advance notice. There are many walking trails in the area including one to Quilotoa.

The small indigenous village of **Zumbahua** lies 500 m north of the main Latacunga-Quevedo road, 65 km from Pujilí. It has a good hospital, a school and a large church with woodcarvings by local artisans. It is quite sleepy for most of the week, but comes alive on weekends, festivals and market day, Saturday. The market starts at 0600, and is only for local produce and animals, interesting and best before 1000. Friday nights involve dancing and drinking.

Zumbahua is the point to turn off to continue along the Quilotoa Circuit and to visit **Quilotoa** ① *the community charges a US$1 entry fee*, a volcanic crater filled by a beautiful emerald lake. The crater is reached by a paved road which runs north from Zumbahua. It's about 12 km (3-5 hrs to walk, 30 mins by car).

Along the access road to the rim of the crater the small community of Lago Verde Quilotoa, which caters to visitors, has sprung up. A number of the houses are basic *residenciales*. The limiting factor here is the lack of water which must be trucked in.

‡ *Bring drinking water as there's none at the top of the crater and the water in the lake is salty and sulphurous.*

Everyone in the village tries to sell the famous naïve Tigua pictures and carved wooden masks (see Tigua above). Try to spread your business as people in this area are very poor.

From the rim of the crater several snow-capped volcanoes can be seen in the distance. During the wet season, the best views are in the early morning. There's a 300-m drop down from the crater rim to the water. The hike down takes about 30 minutes (an hour or more to climb back up). The trail starts to the left of the parking area down a steep, canyon-like cut. You can hire a mule to ride up from the bottom of the crater, but arrange it before heading down.

Quilotoa to Salcedo

Beyond Quilotoa the road is unpaved and can be quite poor at times. It is 22 km from the Quilotoa crater to **Chugchilán**, a small, poor, mainly indigenous village in a beautiful setting. The area offers good trekking, horse riding and cycling. Horses with a guide for a trip to Quilotoa are available at US$20 per horse. Near town is a cheese factory which welcomes visitors, further afield is an area of nice cloud forests. Chugchilán has a Sunday market.

Continuing north from Chugchilán the road runs through **Sigchos**, a somewhat larger town along this circuit. There are beautiful views of both Ilinizas from here, and a Sunday market. Sigchos is the main starting point for hiking in the Río Toachi Canyon, but this can also be done from other towns along the loop. From Sigchos a road goes north and follows the Toachi on its descent towards the town of **Las Pampas** (basic accommodation and meals) and on to Alluriquín and Santo Domingo in the western lowlands.

Southeast from Sigchos and southwest of Toacazo, along secondary roads is **Isinliví**, with its colourful Christmas fiestas. It is a pleasant town populated mainly by mestizos. There are some spectacular hikes and bike rides in the area and several *pucarás* (hill fortresses) to explore. Also here is an excellent carpentry workshop to visit and some birdwatching. The Monday market at nearby **Guantualó** is also an attraction; there is plenty of transport. You can hike from here to Chugchilán, or vice versa, in three to four hours. A longer hike is to Yanaurco volcano, which will take a full day. Alternatively, catch a morning bus to Güingopana and hike the ridge route from the pass. Horses can be hired for riding or carrying luggage, US$15 per horse.

From Chugchilán a cobbled road runs east to the town of **Toacazo** from where there are paved roads to Saquisilí and to the Panamericana near Lasso. There is an inn near town. You can also access Los Ilinizas from here.

Some 16 km south of Lasso, and 6 km west of the Panamericana, is the small but very important market town of **Saquisilí**. Its Thursday market (0700-1400) is famous throughout Ecuador for the way in which its seven plazas and most of its streets become jam-packed with people, the great majority of them local Indians with red ponchos and narrow-brimmed felt hats.

The best time to visit the market is between 0900 and 1200, be sure to bargain. The animal market is a little way out of the village and it's best to be there before 0700. There is accommodation in town and a few simple *comedores*, you will find a much better selection of places to eat in Latacunga.

About 10 kilometres south of Latacunga along the Panamericana is **Salcedo**
(officially San Miguel de Salcedo), with a pleasant main square. The town is known for its unique fruit ice cream, also sold in other parts of Ecuador, give it a try (**Heladería Tiwinza** on the southbound street through town is recommended). The area is also known for its excellent *máchica* (roasted barley flour) and *pinol* (*máchica* with raw sugar and spices, makes a nice hot drink when prepared with milk). The Thursday and Sunday markets are authentic.

From Salcedo a road goes east to Cashaloma and beyond to the northwestern edge of **Parque Nacional Los Llanganates**.

● Sleeping

Latacunga *p208, map p209*
C El Marquez, Roosevelt y Márquez de Maenza, in La Laguna neighbourhood, T03-2811150, F2813487. A bright, quiet, modern hotel, restaurant, parking, good but out of the way.
C Llacta-Cunga, Eloy Alfaro 79-213 (Panamericana, note Los Ilinizas on the same building is not as nice), T03-2802372, F2800635. A multi-storey building near the highway, restaurant, ample parking, comfortable, helpful, fine views.
C Makroz, Valencia 8-56 y Quito, T03-2800907, F2807274. Modern hotel with nicely decorated comfortable rooms, restaurant serves economical meals (closed Sun), parking. Recommended.
C-D Rodelú, Quito 16-31, T03-2800956, rodelu@uio.telconet.net Comfortable popular hotel, good restaurant (closed Sun), nice suites and rooms, except for a few rooms which are small and a bit overpriced.
D Central, Sánchez de Orellana y Padre Salcedo, T03-2802912. A multi-storey hotel in the centre of town, cafeteria, a bit faded but friendly.
D Cotopaxi, Padre Salcedo 5-61 on Parque Vicente León, T03-2801310. Overlooking the main park, cafeteria, hot water after 0700, adequate, rooms to the street are noisy on weekends.
D El Alamo, 2 de Mayo 8-01 y Echeverría, T03-2812043. Multi-storey building in a commercial street, area gets busy on market days, helpful owners.
D Estambul, Belisario Quevedo 6-46 y Padre Salcedo, T03-2800354. Simple quiet hostel, cheaper with shared bath, long popular with travellers, provide transport service to Cotopaxi and Quilotoa. Recommended.
D Quilotoa, Julio Andrade 1-08 y Eloy Alfaro (Panamerican Highway), T03-2801866. A bit

out of the way but good value.
D Rosim, Quito 16-49 y Padre Salcedo, T03-2802172, hotelrosim@hotmail.com Centrally located, breakfast available, carpeted rooms, quiet and comfortable. Discounts in low season and for IYHF members.
D Tilipulo, Guayaquil y Belisario Quevedo, T03-2810611. Comfortable hotel, cafeteria, ample rooms, popular, very helpful owner. Recommended.
D-E Santiago, 2 de Mayo 7-16 y Guayaquil, T03-2800899. Pleasant hotel, cheaper with bath outside the room (not shared), small but comfortable rooms, good value.
E Los Nevados, Av 5 de Junio 53-19 y Eloy Alfaro, near bus terminal, T03-2800407. Clean modern hotel, restaurant, cheaper with shared bath, hot water, parking, spacious rooms, good value but unpleasant area.
E-F Amazonas, Valencia 47-36 y Amazonas on Plaza El Salto, T03-2812673. Simple hotel overlooking the market, cheaper with shared bath, electric shower, adequate rooms, gets noisy early in the morning.

The Quilotoa circuit *p210, map p210*
Pujilí
E Residencial Pujilí, Rocafuerte, half a block from the highway, T03-2723648. A simple, small hotel, restaurant downstairs, private bath, hot water.

Tigua
B Posada de Tigua, 3 km east of Tigua-Chimbacucho, 400 m north of the road, T03- 2813682, laposadadetigua@ latinmail.com Refurbished hacienda house, part of a working dairy ranch. Five rooms, wood- burning stove, includes 3 tasty home-cooked meals, shared bath, pleasant

family atmosphere, horses, trails to river and forest, nice views.

C-D Samana Huasi, In the village of Tigua-Chimbacucho, Km 53 from Latacunga, T03-2814868 or 02-2563175 (Quito), www.tigua.org A nice community-run lodge, includes breakfast and dinner, shared composting toilets, some rooms with fireplace or wood burning stove, cheaper in dorm, nice views.

Zumbahua

There are only a few phone lines in town, which are shared among several people. Expect delays when calling to book a room.

E Cóndor Matzi, overlooking the market area, T03-2814611 (at the hospital). Basic but adequate, serves Fri supper, other meals on request, shared bath, hot water, one of the better choices in town, reserve ahead.

E Hostal Richard, opposite the market on the road in to town, T03-2814605 (at Oro Verde). A modern hotel still missing some finishing touches (eg. floors are still bare cement), some rooms with private toilet, hot water in shared shower, laundry and cooking facilities, parking, clean, family-run, friendly, owners can provide transport to Quilotoa.

E Hotel Quilotoa, at the north side (bottom) of the plaza, next to the abattoir. Refurbished in 2004, it has fancy fixtures but is already a bit run down, private bath, hot water, not too clean.

E-F Residencial Oro Verde, first place on the left as you enter town, T03-2814605, T03-2802548 (Latacunga). A friendly hotel, restaurant serves Fri and Sat with advanced notice at other times, cheaper with shared bath, hot water, shop downstairs.

Quilotoa

Take a good sleeping bag to Quilotoa as it gets very cold. Although there are now 7 hostels in Quilotoa, they are all basic or very basic. There are hopes of improvement with a new *hostería* planned for later in 2005. Better choices are available in other towns along the circuit.

D Cabañas Quilotoa, on the left side of the access road, T03-2814867, T09-8730716 (Latacunga). A basic 2-storey hostel, includes breakfast and dinner, shared bath, electric shower, cold despite fireplace and wool blankets. Owned by Humberto Latacunga who will lead treks and provide mules, he is a good painter and has a small store.

D Hostal Pachamama, at the top of the hill by the rim of the crater, T09-8730716 (Latacunga). The best option in Quilotoa in early 2005. A couple of rooms will have private bath, they were not ready yet, includes breakfast and dinner, electric shower, new in 2004.

D Princesa Toa, at the top of the hill by the rim of the crater. A community-run hostel. Large room with a fireplace and several beds. They intend to subdivide this area, includes breakfast and dinner.

Chugchilán

AL-B The Black Sheep Inn, a few mins below the village on the way to Sigchos, T03-2814587, www.blacksheepinn.com A lovely eco-friendly inn built on a hillside. Nice private rooms with fireplace or cheaper in dorm, includes excellent vegetarian dinner and breakfast, also drinking water and hot drinks all day, composting toilets, book exchange, organic garden, sauna, discount for ISIC, seniors or SAE members, llama treks, horse riding arranged, reservations advised. Highly recommended.

D Hostal Cloud Forest, at the entrance to town, 150 m from the centre, T03-2814808. Simple but nice family-run hostel, private rooms and dorm, includes dinner (good local fare or vegetarian) and breakfast, cheaper with shared bath, parking, very friendly, helpful owners.

D Hostal Mama Hilda, 100 m from centre of village on the way in to town, T03-2814814. A pleasant family-run hostel, homely sitting room with stove, large rooms, includes good dinner and breakfast, shared bath, parking, warm atmosphere, arrange horse riding and walking trips. Good value, highly recommended.

Sigchos

F La Posada, Los Ilinizas y Galo Arteaga, T03-2714224. A modern, simple hotel, restaurant downstairs, private bath, hot water.

F Residencial Sigchos, Carlos Hugo Páez y Rodrigo Iturralde, T03-2714107. Simple but clean, large rooms, cheaper with shared bath, hot water.

F Residencial Turismo, Tungurahua y Los

Ilinizas, T03-2714114. Basic hotel, some rooms with private bath, hot water, parking.

Isinliví

D-E Llullu Llama, ('baby llama', pronounced zhu-zhu-zhama), T03-2814790, www.isinlivi.safari.com.ec Nicely refurbished house, cosy sitting room with woodburning stove, good hardy meals available. Shared composting toilet with great views, abundant hot water, private, semi-private and dorm (cheaper) accommodation, nicely decorated rooms (some are a bit small), organic herb garden, warm and relaxing atmosphere, a lovely spot. Recommended.

Toacazo

D La Quinta Colorada, 3 km east of Toacazo on the road from Lasso, T03-2716122, www.la-quinta-colorada.com Hacienda- style house with courtyard and fountain, option with breakfast and dinner available, 9 rooms with fireplace, cheaper in dorm, free transport to Saquisixi market, economical trips to Cotopaxi, guided walks to Ilinizas. To reach the lodge take a camioneta from Lasso (US$3) or a bus from Saquisilí to Toacazo and walk 3 km.

Saquisilí

B Rancho Muller, 5 de Junio y González Suárez at south end of town, T03-2722320, www.berosareisen.com Expensive restaurant, parking, cabins, German-run, owner organizes tours and rents vehicles.
D San Carlos, Bolívar opposite the parque central, T03-2721057. A multi-storey building overlooking the main square, electric shower, parking, good value, but watch your valuables.
F Pensión Chavela, Bolívar by main park, T03-2721114. Shared bath, cold water, very basic but friendly.
F Salón Pichincha, Bolívar y Pichincha. Restaurant, shared bath, hot water, cheap and basic.

Salcedo

AL Rumipamba de las Rosas, in Rumipamba, 1 km north of town, T03-2726128, rumipamba@rumipamba.com Pleasant country inn, includes breakfast, good expensive restaurant, pool, nice gardens, small lake with boats, sport fields. Recommended.

D La Casona, Bolívar 634 y 24 de Mayo, at the main square, T03-2728224. A nicely restored old home, breakfast available, rooms simple but adequate.
E Residencial Central, Bolívar y Sucre, 1 block from main park, T03-2726099. Small simple rooms, some rooms with private bath, hot water, not too clean.

🍴 Eating

Latacunga *p208, map p209*
A local speciality is *chugchucaras*, a deep-fried assortment of pork, pork skins, potatoes, bananas, corn, popcorn, and *empanadas* – the ultimate high-cholesterol snack! The best are at **Rosita Eloy Alfaro** 31-226 on the Panamericana, very popular; also at **Don Pancho**, Quijano y Ordoñez y Rumiñahui; there are many others. Also try *allullas con queso de hoja*, biscuits with string cheese.
††† Finca Parador Don Diego, South of the train station and the Rumipamba bridge on the Panamericana. Trout, steak, chicken; clean, classy, great service.
††† La Buena Tierra, Opposite Hotel El Marquez, closed Sun. Nice international food.
††† Rodelú, Quito 16-31 at the hotel, closed Sun. Good breakfasts, steaks and pizzas, popular with travellers.
†††-†† Los Copihues, Quito 14-25 y Tarqui, Mon-Sat 1000-2200. Good international food, 4-course set lunch, generous portions.
†† Chifa China, Antonia Vela 6-85 y 5 de Junio, daily 1030-2200. Good Chinese food, large portions, clean. Recommended.
†† Pizzería Buon Giorno, Sánchez de Orellana y Maldonado esquina, Mon-Sat 1300-2300. Great pizzas and lasagne, large selection. Recommended.
†† Pizzería Los Sabores de Italia, Quito 16-57 next to Hotel Rosím, daily 1200-2200. Large selection of pizzas and a few other Italian dishes, popular.

Cafés

Café Precolombino, Belisario Quevedo 6-31 y Padre Salcedo, Mon-Sat 0800-1400, 1500-2200. Breakfast, snacks such as *humitas*, *empanadas* and Mexican tacos, desserts and sweets, pleasant atmosphere.
Café-Libro Volcán, Belisario Quevedo 5-56 y Padre Salcedo, Mon-Fri 1400-2200, Sat

1400-2000. Snacks, tacos, drinks, board games, a place to hang around.
Cafetería El Pasaje, Padre Salcedo 43-16, second floor, on pedestrian mall, Mon-Sat 0830-2030. Snacks, burgers, coffee and other drinks.
Pingüino, Quito 73-106, 1 block from Parque Vicente León. Good milkshakes and coffee.

The Quilotoa circuit p210, map p210
Zumbahua
Meals are available at **Residencial Oro Verde** and **Cóndor Matzi** on Fri evening and Sat breakfast and lunch, at other times advance notice is required. Just below the plaza is a shop selling dairy products and cold drinks.

Quilotoa
Simple meals are available from **Hostal Pachamama** and **Cabañas Quilotoa**. Note that because of the water shortages, hygiene is often compromised. Drink only bottled water and eat only well-cooked food.

Sigchos
There are several simple *comedores* in town serving set meals.

Salcedo
ffff Rumipamba de las Rosas, at the *hostería*. Very good Ecuadorean and international food, set lunch and à la carte. Try their *locro de papas* soup.
ffff Casa del Marquez, García Moreno y Quito, at north end of town, 0800-0000. Very good international food, set lunch and à la carte, bar. Recommended.
ffff Marisquería Tiburón, Sucre opposite main park, 0800-2100. Seafood.

◑ Bars and clubs

Latacunga p208, map p209
Beer Center, Sánchez de Orellana 74-20. Bar and disco. Good atmosphere, young crowd.
Galaxy, Barrio El Calvario, on a hill to the east of the centre. Disco, varied music, nice atmosphere.
Kahlúa Bongo Bar, Padre Salcedo 4-56, on pedestrian mall. Bar. Wed-Sat 1900-0100.
Taberna La Mama Negra, Padre Salcedo 4-49.

❂ Festivals and events

Latacunga p208, map p209
23-25 Sep Fiesta de la Mama Negra The most important festival in Latacunga, held in homage to the Vírgen de las Mercedes and the Santísima Tragedia. There is a very well attended parade in which a man dressed as a black woman, the 'Mama Negra' is the focus of the celebrations. She rides on horse, carries a doll and changes kerchiefs in every corner. Another character is the 'Shanga', also painted as a black person and carrying a pig, a symbol of abundance. There is dancing in the streets with colourful costumes, head-dresses and masks. Market vendors are among the most enthusiastic participants in the Sep event which is open to all.

This festival is a good example of the syncretism of Andean celebrations: the reverence to the Virgen de la Mercedes, the role of the Santísima Tragedia, the saving force of the survivors of one of the eruptions of Cotopaxi, the celebration of freedom among the black slaves who escaped the plantations and moved to this area, the fight between Christians and Moors imported from Spain and probably much more...
Weekend before 11 Nov Fiestas de Latacunga. Similar celebrations to the above. The elected officials of the Municipio participate in this civic festival.

The Quilotoa circuit p210, map p210
Festivals in all the villages are quite lively. Life in these small villages can be very quiet, so people really come alive during their festivals, which are genuine and in no way designed to entertain tourists. These include **Año Nuevo** (New Year), **Domingo de Ramos** (Palm Sunday), **Carnaval** (Mardi Gras), **Semana Santa** (Easter Week), **Corpus Cristi**, **Mama Negra**, and **Finados** (Day of the Dead).
May-Jun Corpus Cristi Very colourful celebrations are held in Pujilí for Corpus Christi (Thu after Trinity Sun and on to the weekend) with parades featuring masked dancers (*danzantes*), fireworks, parties, and *castillos*, 5-20 m high poles which people climb to get prizes suspended from the top (including sacks of potatoes and live sheep!). Saquisilí also has colourful Corpus Christi processions.

21 Jun Inti Raymi Festivities for the summer solstice are held in Zumbahua.
7 Jul Cantonización Celebrations are held in Sigchos the week of 7 Jul.
22 Sep Fiestas Patronales Held in Sigchos in honour of San Miguel, the week of 22 Sep.
1 Nov Mama Negra Festival held on the week of 1 Nov in Salcedo.
Dec Navidad Colourful Christmas celebrations are held in Isinliví.

O Shopping

Latacunga *p208, map p209*
Handicrafts
Regional items include *shigras* (finely stitched colourful straw bags) and 'primitivist' paintings. These are found in the markets, see below.
Azul, Padre Salcedo 4-20, on pedestrian mall, ceramics, bronze and wooden items.
La Mama Negra, Padre Salcedo 4-43, on pedestrian mall, a variety of crafts.

Markets
There is a **Sat market** on the Plaza de San Sebastián at Juan Abel Echeverría. Goods for sale include *shigras*, reed mats, and homespun wool and cotton yarn.
On C Guayaquil, between Sánchez de Orellana and Quito, is the Plaza de Santo Domingo, where a **Tue market** is held. The main **fruit and vegetable market**, the *mercado central* or Plaza El Salto, is between Félix Valencia and 5 de Junio. Market days are Tue and Sat, but there is also daily trading.

Supermarkets
Aki, Av Rumiñahui y Unidad Nacional, southeast of centre, largest.
Rosim, Quito 16-37, in the centre, is also well stocked.

▲ Activities and tours

Latacunga *p208, map p209*
All operators and some hotels offer day-trips to Cotopaxi and Quilotoa (US$35 per person, includes lunch and a visit to a market town if on Thu or Sat); prices for 3 or more people. Enquire about the service they offer and compare, there have been reports of some tours being no more than transport to the site.

Climbing trips to Cotopaxi run US$120-130 per person for 2 days (includes equipment, park entrance fee, meals, refuge fees), minimum 2 people. Trekking trips to Cotopaxi, Ilinizas, etc US$30-40 per person, per day.

Tour operators
Metropolitan Touring, Guayaquil y Quito, T03-2802985, www.metropolitan-touring.com A branch of the large Quito operator, also sells airline tickets.
Neiges, Guayaquil 5-19 y Quito, T/F03-2811199, neigestours@hotmail.com Day trips and climbing.
Ruta de los Volcanes, Padre Salcedo 4-55 y Quito, T03-2812452. Day trips; tour to Cotopaxi follows a secondary road through interesting country, instead of the Panamericana.
Selvanieve, Padre Salcedo 4-38, T03-2812895, selvanieve1@hotmail.com Various tours, climbing, also has an agency in Baños, runs tours throughout Ecuador.
Tovar Expediciones, Guayaquil 5-38 y Quito, T03-2811333. Climbing and trekking, helpful service. Fernando Tovar is a qualified mountain guide.

⊖ Transport

Latacunga *p208, map p209*
For main inter-city routes see bus timetable p52. Note that on Thu many buses to nearby small communities leave from the Saquisilí market instead of Latacunga.
Buses to **Quito, Ambato, Guayaquil, Quevedo** and all regional destinations such a **Saquisili**, **Zumbahua**, **Chugchilán** and **Sigchos** leave from the **Terminal Terrestre** on the Panamericana. Long distance interprovincial buses which pass through Latacunga, such as **Quito-Cuenca**, **Quito-Riobamba**, etc do not go into the terminal. During the day (0600-1700) they go along a bypass road called Av Eloy Alfaro, to the west of the Panamericana. To try to get on one of these buses during daytime you have to ask for the Puente de San Felipe, 4 blocks from the terminal. The bus terminal has some shops, a bakery, cafeteria, restaurant and a tourist information office on the 2nd floor.

Cooperativa Santa, has its own terminal at Eloy Alfaro 28-57 y Vargas Torres, 3 blocks north of the Terminal Terrestre along the Panamericana, T03-2811659, serves **Cuenca**, **Loja**, and **Guayaquil** via Riobamba and Pallatanga.

Parking Parqueadero Central J S, Quito y Echeverría, ample.

The Quilotoa circuit *p210, map p210*
All bus times quoted are approximate, buses sometimes wait to fill before leaving and they can be late owing to the rough roads or too many requests for photo stops.

Zumbahua
From **Latacunga**, many daily buses on the Latacunga-Quevedo road, 0500-1900, 2 hrs, US$2. The noon bus continues up to **Laguna Quilotoa**. Buses on Sat are packed full; ride on roof for best views, get your ticket the day before. A **pick-up** truck can be hired from Zumbahua to Quilotoa for US$5; also to **Chugchilán** for US$30. On Sat mornings there are many trucks leaving the Zumbahua market for Chugchilán which pass Quilotoa. **Taxi**: day trip by taxi to **Zumbahua, Quilotoa**, return to Latacunga is US$40.

Quilotoa
From **Latacunga** Trans Vivero daily at 1000, 1100, 1200 and 1300, US$2.50, 2½ hrs. Note that this leaves from Latacunga, not Saquisilí market, even on Thu. Return bus **to Latacunga** around 1230 and 1330. Buses returning around 1430 and 1530 go only as far as **Zumbahua**, from where you can catch a Latacunga-bound bus at the highway. Note also that in addition to the above, buses going through Zumbahua bound for Chugchilán will drop you at the turn off, 5 mins from the crater, where you can also pick them up on their way to Zumbahua and Latacunga.

Chugchilán
From **Latacunga**, daily at 1130 (except Thu) via Sigchos, at 1200 via Zumbahua; on Thu **from Saquisilí market** via Sigchos around 1130. US$2.50, 3½-4 hrs. Buses return **to Latacunga** daily at 0300 via Sigchos, at 0400 via Zumbahua. On Sun there are 2 extra buses to Latacunga leaving 0900-1000. There are extra buses going as far as

Zumbahua Wed 0500, Fri 0600 and Sun between 0900-1000; these continue towards the coast. Milk truck to **Sigchos** around 0900-1000. From **Sigchos**, through buses as indicated above, US$0.60, 1-1½ hrs.

On Sat also **pick-ups** going to/from market in **Zumbahua** and **Latacunga**. **Taxi** from Latacunga US$60. Taxi from Quito US$100.

Pick-up hire to **Quilotoa** US$25, up to 5 people, US$5 additional person. To **Zumbahua** US$30, up to 5 people, US$6 additional person. To **Sigchos** US$25, up to 5 people, US$5 additional person.

Sigchos
From Latacunga frequent daily service US$1.50, 2-2½ hrs. **From Quito** direct service on Fri and Sun, US$3, 3 hrs.

To Pucayaco off the road to Quevedo, on Wed via **Chugchilán**, **Quilotoa** and **Zumbahua** at 0400, US$3.50, 7 hrs (returns Thu at 0930); and to **La Maná** on the road to Quevedo, via **Chugchilán**, **Quilotoa** and **Zumbahua**, Fri at 0500 and Sun at 0830, US$3.50, 6 hrs (returns Sat at 0730 and Sun at 1530).

To **Las Pampas**, at 0330 and 1400, US$2.50, 3 hrs. From Las Pampas to **Santo Domingo**, at 0300 and 0600, US$2.50, 3 hrs.

Isinliví
From Latacunga daily (except Thu) at 1120 (14 de Octubre) via **Sigchos** and 1300 (Trans Vivero) direct, on Thu both leave from Saquisilí market around 1030, on Sat the direct bus leaves at 1030 instead of 1300. US$1.80, 2 hrs. Both buses return **to Latacunga** at 0330, except Sun one at 0700 via Sigchos, the 2nd at 1300 direct, Mon one at 1430, Wed one at 0700.

Buses going through **Sigchos** can be taken to make a connection to **Chugchilán**, **Quilotoa** and **Zumbahua**.

From Sigchos, through buses as indicated go by Sigchos around 1300, US$0.60, 45 min. Bus schedules are posted on www.isinlivi.safari.com, check for any changes.

Toacazo
From Latacunga, every 30 mins via Saquisilí, US$0.50, 40 min. **From Lasso**, pick-up US$3.

Saquisilí
From Latacunga every 10 mins, US$0.30, 20 mins. **From Quito**, frequent service 0530-1300, US$2, 2 hrs. **Bus tours** from Quito cost about US$45 per person, **taxis** charge about US$60, with 2 hrs wait at market. Buses and trucks to many outlying villages leave from 1000 onwards.

Salcedo
Salcedo is along the Panamericana and is served by buses going through from the north to **Ambato** and from the south to **Latacunga**.

● Directory

Latacunga *p208, map p209*
Banks Banco de Guayaquil, General Maldonado 720 y Sánchez de Orellana, for TCs, Visa and MC. **Mutualista Pichincha**, Quito 1497 y General Maldonado, MC.
Hospital Hospital Provincial General, at southern end of Amazonas y Hermanas Páez, T03-2812505, good service.
Internet Prices around US$1 per hr.
Laundry Lavandería, General Maldonado 5-26, $1 per kg, Mon-Fri 0800-1330, 1500-1800, Sat 0800-1200. **Lavatex**, Av Enrique Vacas Galindo by the Coliseo Chiriboga Jácome, T03-2808293, open daily. **Post office** Belisario Quevedo y Maldonado. **Useful addresses** Immigration office, Juan Abel Echeverría y General Proaño, T03-2802595. **Police**, T101.

Ambato and Guaranda

The capital of the Province of Tungurahua, Ambato is the main commercial hub of the central highlands, and an important centre for the leather industry and a major market for nearby fruit growing valleys. It was almost completely destroyed in the great 1949 earthquake and has therefore lost the colonial charm found in other Andean cities. The city comes alive during festivals, especially Carnival, and market days.

The quaint, quiet town of Guaranda, capital of Bolívar Province, proudly calls itself 'the Rome of Ecuador' because it is built on seven hills. It maintains its colonial flavour, in contrast to Ambato, and there are many fine, though fading, old houses along the cobbled streets with narrow sidewalks. There are nice views of the mountains all around, with Chimborazo towering above. Both towns are good bases for exploring the sites nearby. ▸▸ *For Sleeping, Eating and other listings, see pages 225-230.*

Ins and outs
South of Salcedo the Panamericana goes by the Laguna de Yambo and then descends to the more heavily populated valleys surrounding the city of Ambato. From Ambato, the Panamericana continues south to Riobamba, where an important scenic road goes east to Baños and beyond to Puyo in the Oriente, and another main road, which goes by Chimborazo, runs southwest to Guaranda and beyond to the coast. There is also a road connection between Guaranda and Riobamba.

Getting there Ambato has plenty of transport from all directions. Guaranda is also well served from Ambato, Riobamba and Babahoyo on the coast. In both cities, long distance services run from the Terminal Terrestre.

Getting around Buses to nearby communities are also plentiful, these leave from *paraderos*, bus stops at specific locations for each destination.

Ambato → *Phone code 03   Colour map 4, grid B5   Population 154,000   Altitude 2,700 m*

Because of its many orchards, flower and tree-lined avenues, parks and gardens, Ambato's nickname is 'the city of fruits and flowers'. Since it is the birthplace of the writers Juan Montalvo, Juan León Mera and the artist Juan Benigno Vela, it is also known as the 'city of the three Juanes'. On a clear day Tungurahua, Chimborazo and Carihuayrazo can be seen from the city.

Ins and outs

Getting there and around   The main bus station is on Av Colombia y Paraguay, 2 km north from the centre. City buses go there from Parque Cevallos in the city centre, US$0.18. Ambato is a pleasant town to wander around. Many hotels are conveniently located within a block or two of the centre, while others are in the quiet residential neighbourhood of Miraflores. Motorists driving through Ambato to other cities should avoid going into the centre as traffic is very congested. The *paso lateral*, a new bypass road running east of the city, is due to be completed in 2005.
▸▸ *See Transport, page 229, for further details.*

Information Ministerio de Turismo ⓘ *next to the Hotel Ambato, Guayaquil y Rocafuerte, T03-2821800. Mon-Fri 0830-1300, 1430-1730, helpful, Spanish only.*

Sights

Ambato's modern cathedral faces the pleasant **Parque Montalvo**, where there is a statue of the writer Juan Montalvo (1832-89) who is embalmed in a memorial in a neighbouring street. His house, **La Casa de Montalvo** ⓘ *Montalvo y Bolívar, T03-2824248, US$1, is open to the public.*

In the **Colegio Nacional Bolívar** is the **Museo de Ciencias Naturales Héctor Vásquez** ⓘ *Sucre entre Lalama y Martínez, T03-827395, Mon-Fri 0800-1200 and 1400-1730, closed for school holidays, US$1,* with stuffed birds and other animals, botany samples, a small ethnographic collection and items of local historical interest.

The **Quinta de Mera** ⓘ *Wed-Sun 0830-1600, US$1, Bus from Espejo y 12 de Noviembre,* is an old mansion set in beautiful gardens in Atocha suburb.

Ambato is an important centre for the manufacture of leather goods and has some excellent shops in the centre of town. Out along the Río Ambato, a pleasant walk from the centre, is the prosperous suburb of **Miraflores**, which has several hotels and restaurants. Buses leave from the centre to Avenida Miraflores. Another nice residential neighbourhood is **Ficoa** were more restaurants and shops are found.

A couple kilometres southeast of Ambato is **Picaihua** where you can see the local work from cabuya fibre (frequent buses). To the west of the city is **Pinllo**, famous for its egg-loaves, said to be the only bread which would last the mule trip to the coast in the 1800s. Beyond is **Quisapincha**, a colonial town where nice leather jackets and other garments are produced.

Around Ambato

Píllaro → *Phone code 03*

To the northeast of Ambato, 10 km along a paved road is Píllaro, a colonial town with a pleasant park. At the entrance to town is a statue of Rumiñahui, Atahualpa's general. It is believed that Rumiñahui hid the Inca's treasure in the nearby Llanganates when

● *The Monday market is so busy that the phrase "Lunes de Ambato" (an Ambato Monday)*
● *has become synonymous with an unbearably hectic day anywhere in Ecuador.*

word reached him that Atahualpa had been executed. Píllaro is an important access to the highland portion of **Parque Nacional Los LLanganates**, a remote, harsh and magnificent place. Near Píllaro guitars, charangos and other string instruments are made. There is basic accommodation and places to eat and pick-ups for hire to go to the park. Píllaro has a few interesting festivals, see Festivals and events, page 228.

Salasaca → *Phone code 03*

Salasaca is a small village with some modern constructions, 14 km east from Ambato along the road to Baños. The Salasaca Indians wear distinctive black ponchos with white trousers and broad white hats. Some anthropologists think they might be descendants of *mitimaes,* vassals brought by the Incas from Bolivia. Most are farmers, but they are best known for weaving *tapices*, wall hangings with remarkable bird and animal shapes. Prices are somewhat cheaper than in Quito, and the selection is much better. If you have the time you can order one to be specially made. This takes four to six weeks, but is well worth the wait. You can watch the Indians weaving in the main workshop opposite the church. Fine backstrap weaving can also be seen at Alonso Pilla's, just off the main road (signed). He also runs a small hostel.

Pelileo to Baños → *Phone code 03*

Pelileo, 5 km beyond Salasaca, is a lively little market town which has been almost completely rebuilt on a new site since the 1949 earthquake. In all, Pelileo has been

Ambato

To Bus Terminal (1km) & Train Station
To Quito

Maldonado

Fernández

Sevilla

Alfaro

Darquea

Sevilla

Espejo

Mariano Eguez

Lalama

Luis A Martinez

Museo de Ciencas Naturales

Parque Cevallos

Parque 12 de Noviembre

JL Mera

Bolívar

Cathedral

Juan Montalvo

Casa de Juan Montalvo

Parque Montalvo

Castillo

Quito

Rocafuerte

Sucre

Av Cevallos

B Vela

Guayaquil

12 de Noviembre

Olmedo

Oriente

Manabi

Esmeraldas

Av Bellavista

13 de Abr

Chimborazo

To Baños

To Riobamba

To Hotels Miraflores, Florida & Villa Hilda

N

0 metres 100
0 yards 100

Sleeping
Ambato **1**
Cevallos & El Alamo
Chalet Restaurant **3**
Gran Hotel **4**

Pirámide Inn **6**
San Ignacio **7**
Señorial **8**

Eating
Café Marcelo's **1**
El Coyote Disco Club **2**
El Gaucho **3**

La Buena Mesa **5**
Mama Miche **6**
Nueva Hong Kong **7**

Central Highlands Ambato & Guaranda

destroyed by four earthquakes during its 400-year history. The town springs to life on Saturday, the main market day. This is the blue jean manufacturing capital of Ecuador, with lots of clothing for sale everywhere. There are good views of Tungurahua from the plaza.

About 8 km northeast of Pelileo on a paved side-road is **Patate**, a sleepy little town at the centre of the warm, fruit-growing Patate valley. It has a well-kept main park and a modern church. Its fiestas are worth seeing. Arepas, sweets made of squash (unrelated to the Colombian or Venezuelan variety), are the local delicacy; they are sold around the park. From Patate a road goes north to Píllaro and an older cobbled road goes to the Pelileo-Baños road with a scenic branch to El Triunfo, north of Baños.

⏺ Due to landslides and volcanic activity, the road from Los Pájaros to Riobamba was closed in early 2005.

From Pelileo, the road gradually descends to **Las Juntas**, the meeting point of the Patate and Chambo rivers to form the Río Pastaza. The views of Volcán Tungurahua are quite nice along this stretch. About 1 km east from the Las Juntas bridge, the junction with the road to Riobamba is marked by a large sculpture of a macaw and a toucan – the spot is locally known as *Los Pájaros* (the birds) – and it is a favourite volcano watching site. The road to Baños then continues along the lower slopes of the volcano. Baños is 25 km from Pelileo.

Ambato to Riobamba

From Ambato the Panamericana goes south surrounded by apple and plum orchards and crosses to the next valley, **Mocha**, where guinea-pigs (*cuy*) are raised for the table. You can sample roast *cuy* and other typical Ecuadorean dishes at stalls and restaurants by the roadside (**Mariadiocelina** is recommended). The valley's patchwork of fields gives an impression of greater fertility and prosperity than the Riobamba zone that follows. A small crucifix crowns the roof of many houses, where figurines of domestic animals are also found.

From Mocha the road climbs to a high pass at Urbina, from where there are fine views in the dry season of Chimborazo and its smaller sister mountain, Carihuayrazo. There is fine walking in this area, for excursions and accommodation here, see **Reserva Faunística Chimborazo**, page 247. From Urbina the road descends from the *páramo* through onion and potato fields to Riobamba.

Ambato to Guaranda

To the west of Ambato, a paved road climbs through tilled fields, past the *páramos* of Carihuayrazo and Chimborazo, to the great *arenal*, a high desert at the base of Chimborazo where vicuñas may be seen. Some 50 km from Ambato (44 km before Guaranda) is the access to **Mechahuasca**, one of the areas where vicuñas were reintroduced to the **Reserva Faunística Chimborazo**, see page 247. The turn-off left is marked by a large orange sign. About 13 km further is Cruce del Arenal, the intersection with the Vía del Arenal, to the south it leads to the access to the Chimborazo *refugios* (page 248) before meeting the Guaranda-Riobamba road at **San Juan**. Beyond Cruce del Arenal, the road from Ambato drops down to Guaranda in the Chimbo valley.

Guaranda → *Phone code 03 Colour map 4, grid B5 Population 21,000 Altitude 2,650 m*

Until the beginning of the 20th century, Guaranda was the main crossroads between Quito and Guayaquil, but with the construction of the railway and later the opening of newer, faster roads, it has since stagnated. Although not on the tourist trail, there are many sights worth visiting in the province. The climate in Guaranda can be very pleasant with warm days and cool evenings; however, the area is also subject to rain and fog.

Ins and outs

Getting there The **Terminal Terrestre** is at Eliza Mariño Carvajal, on the way out of town towards Riobamba and Babahoyo. If you are staying in town ask to be dropped off closer to the centre. It is a 15-minute walk uphill from the bus station to the centre.

Getting around The centre of Guaranda is quite compact and easy to get around walking. Most hotels and restaurants are here, although there ae a few by the terminal and along the highway to Ambato.

Information **Oficina Municipal de Información Turística** ① *García Moreno entre 7 de Mayo y Convención de 1884, Mon-Fri 0800-1200, 1400-1800*. Useful local and regional information and maps. It can also arrange guided tours, horse riding and camping in the area. Spanish only.

Sights

Locals traditionally take an evening stroll in the palm-fringed main plaza, **Parque Libertador Simón Bolívar**, with a modern statue of Bolívar. Those with an eye for detail will notice that the blade is missing from his sword; every year during Carnival the city places a new blade, which is promptly removed by the university students. Around the park are the **Municipio** buildings with an attractive courtyard, paintings in the Salón de la Ciudad and good views from the **tower** ① *Mon-Fri 0800-1200, 1400-1800*, several colonial homes, and a large stone **Cathedral**, with a nice marble altar, wooden ceiling and stained-glass windows.

Towering over the city, atop one of the hills, is an impressive statue of '**El Indio Guaranga**', a local Indian leader after whom the city may have been named. The site offers fine views of the city, the surrounding hills and the summit of Chimborazo. A cultural centre at the base of the sculpture includes a regional ethnographic and history **museum** ① *Wed-Sun 0800-1200, 1400-1700. To get there, take a taxi (US$1);*

Guaranda

To Riobamba & Babahoyo

N
0 metres 100
0 yards 100

Sleeping	Hostel de las Flores 8	**Eating**	La Estancia 6
Acapulco 1	La Colina 5	Balcón Cuencano 1	Metuccia 7
Bolívar 2	Marquez 6	Cafeteria 7 Santos 4	Pizza Buon Giorno 8
Cochabamba 3	Sante Fé 7	Casa Vieja 5	Rumipamba 3
Ejecutivo 4		Juad's 2	

take a 'Guanujo' bus to the stadium and walk 10 mins from there; or walk 45 mins from the centre, follow García Moreno to the west end and continue up via the cemetery, art gallery and auditorium. Beyond El Indio Guaranga, 2 km towards the Río Salinas is **El Troje**, where you can camp by the river (make arrangements at the tourist office, see above). Walking two hours upriver along the narrow canyon you reach the 8-m high waterfall of **El Infiernillo**.

The Escuela de Educación de la Cultura Andina (Universidad de Bolívar) has an **anthropology museum** ① *7 de Mayo y Olmedo, Mon-Fri 0800-1200, 1400-1800, free*, with pre-Inca and Inca collections.

There are colourful and interesting **markets** on Friday and Saturday (larger), when many indigenous people from the nearby communities, wearing traditional dress, are in town.

Around Guaranda

Salinas de Guaranda → *Phone code 03 Population 5,000 Altitude 3,550 m*

North of Guaranda, 1½ hours by car along poor roads, in a picturesque setting with interesting geological formations is Salinas. This is the best example in Ecuador of a thoroughly successful community development project. Once a very poor village which lived from salt mining, it now runs very successful cooperative projects including a dairy (*Salinerito* brand cheeses are among the best in the country), a wool spinning and dyeing mill, and a sweets industry. It is a good area for walking, horse riding and fishing.

The **Oficina de Turismo Comunitario** ① *Opposite the main park, T03-2390024, daily 0800-1800. Entry fee to Salinas US$1, guided tour of the community projects US$1 per visitor plus US$10 per group for the guide*, has information about the area and offers tours of the different community projects and walking and horse riding tours.

The success achieved in Salinas is spreading. In the 1980s a group of people from Salinas migrated west and founded the town of **La Palma**, which has established a similar cooperative system. Further west, the village of **Chazo Juan** also has a dairy cooperative and basic accommodation. Just east of La Palma is the **Bosque Peña Blanca**, a native cloud forest reserve with a spectacular 300-m high waterfall, **La Chorrera**. A dirt road links this area west to Echeandía (see below, page 225). Access from Salinas is along a dirt road to Los Arrayanes and then a mule track down to Chazo Juan.

El Sub-trópico

About two thirds of the province of Bolívar is in the foothills of the western *cordillera*, a region known as the **Sub-trópico**. Remnants of cloud forest still cover some of the higher elevations of this transition zone between the slopes of Chimborazo and the coastal plain, while the lower reaches produce sugar cane and citrus. The area sees very little tourism but has great potential; recommended for off-the-beaten-track travellers. Several roads go from the highlands to the coast, all very scenic.

The main road from Guaranda to Babahoyo (see page 374) is beautiful. **Chimbo**, where fireworks and guitars are made, is 24 km south of Guaranda. Nearby there is an interesting church museum in **Huayco** (Santuario de Nuestra Señora de la Natividad), constructed around a 'Vatican Square', with interesting pre-Spanish artefacts. The main road continues through **San Miguel**, not far from the colonial town of **Santiago** with paintings in the church by a local artist and the **Bosque Protector Cashca Totoras**, a nature reserve. It continues to **San Pablo**, skirting the forests of **Bosque de Arrayanes** and **San José de las Palmas**. Further on is **Bilován**, with the caves of **Las Guardias** to the west, and then **Balsapamba**, with waterfall and river beaches, before the road reaches the coastal plain at Babahoyo. The views along the way are magnificent.

An older route known as *el torneado* runs from Chimbo to Balsapamba – it is very steep, narrow, there are innumerable hairpin bends and more wonderful views. At **Santa Lucía**, before reaching Balsapamba, is the interesting, Swiss-run **Museo de las Culturas del Ecuador**.

Another scenic road goes from Guaranda to Guanujo and then down to Echeandía, Ventanas, and Babahoyo. **Echeandía**, a small, quiet supply town on the shores of the Río Chazo Juan, has a Sunday market. Located in a scenic area, it is three hours by bus from Guaranda, and one hour by truck from Chazo Juan, both lovely rides. Echeandía has a couple of basic hotels and eateries.

Yet another nice route goes from Guaranda, just south to Santa Fe, then west to **Caluma** from where it goes to Puebloviejo on the coastal plain and on to Babahoyo.

Guaranda to Riobamba

Two routes connect Guaranda with Riobamba. The direct road is a narrow but spectacular dirt road known as the **Gallo Rumi** (rooster rock), so named because of a rock that is said not only to resemble a rooster but also, in a high wind, to sound like one! It climbs gradually, following the Río Titlag, crosses the Cordillera Occidental to the south of Chimborazo and then descends to the native village of San Juan, where people are dressed in colourful traditional attire. From San Juan a paved road descends to the Panamericana at Licán, just west of Riobamba.

The second route is longer but mostly paved. It involves going from Guaranda along the road to Ambato about 30 km to a crossing with the **via del Arenal** and taking this unfinished road southeast. It crosses the great sand plateau (arenal) at the foot of Chimborazo, goes by the access to the Chimborazo climbing shelter, from where it is paved to San Juan, and it joins the direct route to Riobamba. Crossing the arenal, you are likely to see vicuñas and the views of Chimborazo on a clear day are superb.

Central Highlands Ambato & Guaranda Listings

● Sleeping

Ambato *p220, map p221*
There are several cheap *residenciales* and restaurants around Parque 12 de Noviembre, but this area is not safe at night.
AL Miraflores, Av Miraflores 15-27, T03-2843224, www.hmiraflores.com.ec Nice modern facilities, includes breakfast, good elegant restaurant, parking, heating, suites with jacuzzi.
A Ambato, Guayaquil 01-08 y Rocafuerte, T03-2421791, www.hotelambato.com A modern hotel near the heart of the city, includes breakfast, good restaurant, parking, casino, squash court. Best in the centre of town, recommended.
A Hostería Loren, C Los Taxos, SW of centre in Ficoa neighbourhood, T/F03-2846165, www.cialco.com Nice hotel in a pleasant residential area. Spacious rooms, includes breakfast, elegant restaurant and karaoke bar, parking, comfortable, but out of the way.
A-B Diana Carolina, Av Miraflores 05-175, T03-2822756, F2422500. Modern hotel, includes breakfast, restaurant, good views,

pool and spa open to the public.
A-B Florida, Av Miraflores 1131, T03-2422007. Pleasant hotel in a nice setting, includes breakfast, restaurant with good set meals, parking.
C Cevallos, Montalvo y Cevallos, T03-2824877. Includes breakfast, restaurant, parking, good.
C Colony, 12 de Noviembre 124 y Av El Rey, near the bus terminal, T03-2825789. A modern hotel with large rooms, includes breakfast, parking, very clean.
C Señorial, Cevallos y Quito, T03-2825124, F2829536. In a concrete building, good rooms, restaurant, a bit overpriced.
C-D Gran Hotel, Lalama 10-45 y Rocafuerte, T03-2824235, F2825915. Restaurant serves good set meals, friendly service.
D Imperial Inn, 12 de Noviembre 24-92 y Av El Rey, near bus terminal, T03-2411955. Adequate rooms, restaurant, fridge.
D Pirámide Inn, Cevallos y Mariano Egüez, T03-2421920, F2421066. Comfortaable hotel, includes breakfast, cafeteria, owner speaks English and Italian.

D **Portugal**, Juan Cajas 01-36 y 12 de Noviembre, near bus station, T03-2822476. In a concrete building, convenient to the terminal.

D **Royal**, Cevallos 05-60 y Vargas Torres, T03-2823528. A small modern hotel, rooms are small, comfortable and clean, good value.

D **San Ignacio**, Maldonado y 12 de Noviembre, T03-2844370. Cafeteria, good value.

E-F **Madrid**, Juan Cajas y Cumandá, near bus station, T03-2828679. Adequate hostel convenient to the bus terminal, restaurant, cheaper with shared bath, hot water, disco.

Around Ambato *p220*
Píllaro

F **Hostal Pillareñita**, Rocafuerte by the park. In a multi-storey building, restaurant, private bath, electric shower, simple adequate rooms.

F **Pensión Acapulco**, Bolívar near the park. Family-run basic clean hostel, shared bath, patio with many plants, friendly owners.

Salasaca

D **Runa Huasi**, 1 km north off main highway, look for signs and ask around, T09-9840125, alonsopilla@hotmail.com Simple hostel run by Salasacan Alonso Pilla, includes breakfast, other meals on request, cooking facilities, friendly service, nice views. Alonso's daughter guides walks in the area.

Pelileo

E **Hostal Pelileo**, Eloy Alfaro 641, T03-2871390. A simple hostel, shared bath, hot water.

Patate

AL **Hacienda Leito**, on the road to El Triunfo, T03-2859329, llanganates@andinanet.net A classy refurbished hacienda with common areas and nice spacious rooms. Includes breakfast and dinner, see further information in Essentials, p74.

AL **Hacienda los Manteles**, In the Leito Valley, on the road to El Triunfo, T09-8715632, manteles@interactive.net.ec A nice converted hacienda with great views of Tungurahua and Chimborazo, restaurant, offers hiking and horse riding.

A **Hostería Viña del Río**, 3 km from town along the old road from Patate to Baños,

T03-2870314. Cabins for 4-8 in a 22-ha ranch, includes breakfast, restaurant, pool and spa, games room, horse riding, mini-golf. Busy at weekends, non-residents pay US$3 per day for use of facilities.

D **Jardín del Valle**, M Soria y A Calderón, 1 block from the main park, T03-2870209. Nicely furnished hotel, good breakfast available, good value. Recommended.

E-F **Hospedaje Altamira**, Av Ambato y J Montalvo, on the road from Pelileo. Basic hostel, shared bath, hot water.

Guaranda *p222, map p223*

B **La Colina**, Av Guayaquil 117, on the road to Ambato, T/F03-2980666. Nicely situated on a hillside overlooking the city. Bright and attractive rooms, includes breakfast, restaurant mediocre and expensive but good for Sun lunch, small covered swimming pool, parking, restful, tours available, best in town.

C **Hostal de las Flores**, Pichincha 402 y Rocafuerte esquina, T03-2984396. Renovated colonial house with covered courtyard. Nicely decorated rooms.

D **Bolívar**, Sucre 704 y Rocafuerte, T03-2980547. Simple but pleasant hotel, good cheap restaurant (closed Sun), cheaper with shared bath, small courtyard.

D **Cochabamba**, García Moreno y 7 de Mayo, T03-2981958, vviteriv@gu.pro.ec An older hotel, a bit faded but good service, includes breakfast, very good expensive restaurant (best in town), parking.

D **Ejecutivo**, García Moreno 803 y 9 de Abril, T03-2982044. A simple, adequate hotel, cheaper with shared bath.

D **Marquez**, 10 de Agosto y Eloy Alfaro, T03-2981306, F2981101. A pleasant hotel with family atmosphere, parking, a bit kitsch with grandmother-style furnishings, good value.

D **Santa Fé**, 10 de Agosto y 9 de Abril, T03-2981526. Restaurant, cheaper with shared bath, electric shower, very thin walls, sometimes noisy but friendly.

E **Acapulco**, 10 de Agosto y Amazonas, T03-2981953. A basic hostel with small rooms, restaurant, cheaper with shared bath.

Around Guaranda *p224*
Salinas de Guaranda

D **Hotel Refugio Salinas**, on the road leaving town to the northwest, T03-2390022. Pleasant community-run hotel, economical

meals available, cheaper with shared bath or in dorm, dining-sitting area with fireplace.
E Hostería Samilagua, across the road from the **Hotel Refugio**. Family-run hostel, rooms with 3 beds, shared bath, hot water, very basic.

El Sub-trópico
E Amparito, Bolívar, 2 blocks east of the main park in Echeandía, T03-2970249. Simple, clean hotel, good restaurant downstairs, cheaper with shared bath, fan, friendly service, the best choice in town.

Eating

Ambato p220, map p221
¶¶¶ El Alamo Chalet, Cevallos 1719 y Montalvo, T03-2824704, daily 0800-2300, Sun until 2200. Good quality Ecuadorean and International food, set meals and à la carte, Swiss-owned.
¶¶¶ El Coyote Disco Club, Bolívar y Guayaquil. Mexican-American cuisine, disco on weekends.
¶¶¶ El Gaucho, Bolívar y Quito, T03-2826289, Mon-Sat 1000-0000. Grill.
¶¶¶ Farid, Bolívar 705 y JL Mera, T03-2824664. Grilled meat served in middle eastern sauces.
¶¶¶ La Buena Mesa, Quito 924 y Bolívar, T03-2824332. Elegant French restaurant. Recommended.
¶¶¶ Miramar, Quito y Rocafuerte. Good seafood.
¶¶¶-¶¶ Bom Bocado, Av Los Guaytambos next to Supermaxi supermarket in the susburb of Ficoa, closed Mon. Brazilian *churrascaría*.
¶¶ El Quijote, At Casa de Montalvo, Montalvo y Bolívar. Spanish and Ecuadorean cuisine, à la carte and very good 4-course set meals, nice decor and pleasant atmosphere.
¶¶ Gran Pacífico, Mariano Egüez y 12 de Noviembre. Good economical *chifa*.
¶¶ La Fornace, Cevallos 1728 y Montalvo. Wood oven pizza.
¶¶ Nueva Hong Kong, Bolívar 768 y Martínez. Good Chinese dishes.
¶ Mama Miche, 13 de Abril y JL Mera, Centro Comercial Ambato. 24-hr cafeteria serves economical meals.

Cafés
Café Marcelo´s, Rocafuerte y Castillo, daily 0900-2100. Good cafeteria serves

hamburgers and other snacks, also ice cream.
Pastelería Quito, JL Mera y Cevallos. Nice coffee and pastries, good for breakfast.

Around Ambato p220
Pelileo
There are several simple restaurants near the bus terminal.

Patate
¶¶ Pizza Good, On the road to Pelileo next to Hospedaje Altamira. Simple pizzería.
¶¶ Pollo Stav, Opposite the main park. Very good grilled chicken.
¶ Los Arupos, At the park. Set meals.

Guaranda p222, map p223
¶¶¶ Cochabamba, At the hotel, closed Sat after 1500 and Sun. Good international food, set meals and à la carte, best in town. Recommended.
¶¶¶ La Colina, At Hotel La Colina. International food, best for Sun lunch when they expect local families, otherwise mediocre.
¶¶ Balcón Cuencano, Convención de 1884 entre García Moreno y Azuay. Breakfast, lunch and dinner, set meals and à la carte, good.
¶¶ Bolívar, Sucre 706, at Hotel Bolívar, closed Sun. Good value set meals, has a nice display of Andean musical instruments.
¶¶ La Estancia, García Moreno y Sucre. Good quality and value set meals and à la carte, nicely decorated in wood, pleasant atmosphere.
¶¶ Mentuccia, Olmedo y Convención de 1884. Small cosy Italian restaurant, white linen tablecloths.
¶¶ Pizza Buon Giorno, Sucre at Parque Bolívar and Av Circunvalación 2 blocks from Plaza Roja on the way to the bus terminal. Pizza and salads.
¶ Rumipamba, Gen Enríquez 308, Plaza Roja. Fresh fruit juices, grilled chicken. Set meals and à la carte.
¶ Many simple *comedores* around Plaza Roja serve very cheap set meals.

Cafés
Cafetería 7 Santos, Convención de 1884 y Olmedo, Mon-Sat 0900-2200. A pleasant café and bar with an open courtyard. Good coffee

and snacks, fair prices, nicely decorated, fireplace, live music on weekends. A popular meeting place. Recommended.

Casa Vieja, Convención de 1884 y Olmedo. Bar-cafeteria in an elegant old house, also serve sandwiches and some Italian dishes.

Juad's Pastelería, Convención de 1884 y Azuay, closed 1300-1500 and Sun. Very good, popular cafeteria. Cappuccino, hot chocolate, sandwiches, fruit salad, pastries, best selection early in the day. Recommended.

Salinerito, Plaza Roja, daily 0800-1300, 1430-1900. Salinas' cheese shop also serves coffee and sandwiches.

● Bars and clubs

Ambato *p220, map p221*
El Coyote, Bolívar y Guayaquil, bar-restaurant and disco. The restaurant is open all week, the disco only weekends
Exis, Av El Rey y Floreana, discotheque, varied music.
La Mansión, Bolívar y Quito, discotheque, lots of Latin music.

Guaranda *p222, map p223*
Clubs are open on Thu, Fri and Sat nights.
Balcones de la Pila Disco Bar, Pichincha y García Moreno. Varied music, drinks, snacks.
No Bar, Sucre entre Manuela Cañizares y Azuay. Salsa, rock, drinks.

● Festivals and events

Ambato *p220, map p221*
Feb-Mar Fiesta de frutas y flores Ambato's famous festival is held during **Carnival** when there are 4 days of parades, bullfights and festivities. The parades sometimes have the participation of international groups, and the floats can be fairly elaborate. It is impossible to get a hotel room unless you book ahead. The town has taken the bold step of prohibiting water-throwing at carnival (see Festivals, p64).

Around Ambato *p220*
Píllaro
1 &6 Jan Diablada Colourful festival when thousands of people from the nearby communities parade dressed as devils wearing elaborate masks.

Jul-Aug Fiestas de Píllaro Celebrated with a parade, a bull run and fight and other festivities on the weekend nearest 28 Jul.

Pelileo
22 Jul Fiestas de Pelileo Parades, music and parties.

Patate
Feb Fiestas de Nuestro Señor del Terremoto Held on the weeekend leading to 4 Feb, featuring a parade with beautiful floats made with fruit and flowers, reportedly the most elaborate in Ecuador. The Señor del Terremoto is an image of Christ which was rescued from the rubble after an earthquake in 1797; it gave the survivors the strength to continue.

Guaranda *p222, map p223*
Feb-Mar Carnaval in Guaranda is among the best known in the country. People of all walks of life share the festivities: parades, masks, dances, guitars, poetry and liquor fill the streets. *Taita Carnaval* (Father Carnival), a landowner who sponsors the party, opens the celebrations when he makes his grand entrance into town. As in other parts of the country water-throwing (and at times flour, ink, etc) is common. In the surrounding countryside the celebrations last for 8 days.

● Shopping

Ambato *p220, map p221*
Camping gear
Calzado Piedrahita, Bolívar 15-08 y Lalama, good leather hiking boots.

Leather
Several shops on Vela between Lalama and Montalvo for leather jackets, bags and belts. There are many stores selling leather shoes along Bolívar. Also quality footwear at **Calzados Cáceres**, Cevallos y Mariano Egüez.

Malls
Centro Comercial Caracol, Av de los Capulíes y Mirabeles in Ficoa, small shopping centre.
Mall de Los Andes, Av Atahualpa, on the way out to of town towards Riobamba.

Markets

The **main market**, one of the largest in Ecuador, is held on Mon, and there are smaller markets on Wed and Fri. They are interesting, but have few items specifically for the tourist. Most of the action takes place in the streets, although there are also 2 market buildings in the centre, near Parque 12 de Noviembre and a large wholesale produce market to the southeast of the centre.

Supermarkets

Supermercado, Centro Comercial Ambato, Parque 12 de Noviembre.
Supermaxi, at Centro Comercial El Caracol in Ficoa.

Guaranda *p222, map p223*
Food

There are many well-stocked shops in town.
Salinerito, General Enríquez, Plaza Roja, sells good quality cheese and other products from Salinas. Daily 0800-1300 and 1430-1900.

Handicrafts

Artesanías de PHD, General Enríquez, Plaza Roja. Crafts from cooperative in nearby Salinas, woollens, decorations. Mon-Fri 0900-1300, 1430-1900, Sat 0900-1700.

Markets

Mercado 10 de Noviembre, Sucre y Espejo, is the small daily market, busiest on Wed.
Mercado Mayorista, 9 de Abril y Maldonado, at the east end of Calle Azuay, by Plaza 15 de Mayo, is the wholesale produce market with trading on Fri and Sat (busiest).
Plaza Roja, Av Gen Enríquez, is where clothing and dry goods are sold on Fri and Sat.

Around Guaranda *p220*
Handicrafts

In **Salinas**, the nice woollen garments and crafts produced in town are sold in a community shop.

▲ Activities and tours

Ambato *p220, map p221*
Tour operators
Ecuadorian Tours, Bolívar y Quito. Amex agent, but does not change TCs. A branch of the Quito operator, www.ecuadoriantours.com

Metropolitan Touring, Centro Comercial Caracol, Local 59-62, T03-2820211, www.metropolitan-touring.com
A branch of the large Quito operator, also sells airline tickets.

Guaranda *p222, map p223*
Tour operators
Karvar, Convención de 1884 1112 y García Moreno (no sign), T/F03-2980725, karvar92@latinmail.com Diego Vargas. Guided tours to many destinations in the region including Chimborazo, Salinas, nature reserves.
Delgado Travel, García Moreno y 9 de Abril, T/F03-981719. Airline tickets. Mon-Fri 0900-1700, Sat 0900-1200.

⊙ Transport

Ambato *p220, map p221*
For main inter-city routes see bus timetable p52.
TAME, Sucre 09-62 y Guayaquil, T03-2826601.
   Car hire **Localiza**, Juan Cajas y 12 de Noviembre, near the bus terminal, T03-2849128.

Around Ambato *p220*
Píllaro
From Ambato, corner of Colón and Unidad Nacional, near Parque La Merced in the Ingahurco neighbourhood, frequent buses, US$0.40, 30 mins. Taxi US$6.

Salasaca and Pelileo
From Ambato, frequent service from the Terminal Terrestre, going to **Pelileo** or through to **Baños**. **Salasaca** US$0.25, 20 mins. **Pelileo** US$0.40, 30 mins.

Patate
From **Ambato**, frequent service from the Terminal Terrestre, US$0.70, 45 mins.

Guaranda *p222, map p223*
For main inter-city routes see bus timetable p52.
Note that there is transport to **Riobamba** along both the Gallo Rumi and the Arenal routes (see Guaranda to Riobamba above), both are quite scenic.

Salinas de Guaranda

From **Guaranda**, Transportes Cándido Rada, daily from opposite the Verbo Divino School at the top of Plaza Roja, at about 0600 and from Plaza 15 de Mayo between 1200 and 1300, US$1.25, 2 hrs. A taxi or pick-up truck from Plaza Roja costs US$15 (US$20-25 with wait included). Also enquire at the cooperative office or **Salinerito** cheese shop (Plaza Roja) about their vehicles going to Salinas.

El Sub-trópico

There are frequent buses between **Guaranda** and **Babahoyo** going through the sub-trópico, mainly along the paved road through San Miguel. Along the other routes there is regular service to the main towns such as **Echeandía** and **Caluma**, from where there are connections to Babahoyo.

From **Guaranda**, frequent service to Echeandía, US$3, 3 hrs. **From Echeandía** to **Ventanas**, every 30 mins, US41, 1 hr. From Echeandía to **Chazo Juan**, pick-up trucks, US$1 per person in shared service or about US$10 to hire a vehicle.

⦿ Directory

Ambato *p220, map p221*

Banks Banco de Guayaquil, Sucre y JL Mera. Visa and Tcs. Banco del Pacífico, Cevallos y Lalama, and Cevallos y Unidad Nacional. Visa and TCs. Banco del Pichincha, Lalama y Cevallos, on Parque Cevallos and Av El Rey y Av de las Américas, near the bus terminal. Visa and TCs. Produbanco, Montalvo y Sucre. MasterCard and TCs. **Hospital** Clínica Metropolitana, Primera Imprenta 11-41 y Espejo, T03-2829451. Clínica Tungurahua, Vela 7-17 y JL Mera, T2820644. **Internet** Several in the centre of town, along Castillo, also on Montalvo, price US$0.90-1.20. **Post office** Castillo y Bolívar, at Parque Montalvo, 0730-1930. **Useful addresses** Immigration, Lalama 08-51, T03-2421441. Police, T101.

Guaranda *p222, map p223*

Banks Banco del Pichincha, Azuay y 7 de Mayo. **Internet** Compumás, 10 de Agosto y 7 de Mayo. Another at Sucre y 10 de Agosto, near Parque Bolívar. Price US$1. **Laundry** La Primavera, Ciudadela 1 de Mayo, T03-982538. Call for pick-up from your hotel, ask for Patricio Zurita. **Post office** Azuay y Pichincha. **Useful addresses** Immigration, Guayaquil y Manabí 231, T03-2980108. Police, T101.

Baños and around

→ *Phone code 03 Colour map 4, grid B6 Population 10,500 Altitude 1,800 m*

The town of Baños, with its beautiful setting and pleasant subtropical climate, is a major holiday resort. It is bursting at the seams with hotels, residenciales, restaurants and tour agencies. The sidewalks of the main street, Calle Ambato, are lined with outdoor cafés and teem with visitors on a Saturday night. Ecuadoreans flock here on weekends and holidays for a dip in the hot springs, to visit the basilica, and to enjoy the melcochas (toffees), while escaping the Andean chill. Foreign visitors are also frequent; using Baños as a base for trekking, organizing a visit to the jungle, making local day trips on horseback or by mountain bike, or just plain hanging out. The Río Pastaza rushes past Baños to the Agoyán waterfalls 10 km further down the valley, nearly dry now because of the construction of a hydroelectric dam. Beyond, many beautiful waterfalls can be seen tumbling into the Pastaza in an area well suited for excursions. Nearby are two national parks, Sangay and Llanganates. ➤➤ *For Sleeping, Eating and other listings, see pages 235-241.*

Ins and outs

Getting there → *See also Transport, page 241*

Baños is reached from Ambato or Puyo. The road from Riobamba to Baños remains closed due to landslides and volcanic activity. The road from Ambato enters the city from the west after crossing the Rio Bascún. Past Baños it crosses the Rio Ulba and at the Agoyán dam crosses to the north bank of the Río Pastaza, which it follows east towards Puyo. The bus station is on the Ambato-Puyo road (Av Amazonas) a short way from the centre. Its patio is the scene of vigorous volleyball games most afternoons.

Getting around

Baños is an easy place to get around, with most hotels centrally located. A unique feature is the presence of sidewalk ramps, which make the centre of town wheelchair accessible. City buses run throughout the day from Alfaro y Martínez east to Agoyán and from Rocafuerte by the market, west to El Salado and the zoo.

Information

iTur, the **Oficina Municipal de Turismo** ① *the Municipio, Halflants y Rocafuerte, opposite the Parque Central, Mon-Fri 0830-1230, 1400-1700, Sat and Sun 0800-1600.* Helpful, have colourful maps of the area, some English spoken.

There are also several private 'tourist information offices' run by travel agencies near the bus station. The latter offer high-pressure tour sales, maps and pamphlets. Local artist, **J Urquizo** ① *12 de Noviembre y Ambato*, produces an accurate pictorial map of Baños, also sold in many shops.

Note that because Baños is in the eastern slopes of the Andes its weather is different from most of the highlands. The rainy season is usually May to October, with July and August being the wettest. The dry months are November to April. The whole area has a relaxing subtropical climate, but it can be cool during the rainy season.

Volcanic activity Baños is nestled between the Río Pastaza and the Tungurahua volcano, and is only 8 km from its crater. After over 80 years of inactivity, Tungurahua began venting steam and ash in 1999 and the town was evacuated because of the threat of a major eruption. Volcanic activity gradually diminished during 2000, former residents and tourists returned, and Baños recovered its wonderful resort atmosphere. At the close of this edition (February 2005) volcanic activity continues at a generally low level, but occasionally intensifies to produce notable explosions which affect the upper parts of the cone. Tungurahua is closed to climbers and the road from Baños to Riobamba is impassable because of damage caused by debris flows, but all else is normal. From time to time, after heavy rains, the debris slides down from the volcano and blocks the access to Baños from Ambato. It is usually a matter of hours before it is cleared again.

> ‡ *The National Geophysics Institute provides volcanic activity updates in Spanish at www.igepn.edu.ec*

Sights

The **Manto de la Virgen** waterfall at the southeast end of town is a symbol of Baños. Other landmarks include the **Parque Central** or Parque Palomino where the **Municipio** is located and the **Parque de la Basílica**, where the **Basílica de Nuestra Señora del Agua Santa** ① *0700-1600. US$0.50,* is located. Many pilgrims flock to Baños to visit this shrine. The paintings of miracles performed by Nuestra Señora del Agua Santa are worth seeing and there is a **museum** with stuffed birds and Nuestra Señora's clothing.

The thermal baths which gave Baños its name are a popular attraction and well worth trying. Six sets of baths are located in and around town. On holidays and weekends they can get very crowded. The brown colour of the water is due to its high mineral content. All charge US$1 unless otherwise noted.

The **Baños de la Virgen** ① *0430-1700*, are by the waterfall opposite the **Hotel Sangay**. The water in the hot pools is changed daily, and the cold pool is chlorinated. It's best to visit very early in the morning before the crowds. Two small hot pools are open in the evenings only (1800-2200, US$1.25) and their water is also changed daily. The **Piscinas Modernas** ① *open weekends and holidays only, 0800-1700*, with a water slide, are next door.

The **El Salado** baths ① *0430-1700*, (several hot pools with water changed daily, plus icy-cold river water) are 1½ km from the centre, off the Ambato road. If walking from town, take a trail that starts at the west end of Martínez and crosses the Bascún river; the baths are at the top of the road on the west side of the river. **Note** This is a high risk area during volcanic activity.

The **Santa Clara baths** ① *south end of C Rafael Vieira (formerly Santa Clara), weekends and holidays 0800-1800*, are tepid, popular with children and have a gym and sauna. **Eduardo's baths** ① *next to Santa Clara, 0800-1800, entry to pools only*

Baños

US$1, spa US$2.50, have a 25-m cold pool (the best for swimming laps) and a small 233
warm pool. The **Santa Ana baths** ① *Fri-Sun and holidays, 0800-1700*, with hot and
cold pools, just east of town on the road to Puyo.

To go along with the medicinal baths, there are a growing offer of **spas**. Several
hotels ranging from the more luxurious to more modest establishments have spas
and there are also independent spa centres and massage therapists (see Activities
and tours, page 240). These offer a combination of the following services: sauna,
steam bath (Turkish or box), jacuzzi, clay and other types of baths, a variety of
massage techniques (shiatsu, reiki, Scandinavian) and more. Some spas, such as the
one at **Chalets Bascún**, have medical centres on the premises.

Excursions from Baños

There are a number of nice places which can be reached walking from Baños. The **San
Martín shrine** is a 45-minute easy stroll from town and overlooks a deep rocky canyon
with the Río Pastaza rushing below. Opposite the shrine is the **Insectario San Martín**
① *daily 0900-1800, US$0.50*, where butterflies, beetles and other desiccated insects
can be seen. Beyond the shrine, crossing the San Martín bridge to the north side of
the Pastaza, is the site of the **Ecozoológico San Martín** ① *T03-2740552,
www.sanmartinzoo.org, daily 0800-1700, US$1*, with a large variety of regional
animals, in well-designed enclosures. Recommended. Across the road is the
Serpentario San Martín ① *daily 0900-1800, US$1*, with a collection of snakes. Some
50 m beyond the zoo is a path to the **Inés María waterfall**, a thundering, but sadly
polluted, cascade. The road continues on the north side of the Pastaza to the village
of **Lligua** which straddles the river of the same name. A trail leads uphill from Lligua
two to three hours to **Las Antenas**, a good place for viewing Tungurahua.

You can also cross the Pastaza by the **Puente San Francisco** (vehicular bridge),
behind the kiosks across the main road from the bus station. From here a series of trails
fan out into the surrounding hills, giving great views of Tungurahua from the ridgetops.
A total of six bridges span the Pastaza near Baños, so you can make a round trip.

On the hillside behind Baños, it is a 45-minute hike to **La Virgen**, a statue of the
Virgin, with good views of the valley below. Take the trail at the south end of Calle JL
Mera, before the street ends, take the last street to the right, at the end of which are
stairs leading to the trail. A steep path continues along the ridge, past the statue.
Another trail begins at the south end of JL Mera and leads to the **Hotel Luna Runtún**,
continuing on to the village of **Runtún** (5-6 hr round trip).

Along the same hillside, starting at the south end of Calle Maldonado, the path to
the left leads to the **Bellavista cross**. It's a steep climb (45 mins to 1 hr) and there are
two cafeterias at the cross, both with unpredictable schedules. You can also continue
from the cross to the **Hotel Luna Runtún**.

Just east of Baños is the suburb of **Ulba**, by the river of the same name. Along the
west side of the river a road goes up (south) and winds its way to the village of Runtún;
walking this way takes much longer than along the trail described before. Along the
eastern shore of the Ulba another road goes up a short distance to the lovely waterfall
of **Chamanapamba**, where there are cabins and a café (see Baños listings, page 235).
Trails continue from there along the Ulba. To the south of the main road a secondary
road crosses the Pastaza and follows the Río Verde Chico to the towns of **Vizcaya** and
El Triunfo, from where demanding trails go to **Parque Nacional Llanganates**. Before El
Triunfo is a turn-off to Patate.

Volcano watching

The positive side of the reactivation of Tungurahua is that the Baños area has
acquired an important new attraction: volcano watching, which can be enjoyed

from Baños, Patate, Pelileo and several other nearby locations. With clear weather and a little luck, you can experience the unforgettable sight of mushroom clouds being expelled from the crater by day, and occasionally even red-hot boulders tumbling down the flanks of the volcano at night. In town, you can see the volcano from a small bridge over the Río Bascún, accessed from the top (west) end of Calle Ambato. Several operators in town offer volcano watching tours, both day and night, which take you to viewing spots outside town. *Trekking in Ecuador* (see page 482 for further details) describes an interesting volcano-watching route which can be accessed from Baños or Riobamba.

East of Baños

The road from Baños to Puyo (58 km) is very scenic, with many waterfalls tumbling down to the Pastaza, and has been dubbed *The Avenue of the Waterfalls*. It is paved and goes through seven tunnels between Baños and Río Negro. The area has excellent opportunities for walking and nature observation and the route is popular for cycling (see Activities and tours, page 239).

The first town you reach beyond the Agoyán generating station is Rio Blanco, beyond which is the hamlet of La Merced with a lookout and a trail with a swingbridge over the Pastaza going to the base of the lovely **Manto de La Novia** Waterfall, on the Río Chinchín Chico. About a kilometre beyond is the *tarabita*, a cable car crossing the Pastaza to the village of San Pedro; it is powered by an old lorry engine, US$1. From the cable car you have nice views of the Pastaza and the **San Pedro Waterfall** on the river of the same name. Several other *tarabitas* are being installed along this road.

About 3 km beyond and 17 km from Baños is the town of **Río Verde** at the junction of the Verde and Pastaza rivers, with several snack bars, simple restaurants and a few places to stay. The Río Verde has crystalline green water and it is nice for bathing. North of the highway, the river was dammed forming a small lake where rubber rafts are rented for paddling. Before joining the Pastaza the Río Verde tumbles down several falls, the most spectacular of which is **El Pailón del Diablo** (the Devil's Cauldron). Cross the Río Verde on the old road and take the path to the right after the church, then follow the trail down towards the suspension bridge over the Pastaza, for about 20 minutes. Just before the bridge take a side trail to the right (signposted) which leads you to **Paradero del Pailón**, a viewing platform above the falls; there is a kiosk selling drinks and snacks (they maintain the lookout, a contribution is expected). The **San Miguel Falls**, smaller but also nice, are some five minutes' walk along a different trail. In town cross the old bridge and take the first path to the right.

There are excellent **hiking opportunities** up the Rio Verde. The trail on the west side of the river begins at the town park. This trail makes a good day trip. There is basic lodging three hours up the trail; ask about Angel's cabins at the store just east of the town square.

At 2¼ km east of Río Verde is **Machay**, where several waterfalls can be seen, another lovely area for walking. About 10 km beyond, after passing the Río San Francisco where a hydroelectric project is being built, is the larger village of **Río Negro**. Here a road goes a short distance south providing access to the southeastern region of Parque Nacional Sangay. After crossing the ríos Topo and Zuñac, the land flattens and the Pastaza Valley widens. The next town is **Mera**, where there are very basic accommodation, a tour guide, and a police control (have your papers at hand). North of Mera by 800 m is a dam on the Río Tigre, a good place for swimming which gets crowded on weekends. In the region are also the **Anzú caves** and other natural attractions. Beyond are Shell and Puyo, see page 406 for more details.

🌐 Sleeping

Baños *p230, map p232*

Baños can get very crowded and noisy on public holidays, especially **Carnival** and **Holy Week**, when hotels are fully booked and prices rise. The town is so amply supplied with accommodation in all categories, that we can only list a subset. Many cheaper places are found around both parks, and north of C Ambato toward the bus terminal.

LL Luna Runtún, Caserío Runtún Km 6, T03-2740882, www.lunaruntun.com A classy hotel in a beautiful setting overlooking Baños. All-inclusive packages with meals, spa and adventure tours. Very comfortable rooms with balconies and superb views, lovely gardens. Excellent service, English, French and German spoken, hiking, horse riding and biking tours, nanny service available. Recommended.

A Chalets Bascún, Vía El Salado, W of town, T03-2740334, www.hosteriabascun.com Comfortable cabins for 5, includes breakfast, good restaurant and service, pool, parking, spa, games room.

A Finca Chamanapamba, outside town, a 20 min walk from Ulba on the east shore of the Río Ulba, T032742671, chamanapamba@hotmail.com Two nicely finished wooden cabins in a spectacular location overlooking the Río Ulba and just next to the Chamanapamba waterfalls, very good café-restaurant serves German food.

A Volcano, Rafael Vieira y Montalvo, T03-2742140, www.volcano.com.ec Nice spacious modern hotel, large rooms with fridge, includes breakfast, restaurant, heated pool, massage, nice garden.

A-B Palace, Montalvo 20-03, T03-2740470, hotelpalace@hotmail.com Nicely old-fashioned hotel with older rooms and newer suites, the ones in front have balconies. Includes breakfast, restaurant, pools (1 covered) and spa open to the public US$5, parking, pleasant garden, small museum, friendly.

A-B Sangay, Plazoleta Isidro Ayora 101, next to waterfall and thermal baths, T03-2740490, www.sangayhotel.com A comfortable hotel and spa with 3 types of rooms, includes buffet breakfast, good restaurant specializes in Ecuadorean food, pool and spa open to non-residents 1600-2000 (US$5), parking,

tennis and squash courts, games room, car hire, attentive service, British-Ecuadorean run. Recommended.

B Monte Selva, Halflants y Montalvo, T03-2740566, www.hosteriamonteselva.com Modern cabins on a hillside overlooking town, includes breakfast, restaurant, bar, warm pool, spa, parking, well suited to families.

B-C Isla de Baños, Halflants 1-31 y Montalvo, T/F03-2740609, islabanos@andinanet.net Nicely decorated hotel, includes European breakfast, internet, glass-enclosed spa open when there are enough people, nice atmosphere, pleasant garden. Recommended.

B-C Posada del Arte, Pasaje Velasco Ibarra y Montalvo, T03-2740083, www.posadadelarte.com Nice cosy inn, includes breakfast, restaurant, pleasant sitting room, more expensive rooms have fireplace.

B-D La Petite Auberge, 16 de Diciembre y Montalvo, T/F03-2740936, lepetitbanos@yahoo.com Pleasant hotel. Rooms, some with fireplace, around a patio, includes breakfast, good French restaurant, parking, quiet, French-run.

C La Floresta, Halflants y Montalvo, T03-2741824, la_floresta_hospedaje @hotmail.com Nice hotel with large comfortable rooms set around a lovely garden, includes excellent breakfast, other meals available on request, parking, friendly service. Recommended.

C Villa Gertrudis, Montalvo 2975, T03-2740441, F2740442. Classic old resort, includes breakfast, pool open to non-residents (US$1.50), parking, lovely garden, reserve in advance.

D Acapulco, Rocafuerte y 16 de Diciembre at Parque de la Basílica, T03-2740839. Modern multi-storey hotel, restaurant, very clean, rooms with TV are more expensive.

D D'Anthony, Oriente y Halflants, T03-2741153. Modern multi-storey hotel, parking, comfortable rooms, friendly service, good value.

D El Castillo, Martínez y Rafael Vieira, T03-2740285. Simple, quiet hotel, restaurant serves filling 4-course set meals, parking, friendly.

D El Edén, 12 de Noviembre y Montalvo, T03-2740616, hostaleleden@andinanet.net Pleasant wheelchair-accessible hotel with a patio. Includes breakfast, restaurant, parking, rooms with balconies.

D El Oro, Ambato y JL Mera, T03-2740736. Includes breakfast, bath, laundry and cooking facilities, good value, popular. Recommended.

D Flor de Oriente, Ambato y Maldonado on Parque Central, T03-2740418, www.flordeoriente.banios.com Very good hotel in a multi-storey building, includes breakfast, cafeteria, parking, can get noisy at weekends.

D Gala Inn, Montalvo y 16 de Diciembre, T03-2742870. Four-storey hotel. Good Mexican restaurant, parking, good value.

D Inti Luna, Via a El Salado, below the baths, T03-2741341, F2421717. Two-storey chalets, comfortable rooms, quiet, good value.

D Posada El Marqués, Pasaje Velasco Ibarra y Montalvo, T03-2740053, posada_marques @yahoo.com Spacious, good beds, garden, quiet area. Recommended.

D-E Buena Vista, Martínez y Pastaza, T03-2740263. Simple, multi-storey hotel, includes breakfast, clean, quiet, discounts in low season, helpful, good value.

D-E Casa Nahuazo, Via a El Salado, below the baths, T03-2740315, casanahuazo@yahoo.com Quiet country house, breakfast available, parking, a bit faded but in pleasant surroundings.

D-E Llanovientos, Martínez 1126 y Sebastián Baño, T03-2740682, gvieirah@hotmail.com A modern breezy hostel with wonderful views. Comfortable rooms, cafeteria, plenty of hot water, cooking facilities, parking, very clean, garden. Recommended.

D-E Plantas y Blanco, 12 de Noviembre y Martínez, T/F03-2740044, option3@hotmail.com Pleasant hostel in a multi-storey building decorated with plants, a variety of rooms and prices, cheaper with shared bath and in dorm, internet, excellent breakfast and fruit salads in rooftop cafeteria, steam bath 0730-1100 (US$3), French-run, good value. Recommended.

D-E Timara, Maldonado 381 y Martínez, T03-2740599, arte_con_natura @hotmail.com Small, simple family-run

hostel, shared bath, internet, laundry and cooking facilities, garden.

D-E Villa Santa Clara, 12 de Noviembre y Montalvo, T03-2740349. Simple rooms and cabins in a quiet location, cheaper with shared bath, laundry facilities, basic cooking facilities, parking, clean, garden.

E Carolina, 16 de Diciembre y Martínez, T03-2740592. Private bath, good hot water supply, cooking facilities, very clean, terrace, discounts for longer stays, friendly, good value.

E El Belén, Reyes y Ambato, T03-2741024. Nice hostel, private bath, hot water, cooking facilities, parking, helpful staff.

E Inti Raymi, Maldonado y Espejo, T03-2740332. Nice hostel, private bath, hot water, cooking facilities, garden.

E Jireh, Ambato y León, T03-2740321. A pleasant hostel in a multi-storey building, large rooms, private bath, hot water, laundry and cooking facilities, parking, good, friendly service.

E Montoya, Oriente y Maldonado, T03-2740640. Modern multi-storey building, private bath, hot water, laundry facilities, parking.

E Princesa María, Rocafuerte y Mera, T03-2741035. Clean spacious rooms, private bath, hot water, laundry and cooking facilities, budget travellers' meeting place, popular. Good value, highly recommended.

E Santa Cruz, 16 de Diciembre y Martínez, T03-2740648. Private bath, hot water, modern and comfortable, good value. Recommended.

E Transilvania, 16 de Diciembre y Oriente, T03-2742281, hostal.transilvania@gmail.com Multi-storey building. Simple rooms, includes breakfast, Middle Eastern restaurant, private bath, hot water, nice views from balconies, luggage storage, good value.

Around Baños *p233*
Río Verde

B Pequeño Paraíso, 1½ km east of Río Verde, west of Machay, T09-9819756, www.geocities.com/pequeno_paraiso Comfortable cabins in lovely surroundings. Includes breakfast and dinner, small pool, hot water, tasty vegetarian meals, climbing wall, camping possible. Swiss-run. Recommended.

D Hostería Río Verde, between the road to Puyo and town, T09-9396248, T03-2845977 (Ambato). Simple cabins in a rural setting, restaurant.

🍴 Eating

Baños *p230, map p232*
There are restaurants for all tastes and budgets, many close by 2130.

C Ambato has a few restaurants serving cheap set meals and local fare. The *picanterías* on the outside of the market serve local delicacies such as *cuy* and *fritada*. Also along Ambato between Halflants and 16 de Diciembre are several restaurants intended for foreign visitors, some with outdoor seating, serving international food at mid-range prices.

Local specialities Look out for jaw-sticking toffee (known as *melcocha*) and the less sticky *alfeñique* made in ropes in shop doorways; another local speciality is *caña de azucar* (sugar cane), sold in pieces or as *jugo de caña* (cane juice).

🍴🍴🍴🍴 Le Petit Restaurant, 16 de Diciembre y Montalvo, T03-2740936, Tue-Sun 0800-1500, 1800-2200. Very good French cuisine, their onion soup is particularly recommended, also vegetarian dishes, fondue, great atmosphere, Parisian owner.

🍴🍴🍴 Closerie des Lilas, Alfaro y Oriente, T03-2741430, daily 1100-2300. Simple but good French cooking.

🍴🍴🍴 El Jardín, 16 de Diciembre y Rocafuerte. International and some vegetarian food, juices, also bar, good atmosphere and nice garden.

🍴🍴🍴 Higuerón, Arrayanes y Oriente, daily 0900-2230. Good European, local and vegetarian food, nice garden, friendly.

🍴🍴🍴 Mariane, Halflants y Rocafuerte, daily 1800-2300. Excellent authentic Provençal cuisine, large portions, pleasant atmosphere, good value and attentive service. Highly recommended.

🍴🍴🍴 Quilombo, Montalvo y 12 de Noviembre, Wed-Sun 1200-2200. Good quality Argentinian grill.

🍴🍴🍴-🍴🍴 Buon Giorno, Ambato y Pasaje Ermita de la Vírgen west of the market, and at Rocafuerte y 16 de Diciembre, Tue-Sun 1130-2230. Good, authentic Italian dishes. Recommended.

🍴🍴🍴-🍴🍴 Pancho Villa, Montalvo y 16 de Diciembre, Mon-Sat 1230-2130. Very good quality Mexican food, good service. Recommended.

🍴🍴🍴-🍴🍴 Pizzería de Paolo, Rocafuerte at Parque de la Basílica. Good pizza, pasta and salads.

🍴🍴🍴-🍴🍴 Pizzería El Napolitano, 12 de Noviembre y Martínez. Good pizza, pasta and antipasto. Also some Ecuadorean dishes. Pleasant atmosphere, pool table.

🍴🍴 Café Hood, Maldonado y Ambato, at Parque Central, closed Tue. Mainly vegetarian but also some meat dishes, excellent food, English spoken, always busy. Also rents rooms.

🍴🍴 Casa Hood, Martínez between Halflants and Alfaro, closed Wed. Largely vegetarian, but also serve some meat dishes, economical set lunches, juices, good desserts, varied menu including Indonesian and Thai dishes. Travel books and maps sold, book exchange, repertory cinema. Popular and recommended.

🍴🍴 Chifa Shan He, Oriente y Alfaro, daily 1200-2200. Chinese-run chifa, large portions.

🍴🍴 El Paisano, Rafael Vieira y Martínez. Variety of vegetarian meals and large selection of herbal teas.

🍴 Ambateñito, Ambato y Eloy Alfaro. Set meals and barbecued chicken.

🍴 La Puerta de Alcalá, Av Amazonas (main highway), half a block downhill from the bus terminal. Good set meals.

Cafés & bakeries
Ali Cumba, Maldonado opposite Parque Central, daily 0700-1800. Excellent breakfasts, fruit salads, filtered coffee, espresso, muffins, large sandwiches. Pricey but good, Danish-Ecuadorean run.

Café Blah Blah, Halflants 620 y Ambato, open 0900-2100. Cosy café. Very good breakfast, good coffee, snacks and juices. Popular, friendly meeting place.

Pancho's, Rocafuerte y Maldonado at Parque Central, daily 1200-2200. Hamburgers, snacks, coffee, friendly owner.

Plantas y Blanco, 12 de Noviembre y Martínez, esquina, Mon-Sat 0700-1700. Bakery selling natural wholewheat breads and cakes.

Regine's Café Alemán, At Finca Chamanapamba, see Sleeping, open on weekends and unreliably at other times (a notice is posted by the turn-off in Ulba). Very nice café and restaurant serving snacks, drinks, also trout and a few German dishes.

Rico Pán, Ambato y Maldonado at Parque Central, Mon-Sat 0700-2100, Sun until noon. Good breakfasts, hot bread (including whole wheat), fruit salads and pizzas, also meals, friendly owners.

Rincón de Suiza, Martínez y Halflants, Tue-Sun 0900-0000. Snacks, drinks, good coffee, cappuccino, best cakes and pastries in town. Pleasant atmosphere, books, games, pool table, ping-pong. Swiss-Ecuadorean run, recommended.

❶ Bars and clubs

Baños *p230, map p232*
Many bars are along Eloy Alfaro between Ambato and Oriente. **Córdova Tours** (see Tour operators below) has a *chiva* (open sided bus) cruising town, playing music, it will take you to different night spots.

Bamboos Bar, on a small st at the east end of town near C Oriente, popular for salsa, live on weekends.

Buena Vista, Alfaro y Oriente. A good place for salsa and other Latin music.

Coco Bongo, Montalvo y 16 de Diciembre. Bar, snacks and pool hall.

Jack Rock Café, Alfaro y Ambato, a favourite travellers' hangout, fantastic *piña colada* and juices.

Kasbah, Alfaro y Oriente, open 1900-0200. Latin music, pool table, snacks and pizza.

Mocambo´s Bar, Ambato y Halflants, esquina. Large screen TV, loud, modern music.

❷ Entertainment

Baños *p230, map p232*
Art galleries
Galería de Arte Contemparáneo Huillac Cuna, Rafael Vieira y Montalvo, has modern art exhibits and sells paintings, including some from well-known artists, and coffee-table books.

Cinema
Casa Hood, Martínez y Eloy Alfaro. Shows interesting films.

Mini Cine, Oriente y Halflants. Has an extensive selection of films and screens to view, US$1.

Live music
Peña Ananitay, 16 de Diciembre y Espejo. Good live music and dancing.

❀ Festivals and events

Baños *p230, map p232*
Oct Fiestas de Nuestra Señora de Agua Santa Held throughout Oct with several daily processions, bands, fireworks, sporting events and general partying.
Dec Fiestas de Baños Week long celebrations ending 16 Dec, the town's anniversary, with parades, fairs, sports and cultural events and much partying. On the evening of 15 Dec are the **verbenas** when each barrio hires a band and there are many street parties.

❍ Shopping

Baños *p230, map p232*
Camping gear
Varoxi, Maldonado 651 y Oriente, quality backpacks, repairs luggage. Recommended.

Handicrafts
There are craft stalls at Pasaje Ermita de la Virgen, between C Ambato and Rocafuerte, by the market.
Latino Shop, Ambato y Alfaro and 2 other locations. For T-shirts.
Las Orquídeas, Ambato y Maldonado, also at Halflants y Montalvo (**Hotel La Floresta**), large selection of nice crafts from the area and throughout Ecuador. Also sells some travel and coffee-table books.
La Tienda de Mercedes, 12 de Noviembre y Ambato, good quality handicrafts and T-shirts, reasonable prices.
Leather. A couple of shops on Rocafuerte between Halflants and 16 de Diciembre.
Pusanga Women's Cooperative, Halflants y Martínez. Crafts and musical instruments from the Oriente.
Recuerdos, at the south end of Maldonado. For painted balsa-wood birds. Here you can see crafts-people at work.
Sr. Masaquiza, Halflants y Rocafuerte, next to Andinatel. For Salasacan weaving.

Tagua. Nice tagua (vegetable ivory made of palm nuts) crafts can be found at 3 shops on Maldonado between Oriente and Espejo, where you can see how the tagua is carved.
Tucán Silver, Ambato corner Halflants, for jewellery.

Markets
Plaza 5 de Junio, C Ambato y JL Mera. Fruit and vegetable market all day Sun and Wed morning.
Mercado Central, Ambato y Alfaro. Daily produce market.

Supermarkets
Santa María, Rocafuerte y Alfaro, opposite the Mercado Central.

▲ Activities and tours

Baños p230, map p232
Note A number of potentially hazardous activities are currently in vogue in Baños, including mountaineering and white water rafting, as well as adrenaline-sports like canyoning and bridge jumps. Safety standards cannot be relied upon; you undertake such activities entirely at your own risk.

Canyoning
Canyoning involves rappelling down steep river gorges, above and in the water (see Safety above). Many agencies offer this sport, rates US$25-35. Franco at **Pequeño Paraíso**, Rio Verde (see Sleeping, East of Baños), T09-9819756, is experienced in canyoning.

Climbing and trekking
There are innumerable possibilities for walking and nature observation, near Baños and east towards Oriente. Baños operators offer climbing and trekking tours to several destinations. Note that due to the reactivation of the volcano, Tungurahua has been officially closed to climbers since 1999. There is nobody to stop you from entering the area, but the dangers of being hit by flying volcanic bombs are very real. Those who ignore this warning do so at considerable risk to their lives. Unless volcanic activity has completely ceased, do not be talked into climbing to the *refugio*, crater or summit. To obtain impartial

information, try the municipal tourist office; never rely exclusively on an agency who is trying to sell you a climbing tour. At the same time, remember that Tungurahua was a reasonably safe and popular climb for many decades. If the volcano calms down, then in all likelihood it will be reasonably safe once again. We do not describe details of the climb since these are likely to change once the mountain is re-opened to visitors.

Cycling
A very nice, popular ride is along the scenic road east toward the jungle as far as Río Verde or even Puyo (see East of Baños). Note that cyclists have to go through the first tunnel at Agoyán, but not the following tunnels where you stay along the old road at the river's edge; the views are magnificent and you get away from the traffic for those stretches. At Río Verde you can leave your bike at one of the snack bars (a tip is expected), while you visit the falls. You can continue to Puyo (4-5 hrs from Baños); at any point along the route you can get on a bus to return to Baños,the bike goes on the roof.
Adrián Carrillo, 12 de Noviembre y Martínez, rents mountain bikes and motorcycles (reliable machines with helmets).
Hotel Isla de Baños runs cycling tours with good equipment.
Many other places rent bikes but the quality is variable; check brakes and tyres, find out who has to pay for repairs, and insist on a helmet, puncture repair kit and pump. Bicycles cost from US$4 per day; moped US$5 per hr; motorcycles US$10 per hr.

Horse riding
The countryside around Baños is well suited for riding, several tour operators and independent riding guides offer tours.
Angel Aldaz, Montalvo y JL Mera (on the road to the statue of the Virgin).
Hotel Isla de Baños, horses for rent; 3½ hrs with a guide and jeep transport costs US$25 per person, English and German spoken.
José & Two Dogs, Maldonado y Martínez, T03-2740746, flexible hrs.
Ringo Horses, 12 de Noviembre y Martínez (Pizzeria El Napolitano), nice horses, very well looked after.

There are several others, but check their horses as not all are well cared for. Rates average US$5 per hr, a 3 day tour about US$45 per day.

Massage and spas

El Refugio, a couple of blocks north of the Baños-Puyo road, access opposite the Santa Ana baths. Steam baths, massage, a variety of therapeutic media, meditation, and more. US$5 for a basic set of services and add from there.

Massage and Body Work, Alfaro y Martínez, T03-2741071. Swedish and Thai massage, very good, US$20 per hr.

Stay in Touch, Martínez entre Alfaro y 16 de Diciembre, T09-9208000 (mob). Various techniques, US$20 per hr.

Also at hotels with spas.

Puenting

Puenting, or bridge jumps, are like bungee jumping, but it is done with a harness attached to the torso and supported by three ropes. In a **swing jump** you jump outwards, head first, and you sway back and forth in a pendular movement. A different jump involves jumping straight down, feet first and bobbing up and down. The jumps are done from different bridges around Baños, all of different heights. Many agencies offer jumps, quality and safety varies. US$10-15 per jump.

Rafting

Note that the Chambo, Patate and Pastaza rivers are all polluted. Fatal rafting accidents have taken place here (not with the operators listed).

Geotours, see below, has merged with Río Loco, an operator which for many years ran rafting tours. Half-day US$35, US$60 for full day (rapids and calm water in jungle). See also Rafting, p78.

Tour operators

There are many tour agencies in town, some with several offices, as well as 'independent' guides who seek out tourists on the street, or in hotels and restaurants. The latter are generally not recommended. Quality varies considerably; to obtain a qualified guide and avoid unscrupulous operators, it is best to seek advice from other travellers who have recently returned from a tour. We have received some critical reports of tours out of Baños, but there are also highly respected and qualified operators here. In all cases, insist on a written contract and, if possible, try to pay only half the fare up-front. Most agencies and guides offer trips to the jungle (US$30-$50 per person per day in 2005) and 2-day climbing trips to Cotopaxi (about US$130 per person) and Chimborazo (about US$140 per person). There are also volcano watching, trekking and horse tours, in addition to the day trips and sports mentioned above. The following list is not all-inclusive, there are many others.

Córdova Tours, Maldonado y Espejo esquina, T03-2740923, www.cordovatours.banios.com Tours on board their *chiva Mocambo*, an open-sided bus (reserve ahead): waterfall tour, along the Puyo road to Río Verde, 0930-1430; Tour to Puyo 0930-1830, Baños and environs, 1400-1600; night tour with music and volcano watching, 2100-2300 (they will drop you off at the night spot of your choice).

Deep Forest Adventure, no storefront, contact T09-8374530, deepforestadventure@hotmail.com Eloy Torres speaks German, English and French, jungle and trekking tours, goes to off-the-beaten-path destinations.

Expediciones Amazónicas, Oriente 11-68 y Halflants, T03-2740506, www.amazonicas.banios.com Run by Hernán and Dosto Varela, the latter is a recommended mountain guide.

Explorsierra, Halflants y Oriente esquina, T03-740628, explorsierra1@hotmail.com Guido Sánchez. Tours and equipment rental.

Huilla Cuna, there are 2 agencies of the same name: at Ambato y Halflants, T03-2741292, huilacuna@yahoo.es, Marcelo Mazo organizes jungle trips; and at Rafael Vieira y Montalvo, T03-2740187, Luis Guevara runs jungle and mountain trips.

Rainforestur, Ambato 800 y Maldonado, T/F03-2740743, www.rainforestur.com.ec Run by Santiago Herrera, guides are knowledgeable and environmentally conscious.

Vasco Tours, Alfaro entre Martínez y Montalvo, T03-2741017,

vascotours@andinanet.net Run by Juan Medina, a very experienced guide who speaks English.
Willie Navarrete, at **Café Higuerón**, T03-2741482, T09-932411, is a highly recommended climbing guide.

⊖ Transport

Baños *p230, map p232*
For main inter-city routes see bus timetable p52.

To **Riobamba**, note that the direct Baños-Riobamba road is closed, buses go via Ambato.

To **Puyo**, Puyo-bound buses stop at the corner of Av Amazonas (highway) and Maldonado, across Maldonado from the terminal. Some continue from Puyo to **Tena** or **Macas**.

Car hire **Córdova Tours**, Maldonado y Espejo, hires 4WD vehicles with driver, US$80 a day.

East of Baños *p234*
From Baños to **Río Verde**, take any of the buses bound for Puyo from the corner of Amazonas (main highway) y Maldonado, across from the bus terminal, US$0.50, 20 mins. **Córdova Tours** offer a tour to Río Verde, stopping at several sites along the way, on a *chiva* (see Tour operators above). For a thrill (not without its hazards), ride on the roof.

❶ Directory

Baños *p230, map p232*
Banks Banco del Pacífico, Halflants y Rocafuerte by the Parque Central, Mon-Fri 0845-1600. TCs, VISA and Mastercard cash advances, minimum US$200, and Mastercard ATM, but there have been reports of international cards being rejected at this

ATM. **Banco del Pichincha**, Ambato y Halflants, VISA and Mastercard advances, Mon-Fri 0900-1300. **Cooperativa de Ahorros Ambato**, Maldonado y Espejo. TCs, 2% commission. Mon-Fri 0900-1700. **Don Pedro**, Ambato y Halflants, hardware store opposite Banco del Pichincha, 3% commission on TCs. Also exchanges Euros and other currencies. **Book exchange** Casa Hood, Martínez y Alfaro. Rico Pán, Ambato opposite Parque Central. **Internet** Many in town, US$2 per hour. Note that this is a much higher rate than in most places in Ecuador. **Language schools** Rates for Spanish lessons in 2004 ranged from US$4.50-5 per hr. Baños **Spanish Center**, Oriente 820 y Julio Cañar, esquina, T/F03-2740632, elizbasc@uio.satnet.net Elizabeth Barrionuevo, English and German speaking, flexible, salsa lessons. Recommended. **Instituto de Español Alternativo IDEA**, Montalvo y Alfaro, T/F03-27411315. **International Spanish School**, 16 de Diciembre y Espejo, T/F03-2740612. **Martha Vaca F. Mayra's Spanish School**, Martínez y Halflants, T03-2742850, www.mayraschool.com **Raíces Spanish School**, Av 16 de Diciembre y Pablo A Suárez, T/F03-2740090, racefor@hotmail.com **Laundry** Municipal washhouse next to the Virgen baths, US$1 a bundle, or do it yourself for free. Many laundromats in town, US$0.80-1 per kg, but there is a minimum value per load. Watch the scale. **Post office** Halflants y Ambato across from Parque Central. **Travel agents** Distracturs, Ambato y Halflants, T03-2741273, distractur@hotmail.com National and international flight tickets and can help with confirmations (US$3). **Useful addresses** Immigration office, Halflants y Rocafuerte, opposite Parque Central, T03-2740122. Police, T101.

Riobamba and around

Riobamba is the capital of Chimborazo Province. It is built in the wide Tapi Valley and has broad streets and many ageing but impressive buildings. Because of its central location, Riobamba and the surrounding province are known as Corazón de la Patria, *the heartland of Ecuador. The city also has earned the epithet of* Sultana de los Andes *(the Sultan of the Andes). Located at the foot of the magnificent Chimborazo, the highest mountain in the country, and surrounded by other impressive peaks such as El Altar, Tungurahua, Carihuayrazo and Sangay, it is the perfect base from which to explore Parque Nacional Sangay and the Reserva Chimborazo. The famous Devil's Nose train ride also runs through this area. There are also a number of markets worth visiting.* ▶▶ *For Sleeping, Eating and other listings, see pages 251-258.*

Ins and outs

Riobamba is 190 km south of Quito and 250 km north of Cuenca along the Panamericana. South of Riobamba, by the Laguna de Colta, a paved road goes southwest through Pallatanga to Guayaquil, 225 km from Riobamba. Going west from Riobamba are two access routes to Guaranda, see Guaranda to Riobamba, page 225. Another paved road goes northeast to Penipe and beyond to Baños. At the time of writing (Feb 2005), this road was closed near Baños due to volcanic debris, but you can get from Riobamba to Penipe and a bit further. Another road goes southeast from Riobamba to Cebadas, Atillo and over the Cordillera Oriental to Zuñac; it will eventually continue to Macas.

Getting there Buses from Quito, Guayaquil, Cuenca, Guaranda, Alausí and Ambato arrive at the well-run **Riobamba Terminal Terrestre** on Epiclachima y Av Daniel León Borja. Buses from Baños and the Oriente arrive at the **Terminal Oriental**, at Espejo y Cordovez. Buses to smaller towns within the province leave from specific street corners throughout the city. A taxi between terminals costs US$1. The railway station remains a central landmark, but is used only for tourist rides (see The Devil's Nose train ride, pages 244-245).

Getting around There is a frequent bus service to the larger towns within the region. Some more out-of-the-way communities will usually have one or two buses per day and more transport on market days. Riobamba tour operators offer tours or just transport to the attractions in the area.

Riobamba → *Phone code 03   Colour map 4, grid B5   Population 125,000   Altitude 2,754 m*

Riobamba is a pleasant, friendly city, if somewhat chilly with the breeze blowing down from Chimborazo. The centre has many nice colonial buildings and churches, and magnificent views of five of the great volcanic peaks. On market days (Wednesday and especially Saturday), the city lights up with the bright ponchos and shawls worn by the native people.

Once the home of the Puruhá nation, the Spanish Riobamba was founded in 1534 near the current town of Cajabamba. In 1797, the city was destroyed by a major earthquake in which more than 10,000 people were killed. It was relocated to its current location in 1799.

Ins and outs

The city centre is compact and easy to walk around. City buses and taxis are available out to the Terminal Terrestre, about 1 km from the centre. A taxi ride within the city costs US$1. The **Ministerio de Turismo** ① *Av Daniel León Borja y Pasaje Municipal, in the Centro de Arte y Cultura, T/Fo3-2941213, Mon-Fri 0830-1300, 1430-1800*, is very helpful and knowledgeable, English spoken.

Sights

Riobamba has several attractive plazas and parks. The main plaza is **Parque Maldonado**, with a statue to the local scientist Pedro Vicente Maldonado and some interesting wrought-iron fountains. Around it are the **Santa Bárbara Cathedral,** with a beautiful colonial stone façade and a nice but incongruously modern wooden interior, the **Municipio, Gobernación, Museo de la Ciudad,** and several other colonial buildings with arcades. Worth visiting is the house on the corner of Primera Constituyente and Espejo, beautifully restored in 1996, which houses the **SRI** (internal revenue service). **Parque Sucre** with a Neptune fountain is located two blocks to the southeast. Standing opposite, along Primera Constituyente, is the imposing building of Colegio Maldonado. The **railway station,** undergoing renovation in 2005, is at Av Daniel León Borja y Carabobo.

Four blocks northeast of the railway station is the **Parque 21 de Abril,** named after the city's date of independence. (The Batalla de Tapi was fought in the Riobamba valley, on 21 April 1822, when the Argentine General, Juan de Lavalle and 97 patriots defeated 400 Spanish troops.) The park, also known as **La Loma de Quito,** affords an unobstructed view of Riobamba and its five volcanic peaks. It also has a colourful tile tableau of the history of Ecuador and is especially fine at sunset.

Northwest of the centre, along Avenida Daniel León Borja, is **Parque Guayaquil,** with a small lake, a band-shell and a good playground. A stylized Simón Bolívar, donated by Venezuela, adorns the traffic circle at Avenida Daniel L Borja and Zambrano. On the edge of town, south of the centre is the **Parque Ecológico,** on the shores of the Río Chibunga.

Markets

Riobamba is an important market centre where indigenous people from many communities congregate. Saturday is the main market day when the city fills with colourfully dressed Indians from many different parts of the province of Chimborazo, each wearing their distinctive costume; trading overflows the markets and buying and selling go on all over town. Wednesday is a smaller market day. The 'tourist' market is in the small **Plaza de la Concepción** or **Plaza Roja** ① *Orozco y Colón, south of the Convento de la Concepción, see Museums below, Sat and Wed only, 0800-1500.* It is a good place to buy all sorts of local handicrafts and various types of authentic Indian clothing.

The wholesale **Mercado Mayorista** is to the south of the centre, near the turn-off for Chambo, with busiest trading on Friday. Nearby is the animal market with trade on Saturday morning. In town the main produce market is **San Alfonso** ① *Argentinos y 5 de Junio,* which on Saturday spills over into the nearby streets and also sells clothing, ceramics, baskets and hats. Other markets in the colonial centre are **La Condamine** ① *Carabobo y Colombia, daily, largest market on Fri,* **San Francisco** and **La Merced,** near the churches of the same name, both open daily.

Museums

Convento de la Concepción ① *The convent takes up an entire block, entrance to the museum at Argentinos y J Larrea, T03-2965212, Tue-Sat 0900-1200, 1500-1800, US$2,* has been carefully restored and functions as a religious art museum. It is a veritable treasure chest of 18th-century religious art. The priceless gold *monstrance* (where the Host, holy sacrament for communion, is kept), **Custodia de Riobamba Antigua,** is the museum's greatest treasure, one of the richest of its kind in South America. It is solid gold and about 1 m high, ornately engraved and decorated with precious stones. The museum is well worth a visit. The guides are friendly and knowledgeable (tip expected).

Museo del Banco Central ① *Veloz y Montalvo, T03-2965501, Mon-Sat 0830-1330, 1430-1630, US$0.50,* has well displayed exhibits of archaeology and colonial art, as well as temporary exhibits.

Museo de la Ciudad ① *Primera Constituyente y Espejo esquina, at Parque Maldonado, T03-2951906, Mon-Fri 0800-1230, 1430-1800, Sat 0900-1600, free,* opened in 2004 in a beautifully restored colonial building with a number of inner patios. There are displays about regional national parks, temporary exhibits, and Friday evening concerts.

Museo Histórico Córdoba-Román ① *Velasco 24-25 y Veloz, Mon-Fri, 1000-1200, 1500-1700, US$1*, is a private museum which includes a photo collection, paintings, sculptures, furniture and documents.

Sights near Riobamba

Guano is a quiet sisal-working, leather and carpet-weaving town of 7,000 inhabitants, 8 km north of Riobamba. There are lovely views of El Altar from the well-kept main park. Chimborazo and Tungurahua can also be seen from a nearby hilltop. In the library at the Municipio is a small collection of ceramics of the San Sebastián culture found near town and a mummy of a monk, found in the ruins of an old church. The ruins, with some fading frescoes, can be seen behind the El Rosario church, by the nice children's playground. Rugs have been produced in Guano since colonial times when, under the *encomiendas* system, local Indian slaves were trained in this art. You can have rugs made to your own design. There are a number of shops selling rugs, leather goods, and other crafts. You can see how the rugs are made on Calle Asunción, the access from Riobamba; at times five people synchronize their work across a large loom, quite impressive. There are a couple of places to stay and simple eateries.

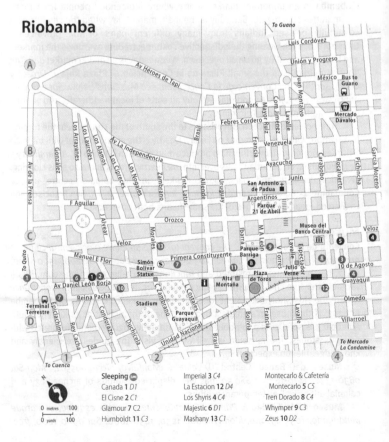

Riobamba

In **Santa Cruz**, just outside Riobamba to the southwest, an agro-tourism project accepts volunteers who assist several communities in a medicinal plants project; information from T03-2951026, www.jambikiwa.org Just after is **Yaruquies**. From the hills above town there are lovely views of Riobamba. Beyond is **Cacha**, a small Indian town, where textiles and excellent honey are sold in the Sunday market and at their shop in Riobamba (see Shopping, page 254).

To the south, 11 km from Riobamba, is the town of **Punín**. In a nearby gully archaeologists uncovered a human skull and animal fossils from the Pliocene. About 30 minutes by car west of Punín is the village of **Salarón** with a small, but very authentic Friday market, worth a visit.

The Devil's Nose train ride → *See also box Railway to the Sierra, page 246.*

ⓘ *The train leaves Riobamba on Wed, Fri and Sun at 0700, arrives in Alausí around 1100, reaches Sibambe about 1130-1200, and returns to Alausí by 1330-1400. It stops for a lunch break and returns to Riobamba by about 1700. From Riobamba to Sibambe and back to Alausí costs US$11; Alausí-Sibambe-Alausí US$7; Alausí back to Riobamba US$3.40. Tickets are sold the day before departure, or the same morning starting around 0600; passport required to purchase tickets.*

Riding the rails from Riobamba over the Devil's Nose (*La Nariz del Diablo*) is extremely popular with tourists and, increasingly, with Ecuadorean families. It makes a great day trip. Seats are not numbered, so it's best to arrive early. Riding on the roof is fun, but hang on tight and remember that it is very chilly early in the morning. Sit away from the engines to avoid getting covered in oil from the exhaust. Since the train changes directions, sit in the middle. The best views are on the right. On the days when the train is not running, you can walk along the tracks down from Alausí; a pleasant day trip. Horseback rides in the area are also offered (see Alausí, page 250).

⁑ *If you plan to ride on the roof of the train, it is a good idea to rent a cushion. It makes the ride warmer and softer.*

The train service has frequent disruptions and timetables often change, best enquire locally about current schedules. **Railway administration office** ⓘ *on Espejo, next to the Post Office, information available during office hours, T03-2960115, or at the station T03-2961909.* At times when there have been heavy rains and minor landslides, a motorized rail-car (*autoferro*) runs as a replacement for the longer train.

Metropolitan Touring (see Tour operators page 256) operates a private *autoferro* on the Riobamba-Sibambe route. They require a minimum number of passengers but will run any day and time convenient to the group. Approximately US$120 per person.

To Baños

Bus to Baños & the Oriente

Av México
Buenos Aires
Alvarado
Mariana de Jesús

España
Larrea

Mercado San Alfonso

Convento de la Concepción
La Concepción
La Basílica

Plaza Roja
Catedral
Santa Bárbara
Parque La Libertad

Parque Maldonado
Municipality San Francisco

Parque Sucre
Museo de la Ciudad
Mercado San Francisco

Colón
Espejo
Velasco

La Merced
La Merced

Benalcázar
Tarqui
5 de Junio

Chile

5   6

Eating ⓕ
Cabaña Montecarlo **2** *C5*
El Delirio **5** *C4*
Gran Havana **1** *D1*
Mónaco Pizzería **8** *C3*

Natural Food **3** *C6*
Sierra Nevada **4** *C4*

⁝ Railway to the Sierra

As you climb aboard for the Devil's Nose, consider the rich history of the train you are about to ride. What is today an exhilarating tourist excursion was once the country's pride and joy, and its construction was an internationally acclaimed achievement.

A spectacular 464 km railway line (1.067 m gauge), which ran from Durán up to Riobamba, was opened in 1908. It passed through 87 km of delta lands and then, in another 80 km, climbed to 3,238 m. The highest point (3,619 m) was reached at Urbina, between Riobamba and Ambato. It then rose and fell before reaching the Quito plateau at 2,857 m.

This was one of the great railway journeys of the world and a fantastic piece of engineering, with a maximum gradient of 5.5%. Rail lines also ran from Riobamba south to Cuenca, and from Quito north to Ibarra, then down to the coast at San Lorenzo. There were even more ambitious plans, never achieved, to push the railhead deep into the Oriente jungle, from Ambato as far as Leticia (then Ecuador, today Colombia).

Sadly, time and neglect have taken their toll and today only a few short rail segments remain in service as tourist rides: from Ibarra to Tulquizán, from Quito to Parque Nacional Cotopaxi, and from Riobamba to Alausí and over the Devil's Nose to Sibambe. There has often been talk of reviving the Ecuadorean railway, and such talk persists. As time passes however, the tracks rust and the ties rot, that seems like an ever more remote possibility. It is a great shame because a working railway could serve Ecuador today as much as, if not more than, it did in the past.

Reserva Faunística Chimborazo → Colour map 4, grid B5

The most outstanding features of this reserve, created to protect the camelids (vicuñas, alpacas and llamas) which were re-introduced here, are the beautiful snow-capped volcano of **Chimborazo** and its neighbour **Carihuayrazo**. Chimborazo, inactive, is the highest peak in Ecuador (6,310 m), and Carihuayrazo is also striking, but dwarfed by its neighbour at 5,020 m. Day visitors can enjoy lovely views, a glimpse of the handsome vicuñas and the rarefied air above 4,800 m. There are great opportunities for trekking in the area and of course climbing Ecuador's highest peak and its neighbour (from where there are great views of Chimborazo). **Horse riding** tours are offered along the Mocha Valley between the two peaks and downhill **cycling** from Chimborazo is a popular activity. Many agencies run tours here. A good map of the reserve, *Mapa Ecoturístico de los Volcanes Chimborazo y Carihuayrazo*, is published by the IGM, see page 58.

Ins and outs

Three roads provide access to the reserve. The Panamericana between Ambato and Riobamba runs along its east side. Along an older road running parallel to the highway are a couple of small communities such as **Urbina, 12 de Octubre, Mochapata,** and **Cuatro Esquinas,** from where the eastern slopes are reached.

To the west of the reserve runs the Vía del Arenal which joins San Juan, along the Riobamba-Guaranda road, with Cruce del Arenal on the Ambato-Guaranda road. A turn-off from this road leads to the main park entrance and beyond to one of the climbing shelters.

The paved Ambato-Guaranda road goes right through the northwest corner of the reserve. It gives access to **Mechahuasca** (50 km from Ambato, 44 km from Guaranda), one of the areas where vicuñas were released and from where you can reach **Carihuayrazo** and the hamlet of **Pogyos** (a couple km east of El Cruce del Arenal) the access for climbing the northwest slopes of Chimborazo. This is also the road to access the Vía del Arenal and main park entrance if coming from Ambato.

Attractions and park services

At the main park entrance from the Vía del Arenal visitors must pay an entrance fee of US$10. From the entrance a gravel road climbs steeply for 5 km and gains 440 m in altitude to reach the **Refugio Hermanos Carrel**, a shelter at 4,800 m. It has a guard, bunk beds with mattresses for 12, includes 1 private room for 2, dining area, cooking facilities, running water, toilet, electricity; bring food and warm gear, it gets very cold at night. In about 45 minutes you can walk up to the **Refugio Edward Whymper**, another shelter at 5,000 m, once at the foot of the Thielman glacier, which is currently receding. The same facilities are available here, with capacity for 45, in 5 separate rooms. Both refuges are managed by **Alta Montaña**, and sell warm soup and drinks, and packaged snacks. Overnight stays are US$10. Take a padlock for the small lockers under the bunks; the guards also have a locked room for valuables, and you can leave your gear with them, but don't take any unnecessary valuables up to the mountain. If there are only a few people, you will be given the key to your room.

❣ Vicuñas are very shy. Make sure to snap that photo before getting too close to them.

The access from Riobamba (51 km, paved to the park entrance) is very beautiful. Along the Vía del Arenal past San Juan are a couple of small native communities which grow a few crops and raise llamas and alpacas. Youngsters of the communities of **Pulinguí San Pablo** (3,850 m) and **La Chorrera**, 15 km north of San Juan on either side of the road, have been trained as *guías nativos*, native guides who lead visitors to the attractions at the base of Chimborazo. They have an interpretation trail and offer tours including a walk right around Chimborazo. See also Activities and tours page 256. Climbing gear is rented at the **Waman Way** shop at the road, but they are not always open. Accommodation and meals are available in Pulinguí, see Sleeping page 252, and there is a shop selling very basic food and some crafts. The Pulinguí school welcomes visitors who want to meet native children. In **Totorillas**, 1 km north of Pulinguí and 7 km south of the turn-off for the main park entrance, is the **Chimborazo Base Camp Lodge**, in a lovely valley at the foot of Chimborazo – you must make advance arrangements through **Expediciones Andinas** in Riobamba. The views are stunning.

The arenal is a large sandy plateau at about 4,400 m, to the west of Chimborazo, just below the main park entrance. It can be a harsh, windy place, but it is also very beautiful; take the time to admire the tiny flowers which grow here. This is the best place to see vicuñas, they hang around either in family groups: one male and its harem, or lone males which have been expelled from the group.

The **eastern slopes** of Chimborazo and Carihuayrazo are good for trekking. There are many walking opportunities here and it is a good place for acclimatization to the altitude. You can make an excursion (Tuesday, Thursday and Friday) to see the *hieleros* who bring ice blocks down from the glacier to sell in the Riobamba market (Riobamba agencies offer this tour). This is also an access to the Mocha Valley. Horses can be hired in **Urbina** (3,619 m), 2 km west of the Panamericana, about halfway between Ambato and Riobamba, and at the village of **12 de Octubre** just north of Urbina, ask for Daniel Villacís. In Urbina is a very good hostel, see Sleeping, page 252.

This is a difficult climb owing to the altitude. No one without mountaineering experience should attempt it before doing other summits; rope, ice-axe, crampon, and helmet must be used, ice screws may be useful, and acclimatization is essential. To make the most of it, consider spending a couple of days at the shelters, before meeting your guide for the climb. The best season is December and June-September. The two routes are up the southwest and northwest faces.

Southwest face From the Whymper refuge to the summit the climb is eight to nine hours and the descent about four hours. The path from the hut to the glacier is marked but difficult to follow at midnight, so it's best to check it out the day before. The route on the glacier is easy to follow as it is marked with flags, though it can be tricky in cloud or mist. There are several crevasses on the route, so you need to rope up. There are three routes depending on your experience and ability. It is highly recommended to go with a guide and start at 0000 or 0100. There are avalanche problems on the entire mountain. *Penitentes* are conical ice formations which can obstruct the final part of the route.

Northwest face (Pogyos route) The climb starts in Pogyos (4,000 m) along the Ambato-Guaranda road. There is a house with a metal roof where you can hire mules to carry your gear. Beware of pilfering from your bags on the ascent. Walk about three hours to the **Refugio Fabián Zurita** (4,900 m) which is uninhabitable. From the refuge to the summit is about an eight-hour climb; descent about three to four hours. It's advisable to start at 2330-0000 at the latest. Take tents and water (obtainable at Pogyos). We are grateful to Enrique Veloz Coronado for much of this information.

Parque Nacional Sangay → *Colour map 4, grid B6*

This is the largest protected area in the Ecuadorean highlands. It spans the Cordillera Oriental descending to the jungle and includes several important peaks: Tungurahua (5,023 m), El Altar (5,315 m) and Sangay (5,230 m). The many landscapes which can be admired in the park are beautiful. There are numerous lakes and waterfalls, not to speak of two active volcanoes: Tungurahua and Sangay. The park is suited for trekking, and experienced climbers will find special challenges in the nine summits of El Altar.

Ins and outs

There are many access routes to the park. The northernmost is from Baños, though beware of the restrictions in this area due to Tungurahua's volcanic activity, see pages 231 and 239. The area south of Tungurahua, and El Altar, are both accessed from Riobamba along the road to Penipe. Sangay is accessed from Riobamba via Chambo, Pungalá and Alao, or via Guarguallá.

A controversial road (known as the Guamote-Macas) which will join Riobamba and Macas in Oriente is missing only a couple kilometres to be completed. This road bisects the park and gives access to the Atillo lakes, among other areas. A turn-off from the Panamericana south of Guamote goes to the village of Totoras and the Lagunas de Osogoche. A small road connects Totoras with Achupallas.

For the lowland access to Parque Nacional Sangay and more park information, see page 406.

Attractions and park services

The park entry fee is US$10, it is charged at a couple of access points, but not all. The many beautiful lakes are an important attraction. The crater lake of **El Altar** is at the end of a popular trek (see Trekking below).

● *Sangay is one of the most active volcanoes in the world and has been in activity for more*
● *than half a century.*

area of lovely *páramo* with several lakes. There is basic, authentic accommodation here and a good restaurant serving local trout.

Sangay, one of the most active volcanoes in the world, has been in activity for over 50 years. It is often shrouded in mist, but when it clears, it is wonderful to see its perfect snow-covered cone and a puff of ash above the summit. It is surrounded by a magnificent, remote area.

Osogoche is a wild, cold and beautiful area of two large lakes and many smaller ones. Access is through the village of **Totoras**, where there is accommodation, and the hamlet of Osogoche, where native people still live in *chozas* (straw huts). The road reaches the edge of Laguna Cubillín, so with a vehicle it is possible to visit in a long day from Riobamba. The best season is November to early March. An unusual phenomenon occurs in some of the larger lakes in the month of September. Thousands of birds, called *cubibigs*, are said to dive into the lakes and die. It is known locally as *El Tributo de los Pájaros*.

Climbing El Altar and Sangay

El Altar Climbs to El Altar are technical. For experienced ice climbers the Ruta Obispo offers grade 4 and 5 mixed ice and rock. **El Obispo** is the highest and most southerly of Altar's nine summits, at 5,315 m. Another technical route is to **El Canónigo** (5,260 m), the northernmost of the summits, mixed ice and rock, grade 4 and 5. Altar's seven other summits are, from north to south: **Fraile Grande** (5,180 m); **Fraile Central** (5,070 m); **Fraile Oriental** (5,060 m); **Fraile Beato** (5,050 m); **Tabernáculo** (5,100 m); **Monja Chica** (5,080 m); and **Monja Grande** (5,160 m). Details are given in *Ecuador: A Climbing Guide*, see page 481. One access route to El Altar is through Candelaria, see Trekking below.

Rapid deglaciation is changing the climbing routes on El Altar.

Sangay Access to the mountain takes at least three days and is only for those who can endure long, hard days of walking and severe weather. Sangay can be dangerous even on a quiet day and protection against falling stones is vital. With a little coaching a *mecánica* can make shields, such as arm loops welded to an oil drum top. December/January is a good time to climb Sangay. Agencies in Quito and Riobamba offer tours or you can organize an expedition independently. A guide is essential. Porters can be hired in the access towns of Alao and Guarguallá. Guarguallá also has a community tourism project with accommodation and native guides.

Trekking in the park

El Altar The most popular trek is to the crater of El Altar. A well-used track (very muddy in the wet season) leads up a steep hill past **Hacienda Releche** (where there is accommodation), outside the little village of **Candelaria** (altitude 3,100 m). There are small signs at the only two turnings on the route. The track leads up a hill to a ridge where it joins a clearer track. This goes south first and then turns east up the valley of the Río Collanes. It is about six hours to the Collanes plain, where there are basic thatched-roof shelters, and another two hours to the crater which is surrounded by magnificent snow-capped peaks. Horses can be hired at Hacienda Releche to carry your gear.

Sangay The access route used by climbers is also a fine trekking route, experience is required.

Lakes The Atillo and Osogoche areas offer excellent trekking and it is possible to trek from one set of lakes to the other. *Trekking in Ecuador* (see page 482) describes a set of four interconnecting routes, for up to three weeks of excellent trekking within the park. Guides are available in all these areas.

South of Riobamba

To the south of Riobamba is a region of windswept plains where desendants of the Puruhá nation grow potatoes, *habas* (broad beans) and barley. The scenery is quite nice and there are some impressive canyons.

Cajabamba → *Phone code 03 Colour map 4, grid B5 Population 18,000 Altitude 3200 m*

In 1534 the original Riobamba was founded on this site, but in 1797 a disastrous earthquake caused a large section of the hill on the north side of the town to collapse in a great landslide, which can still be seen. It killed several thousand of the original inhabitants of Riobamba and the town was moved almost 20 km northeast to its present site. The new Riobamba has prospered, but Cajabamba has stagnated and is now a small, rather poor town. A colourful Indian market on Sunday is small but uncommercialized and interesting. There are few restaurants out of town on the Panamericana towards Cuenca.

The road and railway skirt the shores of **Laguna de Colta**, just after the fertile Cajabamba valley. The lake and surroundings are very beautiful and just a short bus trip from Riobamba. The views of Chimborazo, from the south shore of the lake are special. At the edge of the village along the Panamericana on the shore of Laguna de Colta is a small chapel, **La Balbanera**, dating from 1534, making it the oldest church in Ecuador, although it has been restored several times because of earthquakes.

Pallatanga → *Phone code 03 Population 1,200 Altitude 1,600*

Just south of La Balbanera, 5 km south of Cajabamba, a paved highway branches southwest to **Pallatanga**, a small town with a pleasant subtropical climate on the route to Bucay (Cumandá), Milagro, and Guayaquil. It is a pleasant place to get away in nice surroundings. There is accommodation and many small *comedores* along the highway.

Guamote → *Phone code 03 Colour map 4, grid B5 Population 2,000 Altitude 3,050 m*

Some 28 km south of Cajabamba is Guamote, a mainly indigenous town. It has an interesting and colourful market on Thursday with lots of animals and few tourists. There are good walking possibilities in the area. There is accommodation and some simple eateries. Many buses from Riobamba, especially on Thursday.

South of Guamote is **Tixán**, which has a beautifully restored church and many old houses. It is the home of many workers in the nearby sulphur mines. Between Guamote and Tixán is the well-signed turn-off to Osogoche, 32 km to the southeast, see Parque Nacional Sangay, page 248. The hike to/from the paved road takes at least five hours across windswept *páramos* with views of Sangay on clear days.

Alausí → *Phone code 03 Colour map 4, grid C5 Population 5,500 Altitude 2,350 m*

Some 84 km south of Riobamba, Alausí sits at the foot of Cerro Gampala on a terrace overlooking the deep Chanchán gorge. From a hill, Loma de Llugchi, a large statue of San Pedro overlooks town. The area enjoys a temperate climate and, in the heyday of the railroad, it was a popular holiday destination for Guayaquileños wishing to escape their hottest season. There is also a road going from here to the Pacific lowlands through Huigra (basic lodgings and restaurants). The atmosphere in the town is laid-back and friendly. The colourful Sunday market, in the plaza by the church, just up the hill from the station, draws *campesinos* from the outlying villages.

Many tourists join the train here for the amazing descent to Sibambe, via the famous *Nariz del Diablo* (Devil's Nose). See details about the train on page 245. In Alausí, tickets go on sale around 0900 at the train station, T03-2930126.

Chunchi, a friendly village with a Sunday market, is 37 km south of Alausí along the Panamericana. From here you can hike or cycle down the Huigra road to Chanchán, a scenic area. There are many restaurants along the highway, which are better than those in Alausí.

● Sleeping

Riobamba *p242, map p242*

A Abraspungu, Km 3 on the road to Guano, T03-2940820, www.hosteria-abraspungu.com Beautiful house in a country setting, excellent restaurant, parking, comfortable rooms and attentive service. Recommended.

A El Troje, 4½ km on the road to Chambo, T03-2960826, www.eltroje.com Quiet setting, good restaurant, pool and suana, internet, parking, nice rooms, good views.

A La Andaluza, 16 km north of Riobamba along the Panamericana, T03-2949370, www.hosteria-andaluza.com An old hacienda with modern facilities, good restaurant, parking, nice rooms with heaters and roaring fireplaces, lovely views, good walking in the area. Recommended.

B El Cisne, Av Daniel L Borja y Duchicela, T03-2964573, F2941982. Modern multi-storey building, includes breakfast, restaurant, parking, adequate rooms.

B Rincón Alemán, Remigio Romero y Alfredo Pareja, Ciudadela Arupos del Norte, T03-2603540, arupo@gmx.de Family-run hotel in a quiet residential area. Includes breakfast, laundry and cooking facilities, parking, garden, sauna, fitness room, fireplace. German spoken. Recommended.

B Zeus, Av Daniel L Borja 41-29, T03-2968036, www.hotelzeus.com.ec Restaurant, parking, modern, comfortable and nice. Bathtubs with views of Chimborazo!

B-C Montecarlo, Av 10 de Agosto 25-41 entre García Moreno y España, T03-2960557. Includes breakfast, restaurant, parking, nice house in colonial style, central location.

D Canadá, Av de la Prensa 23-31 y Av Daniel L Borja, near bus terminal, T03-2964677, hotelcanada@lasernet.net Restaurant, parking, clean and modern.

D Glamour, Primera Constituyente 37-85 ente Brazil y Zambrano, T03-2944406, F2944407. Comfortable but a bit out of the way, good value.

D La Estación, Unidad Nacional 2915 y Carabobo, T03-2955226. A nicely refurbished building, coveniently located near the railway station. Nice restaurant, good beds, several sitting rooms, nice wooden floors, terrace with hammocks and good views. Good value.

D Los Shyris, Rocafuerte 21-60 y 10 de Agosto, T/F03-2960323, hshyris@yahoo.com An old-time budget travellers' favourite, cheaper with shared bath, hot water 0500-1100 and 1700-2300, internet, decent rooms, service and value. Rooms at the back are quieter.

D Majestic, Av Daniel L Borja 43-60 y La 44, not far from bus terminal, T03-2968708. Cafeteria, electric shower, parking for a small car, rooms vary, adequate overall.

D Mashany, Veloz 41-73 y Zambrano, T03-2942914, F2964606. Parking, modern and comfortable but a bit out of the way.

D Oasis, Veloz 15-32 y Almagro, T03-2961210, F2941499. A small, pleasant, family-run hostel in a quiet location, laundry facilities, some rooms with kitchen and fridge, parking, nice garden, friendly, pick-up service from the Terminal. Recommended.

D Tren Dorado, Carabobo 22-35 y 10 de Agosto, T/F03-2964890, htrendorado@hotmail.com Conveniently located near the train station, early breakfast available in time to catch the train, restaurant serves good vegetarian lunch, reliable hot water, modern, nice large rooms, friendly, very good value. Recommended.

D Whymper, Av Miguel Angel León 23-10 y Primera Constituyente, T03-2964575, F2968137. Safe parking, spacious rooms, friendly, but a bit run down.

D-E Imperial, Rocafuerte 22-15 y 10 de Agosto, T03-2960429. Cheaper with shared bath, hot water 24 hours, stores luggage, good beds, comfortable, good views from the roof but loud music from bar on Fri and Sat nights, overall good value.

Reserva Faunística Chimborazo *p246*
L Chimborazo Base Camp, at Totorillas along the Vía del Arenal, T03-2964915, www.expediciones-andinas.com A beautiful lodge in a spectacular secluded valley at the foot of Chimborazo. Includes breakfast and dinner, very comfortable rooms, tastful decor, heaters. Caters to groups, advance arrangements necessary.
C Casa Cóndor, at the Pulinguí San Pablo community centre, T09-7584097, Fcea_sanpablo@yahoo.com. A community-run hostel built in the shape of a condor (if viewed from above). Includes 3 meals, shared bath, 2 rooms for 4 and a dorm for 22, bunk beds. Very cold but the bread oven in the dining area helps.
D Cabins, by the roadside at Pulinguí San Pablo, T03-2941481 (Riobamba), twalsh@ch.pro.ec Two nice cabins with capacity of up to 6 each. Common area with fireplace, arrange in advance.
D Posada de la Estación, at Urbina on the eastern slopes of Chimborazo, T03-2942215 (Riobamba), aventurag@ch.pro.ec A pleasant inn located in the converted station of Urbina, at 3,619 m this was the highest point of the Ecuadorean railway, good meals available, shared bath, clean, cold at night but dining room has a fireplace. Tours and treks can be arranged. Slide shows when the owner is in. Recommended.

Parque Nacional Sangay *p248*
D Hostal Capac Urcu, at Hacienda Releche, near the village of Candelaria, T03-2949761 or T03-2960848 (Riobamba). Pleasant and relaxing small working hacienda. Use of kitchen (extra charge) or good meals prepared on request, rents horses for the trek to Collanes, US$6 per horse each way, plus US$6 per muleteer.
 Also runs the **E refugio** at Collanes, by the crater of El Altar: thatched-roof rustic shelters, use of kitchen with gas stove and all utensils US$6. No hot water or blankets, take a warm sleeping bag. A new shelter was under construction in early 2005. Recommended.
E Los Saskines, by the hamlet of Atillo, T03-2601931 (Riobamba). Very basic accommodation in an authentic *choza* (native straw hut). Also runs a pleasant little restaurant serving good meals. The local

speciality is trout, caught when you order. If you are going out for an excursion, order your meal ahead.
F Guarguallá Cabaña, in Guarguallá Chico, T03-2949552 (Licto), agig-ec@yahoo.com Two community-run thatched roof cabins, bunk bed and use of kitchen, meals available. Nice woven and knitted crafts are produced in the village.
E Totoras Cabañas, just above the village of Totoras along the road to Osogoche, T03-2930635 or T03-2930634. Community-run cabins, nicely built and furnished by an NGO but not quite as well cared for by the community. Negotiable price, no running water. Meals may be available in the village if requested in advance.

South of Riobamba *p250*
Pallatanga
B Hostería El Valle, west of town on the road to Bucay, T/F03-2919216. Cabins in a rural setting. Includes 3 meals, pool, popular with *costeños* coming up to the hills to cool off, advance reservations required.
D Hostería El Pedregal, Pilchipamba, 30 min walk from town on the shores of the Río Coco, T03-2919192. Pleasant cabins in nice grounds by the river. Electric shower. Busy on weekends and holidays, otherwise very tranquil.

Guamote
D Inti Sisa, JM Plaza y García Moreno, T03-2916319, www.intisisa.org Part of a community development project run by a Belgian-Ecuadorean couple. Most rooms have private bath, cheaper in dorm, dining room and communal area with fireplace.
D Ramada Inn, Vela y Riobamba, T03-2916242. Some rooms with private bath.

Alausí
D Americano, García Moreno 151, T03-2930159. Hot water on request, a bit run down and out of the way.
D Europa, 5 de Junio 175 y Orozco, T03-2930200. Nicely refurbished in 2004, restaurant, ample parking, rooms vary from functional to comfortable, best in town. Recommended.
D Gampala, 5 de Junio 122, T03-2930138. Restaurant and bar with pool table, electric

shower, run down and barely adequate.
D San Pedro, 5 de junio y 9 de Octubre, T03-2930086. Parking, modern and comfortable but rooms are still a bit bare, friendly owner, new in 2004.
D-E Alausí, 5 de Junio 142 y Orozco, T03-2930361. Cheaper with shared bath, electric shower, simple, clean and friendly.
D-E Panamericano, 5 de Junio y 9 de Octubre, near the bus stop, T03-2930278. Restaurant, cheaper with shared bath, simple to basic, quieter rooms in back.
E Tequendama, 5 de Junio 152, T03-2930123. Incongruous namesake of a Bogotá luxury hotel, shared bath, electric shower, basic but clean and friendly, good value.

Chunchi
D Unnamed Hotel, Bolívar y Manuel Reyes, T03-2936626, F2936658. Modern.
E Residencial Patricia, Bolívar, half a block from the main plaza, T03-2936237. Cheaper with shared bath, adequate.

● Eating

Riobamba *p242, map p244*
Most restaurants close by 2100 and on Sunday.
♥♥♥♥ **El Delirio**, Primera Constituyente 2816 y Rocafuerte, T03-2966441, Tue-Sun 1200-2130. Ecuadorean and international food served in an historical home with patio. Food and location are not bad, but the place is touristy and overpriced.
♥♥♥ **Cafetería Montecarlo**, 10 de Agosto 25-45 y García Moreno, daily 0700-1200, 1600-2200 (0500 breakfast can be arranged before train ride). Ecuadorean and international, good breakfasts, snacks and complete meals, pleasant atmosphere.
♥♥♥ **La Gran Havana**, Daniel León Borja 42-52 y Duchicela, T03-2968088, daily 1100-2300. Economical set lunch, very good Cuban and international food à la carte.
♥♥♥ **Parrillada de Fausto**, Uruguay 2038 y Daniel León Borja, T03-2967876, Mon-Sat 1200-1500, 1800-2300. Good grilled meat and fish, nice atmosphere.
♥♥♥-♥♥ **Bonny**, Villaroel 1558 y Almagro, Mon-Sun 1000-2000. Seafood is their speciality, also serve good value set meals, very popular. Recommended.

♥♥♥-♥♥ **Cabaña Montecarlo**, García Moreno 21-40 y 10 de Agosto, Tue-Sat 1200-2100, Sun-Mon 1200-1500. Good value set lunch, pricier à la carte. Good food and service, large portions, 'old Riobamba' atmosphere, popular with locals, recommended.
♥♥♥-♥♥ **Mónaco Pizzería**, Diego Ibarra y Daniel León Borja, Mon-Fri 1400-2200, Sat-Sun 1200-2300. Delicious pizza and pasta, nice salads, very good food, service and value, recommended.
♥♥♥-♥♥ **Sabores d'Italia**, Lavalle 22-36 y Primera Constituyente, Mon-Sat 1100-2300, Sun 1400-2300. Pizza and pasta, good value, personal service.
♥♥ **Posada San Francisco**, Primera Constituyente 1532 y Almagro, Tue-Sun 1000-2000. Good value set lunch, grill at night.
♥♥ **Restaurante Montecarlo**, Colón y Primera Constituyente, daily 1200-1500, at night to 0100. Cheap set meals at midday and *comida típica* late at night, popular.
♥♥ **Sierra Nevada**, Primera Constituyente y Rocafuerte, Mon-Sat 0800-2200, Sun 0800 - 1600. Excellent value set lunch, vegetarian on request. Nice atmosphere, recommended.
♥♥-♥ **Café VIP**, Rocafuerte entre 10 de Agosto y Primera Constituyente. Vegetarian.
♥ **Natural Food**, Tarqui entre Veloz y Primera Constituyente, Mon-Sat 1200-1430. Set meals only, vegetarian available.

Cafés
Helados de Paila, Espejo y 10 de Agosto, daily 0900-1900. Very good home-made ice cream, coffee and sweets.
La Abuela Rosa, Brasil y Esmeraldas, Tue-Sat 1600-2100. Cafeteria in grandmother's house serving humitas, *quimbolitos* and other typical Ecuadorian snacks. Nice atmosphere and good service.
Pynn's, Espejo 21-20 y Guayaquil, Mon-Sat 0900-1930. Tacos and lasagne, also set lunches.

Bakeries & ice cream parlours
Helados de Paila, Espejo entre Guayaquil y 10 de Agosto. Home-made ice cream, good selection, coffee, sweets, popular.
Pan Van, Primera Constituyente y Colón and Veloz y Epiclachima. Excellent quality and variety.

La Vienesa, Larrea 2116 y Guayaquil and Av Daniel León Borja y Brasil. Try their popular *palanquetas*, water buns.

South of Riobamba *p250*
Alausí

Alausí is not the culinary capital of Ecuador, but a few places serve decent meals.

¶¶-¶ La Diligencia, at the railway station. Set meals and pizza.

¶ El Flamingo, Antonio Mora y 9 de Octubre, behind Hotel Tequendama, lunch only. Good set meal.

¶ Gampala, At the hotel, 0700-2300. Set meals and à la carte, vegetarian on request.

⊙ Bars and clubs

Riobamba *p242, map p244*

Gens-Chop Bar, Av Daniel León Borja 42-17 y Duchicela. Bar, good music and sport videos, open daily, popular. Recommended.

Romeo Bar, Vargas Torres y Av Daniel León Borja, US$2 cover. Popular, nice bar and club, with pleasant sitting area on the second floor. A variety of music from Latin to R&B.

San Valentín, Av Daniel León Borja y Vargas Torres, esquina. A combination restaurant serving good Mexican dishes, pizza, and other snacks, bar and even disco with a mini dance floor. Very popular with locals.

Vieja Guardia, Av Flor 40-43 y Av Zambrano, US$2 cover. Good bar and open air disco.

⊙ Entertainment

Riobamba *p242, map p244*
Live music

Café Concierto, at the Museo de la Ciudad, Primera Costituyente y Espejo, T03-2951906, usually Fri at 1930.

Casa de la Cultura, Rocafuerte y 10 de Agosto, T03-2960219. Sometimes has a good *peña* or other live music Thu-Sat evenings, enquire in advance.

⊛ Festivals and events

Riobamba *p242, map p244*

Jan Fiesta del Niño Rey de Reyes Culminates on 6 Jan after a period of Pases del Niño, parades in honour of the baby Jesus, which are carried out throughout Dec and the first week of Jan. On the eve there are fireworks

and parties and on the 6th a street parade with floats which gathers thousands of people dressed up in costumes.

Mar-Apr Semana Santa, on the Tue of Holy Week, an impressive, well-attended, solemn procession is held in honour of El Señor del Buen Suceso.

21 Apr Fiestas de Abril Riobamba's independence day, celebrated for several days with lively parades, concerts, bullfights and drinking. Hotel prices rise and rooms may be difficult to find during this period.

29 Jun Fiestas Patronales in honour of San Pedro are held with street parties; the daring jump over bonfires.

11 Nov Fiestas del 11 de Noviembre Festivals to celebrate the first attempt at independence from Spain take place for several days around 11 Nov with cultural events.

Reserva Faunística Chimborazo *p246*
La Chorrera and Pulinguí San Pablo

Feb-Mar Carnival Authentic celebrations are held at La Chorrera on the Sun of Carnival and at Pulinguí San Pablo on Ash Wed, with the participation of the local school kids.

Parque Nacional Sangay *p248*
Totoras

Sep Festival de los Cubibigs Held in Totoras and Osogoche on the 3rd weekend of Sep, with music and folkloric presentations.

South of Riobamba *p250*

20 Jan Fiestas de San Sebastián are held in Cajabamba in honour of the patron saint.

24 Jun Fiestas de San Juan Bautista Held in Tixán in honour of the town's patron saint, these are very colourful.

29 Jun Fiestas de San Pedro are held in Alauí in honour of the town's patron saint.

2 Aug Fiestas de Chunchi celebrate the town becoming a canton.

29 Sep Fiestas de Pallatanga Held in honour of patron saint San Miguel Arcángel.

⊙ Shopping

Riobamba *p242, map p244*
Camping gear

Hobby Sport, 10 de Agosto y Rocafuerte, sleeping bags, tents, fishing supplies. Directly opposite is a store which also has some camping supplies, including *Camping Gaz*. **Julio Verne** tour operator also sells Camping Gaz.

Protección Industrial, Rocafuerte 24-51 y Orozco, T03-2963017. For waterproof ponchos and suits, fishing supplies, ropes. Some of the tour operators hire camping and climbing gear.

Handicrafts

Crafts are sold Wed and Sat, 0800-1500, at Plaza Roja, see Markets above.

Almacén Cacha, Orozco next to the Plaza Roja, Tue-Sat. Cooperative of native people from the Cacha area, sells good value woven bags, wool sweaters and other crafts, also excellent honey.

Alta Montaña, Av Daniel León Borja y Diego Ibarra. Nice *tagua* carvings and other crafts, you can also see how the *tagua* is carved.

Artesanías Ecuador, Carabobo y 10 de Agosto. Good selection of crafts, ceramics, wood, *tagua*, straw.

Camari, Espejo y Olmedo esquina, at the supermarket. Small crafts section, especially woollens.

Casa de la Cultura, Rocafuerte y 10 de Agosto. Crafts workshops (which you can visit) and store. Wood, knitted garments, and a variety of other crafts.

Several *tagua* shops on Daniel León Borja near the train station.

Markets

See description in main text, p243.

Supermarkets

Akí, Colón y Olmedo and Costales y Av Daniel León Borja, opposite Parque Guayaquil.

Camari, Espejo y Olmedo esquina, near La Merced church.

La Ibérica, Av Daniel León Borja 37-62.

▲ Activities and tours

Riobamba *p242, map p244*
Ball games

Bolas a game played with large metal balls can be seen at Parque Barriga on Av Miguel A León.

Mamona a local ball game in which a solid leather ball is hit with the palm of the hand, is played in the afternoons at the Plaza Roja and in San Alfonso on Sun.

Climbing and trekking

Riobamba is an excellent starting point for trips to Chimborazo, Carihuayrazo, Altar, Tungurahua, Sangay and the Inca Trail to Ingapirca. For organized tours, transport and gear hire see Tour operators below. For general information see Climbing, p71, and Trekking, p81.

Cycling

There are good cycling routes in the Riobamba area, the most popular is a downhill ride from Chimborazo. Rates from US$10 per day for rentals, from US$35 per day for a tour including transport, guide, meal.

Julio Verne (see Tour operators below).

Pro Bici, Primera Constituyente 23-40 or 23-51 y Larrea (if the bike shop is closed, try

at the clothing shop across the street),
T03-2951759, www.probici.com Run by
guide and mechanic, Galo Brito, bjke trips
and rental, guided tours with support
vehicle, full equipment (use Cannondale
ATBs).

Tour operators

Most companies offer climbing trips (from
US$150 per person for 2 days), trekking
(from US$50 per person per day) and cycling
tours (from US$30 per day). Many hotels also
offer tours, but note that not all are run by
qualified guides.

Alta Montaña, Av Daniel León Borja 35-17 y
Diego Ibarra, T2942215,
aventurag@ch.pro.ec Trekking, climbing,
cycling, birdwatching, photography and
horse-riding tours in the highlands, logistic
support for expeditions, transport,
equipment rental, English spoken.
Recommended.

Andes Trek, Rocafuerte 22-66 y 10 de
Agosto, T2940964,
www.andes-trek.com Climbing, trekking
and mountain-biking tours, transport,
equipment rental, run by Marcelo
Puruncajas a known climber, English and
German spoken.

Expediciones Andinas, Vía a Guano, Km 3,
across from **Hotel Abraspungo**, T2964915,
www.expediciones-andinas.com Climbing
expeditions, operate Chimborazo Base Camp
on south flank of mountain. Caters for
groups, contact well in advance, run by
Marco Cruz, a well-known climber and
certified guide of the German Alpine Club,
German spoken. Recommended.

Julio Verne, El Espectador 22-25 y Av Daniel
León Borja, 2 blocks north of the train
station, T/F03-2963436, www.julioverne-
travel.com Climbing, trekking, cycling,
jungle and Galápagos trips, river rafting,
transport to mountains, good equipment
rental, Ecuadorean-Dutch run, uses official
guides, English spoken. Recommended.

Metropolitan Touring, Lavalle y Av Daniel
León Borja, T03-2969600,
www.metropolitan-touring.com A branch
of the large Quito operator, railway tours,
airline tickets.

Veloz Coronado, Chile 33-21 y Francia,
T/F03-2960916, best reached after 1900.
Enrique Veloz Coronado is a known climber,

his sons are also guides and work with him
on climbing and trekking expeditions.

Reserva Faunística Chimborazo *p246*
Climbing and trekking

1-5 day tours in the Chimborazo area,
including one circumnavigating the
mountain, are offered by the native guides
of the communities of Pulingí San Pablo
and La Chorrera.

Wasi Cóndor, Vía del Arenal, T09-7584097 or
through chief guide Juan Pacheco
T09-7580033, cea_sanpablo@yahoo.com
Climbing and trekking tours in the reserve
are also offered by operators in Riobamba,
Ambato, Guaranda, Baños, and Quito.

Parque Nacional Sangay *p248*
Climbing & trekking

Dora Paña, at Restaurant Los Saskines in the
village of Atillo, is a native guide. She offers
trekking and horse-riding tours in the area.
Arrange in advance leaving a message with
Victor Paña in Riobamba, T03-2601931.
The community of Totoras also has native
guides offering tours to the Osogoche lakes
and other local attractions. You can try to
make advance arrangements, T03-2930634,
but will be easier in person.
Climbing and trekking tours in the park
are also offered by operators in Riobamba
and Quito.

South of Riobamba *p250*
Alausí

Nariz del Diablo Devil's Nose, 5 de Junio
132 y Pedro de Loza, T/F930240. Runs
horseback trips to the Devil's Nose and other
trips in the area.

⊖ Transport

Riobamba *p242, map p244*
For main inter-city routes see the bus
timetable page 52.
To **Guaranda**, the road is paved to San
Juan, from where there are 2 routes, both
very scenic: that via Gallo Rumi is unpaved,
while the one via the arenal is mostly paved
(some **Flota Bolívar** buses take this route),
sit on the right for the beautiful views on
either route.
 To **Guayaquil**, service goes via Pallatanga,
really spectacular for the first 2 hrs.

To **Baños** and **Oriente**, from the Terminal Oriental. Note that because the direct road is closed, buses go via Ambato.

To **Guano** from Mercado Dávalos, García Moreno y New York, every 20 mins, last bus returns to Riobamba at 1800, US$0.25, taxi US$4.

To **Punín** from Av Juan Félix Proaño y Olmedo, by the public hospital, at the south end of town, every 20 mins, US$0.25, 20 mins.

To **Salarón** Transportes Unidos, same stop as Punín, Mon-Fri at 0630, US$0.60, 50 min, returning at 1230.

Reserva Faunística Chimborazo *p246*
Arenal and shelters The easiest way to visit the western side of the reserve is on a tour. There are no buses that will take you to the shelters. You can arrange transport with a tour operator or taxi from Riobamba (about US$25 one way). You can also take a bus travelling between Riobamba and Guaranda which goes on the Vía del Arenal (Flota Bolívar 8 daily, 0700-1800, check that it is taking this route; from Riobamba US$0.90, 1 hr). Alight at the turn-off for the refuges and walk the remaining steep 5 km to the first shelter.

Pulinguí San Pablo Riobamba-Guaranda buses as indicated above, go by Pulinguí San Pablo. From Riobamba US$0.60, 45 min.

Urbina and the eastern slopes There are trekking tours in this area, arrange transport from an agency or take a bus between Riobamba and Ambato, get off at the turn-off for Posada La Estación and Urbina. It is 1.2 km from the Panamericana to the hostel.

Pogyos take a bus between Ambato and Guaranda.

Parque Nacional Sangay *p248*
Candelaria Don't confuse the mountain El Altar with the village of the same name. There is an El Altar signpost on the Riobamba-Baños road but this is not the route to the mountain. From the Terminal Oriental in Riobamba, to Candelaria, Mon-Fri 0600, 1215 and 1700, Sat 1400 and 1800; get there early, sometimes they leave ahead of schedule, US$1, 1½ hrs. Alternatively, take a bus from the same terminal to Penipe, every ½ hr, US$0.40,

40 mins, and hire a pick-up truck from there to Candelaria, US$15, 40 mins.
Alao From Parque La Dolorosa, Puruhá y Primera Constituyente in Riobamba, Mon-Sat 0530, 0630 and hourly 1145-1845, Sun 0630, US$1, 1½ hrs.
Guarguallá A milk truck goes to Guarguallá Chico from Parque La Dolorosa, Puruhá y 10 de Agosto, Riobamba, daily at 0400, returns 0830, US$1.50, 2 hrs. A bus and pickups go from 10 de Agosto y Benalcázar to Guarguallá Grande (from where it is a 25 min walk to Guarguallá Chico), Mon, Wed, Fri, Sat around 1330-1400, US$1.75, 2 hrs.

Atillo Buses from Riobamba, from Juan de Velasco y Olmedo, daily at 0545, goes by Atillo about 0830, US$2.40 and arrives at La Punta, the end of the road about 1000, US$3.50. From corner 10 de Agosto y Benalcázar, 1445-1500 Mon, Tue, Wed, Fri and Sat, from Guamote on Thu and Sun at 1430; this service goes as far as the military camp about 10 min past Atillo. Return service from the military camp at 0500, from La Punta at 1400, going by Atillo at 1530.

Totoras Bus from Riobamba, corner Gaspar de Villarroel y Pichincha, between 1300 and 1400 on Mon, Tue, Wed, Fri and Sat. US$2, 2½ hrs. On Thu a couple buses and pick-ups leave from Guamote around 1300. On Sun trucks from Alausí around 1400. Bus to **Riobamba** at 0500, on Thu it goes to Guamote from where you can transfer.

South of Riobamba *p250*
Cajabamba Frequent service from Av Unidad Nacional y Av de la Prensa, 2 blocks from the Terminal Terrestre in Riobamba, US$0.25, 25 min.

Pallatanga Frequent buses from the Terminal Terrestre Riobamba, US$1.75 2 hrs, and Guayaquil US$3, 3 hrs.

Guamote Frequent service from Av Unidad Nacional y Av de la Prensa, 2 blocks from the Terminal Terrestre in Riobamba, US$1, 1 hr.

Alausí Coop Patria and Trans Alausí have offices along 5 de Junio in Alausí, note that many through buses don't go into town, they have to be caught at the highway. Every 30 min to/from the Terminal Terrestre in **Riobamba**, US$1.50, 1¾ hrs. To **Quito**, 4 direct in AM or buses from Cuenca pass through, about 20 a day, US$5-6, 5½ hrs; or change in Riobamba. To **Cuenca**, US$5, 4 hrs. To **El Tambo** or **Cañar**, buses going through to Cuenca. To **Ambato**, hourly, 3 hrs, US$3. To **Guayaquil via Huigra**, 3 daily US$5, 5 hrs.

Chunchi Buses leave from the plaza, several daily to/from the Terminal in Riobamba.

ℹ Directory

Riobamba *p242, map p244*
Banks Banco del Pacífico, Av Daniel León Borja y Zambrano, esquina. Banco del Pichincha, Primera Constituyente y García Moreno. Banco de Guayaquil, Primera Constituyente 2626 y García Moreno. Produbanco, Veloz y García Moreno esquina.
Internet Rates about US$1 per hr.
Laundry Donini,Villarroel entre España y Larrea, Mon-Sat 0830-1230, 1500-1800, US$0.40/lb. They also have a dry cleaning service on Av Daniel León Borja 37-55 y Brasil. **Hospitals** Metropolitano, Junín, entre España y García Moreno, T03-2941930. **Post office** 10 de Agosto y Espejo, esquina. **Travel agents** Diamante Tours, García Moreno y Veloz, T03-2960124. For airline tickets. **Useful addresses Immigration**, Av Leopoldo Freire (Av de la Policía) by the Police station, Barrio Pucará, T03-2964697. **Ministerio del Ambiente**, Av 9 de Octubre y Quinta Macají, at the western edge of town, north of the roundabout at the end of Av Isabel de Godin, T03-963779. Open Mon-Fri 0800-1300, 1400-1700. For information about Parque Nacional Sangay; rangers are only in the office in the early morning. From town take a city bus San Gerardo-El Batán. **Police**, T101.

South of Riobamba *p250*
Alausí
Banks Banco de Guayaquil, 5 de Junio near train station. TCs, Visa and Mastercard.

Southern Highlands

⁑ Footprint features

Introduction

The convoluted topography of the Southern Highlands, comprising the provinces of Cañar, Azuay and Loja, reveals an ancient non-volcanic past distinct from its northern Sierra neighbours. This region is home to many treasures. Here are Ecuador's prime Inca site, two of its most spectacular national parks, and Cuenca, the focal point of El Austro (as this part of the country is called), which boasts some of the country's finest colonial architecture. The Cuenca basin is a major artesanía centre, producing ceramics, baskets, gold and silver jewellery and textiles, as well as the famous Panama hat.

In addition to cultural attractions, a pleasant climate and magnificent scenery make the Southern Highlands prime walking country. Vilcabamba, south of Loja, is a particularly suitable base for trekking and horseback excursions, with nearby undisturbed páramo and cloud forest, home to many birds and other wildlife.

The Southern Highlands have an extensive road network and there is access to the Peruvian border at several different points. An increasing number of travellers are discovering these out-of-the-way crossings, which link Ecuador with interesting areas in the north of Peru.

★ Don't miss...

1 **Cuenca's architecture** Take a stroll through the colonial past in the heart of the city, page 263.

2 **Ice cream at Heladería Holanda** Get your just desserts at this popular Cuenca institution, page 270.

3 **Ingapirca** Visit the 'Wall of the Inca', Ecuador's most famous archaeological site, page 275.

4 **Parque Nacional Podocarpus** Trek into magical Ecuadorean cloud forest, page 287.

5 **Horseriding around Vilcabamba** Give in to the call of the wild in the magnificent scenery around Vilcabamba, page 302.

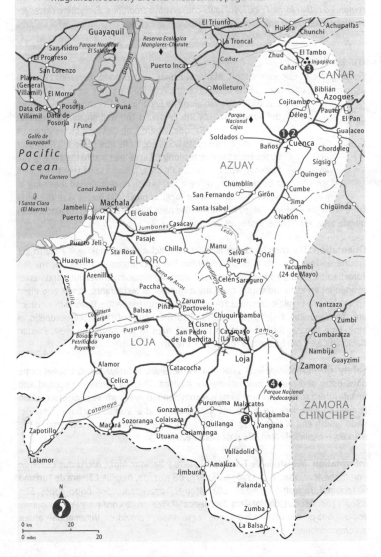

Cuenca → *Phone code 07 Colour map 6, grid A4 Population 300,000 Altitude 2,530 m*

Cuenca is capital of the province of Azuay and the third largest city in Ecuador. The city has preserved much of its colonial ambience, with many of its old buildings constructed of the travertine quarried nearby and recently renovated. Most Ecuadoreans consider this their finest city and few would disagree. Its cobblestone streets, flowering plazas and whitewashed buildings with old wooden doors and ironwork balconies make it a pleasure to explore. In 1999 Cuenca was designated a World Heritage site by UNESCO.

As well as being the economic centre of El Austro, as the Southern Sierra is called, Cuenca is also an intellectual centre. It has a long tradition as the birthplace of notable artists, writers, poets and philosophers, earning it the title 'The Athens of Ecuador'. It remains a rather formal city, loyal to its conservative traditions. Everything closes for lunch between 1300 and 1500 and many places are closed on Sunday. ▸▸ *For Sleeping, Eating and other listings, see pages 265-274.*

Ins and outs

Getting there Cuenca's airport, **Mariscal Lamar** ⓘ *Av España, T07-2862203*, is a 25-minute walk northeast of the colonial centre. A taxi to the centre costs US$2, a city bus US$0.25. Also along Av España and five minutes' walk from the airport towards the centre, is the well-organized **Terminal Terrestre** ⓘ *T07-2827061*, where long-distance buses arrive. A taxi to the centre costs US$1.50, a city bus US$0.25. Note that buses from the centre along C Larga take you to the back of the terminal, which is not a safe area; taking a taxi to the terminal is a better option. Using a taxi is also recommended if arriving at night. The terminal for local or provincial buses is at the **Feria Libre** on Av las Américas. Many city buses also pass here, but note that this, too, is an unsafe area. ▸▸ *For further details, see Transport, page 273.*

● Cuenca has spring-like days with chilly nights, characteristic of interandean valleys. The rainiest months are Mar-May. Aug can be very windy and cold at night.

Orientation The colonial centre is fairly compact and flat, making it easy to get around on foot. The city is bounded by the Río Machángara to the north. The Río Tomebamba separates the colonial heart from the stadium, universities and newer residential areas to the south; there are a number of restaurants, hotels and night spots along Av Remigio Crespo, a 20-minute walk from the centre. Beyond this district are the Yanuncay and Tarqui rivers and to the south of them the *autopista*, a multi-lane bypass. Av las Américas is a ring road to the north and west. Parque Nacional Cajas can be seen to the west of the city.

Safety Cuenca is somewhat safer than either Quito or Guayaquil, but street crime does occur and routine precautions are advised. The city centre is deserted and unsafe after 2200, when using a taxi is recommended. Areas where particular caution is advised after dark are, El Puente Roto (south end of Vargas Machuca), Cruz del Vado (south end of Juan Montalvo), behind the Terminal Terrestre and around the markets – especially Mercado 9 de Octubre.

Information Ministerio de Turismo ⓘ *Sucre y Benigno Malo, on Parque Calderón next to the Municipio, T07-283933, Mon-Fri, 0830-1700,* helpful. **Cámara de Turismo** ⓘ *Terminal Terrestre, T07-2868482, Mon-Fri 0700-2100, Sat 0800-2000, Sun 0800-1300.* **Asociación Hotelera de Cuenca** ⓘ *Presidente Córdova y Padre Aguirre, T07-2836925, Mon-Fri 0830-1300, 1430-1800,* provides information about accommodation.

History

From AD 500 to around 1480, Cuenca was a Cañari settlement, called Guapondeleg, which roughly translates as 'an area as large as heaven'. The suffix 'deleg' is still found in several local place names, a vestige of the now extinct Cañari language.

Owing to its geographical location, this was among the first parts of what is now Ecuador to come under the domination of the Inca empire, which had expanded north. The Incas settled the area around Cuenca and called it Tomebamba, which roughly translates as 'Valley of Knives'. The name survives as one of the region's rivers. Some 70 km north of Cuenca, in an area known as Jatun Cañar, the Incas built the ceremonial centre of Ingapirca, which remains the most important Inca site in the country (see page 275). Ingapirca and Tomebamba were, for a time, the hub of the northern part of the Inca empire.

The city as it is today was founded by the Spanish in 1557 on the site of Tomebamba and named Santa Ana de los Cuatro Ríos de Cuenca. Cuenca then became an important and populous regional centre in the crown colony governed from Quito. The *conquistadores* and the settlers who followed them were interested in the working of precious metals, for which the region's indigenous peoples had earned a well-deserved reputation. Following independence from Spain, Cuenca became capital of one of three provinces that made up the new republic, the others being Quito and Guayaquil.

Sights

City centre

On the main square, **Parque Abdón Calderón**, are both the Old Cathedral, also known as **El Sagrario**, and the immense 'new' **Catedral de la Inmaculada**. The former was begun in 1557, when modern Cuenca was founded, and was built on the foundations of an Inca structure; some of the Inca blocks are still visible facing the plaza. The new cathedral was started in 1885 and contains a famous crowned image of the Virgin. It was the work of the German architect Padre Johannes Baptista Stiehle, who also designed many other buildings in the Cuenca area. It was planned to be the largest cathedral in South America but the architect made some miscalculations with the foundations and the final domes on the front towers could not be built for fear that the whole thing would collapse. Modern stained glass, a beautiful altar and an exceptional play of light and shade inside the cathedral make it worth a visit. The Sunday evening worship is recommended.

Other Cuenca churches that deserve a visit are **San Blas**, **San Francisco**, **El Cenáculo**, and **Santo Domingo**. Many are open at irregular hours and for services only, because of increasing problems with theft. The 17th-century church of **El Carmen de la Asunción** is close to the southwest corner of La Inmaculada and has a flower market in the tiny **Plazoleta El Carmen** in front. The church is open early in the morning and mid-afternoon, but the attached cloister of El Carmen Alto is closed as the nuns inside live in total isolation.

Housed in a cloistered convent founded in 1599, the **Museo del Monasterio de las Conceptas** ① *Hermano Miguel 6-33 between Pdte Córdova and Juan Jaramillo, T07-2830625, Mon-Fri 0900-1730, Sat and public holidays 1000-1300, US$2.50,* has a well-displayed collection of religious and folk art, and an extensive collection of lithographs by Guayasamín.

● *The French Geodesic Mission of 1736-44, which came to Ecuador to measure the Equator,*
● *used El Sagrario as one of the fixed points for their measurements.*

The **Museo de Esqueletología** ① *Sucre y Borrero, Mon-Fri 0900-1330, 1500-1800, US$1*, has a small well-designed collection of bird and animal skeletons, from a hummingbird to an elephant. For live animals, visit the **Amaru Zoológico** ① *Benigno Malo 4-74 y C Larga, by the esclinata, To7-2826337, www.zoologicoamaru.com, Mon-Sat 0900-2000, Sun and holidays 0900-1300*, which has a collection of fish, amphibians and reptiles on display.

> ‼ A lovely, restored colonial house is the Casa Azul at Gran Colombia 10-29 y Padre Aguirre, which houses a travel agency, restaurant and a museum.

West of the centre, the **Museo Municipal de Arte Moderno** ① *Sucre 1527 y Talbot, on the Plaza San Sebastián, To7-2831027, Mon-Fri 0830-1300, 1500-1830, Sat-Sun 0900-1300, free*, has a permanent contemporary art collection and an art library. Some of the exhibits of Cuenca's biennial international painting competition are shown here as well as other cultural activities worth attending.

Along the Río Tomebamba

From the centre, **las esclinatas** (steps) descend towards the river. Along the north shore is **El Barranco**, a bluff with picturesque colonial houses. It can be admired from **Parque de la Madre** and from a linear park along the opposite shore, a pleasant place for a stroll. Construction started in 2005 to revitalize the riverfront.

The excellent **Museo del Banco Central 'Pumapungo'** ① *C Larga y Huayna Capac, entrance on the far left of the building, To7-2831255, Mon-Fri 0900-1800, Sat 0900-1300, US$3*, is on the southeastern edge of the colonial city, at the actual site of the Tomebamba excavations (see page 263). The ruins can be seen at the **Parque Arqueológico Pumapungo**, part of the museum complex. The **Museo Arqueológico** contains all the Cañari and Inca remains and artefacts found here. Although the Ingapirca ruins are more spectacular, it is believed that Tomebamba was the principal Inca administrative centre in southern Ecuador. Other halls in the premises house the **Museo Etnográfico**, with information on different Ecuadorean cultures, including a special collection of *tsantsas* (shrunken heads from Oriente), the **Museo de Arte Religioso**, the **Museo Numismático** and temporary exhibits. There are also book and music libraries and free cultural videos and music events.

About 300 m from the Pumapungo site there are further excavations at the **Museo Manuel Agustín Landívar** ① *C Larga 2-23, To7-2832639*, which reveal traces of Inca and Cañari civilizations and show how the Spanish reused the stonework. It is undergoing restoration in 2005. Nearby, the **Museo de las Culturas Aborígenes** ① *C Larga 5-24 y Mariano Cueva, To7-2839181. Mon-Fri 0830-1230, 1430-1830, Sat 0830-1230, US$2*, the private collection of Dr J Cordero López, has a good selection of pre-Columbian archaeology and is well worth a visit. There are guided tours in English, Spanish and French.

Just to the west, the **Instituto Azuayo de Folklore** ① *Escalinata 303 y C Larga, extension of C Hermano Miguel, To7-2842586, Mon-Fri 0930-1300, 1430-1800, Sat 1000-1300, free*, has an exhibition of popular Latin American arts and crafts. Through **CIDAP** (Centro Interamericano de Desarollo de Artes Populares), it supports research and promotes sales of artisans' works. There is also a library and a recommended crafts shop. Housed in a beautifully restored colonial mansion, the **Museo Remigio Crespo Toral** ① *C Larga 7-07 y Borrero, closed for renovations in 2005*, has various regional history collections, including gold objects from several indigenous cultures.

Beyond the centre

Located on Calle las Herrerías, or the 'blacksmiths' road, across the river from the Museo del Banco Central, the **Museo de Artes de Fuego** ① *Las Herrerías y 10 de Agosto, Mon-Fri (closed for lunch), Sat am*, has a display of wrought-iron work and pottery. Also known as Casa de Chaguarchimbana, it is housed in a beautifully restored old building. Outside is a sculpture of a volcano and on special occasions the god Vulkan, wrapped in flames, comes out of the volcano. There is also a shop.

South of the city, accessed via Avenida Fray Vicente Solano, beyond the football stadium, is **El Turi** church, orphanage and *mirador*, well worth a visit for the great views; a tiled panorama explains what you see. It's a 40-minute walk from the base to the church or two hours from the colonial city (not safe after dark), or take a taxi. There are good walks along attractive country lanes further south but do not take valuables.

The **Universidad de Cuenca**, in Balzaí west of the city, has an **Orquideario** ⓘ *follow Av Ordóñez Lazo, just past the bridge over the Tomebamba (2 blocks west of the Hotel Oro Verde), T07-2842893, Mon-Fri 0830-1130, 1415-1700,* with over 360 species of orchids.

The suburb of **San Joaquín**, out west near the tennis club, is famous for its basketwork. There are many houses where you can see the different types of baskets being made. Some of the styles, in particular the hour-glass shapes, are made only in the Cuenca and Azogues areas.

Baños

There are sulphur baths, 5 km southwest of Cuenca at **Baños**, with its domed, blue church in a delightful landscape. Water temperatures at the source are measured at 76°C, making them the hottest commercial baths in the country. There are three complexes: **Rodas, Merchan** and **Durán** ⓘ *dawn-2100 or 2200, US$3.50.* The latter are by far the largest and best maintained and, although associated with the **Hostería Durán** (see Sleeping), the numerous hot pools and tubs and steam baths are open to the public. They are very crowded at weekends. The country lanes above the village offer some pleasant walks. City buses marked 'Baños' go to and from Cuenca; to walk takes 1½ hrs.

● Sleeping

Cuenca *p262, map p266*
Cuenca is more expensive than other Ecuadorean cities.
L Mansión Alcázar, Bolívar 12-55 y Tarqui, T07-2823918, www.mansionalcazar.com A beautifully restored colonial house, a mansion indeed, includes breakfast, restaurant serves gourmet international food, lovely gardens, quiet relaxed atmosphere, exclusive boutique.
L Oro Verde, Av Ordóñez Lazo, northwest of the centre towards Cajas, T07-2831200, www.oroverdehotels.com Elegant hotel on a lake at the outskirts of town, includes buffet breakfast, excellent international restaurant offers buffet lunch and à la carte dinner, small pool, internet.
AL Crespo, C Larga 793, T07-2842571, www.ecuadorexplorer.com/crespo Modern hotel in the colonial centre, includes breakfast, very good restaurant, internet, parking, some nice rooms overlooking the river, others dark or with no windows, avoid rooms on the side of the hotel by the lane.
AL El Dorado, Gran Colombia 787 y Luis Cordero, T07-2831390, F2831663. Elegant

modern hotel, includes buffet breakfast, cafeteria open 0530-2300, until 0400 Thu-Sat, internet, parking, sauna, gym. A meeting place among Cuencanos.
AL Pinar del Lago, Av Ordóñez Lazo, next door to the **Oro Verde**, T07-2837212, www.hotelpinar.com Modern hotel in a nice setting, includes breakfast, restaurant, parking, carpeted rooms with fridge, good views of lake or river.
AL Santa Lucía, Borrero 8-44 y Sucre, T07-2828000, www.santaluciahotel.com An elegantly restored colonial house with 20 comfortable rooms around a patio, includes breakfast, Italian restaurant in the central courtyard, fridge, safe deposit box. Luxurious and good.
A El Conquistador, Gran Colombia 665 (also at Sucre 6-78 y Borrero), T07-2831788, hconquis@etapaonline.net.ec Modern hotel in the heart of the colonial city, includes buffet breakfast, good restaurant, cafeteria, internet, fridge, includes airport transfers. Avoid back rooms Fri and Sat because of noise from disco, good value.

A Patrimonio, Bolívar 6-22 y Hermano Miguel, T07-2831126, hpatrimo @etapaonline.net.ec Centrally located modern hotel with restaurant, price includes breakfast, internet, transfers from the airport or bus terminal.

A Victoria, C Larga 6-93 y Borrero, T07-2831120, www.grupo-santaana.com Elegant refurbished hotel overlooking the river, includes breakfast, excellent expensive restaurant, comfortable modern rooms, nice views, friendly service.

B El Molino, Km 7.5 on Cuenca-Azogues road, T07-2875367, F2875358. Includes breakfast, restaurant, pool, parking, pleasant location near river, rustic style. Reservations advised. Recommended.

B El Príncipe, J Jaramillo 7-82 y Luis Cordero, T07-2847287, htprince@etapaonline.net.ec A refurbished 3-storey colonial house in the centre of town. Comfortable rooms around a nice patio with plants, includes breakfast, restaurant serves lunch.

B El Quijote, Hermano Miguel 9-58 y Gran Colombia, T07-2843197,

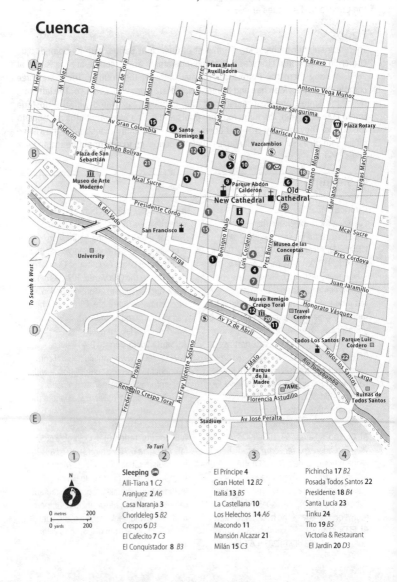

Cuenca

www.hotelquijote.com Nicely restored old building with patio, includes breakfast, restaurant serves à la carte international dishes, carpeted rooms.

B Inca Real, G Torres 8-40 entre Sucre y Bolívar, T07-2823636, incareal @cue.satnet.net Refurbished colonial house with rooms around patios, includes breakfast, restaurant serves Ecuadorean food, internet, parking, comfortable.

B Italia, Av España y Huayna-Cápac, T07-2840060, hitalia@cue.satnet.net Modern hotel near the Terminal Terrestre,

includes buffet breakfast, restaurant, parking, comfortable and nice.

B Nuestra Residencia, Los Pinos 1-100 y Ordoñez Lazo, T07-2831702, www.nuestraresidencia.4t.com Small hotel in a residential area 10 blocks from the centre, includes breakfast, living room, bar, garden, friendly, good atmosphere.

B Posada del Angel, Bolívar 14-11 y Estévez de Toral, T07-2840695, www.hostalposadadelangel.com A nicely restored colonial house, includes breakfast, internet, parking, comfortable rooms, sitting area in patio with plants.

B Presidente, Gran Colombia 659, T07-2831341, F2842127. Comfortable, good-value hotel in a convenient location, includes breakfast, good restaurant, internet, parking, good value.

B Villa del Río, Av Paucarbamba 1-118 y José Peralta, near the stadium, T/F07-2816204, ivegues@etapaonline.net.ec A converted family home in a residential area. Small 6 room hotel, includes breakfast, meals on request, parking, garden with hammocks.

C Alli Tiana, Córdova y Padre Aguirre, T07-2821955, F2821788. A multi-storey hotel, includes breakfast, restaurant on the top floor, small carpeted rooms, nice views.

C Cabañas Yanuncay, Calle Cantón Gualaceo 21-49, between Av Loja and Las Américas (in Yanuncay), 10 min by car from centre, T07-2883716. Rustic cabins and rooms in a nice country setting, includes breakfast, home-cooked meals available, English spoken, friendly and helpful. Recommended.

C Chordeleg, Gran Colombia 11-15 y Gral Torres, T07-2822536, hostalfm @etapaonline.net.ec Charming colonial house with courtyard and fountain, includes breakfast, cafeteria, carpeted rooms.

C Colonial, Gran Colombia 10-13 y Padre Aguirre, T/F07-2841644. Refurbished colonial house with beautiful patio and carpeted rooms, some to the street, others interior. Price includes breakfast, restaurant serves lunch only.

C La Castellana, Luis Cordero 10-47 y Gran Colombia, T/F07-2827293, castelho @etapaonline.net.ec Elegant refurbished colonial house in the centre of town, includes breakfast, restaurant, carpeted rooms, a couple of sitting areas, good service.

C-D Hurtado de Mendoza, Huayna-Cápac y Sangurima, T07-2843611, F2831909. Modern building near the Terminal Terrestre, includes breakfast, restaurant, parking, good rooms and service, discounts Fri-Mon.

C-D La Orquidea, Borrero 9-31 y Bolívar, T07-2824511, F2835844. Nicely refurbished colonial house. Bright rooms, includes breakfast when room at normal rate, restaurant, fridge, discounts in low season, good value.

C-D Macondo, Tarqui 11-64 y Lamar, T07-2840697, www.hostalmacondo.com Nice restored colonial house, includes breakfast, cheaper with shared bath, cooking facilities, pleasant patio with plants, garden, very popular, US run. Highly recommended.

D Aranjuez, Aranjuez 1-31 y Madrid, T07-2820622, isro_5@hotmail.com Modern hotel near the bus terminal. Comfortable and bright,

D Caribe Inn, Gran Colombia 10-51 y Padre Aguirre, T07-2835175, F2834157. Colonial house with balconies, restaurant, adequate rooms, terrace with views of Plazoleta Sto Domingo and the Cathedral.

D Casa Naranja, Lamar 10-38 y Padre Aguirre, T07-2825415, www.casanaranja .galeon.com Restored colonial house, breakfast available weekdays, cheaper with shared bath or in dorm, cooking facilities, motorcycle parking, 2 inner patios, storage room, long stay discounts.

D Gran Hotel, Gral Torres 9-70 y Bolívar, T07-2831934, F2842127. Includes breakfast, restaurant, some rooms dark, nice patio, friendly service, popular meeting place.

D Los Helechos, Gil Ramírez Dávalos y Del Chorro, T07-2863401. Four-storey hotel near the bus terminal, restaurant, cheaper with shared bath, parking, adequate rooms, convenient for late arrivals.

D Milán, Pres Córdova 989 y Padre Aguirre, T07-2831104, hotmilan@etapaonline.net.ec Includes breakfast, restaurant, internet, laundry facilities, view over market, rooms variable, popular.

D Posada Todos Santos, C Larga 3-42 y Tomás Ordóñez, near the Todos Santos Church, T07-2824247. Nice clean and tranquil hostel, includes breakfast, very good, friendly service.

D Tito, Sangurima 1-49 y M Vega, T07-2829734, F2843577. Older refurbished hotel near the bus terminal. Small bright rooms, restaurant very good value.

D Verde Limón, J Jaramillo 4-89 y Mariano Cueva, T07-2820300. Three-storey colonial house. Rooms for 1 to 4 people, very basic breakfast included, larger breakfasts also available, cafeteria-bar in open patio, shared bath, rooms with private bath are planned, sitting room with games and DVDs, will pick up from airport or terminal.

D-E Casa del Barranco, Calle Larga 8-41 entre Benigno Malo y Luis Cordero, T07-2839763, grupobar@etapaonline.net.ec Refurbished colonial house with views over the river, breakfast available, cafeteria, most rooms with bath, a few with shared bath are cheaper, parking, some spacious rooms.

D-E El Cafecito, Honorato Vásquez 7-36 y Luis Cordero, T07-2832337, cuenca @cafecito.net Colonial house, restaurant and bar in nice patio, cheaper in dorm, popular with travellers and noisy.

D-E Norte, Mariano Cueva 11-63 y Sangurima, T07-2827881. In a renovated building, large comfortable rooms, good restaurant, cheaper with shared bath, the hotel is safe but this is not a nice area after dark.

D-E Tinku, Honorato Vázquez 5-66 y Hermano Miguel, T09-7245696, tinkuenca@yahoo.es A friendly popular hostel, most rooms with shared bath, cheaper in dorm, internet, cooking facilities, very clean, sitting room with videos and games, book exchange, helpful. Recommended.

E Pichincha, Gral Torres 8-82 y Bolívar, T07-2823868, karolina@etapaonline.net.ec Shared bath, hot water, cooking facilities, spacious rooms but a little noisy on the street side. Helpful and recommended.

Apart-hotels and suites

Apartamentos Otorongo, Av 12 de Abril y Guayas, T07-2818205, pmontezu @az.pro.ec A 10-15 min walk from centre, fully furnished 1 or 2 bedroom apartments with kitchenette, TV, phone. Cleaning service included, friendly owners, US$375-480 per month.

Baños *p265*

A Hostería Durán, Km 8 Vía Baños,
T07-2892485, www.hosteriaduran.com
Nice hotel in the thermal baths complex.
Includes breakfast and use of all facilities.
Expensive restaurant, well maintained and
very clean pools (US$3.50 for non-residents),
steam bath, gym, tennis courts. There are also
a couple of cheap and basic *residencias*.

⊕ Eating

Cuenca *p262, map p266*
Dining out in Cuenca can be expensive, but
there are cheap *comedores* on the 2nd floor
of **Mercado 10 de Agost**o, open all week. Av
Remigio Crespo, between the stadium and
the coliseum, has a variety of pizzerías,
heladerías, burger and sandwich places,
steak houses, bars and discos. The area is
very popular with young people and lively
at weekends.

A very traditional dish in the Cuenca area
is roast *cuy* (guinea pig). In town you can
find it in one of the many *salones* along Av
Don Bosco between Av Solano and Av Loja.
For a more rural setting, go to Ricaurte, a
20-min ride north of Cuenca (bus along Av
Sangurima), where many places offer this
delicacy, **Mi Escondite** is recommended.

†††† Balcón Quiteño, Sangurima 6-49 y
Borrero, and Av Ordoñez Lazo 311 y los
Pinos, T07-2831926, open until 0200.
Good Ecuadorean food and service,
1960s decor. Popular with the locals
after a night's hard partying.

†††† El Franciscano, Gran Colombia 11-80 y
Tarqui, T07-2850513. Very elegant restaurant
in the centre of the city, excellent
international food. Opened in 2004.

†††† El Jardín, In Hotel Victoria, C Larga 6-93,
T07-2827401, closed Sun-Mon. Lovely
elegant restaurant overlooking the river.
Good international food and service, pricey.

†††† El Jordán, C Larga 6-111, near Hotel
Victoria, T07-2850517. International and
some Middle Eastern dishes. Also serves
an economical set lunch. Belly dancing show
on weekends. Popular.

†††† La Herradura Grill, Remigio Romero
3-55 y Remigio Crespo, T07-2887540. A well
established Cuenca grill. Excellent *parrilladas*
and very good service.

El Vado, T07-2811531. Excellent *comida
típica* Cuencana in a nice setting by the river.

†††† Rancho Chileno, Av España 13-17,
next to airport and a couple other locations,
T07-2864112. A Cuenca tradition. Serves
good steak, seafood and *empanadas
chilenas*, slow service.

†††† Villa Rosa, Gran Colombia 12-22 y
Tarqui, T07-2842443. Very elegant restaurant
in the centre of town, excellent international
food and service. A meeting place for
business people.

††† Café Austria, Benigno Malo 5-99 y J
Jaramillo, T07-2840899, 1100-2200.
A traditional Cuenca café, under new
management and refurbished in 2004.
Now also serves international food but
pastries are still very good here.

††† Café Eucalyptus, Gran Colombia 9-41
y Benigno Malo, T07-2849157,
www.cafeeucalyptus.com, Mon-Fri
1700-2300, Sat 1900-late. A pleasant
restaurant, café and bar in an elegantly
decorated 2-storey house. Large menu with
dishes from all over the world, varied tapas
(try Vietnamese shrimp) and drinks. Ladies
night on Thu, Salsa and dancing on Sat.
Good service, pleasant atmosphere, popular,
reserve in advance for the comfy couch by
the fireplace. British-American run and
recommended.

††† El Mar, Gran Colombia 20-33, T07-
2843522. Good *ceviches* and other seafood.

††† El Pedregal Azteca, Gran Colombia
10-29 y Padre Aguirre, T07-2823652.
Very good Mexican food. In the Casa Azul,
a refurbished colonial house with nice patios,
live music in the evenings.

††† El Tequila, Gran Colombia 20-59,
T07-2831847. Good local food, good value
and service.

††† El Túnel, Gral Torres 8-60, T07-2823109.
Good hamburgers and other snacks, cheap
lunch menu, quick service, romantic.

††† Las Campanitas, Borrero 7-69 y Sucre,
open until 0200. Good Ecuadorean food.

††† Las Tres Caravelas, Gran Colombia 6-65
at Hotel El Conquistador. Good value,
Ecuadorean and international fare. Live
Andean music on weekends.

††† New York Pizza, Gran Colombia 10-43 y
Padre Aguirre, T07-2842792. Good Italian
food, especially the calzones.

Raymipampa, Benigno Malo 8-59, at Parque Calderón, T07-2827435. Very good international food in a nice central location. Fast service, popular, at times it is hard to get a table. Refurbished in 2004.

Shang Dong, Juan Jaramillo 8-38 entre Benigno Malo y Luis Cordero, T07-2822586. Good Chinese food, try spicy *chancho al ají*.

Caos, J Jaramillo y Hermano Miguel, Open Mon-Sat 1800-2400. Italian food, pleasant atmosphere.

La Fornace, Borrero 8-29 y Sucre and other locations. Good pizza.

La Tasca, Pasaje 3 de Noviembre bajos del Puente Roto. Small restaurant-bar, serves Cuban dishes.

Tzar Peter, Presidente Córdova 8-34 y Luis Cordero. Formally decorated restaurant-bar, serves very good international and Russian specialities, also set lunches Mon-Fri 1200-1500. Happy hour 1800-2100.

El Paraíso, Tomás Ordóñez 10-45 y Gran Colombia, Mon-Sat 0800-1600. Good breakfast, vegetarian food, fruit salads and juices, cheap set lunches.

Goura, Juan Jaramillo 7-27 y Borrero. Very good vegetarian restaurant. Nice economical set lunches, tasty pizza, great fruit salad, good choice of à la carte dinners with some Indian dishes. Recommended.

Cafés, bakeries and ice-cream parlours
Traditional Cuenca bread, baked in a wood oven, can be found in several bakeries along Mariano Cueva between C Larga and Honorato Vázquez.

Aguacolla, Bajada de Todos los Santos by Puente Roto, Mon-Fri 1000-2200. Informal café-bar, serves organic food. Shows films, sometimes has live music, climbing cave.

Café Cappuccino, Bolívar y Padre Aguirre, opens 0930. Good hamburgers and other snacks. Real coffee and liqueur coffees.

Cinema Café, Luis Cordero 7-42 y Sucre, above the Teatro Casa de la Cultura. Popular café-bar, serves breakfast, snacks, salads, drinks.

Heladería Holanda, Benigno Malo 9-51, open from 0930. Yoghurt for breakfast, good ice cream, fruit salads, cream cakes. Popular and recommended.

Monte Bianco, Bolívar 2-80 y Ordóñez and a couple of other locations.

Panesa, Benigno Malo entre Gran Colombia y Sucre. Good pastries.

Pity's, Av Remigio Crespo T y Alfonso Borrero. Recommended for hamburgers and sandwiches. Try their *sanduche morlaco* with mushrooms.

The English Café and Bookshop, C Larga 6-69 y Borrero, closed Wed. Pleasant small café, serves good breakfast all day, juices, snacks and sandwiches. Nice atmosphere, British-Ecuadorean run. English books for sale and trade.

Tutto Freddo, Benigno Malo 9-40 y Bolívar and 1 other location. Ice cream, pizza and sandwiches.

⊙ Bars and clubs

Cuenca *p262, map p266*
Along Av Remigio Crespo are many night spots. Most bars and clubs open Wed-Thu until 2300, Fri-Sat until 0200.

Café del Tranquilo, Borrero 7-47 y Presidente Córdova. Pleasant popular bar, live music US$3 cover.

Chaos, Honorato Vásquez y Hermano Miguel. Small popular bar, pool table, young crowd.

La Mesa Salsoteca, Gran Colombia 3-36 entre Vargas Machuca y Tomás Ordóñez, no sign. Latin music, very popular among locals and travellers, young crowd.

Pop Art, Remigio Crespo y Solano. Modern music, young crowd.

Roho, Tarqui entre Gran Colombia y Bolívar. Modern music, young crowd.

Ruby Red, Gran Colombia 11-33 y Gral Torres. Pleasant, centrally located bar-club, good selection of drinks, small dance floor, mature crowd.

San Angel, Hermano Miguel 6-88 y Presidente Córdova esquina. Popular bar and dance spot, live music, for a mixed-age crowd.

Tapas y Canciones, C Larga y Borrero. Small quaint *peña*, live music for a more mature crowd.

Wunderbar, C Larga 3-43 y Hermano Miguel, T07-2831274. A café-bar-restaurant, drinks, good coffee and food including some vegetarian dishes. Nice atmosphere, a popular travellers' hangout with games, German magazines and book exchange, German-run.

♻ Entertainment

Cuenca *p262, map p266*
Art galleries
Galería Pulla, Jaramillo 6-90. Works by this famous painter, also sculpture and jewellery.
Prohibido Centro Cultural, La Condamine 12-102 in the Cruz del Vado area, T07-2828094. Mon-Thu 0900-2100, Fri-Sat 0900-2300. Gothic style gallery and bar. A striking place where artist Eduardo Moscoso presents his paintings of all the taboos of society: sex, death and religion, to the sounds of heavy metal rock.

Cinema
Casa de la Cultura, Luis Cordero y Sucre.
Multicines, Av José Peralta, complex of 5 theatres and food court, also at Mall del Río.

Dance classes
Cachumbambe, Remigio Crespo 7-79 y Guayas, above **Restaurante Charito**, T07-2882023. Salsa, merengue and a variety of other rhythms.

♻ Festivals and events

Cuenca *p262, map p266*
Bienal de Cuenca Cuenca hosts an internationally famous biennial international painting competition. Exhibitions occupy museums and galleries around the city for three months starting either during the Apr or Nov festivities. The next *bienal* is due in 2006. Information from Bolivar 13-89, T07-2831778.
Mar-Apr Semana Santa On **Good Fri** there is a fine procession through the city and up to the Mirador Turi.
12 Apr Fundación is the anniversary of the foundation of Cuenca. Celebrations include fireworks at the Parque Calderón and various exhibits throughout the city including crafts and, on some years, the Bienal, see above.
May-Jun Septenario is a religious festival in the week leading up to **Corpus Christi**. On Parque Calderón a decorated tower with fireworks attached, known as 'castillo', is burnt every night after a mass, 'vacas locas' or mad cows (people carrying a reed structure in the shape of a cow, with lit fireworks) run across the park, and hundreds of hot air paper balloons are released. A

spectacular sight which is not to be missed. There are also dozens of dessert sellers and games in the streets. A traditional drink for this holiday is *rosero*, prepared with *babaco*, *chamburo* (star-fruit) strawberries, *mote*, orange leaves and cloves.
3 Nov Independencia celebrates the independence of Cuenca, with street theatre, art exhibitions and night-time dances all over the city, including the **Puente Roto**, east of the Escalinata.
24 Dec Pase del Niño Viajero This outstanding parade is probably the largest and finest Christmas parade in all Ecuador. Children and adults from all the barrios and surrounding villages decorate donkeys, horses, cars and trucks with symbols of abundance. Young children dressed in colourful Indian costumes or as Biblical figures ride through the streets accompanied by musicians. The parade starts about 1000 at San Sebastián, proceeds along C Simón Bolívar, past Parque Calderón and ends at San Blas. On other days around Christmas there are also smaller Pase del Niño parades.

○ Shopping

Cuenca *p262, map p266*
Books
The English Café & Bookshop, C Larga 6-69. See Cafés above.

Camping gear
Apullacta, see Tour operators, also hires out camping gear. To buy equipment try:
Bermeo Hnos, Borrero 8-35 y Sucre, T07-2831522
Créditos y Negocios, Benigno Malo y Presidente Córdova, T07-2829583.
Explorador Andino, Borrero 7-52 y Sucre, T07-2847320.

Handicrafts
The Cuenca region is noted for its *artesanía*. Good souvenirs are carvings, leather, basketwork, ceramics, painted wood, onyx, woven stuffs, embroidered shirts and jewellery. There are many craftware shops along Gran Colombia, Benigno Malo and Juan Jaramillo alongside Las Conceptas. There are several good leather shops in the arcade off Bolívar between Benigno Malo

and Luis Cordero. At Plaza Rotary (see markets below) baskets, pottery and wooden objects are sold.

Altany, Juan Jaramillo 5-42 y Hermano Miguel, T07-2839949. Artistic ceramics.

Arte, Artesanías y Antigüedades, Borrero y Córdova. Textiles, jewellery and antiques.

Artesa, L Cordero 10-31 y Gran Colombia, modern Ecuadorean ceramics at good prices. Several other branches around the city.

Centro Artesanal Municipal 'Casa de la Mujer', Gral Torres 7-33, T07-2845854. Market with a great variety of handicrafts.

Colecciones Jorge Moscoso, Juan Jaramillo 6-80 y Borrero, T07-2822114. Weaving exhibitions, ethnographic museum, antiques and handicrafts.

El Barranco, Hermano Miguel 3-23 y Av 3 de Noviembre. Artisans' cooperative selling a wide variety of crafts.

El Tucán, Borrero 7-35. Recommended.

Galápagos, Borrero 6-75, excellent selection.

Torres, between Sucre y Córdova, or **Tarqui**, between Córdova and the river, for *polleras*, traditional Indian women's skirts.

E Vega, on the road up to Turi, T07-2881407. Nice artistic ceramics.

Jewellery

Prices are reported as high, so shop around.

Galería Claudio Maldonado, Bolívar 7-75, has unique pre-Columbian designs in silver and precious stones.

Joyería Turismo, Gran Colombia 9-31. Recommended.

Unicornio, Gran Colombia y Luis Cordero. Good jewellery, ceramics and candelabras.

Markets

The municipality is in the process of rehabilitating the city's markets with good results already seen at Mercado 10 de Agosto. Markets sell mostly produce, but some crafts can also be found. Only a few are listed here.

Feria Libre, Av de las Américas y Av Remigio Crespo, west of the centre. The largest market, also has dry goods and clothing. Most activity on Wed and Sat, when people from outlying communities come to trade.

Mercado 9 de Octubre, Sangurima y Mariano Cueva, busiest on Thu. Crafts are sold nearby at Plaza Rotary, Sangurima y Vargas Machuca; best selection on Thu.

Mercado 10 de Agosto, C Larga y Gral Torres. A daily produce market with a prepared foods and drinks section on the second floor, which is looking good after refurbishing.

Panama hats

Cuenca is a centre of the Panama hat industry. Manufacturers have museums explaining the hat-making process and offer factory tours followed by visits to their showrooms where purchases can be made. Note there is a wide range of quality and prices; the finer the fibres used, the more supple, the higher the price and the longer it will last. Check the quality of Panama hats very carefully as some tend to unravel and shops are unwilling to replace or refund. Outlets include:

El Barranco, C Larga 10-41 y Gral Torres; Exportadora Cuenca, Mcal Lamar 3-80.

Kurt Dorfzaun, Av Gil Ramírez Dávalos 4-34, near the bus terminal, T07-2807563, www.kdorfzaun.com, Mon-Fri 0830-1200, 1500-1830, nice selection.

Homero Ortega P e Hijos, Av Gil Ramírez Dávalos 3-86, T07-2801288, www.homeroortega.com

▲ Activities and tours

Cuenca *p262, map p266*
For cycling and horseriding, see the **Travel Center**, below.

Trekking

There are excellent hiking opportunities at **Parque Nacional Cajas** (see p278) and other areas around Cuenca, such as **Jima** (see p278). Cuenca operators offer trekking tours for about US$35 per day. **Club Sangay** (Victor Hugo Dávila), Gran Colombia 7-39, p 1E, T07-2868468 clubsangay@hotmail.com, is a walking and climbing club that organizes outings 2 to 3 times per month and welcomes visitors. Arrangements through **Explorador Andino**, see Shopping, Camping gear.

Tour operators

All operators offer city tours, trips to **Ingapirca** (US$35-45), trekking in **Cajas** (about US$35 per person per day), **Gualaceo-Chordeleg** crafts towns (US$45), the **Yunguilla-Girón** area (US$45, see p280). Some also sell jungle and Galápagos tours.

Almíbar, Presidente Córdova 5-33
y Mariano Cueva, T07-2826006,
megajuancho@hotmail.com
Local and regional tours.

Apullacta, Gran Colombia 11-02 y Gral
Torres, T2837815, info@apullacta.com
Offers the usual tours and also hires tents,
sleeping bags and other camping
equipment.

Ecotrek, C Larga 7-108 y Luis Cordero,
T07-2834677, ecotrek@az.pro.ec Manager
Juan Gabriel Carrasco specializes in shaman
trips and climbing tours in addition to the
standard trips.

Hualambari, Borrero 9-69, T07-2848768.
Regional and country-wide tours.

Metropolitan Touring, C Larga 6-96, T07-
2837000, www.metropolitan-touring.com
A branch of the large Quito operator, also
sells airline tickets.

Río Arriba, Hermano Miguel 7-14 y
Presidente Córdova, T07-2830116,
negro@az.pro.ec Specializes in trips to
Girón. Recommended.

The Travel Center, Hermano Miguel 5-42
entre Honorato Vázquez y Juan Jaramillo,
T07-2823782, F2820082. Two operators under
one roof with lots of useful information,
helpful staff, a pleasant sitting area, small
library and bulletin boards. Recommended.

Montaruna Tours, www.montaruna.ch, offer
excellent 1- to 10-day horse-riding trips with
overnight stays in haciendas. A single day
costs US$45.

Terra Diversa, www.terradiversa.com, offers
regular tours plus mountain biking trips to
Ingapirca, Cajas and other sites, US$39-47 per
person per day, with fixed departures. Also
jungle trips, Galápagos tours and flight tickets.

⊝ Transport

Cuenca *p262, map p266*
Air
TAME, Icaro and Aerogal fly from Cuenca
to Quito, US$63, and Guayaquil, US$49,
several flights daily, schedules change often
so ask locally.

Southern Highlands Cuenca Listings

For main inter-city routes see the Ecuador bus timetable, p52. For destinations around Cuenca, see p283. To **Guayaquil**, US$8, either via Zhud, 5 hrs, or via Cajas and Molleturo, 3½ hrs. There are 2 routes to **Gualaquiza**, in the southern Oriente, either via Gualaceo (p283) and Plan de Milagro or via Sígsig (p283).

ⓘ Directory

Cuenca *p262, map p266*
Airline offices Aerogal, Aurelio Aguilar y Solano, T07-2861041. **American Airlines**, Hermano Miguel 8-63, T07-2831699. **Continental**, Padre Aguirre 10-96 y Lamar, T2847374. **Icaro**, Av España 1114, T07-2802700. **TAME**, Florencia Astudillo 2-22, T07-2889581. **Banks** Banco de Guayaquil, Sucre y Hermano Miguel, T07-2837700. **Banco del Austro**, Sucre y Borrero, T07-2842492. **MasterCard** office at Bolívar y T Ordóñez, T07-2883577. **Produbanco**, Padre Aguirre 9-72 y Gran Colombia, T07-2836000. **Vaz Corp**, Gran Colombia 7-98 y Cordero, T07-2833434. Mon-Fri 0830-1300, 1430-1745, Sat 0900-1230. TCs 1.80-2% commission, also change Euros, Peruvian *soles* and other currencies, efficient. **Consulates** Great Britain, Plazoleta de San Alfonso, P Baja 9A, CAsa 56, T07-2831996. **Car hire** Inter, Av España, opposite the airport, T07-2801892. **Localiza**, at the airport, T07-2863902, www.localiza.com.ec **Hospitals** Clínica Santa Ana, Av Manuel J Calle 1-104,

T07-2814068. **Clínica Santa Inés**, Av Daniel Córdova Toral 2-113, T2817888, Dr Jaime Moreno Aguilar speaks English. **Hospital Monte Sinai**, Miguel Cordero 6-111 y Av Solano, near the stadium, T07-2885595. **Internet** Rates US$0.70-US$1 per hr. **Language schools** Hourly rates for Spanish classes US$6-10. **Centro Abraham Lincoln**, Borrero y Honorato Vásquez, T07-2830373. Small Spanish language section. **Estudio Internacional Sampere**, Hermano Miguel 3-43 y Calle Larga, T/F07-841986, samperec@samperecen.com.ec At the high end of the price range. **Fundación Centro de Estudios Interamericanos**, Tarqui 13-45 y Pío Bravo, T07-2839003, www.cedei.org Spanish and Quichua, free email service for students, accommodation at short notice, Hostal Macondo attached. Recommended. **Sí Centro de Español e Inglés**, Juan Jaramillo 7-27, T07-2846932, www.sicentrospanishschool.com Good teachers, competitive prices, helpful, tourist information available. Recommended. **Laundry** Fast Klin, Hermano Miguel 4-21 y Calle Larga. **Lavandería**, Manuel Vega y Sucre. A self-service laundromat. **Pharmacies** Farmacia Botica Internacional, Gran Colombia 7-20 y Borrero. Experienced staff, wide selection. **Post office** Corner Gran Colombia y Borrero, T07-2838311. **Useful addresses** Emergencies, T911. **Immigration**, Av Ordóñez Lazo y Los Cipreces, Edificio Astudillo. For tourist visa extensions, Mon-Fri 0800-1230, 1500-1830. **Police**, T101.

Around Cuenca

Cuenca is surrounded by scenic countryside, where you are likely to see the 'chola cuencana' – women dressed in traditional costume, with colourful pleated skirt, lace blouse and Panama hat. To the north live the Cañari people, who wear bright attire and small white felt hats. They are the custodians of Ingapirca, Ecuador's most important archaeological site. Beyond, approaching the province of Chimborazo, the countryside is poor, dry, chilly and windswept, and the Indians withdrawn and wrapped-up.

There is much to explore in the area around Cuenca. Beautiful Parque Nacional Cajas, with over 200 lakes, is a short ride from the city. Here, and in several other locations, are very good opportunities for trekking. There are also craft towns producing weavings, jewellery, basketry and Panama hats. ►► *For Sleeping, Eating and other listings, see pages 281-284.*

Ins and outs

Getting there The Panamericana connects Cuenca with the province of **Cañar** and the central highlands to the north and with the province of **Loja** to the south. Three roads lead from Cuenca to the coast: one leaves the Panamericana at **Zhud** and goes to La Troncal; the second goes through **Parque Nacional Cajas** to Molleturo and Puerto Inca; the third runs southwest to Girón, Santa Isabel and Pasaje. From all these towns there are roads to Guayaquil and Machala. There are also three roads east to Oriente: one via **Paute** and Guarumales to Méndez; the second through **Gualaceo** to Plan de Milagro and Limón; the third through **Sigsig** to Gualaquiza. These towns are all along the main Oriente road, between Macas and Zamora. There is regular public transport from Cuenca along all these routes. ▶▶ *For further information, see Transport, p283.*

Towards Ingapirca → *Colour map 6, A4*

Azogues and around

The capital of the province of Cañar, Azogues is a busy city perched at 2,500 m on a steep hillside above the Río Burgay, 31 km northeast of Cuenca along a four-lane highway. The Saturday market is colourful. Beautifully situated on the hill is the city's huge church and convent **San Francisco de la Virgen de las Nubes**.

A pleasant excursion from Azogues is to the village **Cojitambo**, 20 minutes west on the road to Deleg. Small Inca/Cañari ruins are being restored near the top of the hill above the village (free admission, no services or facilities) and there are grand views. Walk 1½ km along the road towards Deleg and take a turn-off left to follow trails to the summit or take a bus from the Terminal Terrestre. There is good technical rock climbing on the cliffs behind Cojitambo; bring all your own gear.

Just 6 km north of Azogues along the Panamericana is **Biblián**, with a sanctuary to **La Virgen del Rocío**, built into the rocks high above the village. It's a pleasant walk up with impressive views of the river valley and surrounding countryside.

Cañar → *Population 11,000 Altitude 3,175 m*

Some 67 km north of Cuenca and 36 km north of Azogues, Cañar is a cold colonial town and one of the access points for Ingapirca. It is famous for double-faced weaving, although this is now difficult to find. The jail, **Centro de Rehabilitación Social**, Colón y 3 de Noviembre, sells weavings made by prisoners. The market on Sunday, when indigenous inhabitants of surrounding rural communities flock to town, is very colourful and it is still relatively easy to find the Cañar hats for sale in several of the small stores in town.

El Tambo

Some 7 km north of Cañar along the Panamericana, **El Tambo** is the most frequently used access point for Ingapirca. Note the stonework on the façade of the church on the main square. There is some very basic accommodation and a few simple eateries in town and a better option on the road to Cañar. About 1 km down the hill off the El Tambo-Ingapirca road, or 30 minutes' walk along the disused rail line from El Tambo, are Inca ruins called **Baños del Inca** or **Coyoctor**. This massive rock outcrop has been carved to form baths, showers, water channels and seats overlooking a small plaza or amphitheatre. It's worth visiting but not easy to find, so ask around.

Ingapirca → *Altitude 3,160 m*

① *8½ km east of Cañar. Daily 0800-1800. US$6, including entry to the museum and a guided tour in Spanish 0800-1700.*

Ecuador's most important Inca site lies just uphill from the village of Ingapirca, where there is an interesting Friday market and a good cooperative craft shop next to the

Southern Highlands Around Cuenca

church. Access is from Cañar or El Tambo. The road from El Tambo is paved and faster, while the Cañar road is recommended for the beautiful four-hour, 16-km walk down from Ingapirca to Cañar; take water. The site is administered by the local Cañari community. A small café serves very cheap set lunches and photogenic llamas graze the grounds. Camping is permitted at no extra cost; there are bathrooms but no showers.

Although it is famed as a classic Inca site, Ingapirca, which translates as 'Wall of the Inca', had probably already been sacred to the native Cañari people for many centuries. It is also known as 'Jatun Cañar' (great Cañar). The Inca Huayna Capac took over the site from the conquered Cañaris when his empire expanded north into Ecuador in the third quarter of the 15th century. Ingapirca was strategically placed on the Royal Highway that ran from Cusco to Quito and soldiers may have been stationed there to keep the troublesome Cañaris under control.

The site, first described by the French scientist Charles-Marie de la Condamine in 1748, shows typical imperial Cusco-style architecture, such as tightly fitting stonework and trapezoidal doorways, which can be seen on the **Castillo** and **Governor's House**. The central structure may have been a **solar observatory**. There is considerable debate as to Ingapirca's precise function. Although it is popularly considered a fortress complex, this is contradicted by archaeologists. From what remains of the site, it probably consisted of storehouses, baths and dwellings for soldiers and other staff, suggesting it could have been a royal tambo, or inn. It could also have been used as a sun temple, judging by the beautiful ellipse, modelled on the Qoricancha in Cusco. Furthermore, John Hemming has noted that the length of the site is exactly three times the diameter of the semi-circular ends, which may have been connected with worship of the sun in its morning, midday and afternoon positions.

A 10-minute walk from the main site is the **Cara del Inca** (face of the Inca), an immense natural formation in the rock looking over the landscape. Nearby is a throne cut into the rock, the **Sillón del Inga** (Inca's Chair) and the **Ingachugana**, a large rock with carved channels. This may have been used for offerings and divination with water, chicha or the blood of various sacrificial animals.

Inca trail to Ingapirca

The popular three-day hike to Ingapirca on the Inca road starts north of the site at **Achupallas**, 25 km from Alausí, altitude 3,300 m. The route climbs to **Laguna Las Tres Cruces**, then goes past the peak of **Quilloloma**, the shore of **Laguna Culebrillas** and the ruins of **Paredones**. The walk is covered by three 1:50,000 IGM sheets: Alausí, Juncal (the most important) and Cañar. The name 'Ingapirca' does not appear on the latter, so you may have to ask directions near the end. A compass and good camping equipment are essential. Take all food and drink with you as there is nothing along the way. A shop in Achupallas sells basic foodstuffs and on Saturday you can buy fresh vegetables at the market.

‡ *There are persistent beggars, especially children, the length of the hike. Don't encourage them with gifts, rather make a donation to a recognized project or charity, see p46.*

East of Cuenca → *Colour map 6, A4*

To the east of Cuenca lie a series of warm valleys with fruit orchards, flower plantations and the country's largest orchid nursery. The area has long been a favourite weekend recreation zone among Cuencanos and improved access roads mean that many of the original orchards and cane fields have now been converted into weekend home developments. Subsistence farming has been pushed onto the higher slopes, contributing to deforestation, with many hills now eroded. Beautiful crafts are produced in this area.

Paute → *Population 5,100 Altitude 2,230 m*

Some 42 km northeast of Cuenca and 24 km north of Gualaceo is the busy market town of Paute, built on the shores of the Río Cutilcay at its confluence with the Río Paute. The town has a pleasant park with a modern church and, although they are not as common as before, fruit preserves and other local delicacies can still be found. On Sucre by the river's edge is a small plaza with a stone fountain.

From Paute the road to Oriente, partly paved, follows the Río Paute through **Guachapala**, **El Pan** (one hotel), **Sevilla de Oro**, **Amaluza** (dam), **Guarumales** (generating station) and **Méndez**. It is a beautiful ride, passing cloud forest and several waterfalls along the way. There is bus service along this route between Cuenca and Macas. ▸▸ *For further information, see Transport, page 283.*

Gualaceo → *Colour map 6, grid A4 Population 11,000 Altitude: 2,220 m*

Gualaceo is a thriving, modern town set in pleasant landscape along the Santa Bárbara and Gualaceo rivers. It is the largest town in the area and the centre of a craft-producing region, although the Sunday market doesn't cater to tourists. The town has a charming plaza and fine church, with splendid modern stained glass. Also here is the very helpful **Oficina Municipal de Turismo** ① *Municipio, Gran Colombia y 3 de Noviembre, Parque Central, T07-2255131, Mon-Fri 0800-1300, 1400-1700, information in Spanish only.* There is a small **Museo Artesanal** ① *Tue-Sat 0800-1700, Sun 0800-1200, free,* at the entrance to the **Parador Turístico** (see Sleeping), with good displays about the weaving of Panama hats and *macanas* (Ikat-dyed shawls).

Many of Ecuador's over 4000 species of orchids can be seen in the 18 greenhouses at **Ecuagénera** ① *Km 2 on the road to Cuenca, T07-2255237, www.ecuagenera.com, Mon-Sat 0900-1500, advance arrangements required, US$2.* This is the country's biggest orchid-growing facility and among the largest in South America. It welcomes visitors and organizes interesting tours to private cloud forest reserves. From Gualaceo a scenic road goes to **Limón** in Oriente, see page 407.

Around Gualaceo

Among the crafts produced in this area are *macanas*, Ikat-dyed shawls, woven on backstrap looms. These are found in the communities of **Bulcay**, 3 km from Gualaceo on the main road to Cuenca, and in nearby **Bulzhun** on a secondary road. The community of **San Juan**, 15 km south of Gualaceo, where Panama hats are woven, has developed a tourism project offering accommodation with rural families. Beyond is **San Bartolomé**, a lovely colonial town, where guitars are made.

A paved road runs 4 km south from Gualaceo to **Chordeleg**, a village famous for its crafts in wood, silver and gold filigree, pottery and for Panama hats. The village can be very touristy but it has a pleasant park surrounded by houses with pleasing wooden balconies and an interesting church, with some lovely modern stained glass. The helpful **Oficina Municipal de Turismo** ① *Municipio, C 23 de Enero, at the main square, T07-2223223, Mon-Fri 0800-1300, 1400-1700,* organizes tours to attractions in the area, including a trip through cloud forest to Las Tres Lagunas. Also in the Municipio is the **Centro de Interpretación** ① *C 23 de Enero, Mon-Fri 0800-1300, 1400-1700,* an exhibit hall with fascinating local textiles, ceramics and straw work, some of which are on sale at reasonable prices.

It's a good uphill walk from Gualaceo to Chordeleg, or a pleasant hour downhill in the other direction. With your own vehicle, you can drive back to Cuenca through San Juan and San Bartolomé, see above. South of Chordeleg is the isolated community of **Principal** which has a tourism project.

● *Ecuador's largest hydroelectric plant is located 75 km downriver from Paute. Massive deforestation in the area means that the rainwater run-off carries mud and soil, which silts up the Paute dam. The dam has to be continually dredged to function.*

Some 26 km south of Gualaceo and 83 km from Cuenca, is Sígsig, an authentic highland town where women can be seen weaving hats 'on the move'. The main square, **Parque 3 de Noviembre** has the modern **Iglesia de San Sebastián** and a statue to Duma, the local Cañari chief who defeated the conquering Inca Tupac Yupanqui. At **Plaza Tudul**, where the buses stop, is the **Iglesia de María Auxiliadora,** with an interesting stone façade, blue domes and a Moorish tower; there are pleasant views of the surrounding hills from here. On the shore of the Río Zhingate is a recreation area. Market day is Sunday.

This area is rich in archaeology, with caves and several undeveloped ruins to explore. At the Municipio is the **Museo Cantonal** ① *Parque 3 de Noviembre, T07-2266106, Mon-Fri 0800-1600, free*, with objects from the Talcazhapa culture (700 BC-AD 1100) and information in Spanish about the area's archaeological sites.

A very scenic but poor road goes from Sígsig, 5 km to **Cutchil**, a hat weavers town, and on to a pass at 3,360 m, from where it drops to **Chigüinda**, **El Aguacate** and **Gualaquiza** in southern Oriente, see page 407. This route is prone to landslides and may be impassable after heavy rain.

Jima

Southeast of Cuenca, along a secondary road off the Panamericana, is the village of **Jima** (written Gima on some maps), where a tourism project has been developed. **Centro de Información Turística** ① *T07-2418270, www.projectsforpeace.org/jima*, offers information and can arrange guides, horses and accommodation with local families. The area is off the beaten track and has very good walking opportunities, including a three- to four-day trek to **La Florida** and **Nueva Tarqui** near Gualaquiza in Oriente (see page 407). Beyond Jima, the road continues for 25 km to the **Bosque Tambillo** cloud forest. **Laguna Zhirigüina** is also in this area.

Parque Nacional Cajas → *Colour map 6, grid A3*

This beautiful national park, located 29 km west of Cuenca, encompasses easily accessible *páramo* and high-elevation forest. It is speckled with over 230 lakes, separated by rocky ridges, and has been a **Ramsar** wetland site since 2002 (www.ramsar.org). It is well managed because it is the source of Cuenca's drinking water. The park is relatively small (29,000 ha) but, although hundreds of Cuencanos go there at weekends, it is possible to find solitude, since most tourists do not travel far from the road. The park is a favourite with birdwatchers, trekkers and trout fishermen. Cajas is very rich in birdlife; 125 species have been identified here, including the condor and many varieties of hummingbird. The violet-tailed metaltail is a hummingbird endemic to this area; others include the shining sunbeam, veridean metaltail, sparkling violet-ear and the sword-billed hummingbird. The lakes harbour andean gulls, speckled teal and yellow-billed pintails.

Ins and outs

Getting there There are two access roads into the park. The paved road from Cuenca to Guayaquil via Molleturo goes through the northern section and is the main route for Laguna Toreadora, the visitors' centre and Laguna Llaviuco. Skirting the southern edge of the park is a poor secondary road, which goes from Cuenca via San Joaquín to the Soldados entrance and the community of Angas beyond. ▶▶ *For further details, see Transport, page 283.*

● *The magnificent gold sun with curly rays, which is the symbol of the Banco Central del*
● *Ecuador, is a Cañari piece found in Chunucari, just north of Sigsig.*

Getting around Travel is largely cross country, along way-trails or through the *páramo* grasses, so good maps are necessary. The following IGM 1:50,000 maps cover the whole park: Chaucha, Cuenca, San Felipe de Mollerturo and Chiquintad; printed copies are not always available and getting plotted maps is expensive. The park office in Cuenca has a 1:70,000 map of the park. Access to some drainages on the eastern edge of the park is restricted.

Best time to visit The park ranges in altitude from 3,150 to 4,450 metres, so there is no permanent snow, but it is cold, especially at night, and it can rain, hail or snow. August and September are the driest months but hiking is possible all year round. The best time is August to January, when you can expect clear days, strong winds, night-time temperatures of -8°C and occasional mist. From February to July temperatures are higher but there is much more fog, rain and snow. It is best to arrive in the early morning as it can get very cloudy, wet and cool after about 1300.

Information and admission The park office is in Cuenca at **ETAPA** ① *Empresa de Telefonos, Agua Potable y Alcantarillado, Presidente Córdova 9-06 y Benigno Malo, p2, T07-2829853/2826501, www.etapa.com.ec, Mon-Fri 0800-1300, 1500-1800.* Park entry is US$10, payable at the entrance gates at Laguna Toreadora, Laguna Llaviuco or Soldados.

Attractions and park services
Laguna Toreadora is in a high *páramo* area at 3,870 m, with some attractive polylepis (quinoa) forest fragments around the shore. Along the main road is the **Centro de Visitantes** ① *Tue-Sun 0800-1630, also Mon in high season,* the Centro de Interpretación Ambiental, a cafeteria with snacks and warm drinks (it also serves meals at weekends, including local trout) and the *refugio,* a basic shelter with bathrooms but no beds. ►► *For further details, see Sleeping, page 282.*

    Laguna Llaviuco is in a cloud forest area at 3,150 m, on the eastern side of the park. Three kilometres off the main road is a camping area, a dock and a cafeteria. There are no facilities at **Soldados**, the southern access point into the park.

Parque Nacional Cajas

For day walks, there are some marked trails near the visitors' centre but they tend to peter out quickly. For overnight treks, adequate experience and equipment are necessary. Open fires are not permitted, so take a stove. A very strong hiker with a good sense of direction can cross the park in two days. Groups of eight or more must be accompanied by a naturalist guide, arranged through a Cuenca operator. Independent trekkers must register with the rangers, indicate the exact route they are planning and show a GPS and compass.

‡ There have been deaths from exposure in the park, so it is important to be prepared for wet and cold, with proper clothing and equipment.

On the opposite side of Laguna Toreadora from the refugio is **Cerro San Luis** (4,200 m), which may be climbed in a day, with excellent views. From the visitors' centre go anticlockwise around the lake; after crossing the outflow look for a sign 'Al San Luis', follow the yellow and black stakes to the summit and beware of a side trail to dangerous ledges. Beyond **Laguna Toreadora** on a paved road is the village of **Migüir**, from where you can follow a trail past several lakes and over a pass to **Soldados** (two days). It is also possible to follow the **Ingañan Trail**, an old Inca pathway that used to connect Cuenca with the coast. It is in ill-repair or lost in places but there are interesting ruins above **Laguna Mamamag**. You can access the Ingañan from the park headquarters or from **Migüir**, from where it is two to three days' trekking to **Laguna Llaviuco**. From Llaviuco you might get a ride with fishermen back to Cuenca or you can walk to the main road in about an hour.

Cuenca to Machala

From Cuenca the Panamericana runs south to La Y, about 20 km away. Here the road divides: the left branch continues as the Panamericana south to Loja and the right branch runs southwest through sugar cane fields to Pasaje and Machala on the coast. Although this is a major intersection it is not well signposted.

Girón

One hour from Cuenca along the road to the coast is **Girón** (altitude: 2,100 m), whose beauty is spoiled only by a modern concrete church. After the battle on 27 February 1829 between the troops of Gran Colombia, led by Sucre, and those of Peru under Lamar, at nearby Portete de Tarqui, a treaty was signed in Girón. The building, **Casa de los Tratados** ① *daily 0800-1600, US$1,* is shown to visitors, as is the site of the Peruvians' capitulation. Ask directions to the beautiful **El Chorro de Girón** waterfall, a 6-km walk or 20-minute ride (pick-up taxi US$5), with cloud forest above. Agencies in Cuenca offer tours here. From Girón, trucks take passengers up a winding road to the hamlets of **San Fernando** (rooms at La Posada) and **Chumblín**. Friendly inhabitants will act as guides to three lakes with excellent trout fishing high in the *páramo*. There is also rock-climbing on San Pablo, overlooking Lago Busa. Take camping gear. Return to the main road through **Asunción**; it's a beautiful downhill stretch for cyclists.

To the coast

Beyond Girón, the route to the coast goes through the warm **Yunguilla Valley**, where sugar cane is grown; it's a popular weekend destination for Cuencanos. Here is the town of **Santa Isabel** (altitude: 1,800 m) with a pleasant park and modern church. The road then descends through desert to the stark, rocky canyon of the Río Jubones. At a military checkpoint, a road climbs south to **Chilla** (see below). In the Province of El Oro is the lowland town of **Casacay**, after which the road passes through lush banana plantations. Further along is the market town of **Pasaje** (population: 45,000), 18 km east of Machala. From here roads go north to Guayaquil via La Troncal, or south down the coast to Huaquillas on the Peruvian border (see page 329).

Azogues *p275*

C Paraiso, Váscones y Veintimilla, in
La Playa sector N of town, T07-2244729,
hparaiso@easynet.net.ec Modern
comfortable hotel, includes breakfast,
restaurant, pool and spa, parking, quiet
neighbourhood, good value.

D Cordillera, Azuay y Malo, by former
bus terminal, T07-2240587. Simple,
adequate hotel.

D Hostería El Camping, in Sageo, 3 km
north of Azogues, 2½ km south of Biblián,
T07-2240445. A popular place for weekend
outings, meals available on request, pool and
steam bath open weekends only, US$2.

D Rivera, 24 de Mayo y 10 de Agosto,
T07-2248113. Multi-storey hotel, modern
rooms, restaurant, parking for small vehicles.

D Santa María, Serrano y Emilio Abad,
T07-2241883, F2241210. Simple, adequate
hotel, restaurant.

Cañar *p275*

D-E Ingapirca, Sucre y 5 de Junio, on the
plaza, T07-2235201. Simple hostel with
carpeted rooms, cheaper with shared bath.

E Irene, 24 de Mayo, in the upper part of
town. Shared bath, dodgy electric shower,
parking, basic but adequate.

El Tambo *p275*

C-D Cuna del Sol, 1 km south of El Tambo
along the Panamericana, T07-2233633. Nice
rustic cabins in a tourist complex, includes
breakfast, restaurant with Ecuadorean and
international food open Tue-Sun, pool,
steam bath, horse riding, sports fields.

Ingapirca *p275*

A Posada Ingapirca, 500 m uphill from
the archaeological site, T07-2215116,
or T07-2838508 in Cuenca, www.grupo
-santaana.com A nice converted hacienda
with superb views, includes typical breakfast
with dishes such as *mote pillo* and *morocho*,
good expensive restaurant and well-stocked
bar, good service.

D Inti Huasi, in the village, T07-2215171.
Simple adequate hostel, restaurant serves
cheap set meals.

E Huasipungo, in the village. Basic hostel,
restaurant, shared bath, electric shower.

For trekkers, there is a basic hostel in
Achupallas: **E Ingañán**, T03-2930663, with
shared bath and hot water.

Paute *p277*

A Hostería Uzhupud, 10 km from Paute on
the opposite shore of the river, T07-2250329,
huzhupud@cue.satnet.net Very nice
converted farm in beautiful grounds with
orchids. Comfortable rooms, those in back
have the best views, includes breakfast,
restaurant at mid-range to expensive prices,
pool and sauna open to non-residents US$5,
sports fields, horse riding extra. Quiet,
relaxing. Recommended.

D Cabañas de San Luis, at the entrance to
town from Cuenca, T07-2250165. Small
simple cabins in nice grounds at the edge of
town. Restaurant open on weekends, electric
shower, dirty pool.

D-F Cutilcay, Abdón Calderón, by the river,
T07-2250133. Older hostel with basic rooms,
cheaper with shared bath and cold water.

Gualaceo *p277*

B Parador Turístico Gualaceo, Av del
Parador y Loja, on the outskirts of town,
T07-2255010, T07-2842443 (Cuenca).
Pleasant chalets and rooms in nice grounds,
good restaurant at mid-range prices, pool
open to non-residents US$1.60, parking,
ageing but still fine. At the entrance is the
Museo Artesanal de Gualaceo.

D Belén, Jaime Roldós y 3 de Noviembre,
T07-2255212. Modern multi-storey hotel,
cheaper with shared bath, convenient to
the bus station, friendly, good value, opened
in 2004. There are several others in town.

Sígsig *p278*

There are several *residenciales* in town.

Jima *p278*

E Centro de Capacitación, T07-2418397.
The local high school offers clean, simple
rooms and dorms, shared bath, electric
shower, proceeds go into improving
education in the Jima area.

E La Casita Blanca, T07-2418046. A beautiful
house in the centre of town, shared bath,
electric shower, large balcony with wonderful
mountain views, owner speaks some English.

Parque Nacional Cajas *p278, map p279*
There is a *refugio* at **Laguna Toreadora** and camping at **Laguna Llaviuco**. Other shelters in the park are very primitive. The cost of overnight stays is US$4.
B Hostería Dos Chorreras, Km 14½ vía al Cajas, sector Sayausí, T07-2853154, www.doschorreras.com Hacienda-style inn, outside the park. Carpeted rooms with heating, includes breakfast, restaurant serves excellent fresh trout, reservations recommended, horse rentals with advanced notice, trout farm.
C Hacienda Sustag, 11 km from San Joaquín and 16 km from Soldados on the southern road to the park, T07-2830834, T07-2831120 (Cuenca), www.grupo-santaana.com Large family-sized cabin in a working dairy farm with beautiful landscapes. Includes breakfast and dinner, restaurant serves delicious Ecuadorean food, local trout and some international dishes, horse rentals, sports fields, games, camping possible if taking meals in the restaurant. Advanced reservations required. The road is poor during the rainy season.

Girón *p280*
E El Chorro de Girón, 20 min drive from town, by the waterfall, T07-2275782, T07-2883711 (Cuenca). Basic shelter with mattresses and sheets, meals available with previous arrangement.

To the coast *p280*
D Hostería San Luis, Casacay, T07-2915904. Simple rooms, with private bath, fan, pool.
C Hostería Sol y Agua, below Santa Isabel on the Cuenca side, T07-2270596, F2270436. Cabins in a pleasant location with good views, good restaurant, pool and water slide, fridge, good service.
D San Martín, Bolívar 616 y Olmedo, Pasaje, T07-2915434. Some interior rooms, others with window, restaurant, cold water, a/c, parking, clean, best in town.

Eating

Azogues *p275*
Chifa Oriental, 24 de Mayo y Gral Enríquez. Chinese food.
El Padrino, Bolívar 609 y 10 de Agosto, Mon-Sat 0700-2100, Sun 0700-1500.

Extensive menu of à la carte dishes and set meals, also serves breakfast. Popular.
Peleusí, Emilio Abad y Sucre, Mon-Sat 0900-1900. Pleasant cafeteria, snacks, nice atmosphere. Several others in town.

Cañar *p275*
Casa Grande, Panamericana y Colón. A choice of several set meals (very cheap) and à la carte dishes. Good and popular.

Paute *p277*
Gabita, Bolívar y Matovelle. Nice set meals and grilled chicken.

Gualaceo *p277*
Borin Cuba, Av Jaime Roldós y Fidel A Piedra. International food, grill on weekends.
Don Q, Gran Colombia y 9 de Octubre, near Parque Central, open lunch time only. Good economical set meals and à la carte, the best place to eat in town, fast service.

Sígsig *p278*
Turismo, Opposite the market. Set meals.

Jima *p278*
Descanso, 1 block from the plaza, daily 0700-2000. All meals (vegetarian available) and nice home-made cheese.
Ruben's, On the main plaza. Breakfast, lunch and dinner including local trout, vegetarian available.

Parque Nacional Cajas *p278, map p279*
There are 2 cafeterias in the park, at **Laguna Toreador** and **Laguna Llaviuco**. The inns near the park (see Sleeping) have very good restaurants but advanced booking is necessary for **Hacienda Sustag**, which is only open on weekends during the summer months and when they have guests.

Shopping

Paute *p277*
Tienda de la Familia Rivera Ochoa, Abdón Calderón y García Moreno, T07-2250312. Fruit preserves, pickles, home-made bread.

Gualaceo *p277*
The **feria artesanal**, across the suspension bridge at the junction of the Santa Bárbara and San Francisco rivers, sells various crafts.

Woollen goods are sold on Av Jaime Roldós, the main street, near the bus station. Embroidered goods are sold from a private home above the pharmacy on the main square, corner 3 de Noviembre y Gran Colombia. Nice baskets are sold at the **Museo Artesanal**, at the Parador Turístico.

Around Gualaceo *p277*
Good shops in **Chordeleg** sell beautiful ceramics. **Joyería Dorita** and **Joyería Puerta del Sol**, on Juan B Cobos y Eloy Alfaro, have been recommended for jewellery; watch out for fake jewellery elsewhere.

▲ Activities and tours

Cuenca tour operators offer trips to destinations throughout this region, p272.

Inca trail to Ingapirca *p276*
Tour operators in Riobamba (see p256) offer this 3-day trek for US$180 per person for a group of 4, everything included. **Sr Alonso Zea**, T07-2930663 in Achupallas can provide pack animals but you must provide all the gear and food for yourself and the muleteers.

East of Cuenca *p276*
Chordelg's **Oficina Municipal de Turismo** arranges tours to **Las Tres Lagunas**, a high *páramo* area, and other local destinations. Jima's **Centro de Información Turística** arranges tours to all the attractions in the area, including the trek to **Oriente**.

● Transport

Azogues *p275*
The **Terminal Terrestre** is at the south end of town, near the highway. To **Cuenca**, every 10 mins, US$0.50, 30 mins. To **Guayaquil**, US$6, 4 hrs. To **Quito**, US$10, 8 hrs.

Cañar *p275*
Buses run from C 24 de Mayo near the Panamericana to **Cuenca**, every 15 min, US$2, 2 hrs. There are also many through buses along the Panamericana heading towards Guayaquil and points north.

Ingapirca *p275*
There 2 direct daily buses from **Cuenca**, with **Transportes Cañar**, 0900 and 1300, returning

1300 and 1600, US$2.50, 2½ hrs. Also from **Cañar**, corner 24 de Mayo and Borrero, every 20 mins, 0600-1800, US$0.50, 30 min; last bus returns from Ingapirca to Cañar at 1700. The buses from Cañar go through **El Tambo**, from where it is 20 min, US$0.40, to the ruins. If coming from the north, transfer in El Tambo.

Inca trail to Ingapirca *p276*
There is a pick-up from Alausí to **Achupallas**, daily except Sat at 1130-1200; also a small bus Thu and Sun about 1300, other days about 1400, US$1, 1 hr, a nice ride. On Sat trucks go to market in Achupallas early in the morning. Alternatively, take any bus along the Panamericana to **La Moya**, south of Alausí, at the turn-off for Achupallas, and a pick-up from there (best on Thu and Sun). To hire a pick-up from Alausí costs US$15, from La Moya US$10.

Paute *p277*
The terminal is on Sucre by the river. From **Cuenca**, every 15 min, US$0.75, 1 hr. Buses between Cuenca and **Macas** also stop here; journey Paute-Macas, US$7.50, 7-8 hrs.

Gualaceo *p277*
The terminal is on Av Jaime Roldós y Luis Cordero, esquina. There are buses from the Terminal Terrestre in **Cuenca**, every 15 min via El Descanso, US$0.55, 50 min; also via Jadán, a more scenic route, US$1, 2 hrs. Buses between Cuenca and **Macas** also stop here; journey Gaulaceo-Macas, US$8, 9 hrs. There are buses from Gualaceo to **Chordeleg**, every 15 min, US$0.20, 15 min. Also from Cuenca, US$0.80, 1 hr.

Sígsig *p278*
Buses from **Cuenca**, US$1.25, 1½ hrs, via Gualaceo and Chordeleg, every 20 min in the morning, every 30 min in the afternoon; or 8 daily via San Bartolo. A road has been built from Sígsig to **Gualaquiza**, along a beautiful and unspoilt route (see p407). It is served by 2 buses daily, passing through from Cuenca, US$5.25, 4½ hrs.

Jima *p278*
Buses from **Cuenca** depart from opposite the Feria Libre market, Av de las Américas, daily at 0830, 1100, 1430 and 1530, US$1, 1½ hrs.

Parque Nacional Cajas *p278, map p279*
From the **Terminal Terrestre** in Cuenca take
a Guayaquil-bound bus via Molleturo (not
Zhud), US$1-1.50, 30 min to the turn-off for
Laguna Llaviuco, 45 min to **Laguna
Toreadora**. Cooperativa Occidental to
Molleturo leaves from its own station in
Cuenca, at Lamar y M Heredia, west of the
centre. For the **Soldados entrance**, catch a
bus from Puente del Vado in Cuenca, daily at
0600, US$1.25, 1½ hrs; the return bus passes
the Soldados gate at about 1600.

Cuenca to Machala *p280*
From the **Terminal Terrestre** in Cuenca there
is a frequent service, to **Girón** US$1, 45 min;
to **Santa Isabel**, US$1.50, 1½ hrs; to **Pasaje**,
US$4, 3½ hrs and to **Machala** US$4.50, 4 hrs.

❻ Directory

Towards Ingapirca *p275*
Banks Banco del Austro, Matovelle y
Azuay, Azogues, T07-2240860, cash
advances on Visa and MasterCard, Mon-Fri,
morning only. Banco del Austro, on plaza,
Cañar, T07-2235256, cash advances on Visa
and MasterCard, Mon-Fri, morning only.

Gualaceo *p277*
Banks Banco del Austro, 3 de Noviembre
y Colón; Vaz Corp, 3 de Noviembre y Colón,
Mon-Fri 0830-1300, 1400-1630, Sun
0830-1300, cashes TCs at 1.8%, also
currency exchange.

Province of Loja

*Loja is a land of irregular topography, where the two distinct cordilleras further north
give way to a maze of smaller ranges which barely reach 3,000 metres. Many warm
valleys lie between these hills. Beautiful Parque Nacional Podocarpus is the ideal
place to visit the cloud forests, which has made Loja famous since colonial days, when
chinchona, the bark from which quinine is extracted, was first described here.*

*Long isolated from the rest of the country, the south developed its own unique
character. Loja is functionally and culturally self sufficient, home to important
universities and cultural centres. The Saraguros, proud people who maintain their
traditions, are today the only indigenous group in the province. The Palta natives
disappeared long ago and many Lojanos are of European stock, dating back to early
colonial times.*

*The province has a bad reputation for unsustainable agricultural practices. These
combined with cyclical droughts have made many Lojanos migrate over the years.
Some became colonists in Oriente, hence the official name of Lago Agrio, capital of the
province of Sucumbíos, is Nueva Loja. Today Lojanos are migrating further afield, to
Europe and North America, in search of better economic opportunities.* ▸▸ *For Sleeping,
Eating and other listings, see pages 294-304.*

Ins and outs
Getting there The Panamericana goes south from Cuenca for 204 km to the city of
Loja from where it turns west to **Catamayo** (La Toma), where the regional airport,
Aeropuerto Camilo Ponce Enríquez, is located, with services to Quito and Guayaquil.
The Panamericana continues to **Macará**, on the Peruvian border. From Loja, another
road heads south to **Vilcabamba** and on to **Zumba**, also near the border with Peru. Yet
another road goes east to **Zamora** in Oriente. From Catamayo several routes go to the
coastal province of **El Oro** and the city of **Machala** and a couple of roads go to
alternative border crossings at **Jimbura** and **Lalamor**. There are very good bus services
on all routes. ▸▸ *For further details, see Transport, page 302.*

South of Cuenca

The road from Cuenca south to Loja is fully paved, though a few spots are prone to landslides. It passes through bare, sparsely populated country and offers lovely views. The road climbs south from La Y (where a branch goes to Pasaje and Machala) to the village of **Cumbe**, with its small, colourful Wednesday market. The road then rises to the Tinajillas pass (3,527 m). Further south at La Ramada a branch road forks left to the lovely, sleepy colonial town of **Nabón**, with its weekend market. There is fine hiking in the nearby valleys and several unexcavated ruins. A small *pensión* offers accommodation.

With a rental car or a bike, it is possible to do a loop through Nabón, to rejoin the Panamericana at Oña. This trip is best done in the dry season (Jun-Sep).

The road descends sharply into the warm valley of the Río León, 95 km from Cuenca. This is the 'Grand Canyon' of Ecuador. The bridge over the Río León is 1,900 m above sea level and the surrounding hills rise to 3,300 m. Beyond the valley the road ascends again to the small, quiet town of **Oña** at 2,300 m, 105 km from Cuenca. The town has a pleasant park and a couple of places to sleep and eat, and is the starting point for the five- to seven-day, 65-km **Gold Rush Trail** to Zaruma (see page 327). This difficult and rewarding trek climbs 2,600 m from the valley of the Río León to mysterious rock formations atop Cerro de Arcos. For details, refer to *Trekking in Ecuador* (see page 482).

From Oña the road crosses into the province of Loja, weaving and climbing through highland *páramo* pastures, before descending to Saraguro, 144 km from Cuenca.

Saraguro → *Colour map 6, B3   Population 3,100   Altitude 2,500 m   www.saraguros.com*

This is a cold town, famed for its weaving and for its distinctive indigenous population, the most southerly Andean group in Ecuador. Saraguros dress all in black and wear very broad flat-brimmed hard felt hats. The men are notable for their black shorts, sometimes covered by a pale divided apron, and for a particular kind of saddle bag, the *alforja*, and the women for their pleated black skirts, necklaces of coloured beads and silver *topos*, ornate pins fastening their shawls. Many of them take cattle across the mountains east to the tropical pastures above the Amazonian jungle. The town has a picturesque Sunday market and interesting mass. Above the altar of the church, with its imposing stone façade, are inscribed the three Inca commandments in Quichua: "Ama Killa, Ama Llulla, Ama Shua". Do not be lazy, do not lie, do not steal. In the area surrounding Saraguro are several remnants of high-elevation forest, in which 145 species of birds have been identified. Birdwatching is good even along the main road both north and south of town.

North of Saraguro by about 5 km is **Paquizhapa** or **Urdaneta**. A 2002 study by Dennis Osburn of the University of California, Berkeley, USA, suggests that some large stones, found at the base of the church here, came from Cusco, 1,600 km away. Accounts of early colonial chroniclers suggest that the Incas transported these 200-500 kg stones for construction of the palace at Tomebamba in Cuenca (see page 263); they were abandoned at this site when lightning hit the lintel piece.

West from Saraguro

From Saraguro a spectacular road (subject to landslides in the rainy season) runs through El Paraíso de Celén, Selva Alegre, Manu, Guanazán and Chilla down to the coast. A bus goes to Manu throughout the year and to Guanazán in the dry season. **Chilla** is famous for its Santuario de la Virgen de Chilla and pilgrims flock here in September from all over the country. The only place to stay is the **Casa de Huéspedes** (Pilgrims' Guest House) which is empty the rest of the year. This area has remnants of native forest between 2,800 and 3,000 m and good birdwatching possibilities.

The trail from Saraguro to the jungle town of **Yacuambi** (also called 28 de Mayo on some maps), is a classic old trading route down the eastern slope of the Andes to the jungle. It is among the most delightful two- to three-day walks in Ecuador, with magnificent views from **Cerro Condorcillo**, where you can spend the first night. The route is prone to landslides in the rainy season, so ask about conditions before starting. In 2005 a gravel road went 10 km to the Río Quingueado and an unfinished road 4 km beyond to the higher plateau. There has also been road construction on the Yacuambi side, but not directly along the trekking route. The trek starts in **Paquizhapa** (see above) and is covered by the Saraguro and San José de Yacuambi 1:50,000 IGM maps. There are a couple of places to stay and eat in **Yacuambi** at the end of the route. ▸▸ *For Transport at the beginning and end of the route, see page 302.*

> ✷ *The best time to do this trek is during the dry season (Aug-Dec) but be prepared for cold, rain and mud at all times of year.*

Loja → *Colour map 6, grid B3 Population 118,500 Altitude: 2,063 m*

This friendly pleasant city, encircled by hills, is the provincial capital. It is a colonial city, founded on its present site in 1548, having been moved from La Toma, and was rebuilt twice after earthquakes, the last of which occurred in the 1880s. The town has the distinction of being the first in the country to have electricity and it remains a progressive place. The central market is the cleanest in all of Ecuador and, in recent years, Loja has won several international awards for its beautiful parks and for its rubbish recycling programme.

Ins and outs

Getting there The city can be reached by air from Quito or Guayaquil to **Catamayo** (also known as La Toma), which is 35 km away by paved road (see page 292). Shared taxis between the airport and Loja charge US$4 per person; to hire a taxi is US$15. Taxi drivers going to the airport are often found outside the **TAME** office in Loja. Arrange the day before and they will pick you up at your hotel. Loja is a transportation hub, the gateway to Zamora in Oriente and to several areas in northern Peru. The well organized **Terminal Terrestre**, at Av Gran Colombia y Isidro Ayora, is to the north of the centre. At the terminal are a tourist information office, left luggage, a bus information desk, shops and **Pacifictel** office. There are frequent city buses to the centre; a taxi costs US$1. ▸▸ *For further information, see Transport, page 302.*

Getting around The centre of Loja, which has most hotels and services, is compact and easy to walk around. City buses cost US$0.25. *Taxirutas* are shared taxis that run on a set route, US$0.25. A taxi ride within the city costs US$1.

Information i Tur ① *Unidad Municipal de Turismo, José Antonio Eguiguren y Bolívar, Parque Central, T07-2570407 ext 220, www.municipiodeloja.gov.ec, Mon-Fri 0800- 1300, 1500-1830, Sat 0900-1300,* provides local and regional information and maps. The staff are helpful and speak some English. There are also offices at the Terminal Terrestre and the airport. The **Ministerio de Turismo** ① *Bolívar 12-39 entre Mercadillo y Lourdes, p3, Parque San Sebastián, T07-2572964, fronterasur@turismo.gov.ec, Mon-Fri 0830-1700,* which has information and pamphlets for all of Ecuador, Spanish only.

Sights

Loja has a reasonably preserved centre, bound by the Río Malacatos and Río Zamora. Around the **Parque Central** are the Cathedral, with painted interior and carved wooden choir, the Municipio, Concejo Provincial, Gobernación and the **Centro Cultural Loja**. The latter is housed in a beautifully restored house and is home to the

Museo del Banco Central ① *10 de Agosto 13-30 y Bolívar, T07-2573004. Mon-Fri 0900-1300, 1400-1700, US$0.40*, with well-displayed archaeology, ethnography, art and history halls. There are also temporary exhibits, a library and an auditorium. Nearby, the Monasterio de las Concepcionistas de Loja ① *10 de Agosto y Bernardo Valdivieso, T07-2584032. Mon-Sat 0900-1700, US$1*, has a religious art museum with paintings and sculptures.

The small Parque de Santo Domingo is at Bolívar y Rocafuerte, its church has over 100 paintings by Fray Enrique Mideros. The Parque de San Sebastián, at Bolívar y Mercadillo, has a tall Moorish clock tower. This square and the adjoining Calle Lourdes preserve the flavour of the old Loja and are worth a visit. The Parque de El Valle is along Av Salvador Bustamante Celi, to the north of the centre; its colonial church has a lovely interior. This is the traditional place to go for *comida típica*. At Puente Bolívar, by the northern entrance to town, is a fortress-like monument and a lookout over the city, known as La Puerta de la Ciudad ① *Mon-Fri 0830-2130, Sat and Sun 0900-2130*. It has art exhibits at ground level and a small café upstairs, a good place to take pictures.

Loja is famed for its musicians: it has one of the few musical academies in the country and two symphonic orchestras. Musical evenings and concerts are often held around the town. The Museo de Música ① *Valdivieso 09-42 y Rocafuerte, T07-2561342, Mon-Fri 0900-1300, 1500-1900, free*, housed in the restored Colegio Bernardo Valdivieso, honours ten Lojano composers. It also has rotating exhibits, not necessarily about music. The city also boasts two universities, with a well-known law school. The Universidad Nacional has good murals on some of its buildings. The Universidad Técnica, on the hill to the northeast of the centre, is the Open University for Ecuador, having correspondence students and testing centres scattered across the country and even in Spain and the USA. On the campus is the Museo de Arqueología y de la Lojanidad ① *Sector San Cayetano, T07-2570275, ext 2642, Mon-Sat 0900-1230, 1500-1830*, with archaeological pieces from several Ecuadorean native groups and information about contemporary cultural groups.

Parks

In the north of the city, a couple of blocks east of the bus terminal is the Parque Recreacional Jipiro ① *information T07-2583357 (ext 251), 5 mins from the centre by bus, marked 'Jipiro', camping is possible here*, a good place to walk and relax. A well maintained, clean park, with a small lake, sports fields, pools, a zoo complete with giraffe, an observatory and replicas of different cities. It is popular with Lojanos at weekends, when there are puppet shows, theatre and other activities.

On the road south to Vilcabamba is the Parque Universitario Argelia ① *opposite the first gate for the botanical gardens, no sign, look for a red and white gate, daily 0800-1200, 1400-1800, US$1, city bus marked 'Capulí-Dos Puentes' to the park or 'Argelia' to the Universidad Nacional and walk from there*. This 90-ha reserve has 7 km of trails through the forest and going up to the *páramo*. Across the road and 100 m south, the Jardín Botánico Reynaldo Espinosa ① *Mon-Fri 0900-1600, Sat and Sun 1300-1800, US$0.60*, has very nice grounds. There are native species including several cinchona trees, medicinal plants, an orchid garden and an Andean crop section. There are also linear parks following the rivers.

Parque Nacional Podocarpus → *Colour map 6, grid C4*

Spanning elevations between 950 and 3,700 m, Podocarpus is one of the most diverse protected areas in the world. It is particularly rich in birdlife, including many rarities and some newly discovered species; there could be up to 800 species in the park. It also includes one of the last major habitats for the spectacled bear. The park protects stands of romerillo or podocarpus, a native conifer. Podocarpus is divided into two areas, an upper premontane section with spectacular walking country, lush tropical cloud forest and excellent birdwatching, and a lower subtropical section, with remote areas of virgin rainforest and unmatched quantities of flora and fauna.

Ins and outs

Getting there The park is easily accessed at several points. From Loja, entrance to the upper section of the park is easiest at **Cajanuma**, 8 km south, or **San Francisco**, 24 km east. For Cajanuma, take a Vilcabamba-bound van or *taxiruta*, and get off at the turn-off, US$1-1.20, from where it is a 8 km walk. Direct transport by taxi to the park gate is about US$10 but may not be feasible in the rainy season. Alternatively, take a tour from Loja. You can arrange a pick-up later from the guard station.

The southwestern section of the park can also be accessed via trails from Vilcabamba (see page 290), Yangana and Valladolid. There are also two possible entrances to the lower subtropical section of the park in Oriente: **Bombuscara**, which can be reached from Zamora (see page 408) and **Romerillos**, two hours south.

Admission and information Park entry is US$10, valid for five days at all entrances. Information is provided by the **Ministerio del Ambiente** ① *Sucre entre Quito e Imbabura, Loja, T/F07-2585421, podocam@easynet.net.ec, also in Zamora T/F07-2605606.* They have a general map of the park, not adequate for navigation. Conservation groups working in and around the park include: **Arcoiris** ① *Segundo Cueva Celi 03-15 y Clodoveo Carrión, T/F07-2577499, www.arcoiris.org.ec;* **Fundación Ecológica Podocarpus** ① *Catacocha entre Olmedo y Juan José Peña, T07-2585924, podofund@loja.telconet.net;* **Naturaleza y Cultura Internacional** ① *Av Pío Jaramillo y Venezuela, T07-2573691, www.natureandculture.org*

Attractions and park services

Both the highland and lowland areas are quite wet, making hiking or rubber boots essential. There are sometimes periods of dry weather from October to January. The upper section is also very cold, so warm clothing and waterproofs are indispensable year-round.

Cajanuma is about 8 km south of Loja on the Vilcabamba road. From the turn-off it is 8 km uphill to the guard station, where there are cabins with beds and mattresses. Cajanuma is the trailhead for the 8-hr hike to **Lagunas del Compadre**, 12 lakes set amidst rock cliffs; camping is possible there.

Access to the upper section of the park is also possible at **San Francisco**, 24 km from Loja along the road to Zamora. The *guardianía* (ranger's station), operated by **Fundación Arcoiris**, offers nice accommodation. This section of the park is a transition cloud forest area at around 2,160 m, very rich in birdlife. It is also the best place to see the podocarpus trees, a very slow-growing conifer which is in danger of extinction. A trail (4 hrs return) goes from the *guardianía* to the podocarpus. Next to the *guardianía* is the **Estación Científica San Francisco** (not open to the public), run by **Naturaleza y Cultura Internacional**, who carry out tropical forest research.

In the **Vilcabamba** area, abutting the park, are several private reserves with shelters, which provide access to the cloud forest within the park (see page 290).
>> *For details of accommodation in the park, see Sleeping page 294.*

Vilcabamba → *Colour map 6, grid C3   Population 1,300   Altitude 1,520 m.*

From Loja the road climbs past the entrance to Parque Nacional Podocarpus to a pass at 2,390 m and then gradually descends to **Malacatos**, which has an impressive church, and then continues one valley over to Vilcabamba. Once an isolated village, Vilcabamba has become increasingly popular with Lojanos on a

Ecuador to Peru or vice versa. There are many excellent places to stay and several
good restaurants. The town has a pleasant well kept plaza where
you can find orchids on the trees. Around it are the church, which
has an attractive wooden interior, several pavement cafés and
restaurants, and well stocked shops. The area   around
Vilcabamba is very beautiful and tranquil, with an agreeable
climate. There are many great day-walks and longer treks
throughout the area, as well as ample opportunities for horse
riding. A number of lovely private nature reserves are situated east of Vilcabamba,
towards Parque Nacional Podocarpus. Above all, Vilcabamba is a great place to relax,
pamper yourself and enjoy nature.

‡ Vilcabamba is infamous for its local hallucinogenic cactus juice, called San Pedrillo. As well as being illegal, the juice can cause flashbacks years after use.

Ins and outs

Getting there and around Vilcabamba is 38 km south of Loja along a paved road
and about 150 km on a rough gravel road from the border with Peru at La Balsa (south
of Zumba). The bus terminal is behind the market, three blocks from the main square.
There are vans and shared taxis from Loja and a bus service from Zumba. Everything
in town is within walking distance but pick-up trucks are available at the main plaza
and by the bus terminal for excursions to the surrounding area. ▸▸ *For further information,
see Transport, page 302.*

When to visit Vilcabamba has a pleasant climate year-round. The rainy season is
October to May; March and April are the rainiest; July and August can be very windy.

Information i Tur ① *Unidad Municipal de Turismo, Diego Vaca de Vega y Bolívar
esquina,   at   the   Casa   Comunal   on   the   main   plaza,   T07-2580890,
www.vilcabamba.org, daily 0800-1300, 1500-1800,* has a sketch map of Vilcabamba
and surroundings; staff are friendly and helpful.

Around Vilcabamba

The area around Vilcabamba is splendid for excursions, with crystal-clear rivers that
are very inviting for a dip. Follow any of the roads out of town and discover how the
locals stay young in their cane fields, coffee plantations or fruit orchards. You will be
rewarded with lovely views and you might stumble onto a working *trapiche*, where
you can sample the freshly squeezed cane juice. Horseback or walking tours are
offered to lookouts and waterfalls near town as well as longer trips to private
reserves in the foothills to the east (see page 290). Trekkers can continue on foot
through orchid-clad cloud forests to the high cold *páramos* of **Parque Nacional
Podocarpus** (see page 287)

Rumi Wilco ① *10-min walk northeast of town, take C Agua de Hierro towards C La
Paz and turn left, following the signs from there, admission US$2, valid for the
duration of your stay in Vilcabamba,* is a 40-hectare private nature reserve, a short
walk from town. It has several signed trails and many of the trees and shrubs are
labelled with their scientific and common names. There are great views of town from
the higher trails, and it is a very good place to go for a walk. Over 100 species of birds
have been identified here. Volunteers are welcome.

Climbing **Mandango**, the 'sleeping woman', ① *signed access along the highway,
250 m south of the bus terminal, US$1.50, includes a small bottle of mineral water and
a small bag of panela, local raw sugar,* is a popular and scenic half-day walk. For a
pleasant two- to three-hour walk and a good view of Mandango's sleeping woman
profile, follow Calle Hatillo to the **Hotel Parador Turístico**, turn right just after the
Parador and continue up hill. You will pass **Hacienda Mollepamba** and the hamlet of
Mollepamba, before reaching the end of the road. Follow the trail that continues from

⁝ Valley of the immortals?

The tiny, isolated village of Vilcabamba gained a certain fame in the 1960s when doctors announced that it was home to one of the oldest living populations in the world. It was said that people here often lived to well over 100 years old, some as old as 135. It was subsequently revealed that researchers had been given parish records which corresponded to the subjects' parents. However, given that first children were often born to parents in their teenage years, this still meant that there were some very old people living in these parts.

There is still a high incidence of healthy, active elders in Vilcabamba. It is not unusual to find people in their 70s and 80s working in the fields and covering several miles a day to get there. Such longevity and vitality has been ascribed to the area's famously healthy climate and excellent drinking water, but other factors must also be at play: physical activity, diet and lack of stress.

Attracted in part by Vilcabamba's reputation for nurturing a long and tranquil life, a number of outsiders – both Ecuadoreans and foreigners – have settled in the area. The first trickle of such immigrants arrived in the 1970s, following the lead of a North American ascetic called Dr Johnny Lovewisedom. A lot more have arrived since, each for their own reasons. Many work in the tourist trade, while the exploits of others have become local lore. Will the gringos benefit from the unique serenity of the 'valley of the immortals' or have we brought with us the seeds of our own destruction?

there towards a power-line which you can see in the distance. From the power-line you descend to the highway and turn right to return to Vilcabamba. You may be able to catch an infrequent bus to town, or walk back along the winding paved road. Consider stopping at **Hostería Izhcayluma** for a late breakfast on your way down. The route climbs 400 m, so take water.

A longer, but easy 10-km walk, mostly downhill, starts from **Caxarumi** just south of the turn-off for Cajanuma along the Loja-Vilcabamba road. It goes to **Rumizhitana**, north of Malacatos, along the same road. The begining of the route is signposted and there are a couple of places along the way where you can access the main road. Take a van to the trailhead and then back from Rumizhitana.

Towards Parque Nacional Podocarpus

The following private reserves abut **Parque Nacional Podocarpus** and provide access to it. They all have shelters, open to people taking a tour from town. From north to south they are: **Solomaco**, above Quebrada de Solomaco, run by **Monta Tours**; **Las Palmas**, between Quebrada de Solomaco and Quebrada Las Palmas, run by **Cabañas Río Yambala**; **Refugio Comunitario**, at Cerro Los Helechos by Quebrada Palto, used by various operators; **Los Helechos**, at Cerro Los Helechos on the Capamaco side, run by **La Tasca Tours**, and **Gavin's**, along the Río Capamaco, run by **Caballos Gavilán**. ▸▸ *For further details, see Activities and tours, page 302.*

Vilcabamba to Peru → *Colour map 6, grid C3*

South of Vilcabamba is a transition zone going from highlands to tropical foothills of Oriente; the scenery is wild and beautiful, but marred by deforestation. A secondary road leads to Zumba and the border with Peru.

From Vilcabamba the road, paved at first and then gravel, heads first to the cheese-producing valley and pleasant town of **Yangana** (population: 1,500, altitude: 1,900 m), which has a nice park, a basic hostel and a place to eat on either side of the church. From Yangana, the road climbs to a pass at at 2,660 m. Here is the **Tapichalaca Reserve** ① *T02-2272013 (Quito), www.jocotoco.com, day visit US$15*, a beautiful cloud forest area very rich in birdlife and epiphytes. It is run by the **Jocotoco Foundation** and has a few trails and a beautiful lodge. ►► *For further details, see Sleeping, page 294.*

In the next valley is **Valladolid** (population: 1,300, altitude: 1,650 m), from where there is access to the southern edge of Parque Nacional Podocarpus (see page 287). Then comes **Palanda**, (population: 1,500, altitude: 1,200 m), about three hours from Vilcabamba, an important regional supply town. It has a nice park and several basic places to sleep and eat. Beyond Palanda the road crosses several low river valleys. After a further two hours, you reach a military control (have your passport at hand) and, just beyond it, Zumba.

Zumba → *Phone code 07 Colour map 6, grid C3 Population 2,500 Altitude 1,300 m*

Zumba is a small end-of-the-road town built around a hillside garrison. Shops are well stocked. Transport leaves from the small plaza near the modern church, where several bus companies have offices. The small **Museo Arqueológico del Cantón Chinchipe** ① *12 de Febrero opposite the Municipio, T07-2308193, open from 1000, US$1*, has a collection of ceramics found in the area.

From Zumba a poor road climbs northwest to San Andrés and beyond to a high *páramo* area with lakes. It crosses the continental divide and continues to **Jimbura**, (see page 293). Another road goes south to the border.

La Balsa and into Peru

A poor dirt road runs south from Zumba towards Peru. It goes by the village of **El Chorro** and a military post at **Pucapamba**, have your passport at hand. The frontier is at **La Balsa**, just a handful of houses on either side of the modern concrete international bridge over the Río Canchis.

This is a very small, tranquil border crossing. The Ecuadorean **Migración** office, where passports are stamped, is about 80 m from the bridge. In principle, it is open 24 hrs; knock on the door or ask around for the officer if he is not in sight. Entering Peru from Ecuador, passports are stamped at **Peruvian immigration** to the right of the bridge, open 0800-1300 and 1500-2000. Once you have cleared immigration, you must register with the **Policía Nacional del Perú** (PNP), next door. (When leaving Peru, there is no need to stop at the PNP, only at immigration.)

There is no accommodation at the border, only a few shops selling drinks and basic items, but **Namballe**, a small Peruvian town is just 15 minutes from La Balsa. It has several basic places to stay and a better place was under construction in late 2004, outside town towards the border.

San Ignacio is a pleasant town 1¾ hours from Namballe, with reasonable accommodation and eateries. From San Ignacio there are minivans to **Jaén**, a city with all services. San Ignacio is by far the best place to break a trip between Vilcabamba and Chachapoyas. If you leave Vilcabamba on the southbound bus that passes through around 0615, then you can make it to San Ignacio the same day and reach Chachapoyas the following day. This is faster and more interesting than going along the coast but it is a rough ride. For further details, see *Footprint Peru* and the *South American Handbook*.

Exchange Shopkeepers in Zumba or the *ranchera* driver will exchange US$ cash and *soles*. Once you're in Peru the **Centro Comercial Unión**, Av San Ignacio 393, in San Ignacio, usually changes *soles*; otherwise there are banks in Jaén.

Western Loja and the Peru border

Western Loja Province is a land of dry hot valleys, grand views and friendly people; this part of Ecuador is far off the tourist trail and home of El Cisne, one of the most important pilgrimage shrines in the country. Criss-crossed by roads, this area provides good access to the southern coast and to several locations in Peru.

An established alternative to the Huaquillas border crossing is the more scenic route from Loja to Piura (Peru), via Macará (see page 294), where the crossing is also more relaxed. Other smaller border posts include **La Balsa** south of Zumba (see page 291) as well as **Jimbura** (see page 293) and **Alamor** (see page 293). Facilities are limited in these small towns and immigration officers may not always be available to stamp passports at the latter two crossings.

Ins and outs

Getting there and around Due west of the city of Loja is **Catamayo**, where the regional airport is located and where the road divides into two main branches, both of which later subdivide several times. One branch goes west, providing access to the coast, the western extreme of the province and the border crossing at Macará (see page 294). The second unpaved branch goes south and leads to the Jimbura border post (see page 293). There is good bus service throughout the region; most towns have several daily buses to Loja and often direct services to Quito. International buses go from Loja to Piura through Macará. ▸▸ *For further details, see Transport, page 302.*

Catamayo and around → *Colour map 6, grid B3 Population 17,000 Altitude 1,250 m*

Catamayo, also known as **La Toma**, lies in a warm subtropical valley. Just outside town is the regional airport, which serves the city of Loja; a taxi from the airport to Catamayo centre is US$1, or it's a 20-minute walk. If flying from here, you can stay at one of the weekend resorts around Catamayo, where you can relax by the pool in a warmer climate than Loja. To the northwest of town is **Ingenio Monterrey**, one of the largest sugar-processing plants in Ecuador.

From Catamayo, the fully paved western road climbs steeply to **San Pedro de La Bendita,** from where a secondary road climbs to the small village and much venerated pilgrimage site of **El Cisne**, dominated by its large, incongruous French-style Gothic church. There is a small museum here housing religious part pieces as well as the sequinned, jewelled clothes, which dress the statue of the Virgen del Cisne for every conceivable occasion. The village has a basic *pensión* and places to eat, as well as countless vendors and beggars. ▸▸ *For details of the Fiesta, see Festivals and events, page 301.*

Ahead on the western branch, at **Las Chinchas**, an unpaved road branches north to the magnificent area of **Portovelo**, **Zaruma** and **Piñas** (see page 327). Beyond, the paved road again divides at **Velacruz**, heading northwest to **Balsas** and **Machala** (see page 325), or southwest to Catacocha (see page 293).

South from Catamayo

The road running south from Catamayo, meanwhile, first reaches **Gonzanamá** (phone code: 07, population: 1,500, altitude: 1,980 m), a pleasant, sleepy little town famed for the weaving of beautiful *alforjas* (multi-purpose saddlebags), also made in nearby **Quilanga**. Ask around and buy direct from the weavers as there are no handicraft shops. Gonzanamá also produces a good soft cheese.

From Gonzanamá there is an old and poorly maintained road over a mountain range to **Malacatos**, near Vilcabamba (see page 288), passing through the isolated village of **Purunuma**. There is almost no traffic but the views are great. It may be possible to get a ride in the morning up to the village, then it's a long hike down to the river and back up to Malacatos.

Cariamanga (phone code:07, population: 11,000, altitude: 1,950 m), about 27 km southwest from Gonzanamá, is an important regional centre with several hotels and reasonable services. Near town is **Cerro Ahuaca**, which has interesting rock formations. Beyond Cariamanga the roads are unpaved and poor. One heads southeast via **El Lucero** and Amaluza into one of the least visited parts of the country. **Amaluza** (phone code: 07, population: 1,400, altitude: 1,724 m) has a pleasant park with a nice, well-attended church. From Amaluza a poor road climbs about one hour to **Jimbura**, an authentic village where time has stood still for the past century. From here a road leads over mountains, where the beautiful Laguna de Jimbura is located, across the continental divide to **Zumba** (see page 291). About 5 km from Jimbura is a small border crossing to **Espíndola** in Peru, with connections to **Ayabaca**. Ecuadorean immigration is located a little way outside the town, on the road to the frontier.

Another road twists its way westwards from Cariamanga to **Colaisaca**, then follows a steep, rough descent through 2,000 m to **Utuana**. Nearby is the **Utuana Reserve**, run by the Jocotoco Foundation and the **Bosque Protector El Guabo**. From there, the road continues to **Sozoranga** (75 km from Gonzanamá) and on to Macará on the border (see page 294). North of Sozoranga, a road gives access to the **Jatunpamba-Jorupe Reserve** (see page 294).

Catacocha → *Colour map 6, grid B2 Population 5,400 Altitude 1,800 m*

Catacocha is a spectacularly placed town perched on a hilltop overlooking the surrounding valleys. It is authentic and very friendly. Behind the hospital is Shiriculapo, a notorious 'lover's leap', affording marvellous views. Ask to walk through the hospital grounds to see it. There are pre-Inca ruins around the town, which was once inhabited by the Palta Indians, a group which now only exists in history books. There is an archaeology museum in the high school, **Colegio Marista**.

Celica and around → *Population 3,700 Altitude 2,000 m*

From Catacocha, the paved road runs west and then south towards the border at Macará (see below). A turn-off 48 km from Catacocha, at the military checkpoint of **El Empalme** (have your passport at hand), leads west to **Celica**, a charming town perched on a hill. It has a nice church, very friendly people and lovely views of the surrounding valleys. North of town is the Guachanamá Ridge, between 2,000 and 2,800 m, where many rare southwestern endemic birds are found. **Alamor** (population: 3,800, altitude: 1,150 m) is a warm market town, 26 km northwest of Celica. It has a busy agricultural fair around the 15th of each month. It is a convenient place to stay in order to visit the petrified forest at **Puyango** (see page 329), but Celica is more attractive. There are hourly *rancheras* to Arenillas, which take you to the turn-off for Puyango, 29 km north. Several buses bound for Machala or Huaquillas also go this way.

South of Celica, a road heads southwest to **Zapotillo** (phone code: 07, population: 2,000, altitude: 325 m), a hot riverside town on the Peruvian border, also reached by a paved road from Macará. It feels like and is the end of the line. Nearby is the **Ceiba Grande Reserve**, which protects a 6,600-ha tract of Tumbesian forest, information is available from **Hotel Los Charanes**. Southwest of Zapotillo, 21 km along a dirt road, is the hamlet of **Lalamor**, with a tiny border post (not always staffed). Hire a rowboat for US$0.20 or wade across the river. On the Peruvian side you can get a vehicle to **Lancones** and on to **Sullana**, three hours away, US$3 per person or US$18 to have the car to yourself. There is hardly any traffic.

● *Travellers should note that Gonzanamá has a reputation in the south for the high*
● *incidence of deafness, so don't be paranoid if everyone seems to be ignoring you!*

Southern Highlands Province of Loja

This hot, noisy town with convoluted streets is the centre of a rice-farming area along the border with Peru. Although Macará is growing and sees increasing border traffic, it remains a much more relaxed place to cross to Peru than Huaquillas, with good road connections to Sullana north of Piura on the Peruvian coast. To the northeast of town is the **Jatunpamba-Jorupe Reserve**, run by the **Jocotoco Foundation**, which protects remnants of a wide variety of native forests between 1,300 and 2,600 m, rich in bird life. A total of 190 species of birds are known in this area, including many southwestern endemics.

> ❗ *Border formalities are reported to be much easier at Macará than at Huaquillas (see p329).*

The international bridge over the Río Macará is 2½ km from Macará. **Ecuadorean Migración**, open 24 hrs, is a few metres from the bridge. On the Peruvian side is **La Tina**, which consists of just a few houses and a public phone but no other services. Peruvian immigration is a few metres from the bridge, open 24 hrs. After clearing immigration, you have to register with the **Policía Nacional de Perú** (PNP) across the street. When leaving Peru, there is no need to stop at the PNP, only at immigration.

➤ *For transport from La Tina, see page 304; also see Footprint Peru or the South American Handbook.*

Exchange During the day there are moneychangers dealing in *soles* at the the international bridge, and in Macará at the park where taxis leave for the border. There is also a bank on the Peruvian side of the bridge which changes *soles*, Mon-Fri 0900-1300, 1430-1800, Sat 0900-1200. All transactions are US$ cash only; there is nowhere to change TCs.

⊜ Sleeping

South of Cuenca *p285*

D Buenos Aires, Oña, near the highway, off the southern access to town, T07-2434124. Basic hotel with nice views of the area, shared bath, electric shower, parking, mosquitoes at night. It is often closed so call ahead, the owner lives north along the highway, past the petrol station.

Saraguro *p285*

D Samana Wasi, 10 de Marzo near the Panamericana, T07-2200315. Modern hotel, a few blocks from the centre.

E Sara Allpa, Antonio Castro y Loja, T2200272. Adequate family-run hostel, several types of rooms and prices, cheaper with shared bath, electric shower.

F Saraguro, Loja 03-2 y Antonio Castro, T07-2200286. Clean basic hostel, cheaper with shared bath, electric shower, friendly, good value. Recommended.

Saraguro to Yacuambi trek *p286*

E-F Torres, Zamora 13-28, near the entrance to Yacuambi from Zamora, T04-2527003. Simple adequate rooms, 1 room with private bath, cold water, friendly.

Loja *p286, map p295*

L-AL La Casa Lojana, París 00-08 y Zoilo Rodríguez, T07-2585984, casalojanahotel@utpl.edu.ec A refurbished residence elaborately decorated in colonial style. Rooms are plain compared to the opulent common areas. Includes breakfast, elegant dining room, lovely grounds and views of the city. Run by the Universidad Particular de Loja and staffed by their Hotel School students, new in 2004.

A Andes del Prado, Mariana de Jesús entre 10 de Agosto y Rocafuerte, T07-2588271. A refurbished modern home overlooking the city. Bright comfortable carpeted rooms, includes breakfast, internet, parking, sitting area, terrace, new in 2004.

A Grand Hotel Loja, Av Iberoamérica y Rocafuerte, T07-2586600, www.grandhotelloja.com Nice hotel, popular with business people, includes breakfast, restaurant, spa, parking, weekend discounts.

A Libertador, Colón 14-30 y Bolívar, T07-2570344, hlibloja@impsat.net.ec A comfortable hotel in the centre of town, includes buffet breakfast, good restaurant, pool and spa, parking, suites available.

A-B Bombuscaro, 10 de Agosto y Av Universitaria, T07-2577021, www.bombuscaro.com.ec Comfortable rooms and suites, includes buffet breakfast, restaurant, internet, airport transfers, car rental, good service. Recommended.

B Hostal del Bus, Av 8 de Diciembre y Flores, across from bus station, T07-2575100, hdelbus@easynet.net.ec Modern carpeted rooms and suites, includes breakfast, restaurant serves set meals and à la carte.

B Ramsés, Colón 14-31 y Bolívar, T07-2562290, F2571402. Nice, modern rooms, includes breakfast, good restaurant, parking.

B Vilcabamba Internacional, Iberoamérica y Pasaje la FEUE, T07-2573393, F2561483. Pleasant multi-storey hotel, comfortable carpeted rooms, includes breakfast, restaurant, discount for Footprint readers.

C Acapulco, Sucre 07-61 y 10 de Agosto, T07-2570651, F2571103. Pleasant hotel in the centre of town. Nicely furnished small rooms, includes breakfast, cafeteria, first floor rooms are quieter.

C Aguilera Internacional, Sucre 01-08 y Emiliano Ortega, T07-2572894, F2584660. Comfortable hotel to the north of the centre. Nice rooms, includes breakfast, restaurant and bar, parking, gym, steam bath and sauna. Recommended.

C América, 18 de Noviembre entre Imbabura y Quito, T07-2576593. Modern multi-storey hotel with spacious, comfortable rooms, includes breakfast, opened in 2003.

C Apart-hotel Iberoamérica, Av Iberoamérica y Manuel Ignacio Monteros, T07-2574432, F2570587. One- and two-bedroom furnished apartments, US$380-$450 per month.

C Podocarpus, José Antonio Eguiguren 16-50 y 18 de Noviembre, T07-2581428, F2548912. Modern comfortable hotel, includes breakfast, restaurant, parking.

C-D Metropolitano, 18 de Noviembre 6-31 y Colón, T07-2570244. Multi-storey building with adequate rooms, parking, interior rooms without a window are cheaper.

D Chandelier, Imbabura 14-82 y Sucre, T07-2563061, chandelierhotel @hotmail.com Friendly hotel wirh adequate rooms, cheaper with shared bath, electric shower, parking, reasonably clean.

D San Luis, Sucre 04-62 y Quito, T07-2570370. Large adequate rooms, parking for small car, simple but clean.

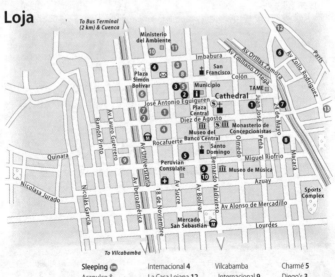

Loja

E **Internacional**, 10 de Agosto 15-30 entre Sucre y 18 de Noviembre, T07-2578486. Private bath, electric shower, older place but refurbished and adequate.

E **Londres**, Sucre 7-51 y 10 de Agosto, T07-2561936. Hostel in a well- maintained old house, shared bath, hot water, basic but clean, good value.

Parque Nacional Podocarpus p287

E **San Francisco**, pleasant accommodation in the ranger's station, with shared bath, hot water and kitchen facilities, US$8 per person if you bring a sleeping bag, US$10 if they provide sheets.

G **Bombuscara**, cabin with kitchen facilities, US$3 per person.

G **Cajanuma**, cabins with beds and mattresses. Overnight stay US$3 per person, bring warm sleeping bag, stove and food.

Vilcabamba p288, map p296

You may be approached on arrival by people touting for hotels. For its size, Vilcabamba has one of the best selections of rooms in all of Ecuador, so you are better off looking around and choosing on your own.

AL-C **Madre Tierra**, 2 km north on road to Loja, then follow signs west, T07-2580269, www.madretierra1.com A variety of rooms from elaborate suites to simple cabins and dorms, each one nicely decorated with its own character. Includes breakfast and dinner, superb home cooking, vegetarian to order, non-residents must reserve meals a day in advance. Nice grounds, pool, spa

Vilcabamba

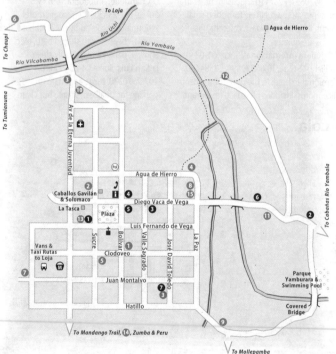

Not to scale

Sleeping
Don Germán **1**
El Jardín Esondido
  & Restaurant **2**
Hostería Vilcabamba **3**
Izhcayluma **14**
Las Margaritas **5**
Madre Tierra **6**
Mandango **7**
Parador Turístico **9**
Paraíso **10**
Pinar del Río **8**
Rendez-Vous **15**

Ruinas de Quinara **11**
Rumi Wilco **12**
Solomaco **4**
Valle Sagrado **13**

Eating
El Ché & Craig's
  Book Exchange **2**
El Punto **4**
La Terraza **4**
Natural Yogurt
  & Campary **5**
Shanta's **6**
Vegetariano **7**

Bars & clubs
Sonic's **3**

(extra charge), videos, ping-pong. Under new US management since 2004, English and French spoken, popular. Recommended. **B Hostería Vilcabamba**, by the bridge at the northern entrance to town, T07-2580271, F2580273. Spacious modern rooms and family bungalows, includes breakfast, good restaurant and bar, parking, comfortable, nice grounds, pool and spa. Popular with Ecuadorean families.

C-D Izhcayluma, 2 km south on road to Zumba, T07-2580895, www.izhcayluma.com Comfortable cabins with terrace and hammocks. Includes a very good breakfast available all day, excellent restaurant with European specialities. Nice grounds, pool, dining area with wonderful views of Vilcabamba, pleasant bar, billards, ping-pong and other games. Cheaper with shared bath. A bit out of the way but includes use of bikes to get to town. English and German spoken, friendly and helpful. Highly recommended.

D Cabañas Río Yambala, Yamburara Alto, 4 km east of town, www.vilcabamba.cwc.net Cabins in a beautiful tranquil setting on the shores of the Río Yambala. Some with kitchen facilities, meals also available, cheaper with shared bath, one simple cabin across the river with kitchen facilities is in the **F** range. Access to Las Palmas private nature reserve with good birdwatching. English spoken, friendly owners: Charlie and Sarah. Recommended.

D El Jardín Escondido (Hidden Garden), Sucre y Diego Vaca de Vega, T/F07-2580281, www.vilcabamba.org/jardinescondido.html A nicely refurbished old house around a lovely patio. Brightly decorated comfortable rooms, includes very good and generous breakfast, excellent restaurant, small pool,

jacuzzi extra. Recommended.

D Las Margaritas, Sucre y Clodoveo Jaramillo esquina, www.vilcabamba.org /lasmargaritas.html Small family-run hotel with very comfortable rooms, includes good breakfast, small pool, parking, solar heated water, nice garden. Good value.

D Le Rendez-Vous, Diego Vaca de Vega 06-43 y La Paz, rendezvousecuador @yahoo.com Very nice adobe cabins with terrace and hammocks around a lovely garden. Comfortable modern rooms, includes breakfast, pleasant atmosphere, friendly service, French run by Isabelle and Serge, English also spoken, opened in 2003.

D Paraíso, Av Eterna Juventud (the main highway) 500 m north of the centre, T07-2580266, F2575429. Comfortable cabins in nice grounds, includes breakfast, restaurant, pool and spa, parking, massage availale in an 'energized' pyramid.

D Pinar del Río, La Paz y Agua de Hierro. Small family-run hostel with a variety of rooms for different prices. Includes breakfast, cheaper in dorm, clean, small patio with hammocks, discounts for longer stays.

D Ruinas de Quinara, Diego Vaca de Vega east of centre, T07-2580301, www.lasruinasdequinara.com Includes breakfast, restaurant, cheaper with shared bath, pool and sauna, internet, laundry facilities, parking, hammocks, videos, sports facilities. Looks OK and offers good value, but we have received some negative reports.

D Solomaco, Agua del Hierro y La Paz, at northeast end of town, T07-2580904, martinesolomaco@yahoo.fr A large house on a tranquil corner by the stream, away from the centre. Includes good breakfast, most rooms

with private bath, parking, nice wooden floors and ceilings. Under new French management in 2005, some English spoken, good friendly service, also runs tours.

D-E Rumi Wilco Ecolodge, Rumi Wilco Reserve, see p289, http://koberpress.home. mindspring.com/vilcabamba/ Nice adobe cabins and a wooden one on stilts (the 'Pole House') located in the Rumi Wilco reserve. Lovely setting on the shores of the river, very tranquil, cheaper with shared bath, laundry facilities, fully furnished kitchens, discounts for long stays, friendly owners. Recommended.

E Don Germán, Bolívar y Clodoveo Jaramillo (no sign), T07-2673130. Shared bath, electric shower, laundry and cooking facilities, simple, family run, friendly owner: Sra Líbia Toledo.

E La Florida, 1 km east on road to Yamburara. Basic wooden cabin in a quiet location, shared bath, hot water, cooking facilities, friendly, caters to long stays.

E Mandango, Guilcopamba y Juan Montalvo behind the market. A multi-storey building with lovely views from the top-floor balconies. Simple clean rooms, cheaper with shared bath, electric shower, small pool, internet, laundry and cooking facilities, friendly.

E Parador Turístico, at the southeast end of town, T/F07-2673122. One of Vilcabamba's first hotels, lovely grounds and views. With breakfast, restaurant and bar, private bath, electric shower, pool, parking, a bit faded but very good value outside holiday times.

E Valle Sagrado, Luis Fernando de Vega y Av de la Eterna Juventud, T07-2580686, www.vilcabamba.org/vallesagrado.html Nice ample grounds, clean basic rooms, cheaper with shared bath, electric shower, laundry and cooking facilities, parking.

South of Vilcabamba p291

LL Tapichalaca Reserve. Comfortable rooms in a beautiful lodge, with private bath, hot water, nice sitting room with fireplace and a professional cook who prepares great meals. Prices are for full board.

E-F Residencial Palanda, 12 de Febrero at the plaza, Palanda. Basic but adequate, shared bath, electric shower, friendly.

Zumba p291

F San Luis, 12 de Febrero y Brasil, T07-2308121. Simple hotel, shared bath, cold water, the only halfway decent place in town.

Catamayo p292

C-D Los Almendros, 500 m past the bridge on the main road west of town, T07-2677293, F2570393. Pleasant family resort with a range of rooms. More expensive ones include breakfast and fridge, restaurant and bar, 2 pools, parking.

D-F Rosanna, Isidro Ayora y 24 de Mayo, near the Transportes Loja station, T07-2677006. A variety of rooms and prices, cheaper with shared bath, cold water, also cheaper annexe next door.

South from Catamayo p292

D San Francisco, Chile y Estéban Narváez, Cariamanga, T07-2687268. Restaurant, cheaper with shared bath, electric shower, refurbished in 2004.

E-F El Rocío, on the main park in Amaluza, T07-2653025. Basic friendly hostel, cheaper with shared bath, electric shower doesn´t always work, best choice in town.

E-F Sozoranga, on the main park inSozoranga, T07-2699125. Basic hostel, cheaper with shared bath, cold water.

F Residencial Jiménez, on 10 de Agosto, Gonzanamá, T07-2679146. Basic hostel, cheaper with shared bath, cold water.

Catacocha p293

D Tambococha, opposite the church, T07-2683551. Modern hotel with comfortable rooms, cafeteria, electric shower, friendly.

D-E Buena Esperanza, Vivanco y Celi, T07-2683031. Simple older place but very friendly, cheaper with shared bath and cold water.

Celica and around p293

Alamor D SICA, 10 de Agosto, 2 blocks from the park, T07-2680230. Comfortable rooms, electric shower, parking.

E Puyango, 10 de Agosto 7-34 at the main park, T07-2680137. Nice friendly hostel, cheaper with shared bath, cold water, karaoke bar.

Celica E Central, on the main park, T07-2657120. Comfortable rooms, cheaper with shared bath and cold water.

E-F Pucará, Manuela Cañizares half a block from the main park, T07-2657159. Nice place with comfortable rooms, cheaper with shared bath, electric shower, friendly.

Zapotillo **D Los Charanes**, Quito y Roldós, across from Transportes Loja, Zapotillo, T07-2659249. Pleasant modern hotel, includes breakfast, cold water, fan.

Macará *p294, map p299*
D El Conquistador, Bolívar y Abdón Calderón, T07-2694057. Modern comfortable hotel, includes breakfast, fan, parking.
D Espiga de Oro, Calle Ante opposite the market, T07-2695089. Adequate rooms, cold water, a/c, cheaper with fan, parking.
D Santigyn, Bolívar y Rengel, T07-2695035. Modern comfortable hotel, includes breakfast, fan, some rooms with fridge.
D Terra Verde, Lazaro Vaca s/n, near the Hospital Civil, T07-2694540, patricioluzuriaga @hotmail.com   Nice hotel in a quiet location 2 blocks from the Cooperativa Loja bus station. Includes breakfast, a/c, very clean, rooftop terrace, helpful, opened in 2003.
D-E Bekalus, Bernardo Valdivieso entre 10 de Agosto y Rengel, T07-2694043. Cheaper with shared bath, cold water, parking, simple but adequate, good value.
E Hostal del Sur, Veintimilla y Loja, T07-2694189. Modern hotel with small rooms, private bath, cold water, fan.

● Eating

South of Cuenca *p285*
Ψ Restaurant Pana, near the highway in Oña, reached from the southern access to town. Here the four Alvarado sisters offer good traditional cooking and lots of friendly chatter in their outdoor kitchen; recommended both for the food and the experience.

Saraguro *p285*
There are several restaurants around the main square, serving economical set meals.

Loja *p286, map p295*
Tamales lojanos are made of corn meal with chicken or pork, onions, raisins and spices, steamed wrapped in achira leaves; very good. Another local dish is *repe*, a soup made from cheese and a special type of green banana which only grows in the south. *Cecina* is thinly cut meat, usually pork, cooked over open flames. Local buns made with raw sugar are called *bollos*. El Valle, northeast of the centre, is the district to try typical *comida lojana*. La Delicia del Valle and La Lolita have been recommended, try their *cuy*.
ΨΨΨ Charme, Riofrío 14-55 entre Sucre y Bolívar, T07-2585819, Mon-Sat 1100-2200. Elegant French restaurant, a bit pretentious. Also café in the afternoon.
ΨΨΨ 200 Millas, Juan José Peña 07-41 y 10 de Agosto, T07-2573563, 0900-1500 daily. Good fish and seafood.
ΨΨΨ José Antonio's, José Antonio Eguiguren 12-24 y Olmedo, second floor, daily 1000-2200. Excellent French and other international food. Enthusiastic chef.

Macará

To Loja & Cariamanga

To International Bridge (2 km)

N

0 metres 200
0 yards 200

Sleeping ●
Bekalus **2**
El Conquistador
& Santigyn **3**
Espiga de Oro **4**
Gran Hotel Macará **5**
Terra Verde **1**

Eating ●
Chifa Internacional **1**
Colonial Macará **2**
Emperador **3**

Mar y Cuba, Rocafuerte 09-00 y 24 de Mayo, T07-2585154, Wed-Sun 0930-1630, 1830-2300. Seafood and Cuban specialities, friendly service.

Parrilladas El Fogón, 8 de Diciembre y Flores, across from the bus station. Grill and salad bar.

Parrilladas Uruguayas, Juan de Salinas y Av Universitaria, T07-2570260, Mon 1800-0000, Tue-Sat 1100-0000, Sun 1100-1800. Good grilled meat, helpful.

Café Azul, José Antonio Eguiguren entre Bolívar y Sucre, Mon-Fri 0900-1230, 1500-2200, Sat 1500-2100. Breakfasts, crêpes, salads, sandwiches, lasagna and other pasta, drinks.

Cevichería Las Redes, 18 de Noviembre 12-34 y Mercadillo, Mon-Sat 0900-2100, Sun 0900-1500. Seafood and some meat dishes, some tables on patio.

Casa Sol, 24 de Mayo 07-04 y José Antonio Eguiguren, daily 0900-0000. Economical set meals and à la carte. Pleasant seating on a balcony overlooking the small Parque Cristóbal Ojeda.

Diego's, Colón 14-88 y Sucre, 2nd floor, Mon-Sat 0800-2130, Sun 0800-1530. Pleasant restaurant on the second floor of a colonial house, seating on balconies around a courtyard. Good filling set lunches and international à la carte dishes, very popular.

El Arbol de Oro, Bolívar y Lourdes, opposite Parque San Sebastián. Good economical Chinese food.

Mi Tierra, Zoilo Rodríguez y 24 de Mayo, Tue-Sun 1000-2200. Typical *comida lojana* and international dishes in a very nice setting. Great views of the city.

Pizzería Forno di Fango, Bolívar 10-98 y Azuay, Tue-Sun 1200-2230. Excellent wood-oven pizza, salads and lasagne. Large portions, friendly service, good value. Recommended.

Plaza Inn, Bolívar 07-57, at main park, Mon-Sat 0900-2300, Sun 1600-2200. Cheap fast food.

El Paraíso, Quito 14-50 y Bolívar, daily 0700-2100. Good vegetarian food. Set breakfast, lunch and dinner and some à la carte dishes.

Tamal Lojano, 18 de Noviembre e Imbabura, Mon-Sat 0930-1330, 1630-2000. Set lunches, very good *tamales* and other local snacks in the evening.

Cafés

Loja has many excellent bakeries and cafés. Lojanos often enjoy a warm drink and sweets in the evening, or one of the very popular *tamales*.

Café del Museo, Bernardo Valdivieso 09-42 y Rocafuerte, at the Museo de Música, Mon-Sat 1000-1300, 1500-1900. Local snacks such as *tamales* and *quesadillas*, fruit salads, coffee and other drinks.

El Jugo Natural, José Antonio Eguiguren 14-18 y Bolívar, Closed Sun. Very good fresh juices and breakfast.

Topoli, Bolívar 13-78 y Riofrío esquina, Mon-Fri 0800-2100, Sat 0800-2000. Best coffee and yoghurt in town, good for breakfast, sandwiches, snacks, nice sweets. Very popular with young and old, can get crowded and noisy.

Vilcabamba *p288, map p296*

El Jardín, Sucre y Agua de Hierro, at Jardín Escondido hotel, 0800-2000. Excellent authentic Mexican food and drinks (Mexican chef), also international dishes and very good breakfasts. Pleasant atmosphere in a garden setting, attentive service, live music some Sat nights. Highly recommended.

Izhcayluma, At Hostería Izhcayluma south of town (don´t confuse with El Molino de Izhcayluma next door), T07-2580895, Mon 1700-2000, Tue-Sun 0800-2000. Excellent international dishes with some German specialities, also serve nice breakfasts. Lovely terrace dining room with wonderful views. Highly recommended.

Shanta's, 800 m from town on the road to Yamburara, daily 1230-2200. Good international food with specialities such as trout and frog legs, tasty pizza, nicely decorated, rustic setting just outside town, pleasant atmosphere, friendly service.

La Terraza, D Vaca de Vega y Bolívar, esquina, daily 1000-2100. Popular restaurant with sidewalk seating, right at the main park. A variety of international dishes, good fajitas.

Campary, Bolívar at the main park, daily 0800-2200. A sidewalk restaurant by the park. International food.

El Ché, moving at the close of this edition and due to re-open in Yamburara next to Craig's Book exchange, 1½ km from town. Terrace restaurant serving Argentine specialities. Tasty meat, pasta and pizza, good quality and generous portions, friendly owner. Recommended.

¶¶ La Cumbre, J Montalvo 07-36 y J D Toledo, Sun-Tue 1200-11800, Wed-Fri 1200-2200, Sat 1200-0100. Cultural centre and language school. Ecuadorean and international food in a covered patio setting. Films shown some evenings, dancing on Sat night if not booked for private events.

¶¶-¶ Vegetariano, Valle Sagrado y Diego Vaca de Vega, daily 0830-2030. Small vegetarian restaurant in a garden setting. Very good 3-course set meals and a few à la carte dishes, also breakfasts. Recommended.

¶ Along C Sucre, between Clodoveo Jaramillo and Agua de Hierro, are several simple places serving economical set meals.

Cafés

El Punto, Sucre y Luis Fernando de Vega, esquina, 0800-2100, closed Tue. A pleasant pavement café on the main park. Breakfast, snacks, pizza, sandwiches, home-made bread, sweets, coffee and drinks.

Natural Yogurt, Bolívar, at the main park, daily 0800-2200. Home-made yoghurt, a variety of savoury and sweet crêpes, some pasta dishes, pavement seating.

South of Vilcabamba *p291*

¶ El Turista, main plaza in Palanda. Good set meals, try, *pollo ahumado* (smoked chicken).

Zumba *p291*

¶ Las Cañitas, 24 de Mayo y 12 de Febrero. Simple set meals.

Catacocha *p293*

¶ Salón Macará, on Vivanco. Cheap set meals.

Macará *p294, map p299*

¶ Chifa Internacional, Sucre y Bolívar. Chinese.

¶ Colonial Macará, Rengel y Bolívar. Set meals and some à la carte dishes.

¶ El Emperador, Carlos Veintimilla. Set meals.

① Bars and clubs

Loja *p286, map p295*

Casa Tinku, Mercadillo entre Bolívar y Bernardo Valdivieso. Bar-café, live music on Fri night, also crafts shop.

El Viejo Minero, Sucre 10-76 y Azuay, T07-

2585878. Mon-Sat 1500-0000. Bar and café, popular with foreigners. Recommended.

Vilcabamba *p288, map p296*

La Cumbre, see Eating. Dancing on Sat nights when not catering private events.

Sonic's, José David Toledo y Hatillo. Thu-Sat from 2000. Drinks and dancing, varied music, popular with local youth.

◉ Entertainment

Loja *p286, map p295*

The Municipio organizes live music on Thu evenings. Ask at the information office.

Vilcabamba *p288, map p296*

Occasional films are shown at **La Cumbre**, see Eating, and there are concerts on Sat nights at the **Jardín Escondido**, Sucre y Agua del Hierro, featuring a variety of music from classical to modern, pleasant atmosphere.

❀ Festivals and events

Feb-Mar Carnival This is when normally sedate and tranquil **Vilcabamba** runs riot. The town is crowded, noisy and prices go up. Parade, concerts and lots of water throwing.

Mar/Apr Interesting **Semana Santa** celebrations are held in **Saraguro**, with the participation of people from the surrounding villages. There are processions on Palm Sun, Mon, Maundy Thu, Good Fri and Easter Sun. Watchmen stay in the church with the image of Christ from Maundy Thu to Easter Sun.

Aug-Sep Fiesta de la Virgen del Cisne Loja, Catamayo and El Cisne are crowded with religious pilgrims and Ecuadorean tourists during the last 2 weeks of Aug and the first 2 weeks of Sep, when it is very difficult to find a room and all prices rise. The main festival in honour of the Virgen is **15 Aug**, when hundreds of pilgrims from Ecuador and Peru gather in **El Cisne**. On **16-20 Aug**, the faithful walk in procession with the image of the Virgin, 74 km from El Cisne to the cathedral in **Loja**. A religious festival is then held in honour of the Virgin on **8 Sep**, with serenades at the cathedral. The image remains in Loja until **1 Nov**, after which devotees return the image to El Cisne in another 3-day procession. Also starting on **8 Sep** and continuing for 1 week is the **Feria**

de Loja/Feria de Integración Fronteriza, a commercial and agricultural exhibition which has Peruvian participants every second year. Dances and other festivities.
17-19 Nov **Independencia**, celebrated with dances and parades.

O Shopping

Loja *p286, map p295*
Handicrafts
Regional crafts include Saraguro bead necklaces, *alforjas* (woven saddlebags), ceramics and woodwork. Several craft shops on Lourdes, near Parque San Sebastián.
Cer-Art, pre-Columbian designs on mostly high-gloss ceramics, which are produced at the Universidad Técnica. Above the university is the 'Ceramics Plaza', where you can buy directly from the crafts studio. Mon-Fri 0800-1200, 1500-1800.
La Negrita, 18 de Noviembre y 10 de Agosto, opposite the market, for saddlebags.
Patronato Municipal, Bolívar y 10 de Agosto. Tue-Sat 0900-1300, 1500-1900.

Markets
Mercado Centro Comercial Loja, 18 de Noviembre y 10 de Agosto, Mon-Sat 0600-1630, Sun 0600-1330. Clean, efficient and attractive. Crafts are found near where flowers are sold.

Vilcabamba *p288, map p296*
Handicrafts
Artesanal Primavera, Diego Vaca de Vega y Sucre, at the main square, Mon, Wed and Fri 1500-1730, Tue and Sat 0930-1300, Thu 0900-1030. T-shirts and crafts.
Artesanías Tucán, Fernando de la Vega y Sucre, daily 1000-1300, 1400-1800. A selection of crafts, T-shirts and postcards.

▲ Activities and tours

Loja *p286, map p295*
Tour operators
Aratinga Aventuras, Lourdes 14-80 y Sucre, T/F07-2582434, aratinga@loja.telconet.net Specializes in birdwatching tours, overnight trips to cloud forest, rainforest, dry forest or Tumbesian forest. Pablo Andrade is a knowlegeable guide.

Biotours, Pasaje E, off Emiliano Ortega entre Colón y Azuay, T07-2579387. City, regional, cycling and jungle tours, flight tickets. Friendly.
Franky Tours, Bolívar y Azuay, T07-2560084, fhidalgo@loja.telconet.net Local and regional tours, airline tickets.

Vilcabamba *p288, map p296*
Tour operators
Many operators offer horse riding: short trips US$5 per hour, half day US$15, full day with lunch US$25. Overnight trips cost US$25-35 per day, including accommodation and meals. Some operators offer trekking to their own shelters in private reserves.
Caballos Gavilán, Sucre y Diego Vaca de Vega, T07-2580281, gavilanhorse @yahoo.com Run by New Zealander Gavin Moore, lots of experience, good horseman, good food in his lodge.
Caminatas Andes Sureños, Bolívar, 3 blocks from the plaza towards Loja, jorgeluis222 @latinmail.com Specialist trekking tours run by Jorge Mendieta, friendly.
Centro Ecuestre, Diego Vaca de Vega y Bolívar, centroecuestre@hotmail.com A group of local guides, friendly and helpful.
Monta Tours, Sucre y Diego Vaca de Vega, T/F07-2580916, solomaco@hotmail.com French-run, friendly and helpful.
Orlando Falco. Experienced English-speaking guide. Contact through **Rumi Wilco Ecolodge** (see Sleeping above) or Primavera craft shop on plaza.
Las Palmas, at Cabañas Río Yambala (see Sleeping above), riding tours to their reserve.
La Tasca Tours, Diego Vaca de Vega y Sucre, T07-2580888, latascatours@yahoo.fr Riding with René León an experienced horseman.

⊖ Transport

For main inter-city bus routes, see p52.

South of Cuenca *p285*
Oña is served by frequent buses to/from **Cuenca**, US$3-3.50, 2 hrs, and **Loja**, US$3-3.50, 2½ hrs.

Saraguro *p285*
Frequent buses to/from **Cuenca**, US$4.50, 3 hrs, and **Loja**, US$1.50, 2 hrs. Also services to **Quito**, US$12, 12 hrs.

Saraguro to Yacuambi trek *p286*

To the trailhead, take any bus along the Panamericana to **Paquizhapa** (Urdaneta). Hire a pick-up truck from there, depending on road conditions and how far they can get it will cost US$5-8. A pick-up from Saraguro is US$10, one option is Jaime Castro, T07-2200125. To return from **Yacuambi**, there are several daily buses, most in the early morning, to **Zamora**, US$2.50, 3½ hrs; from Zamora there is frequent service to Loja. There is also an overnight bus from Yacuambi to **Saraguro**.

Loja *p286, map p295*
Air

Aeropuerto Camilo Ponce Enríquez at Catamayo (1 hr from Loja) is served by TAME, with 1-2 daily flights to **Quito**, US$63 and 3 weekly to **Guayaquil**, US$49. Flights are sometimes cancelled due to strong winds or fog. For buses to the airport, see below.

Bus

To **Catamayo** (for the airport) every 30 min, 0600-2000, US$1, 50 min; note that none of the buses arrive in Catamayo early enough to connect with the morning flight to Quito.

There are 3 different routes from Loja to **Machala** on the coast, each with its own bus service; ask for the one you need. They are, from north to south: via Piñas, for **Zaruma** (p327) unpaved and rough but very scenic; via **Balsas**, fully paved and also scenic; and via **Alamor**, for Puyango petrified forest (p329), military checkpoints on route.

To **Vilcabamba**, Vilcabambaturis vans and mini-buses from the Terminal Terrestre in Loja, every 15 min, 0545-2045, US$1, 1 hr; or *taxirutas* (shared taxis) from La Tebaida, south of Loja centre, near Av Iberoamérica y Chile, US$1.20, 45 min.

To **Zumba**, via Vilcabamba, US$5-6, 6-7 hrs, a rough but beautiful ride, worth doing in daylight, prone to landslides with heavy rain, **Sur Oriente**, 0800, 1730, 2130, or **Unión Cariamanga**, 0530, 0900, 1200, 1600, 2330, or **Unión Yantzatza**, 1045, 2145, or **Nambija**, 2400 and 1230. The 2400 bus reaches Zumba about 0600 and continues to **La Balsa** (border crossing), if the road is passable; Loja-La Balsa, US$7.50, 8 hrs.

To **Catacocha**, US$2.25, 2½ hrs; to **Gonzanamá**, US$2.20, 2½ hrs; to

Cariamanga, US$3, 3 hrs; to **Amaluza**, US$4.75, 6 hrs; to **Sozoranga**, US$4.50, 4½ hrs; to **Celica**, US$4.70, 4 hrs; to **Alamor**, US$5.80, 6 hrs; to **Zapotillo**, US$7.75, 8 hrs; to **Macará**, frequent service with Transportes Loja and Unión Cariamanga, US$5.80, 6 hrs.

International buses To **Piura** (Peru), via Macará, **Loja Internacional** departs 0700, 1300, 2030 and 2230 daily, US$8, 8 hrs including border formalities. Return from Piura at 0930, 1300, 2130 and 2230; office in Piura at Av Sánchez y Cerro 2-28 y Av Vice.

Vilcabamba *p288, map p296*

To **Loja**, all transport leaves from the small terminal behind the market. Buses to **Zumba** pass through Vilcabamba about 45-60 min after departing Loja, US$5-6, 5-6 hrs. They stop along the highway, outside the market. Note that some of the buses go only as far as **Palanda**. To **Catamayo airport**, direct taxi US$25, or take a van to Loja, a bus to the centre of Catamayo (see Loja transport, above) and a taxi from there.

Zumba *p291*

To **Vilcabamba** and **Loja**, Sur Oriente, 1000, 1330, 2100, or **Unión Cariamanga**, 0700, 1230, 1600, 2200, 0030, or **Unión Yantzatza**, 2000, 2330, or **Nambija**, 0500 and 2245; note the 2245 bus comes from La Balsa if the road is passable. There are 2 daily *rancheras* (open-sided trucks with benches) to **La Balsa** (border crossing) at 0800 and 1430, US$1.75, 1½-2 hrs. For onward transport into Peru, see La Balsa transport, below.

La Balsa *p291*

There are 2 daily *rancheras* (open-sided trucks with benches) to **Zumba**, at about 1230 and 1730, US$1.75, 1½-2 hrs. To **Loja**, via Vilcabamba and Zumba, Transportes Nambija, 2030. Shared taxis go from La Balsa to **San Ignacio** (Peru), US$3, 2 hrs.

Catamayo *p292*

For flight information, see Loja transport, above. To **Loja**, bus every 30 min, 0600-2000, US$1, 50 min, also shared taxi US$4 per person or private taxi US$15. To **Macará**, $4.80, 5 hrs. International buses to **Piura** (Peru) can also be borded in Catamayo.

Macará and into Peru *p294, map p299*
To **Loja**, frequent service with Transportes
Loja and **Unión Cariamanga**, US$5.80, 6 hrs.
To **Quito**, US$15, 15 hrs; to **Guayaquil**,
US$11-12, 8 hrs.

Into Peru Taxi (US$0.25 shared, US$1
private) or pick-up from the small park near
the market to the **border**. Once in Peru, cars
and minivans run from La Tina to **Sullana**,
US$3 per person or US$12 for a private car,
1½-2 hrs. From Sullana there is onward
transport to **Piura**. Also direct international
buses to **Piura** can be boarded in Macará at
0030, 0300, 1300 and 1800, US$3.50, 3 hrs.

❶ Directory

Loja *p286, map p295*
Airline offices TAME, 24 de Mayo y
Emiliano Ortega, T07-2570248, Mon-Fri
0830-1300, 1430-1800, Sat 0900-1300.
Banks Banco de Guayaquil, José Antonio
Eguiguren y Bernardo Valdivieso, Mon-Fri
0830-1630. Amex TCs 1% commission, Euros,
Visa, Mastercard credit cards (not debit).
Banco del Austro, José Antonio Eguiguren
14-12 y Bolívar, Mon-Fri 0830-1600. Visa and
MasterCard, 4% commission. Mutualista
Pichincha, Bolívar y José Antonio Eguiguren,
on plaza, Mon-Fri 0900-1600. Mastercard.
Produbanco, Bernardo Valdivieso y José
Antonio Eguiguren, on plaza, Mon-Fri
0830-1600. TCs, Euros. **Comercial Karen's**,
18 de Noviembre 06-80 y José Antonio
Eguiguren, T07-2572140, Mon-Sat
0900-1300, 1500-1900. Changes Peruvian
soles and Euros. **Car hire** Arricar, in Hotel
Libertador, T07-2571443. Bombuscaro
Rent-a-Car, in hotel of the same name,
T/F07-2577021. **Consulates** Peru, Sucre
10-64 y Azuay, T07-2571668, Mon-Fri
0830-1300. **Hospital** Clínica San Agustín,
18 de Noviembre 10-72 y Azuay, T2573002.
Internet US$1 per hr. **Laundry**

Lavandería, 24 de Mayo y José Antonio
Eguiguren, Mon-Sat 0830-1300, 1430-1930,
Sun 0830-1300. **Post office** Colón y Sucre.

Vilcabamba *p288, map p296*
Banks There are no banks, ATMs or places
to exchange TCs in Vilcabamba. **Book
exchange** Craig's Book Exchange,
Yamburara Bajo, follow Diego Vaca de Vega,
1 km from town. Impressive collection, 2,500
books in 12 languages, 2 for 1 exchange.
Hospital Hospital Kokichi Otani, Av Eterna
Juventud (main highway), T07-2673188.
Internet US$1-1.20 per hour. Mandango,
at the hostel, 0900-2100. **Language
schools** La Cumbre, Juan Montalvo 07-36
y José David Toledo, T07-2580283,
www.cumbrevilcabamba.com, Spanish
lessons, US$4.50-US$8 per person per hr,
depending on size of group. Also German
lessons. **Laundry** Laundry Services, Diego
Vaca de Vega y Bolívar, opposite the park,
daily 0800-2200, US$3 up to 4 kg. Lava Listo,
Luis Fernando de la Vega 07-42 y Valle
Sagrado, daily 0800-1200, 1400-1700,
US$0.80 per kg. Shanta's, see Eating above,
daily 0800-1800, US$3.50 per load.
Massage Beauty Care, Bolívar y Diego
Vaca de Vega, daily 1000-1800. Karina
Zumba, facials, waxing, Reiki, 1 hr US$10.
Nicole Falardeau, weekends at Hostería
Paraíso, see Sleeping, weekdays at Av Eterna
Juventud, entre Juan Montalvo y Hatillo.
Therapeutic massage, Reiki, reflexology, 1½
hr US$15. **Telephone** Pacifictel, Bolívar y
Diego Vaca de Vega, near the park, but due to
move to Sucre y Clodoveo Jaramillo. One of
the worst services in the country, frequently
out of order, with long queues. Make your
calls before arriving in Vilcabamba.

Zumba *p291*
Internet Cybernet, 12 de Febrero next to
Hotel San Luis, US$1.50 per hr.

Guayaquil and Southern Pacific

❗ Footprint features

Introduction

The coastal plains are the agro-industrial heartland of Ecuador. Rice, sugar, coffee, African palm, mango, cacao, and shrimp are produced in these hot and humid lowlands and processed or exported through Guayaquil. The largest and most dynamic commercial centre in the country, Guayaquil is also Ecuador's main port and the city's influence extends throughout the coast and beyond. This 'working Ecuador' is most frequently seen by business visitors rather than tourists, but Guayaquil has experienced a civic revival in recent years and has some attractions to offer. Trips to Galápagos can be organized from here, and the city is a logical starting point for travels north along the coast.

In the opposite direction, south to the Peruvian border, the land gives the impression of being one giant banana plantation. Machala is the main centre here, and nearby Puerto Bolívar the port through which the *oro verde* (green gold) is shipped out to the world. With the opening of new inland routes south to the border, fewer travellers are passing through this area but it still provides good access to the beaches of northern Peru. And inland from Machala, in the uplands of El Oro, is one of the best hidden treasures of Ecuador – the colonial mining town of Zaruma.

In Guayaquil and along the coast, the climate from May to December is dry with often overcast days but pleasantly cool nights, whereas the hot rainy season from January to April can be oppressively humid.

★ Don't miss

1 **Malecón 2000** Stroll along Guayaquil's pride and joy, page 310.
2 **Giant iguanas** Check out these prehistoric creatures in Parque Bolívar, page 311.
3 **Botanical Gardens** Enjoy a stroll and admire the orchids in this urban oasis, page 312.
4 **Bosque Protector Cerro Blanco** Tour the nature reserve, page 312.
5 **Uplands of El Oro** Discover the romance of this seldom-visited gold mining of this gold-mining region, page 327.

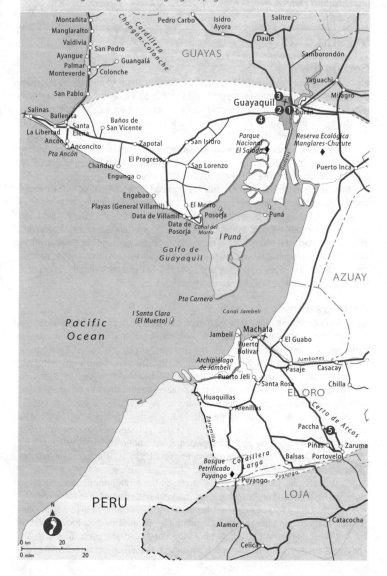

Guayaquil & Southern Pacific

Guayaquil

→ *Phone code 04 Colour map 4, grid C3 Population 2,000,00 Altitude sea level*

Ecuador's largest city and the country's chief sea port and industrial and commercial centre lies on the west bank of the chocolate-brown Río Guayas, some 56 km from its outflow into the Gulf of Guayaquil. The city couldn't be more different from its highland counterpart and political rival, Quito. It is hot, sticky, fast-paced, bold and brash. It may lack the capital's colonial charm, but Guayaquileños are certainly more lively, colourful and open than Quiteños. Since 2000, Guayaquil has cleaned-up and 'renewed' some of its most frequented downtown areas, and the authorities are trying hard to attract tourism. ▶▶ *For Sleeping, Eating and other listings, see pages 313-319.*

Ins and outs

Getting there

Air Simón Bolívar International Airport is to the north, about 10 minutes by taxi from the city centre. Buses to the centre (eg Linea 130 'Full 2') are neither safe nor practical with luggage. If you are going straight on to another city, take a cab from the airport directly to the bus station, which is close by. If you are arriving in Guayaquil by air during the daytime, you can walk from the terminal out to Av de las Américas to hail a cab. The fare will be about half of what you would be charged for the same trip by one of the drivers who belong to the airport taxi cooperative, but it is not safe to leave the terminal area at night. See below for bus and taxi fares.

    Bus The Terminal Terrestre is north of the airport, just off the road to the Guayas bridge. The company offices are on the ground floor, long-distance buses leave from the top floor and regional buses (for Playas, Salinas, etc) leave from the ground floor. When you purchase a ticket, ask where your bus leaves from. There are restaurants, shops and a **Pacifictel** office for calls but no left-luggage depot; do not leave anything unattended. The terminal is busy at weekends and holidays. Lots of local buses go from the bus station to the city centre, (eg Linea 84 to Plaza Centenario) but this is not safe with luggage; take a taxi. ▶▶ *See also Transport, page 318.*

Getting around

A much-needed street numbering system was introduced in 2001, which divides the city into four quadrants separated by a north-south axis and an east-west axis. All north-south streets are 'avenidas' and the east-west streets are 'calles'. Each has an alpha-numeric designation such as Av 12 south-east. The airport and bus terminal are in the northeastern quadrant, the commercial heartland in the southeastern quadrant. Although this system is officially in place, the old street names persist and almost everybody uses the old nomenclature.

    Not surprisingly for a city of this size, you will need to get around by public transport. A number of hotels, however, are centrally located near the riverfront. City buses are often confusing and overcrowded at rush hour; US$0.25, watch out for pickpockets. There are also *furgonetas* (minibuses), US$0.25, which post their routes in the windscreen.

    Buses are only permitted in a few streets in the centre; northbound buses go along the Malecón and on Rumichaca, southbound along Boyacá. Bus No 15 will take you from the centre to Urdesa, 13 to Policentro, 14 to Albanborja, 74 to La Garzota and Sauces. **Taxis** are the safest and most comfortable option. They must have meters by law but these are seldom used, so prices are negotiable and overcharging is rife. Always agree on the fare in advance. From outside the airport or bus terminal to the centre is US$3-4; same fare from the centre to Urdesa, Policentro or Alborada. From the airport to the bus terminal and short trips costs US$2. It is often quicker to walk short distances in the centre, rather than taking a bus or taxi, but on no account walk around after dark except in the city's few 'renewed' areas such as the Malecón 2000.

Orientation and safety

Guayaquil's suburbs sprawl to the north and south of the centre, with middle-class neighbourhoods and some very upscale areas in the north and poorer working class neighbourhoods and slums to the south. Rapid growth has stretched the city's services, at times beyond the limit, but things are currently on the mend. A road tunnel under Cerro Santa Ana was opened in 2004, linking the northern suburbs to downtown, and greatly improving traffic flow. Garbage collection is also better than it used to be, but remains a problem in some areas.

Safety is also an important issue. Despite an ongoing public safety campaign by the municipal authorities, residential neighbourhoods hide behind bars and protect

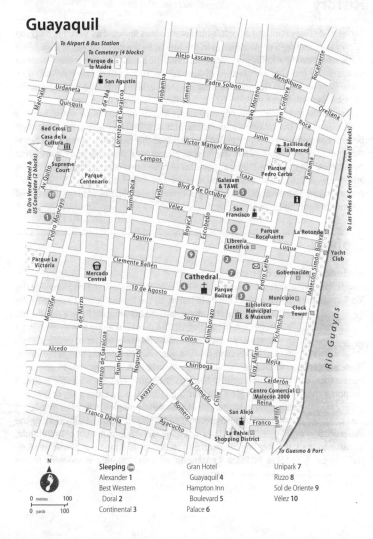

Guayaquil

Sleeping		Gran Hotel		Unipark **7**
Alexander **1**		Guayaquil **4**		Rizzo **8**
Best Western		Hampton Inn		Sol de Oriente **9**
Doral **2**		Boulevard **5**		Vélez **10**
Continental **3**		Palace **6**		

themselves with armed guards. Gangs are an important problem. The Malecón, parts of Av 9 de Octubre and the Las Peñas neighbourhood are heavily patrolled and safe. The rest of the city carries the usual risks of a large seaport and metropolis. Don't walk around with valuables and always take taxis at night.

Information

Dirección Municipal de Turismo ① *Municipio, 4th floor, T04-2524200 ext 3479, Mon-Fri 0830-1230, 1300-1630*. Information about the city, English and French spoken, friendly and helpful. **Ministerio de Turismo** ① *P Ycaza 203 y Pichincha, 5th and 6th floors, T04-2568764, Mon-Fri 0830-1700*. Information about the coastal provinces of Ecuador, friendly, Spanish only. **Websites** with information about Guayaquil and the coast include **www.visitaguayaquil.com, www.guayaquil.gov.ec**, and **www.turismoguayas.com**.

History

Santiago de Guayaquil had a complicated start. It was founded as Santiago de Quito (*sic*) in 1534 by Diego de Almagro up in the Sierra, by the chilly shores of Laguna de Colta, and moved the following year by Sebastián de Benalcázar to its current warmer location near the native settlement of Guayaquile. This, in turn, may have taken its name from two native Huancavilca rulers: Guayas and his wife Quil. Throughout the colonial and republican periods, Guayaquil always retained its strategic importance as Ecuador's main port. The current Puerto Marítimo, opened in 1964, handles three-quarters of the country's imports and almost half of its exports. It is a constant bone of contention between *costeños* and *serranos* that Guayaquil is not given better recognition of its importance in the form of greater local authority and more central government funds. Since the late 1990s there have been organized movements for autonomy of Ecuador's coastal provinces, spearheaded by Guayaquil. The city's current mayor, Jaime Nebot, is a leading national figure who has at times challenged the authority of the Quito government.

Sights

Malecón Simón Bolívar

A wide, tree-lined waterfront avenue, the Malecón Simón Bolívar runs alongside the Río Guayas from the exclusive **Club de la Unión**, by the Moorish clock tower, past the imposing **Palacio Municipal** and **Government Palace** and the old Yacht Club to Las Peñas. The riverfront along this avenue is an attractive promenade, known as **Malecón 2000**, where visitors and locals can enjoy the fresh river breeze and take in the views.

❢ *The Malecón is patrolled and safe, and a favourite place to stroll.*

There are gardens, fountains, monuments and walkways. You can dine at upmarket restaurants, cafés and food courts. Towards the south end are souvenir shops, a shopping mall and the old **Mercado Sur** (prefabricated by Eiffel 1905-07), now a gallery housing temporary exhibits. The **Museo Antropológico** is housed in modern new premises at north end of the Malecón (see Museums, below). Halfway along the Malecón, Boulevard 9 de Octubre, the city's main street, starts in front of **La Rotonda**, a statue to mark the meeting between Simón Bolívar and José San Martín in 1822. Halfway up 9 Octubre is **Plaza Centenario** with its towering monument to the liberation of the city erected in 1920.

Guayaquil's second showpiece is the old district of Las Peñas, a vestige of old Guayaquil at the north end of the Malecón. This picturesque neighbourhood, built on the Cerro Santa Ana hill, at the edge of the river, is one of the areas that has undergone gentrification. Visitors can walk up its steep stairway amid the brightly painted wooden houses. There are cafés, bars and lovely views from the top. The area is heavily guarded and safe. During the *fiestas julianas* (24-25 July), young painters exhibit their art at Las Peñas. The main artery is a narrow cobbled street (Numa Pompilio Llona). The entrance is guarded by two cannon pointing riverward, a reminder of the days when pirates sailed up the Guayas to attack the city. Guayaquil was sacked and destroyed by fire a number of times, so almost none of its original wooden buildings remain. There are several important churches which were rebuilt on several occasions, otherwise, most of its colonial history is confined to the history books.

Churches

There are several noteworthy churches. **Santo Domingo**, founded by the Dominicans in 1548, stands just by Las Peñas. It was sacked and burned by pirates in 1624. Its present form was built in 1938, replacing the wooden structure with concrete in classical style. Pirates also sacked the original church of **San Agustín**; the present building dates from 1931.

The original wooden structure of the **Cathedral**, built in 1695, survived both sackings and fire, but the years took their toll and a new building was completed in 1822. In 1924 construction on the present building was started, in the classical Gothic style, and it was inaugurated in the 1950s. The pleasant, shady **Parque Bolívar** (officially called Parque Seminario but best known as Parque de las Iguanas) in front of the Cathedral is filled with large tame iguanas which scuttle out of the trees for scraps.

Other notable churches are **San Francisco**, with its restored colonial interior, off 9 de Octubre and Pedro Carbo, and the beautiful **La Merced**.

At the north end of the centre, below Cerro El Carmen, the huge, spreading **Cemetery**, with its dazzling, high-rise tombs and the ostentatious mausoleums of the rich, is worth a visit. A flower market over the road sells the best blooms in the city. Go on a Sunday when there are plenty of people about.

Museums

The **Museo Municipal** ⓘ *Sucre y Chile, Tue-Sat 0900-1700, guided tours available, free*, is housed in the Biblioteca Municipal, where there are paintings, gold and archaeological collections, shrunken Shuar heads, a section on the history of Guayaquil and a good newspaper library.

Museo Antropológico y de Arte Contemporaneo ⓘ *Tue-Fri 0900-1800, Sat and Sun 0900-1300, US$1, located at the north end of the Malecón 2000*, has excellent collections of ceramics, gold objects and paintings. It also houses the collection of religious art from the former **Museo Nahim Isaías**.

Museo del Banco del Pacífico ⓘ *Ycaza 200 y Pichincha, 3rd floor, T04-2328333, Mon-Fri 0900-1700, free*, is a beautiful small museum that displays mainly archaeological exhibits.

Museo de la Casa de la Cultura ⓘ *9 de Octubre 1200 y P Moncayo, Tue-Fri 1000-1800, Sat 0900-1500. US$0.50. English-speaking guides available*, has an impressive collection of prehistoric gold items in its archaeological museum. Also at the Casa de la Cultura is the **Pinacoteca Manuel Rendón Seminario**, a photo collection of old Guayaquil.

Guayaquil & Southern Pacific Guayaquil

The **Botanical Gardens** ⓘ *Av Francisco de Orellana, Las Orquídeas (bus line 63 or furgoneta Orquídeas), T04-2560498, 0800-1600 daily, US$3, English-speaking guides available for about US$5*, are in the Ciudadela Las Orquídeas to the northwest. There are over 3,000 plants, including 150 species of Ecuadorean and foreign orchids. The views are good and it is the ideal place for a pleasant stroll. Recommended.

A second *malecón* has been built by the **Estero Salado**, a brackish estuary which flanks the west side of the city. This **Malecón del Salado** is another spot for a pleasant stroll and is popular with locals. It has various monuments, and eateries specializing in seafood. Rowboats and pedal-boats can be hired.

You can take in the city's sights on a **double-decker bus tour** ⓘ *US$5-17 depending on route, departs from Plaza Olmedo, the Rotonda or IMAX cinema on the Malecón 2000. Office: VM Rendón 401 y Córdova, T04-2306444, www.guayaquilvision.com*, ranging from 90 minutes to three hours in length. They also offer full-day tours to the Parque Histórico (see Excursions below) and night-time party tours.

The **Pirata** ⓘ *US$5*, a tour and party boat, sails from the Malecón every evening. It offers pricey drinks, snacks, music and dancing, with nice views of the city.

Guayaquil is a city of suburban **shopping malls**, where consumerism flourishes in air-conditioned comfort. Here you will find many banks, restaurants, bars, discos, cinemas, cybercafés and of course shops. For a complete list see Shopping, page 317.

Excursions

Bosque Protector Cerro Blanco

ⓘ *US$5, additional fee charged for each trail visited, US$4 for 1 trail, US$5 for 2, US$8 for 3, camping $7 per person. Guides can be hired. Reservations required during weekdays and for groups larger than 8 on the weekends, and for birders wishing to arrive before or stay after normal opening hours (0800-1530). On the Vía a la Costa, Km 16, the entrance is beyond the Club Rocafuerte. Taxi from Guayaquil US$10-20. The yellow and green 'Chongonera' buses leave every 30 mins from Parque Victoria and pass the park entrance on the way to Puerto Hondo.*

‡ *Remember to take water, sun protection and insect repellent on all excursions from Guayaquil.*

This nature reserve is set in tropical dry forest along the Río Blanco with an impressive variety of birds (over 190 species), such as the Guayaquil Green-Macaw (symbol of the reserve), Crane Hawk, Snail Kite and so on, and with sightings of Howler Monkeys, ocelot, puma, jaguar and peccaries, many reptiles, among others. The reserve is run by **Fundación Pro-Bosque** ⓘ *edif Promocentro, local 16, Eloy Alfaro y Cuenca, T04-2871900*.

Manglares de Puerto Hondo

On the other side of the road from Cerro Blanco, at Km 17 on the Vía a la Costa, is **Puerto Hondo** ⓘ *Boat rentals can be arranged on the spot at weekends from the Fundación Pro-Bosque kiosk for US$7 per person with guides, or during the week with their Guayaquil office (see Cerro Blanco, above)*. Canoe trips through the mangroves can be made from here, which is a good way to see many migratory birds. This is also a good place to try local seafood specialities.

Parque El Lago

ⓘ *T04-2872033, 0800-1700, US$0.40 per vehicle, boat rentals US$1.60, bicycle rentals US$0.80*. Also along the road to the coast, at Km 26, is El Lago, a national recreation area with a lake for boating, walking paths and picnic areas.

Reserva Ecológica Manglares Churute

ⓘ *US$10 per person, basic cabins US$5, camping US$3. Boat tour (2 hrs), US$40 for group up to 15 passengers; arrange several days ahead through the Ministerio del Ambiente office in Guayaquil, Dept Forestal, Av Quito 402 y Padre Solano, p 10, T04-2293131; or Biólogo Fernando Cedeño, T09-9619815 (mob). Entrance to the reserve is at Km 50 of the Guayaquil-Naranjal-Machala road. Buses (CIFA, Ecuatoriano Pullman, 16 de Junio) leave the terminal terrestre every 30 mins, going to Naranjal or Machala. Ask to be let off at the Churute information centre. The reserve can also be reached by river.*

About 45 minutes southeast of Guayaquil is Reserva Ecológica Manglares Churute, part of the national park system, preserving mangroves in the Gulf of Guayaquil and forests of the Cordillera Churute. It is a rich natural area with five different ecosystems. There is a trail through the dry tropical forest (1½ hours' walk) and you can also walk (one hour) to Laguna Canclón or Churute, a large lake where ducks nest. Many waterbirds, animals and dolphins can be seen.

Parque Histórico

ⓘ *T04-2833807, Tue-Sun 0900-1700. US$3, Sun US$4.50 with show, www.parquehistorico.com CISA buses to Samborondón leave from the Terminal Terrestre every 20 mins, US$0.25.*

The Parque Histórico is north of the city in Entreríos, on the way to Samborondón. It recreates Guayaquil and its rural surroundings at the end of the 19th century. There is a natural area with native flora and fauna, a traditions section where you can learn about rural life and how crafts are made, an urban section with wooden architecture and an educational farm. A pleasant place for a stroll.

Zoo El Pantanal

ⓘ *Km 23 Vía a Daule, T04-2267047, daily 0900-1700, US$3.* This zoo has some 60 different species of animals and is popular with locals, school groups during the week and families at weekends.

🛌 Sleeping

Guayaquil *p308, maps p309 and p314*
Most hotels are downtown, so take a taxi from the airport or bus station. The cheapest hotels are pretty basic and many cater to short-stay customers. Around Plaza Centenario is the best bet for budget travellers wishing to stay downtown. Note however that this area is unsafe, especially at night. As an alternative, there are a few good places in residential neighbourhoods in our **B-C** range.

LL Hilton Colón, Av Francisco de Orellana in Kennedy Norte (outside downtown), T04-2689000, F2689149. 5 restaurants and bars, 2 pools, largest luxury hotel in town, all facilities, provides airport transfers.

L Continental, Chile y 10 de Agosto, T04-2329270, F2325454. Includes breakfast, 24 hr restaurant and good coffee shop, gym and sauna, a KLM Golden Tulip hotel, 5-star, centrally located.

L Oro Verde, 9 de Octubre y Gracía Moreno, T04-2327999, www.oroverdehotels.com 4 restaurants (El Patio open 24 hrs), deli and bar, pool, gym, business centre, limo service, airport transfers, top class.

L Unipark, Clemente Ballén 406 y Chile, T04-2327100, uni_gye@oroverdehotels.com Includes breakfast, good restaurants, café and bar, meeting and banquet facilities, gym, golf and tennis, 5-star luxury, some rooms being refurbished in early 2005.

L-AL Hampton Inn Boulevard, 9 de Octubre 432 y Baquerizo Moreno, T04-2566700, www.hampton.com.ec Buffet breakfast, restaurant, internet, central location, very good facilities, weekend discounts.

AL Gran Hotel Guayaquil, Boyacá 1600 y 10 de Agosto, T04-2329690, www.grandhotelguayaquil.com Includes buffet breakfast, good restaurants, a/c, pool

(US$6 for non-residents), gym and sauna, traditional Guayaquil luxury hotel.

AL Marcelius, Ciudadela Kenedy Norte, José Falconí Mz 102 S 12 y José Alavedra Tama, T04-2296044, marcelius_hotel@hotmail.com Restaurant, a/c, pool, parking, modern luxury hotel in the north of the city.

AL Ramada, Malecón 606 y Orellana, T04-2565555, www.hotelramada.com Incudes buffet breakfast, a/c, pool, internet, excellent location right on the Malecón.

A Best Western Doral, Chile 402 y Aguirre, T04-2328002, www.hdoral.com Centrally located modern hotel, includes breakfast, restaurant, a/c, internet, comfortable quiet rooms, good value. Recommended.

A Castel, Av Miguel H Alcivar y Calle Ulloa, by the Parque Japonés, Kennedy Norte, T04-2680190, www.hotelcastell.com Includes breakfast, restaurant, a/c, modern comfortable hotel in the north of the city.

A Gold Center, Alborada 5ta Etapa NE, Av Rodolfo Baquerizo Nazur y José María Egas, T04-2241736, goldcenterhotel@hotmail.com Includes breakfast, cafeteria, a/c, parking, modern comfortable hotel in the north of the city. *matrimonial $60*

A Las Peñas, Escobedo 1215 y Vélez, T04-2323355, www.hlpgye.com Includes breakfast, cafeteria, a/c, good location in a refurbished part of downtown.

A Palace, Chile 214 y Luque, T04-2321080, www.hotelpalaceguayaquil.com.ec Includes breakfast, 24 hr cafeteria, a/c, modern, traffic noise on Av Chile side, good value for business travellers. Recommended.

A Sol de Oriente, Aguirre 603 y Escobedo, T04-2325500, hsolorie@gye.satnet.net Includes breakfast, cafeteria, a/c, minibar, gym, excellent value. Recommended.

B Del Rey, Aguirre y Marín, behind tennis club, T04-2452909. Includes breakfast, cafeteria, a/c, quiet and friendly. Recommended.

B Rizzo, Clemente Ballén 319 y Chile, T04-2325210, F2326209. Includes breakfast, **Café Jambelí** downstairs for seafood, a/c, centrally located, comfortable rooms but some have no windows.

B San Rafael, Chile 414 y Clemente Ballén, T04-2324006, hotelsanrafael@hotmail.com Includes breakfast, cafeteria, a/c, comfortable rooms, central location.

B Tangara Guest House, Manuela Sáenz y O'Leary, Manzana F, Villa 1, Ciudadela Bolivariana (a residential area between the airport and downtown), T04-2284445, F2284039. Includes breakfast, a/c, fridge, nice and friendly. Recommended.

B-C Alexander, Luque 1107 y Pedro Moncayo, T04-2532000, F2514161. Cafeteria, a/c, comfortable and good value but can be noisy, some rooms without windows.

B-C Hostal de La Alborada, Alborada IX, Manzana 935, Villa 8, near airport, T04-2237251. A/c, friendly.

C La Torre, Chile 303 y Luque, T04-2531316, www.latorrehotel.com.ec Includes breakfast, cafeteria, centrally located.

C-D Casa Alianza, Av Segunda 318 y Calle 12, Los Ceibos, T04-2351261, www.casaalianza.com Cafeteria, a/c, cheaper with shared bath and fan, very far from centre, run by a Norwegian NGO.

C-D Ecuahogar, Av Isidro Ayora, Mz-F 31, V 20, opposite Banco Ecuatoriano de La Vivienda, Sauces I, T04-2248357, youthost@telconet.net Poor breakfast, restaurant, cheaper in dorm with shared bath, overpriced, frequent negative reports.

C-D Europa, Presidente Jaime Roldós 4 NE, primer paseo 14A-NE, T04-2284751, imporras@uio.telconet.net A/c, cheaper

Guayaquil northern suburbs

Av Jaime Roldós
Av Parra
Rolando
Av B Carrión
Av Isidro Ayora
Av Egas

ALBORADA
Shopping Mall La Rotonda
ShoppingMall Plaza Mayor
SAUCES
BEV
Roldós Statue
Av Freire
Av Orellana
Shopping Mall Garzo Centro
Terminal Terrestre
GARZOTA
Av Juan Tanca Marengo
Av Las Americas
To Urdesa
Bridge to Durán
Shopping Mall Plaza Quil
Policentro
Shopping Mall San Marino
Plaza Danín
Clínica Kennedy
To City Centre

N
Not to scale

Sleeping 🛏
Ecuahogar 1
Europa 2
Gold Center 3

Eating 🍴
Cangrejo Criollo 1

✸ Festivals and events

Guayaquil *p308, map p309*
24-25 Jul Fiestas Julianas The foundation of Guayaquil (actually its relocation from a previous site) is celebrated. There are parades and many public events.
9-12 Oct The city's **independence** is commemorated and cultural events take place throughout the month.

◐ Shopping

Guayaquil *p308, map p309*
Books
El Librero, in the Ríocentro, English books.
Librería Científica, Luque 223 y Chile and Plaza Triángulo on Av Estrada in Urdesa. English books, field guides to flora and fauna, travel in general.
Nuevos Horizontes, 6 de Marzo 924, book exchange.
Sagitario, at Mall del Sol. Excellent bookstore, has English books.
Selecciones, at Av 9 de Octubre 830 and in **Albán Borja Mall**, expensive novels and lots of magazines in English.

Camping gear
Casa Maspons, Ballén 517 y Boyacá, sells camping gaz.
Kao Policentro, for fishing, camping and sports gear.

Handicrafts
Albán Borja Mall has **El Telar**, which is expensive but of superb quality, especially ceramics, jewellery and embroidery, and **Ramayana**, for reasonably priced ceramics.
Cerámica Vega, VE Estrada 1200 y Laureles, Urdesa, for brightly painted Cuenca ceramics.
Mall del Sol, has more than 20 crafts shops in the Plaza de Integración section.
Manos, Cedros 305 y Primera, Urdesa. Closes until 1530 for lunch.
Mercado Artesanal, between Loja y Montalvo and Córdova y Chimborazo. Greatest variety, almost a whole block of permanent stalls with good prices.
Mercado Artesanal del Malecón 2000, at the south end of the malecón, has many small kiosks selling varied crafts.
Otavalo Indians, sell their crafts along Chile between 9 Octubre y Vélez.

Las Bahías
This is a huge bazaar area on either side of Olmedo from Villamil to Chile, by the south end of the Malecón. It was traditionally where contraband was sold from boats which put into the bay and is one of the city's oldest marketplaces. It's still very popular for electrical appliances, clothing and shoes. It has been cleaned up a bit in recent years but you must watch your valuables and be prepared to bargain. Here and throughout the city are many very cheap 'dump' stores selling very cheap clothing. You can find great bargains, but you can also be badly cheated.

Malls
Albán Borja, Av Arosemena Km 2.7.
Centro Comercial Malecón 2000, at the south end of the Malecón.
Centro Comercial San Marino, Av Francisco de Orellana y L Plaza Dañín. Huge, one of the largest in South America.
Garzocentro 2000, Av R Pareja, La Garzota.
Mall del Sol, Av Constitución y Juan Tanca Marengo, near the airport.
Mall del Sur, Av 25 de Julio. New in 2004.
Plaza Mayor and Albocentro, Av R Pareja, La Alborada.
Policentro and Plaza Quil, both on Av San Jorge, Kennedy Norte.
La Rotonda, entrance to La Garzota.

▲ Activities and tours

Guayaquil *p308, map p309*
Many operators run regional tours to the beaches and whale-watching tours in season (Jun-Sep). A number of the agencies listed operate Galápagos cruises and also have offices in Quito. There are many travel agencies for airline bookings, at the Malecón 2000 and in the large shopping centres. For city tours in double-decker buses and river cruises see Sights, p312.

Hacienda tours
Tours can be made to coastal haciendas, large plantations growing sugar cane or cacao, for a glimpse of rural life. The following cater to groups and may include meals, snacks or folklore shows. Try booking through hotels, tour agencies, or contact them directly well in advance.

Hacienda Jambelí, T04-2205401.
Hacienda Cañas, T04-2447448, F2441851.

Ice skating
Zona Fría, at Km 2.5 on the autopista La Puntilla-Samborondón.

Tour operators
Canodros S A, Urb Santa Leonor, Mz 5, local 10, T04-2285711, www.galapagosexplorer.com Runs luxury Galápagos cruises and also operates the Kapawi Ecological Reserve in the southern Oriente (see p403).
Centro Viajero, Baquerizo Moreno 1119 y 9 de Octubre, No 805, T04-2562565, centrovi@telconet.net Custom-designed tours to all regions, travel information and bookings, car and driver service, well informed about good value options for Galápagos, English spoken, very friendly, open daily. Highly recommended.
Ecoventura, Av Francisco de Orellana 222, Mz 12, Solar 22, Kennedy Norte, T04-2283182, www.ecoventura.com Excellent high-end Galápagos tours.
Ecuadorian Tours, 9 Octubre 1900 y Esmeraldas, T04-2286900, www.ecuadorian toursgye.com.ec Sells land tours and Galápagos cruises. Amex representative.
Galapagos Tours, Edificio Gran Pasaje, Av 9 Octubre 424, office 9, T04-2304488, www.galapagos-islands.com Has a large fleet of boats in different categories for Galápagos cruises, city tours, tours to reserves near Guayaquil, diving trips, also run highland and jungle tours.
Kleintours, Av Alcívar, Mz 410, Solar 11, Kennedy Norte, T04-2681700, F2681705, www.kleintours.com Runs land and Galápagos tours.
La Moneda, Av de las Américas 809 y C 2, and P Icaza 115 y Pichincha, T04-2690900, www.lamoneda.com.ec City and coastal tours, whale-watching, tours to other areas.
Macchiavello Tours, Antepara 802-A y 9 Octubre, T04-2286079. Very good whale and dolphin watching tours, for more details see Calypsso tour operator in Salinas, p323.
Metropolitan Touring, Antepara 915 y 9 de Octubre and at **Hotel Hilton Colón**, T04-2320300, www.metropolitan -touring.com High-end land tours and Galápagos cruises.

Pescatours, Domingo Comín 135 y El Oro, T04-2443365, www.pescatours.com.ec Fishing, see Tour operators in Salinas, p323.

 Transport

Guayaquil *p308, map p309*
Air
For facilities and ground transportation to/from **Simón Bolívar Airport**, see p308. For information on national flights see Getting around by air, p49.

Airline offices
Aerogal, at the airport, T04-2289313.
Air Europa, José Mascote 701 y Quisquis, p1, T04-2399103.
Air Madrid, office in Edifico Banco Amazonas, airport, T04-2549844.
American Airlines, Gen Córdova y Av 9 de Octubre, edif San Francisco, 20th Floor, T04-2564111.
Continental, 9 de Octubre 100 y Malecón, T1800-266846 or T04-2288987.
Copa, Circunvalación Sur 631 A y Ficus, Urdesa, T2888127.
Iberia, Av 9 de Octubre 101 y Malecón, T04-2320664.
Icaro, Av Francisco de Orellana, edif World Trade Centre, T04-2294265.
KLM, at the airport, T04-2282713.
TACA, 9 de Octubre y Malecón, edif Banco de la Previsora, T04-2562950.
TAME, 9 de Octubre 424, edif Gran Pasaje, T04-2692500.

Bus
For main inter-city routes see the bus timetable p52.
  Local To Santa Elena Peninsula and beaches Frequent service to all destinations, crowded on weekends and holidays. To **Playas**, 2 hrs, US$2. To **Salinas**, 2½ hrs, US$3. To **Santa Elena**, 2¼ hrs, US$3; change here for Puerto López. To **Olón**, also for Montañita, CLP at 0500, 1300, 1630, 3½ hrs, US$5.
  International To Huaquillas for the **Peruvian border**, direct, US$6, 4½ hrs; or via Machala, 6 hrs. To **Piura**, CIFA at 0550, 0650, 1120 and 2100, 10 hrs, US$9. In the Terminal Terrestre, T04-2140379. To **Lima**, Ormeño daily at 1330, 24 hrs, US$60. Offices in Centro de Negocios El Terminal, near the Terminal Terrestre but not inside it, T04-2140362.

Car hire

There are several car hire firms in booths outside the national terminal of the airport. For prices and procedures see Car hire, p55. **Avis**, T04-2287906 (airport), T04-2692884 (at **Hotel Hilton Colón**).
Budget, T04-2288510 (airport), T04-2328571 (by **Hotel Oro Verde**).
Expo, T04-2282467 (airport).
Localiza, T04-2811462 (airport).

❶ Directory

Guayaquil *p308, map p309*

Banks **American Express**, Ecuadorian Tours, 9 de Octubre 1900 y Esmeraldas. Replaces lost Amex TCs and sells TCs to Amex card holders, but does not exchange TCs or sell them for cash. Open Mon-Fri 0900-1300, 1400-1800. **Banco del Pacífico**, Icaza 200, p 4. Amex TCs in US$ only, maximum US$200 per day, US$5 charge per transaction, also some Mastercard and Visa through·ATMs. **Banco de Guayaquil**, head office at P Carbo y 9 de Octubre, edif San Francisco 300, 7th Floor, for Amex and Visa TCs, 1% commission. ATMs and cash advances on Visa, fast and efficient. **Cambiosa**, 9 de Octubre y Pichincha. **Wander Cambios**, at the airport.

Consulates **Argentina**, Aguirre 104 y Malecón, T04-2323574. **Austria**, 9 de Octubre 1312 y Quito, No 1, T04-2282303. **Belgium**, Lizardo García 301 y Vélez, T04-2364429. **Bolivia**, Cedros 400 y la 5ta, Urdesa, T04-2889955. **Brazil**, Av San Jorge 312 y Calle 3 Este, Nueva Kennedy, T04-2293046. **Canada**, Córdova 808 y VM Rendón, edif Torre de la Merced, p 21, T04-2563580. **Colombia**, 9 de Octubre y Córdova, edif San Francisco, p 2, T04-2568753. **Denmark**, Gen Córdova 604 y Mendiburo, p 3, T04-2308020. **France**, José Mascote 909 y Hurtado, T04-2294334. **Germany**, Av Carlos Julio Arosemena Km 2, Ed Berlín, T04-2200500. **Italy**, Baquerizo Moreno 1120, T04-2312523. **Netherlands**, P Ycaza 454 y Baquerizo Moreno, edif ABN-AMRO Bank, T04-2563857. **Panama**, Aguirre 509, T04-2512158. **Peru**, Av Francisco de Orellana y Alberto Borges, Edificio Porta, 14th floor, Kennedy Norte, T04-2280135. **Spain**, Urdesa

calle Circunvalación, Solar 118 y Calle Unica, T04-2881691. **Sweden**, Km 6.5 vía a Daule, T04-2254111. **Switzerland**, 9 de Octubre 2105, T04-2453607. **UK**, Gen Córdova 623 y Padre Solano, T04-2560400. **USA**, 9 de Octubre 1571 y García Moreno, T04-2323570. **Venezuela**, Chile 329 y Aguirre, T04-2326566.

Doctors Dr Angel Serrano Sáenz, Boyacá 821 y Junín, T04-2301373. English- speaking. **Clínica Santa Marianita**, Boyacá 1915 entre Colón y Av Olmedo, T04-2322500. Some doctors speak English. **Dr James Peterson**, C Acacias 608 y Av Las Monjas, Urdesa, T04-2888718, T09-9770670 (mob). Homeopath and chiropractor, speaks English.

Hospitals **Clínica Kennedy**, Av San Jorge y la 9na, T04-2289666. The main hospital used by the foreign community. Also has a branch in Ciudadela La Alborada XII Mz-1227. (Dr Roberto Morla speaks German, T04-2293470). Very competent emergency department. **Clínica Alcívar**, Coronel 2301 y Azuay, T04-2580030. **Clínica Guayaquil**, Padre Aguirre 401 y General Córdova, T04-2563555 (Dr Roberto Gilbert speaks English and German).

Internet There are many cyber cafés in the centre and suburbs, mainly concentrated in shopping malls. Prices around US$1 per hr for internet, U$0.25 per min for Net to Phone.

Laundry **Sistematic**, F Segura y Av Quito, or C 6a y Las Lomas, Urdesa. **Martinizing**, Sucre 517 y Boyacá, and in CC La Gazota, for dry cleaning, many other outlets, but don't rely on their 1-hr service.

Post and courier Main post office, Pedro Carbo y Aguirre. **DHL**, Pichincha y Luque, T04-2287044. Recommended for international service **Servientrega**, offices throughout the city, for deliveries within Ecuador. **Shipping agents** Isaac Alvia, Elizalde 119 y Pichincha, Oficina 2-4, T04-2517215, isaacalviao@andinanet.net Speaks English, helpful. **Luis Arteaga**, Aguirre 324 y Chile, 3rd floor, T04-2533592, F2533445. Fast, variable prices but generally expensive.

Useful addresses Immigration, Av Río Daule, near the bus terminal, T04-2297010. For visa extensions.

Santa Elena and the beaches

Southwest of Guayaquil is the beach resort of Playas and, west of it, the Santa Elena Peninsula, with Salinas at its tip. The resorts of Salinas and Playas are very popular with Guayaquileños. Playas is the blue-collar beach and receives huge numbers of day visitors, yet retains something of its former fishing village atmosphere in the low season. Salinas is more highbrow, the place to be seen during 'la temporada'. Both resorts are reached along a paved toll highway from Guayaquil, and are busy and expensive during the high season (Christmas to Easter). ▶▶ *For Sleeping, Eating and other listings, see page 322-324.*

Playas → *Phone code 04 Colour map 4, grid C2 Population 25,000*

One branch of the highway from Guayaquil leads to General Villamil, normally known as Playas, the nearest seaside resort to Guayaquil. Look out for the bottle-shaped ceibo (*kapok*) trees between Guayaquil and Playas as the landscape becomes drier, turning into tropical thorn scrub. Fishing is important in Playas and a few single-sailed balsa rafts can still be seen among the motor launches returning laden with fish. These rafts are unique, highly ingenious and very simple. Without sails, they are used to spread nets close to the shore, then two gangs of men take two to three hours to haul them in.

As the closest resort to Guayaquil, Playas is popular with city dwellers and prone to severe crowding, especially during the high season, when there are frequent promotional beach parties. The beach shelves gently, is 200-400 m wide, lined with square canvas tents hired out for the day (US$3). It is very nice for bathing. There are cafés, showers, toilets and changing rooms along the beach, with fresh water, for a fee. Local authorities work at keeping the beach clean, but it is difficult when busy. Beware of thieves when it is crowded and don't walk along the beach at night, it is not safe. Out of season, when it is cloudier, or midweek the beaches are almost empty especially for anyone who walks north up the beach towards Punta Pelado (5 km). Playas is also a popular surfing resort with six good breaks. **Tourist information** ⓘ *Av Pedro Menéndez Gilbert y 10 de Agosto opposite the church, T04-2760758*, is helpful and friendly.

Excursions

An interesting walk, or short drive, is to the village of **El Morro**, east of Playas. It has a disproportionately large wooden church built in 1737, with an impressive façade (under 'permanent' repair), and nearby there is the mysterious rock formation of the **Virgen de la Roca**, where there are a small shrine and marble stations of the cross. There is regular pick-up service from the crossroads of Av Guayaquil y Av Paquisha.

Some 3 km further down the road is **Puerto del Morro**, up a scenic mangrove estuary in the Gulf of Guayaquil, where there are several working wooden trawlers and other traditional boats. It is possible to rent a canoe for three hours to visit the mangroves and probably see dolphins (about US$25). There's no accommodation, but a few basic eating places.

Following the coast southeast, a road goes to the quiet beaches of **Data de Villamil** and **Data de Posorja**, then crosses the peninsula east to **Posorja**, an important fishing port on the Gulf of Guayaquil. Guayaquil-Playas buses continue to Posorja.

Northwest up the coast is **Engabao**, a small settlement where you can find deserted beaches and wooden fishing boats along the coast. There's no food or lodging here, but there are some surf spots. A pick-up goes here from the crossroads, a 30-minute bumpy ride down sandy tracks. Along this road, 1 km from Playas, is the **Centro Ecológico de Playas**, where you can hire horses.

Santa Elena and around → *Phone code 04 Population 27,000*

West of El Progreso (Gómez Rendón), a good road runs to Santa Elena and then forks west for Salinas or north for the coastal road. About halfway between these towns is Zapotal, west of which is the turn-off for **Chanduy**, a tiny, picturesque port with accommodation at the restaurant on the east side of the bay. About 12 km along is the **Museo Real Alto** ① *T09-9772699 (mob), daily 1000-1700, US$1*, which has a well laid-out explanation of the peoples, archaeology and customs of the area.

In Santa Elena are a **tourist information office** ① *at the entrance to town, open daily 0800-1700*, **Hostal El Cisne** on the plaza, restaurant **Echeverría**, and **Bambú Arte** (on Rocafuerte y Félix Sarmiento, regional crafts). Near Santa Elena is the **Museo de los Amantes de Sumpa** ① *Wed-Sun 0900-1230, 1330-1700. US$1. From Santa Elena follow the road to Salinas, past the Shell gas station on your left, take the first street left, follow it for 2 blocks and turn left again to the museum*, which has a very interesting display on the Las Vegas culture, which lived in this area between 8,800 and 4,600 BC. A burial site with 200 skeletons was found in this spot, including an embracing couple, which is displayed in situ, hence the name of the site. These are the oldest remains to have been discovered in Ecuador. The interesting museum also includes information about other ancient cultures of the Península de Santa Elena and the history of this region. There is also a native dwelling where the old-timers' way of life is demonstrated.

Around Santa Elena

About 7 km before Santa Elena, a well signed turn-off leads 8 km to **Baños de San Vicente** ① *0600-1800, US$0.30, massages extra*, hot thermal baths which consist of a swimming pool and a big mudhole which claim to cure assorted ailments. It's best to go early or late to avoid the crowds.

To the west of Santa Elena the road passes a petroleum refinery and enters the busy port and regional market centre of **La Libertad**. It's not the most appealing of towns, and you'll be eager to jump on the first bus out. Thankfully, these are frequent, so there's no need to spend the night here.

Salinas → *Phone code 04 Population 30,000*

A few kilometres west of La Libertad, surrounded by miles of salt flats, is Salinas, Ecuador's answer to Miami Beach. Upscale hotels, high-rise holiday flats, restaurants, bars, and shops line the attractive *malecón*, while a few more modest establishments are to be found in the back streets. There is safe **swimming** in the bay, though the beach is narrow, with coarse sand and not too clean. More appealing is the (still urban) beach of Chipipe, south of the well-equipped and very exclusive Salinas Yacht Club. There are some decent **surf breaks** at the east end of the bay, by an old shipwreck and also by Mar Bravo and near the Chocolatera (see Excursions below). Whale-watching, birdwatching and fishing trips can be arranged here (see Tour operators page 323).

During *temporada* (December to April) it can be overcrowded, overpriced, noisy, with traffic jams, rubbish-strewn beaches and water shortages. At this time the highway from Guayaquil becomes one-way, depending on the time of day, and is said to resemble a Grand Prix racetrack, especially on Sunday. During the off season it is cheaper, quieter, but still not the best place for 'getting away from it all'.

Museo Salinas Siglo XXI ① *Malecón corner Guayas y Quil, Wed-Fri 0800-1200, 1500-1800, Sat-Sun 1000-1300, 1500-1900, US$2*, has well-displayed collections of naval history and regional archaeology. There is another interesting collection in Ballenita, see page 336. At the entrance to town there is a crafts cooperative. **Turismo Municipal** ① *Av Rafael Serrano, behind the Municipio, T/F04-2773931*, is friendly.

Beyond Chipipe, the western end of the peninsula is occupied by a navy base. Within it, at the westernmost point of Ecuador, is **La Chocolatera**, a blow hole in the rocky cliffs. Although erosion has diminished the once very impressive jet stream, it is still a magnificent spot with wild surf stirring the turquoise waters. Ask for permission to enter at the gate on the naval base, it is 2½ km from there.

On the southern shore of the Santa Elena peninsula, 8 km south of La Libertad, is **Punta Carnero**, built on headlands high above the sea. West of it stretches a magnificent 15-km beach with wild surf and heavy undertow (not suitable for swimming), which is virtually empty during the week. There are a couple of upmarket places to stay and, in July, August and September, great whale-watching from shore. Buses (US$0.50) and *taxirutas* (US$1), between La Libertad and Anconcito, take you to within walking distance of Punta Carnero.

Between Punta Carnero and **Mar Bravo**, just east of Salinas along the southern shore of the peninsula, are the **Ecuasal Ponds** (commercial salt pans), which offer the spectacle of thousands, at times tens of thousands, of shorebirds and water birds. More than 100 species have been identified here, sometimes there are even Chilean Flamingos, visiting from their breeding grounds near Piura, Peru. Birds can be seen from the road, but if you wish to get a closer look, you must go with Ben Haase, the naturalist guide who studies the birds (see Salinas tour operators, page 323). Independent visits are not permited by **Ecuasal,** the company which owns the 500-ha property.

A few kilometres to the east of Punta Carnero, along the coast, lies **Anconcito**, a scenic fishing port at the foot of steep cliffs. Pelicans and frigate birds gather round the colourful boats when the catch is brought in. There's nowhere in town to stay. Further on is **Ancón**, centre of the declining local oilfield, where a few houses built by the American oil company in the 1920s can still be seen.

⊙ Sleeping

Playas *p320*
A Bellavista, Km 2 on road to Data, T04-2760600. Restaurant, a/c, rooms or suites (some with fridge) in comfortable bungalows on the beach, Swiss-run, advance booking necessary.
B Arena Caliente, in town, one block from beach, T04-2761580. Restaurant, a/c, pool, modern, clean and comfortable.
B-D Dorado, on the Malecón, T04-2760402, doradoplayas@hotmail.com A/c, cheaper with fan, adequate, some rooms with sea view.
C-D Las Redes, 300 m on the road to Data, T04-2760222. A/c, cheaper with fan, some rooms with fridge, the more expensive rooms are nice, otherwise fair.
C-D Rey David, Malecón y Calle 9a, T04-2760024. A/c, cheaper with fan, centrally located, clean and functional.
D El Delfín, 1½ km south on the road to Data, T04-2760125. Restaurant, electric showers, fan, pool, parking, old-fashioned hacienda type building on the beach, big rooms, very friendly and good value.

D Playas, on the Malecón, T04-2760121. Restaurant, a/c, cheaper with fan, parking, older place but clean and good value.

Santa Elena and around *p321*
C Las Gaviotas, Av Solórzano y la Y, Vía a Salinas, La Libertad, T04-2784456, F2782841. Restaurant, a/c, cheaper with fan, adequate. There are also several other cheap and basic places in La Livertad.
E El Cisne, plaza in Santa Elena. Adequate.
E Florida, next to the baths in Baños de San Vicente. Basic but clean.

Salinas *p321*
There are almost 50 hotels in Salinas, of which we list only a few. Quality varies but price is determined more by the season than by the facilities provided. Good places are expensive year round and nothing is cheap during *temporada*. High-season prices are listed below, lower rates may be available at other times.
LL Barceló Colón Miramar, Malecón entre C 38 y C 40, T04-2771610, www.barcelo.com Includes 3 meals, slightly cheaper for room

only, restaurant, pool and spa, highrise by the sea, most luxurious in town.

AL Calypsso, Malecón near Capitanía de Puerto, T04-2772435, www.hotelcalypsso.com Restaurant, a/c, pool and gym, casino, crafts shop, full facilities.

AL Francisco II, Malecón y Las Palmeras, T04-2773471. A/c, pool, fridge, modern and comfortable.

A El Carruaje, Malecón 517, T/F04-2774282. Includes breakfast, good restaurant, a/c, fridge, comfortable rooms, some with ocean view, all facilities.

A Francisco I, Enríquez Gallo y Rumiñahui, T04-2774106. Restaurant, a/c, pool, comfortable and very nice.

B Cocos, on the Malecón, T04-2774349. A/c, comfortable rooms, nice terrace overlooking the bay, noisy restaurant/bar downstairs.

B Salinas, Enríquez Gallo y Estrella, T/F04-2772993. A/c, cheaper with fan, small rooms.

B Salinas Costa Azul, C 27 y Enríquez Gallo, T04-2774269, hotelsalinas@porta.net Includes breakfast, a/c, cheaper with fan, pool, plain but adequate.

B-C Suites Salinas, Gral Henríquez Gallo y 27, T04-2772759, hotelsalinas@porta.net Restaurant, a/c, cheaper with fan, pool, internet, fridge, parking, modern.

B-D Yulee, downhill from church, near the baech, T04-2772028. Restaurant, a/c, cheaper with fan and shared bath, older place but well maintained. Different types of rooms, the cheaper ones are simple and good value.

C-D La Olas, C 17 y Av Quinta, T04-2772526. A/c, cheaper with fan and shared bath, very clean and good value.

Around Salinas *p322*
AL Punta Carnero, Punta Carnero, T/F04-2948477, info@hotelpuntacarnero.com A/c, swimming pool (day use US$2), fridge, all rooms with lovely sea view.

A Hostería del Mar, Punta Carnero, T04-2948370, F2948480. Restaurant, pool, family suites to let on a weekly basis.

① Eating

Playas *p320*
There are many simple restaurants, some on the beach, most closed out of season. Fish and seafood are the specialities but keep an eye on cleanliness.

𝖸𝖸𝖸𝖸 **La Bella Italia**, Malecón y C 17, near Hotel El Carruaje. Good pizza and international food, recommended.

𝖸𝖸𝖸𝖸-𝖸𝖸𝖸 **Mar y Tierra**, Malecón y Valverde. Excellent seafood and some meat dishes.

𝖸𝖸𝖸 **Cozzoli's**, Malecón y Valverde. Pizzeria.

𝖸𝖸𝖸 **Pescao Mojao**, Malecón y José de la Cuadra. Meals, bar, pool table.

𝖸𝖸 **El Colonial**, Malecón y Guayas y Quil. Live music at weekends in season.

𝖸𝖸 **Nuevo Flipper**, Malecón y 24 de Mayo. Simple, clean and friendly.

𝖸𝖸-𝖸 **La Ostra Nostra**, Eloy Alfaro y Los Almendros. Good set meals.

𝖸𝖸-𝖸 **Menú de Yiyín**, Eloy Alfaro y Los Almendros. Good set meals.

𝖸𝖸-𝖸 **Selva del Mar**, Enríquez Gallo y 24 de Mayo. Good *pescado con menestra*. A couple of blocks inland from the Malecón are some complexes with food stalls serving good *ceviches* and freshly cooked seafood, a *ceviche* costs US$4-5; **Cevichelandia** is on María González y Las Palmeras; **La Lojanita**, Enríquez Gallo y Leonardo Avilés, is popular and recommended; others are around the **Libertad Peninsular** bus station, María González y León Avilés.

① Bars and clubs

Salinas *p321*
Oyster-catcher, Enríquez Gallo entre C 47 and C 50. Friendly place, safe oysters. Enquire here here about birdwatching tours with local expert Ben Haase.

▲ Activities and tours

Salinas *p321*
Tour operators
Whale-watching tours (Jun-Sep, see p340), birdwatching and deep-sea fishing are offered by the following agencies.
Calypsso, at the hotel, T04-2772435. Whale-watching tours with specialist guides, US$25 per person. Fernando Félix, a recommended guide, is a marine biologist who has studied whales in the area for many years, he is fluent in English.
Centro Informativo Natural Peninsular, T04-2778329, bhaase@ecua.net.ec Naturalist guide Ben Haase runs birdwatching tours at the Ecuasal ponds

(see Around Salinas below), US$20 per group of up to 10 people. He is very knowledgeable about birds and also whales. You can ask for Ben at the Oyster-catcher bar (see above). **Pesca Tour**, Malecón 577 y 24 de Mayo, T04-2772391, www.pescatours.com.ec Regional tours, fishing trips (US$350 per day for up to 6 passengers), sailboat and water-skis rental.

⊖ Transport

For main inter-city routes see the bus timetable p52.

Playas *p320*
Transportes Posorja and Transportes Villamil leave from stations along Av Menéndez Gílbert, a couple of blocks back from the beach. To Guayaquil, frequent, 2 hrs, US$2; taxi costs US$25.

Santa Elena and around *p320*
La Libertad
Note Muggings are frequent, take a taxi between bus terminals. If travelling between Guayaquil and Montañita or other points north along the coast, then you can avoid La Libertad altogether by changing buses at the crossroads in Santa Elena, but you may not get a seat.

Buses to **Guayaquil**, with Coop Libertad Peninsular (CLP), on 9 de Octubre y C 19, and CICA across the street, every 15 mins

(the 2 companies alternate departures), US$3, 2½ hrs. Get off at Progreso for **Playas**, 1 hr, US$1.15.

Buses leave every 30 mins until 1715 to **Manglaralto**, US$2; **Puerto López**, US$4, 2½ hr; **Jipijapa**, US$4; and **Manta**, US$5, from the terminal on Dagoberto Montenegro y C 10, 1 km from town. To **Quito**, with Trans Esmeraldas (opposite Coop Libertad Peninsular), 2 nightly, US$10, 9½ hrs.

Salinas *p321*
City buses (US$0.20), minivans (US$0.20) and shared taxis (*taxirutas*, US$0.40) run 1 and 2 streets back from the Malecón and continue to **La Libertad**. For **Montañita**, **Puerto López** and points north, transfer at La Libertad or Santa Elena (see above and p321). To **Guayaquil**, Coop Libertad Peninsular, María González y León Avilés, every 10 mins, US$3, 2½ hrs. For **Playas** transfer in El Progreso.

⊕ Directory

Playas *p320*
Banks Banco de Guayaquil.
Internet Several places, US$2/hr.

Salinas *p321*
Banks Banco de Guayaquil, Malecón y 24 de Mayo. Banco del Pichincha, Malecón y Armando Barreto. **Internet** Several places, US$2/hr.

South to Peru

For most visitors, the area leading south to Peru is of interest principally as a transport route. The sweltering city of Machala has little to recommend it and nearby beaches are dirty and overpriced. Huaquillas is a hot and frantic border town. The exceptions to the rule are the Uplands of El Oro, a tranquil backwater with friendly people, a fresh climate and lovely scenery. This pleasant hill country features forests and waterfalls, as well as the charming colonial town of Zaruma with the largest wooden church in Ecuador. ➤➤ *For Sleeping, Eating and other listings, see pages 322-324.*

Ins and outs

From Durán, across the river from Guayaquil, an excellent four-lane road heads south to Puerto Inca, Naranjal and on to Machala, centre of Ecuador's most important banana-producing region, and a useful stopover if heading on to Huaquillas at the Peruvian frontier. At Puerto Inca, one road goes inland to La Troncal, then climbs to Zhud and the Panamericana near El Tambo, a good route to Ingapirca and on to Cuenca. Just south of Puerto Inca another road goes southeast and climbs to

Molleturo, goes through Parque Nacional Cajas and on to Cuenca. This is the fastest route between Guayaquil and Cuenca. From Machala, roads also run through Pasaje and Girón to Cuenca (188 km), and via Arenillas to Loja (216 km). **Warning** The Guayaquil-Machala road has been among the worst in the country for bus hold-ups, never travel this route at night.

Machala and around → *Phone code 07 Colour map 6, grid B2 Population 210,000*

The capital of the province of El Oro, this booming agricultural city is the centre of the surrounding banana and shrimp producing region. There is an annual international banana fair in September. The city is not particularly clean, safe or attractive, but it is a logical stopping point along the coastal route to Peru. Machala has more and better facilities than Huaquillas, at the border.

The main square, Parque Juan Montalvo, is spacious and has a nice church. There aren't many sights in Machala and the nearest beaches, at Jambelí, are dirty. Puerto Bolívar, the banana export port, can be visited as can mangrove islands in the Archipiélago de Jambelí. Much more interesting, however, are the beautiful uplands of El Oro as well as Puyango petrified forest. For details see below.

Information and safety
Dirección Municipal de Turismo ① *9 de Mayo y 9 de Octubre, at the Municipio, 2nd floor, T07-2920400, Mon-Fri 0800-1230, 1500-1800*. **Note** Machala has serious public safety problems, mind your valuables and avoid deserted areas. Do not leave your hotel late at night.

Puerto Bolívar
Built on the Canal de Santa Rosa among mangroves, and 9 km west of Machala, this is Ecuador's main banana exporting port. There is a pleasant waterfront and from the old pier a motorized canoe service crosses to the beaches of **Jambelí** on the far side of the mangrove islands which shelter Puerto Bolívar from the Pacific. Three daily canoes make the return trip to Jambelí, US$2 per person. The beaches of Jambelí are safe and long with straw beach umbrellas for shade (the sun is fierce), but unfortunately dirty and the accommodation here is poor.

The **Archipiélago de Jambelí** is a maze of islands and channels just offshore, stretching south between Puerto Bolívar and the Peruvian border. These mangrove islands are rich in birdlife (and insects for them to feed on, take repellent), the water is very clear and you may also see fish and reefs. Boats can be rented for excursions

Guayaquil & Southern Pacific South to Peru

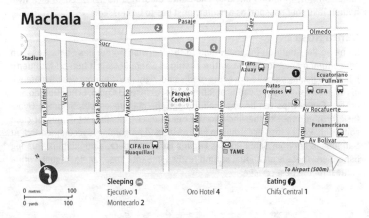

Machala

| 0 metres | 100 |
| 0 yards | 100 |

Sleeping 🛏
Ejecutivo 1
Montecarlo 2
Oro Hotel 4

Eating 🍴
Chifa Central 1

To Airport (500m)

⁞ Boom and bust agriculture

In the late 18th century the Guayas basin, with its fertile soils, hot climate, abundant rainfall and easy river transport, became the most important area in the world for the production and export of cacao, a plant native to the Americas. At the time of independence this was the new Republic's only major export. Half a century later, when chocolate ceased to be an expensive luxury and world consumption multiplied eightfold, cocoa plantations expanded rapidly around the Río Guayas estuary, replacing the tropical forests of the area.

Grown on large plantations, cocoa made fortunes for a new coastal élite, who backed the Radical Liberal Party which seized power in 1895. By 1900 over 60% of government income came from taxes on cocoa exports. Great development schemes were begun, building roads, ports and railway lines, the most important of which, between Guayaquil and Quito, was completed in 1908. After the First World War, however, competition from Africa lowered the world cocoa price while witch broom disease swept through Ecuadorean plantations. Large areas of land were abandoned, most of the grand building projects were left incomplete and the Guayaquil élite was driven from power by a group of young army officers in the 1925 Revolution.

Today, cacao continues to be produced and exported on a more modest scale. The Ecuadorean variety is prized for its aroma and a small amount is a necessary ingredient in the world's finest chocolates. Meanwhile, the boom and bust cycle of Ecuadorean export agriculture continues. Vast banana plantations occupy much of the land where cacao was once grown. They have drawn international criticism for the use of child labour and they dump about one million pesticide-impregnated plastic bags every week, into rivers and open pits. Shrimp was the great miracle crop of the 1980s and 90s, until pollution from the banana plantations and *mancha blanca* (white spot disease) wiped out many producers.

At the start of the 21st century, the industrial flower plantations around Cayambe in the northern highlands seem destined for endless growth, until... (see if you can guess what happens next...)

here, to explore the narrow channels near Puerto Bolívar and go to Isla del Amor, a few minutes away, or further afield to **Isla Santa Clara** (1½ hours) or Costa Rica (two hours). Take your passport as a military post has to be crossed.

Santa Rosa

Some 30 km south on the main road to the Peruvian border lies Santa Rosa, an agricultural market town. Just by the airstrip at Santa Rosa is a turn-off for **Puerto Jelí**, a tiny fishing village 4 km at the road's end, right in the mangroves on a branch of the main *estero*. Good eating at **Riberas del Pacífico, El Chino, El Pez Dorado** and others. **Canoe trips** can be arranged through the mangroves with Segundo Oyola (ask for him opposite the dock) to the beach of Las Casitas, for fishing or clam collecting. Price varies according to group size and bargaining is recommended. At **San José**, 8 km from Santa Rosa is **Laguna La Tembladera**, a popular lake among fishermen. There is an annual shrimp festival in Santa Rosa, 24-30 August, with a contest for the best *ceviche*.

Uplands of El Oro

Inland from Machala is a tranquil corner of Ecuador overlooked by most travellers. This is a great area in which to get off the beaten path. A transition zone between the great coastal plain and the Andes, it has forests (live and petrified), waterfalls, charming colonial cities, gold mines that give the province its name, good walking, friendly people and a very pleasant climate.

A number of scenic roads cross this green hilly country connecting the lowlands and highlands. From Machala to Loja, the most direct road starts near Santa Rosa and goes through Balsas. A second road branches off the Balsas road, goes through Piñas and Zaruma from where an unpaved road rejoins the Balsas route higher up in the highlands. Zaruma can also be reached through a secondary unpaved road from Pasaje, on the Machala-Cuenca road. A more southerly route starts by **Arenillas**, between Santa Rosa and Huaquillas, goes near the **Bosque Petrificado Puyango** (see below), then climbs to Alamor and Celica (see page 293), from where you can go to Catacocha and Loja or to the Peruvian border at Macará.

Balsas and around → *Phone code 07 Colour map 6, grid B2 Population 3,100 Altitude 700 m*

The main Machala-Loja road starts 33 km south of Machala, just south of Santa Rosa, on the road to Huaquillas. The winding road follows the Río Santa Rosa southeast, passing several river beaches and a couple of villages. At **Saracay** (also known as Zapote), 22 km from the turn-off, a paved road branches east to Piñas (29 km) and Zaruma (48 km). The main road continues to climb 13 km to **Balsas**. Just west of town is a lookout with lovely views.

Balsas is at the centre of a coffee, cattle and poultry producing area. It is a pleasant town, with a colourful tiled church, nestling amid green hills. A secondary road goes southwest from Balsas to **Marcabelí**. Nearby is the La Chorrera river bathing beach. A very poor road continues from Marcabelí to the Arenillas-Puyango road.

After Balsas the road crosses into the province of Loja and climbs steeply to **Chaguarpamba, Olmedo** (two *residenciales* and some *comedores*) and **Velacruz** (78 km from Balsas) where a road goes southwest to Catacocha and Macará (see page 293). About 16 km ahead is another turn-off, a dirt road going northwest to Portovelo and Zaruma. From here the road continues 23 km to Catamayo and 34 km from there to Loja.

Zaruma → *Phone code 07 Colour map 6, grid B2 Population 8,700 Altitude 1,170 m*

Some 100 km southeast from Machala is the lovely colonial town of Zaruma, perched on a hilltop at the heart of a pre-Hispanic gold-mining area. It is reached from Machala by paved road via Piñas, by a scenic dirt road off the main Loja-Machala road, or via Pasaje and Paccha on another scenic, dirt road off the Machala-Cuenca road.

Founded in 1549 on the orders of Felipe II to try to control the gold extraction, Zaruma is characterized by steep, twisting streets and painted wooden buildings. The beautiful main plaza is marred by the cement municipality, facing one of Ecuador's loveliest wooden churches. A preservation order now protects the town centre from similar acts of architectural vandalism. Many of the noticeably white-skinned inhabitants of direct Spanish stock still work as independent gold miners; there are a few industrial companies too. On the outskirts of town you can see large *chancadoras*, primitive rock-crushing operations, where independent miners take their gold-bearing rocks to be crushed then passed through sluices to wash off the mud. It is possible to visit some of the small roadside mining operations and watch the whole process. **Mina del Sexmo**, one of the oldest mines in the area (exploited by the Spanish since 1539 and the natives before that), is an easy walk from the centre (access at the end of Calle El Sexmo). At the entrance to town is **Compañía Bira**, a more technified mine, which can also be seen. Other mines are in Portovelo (see below).

Agricultural production in this area includes coffee (some of the best in the country), citrus and cattle ranching. **El Cafetal** shop in Zaruma roasts its own for sale and sends weekly shipments to Quito.

The **Museo Municipal** ① *2nd floor of the Municipio, at the main square, Wed-Sat 0800-1200, 1400-1800, Sun 0800-1200, free*, has a small collection of local historical artefacts. There is another museum at Colegio Nacional 26 de Noviembre. The Zaruma area has a number of pre-Hispanic archaeological sites and petroglyphs are also found in this area.

On top of the small hill beyond the market (follow Calle Pichincha) is a public swimming pool, from where there are amazing views over the nearby valleys. For even grander views, walk up **Cerro del Calvario** (follow Calle San Francisco); go early in the morning as it gets very hot.

A worthwhile excursion is to **Orquideario Gálvez** ① *on the road north to Malvas, 4 km from Zaruma, T07-2964063*. They have a collection of orchids and also a tree house to rent (see Sleeping, page 330). It's a pleasant relaxing place, with friendly people. Northeast of Zaruma is **Salvias**, one of the access points to Cerro de Arcos, along the 'Gold Rush Trail' from Oña, see page 285.

Piñas and around → *Phone code 07 Colour map 6, grid B2 Population 12,600*

About 19 km west of Zaruma, along the road to Machala is Piñas, a pleasant town which conserves just a few of its colonial-era wooden buildings. There are buses along scenic secondary roads to **Paccha**, up in the hills to the north, and to **Ayapamba** and many other old gold mining villages. Northwest of Piñas, 20 minutes along the road to Saracay and Machala, is **Buenaventura**, to the north of which lies an important area for bird conservation. Many rare birds have been found in the few remaining tracts of forest, with over 310 bird species recorded in the area. **The Jocotoco Foundation** ① *www.jocotoco.com*, protects a 300-ha forest in this region. The Piñas area is also rich in orchids. Along the road to Portovelo are several *complejos turísticos* with river beaches. **Museo Rubén Torres** ① *8 de Noviembre 25-82, Piñas*, has a private collection of archaeological and historical artefacts. The owner, a school teacher, is also knowledgeable about orchids. Local tour operator **Contac-tour** ① *García Moreno entre Loja y Rumiñahui, Piñas*, know the region well and are very helpful.

Portovelo → *Phone code 07 Colour map 6, grid B2 Population 6,600*

South of Zaruma and in the lower valley of the Río Amarillo, Portovelo is the site of the largest gold mine in the area. It was exploited by French and British companies in the early 1800s, followed by American companies until 1949. The huge gold mine took many hundreds of tonnes of gold out of the country but allegedly never paid any taxes.

Portovelo was deemed too hot and unhealthy so the miners' families were moved to the top of the neighbouring hill and the beautiful wooden town of Zaruma. There are numerous tiny chapels scattered across the surrounding hills and, in the times when the mines were functioning, it was fashionable to take a trip by horse and carriage to these outlying chapels for the Sunday services. In recent years, the mine was being exploited by 'Río Amarillo', once again a large company. Enquire locally about visits.

The **Museo Magner Turner** ① *at the old Campamento Americano, in the hills above town, T07-2949345, daily 0900-1100, 1400-1700, US$1*, run by the grandson of one of the early US geologists, is set inside a mine shaft. It has an interesting, eclectic collection of minerals, historical documents and paraphernalia.

There are hot thermal springs at **Aguas Calientes**, 6 km from Portovelo, but no facilities. From Portovelo, the very scenic road to Loja follows the Río Amarillo, then climbs steeply to join the Balsas road on the ridge top west of San Pedro de la Bendita and Catamayo. A nice walk is 5 km on this road to Río Pindo or Río Luís.

ⓘ *US$5 includes tour, camping US$5 per person. For further information, contact the Dirección Provincial de Turismo, Machala T07-2932106. For transport, see page 332.*

The 2,659-ha Bosque Petrificado Puyango is 110 km south of Machala, west off the Arenillas-Alamor road; the turn-off is at the bridge over the Río Puyango, where there is a military control. A great number of petrified trees, ferns, fruits and molluscs, 65 to 120 million years old, have been found here. A deciduous dry tropical forest at elevations between 270 m and 750 m covers the area. Over 120 species of birds can be seen here, including several endemics. There are good Spanish-speaking guides who do an interesting tour of a small segment of the reserve. The village of Puyango is 5 km from the Arenillas road; the reserve's information centre and a small museum with interesting fossils is 250 m past the village; the *mirador*, a gazebo at the entrance to the trails, is 1 km beyond. There is no accommodation in the village, camping is permited by the *mirador*, where there are toilets and water; you can also ask around for floor space in town or at the information centre. There is one basic residencial in **Las Lajas**, 30 minutes towards Arenillas, and several options in Alamor.

❢ This petrified forest is supposedly the most extensive outside Arizona.

Huaquillas → *Phone code 07   Colour map 6, grid B1   Population 40,000*

The border town of Huaquillas was for many decades the only major land crossing to Peru, but Macará (see page 294) is currently a better choice for most travellers unless you are headed to the beaches around Máncora. Huaquillas has grown into a small bustling commercial city; it can be harrowing, made worse by the crowds and heat. You must always watch your gear carefully. In addition to cheating by money changers and cab drivers (see below), this border is known for its minor shakedowns of travellers. These are annoying but seldom serious. Those seeking a more relaxed crossing to or from Peru should consider other more out-of-the-way border posts (see page 292).

Frontier with Peru

The border runs along the Río Zarumilla and is crossed by the international bridge at the western end of Avenida La República. It is a shortish walk from the bus terminals which are just off the main street. Tricycle taxis are available to help with luggage. Keep an eye on your belongings at all times and deal only with border officials or transport drivers.

❢ It is not uncommon to be asked for a small bribe by one of the many officials here.

Ecuadorean immigration Passports are stamped 3 km north of Huaquillas along the road to Machala. There is no urban transport; take an inter-city bus or taxi, US$1. Immigration is open 24 hours. Allow an hour to complete formalities. To cross to Peru, walk along the main street in Huaquillas and across the international bridge to Aguas Verdes; police may check passports.

Peruvian immigration Passports are stamped at the main Peruvian immigration and customs complex outside Zarumilla, about 3 km past the international bridge. It is open 24 hours.

Exchange There are a couple of banks along the main street of Huaquillas but these generally do not change *soles* nor TCs. Many street changers, recognized by their black briefcases, deal in *soles* and US$ cash. Check the rate beforehand on the internet or with travellers leaving Peru, as there are many tricks and travellers are often cheated. Do not change more US$ than you need to get to Tumbes, where there are reliable *cambios*, but get rid of all your *soles* here as they are difficult to exchange further inside Ecuador. Ask around for the best rate before changing and do your own arithmetic (there have been reports of 'doctored' calculators), count your change carefully and watch out for counterfeit bills. Especially avoid those changers who chase after you.

Aguas Verdes is the Peruvian border town, a small place with basic facilities. There are various forms of transport between it and **Tumbes**, the first city 27 km into Peru. Some *colectivos* (shared taxis) leave from right near the international bridge; they charge higher prices, especially for foreigners, so beware of rip-offs. Others leave from further along the main street into Aguas Verdes. All *colectivos* should stop and wait at the immigration complex in Zarumilla but they are not always willing to do so, ask in advance. There are also *combis* (vans) to Tumbes and *mototaxis* to Zarumilla. Tumbes has a decent range of hotels, places to eat, and good transport links including flights south down the coast as far as Lima. Details are given in *Footprint Peru* and the *South American Handbook*. Coming from Peru into Ecuador, take a bus to Tumbes and a *colectivo* from there to immigration at Zarumilla and on to the border at Aguas Verdes.

● Sleeping

Machala *p325, map p325*
LL Oro Verde, Circunvalación Norte in Urbanización Unioro, T07-2933140, www.oroverdehotels.com Includes buffet breakfast, 2 restaurants, nice pool (US$6 for non-residents), beautiful gardens, tennis courts, casino, full luxury. Best in town.
B Centro Hotel, Sucre y Guayas, T07-2931640, F2935110. Includes breakfast, a/c, parking, cafeteria, modern and comfortable.
B Oro Hotel, Sucre y Juan Montalvo, T07-2930032, orohotel@oro.satnet.net Includes breakfast, pricey restaurant and cheaper café downstairs, a/c, fridge, parking, refurbished and good, helpful, rooms to street are noisy. Recommended.
C Ejecutivo, Sucre y 9 de Mayo, T07-2923162, F2933992. Cafeteria, a/c, parking, modern and good.
C Montecarlo, Guayas y Olmedo, T07-2931901, F2933104. Restaurant, a/c, parking, modern.
D Araujo, 9 de Mayo y Boyacá, T07-2931464. A/c, cheaper with fan, parking, some rooms are small, good value but disco next door.
D Julio César, 9 de Mayo 1319 entre Pasaje y Boyacá, T07-2937978, F2923485. Cold water, a/c, cheaper with fan, adequate and friendly.
D San Miguel, 9 de Mayo y Sucre, by market, T07-2935488. Cheaper with cold water, a/c, cheaper with fan, fridge, good value.
E Pesántez, 9 de Mayo y Pasaje, T07-2920154. Private bath, cold water, fan, basic but clean.

Puerto Bolívar *p325*
B-C Solar del Puerto, Córdova y Rocafuerte, T07-2928793, solarpto@ecua.net.ec Restaurant, a/c or fan, best in town.

C-D Acosta, Municipalidad y Córdova, T07-2928443. A/c, cheaper with fan, adequate, but noisy disco next door.

Santa Rosa *p326*
D Santa Rosa, 1 block from plaza. A/c, good.

Balsas and around *p327*
D Casa Grande, on the right, 100 m past the traffic light. Includes breakfast, restaurant, pool, nice views, disco on weekends.
E Café, on the highway. Private bath with cold water.
E Express, on the highway. Private bath, cold water, clean and friendly.
E-F Residencial Alexander, at the park in Marcabelí, T07-2956251. Cheaper with shared bath, basic.

Zaruma *p327*
C Roland, at entrance to town on road from Portovelo, T07-2972800. Comfortable rooms and a nice cabin, lovely views.
D Cerro de Oro, Sucre 40, T/F07-2972505. Modern and nice.
D Colombia, on main plaza next to municipio, T07-2972173. Very basic.
D Finca Gálvez, Santa Marianita, vía a Paccha km 3, (enquire at Bazar María Alejandra, Sucre 005), T07-2964063. Includes breakfast, meals on request, nice tree house on a coffee plantation, orchid garden, family run, quiet and friendly, a lovely out-of-the-way spot. Recommended.

Piñas *p328*
D Las Orquídeas, Abdón Calderón y Montalvo, T07-2976355. Shower, adequate.

D-E **Dumari**, 8 de Noviembre y Loja,
T07-2976118. Cheaper with shared bath.
E **Residencial Reina del Cisne**, in Paccha.
Clean and pleasant.

Portovelo *p328*
E **Residencial Mónica**, near the Iglesia de
Fátima, Barrio Machala. Basic.

Huaquillas *p329, map p331*
D **Hernancor**, Primero de Mayo y Hualtaco.
Cafeteria, a/c, best in town.
D **Vanessa**, 1 de Mayo y Hualtaco. A/c,
fridge, parking, adequate.
E **San Martín**, Av la República opposite the
church. Private bath, fan, mosquito net.
There are several other basic hotels in town.

🍴 Eating

Machala *p325, map p325*
The best food is found in upmarket hotels.
🍴 **200 Millas**, 9 de Octubre entre Santa Rosa
y Vela. Seafood specialities.
🍴 **Aquí es Correita**, Av Arízaga y 9 de Mayo,
closed Sun. Popular, clean and good.
🍴 **Cafetería San Francisco**, Sucre block 6.
Good filling breakfast.
🍴 **Chifa Central**, Tarqui y 9 de Octubre.
Good Chinese.
🍴 **Chifa Gran Oriental**, 9 de Octubre entre
Guayas y Ayacucho. Good food and service,
clean place. Recommended.
🍴 **Copa Cabana**, On the main plaza. Good
clean snack bar.
🍴 **Mesón Hispano**, Av Las Palmeras y Sucre.
Very good grill, attentive service.
🍴 **Palacio Real**, 9 de Octubre y Ayacucho.
Good set meals.

Puerto Bolívar *p325*
Lots of seafood kiosks between the piers.
Food is better and cheaper than in Machala.
🍴 **Acuario**, Rocafuerte 120, half block from
the Malecón. English spoken, good source of
information. Recommended.

Balsas *p327*
🍴 **Don Pepe**, 2 km east of town. Good set
meals. Several others along the highway.

Zaruma *p327*
Zaruma specialities often include plantain.
Try *tigrillo*, ground plantain fried with eggs,
cheese and onions.
🍴 **Barcelona**, Bolívar by the steps to the
church. Varied à la carte and set lunches.
🍴 **Cafetería Uno**, C Sucre. Very good Zaruma
specialities.
🍴 **Chamizal**, Bolívar y San Francisco, also on
C Sucre. Variety of à la carte dishes, some
Chinese, also set meals.
🍴 **Mesón de Joselito**, At the entrance to
town from Portovelo. Good for seafood.
🍴 **Sabor Tropical**, C Colón. Encebollados
(fish with onions and yuca).
🍴 **Veros**, Colón y Pichincha. Local dishes, set
meals, breakfast.

Piñas *p328*
🍴 **Punto del Sabor**, Sucre y Montalvo, by the
main park. Good choice of set meals. There
are also several restaurants along C Angel
Salvador Ochoa.

Huaquillas *p329, map p331*
🍴 **Flamingo**, Tnte Córdovez y 10 de Agosto.
Simple set meals. Several other basic
comedores in town.

Huaquillas

PERU

International
Bridge

Río Zarumilla

Arenillas
Portovelo
Av Tnte Córdovez
Azuay
Panamericana
Transportes
Occidental
R Gómez
Customs
Av La República
Ecuatoriano
Portovelo
19 de Octubre
Machala
Santa Rosa
Costa Rica
CIFA
Municipalidad
10 de Agosto
1 de Mayo
Av Hualtaco
To Immigration (3 km)
& Machala

N

Not to scale

Sleeping
Hernancor **3**   San Martín **6**
Vanessa **7**

⊙ Entertainment

Machala *p325, map325*
Cinema Unioro, Ubanización Unioro, near the Hotel Oro Verde, has a/c, cushioned seats and good sound.

⊙ Transport

For main inter-city routes see the bus timetable p52.

Machala *p325, map p325*
Air The airport is at the south end of the city, less than 1 km from the centre of town. TAME, Juan Montalvo y Bolívar, T07-2930139, 0830-1800, flies to **Guayaquil** on Mon, Wed, Fri, US$34; connecting to **Quito**, US$80.

Bus Most of the bus company offices are quite central, but there is no **Terminal Terrestre**. Do not take night buses into or out of Machala as they are prone to hold-ups. There are 3 different routes from Machala to **Loja**, with bus service along all of them; ask for the one you need. They are, from north to south: via **Piñas** and **Zaruma**, partly unpaved and rough but very scenic; via **Balsas**, fully paved and also scenic; and via **Arenillas** and **Alamor**, for **Puyango** petrified forest.

To **Piura (Peru)**, CIFA at 1040, 1420, 2200 and 0000, 7 hrs, US$6; also with Transportes Loja, 1230 daily.

Zaruma *p327*
Bus companies are along Av Honorato Márquez, some local service goes from C Pichincha near Banco del Pichincha. To **Machala**, with TAC or Trans Piñas, hourly, US$3, 3 hrs. To **Piñas**, take a Machala bound bus, US$1, 1 hr. To **Guayaquil**, with TAC, 5 daily, US$6, 6 hrs. To **Quito**, with TAC, 4 daily, US$10, 12 hrs. To **Loja**, with TAC or Trans Piñas, 7 daily, may have to change at Portovelo, US$5, 5 hrs. To **Cuenca**, with TAC at 0030, Trans Piñas at 0315 and Azuay at 0730, US$6, 6 hrs. *Rancheras* to **Portovelo**, with 24 de Julio, every 30 min 0600-1830, US$0.50, 20 mins.

Portovelo *p328*
Rancheras to **Zaruma**, every 30 min 0600-1830, US$0.50, 20 mins. Frequent buses to **Piñas** and **Machala**, several daily departures to **Loja**.

Bosque Petrificado Puyango *p329*
There are hourly *rancheras* between Arenillas and Alamor. Buses from **Machala**, with Transportes Loja at 0930, 1315 and 2130, US$3, 2½ hrs. From **Loja**, with Transportes Loja at 0900, 1430 and 1930, US$5, 5 hrs. From **Huaquillas**, with Transportes Loja at 0730, US$2, 1½ hrs. Returning to **Machala**, buses pass the bridge about 1100, 1330 and 1700, their final destination may not be Machala, so ask. To **Huaquillas**, about 1000. There are several military checkpoints between Puyango and Machala, have your passport at hand.

Huaquillas *p329, map p331*
There is no **Terminal Terrestre**, each bus company has its own station. If in a hurry to reach Quito or other highland destinations, it can be faster to change buses in Machala or Guayaquil rather than waiting for the next departure from Huaquillas. There are checkpoints along the road north from Huaquillas to Machala, so keep your passport to hand. To **Machala**, with CIFA (Santa Rosa y Machala) and **Ecuatoriano Pullman** (Av la República y 19 de Octubre), direct, 1 hr, US$2, every hr from 0400-2000; via Arenillas and Santa Rosa, 2 hrs, every 10 mins. To **Guayaquil**, frequent service with CIFA and Ecuatoriano Pullman, 5 hrs, US$5. To **Quito**, with Occidental (Remigio Gómez 129 y Portovelo), 12 hrs, US$10; with Panamericana (on Remigio Gómez), slightly fancier service, US$12. To **Cuenca**, with Trans Azuay or Sucre (Cordovez y 10 de Agosto), 5 hrs, US$5. To **Loja**, with Transportes Loja (Tnte Córdovez y Arenillas), 6 hrs, US$5. Direct to **Piura (Peru)**, with CIFA or Transportes Loja, 5 hrs, US$5.

⊙ Directory

Machala *p325, map p325*
Banks Banco del Austro, Rocafuerte y Guayas. Banco de Guayaquil, Rocafuerte y Guayas. Banco de Machala, Rocafuerte y 9 de Mayo. **Consulates** Peru, Urb Unioro, Mz 14, V 11, near *Hotel Oro Verde*, T07-2930680, Mon-Fri 0900-1800. **Internet** Many places, US$1/hr. **Post office** Bolívar y Montalvo.

Zaruma *p327*
Banks Banco del Pichincha, Pichincha y Luis Crespo. Banco de Machala, at the main square. **Internet** US$2/hr.

⁞ Footprint features

Introduction

The coastal region covers a third of Ecuador's total area. Though popular with Quiteños and Guayaquileños, who come here in their droves for weekends and holidays, the Northern Pacific lowlands receive relatively few foreign visitors, which is surprising given the natural beauty, diversity and rich cultural heritage of the coast. You can surf, watch whales at play, visit ancient archaeological sites, or just relax and enjoy the best food that this country has to offer. The jewel in the coastal crown, Parque Nacional Machalilla, protects an important area of primary tropical dry forest, pre-Columbian ruins, coral reef and a wide variety of wildlife. Further north, in the province of Esmeraldas, there are not only well-known party beaches, but also opportunities to visit the remaining mangroves and experience two unique lifestyles: Afro-Ecuadorean on the coast and native Cayapa further inland.

Even if your time is limited, the coast is easily accessible from Quito, making it the ideal short break from the Andean chill. The water is warm for bathing and the beaches, many of them deserted, are generally attractive.

★ Don't miss...

1 **Whale watching** Observe migrating humpback whales from Puerto López or other coastal towns, page 340.
2 **Parque Nacional Machalilla** Spot birds and marine wildlife on the mainland and on Isla de La Plata, page 340.
3 **Bahía de Caráquez** Support the town's environmentally friendly reputation by taking an eco-tour, page 350.
4 **Canoa** Be a beach bum or make the most of activities, such as surfing, horse riding and cycling, page 353.
5 **Getting back to the roots** Visit endangered mangroves and experience Afro-Ecuador to the north of Esmeraldas, page 363.

Ruta del Sol: Santa Elena to Manta → www.rutadelsol.com.ec

North of the Santa Elena Peninsula (see page 320), the coastal road stretches for 737 km to Mataje on the Colombian border; along the way are countless beaches and fishing villages, and a few cities. The coastal strip is known as the 'Ruta del Sol' about as far north as Manta. Along it are several archaeological sites and museums, scenic beaches like Ballenita and Olón, the popular surfing beach of Montañita, the forested hills of the Cordillera Chongón-Colonche, not to mention Puerto López, the perfect base from which to explore the beautiful Parque Nacional Machalilla. Seaside resorts are busy and more expensive during the temporada de playa, *December to April.* ➤➤ *For Sleeping, Eating and other listings, see pages 342-347.*

Ins and outs

The coastal road is fully paved and well supplied with buses. Access to the region is either from Guayaquil in the south or Manta in the north. There are also direct buses from Quito to Puerto López.

North from Santa Elena → *Phone code 04*

The coastal road north from Santa Elena parallels the coastline, provides access to some beautiful beaches, and crosses the Chongón-Colonche coastal range. Note that not all beaches are suitable for bathing: the surf and undertow can be strong in some places. Between June and September whales may be seen in this area.

The northern fork of the road at Santa Elena leads past **Ballenita**, which has a pleasant beach. At Lomas de Ballenita is **Hostería Farallón Dillon** (see page 374), run by Douglas Dillon who is knowledgeable about the area. On the premises is **Galería Náutica**, an interesting, eclectic collection of nautical objects from many countries; antiques are restored and sold.

North of Ballenita are a couple of luxury private beach-side developments, with exclusive yacht clubs at **Punta Centinela** and **Punta Blanca**. The road then hugs the coast, passing **Monteverde**, and then **Palmar**, with popular beaches and beach cafés, but no accommodation.

Continuing north is **Ayangue**, in a beautiful horseshoe bay, 2.7 km from the main highway. There is snorkelling and diving by **Islote El Pelado** and **Islote El Viejo**, two small islands offshore. It is a good area for snorkelling (bring your own gear) and whales may be seen in season. There are a couple of places to stay but it gets very crowded and dirty at peak weekends and holidays.

Valdivia → *Phone code 04*

San Pedro and Valdivia are two unattractive fishing villages which merge together. There is accommodation nearby at **Valdivia Ecolodge** (see page 342) and many fish stalls for *ceviche* and simple meals.

This is the site of the 5,000 year-old Valdivia culture (see box page 337). Many houses offer 'genuine' artefacts and one resident at the north end of the village will show you the skeletons and burial urns dug up in his back garden. It is illegal to export pre-Columbian artefacts from Ecuador. The replicas are made in exactly the same manner as their predecessors and copied from genuine designs, so they may not be the real thing, but at least you're not breaking the law and at the same time you

The Valdivia culture

The village of Valdivia gave its name to one of the earliest of Ecuador's cultures, famed for its ceramics and dating back to 3300 BC. In the 1950s and 1960s these were the earliest ceramics known in the Americas. The superficial similarities between Valdivia ceramics and those of the Jomon Culture of Japan led many archaeologists to the conclusion that the Valdivia ceramics were first introduced to the Americas by Japanese fishermen.

However, discoveries over the past 35 years show that ceramic manufacture in the Americas has its own long path of development and that the idea of a Japanese contribution to pre-European cultures in South America should be discarded.

A much more compelling notion is that ceramic production in Ecuador had its origins in the non-Ecuadorean eastern Amazon basin. New claims from Brazilian sites place early pottery there at between 6000-5000 BC. It is possible that ceramic technology was transmitted from the Amazon basin through commerce or movement of people.

The third alternative is that the development of pottery occurred locally and may have accompanied the development of a more sedentary lifestyle on the Colombian, Venezuelan and Ecuadorean coasts.

The impressive Valdivia figurines are, in most cases, female representations and are nude and display breasts and a prominent pubic area. Some show pregnancy and in the womb of these are placed one or more seeds or small stones. Others have infants in their hands and some have two heads.

These figurines fill museum cases throughout the country (notably the excellent museums of the Banco Central in Guayaquil, Quito and Cuenca). They are still being produced by artisans in the fishing village of Valdivia today and can be purchased here or at the site museum in Salango, further north near Puerto López. In fact, according to the research of several Ecuadorean archaeologists, many of the figurines housed in the museum collections were made in the 1950s and 1960s because the archaeologists working at that time would pay for any figurines that were found.

(Jonathan D Kent, PhD, Associate Professor, Metropolitan State College of Denver).

can provide some income for the locals. Ask for Juan Orrala, who makes excellent copies, and lives up the hill from the museum. Most of the genuine artefacts discovered at the site are in museums in Quito and Guayaquil. Some pieces remain in the small, local **Ecomuseo Valdivia** ① *daily, US$0.60*, which also has artefacts from other coastal cultures and in-situ remains. There is also a **handicraft section**, where artisans may be seen at work, and lots of local information. At the museum there is also a restaurant and five basic rooms with bath to let.

There is a simple **aquarium** ① *T04-2780375, daily 0900-1800, US$1, local children will guide you and expect a tip,* with three tanks and several huts with exhibits about marine life. You can also rent a boat here for excursions to **Islote El Pelado** or **Islote El Viejo**.

About 8 km northeast of Valdivia is **Reserva Comunal Loma Alta**, a reserve which protects a tract of *garúa* forest in the Cordillera Chongón-Colonche. Access is via a secondary road from Valdivia, through Sinchal, Barcelona and Loma Alta to El Suspiro, one hour by car. From there it is three to four hours on foot to the shelter. Guides are available at the Comunal Loma Alta.

North of Valdivia is the village of **Libertador Bolívar**, where hammocks and crafts made of wood, *paja toquilla* and banana fibres are produced. There is lodging at a **Hospedería Comunitaria**, see Mamglaralto below.

Manglaralto → *Phone code 04   Regional population 23,500*

This sleepy little town is the main centre of the region north of Santa Elena, 180 km northwest of Guayaquil. There is a *tagua* nursery and you can ask to see examples of these 'vegetable ivory' nuts being turned into intricate works of art. It is a pleasant place, with a quiet beach and good surf. There's little shelter, so take plenty of sun screen.

Pro-pueblo is an organization working with local communities to foster family-run orchards and cottage craft industry, using *tagua* nuts, *paja toquilla* (used to make Panama hats) and other local products. They have a **craft shop** in town (opposite the park); an office in San Antonio south of Manglaralto, Mon-Fri 0800-1300 and 1400-1700, T04-2780230; and headquarters in Guayaquil, T04-2683569, www.propueblo.com **Proyecto de Desarollo Ecoturístico Comunitario** ① *contact Paquita Jara in Manglaralto, T04-2901114, or the Guayaquil office T04-2360896*, is another organization promoting ecotourism in the local communities. They have a network of simple community lodgings (US$5 per person) and many interesting routes into the interior have been set up.

Inland, 4 km northeast of Manglaralto, is **Dos Mangas**, in the Cordillera Chongón Colonche. Crafts are produced here and it is a good area for walking.

Montañita → *Phone code 04*

A popular destination among travellers with a good surfing beach, Montañita is 3 km north of Manglaralto. The main village has experienced haphazard growth and is crowded with small hotels. There are also restaurants, surf-board rentals, tattoo parlours, craft/jewellery vendors and sundry other services. At the north end of the bay, 1 km away, is another hotel area with more elbow-room, referred to as **Baja Montañita**, after one of the hotels. Between the two is a lovely beach where you'll find some of the best **surfing** in Ecuador. Various competitions are held during the year and at weekends in season, when the town is noisy and packed with Guayaquileños. There are many street dogs; don't contribute to the problem by feeding them.

Warning Drugs are a problem in Montañita. There are periodic police raids and several people, including foreigners, are serving long sentences in jail.

Olón → *Phone code 04*

About 3 km further north, Olón has a spectacular long beach. Starting here and continuing to the north, the surroundings get greener. On the headland between Montañita and Olón, built atop a cliff by the sea, is the **Sanctuary of Santa María de Fíat**. There is access from either side and the views are spectacular. Nearby, 1 km north of Olón, past the bridge is **El Cangrejal de Olón** ① *to visit contact Eustacio Salinas, at the copy shop on the highway*, a 7-ha dry tropical forest, with mangroves, and the home of the blue crab (*Cardisoma crasum-smith*), a species in danger of extinction. Horse-riding tours in the area are available from Dr Wilmer Cevallos, ask around for him.

A beautiful beach continues 10 km north by the villages of Curía, San José and La Núñez, to **La Entrada**, where the Cordillera Chongón Colonche comes out to the sea. This is the provincial boundary between Guayas and Manabí. There are good walking possibilities in this area. North of La Entrada, a road goes inland to Guale, 3½ km along it is the access to **Cantalapiedra Cabins**, run by **Alandaluz** (see Sleeping, page 343).

Ayampe → *Phone code 04*

Located at the foot of the Cordillera Chongón Colonche, on the south shore of the river of the same name, Ayampe is a small, poor village, with friendly people, but no services. Just south of it are a group of hotels offering a good option for those seeking tranquillity. This is a base for trips up to the **Cordillera Chongón Colonche**, which has tropical forest and good birdwatching. The area produces crafts with banana fibres, known as *sapán*.

Alandaluz and surroundings → *Phone code 04*

North of Ayampe are the villages of Las Tunas, Puerto Rico and Río Chico; there are places to stay all along this stretch of beach. In **Las Tunas** you can arrange for horse tours with **Kankagua**, opposite **Hotel La Barquita**. Just south of **Puerto Rico** is the **Alandaluz Ecological Centre**, an organization involved in promoting ecologically sound practices in nearby communities, including recycling of rubbish, water and organic agriculture. It is also a very good *hostería* (see below), which gives working demonstrations of its innovative practices. Near **Río Chico**, at Hostería Piqueros Patas Azules, there is a small private **museum** displaying ceramics, stone artefacts and funerary urns found at the site by archaeologist Presley Norton. These correspond to the Manteña, Valdivia, Machalilla and other prehistoric coastal cultures. A prize piece is the 2-cm-high 'Venus de Valdivia' statue, the smallest of its kind.

Salango → *Phone code 04   Population 3,600*

Just north of Río Chico and 5 km south of Puerto López is Salango, a commercial fishing port with a fish meal plant. It is worth visiting for its excellent **Presley Norton archaeological museum** ① *towards the north end of town, daily 0900-1200, 1300-1700, US$1*, housing artefacts from the excavations in town, and with a craft shop. Just offshore is **Isla Salango**, a good place for snorkelling.

Puerto López

→ *Phone code 05   Colour map 4, grid B1   Population 7,700   Altitude Sea level*

This pleasant little fishing town is beautifully set on a turquoise horseshoe bay, with a broad sweep of beach enclosed by headlands to the north and south. The beach is cleanest at the far north and south ends, away from the fleet of small fishing boats moored offshore. The streets are either dusty or muddy, depending on the season. A lookout above the south end of the bay along the main road offers great views.

> ‡ *Puerto López is the whale-watching capital of Ecuador.*

Excursions

Tourism is second only to fishing in Puerto López, with a wide array of hotels, restaurants and tour operators catering to the many foreign and Ecuadorean visitors who flock here every year during 'whale season' or *temporada de ballenas*, approximately mid-June to September (see box, A whale of a time, page 340). **Whale watching** is reasonably well organized, but things can get out of hand during the height of the season in July and August, when prices rise and touts await tourists arriving in town. During these peak months, fishermen may offer whale-watching trips for less than authorized tour operators. Such improvised excursions are seldom recommended, your safety may be compromised and the whales can be threatened by boatmen who have not been trained how to best approach them. You may wish to reserve accommodation and tours in advance during high season. Whales can also be seen from other points along the coast where tours are likewise available.

A year-round attraction is **Parque Nacional Machalilla**, which incorporates mainland sites and **Isla de la Plata** offshore, an island with bird colonies and good snorkelling. Excursions here are combined with whale watching in season. This has been called a 'cheap alternative to Galápagos', which is overstating the case; excursions to Isla de la Plata are definitely worthwhile, but your expectations should be reasonable. In town there is a **national park information centre** ① *C Eloy Alfaro y García Moreno, open daily*.

⁞ A whale of a time

Whale watching has taken off as a major tourist attraction along the coast of Ecuador. One of the prime sites to see these massive mammals is around Isla de La Plata but whales do travel the entire length of Ecuador's shores and well beyond.

Between June and September, each year, groups of up to 10 individuals of this gregarious species make the 8,000 km-long trip from their Antarctic feeding grounds to the equator. They head for these warmer waters to mate and calve. Inspired by love, we presume, the humpbacks become real acrobats. Watching them breach (jump almost completely out of the water) is the most exciting moment of any tour. Not far behind, though, is listening to them 'sing'. Chirrups, snores, purrs and haunting moans are all emitted by solitary males eager to use their chat-up techniques on a prospective mating partner. These vocal performances can last half an hour or more.

Adult humpbacks reach a length of over 15 m and can exceed 30 tonnes in weight. The gestation period is about one year and newborn calves are 5-6 m long. The ventral side of the tail has a distinctive series of stripes which allows scientists to identify and track individual whales.

Humpbacks got their English name from their humped dorsal fins and the way they arch when diving. Their scientific name, *Megaptera novaeangliae*, which translates roughly as 'large-winged New Englanders', comes from the fact that they were first identified off the coast of New England, and from their very large wing-like pectoral fins. In Spanish they are called *ballena jorobada* or *Yubarta*.

These whales have blubber up to 20-cm thick. Combined with their slow swimming, this made them all too attractive for whalers during the 19th and 20th centuries. During that period their numbers are estimated to have fallen from 100,000 to 2,500 worldwide. Protected by international whaling treaties since 1966, the humpbacks are making a gradual recovery. Ironically, the same behaviour that once allowed them to be harpooned so easily makes the humpbacks particularly appealing to whale watchers today. The difference is that each sighting is now greeted with the shooting of film instead of lethal harpoons.

Parque Nacional Machalilla

ⓘ *Entrance fee for Isla de la Plata, US$15. For mainland part only, US$12. For both mainland and Isla de la Plata, US$20. Children under 11 and seniors pay half price. Fee is payable at the park office next to the market in Puerto López (open 0700-1800) or directly to the park rangers (insist on a receipt). The ticket is valid for several days so you can visit the different areas.*

The park extends over 55,000 ha, including Isla de la Plata and Isla Salango offshore, as well as the magnificent beach of Los Frailes. It preserves marine ecosystems as well as the dry tropical forest and archaeological sites on shore. The park is recommended for birdwatching, especially in the cloud forest of Cerro San Sebastián, and there are also several species of mammals and reptiles. The continental portion of the park is divided into three sections which are separated by private land, including the town of Machalilla.

ⓘ *To get there, take a tour, a bus bound for Jipijapa (US$0.25) or a pick-up (US$5), the beach is a 30-min walk from the turn-off. Camping is only permitted by the ranger's house where you can get some water, US$5 per tent. The park gates close at 1700.*

This stunning beach, one of the nicest on the entire coast, is 11 km north of Puerto López and and 1 km south of the town of Machalilla. At the north end of the beach is a trail through the forest leading to a lookout with great views. You can continue along this trail to the town of Machalilla. Bathing at Los Frailes is best at the ends of the bay; in the centre there is a strong undertow.

❗ *There are poisonwood trees (manzanillo) by the beach, do not shelter from the sun under them.*

Agua Blanca

ⓘ *0800-1800. The commune charges US$3 for a 2-3 hr guided tour of the museum, ruins (a 45-min walk), funerary urns and sulphur lake. Horses can be hired for the visit. To get there, take tour, a pick-up (US$5) or a bus bound for Jipijapa (US$0.20); it is a hot walk of more than 1 hr from the turning to the village. Camping is possible and there's a cabin and 1 very basic room for rent above the museum for US$5 per person.*

About 5 km north of Puerto López, at Buena Vista, on the road to Machalilla, there is a dirt road to the east marked to Agua Blanca. Here, 5 km from the main road, amid hot, arid scrub in the national park, is a small village and a fine, small **archaeological museum** containing some fascinating ceramics from the Manteño civilization.

San Sebastián

ⓘ *A 5 hr trip on foot or by horse. A tour to the forest costs US$20 per day for the guide (fixed rate, minimun 2 days). You can camp (US$2), otherwise lodging is with a family at extra cost. Horses are also extra and you have to pay to get to Agua Blanca to start the excursion.*

A recommended trip is to San Sebastián, 9 km from Agua Blanca up in tropical moist forest (altitude 800 m), for sightings of orchids and possibly howler monkeys. This is the best nature hike in the park, going through successively more humid forests until reaching true cloud forest at Cerro San Sebastián. Although part of the national park, this area is administered by the *Comuna* of Agua Blanca, which charges its own fees in addition to the park entrance (see above). You are not allowed to go without one of their guides. You can also make alternative excursions in the Cordillera Chongón Colonche further south, which might prove to be less expensive.

Isla de la Plata

On this island, about 24 km offshore, there are nesting colonies of waved albatross, frigates and three different booby species. A small colony of sea lions also makes its home here and whales can be seen from June to September. As in Galápagos, it is easy to see the bird life – you will walk just by their nests. It is also a pre-Columbian site with substantial pottery finds, and there is good diving and snorkelling (most agencies provide snorkelling equipment).

The island must be visited in a day trip, staying overnight is not permitted. There are two walks, of three and five hours (take water); the national park controls access to these and you will probably be taken along only one of the two loops. See Puerto López tour operators, page 346, for details of tours and agencies. Take dry clothes, water, and precautions against sun and seasickness.

North of Parque Nacional Machalilla → *Phone code 05*

Machalilla is a small fishing village just north of Los Frailes beach. Neither the town nor its beach are particularly attractive. North from Machalilla is **Puerto Cayo**. The beach here is also dirty, but improves a bit as you walk away from town. Puerto Cayo promotes itself as a whale-watching destination, but it can be hard to organize a trip outside July and August. Town is completely dead outside these two months.

The road forks at Puerto Cayo, one branch turns inland for Jipijapa and the other continues northwest along the coast to Manta. The inland road climbs over humid hills to descend to the dry scrub around **Jipijapa**, an unattractive town but an important centre for the region's trade in cotton, cocoa, coffee and kapok. The *paja toquilla* from which Panama hats are made is also grown in the surrounding hills. At **La Pila**, due north of Jipijapa, the road turns east for Portoviejo. The village's main industry is fake pre-Columbian pottery, with a thriving by-line in erotic ceramics. Eleven kilometres northwest from La Pila is **Montecristi**, famous for weaving Panama hats, see page 349.

The coast road, scenic and paved, goes northwest from Puerto Cayo travelling slightly away from the beach through wooded hills. In 17 km is a turn-off for the undeveloped beach of **San José**. Another 12 km further north, by the village of **Santa Rosa** where there are food stalls serving seafood, the road returns to the seashore and follows a beautiful stretch of beach 6 km to **San Lorenzo**, by the cape of the same name. North of San Lorenzo the road again goes inland to an area of forested hills known as **Bosque de Pacoche**, before reaching Manta.

● Sleeping

Ballenita *p336*
B Hostería Farallón Dillon, T2953611, www.farallondillon.com.ec Lovely setting high above the sea, good restaurant, comfortable rooms with a/c, nice views. Recommended.

Valdivia *p336*
B Valdivia Ecolodge, at Km 40, just south of San Pedro, T04-2916128, valdiviaecolodge@hotmail.com Screened cabins without walls in a nice location above the ocean, fresh and interesting. Includes breakfast, restaurant, pool and access to nice bathing beach.

Manglaralto *p338*
The town suffers from water shortages. To stay with a local family, see **Proyecto de Desarollo de Ecoturístico Comunitario**, p338.
C Marakaya, 2 blocks south of the main plaza, 1 block from the beach, T04-2901294. A/c, mosquito net, clean and comfortable.
D Kamala, north of town after crossing the river, T09-9423754. Cabins by the sea, 2 are nice, the others simpler. Offers scuba diving tours and courses.

D Manglaralto, half a block north of the plaza, T04-2901369, hotel@espol.edu.ec Restaurant, fan, clean and pleasant.
D Manglaralto Sunset, a block from the Plaza, T04-2901405, manglaralto_beach @yahoo.com Nice modern place, comfortable rooms, hammocks, cafeteria bar, electric shower, parking, new in 2004.

Montañita *p338*
C Baja Montañita, in Baja Montañita, T04-2901107. Includes breakfast, restaurant, pool, parking, comfortable rooms; a small resort off on its own.
C-D La Casa del Sol, in Baja Montañita, T09-9423922, www.casasol.com Restaurant, a/c, cheaper with fan, large rooms available, surfing packages.
D Hotel Montañita, on beach at north end of village, T04-2901296, www.hotelmontanita.com Restaurant, cheaper with cold water, fan, pool, parking, mosquito net. Larger place, nice courtyard with plants, better rooms upstairs, cheaper ones are musty.
D Paradise South, just north of town across bridge, T04-2901185, paradise_south@hotmail.com Restaurant,

cheaper with shared bath, pool, pleasant grounds, fields and ping-pong tables, quiet. **D Tabuba**, away from centre at south end of town, T09-7486215, T04-2238603 (Guayaquil). Parking, modern place with large rooms, quiet and good.
D-E Tierra Prometida, T09-9446363, hoteltierraprometida@hotmail.com Cheaper with shared bath, fan, popular.
D-F Funky Monkey, in town, T09-4911545. Popular restaurant and bar, cheaper with shared bath or in dorm, simple rooms with mosquito nets.
E Casa Blanca, C Guido Chiriboga, T09-9182501, lacasablan@hotmail.com Good restaurant, private bath, sporadic hot water, mosquito nets, hammocks, clean.
E Pakaloro, at north end of town, next to the river estuary, T09-7415413, pakaloro@hotmail.com Private bath, hot water, mosquito net, small garden, hammocks on porch.
E Rickie, in town, T09-4139036. Cheaper with shared bath, electric shower, cooking facilities, mosquito net, basic, clean, friendly and relaxed. Good meeting place, free surfing lessons.

There are many other places to stay in town, all quite similar. The quieter ones are on the outskirts of the village.

Olón p338
D N & J, on the beach, T04-2390643. Cold water, fan, parking, simple rooms.
E Olón Beach, T04-2780200. Basic but clean.

Rooms are also available in private homes, see **Proyecto de Desarollo Ecoturístico Comunitario** in Manglaralto, p338.

Ayampe p338
L Hotel Atamari, on the headland south of Ayampe, a 15-min walk from the highway, T04-2780430, atamari@hoy.net Restaurant with wonderful food, pool, beautiful, cabins with rooms and suites, in spectacular surroundings on cliffs above the sea.
B Hotel Almare, T04-2780611, hotelalmare@yahoo.com Fan, wooden construction with porch, comfortable rooms and suites, English spoken. Fine views especially at sunset.
C Cabañas La Tortuga, T04-2780708, www.la tortuga.com.ec Restaurant, bar, fan, cabins in nice grounds, ping pong and billiards.

D Cabañas de la Iguana, T04-2780611, ayampeiguana@hotmail.com Meals with advance notice, cooking facilities, cabins for 4, mosquito nets, quiet. Swiss-Ecuadorian-run, family atmosphere, very friendly, helpful and knowledgeable, organizes excursions. Recommended.
D Finca Punta Ayampe, on a hill south of the other hotels, T04-2780616, info@fincapuntaayampe.com Restaurant, bamboo structure built high on a hill with great ocean views, mosquito nets, helpful.

Alanadluz and surroundings p339
B Piqueros Patas Azules, A 10-min drive from Río Chico toward the beach, T04-2780279. Restaurant, fan, cabins overlooking the beach. Price includes entry to the local museum.
B-C Hostería Alandaluz, part of the ecological centre, T04-2780690, www.alandaluz.com Cheaper with shared bath, a variety of cabins ranging from bamboo with thatched roofs and compost toilets to more luxurious with flush toilets, all with private bath. Good homegrown organic food, vegetarian or seafood, and there is a bar; all at extra cost. It is a very peaceful place, with a clean beach and stunning organic vegetable and flower gardens in the middle of the desert. 10% student discount with ISIC, camping with your own tent US$4 per person. Tours to **Cantalapiedra Cabins**, in lovely forest by the Río Ayampe and other locations; not cheap. Often busy, advance bookings required. Friendly and highly recommended.
C Hostería La Barquita, by Las Tunas, 4 km north of Ayampe and 1 km south of Alandaluz, T04-2780683, www.labarquita-ec.com The restaurant and bar are in a boat on the beach with good ocean views, a unique concept. Rooms with fan and mosquito nets, tours, ping pong and billards. Swiss-run; French, English and German spoken, friendly.

Salango p339
E Cabaña Mar, on the Malecón, T04-2780722. Shared bath, hot water, bamboo cabin, with shared bath, simple, clean, friendly and helpful, good value. Offers snorkelling tours to Isla Salango, US$10 per person, minimum 4 people.

Puerto López has many hotels, but may nonetheless fill during July and August. Reserve in advance if you want to stay in a particular establishment.

A Manta Raya Lodge, 3 km south of town on a hill overlooking the ocean, T/F05-2300233, www.advantagecuador.com Located away from the beach. Restaurant and bar, pool, comfortable rooms, nice views, colourful decor. Horse riding, fishing and diving trips organized. Credit cards and TCs accepted.

B-E Pacífico, Malecón y González Suárez, T05-2300147, hpacific@manta.ecua.net.ec Restaurant, a/c, much cheaper in old wing with fan and shared bath but full use of facilities, pool, parking. New rooms are comfortable, older ones are good value, nice grounds, boat tours, friendly and helpful. Recommended.

C La Terraza, on hill north of centre, behind the clinic, T05-2300235. Meals available on request, 6 cabins with great views over the bay, gardens, spacious, run by German Peter Bernhard. Free car service to/from town if called in advance. Highly recommended.

C Mandala, Malecón at north end of the beach, T/F05-2300181, hosteriamandala @yahoo.com Excellent restaurant, nice cabins, mosquito nets, lovely grounds, Swiss-Italian run, English spoken, owners knowledgeable about whales, TCs accepted. Recommended.

D Itapoa, on a lane off Abdón Calderón, between the Malecón and Montalvo, T09-9843042. Breakfast available, cabins around large garden, includes use of sauna and jacuzzi.

D Los Islotes, Malecón 532 y Gen Córdova, T05-2300108, hostallosislotes@hotmail.com Fan, modern, clean, rooftop terrace with ocean views, cheaper in dorm, friendly. Good value, recommended.

D Punta Piedrero, at the south end of the beach, beyond the Malecón, T04-2823225. Fan, concrete building on the beach, large somewhat dark rooms, balcony with ocean views, new in 2003.

D Tuzco, Gen Córdova y JL Mera, 3 blocks uphill from market, T05-2300120, jgsalazar_b@hotmail.com Meals on request, fan, large rooms available for families or groups, simple but adequate, pool table.

D-E Cueva del Oso, Lascano 116 y Juan Montalvo, T05-2300124. Includes breakfast, shared bath, cooking facilities, small place with family atmosphere, good dormitory accommodation. Recommended.

D-E Máxima, Gonzáles Suárez y Machalilla. Restaurant and bar, cheaper with shared bath, laundry and cooking facilities, parking, modern and comfortable, friendly, English spoken, good value.

D-E Monte Líbano, Southern extreme of Malecón, T05-2300231. Breakfast available, cheaper with shared bath, cooking facilities, renovated in 2004, very clean, nice terrace with views, popular and friendly.

D-E Sol Inn, Montalvo entre Eloy Alfaro y Lascano, hostal_solinn@hotmail.com Cheaper with shared bath, laundry and cooking facilities, parking, popular, nice atmosphere, English and French spoken, good value.

Puerto López

Not to scale

Sleeping 📛	
Cueva del Oso **1**	Sol Inn **7**
Itapoa **11**	Tuzco **12**
La Terraza **4**	Villa Colombia **9**
Los Islotes & Carnita	Yubarta **10**
Restaurant **2**	
Mandala **3**	**Eating** 🍴
Máxima **5**	Bellitalia **1**
Monte Líbano **13**	Flipper **2**
Pacífico **6**	Spondylus **3**
Punta Piedrero **14**	Whale Café **8**

E Villa Colombia, on García Moreno behind market, T05-2300105, F2300189. Private bath, hot water, fan, cooking facilities, cheaper in dorm, mosquito nets, garden with hammocks, clean and very friendly.
E Yubarta, on Malecón north of river. Bar, private bath, cold water, mosquito net, simple.

North of P N Machalilla *p342*
A Luz de Luna, 5 km north of Puerto Cayo on the coastal road, T05-2616031, T02-2400562 (Quito). Includes 3 meals, restaurant, fan, pool, comfortable spacious rooms with balcony, nice clean beach, disco, quieter in low season when discounts are also available.
C Puerto Cayo, south end of beach at Puerto Cayo, T05-2616019, T09-7521538, cayos@puertocayo.com Good restaurant, fan, comfortable rooms with and hammocks and terrace overlooking the sea. Friendly. There are several other places to stay, but many are closed outside high season.
C Hostal Jipijapa, Santiesteban y Eloy Alfaro, 2 blocks south of the cemetery, Jipijapa, T05-2601365. Restaurant, a/c, fridge, clean.
D Agua Blanca, Km 1 via a Puerto Cayo, Jipijapa, T05-2600759. A/c, cheaper with fan and cold water, adequate.

🍴 Eating

Manglaralto *p338*
¶¶¶ La Calderada, at the Plaza, closed Tue. Very good seafood, try *calderada* (fish soup).
¶ Laurita, at the Plaza. Home cooking.

Montañita *p338*
¶¶¶ Zoociedad, rustic setting, Italian and international dishes, wine list.
¶¶¶-¶¶ La Lojanita, *ceviches*.
¶¶¶-¶¶ Tres Palmas, in Baja Montañita. Grill and Tex-Mex, generous portions, friendly.
¶¶ Bob Marley Café, Southwest corner of square. Good breakfast and set meals.
¶¶ Desde Montanita con Amor, C Guido Chiriboga, opposite Hotel Casa Blanca. Good vegetarian.
¶¶ Ebeneezer, good set meals.
¶¶ Manuel, pizzas, fruit juices and milkshakes.
¶¶ Tiburón, good pizza.

There are many other small restaurants, with quite uniform food and prices.

Olón *p338*
Several cheap and simple places to eat, including **Flor de Olón** and **María Verónica**.

Salango *p339*
¶¶¶ El Delfín Mágico, excellent food but chronically slow service, so it's best to order your meal before visiting the museum. Try the *spondilus* (spiny oyster) in fresh coriander and peanut sauce with garlic-coated *patacones*. Recommended.
¶¶ El Pelícano, Behind the church. Excellent seafood and also caters to vegetarians.

Puerto López *p339, map p344*
¶¶¶ Bellitalia, Montalvo y Abdón Calderón, 1 block back from the Malecón and near the river, open from 1800. Excellent Italian food, try their spinach soup. Pleasant garden setting, Italian run. Highly recommended.
¶¶ The Whale Café, towards the south end of the Malecón. Good pizza, sandwiches and meals, cakes and pies. Nice breakfast, famous for pancakes. US-run, owners Diana and Kevin are very helpful and provide travel information. Recommended.
¶¶ There are many good places along the Malecón serving local fare, fish and seafood, all quite similar; they usually have an economical set meal which isn't necessarily listed (ask for it, if that is what you want) and slightly more expensive à la carte. These include: **Carmita, Myflower, Spondylus, Soda Bar Danny**.
¶¶-¶ Araza, Gen Córdova ½ block from the Malecón, open from 1600. Vegetarian food with Arab and Indian dishes.
¶ Flipper, Gen Córdova next to Banco del Pichincha. Good set meals, friendly. Recommended.

The *panadería* behind the church serves good banana bread and other sweets.

🍸 Bars and clubs

Puerto López *p339, map p344*
La Resaca, on the beach opposite **Whale Café**, in a converted old fishing boat.

● *For an explanation of the Sleeping and Eating price codes used in this guide, see the*
● *inside front cover. Other relevant information is provided in Essentials, pages 58-64.*

○ Shopping

Puerto López *p339, map p344*
There are several craft shops along the Malecón, including **Palo Santo** for candles. **Yaguarundi** is a cooperative, T05-2780184, selling *tagua* (vegetable ivory), cactus fibre baskets and pottery. They can arrange visits to homes to see handicrafts being made.

▲ Activities and tours

Montañita *p338*
Surfboard rentals US$2 per hr, US$10 per day. **Tatoo** also sells boards. **Balsa House**, opposite **Hotel Tierra Prometida**.

Puerto López *p339, map p344*
Whale watching is possible Jun-Sep or early Oct, and high season is Jul-Aug. There is a good fleet of small boats (16-20 passengers) running excursions, all have life jackets and a toilet; but avoid those boats with a single outboard motor. All agencies offer the same tours for the same price. In high season: US$30 per person for whale watching, Isla de la Plata and snorkelling, including a snack and drinks, US$25 for whale watching only. In low season tours to Isla de la Plata and snorkelling cost US$25 per person, US$20 for whale watching only. These rates don't include the National Park fee (see p340). Trips start about 0800 and return around 1700. Agencies also offer tours to the mainland sites of the national park. A day tour combining Agua Blanca and Los Frailes costs US$25 per person. There are very many agencies; not all are listed here.

For **deep sea fishing**, contact Kevin at the Whale Café, US$40 per trip.

Tour operators
Bosque Marino, on the highway, near the bus stop, T09-9173556 (mob). Experienced guides, some of whom speak English. They also offer hikes through the forest and birdwatching tours to Agua Blanca and Las Goteras for US$20 per day for groups of 2-3.
Ecuador Amazing, Gen Córdova, T05-2300239 Tours to Isla de la Plata and whale watching.
Excursiones Pacífico, Malecón at Hotel Pacífico, T/F05-2300133. Comfortable boat and good service. Also tours to San

Sebastián, Agua Blanca, Los Frailes.
Exploramar Diving, on Malecón next to Spondylus restaurant, T05-2300123, T02-2563905 (Quito), www.exploradiving.com French-run outfit based in Quito. They have 2 boats for 8-12 people and their own compressor to fill dive tanks. PADI divemaster accompanies qualified divers to various sites, but advance notice is required, US$85 per person for all-inclusive diving day tour (2 tanks). Also offer diving lessons.
Machalilla Tours, on Malecón next to Viña del Mar restaurant, T05-2300206. They also offer horse riding, surfing and fishing tours; all cost US$25 per person for a day trip.
Manta Raya, on Malecón Norte, T05-2300233. They have a comfortable and spacious boat. They also have diving equipment and charge US$100.00 per person, all inclusive.
Sercapez, Gen Córdova, T05-2300173. All inclusive trips to San Sebastián, with camping, local guide and food run US$30 per person, per day. They also work with **Guacamayo Bahía Tours** and organize trips further north (see Bahía de Caráquez, p350). They also offer transfers to the airport in Manta or Portoviejo and to other cities.

⊖ Transport

For main inter-city routes see the bus timetable p52.

Manglaralto *p338*
To **Santa Elena** or **La Libertad**, US$2, 1½ hrs, change in Santa Elena for **Guayaquil.** To **Guayaquil direct**, see Olón schedule below. To **Puerto López**, US$1.50, 1 hr.

Montañita and Olón *p338*
Montañita is just a few mins south of Olón, from where there are buses to **Santa Elena** or **La Libertad**, US$2.50, 2 hrs. CLP have daily direct buses starting in Olón going to **Guayaquil**, at 0500, 1300, 1630 (same schedule from Guayaquil), US$5, 3½ hrs; or transfer in Santa Elena. To Puerto López, US$1.50, 45 mins.

Puerto López *p339, map p344*
To **Santa Elena** or **La Libertad**, every 30 mins, US$3.40, 2½ hrs. To **Montañita** and **Manglaralto**, US$1.50, 1 hr. There are

pick-ups for hire to nearby sites are by the market, east of the highway.

North of PN Machalilla *p342*
There is a **Terminal Terrestre** on the outskirts of Jipijapa, with buses to **Puerto López**, US$1, 1 hr; to **Manglaralto**, US$2, 2 hrs; to **Manta**, US$1, 1 hr; to **Quito**, US$9, 10 hrs.

---

❶ Directory

Montañita *p338*
Banks No banks in town, the pharmacy will exchange TCs for a high commission.
Internet On street closest to the river,

US$2 per hr. **Laundry** Lavandería
Espumita, near the church, charges by piece.
Telephone Movistar, public cell phones, daily 0800-2100.

Puerto López *p339, map p344*
Banks Banco del Pichincha, Gen Córdova y Machalilla. **Internet** Malecón next to Myflower restaurant, US$2 per hr. **Language schools** La Lengua, Abdón Calderón y García Moreno, next to the Municipio, east of the highway, same school as in Quito. Puerto López e-mail costamar25@hotmail.com, Quito T02-2543521, www.la-lengua.com US$6 per hr, can organize homestays.

Manta to Pedernales → *Colour map 4, A1-map 2, B1*

The province of Manabí has many different faces. Manta is a bustling city, a fishing and cargo port with a strategic and controversial US airforce base. North along the coast are countless seaside villages, some half-forgotten, others popular beach destinations. The largest resort area is around Bahía de Caráquez, which has dubbed itself an 'eco-city'. Just beyond Bahía, on the other side of the Río Chone estuary, is the little village of Canoa, boasting some of the finest beaches in Ecuador. Northward still, to Pedernales and Cojimies, the coast is less developed for tourism. The country inland is even less visited, with Montubio villages amid the dry hills offering ample scope for exploration. ➤➤ *For Sleeping, Eating and other listings, see pages 354-360.*

Ins and outs
There are several daily flights between Manta and Quito; Manta airport is also convenient for Portoviejo. A paved road runs all along the coast from Manta to Pedernales and connects at Manta, Bahía de Caráquez and Pedernales, with roads to Santo Domingo de los Colorados and the highlands. There is also an inland route from Manta to Guayaquil via Jipijapa, and a frequent bus service throughout the region.

Manta → *Phone code 05   Colour map 4, grid A1   Population 183,000   Altitude sea level*

Manta is the quintessential maritime city. Ecuador's second port after Guayaquil and home to the county's largest fishing fleet, it has hundreds of boats of all sizes moored offshore. This busy lively city has grown and prospered over the past decade. The thriving port and a US airforce base (ostensibly for drug surveillance) give the city a cosmopolitan flavour and have driven up prices, but not diminished friendliness. Cruise ships call on Manta from time to time.

Information
Ministerio de Turismo ① *Paseo José María Egas 1034 (Av 3) y Calle 11, T05-2622944, Mon-Fri 0900-1230, 1400-1700*, very helpful, some English spoken. **Cámara de Turismo** ① *Centro Comercial Cocco Manta, Malecón y C 23, T05-2620478, Mon-Fri 0900-1300, 1500-1800*, helpful, map available, English spoken. **Oficina de Información ULEAM** ① *Malecón Escénico by Playa Murcielago, T05-2624099, daily 0900-1700*, staffed by tourism students from the Universidad Laica Eloy Alfaro.

Northern Pacific Lowlands Manta to Pedernales

A constant sea breeze tempers the intense sun and makes the city's *malecones* (oceanfront avenues) pleasant places to stroll. The **Malecón Escénico**, at the gentrified west end of town, has a cluster of bars and seafood restaurants. It is a lively place especially at weekends, when there is good music, free beach aerobics and lots of action. This promenade is built along **Playa Murciélago**, a popular beach with wild surf (enquire locally before bathing, flags are placed on the beach to indicate whether it is safe or not). It is also a good surfing beach from December to April. Manta's

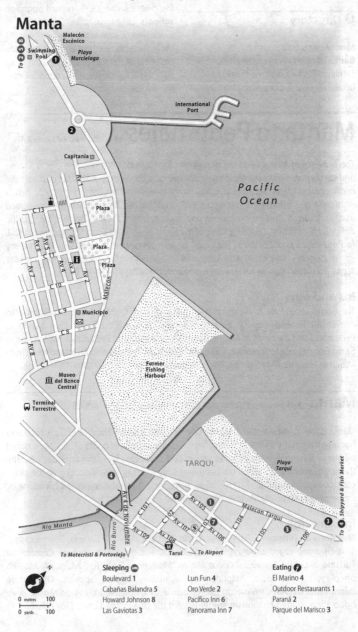

Manta

Sleeping 🛌
Boulevard 1
Cabañas Balandra 5
Howard Johnson 8
Las Gaviotas 3

Lun Fun 4
Oro Verde 2
Pacífico Inn 6
Panorama Inn 7

Eating 🍴
El Marino 4
Outdoor Restaurants 1
Paraná 2
Parque del Marisco 3

growing number of upmarket hotels and restaurants are found in the neighbourhoods near Playa Murciélago. Further west is **Playa Barbasquillo**.

The **centre of town**, built on a hill, conserves some older wooden buildings and a bazaar-like atmosphere. Shops, banks, the *terminal terrestre*, the **Banco Central museum** and a **tourist information office** are here, but no hotels and few restaurants.

Two bridges join the main town with **Tarqui** on the east side of the Río Manta. Many hotels, including all the economy ones, are located near the sea here. This is not a safe area at night (take a taxi to your hotel), but a stroll along the Tarqui Malecón can be interesting during the day (do not take valuables). Visit the **fish market** and *astillero* around Calle 110, where large wooden fishing boats are built. At the Malecón y Calle 106 is the **Parque del Marisco**, with many small seafood restaurants, but mind the hygiene. Tarqui beach is too polluted for swimming and east of Calle 110 it is unsafe at all hours.

The **Museo del Banco Central** ① *Tue-Sat 1000-1800, US$1, Av 8 y C 7, behind the bus station*, has an excellent collection of archaeological pieces from seven different civilizations that flourished on the coast of Manabí between 3500 BC and AD 1530. It is well displayed, with Spanish explanations.

Excursions

Located 11 km southeast of Manta, **Montecristi** (population 15,000) is a quiet, dusty town, set on the lower slopes of an imposing hill. It is just high enough to be watered by low cloud which gives the region its only source of drinking water. The town is one of the main centres of Panama hat production and is renowned for the high quality of its output (see Arts and Crafts, on page 466). Varied straw and basketware is also produced here (much cheaper than in Quito), and wooden barrels which are strapped to donkeys for carrying water. Ask for José Chávez Franco, Rocafuerte 203, where you can see Panama hats being made; he sells wholesale and retail. Montecristi is also famous as the birthplace of the statesman Eloy Alfaro.

Nine kilometres west of Manta along the coast road is **San Mateo**, a fishing village with good surfing, especially from December to April. Ten kilometres beyond is **San Lorenzo**, on a cape jutting into the ocean. Here you'll find a lighthouse atop towering headlands, with lovely views (but beware of the cliffs below), and a waterfall. There several eateries and accommodation in town, see page 355.

In the hills near the village of **El Aromo,** some 15 km south of Manta, is Hostería San Antonio (see page 354), a popular spot with Manteños and busy on weekends and holidays. At other times this is a nice place to escape the heat of the city.

Portoviejo → *Phone code 05   Colour map 4, grid B2   Population 172,000*

Some 40 km inland from Manta and 65 km northeast from Jipijapa, Portoviejo is the capital of Manabí province and a major commercial centre. It was once a port on the Río Rocafuerte, but as a result of severe deforestation the river has silted and almost completely dried up. In the rainy season, however, it floods badly, often breaking its banks. **Information   Ministerio de Turismo** ① *Pedro Gual y J Montalvo, T05-2630877.*

> ‼ *Portoviejo is not a safe city, take precautions here at all hours.*

Sights

The cathedral overlooks **Parque Eloy Alfaro** where you can see sloths taking it easy in the plaza's trees: you may be tempted to do the same in this, Ecuador's hottest city! Portoviejo is one of the main places where kapok mattresses and pillows are made from the fluffy fibre of the seed capsule of the *ceibo*. In **Calle Alajuela** you can buy *montubio* hammocks, bags, hats etc made by the coastal farmers, or *montubios*, as they are known. The **Jardín Botánico** is along Av Universitaria in the north of the city.

About 10 minutes from town, on the road that later branches to Bahía, is the village of **Sosote**; its main street is lined with workshops where figurines are carved out of *tagua* nuts (vegetable ivory) into innumerable shapes.

North of Portoviejo

Crucita → *Phone code 05 Colour map 4, grid A2 Population 11,000*

Crucita is an oceanside playground for folks from Portoviejo and Manta, less than an hour's ride from either city. It gets busy at weekends and holidays. The beach is long, with gentle surf, and small hotels and restaurants line the Malecón. What makes Crucita special, however, are its ideal conditions for several aeronautical sports: paragliding, hang-gliding and kite-surfing. Tandem paragliding flights for novices (US$15), equipment rental (US$25 per day), and courses (US$250 for four to six days) can be arranged through Luis Tobar at **Hostal Los Voladores**, see page 355. The best season for flights is July to December.

For those who prefer to keep their feet on the ground, a walk north along the beach to the village of **Arenales** allows you to see how millions of sardines are brought ashore each day, and are processed by hand before being trucked to the cannery. Further north is **Las Gilces**, another quiet fishing village where accommodation may be available. There is an abundance of seabirds in the area, including brown pelicans, frigates, blue-footed boobies, gulls and sandpipers.

San Clemente and San Jacinto → *Phone code 05 Colour map 4, grid A2*

About 60 km north of Portoviejo (60 km northeast of Manta, 30 km south of Bahía de Caráquez) are San Clemente and, 3 km south, San Jacinto, in an area known for its salt production. Both can get crowded during the holiday season (July and August) but, as resorts, these towns have seen better days and are deserted the rest of the year. The long beach between them is nice enough, as is the ocean, but be wary of strong undertow when swimming.

Bahía de Caráquez → *Phone code 05 Colour map 4, grid A2 Population 20,000*

Set on the southern shore at the seaward end of the Chone estuary, Bahía is a friendly, relaxed resort town and a pleasant place in which to spend some time. The riverfront is attractively laid out with parks on the Malecón Alberto Santos. This becomes Circunvalación Dr Virgilio Ratti and goes right around the point along the ocean side of the peninsula, which is also very nice. The beaches right in Bahia are nothing special, but there are excellent beaches nearby between San Vicente and Canoa as well as at Punta Bellaca, see Excursions below. High season for Bahía and surroundings is July and August. **Information Ministerio de Turismo** ① *Bolívar y Circunvalación*. Spanish only, unhelpful.

Bahía has declared itself an **'eco-city'**, where recycling projects, organic gardens and ecoclubs are common. The city is also a centre of the less than ecologically friendly shrimp farming industry, which has boosted the local economy but also destroyed much of the estuary's precious mangroves. With awareness of the damage done, there is now a drive for alternative methods. Bahía boasts the first certified organic shrimp farm in the world, and a paper recycling scheme, involving communities who previously lived from the mangrove forests. The town recycles all organic waste and has published a residents' guide to living in an eco-city. Tricycle rickshaws called 'eco-taxis' have become a popular form of local transport. Information about the eco-city concept can be obtained from the **Planet Drum Foundation** ① *www.planetdrum.org*

The **Museo Bahía de Caráquez of the Banco Central** ① *Malecón Alberto Santos y Aguilera, Tue-Fri 1000-1700, Sat-Sun 1100-1500, US$1,* has an interesting collection of arcaeological artefacts from various pre-Hispanic coastal cultures. The well organized display includes a very impressive life-size balsa raft. Another section of the museum is devoted to modern sculpture.

Excursions

The **Rio Chone estuary** has several islands with mangrove forest. The area is rich in birdlife, dolphins may also be seen, and conditions are ideal for photographers because you can get really close, even under the mangrove trees where birds nest. The male frigate birds can be seen displaying their inflated red sacks as part of the mating ritual; best from August to January. At **Isla Corazón**, a boardwalk has been built through an area of protected mangrove forest. At the end of the island are a large colony of frigate birds that can only be accessed by boat.

The village of **Puerto Portovelo** ① *US$5 pp for a tour with a native guide. You can visit independently, taking a Chone-bound bus from San Vicente (allow enough time*

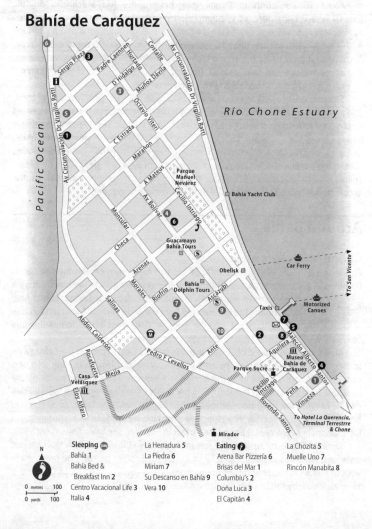

Bahía de Caráquez

Northern Pacific Lowlands Manta to Pedernales

Sleeping
Bahía 1
Bahía Bed &
Breakfast Inn 2
Centro Vacacional Life 3
Italia 4

La Herradura 5
La Piedra 6
Miriam 7
Su Descanso en Bahía 9
Vera 10

Eating
Arena Bar Pizzería 6
Brisas del Mar 1
Columbiu's 2
Doña Luca 3
El Capitán 4

La Chozita 5
Muelle Uno 7
Rincón Manabita 8

N
0 metres 100
0 yards 100

to get back to San Vicente before dark) or with an agency. Agency tours might do part of the trip by boat, which has the advantage of travelling through the estuary and seeing several islands. Visits here are tide-sensitive, so even if you go independently, it is best to check with the agencies about the best time to visit. The agencies are in radio contact with Puerto Portovelo, so they will advise the guides to expect you and sell you the entry ticket; agency tours are US$15-20 per person, reached by bus from San Vicente, has an information centre for the estuary, including an interesting video. The community is involved in mangrove reforestation and runs an ecotourism project.

The **Chirije archaeological site** is a 45-minute ride south of Bahía. This site was a seaport of the Bahía culture (500 BC to AD 500), which traded as far north as Mexico and south to Chile. There is a museum on site, as well as cabins and a restaurant. It is surrounded by dry tropical forest, good beaches, walking and birdwatching possibilities. Tours from Bahía take you in an open-sided *chiva* along the beach (US$30 per person, includes lunch). On the way to Chirije is the scenic **Punta Bellaca**; near it is the **Cerro Viejo** or **Cerro de las Orquídeas** hill, with dry tropical forest, which is worth exploring. A walking tour through the forest to Punta Bellaca costs US$14.

About 10 km north of Canoa (see below), the **Río Muchacho organic farm** ① *Reservations necessary, contact Guacamayo Bahía Tours, p358,* promotes agro-ecology and reforestation in the area and runs an environmental primary school. A three-day visit to the farm is recommended in order to explore the area. Accommodation is rustic but comfortable, and the food is good, mainly vegetarian. It's an eye-opener to rural coastal (*montubio*) culture and to organic farming. Volunteer programmes available. Highly recommended.

Saiananda ① *T05-2398331, reached by taxi or any bus heading out of town, US$2. A visit here is included in some agency tours of the area,* is a private park owned by biologist Alfredo Harmsen, 5 km from Bahía along the bay. The waterfront setting is striking, as is the unusual combination of native and domestic animals and birds, many of which interact freely with each other and humans. There are sloths, coatimundi, deer, ostriches, rabbits, macaws, a donkey, a cow, peacocks and geese. There is also a Japanese bonsai garden, cactus collection, spiritual centre, accommodation and restaurant. The food is first-class vegetarian.

Around Bahía

Chone → *Phone code 05   Population 45,000*

Chone is 1½ hours east from Bahía. At the exit from town on the road to Santo Domingo is a strange sculpture of four people suspending a car on wires across a gorge. It represents the difficulties faced by Carlos Alberto Aray during the first ever trip from Bahía de Caráquez to Quito by car – with many missing bridges. Aray went on to found the bus company which carries his name, and still exists.

‼ *There are several simple comedores in town.*

About 20 minutes west of Chone, in the Parroquia San Antonio, is the **Ciénega de la Segua**, a huge marshland home to 158 species of birds, including 250,000 waterbirds. Another wetland in this region is **Simbocal**. Tours to the wetlands are available from agencies in Bahía (US$25 per person, see page 358, and local guides can be hired in the neighbouring towns of La Segua and La Sabana. La Segua has been designated a **Ramsar site** (specially protected wetlands area according to an international governmental treaty), one of six in Ecuador, see www.ramsar.org

North of Chone, by an attractive stream, is **La Cueva Dibujada**, a cave with ancient drawings. Agencies in Bahía can take you there (US$30 per person); be prepared to walk or ride a horse uphill for 1½ hours. Northeast of town is Cascada **La Guabina**, a 17-m waterfall, by the town of the same name.

North to Esmeraldas

San Vicente → *Phone code 05   Colour map 4, grid A2   Population 8,300*

The market town of San Vicente, on the north side of the Río Chone, can be reached by taking the ferry from Bahía de Caráquez, or the road west from Chone. Its attractive waterfront and wide sandy beach were lost to El Niño in 1998. However it is still popular with some vacationing Ecuadorean families, and is the access point for the impressive stretch of beach north to Canoa. The **Santa Rosa church**, 100 m to the north of the wharf, is worth checking out for the excellent mosaic and glass work by José María Peli Romeratigui (better known as Peli). The views of Bahía from town, especially from the hill, are excellent.

Canoa → *Phone code 05   Colour map 4, grid A2   Rural population 6,100*

Canoa is a quiet fishing and tourist town, with a 200-m wide, clean and relatively isolated beach, one of the nicest in Ecuador. The choice of accommodation is very good and this, along with the lovely setting, has made it especially popular with travellers. The beautiful 17-km beach between San Vicente and Canoa is a good walk, horse or bike ride. Horses and bicycles can be hired through several hotels. Just north of Canoa along the beach is **Cueva del Murciélago**, a

> *Canoa has the widest beach in Ecuador, with good surfing and great bathing.*

natural cave at the cliff base. You can walk there at low tide but allow time to return. Surfing is good, particularly during the wet season, December to April. In the dry season there is good wind for windsurfing. Canoa is also a good place for hang-gliding and paragliding; flights can be arranged through the **Hotel Sol y Luna**, see page 356. Tents for shade and chairs are rented at the beach for US$3 a day.

Jama → *Phone code 05   Population 4,700*

North of Canoa along the shore is **Cabo Pasado**, where howler monkeys might be seen in the forest; it was a stopping point for whalers who used to resupply with water at a spring. The road, however, goes inland from Canoa, through the more humid pasture-lands, north to the small market centre of Jama, 1½ hours from San Vicente. South of town is El Matal, a fishing village and beach (not clean), reached by pick-up from the park.

North of Jama the road gets closer to the shore once again. About 10 km ahead is the village of **Don Juan**, where there is very basic accommodation at the highway. North of Don Juan is **Playa de Tasate**, a beach with interesting rock formations. Also near Don Juan is **Reserva Don Lalo**, a dry forest reserve run by the **Jatun Sacha Foundation** (see Volunteer opportunities, page 84). Another 4 km north is **Punta Prieta** and 3 km beyond, at the next headland, **Punta Blanca**; the black and white promontories, respectively. This area has a handful of interesting and very tranquil places to stay, see page 356. North of Punta Blanca the road goes by the villages of Tabuga and La Cabuya before crossing the equator and reaching Pedernales, 37 km from Punta Blanca.

Pedernales → *Phone code 05   Colour map 2, grid B1   Population 15,000*

Pedernales, a market town and crossroads, is the closest bathing beach to Quito and is doing its best to attract tourism. To the north are good undeveloped beaches, while those in town are less attractive, despite new development and efforts to keep them clean. Pedernales feels more like a commercial lowland city than a beach resort. A mosaic mural on the church overlooking the plaza is one of the best pieces of work by Peli (see San Vicente above), and lovely examples of his stained glass can be seen inside the airy church.

From Pedernales, the main coastal highway goes south to San Vicente, and north to Chamanga, El Salto and Esmeraldas. Another important road goes inland to El Carmen and Santo Domingo de los Colorados; this is the most direct route to Quito.

A small unpaved road runs north of Pedernales through cattle ranches, but at low tide all traffic here goes along the beach. Some 20 km north along this route is **Cocosolo**, a lovely hideaway set among palm trees, see page 356. Twenty kilometres further, the end of the line is **Cojimíes**, a friendly one-horse town with unpaved streets. It is continually being eroded by the sea and has been moved about three times in as many decades. Far from the beaten path, this is a poor and forgotten corner of the coast. There are a couple of basic places to stay and eat, and you might be able to hire a canoe to visit the mangroves around town for about US$10 per hour. Motorized canoes can also be hired to Daule, across the bay in the province of Esmeraldas, from where you can access the main coastal highway. This involves a long walk on the beach.

● Sleeping

Manta *p347, map p348*
Manta's hotels are more expensive than those in other parts of coastal Ecuador.

North of the centre
L Howard Johnson Plaza, Barrio Umiña, 1½ km on the way to Barbasquillo, T05-2629999, www.hojo.com Includes breakfast, restaurant, pool and gym, modern, full facilities.
L Oro Verde, Malecón y C 23, T05-2629200, www.oroverdehotels.com Includes buffet breakfast, restaurant, pool, all luxuries, best in town.
L-AL Cabañas Balandra, Av 8 y C 20, Barrio Córdova, T05-2620316, F2620545. Includes breakfast, comfortable cabins and rooms.
AL Costa del Sol, Malecón y Av 25, T05-2620025, F2620019. Includes breakfast, a/c, pool, parking, modern, comfortable, seaside rooms with balconies are very nice.
AL Lun Fun, Av 11 y C 2, near bridge to Tarqui, T05-2622966, F2610601. Includes breakfast, upmarket Chinese restaurant, a/c, parking, comfortable and nice but in unpleasant area.
A María José, Av Flavio Reyes y C 29 #110, Barrio Umiña, T05-2628562. Includes breakfast, a/c, in private home with nice terrace, quiet residential neighbourhood, far from everything.
A-C Barbasquillo, at Playa Barbasquillo, T05-2620718, F2628111. Includes breakfast, restaurant, a/c, pool and gym, fridge, parking, nice place with a variety of different rooms at different prices.

B Aeropuerto, C M3 y Av 24, Ciudadela el Murcielago (nowhere near the airport), T05-2628040. Includes breakfast, a/c, in converted private home, quiet residential neighbourhood, out of the way.

Tarqui
A-B Las Gaviotas, Malecón 1109 y C 106, T05-2620140, F2620940. Includes breakfast, restaurant, a/c, pool, the best in Tarqui.
B-C Panorama Inn, C 103 y Av 105, T05-2622996, F2611552. Includes breakfast, restaurant, cold water, a/c, cheaper with fan, pool, parking, nice new section across the street, older rooms fair, friendly and helpful.
D Boulevard, Av 105 y C 103, T05-2625333. Cold water, a/c, cheaper with fan, parking, sea view, adequate, also has a newer section: Boulevard III.
D Pacífico Inn, Av 106 y C 101, T05-2623584, F2622475. A/c, cheaper with fan, adequate. There are many other cheap places to stay in Tarqui, but be mindful of safety here.

Out of town
A Hostería San Antonio, near the village El Aromo, about 20 km south of Manta, T09-4138284, T05-2622813 (**Delgado Travel** in Manta), www.sanantoniohotel.com.ec Up in the hills with a refreshingly cool climate. Includes breakfast, 2 restaurants, 2 pools, sports fields, nice rooms with balconies, popular with Manteños and busy on weekends and holidays.

San Lorenzo
B La Cueva, toward the north end of the bay in San Lorenzo, about 20 km south of Manta on the coast road, T05-2615902, T05-2623497 (evenings only). Includes breakfast, good restauarnt, a/c, pool, modern cabins, popular with Manteños on weekends, friendly and helpful, advance booking advised.

Portoviejo *p349*
B-C Máximo, C Cumaná y 5 de Junio. Restaurant, a/c, cheaper with fan, fridge, slightly upmarket.
C-D El Gato, Pedro Gual y 9 de Octubre, T05-2632856. A/c, cheaper with fan, adequate.
D Conquistador, 18 de Octubre y 10 de Agosto, T05-2633259, F2631481. A/c, cheaper with fan, friendly.
F París, Plaza Central, T05-2652727. Private bath, cold water, fan, one of the oldest hotels in town, a faded classic, also for short stays.

Crucita *p350*
Most hotels are along the beach.
C Venecia, T05-2340301. Includes breakfast, a/c, small indoor pool, some rooms with fridge, modern building, rooms with balcony and hammocks.
C Zucasa, T05-2340133. Cold water, fan, 2 pools, fully equipped cabins for up to 6, very nice and friendly.
C-D Hostal Voladores, south end of beach, away from town, T05-2340200, hvoladores@hotmail.com Restaurant, cheaper with shared bath, small pool, simple but nice place, sea kayaks available. Owner Luis Tobar is very friendly and helpful, organizes paragliding flights and lessons.
D Sol Alondra, 150 m back from the beach, T05-2340246. Cold water, pool, some rooms with fridge, parking, friendly.

San Clemente and San Jacinto *p350*
There are various other places to stay in the area but many close in low season.
C Cabañas Tío Gerard, between San Clemente and San Jacinto, T05-2615517. Cold water, fan, small, simple and clean.
C Chediak, between San Clemente and San Jacinto, T05-2615499. Restaurant, fan, mosquito net, parking, comfortable, great views from upper-floor balconies.

D Briggitte, in the centre of San Jacinto, T05-2615505. Cold water, fan, adequate place with tiled floors.
D Cabañas Rocío, in San Jacinto, T05-2615476. Cold water, fan, fridge, small but nice cabins with well-equipped kitchen.

Bahía de Caráquez *p350, map p351*
A La Piedra, Circunvalación near Bolívar, T05-2690780, piedraturi@easynet.net.ec Good expensive restaurant, a/c, pool, modern, good service, access to beach, lovely views.
C Italia, Bolívar y Checa, T/F05-2691137. Restaurant, a/c, older but comfortable.
C-D La Herradura, Bolívar e Hidalgo, T05-2690446, F2690265. Restaurant, a/c, cheaper with fan and cold water, older but very well maintained, cheaper rooms are good value.
D Bahía Bed & Breakfast Inn, Ascázubi 322 y Morales, T05-2690146. Includes breakfast, cheaper with shared bath, cold water, older place with renovated common area, basic rooms, discount for Canadians.
D Bahía Hotel, Malecón y Vinueza, T05-2690509, F2693833. Fan, parking, variety of different rooms, those in back are nicer and more quiet. Good value, recommended.
D Centro Vacacional Life, Cecilio Intriago y Muñoz Dávila, T05-2690496. Cooking facilities, parking, fully furnished cottages. Private facilities for company employees, but may rent to public if there is space available.
D Su Descanso en Bahía, Bolívar y Azcázubi, T05-2691213. Cold water, small, simple rooms.
E La Querencia, Malecón 1800, one block from the *terminal terrestre*, T05-2690009. Private bath, cold water, fan, simple, clean and adequate.
E-F Vera, Ante 112 y Montúfar, T05-2691581. Cheaper with shared bath, cold water, very basic but adequate.
F Miriam, Montúfar entre Ascázubi y Riofrío. Shared bath, cold water, very basic but clean.

Chone *p352*
A-B Atahualpa de Oro, Av Atahualpa y Páez, T05-2696627. Includes breakfast, restaurant, a/c, parking, variety of rooms and suites at different prices, clean and very good.
D Chonanas, C Washington entre Atahualpa y Pichincha, T05-2695236. Cold water, a/c, adequate.

C Cabañas Alcatraz, on the road to Canoa, T05-2674566. Cold water, a/c, cheaper with fan, clean pool, older place but still nice.

C-D Monte Mar, on the road to Canoa, T05-2674197, F2674357. Good restaurant, pool, simple cabins for 5.

D Hostal del Mar, Malecón y Juan Montalvo, across from the park, T05-2674778. Cafeteria, nicely furnished modern rooms, very clean and good value, new in 2004.

D Toronto, on the road to Canoa, T05-2674450. Cold water, fan, modern and friendly.

Canoa *p353*

A Hostería Canoa, 1 km south of town, T05-2616380, ecocanoa@mnb.satnet.net Includes breakfast, good restaurant and bar, a/c, pool, sauna, whirlpool, comfortable cabins and rooms.

B País Libre, 3 blocks from the beach, T05-2616387, www.paislibre.net A 'high-rise' by Canoa standards. Includes breakfast, restaurant, disco in high season, cheaper with shared bath, pool, spacious rooms, upper floors have pleasant breeze and good views, surf board rentals. Recommended.

C Sol y Luna, 2 km south of town, T05-2616363. Includes breakfast, restaurant, fan, small pool, large comfortable rooms.

C-E Bambú, on the beach, T05-2616370. Good restaurant including vegetarian options, cheaper with shared bath and in dorm, camping is also possible, fan, variety of rooms and prices. Pleasant location and atmosphere, surfing classes and board rentals. Dutch-Ecuadorean run, very popular and highly recommended.

D Canoa's Inn, in town, just back from the beach, T05-2616371, drmaurotorres@hotmail.com Clean and quiet, new in 2004.

D Coconut Bungalow, on the baech, 1½ km south of town, T09-9251373. Includes breakfast, restaurant and bar, cheaper with shared bath, bright spacious rooms, nice views, bicycle rentals, camping possible. French spoken, reservations advised.

D Posada de Daniel, at back of the village, a couple of blocks from the beach, T05-2616373. An attractive renovated homestead on nice grounds. Fan, pool,

internet (US$2/hr), pleasant cabins with good views, friendly owner can organize tours. Discounts for long stays.

D-E Palmeras Beach, C 30 de Noviembre by the soccer field, T05-2616339. Cheaper with shared bath, simple bamboo cabins amid palm trees, good value.

D-E Shelmar, 1 block from the beach, T09-8644892, shelmar66@hotmail.com Restaurant, cheaper with shared bath, basic but clean, bike rentals, English and French spoken.

Jama *p353*

B Punta Blanca Tent Camp, by Punta Blanca, 17 km north of Jama and 37 km south of Pedernales, T09-9227559, T02-2342763 (Quito). Restaurant, furnished tents 20 m above the beach, nice views.

B Punta Prieta Guest House, by Punta Prieta, 14 km north of Jama and 40 km south of Pedernales, T09-9837056, T02-2862986 (Quito), puntaprieta@yahoo.com Gorgeous setting on a headland high above the ocean with access to pristine beaches. Meals available, comfortable cabins with fridge, balcony with hammocks, nice grounds. A perfect place to get away from it all.

C-D Latitud 7, north of Jama at Km 379 on the highway. Good restaurant serving crêpes, pizza, and a big breakfast. Rooms and cabins in a very tranquil setting, French-run.

D Cabañas Barbudo, 5 blocks from the park. Good restaurant, bamboo cabins with hammocks, clean and good value.

D-E Palo Santo, C Marco Cevallos 4 blocks from centre, by the Río Jama. Restaurant open in season, cabins by the river.

Pedernales *p353*

B Catedral del Mar, Pereira y Malecon, near the beach, T05-2681136. A/c, fridge, parking, spacious and comfortable rooms.

C-D Arena, Eloy Alfaro y Gonzalez Suárez, T05-2681170. Cold water, a/c, cheaper with fan, modern and adequate.

D Albelo, Plaza Acosta y Malecón, near the beach, T05-2681372. Cold water, fan, simple and friendly.

D Cocosolo, on a secluded beach 20 km north of Pedernales, T09-9215078, T05-2681156 (Pedernales). A lovely hideaway set among palm trees. Restaurant, cheaper with shared bath, clean cabins and rooms, camping possibie, horses for hire. French and English spoken.

D Mr John, Plaza Acosta y Malecón, 1 block from the beach, T05-2681107. Cold water, fan, parking, modern and good value. Recommended.

D Playas, Juan Pereira y Manabí, near the air strip, T05-2681125. Cold water, fan, mosquito net, clean and comfortable. There are many other places to stay, including various cheap and basic options.

🍴 Eating

Manta *p347, map p348*
The **Malecón Escénico** has various restaurants, most serve local seafood. The **Parque del Marisco**, at the beach in Tarqui, also has many *comedores* serving cheap seafood, but keep an eye on hygiene.

††† Chavecito, C 106 y Av 106, Tarqui. *Ceviches* and fish.

††† Club Ejecutivo, Av 2 y C 12, top of the Banco del Pichincha building. First-class international food and service, great view.

††† El Marino, Malecón y C 110, Tarqui. Classic fish and seafood restaurant, for *ceviches, sopa marinera* and other delicacies. Recommended.

††† Mamma Rosa, Flavio Reyes y C26. Italian.

††† Martinica, Via Barbasquillo, near Howard Johnson Plaza. Elegant place, varied menu, good food.

††† Palmeira's, Circunvalación y Av 29. Grill and also Italian dishes.

†††-†† American Deli, Centro Comercial Cocco Centro. Sandwiches and meals.

†††-†† Beachcomber, C 20 y Av Flavio Reyes. Set lunch and grill in the evening.

†††-†† Ch'Farina, El Paseo shopping centre. Good pizza.

†† Chifa Macau, Av 15 y C 13. Good Chinese.

†† Delfín, C 8 y Av 24. Inexpensive seafood.

†† El Rincón de Fey, Av Flavio Reyes y C 26. Colombian home cooking.

†† Paraná, Malecón y C 17 near the port. Excellent quality and value set lunch, also grill in the evening. Highly recommended.

†† Rincón Criollo, Av Flavio Reyes y C 20. Regional cooking, set lunch, a/c.

Cafés

Fruta del Tiempo, Malecón y C 13. Fruit salads, sandwiches, snacks.

††† El Tomate, on the road to Crucita and Bahía. Excellent traditional Manabí food, one of the best places to get *comida típica* in the province.

†† El Galpón, C Quito. Very good food and prices, local music at night, very popular.

†† La Carreta, C Olmedo y Alajuela and at Andrés Vera near the terminal. Good food and service.

†† La Fruta Prohibida, C Chile. Fast food, a popular hang-out.

†† Wing Wat, Pacheco y Pedro Gual. Good Chinese.

† La Crema, Central Park. Clean and cheap, serves lunch and dinner.

† Zalita, Primera Transversal entre Duarte y Alajuela, lunch only. Popular.

North of Portoviejo *p350*

†††-†† Alas Delta 2, at the south end of the Malecón in Crucita. Terrace seating with good ocean views. *Conchas asadas* (grilled shellfish) are the speciality. There are many simple restaurants and kiosks serving mainly fish and seafood along the seafront.

Many simple restaurants serve seafood in **San Clemente** and **San Jacinto** .

Bahía de Caráquez *p350, map p351*

†††-†† Muelie Uno, by the pier where canoes leave for San Vicente. Good grill and seafood, lovely setting over the water. Recommended.

†† Brisas del Mar, Hidalgo y Circunvalación. Good *ceviches* and fish.

†† Chifa Lau, Malecón y Ascázubi. Chinese.

†† Columbiu's, Av Bolívar y Ante. Cheap set meals and à la carte, try the *corvina al pimentón* or the dishes *al ajillo*, good service and value. Recommended.

†† El Capitán, Malecón opposite the Hotel Bahía. Chicken and seafood dishes.

†† La Chozita, On the Malecón south of the pier where canoes leave for San Vicente. Barbecue-style food and cheap set lunch.

†† La Terraza, On the Malecón. Varied menu including vegetarian, good.

†† Rincón Manabita, Malecón y Aguilera. Cheap set lunch and good *comida criolla*.

† Doña Luca, Cecilio Intriago y Sergio Plaza, towards the tip of the peninsula. Simple place serving excellent local fare, *ceviches, desayuno manabita* (a wholesome breakfast), and lunches. Recommended.

San Vicente *p353*
Several simple *comedores* in town and
slightly more upmarket fare at the hotels.

Canoa *p353*
♦♦♦-♦♦ **Molle 1**, on the road south to San
Vicente. Grill, seafood, international dishes.
♦♦♦-♦♦ **Sunset Beach**, next to Hotel Bambú.
Pizza.
♦♦-♦ **Comedor Jixsy**, on main street
near the beach. Set meals, fish dishes.
♦♦-♦ **El Torbellino**, 4 blocks from the beach
along the main street. Good for typical
dishes. Set meals and à la carte, popular
with locals, huge servings, lunch only.

Pedernales *p353*
Many simple *comedores* in town as well as
bamboo huts at the beach selling drinks and
playing music, plus several good soda bars
on Eloy Alfaro.

♦ Bars and clubs

Manta *p347, map p348*
Several bars and clubs are clustered on
Av Flavio Reyes.
Black Daddy, Av Flavio Reyes near Krug bar
(above). Disco; Wed-Sat, young crowd.
Grepy, Av 3 y C 12. Bar with snacks, pleasant
atmosphere, soft music.
Krug, Av Flavio Reyes, across from Velboni
supermarket, Tue-Sun. Bar with varied music,
good atmosphere, very nice place.
Santa Fe, Av 22 y Av Flavio Reyes. Disco;
varied music, occasional shows, mature
crowd.

Bahía de Caráquez *p350, map p351*
Arena Bar Pizerría, Av Bolívar y Arenas.
Great pizza, snacks, coffee, drinks, cake
and music.
Gordon Blues, Arenas y Morales, good
music and atmosphere.
Palma Morena, Morales y Ascázubi. Bar,
good soft music and atmosphere.
Insomnio, Av Unidad Nacional y Riofrío,
on the Pacific side. Disco with Latin music,
open on long weekends.

Canoa *p353*
Coco Bar, 1 block from the beach,
disco and bar.

♦ Entertainment

Manta *p347, map p348*
Super Cines, at El Paseo Shopping. Cinema
with films at 1400.

♦ Shopping

Manta *p347, map p348*
There are several shopping centres in town.
El Paseo Shopping, on Av 4 de Noviembre,
the main road entering town from Portoviejo
(buses run there from the beach end of
town), large mall where you can find some
crafts shops, supermarket, restaurants and
everything else.
Manta Shopping, Av Flavio Reyes y C 23,
supermarket, restaurant and other shops.

▲ Activities and tours

Manta *p347, map p348*
Delgado Travel, Av 6 y C 13, T05-2622813,
vtdelgad@hotmail.com   City and regional
tours, run **Hostería San Antonio** (see p354,
whale-watching trips, Parque Nacional
Machalilla.
Metropolitan Touring, Av 4 y C 13,
and at **Hotel Oro Verde**, T05-2623090.
Local, regional and nationwide tours (see
Quito operators, p136).

Bahía de Caráquez *p350, map p*
Tours available to the estuary islands,
wetlands (see Chone p352), environmental
projects in the area, the Chirije archaeological
site, Punta Bellaca dry forest, beaches and
whale watching. See Excursions, p351.

Tour operators
Bahía Dolphin Tours, Av Bolívar 1004
y Riofrío, T05-2692086 Runs tours and
manages the Chirije site.
E Ceibos Tours, Av Bolívar 200 y Checa,
T05-2690801. Runs tours to Isla Corazón.
Guacamayo Bahía Tours, Av Bolívar y Arenas,
T05-2691107, www.riomuchacho.com Runs
tours, rents bikes, sells crafts and is involved
in environmental work in Río Muchacho. Part
of tour fees go to community environmental
programmes. Also has a small office at **La
Posada de Daniel** in Canoa, where you can
be picked up for trips to Rio Muchacho.

⊖ Transport

For main inter-city routes see the bus timetable p52.

Manta *p347, map p348*
Air
Eloy Alfaro airport is east of Tarqui, along the route to Jaramijó, T05-2622590. To **Quito**, 2-4 flights daily with **TAME** and Icaro, US$55.

Airline offices American Airlines, Av 1 y C 12, T05-2622284. **Icaro**, in **Hotel Oro Verde**, T05-2627484. TAME, Malecón y C El Vigía in the centre, T05-2622006.

Bus
The **Terminal Terrestre** is on C 7 y Av 8 in the centre, mind your belongings here. A couple of companies have their own private terminals nearby and run services to their own terminals in Quito. To **Portoviejo**, every 10 mins, US$0.75, 45 mins. To **Jipijapa**, every 20 mins, US$1, 1 hr. To **Pedernales**, 6 daily, US$4.60, 6 hrs. To **Montecristi**, local buses throughout the day from the *Terminal Terrestre*, US$0.30, 15 min; taxis charge up to US$10, negotiable.

Car hire
Budget, Malecón y C 16, T05-2629919. Localiza, Av Flavio Reyes y Av 21, T05-2622434.

Portoviejo *p349*
Air
Service through Manta airport, 30 km away, see above.

Bus The bus station is 1 km south of the centre, on the opposite side of the Río Portoviejo. Take a taxi in the heat, US$1. To **Manta**, US$0.75, 45 mins. To **Bahía de Caráquez**, US$2, 2 hrs. To **Guayaquil**, US$3, 3 hrs. To **Quito**, US$9, 8 hrs.

Crucita *p350*
Buses run along the malecón, there is frequent service to **Portoviejo**, US$1, 45 mins and **Manta**, US$1.50, 1½ hrs.

San Clemente and San Jacinto *p350*
To **Portoviejo**, every 15 mins, US$1.50, 1¼ hrs. To **Bahía de Caráquez**, US$0.50, 30 mins; a few start in San Clemente in the morning, or wait at the highway for a bus.

Bahía de Caráquez *p350, map p351*
Eco-taxi **tricycles** are available for short trips during the daytime, US$0.40.

Air There is an airport at San Vicente across the estuary, but no commercial flights. For charters contact **NICA**, T05-2690332 or **AECA**, T05-2674198.

Boat Motorized canoes (*lanchas* or *pangas*) cross the estuary to San Vicente, from the dock by the Malecón opposite C Ante, by **Muelle 1 Restaurant**. Frequent service 0615-1800, US$0.29; from 1800-2300, larger and slower boats make the crossing when they fill, US$0.35. A **car ferry** runs from a ramp near the obelisk, next to the Repsol gasoline station, at the end of C Ascázubi. It crosses every 20 mins or so, 0630-2000, US$2 for small vehicles, US$0.50 for motorcycles, free for foot passengers. Depending on the tide, the very steep ramps may be difficult for low clearance cars.

Bus The Terminal Terrestre is located at the entrance to town. To **Chone**, *ejecutivo*, US$2, 1½ hrs. To **Portoviejo**, US$2, 2 hrs, every 30 mins. To **Puerto López**, go to Manta, Portoviejo or Jipijapa and change buses. To **Quito**, 2 *ejecutivos* daily at 0900 and 2240, US$9, 6 hrs; plus regular service.

San Vicente *p353*
Boat Motorized canoes and a car ferry cross the estuary to **Bahía**. See Bahía transport above for details.

Bus San Vicente is a local transport hub for points north along the coast, and larger centres inland. Bus companies have offices at the market on the road to San Isidro, take an eco-taxi tricycle to get there. To **Chone**, US$1.50, 1¼ hrs. To **Guayaquil**, US$7, 7 hrs. To **Pedernales**, US$3, 2½ hrs. To **Portoviejo**, US$2.50, 2½ hrs. To **Quito**, with **Reina del Camino**, US$8, 8½ hrs, more service from Bahía, or take a bus to Pedernales and transfer there. For **Esmeraldas** and **northern beaches**, take a bus to Chamanga, at 0810, 1430 or 1700, US$4.50, 3¼ hrs, and transfer.

Canoa *p353*
To **San Vicente**, every 30 mins, 0700-1730, US$0.50, 30 mins; taxi US$5. To **Pedernales**, every hr, 0600-1800, US$2.50, 2 hrs.

To **Santo Domingo** where you can transfer
for Quito, every 15 mins, US$4, 3 hrs. To **Quito**
direct, 4 daily, US$6, 5½ hrs. To **Chamanga**,
US$1.60, 1½ hrs, continuing to **El Salto**, where
you can make a connection for **Muisne**, or
continue to **Esmeraldas**, US$2.50, 2 hrs from
Chamanga. To **San Vicente**, US$3, 2½ hrs. To
Guayaquil, US$9, 10 hrs. To **Cojimies**,
pick-ups leave from the main park, US$1, 45
mins along the beach at low tide.

❶ Directory

Manta *p347, map p348*
Banks Banco del Pichincha, Av 2 y C 11,
2nd floor. Banco del Pacífico, Av 2 y C 13.
Hospitals Clínica Manta, Av 4 de
Noviembre, T05-2921566, is a good private
hospital, open 24 hrs, expensive. Hospital

Rodríguez Zambrano, Vía a San Mateo,
T05-2611849, is a public hospital. **Internet**
US$1.20 per hr. **Language schools**
Academia Sur Pacífico, Av 24 y C 15,
Edificio Barre, 3rd floor, T05-2610838,
www.ecuadorspanishschools.com US$4 per
hr for group lessons, US$6 for one-on-one.
Shipping agents The Ministerio de
Turismo maintains a list of shipping agents,
see Information p347.

Bahía de Caráquez *p350, map p351*
Banks Banco de Guayaquil, Av Bolívar y
Riofrío. Banco del Pichincha, Bolívar y
Ascázubi. **Internet** US$1.60 per hr.

Pedernales *p353*
Banks Several in town including Banco del
Pichincha and Banco del Pacífico.

Esmeraldas Province → *Colour map 2, grid A2*

*Geographically as well as culturally, Esmeraldas is a unique corner of Ecuador. Here the
dry Manabí coastline turns green with palm trees. Inland, the rainforests of Esmeraldas
are part of the Chocó bio-geographic region, shared with neighbouring Colombia. And
most Esmeraldeños are Afro-Ecuadoreans whose ancestors were brought as slaves to
work the cane fields. Their cultural heritage includes marimba music and dance, as well
as a special cuisine which makes extensive use of coconut and plantain. You can explore
little African and Amerindian villages along the northern coast of the province, and the
last remnants of jungle by the Ríos Cayapas and Santiago.*

*Today, there are gold mines in the province, plus tobacco, cacao and cattle ranching.
Shrimp farms have destroyed much of the region's mangroves, and uncontrolled
lumbering is decimating the rainforest in one of the worst ecological catastrophes in
Ecuador. Despite its wealth in natural resources, Esmeraldas is among the poorest
provinces in the country.* ▸▸ *For Sleeping, Eating and other listings, see pages 366-371.*

Ins and outs

There are four flights a week between Esmeraldas and Quito, as well as very good
road connections to the highlands. Two paved roads run from Quito to Esmeraldas via
Santo Domingo de los Colorados and La Independencia, respectively; another
connects San Lorenzo to Ibarra. The coastal road is also fully paved to the Colombian
border, and there is frequent bus service throughout the region.

Health Mosquitoes and malaria are a serious problem throughout the province,
especially in the rainy season (January-May). Take plenty of insect repellent. Most
residenciales provide mosquito nets (*toldos* or *mosquiteros*), be sure to use them.

Mompiche

North of Pedernales the coastal highway veers northeast, going slightly inland, then
crosses into the province of Esmeraldas near **Chamanga** (San José de Chamanga,

population 3,600), a thriving little hub with houses built on stilts on the freshwater estuary. This is a good spot from which to explore the nearby mangroves, there is one basic *pensión* to stay at and frequent buses north and south. Town is 1 km from the highway. Inland, and spanning the provincial border is the **Reserva Ecológica Mache-Chindul**, administered by the **Jatun Sacha Foundation**, see Volunteer opportunities page 84. North of Chamanga is **Portete**, with nice estuary and beach. It is a long walk along an undisturbed beach to **Daule** (popultaion 1,800), where a canoe crosses to Cojimíes. When there are no passengers, you can hire the canoe for a ride in the estuary (US$10 per hour). Beyond Portete and 7 km from the main road along a poor side road is **Mompiche**, one of Ecuador's best surfing spots. Once a few shacks at the end of the beach, this fishing village is undergoing rapid development.

Muisne → *Phone code 06   Colour map 2, grid B1   Population 6,200*

North of Mompiche and inland is **El Salto**, a crossroads with a few *comedores* and the place to wait for a bus connection to Muisne. A road west from El Salto leads to **El Relleno**, from where motorized canoes cross the river to Muisne. There are a few basic hotels in El Relleno (in case you arrive too late to cross) and boat service to other villages in the area.

Muisne is on an island across a narrow stretch of water called the Río Musine. The town is a bit run down and tourism here has seen better days, but it's a friendly relaxed place. About 15 minutes' walk away (or a tricycle ride for US$0.50), is a long expanse of clean beach, which makes for a pleasant stroll at low tide but practically disappears at high tide. The main streets in town are Calle Manabí and Calle Isidro Ayora, which run about 500 m between the Río Muisne and the beach. Behind the church is a tourist information office, friendly and helpful. You can take **Spanish lessons** in Muisne, see **Hotel Marango** page 366.

Between 1987 and 2000, over 97% of the 20,000 ha of mangrove forest in the area was destroyed and replaced by shrimp ponds. There are now reforestation efforts underway by the **Fundación de Defensa Ecológica** which works with local communities; this is a slow and difficult process. Boat trips can be made to see the mangrove reforestation, also trips to the **Reserva Ecológica Mache Chindul** (see above); enquire at the tourist office. On the Río Sucio, inland from Muisne and Cojimíes, is an isolated group of Cayapa Indians, some of whom visit the town on Sunday.

Tonchigüe and Punta Galera

Tonchigüe is a quiet little fishing village with an adequate beach, two hours north from Muisne and 1½ hours southwest of Esmeraldas. There are a couple of simple places to stay, good *comedores* and transportation to Atacames (US$0.70) and Esmeraldas (US$1.50). About 2 km south of Tonchigüe a road goes west and follows the shore to **Punta Galera**; along the way are two very good places to stay, each on its own beach, see page 366. From Punta Galera the road continues south to **Quingüe**, **Estero del Plátano**, **San Francisco** and **Bunche**. This area is off the beaten path and has some natural wonders to offer, including forests and waterfalls. Bunche has a community hall where you might be able to stay. Between June and September, whales are sometimes seen from the shore at Estero del Plátano.

Same → *Phone code 06   Colour map 2, grid A2*

Northeast of Tonchigüe is **Playa de Same**, with a beautiful, long, clean, grey sandy beach lined with palms, safe for swimming. There's little cheap accommodation here; mostly upmarket hotels and high-rise apartments for rich Quiteños, see page 366.

Súa → *Phone code 06 Colour map 2, grid A2 Population 3,100*

Seven kilometres east of Same and 4 km west of Atacames, Súa is a beach resort set in a beautiful bay with pelicans and frigate birds wheeling overhead when the fishing boats land their catch. Except in the high season (July to September when hotel prices rise) it is a very quiet and friendly little place. Between June and September there are **whale-watching excursions** ① *departures 0800-1100, about US$20 per person*, from Súa. The sighting area is to the south of Punta Galera (see above), 40-60 minutes by boat.

Atacames → *Phone code 06 Colour map 2, grid A2 Population 9,800 Altitude sea level*

Four kilometres east of Same and 30 km from Esmeraldas, Atacames is one of the main resorts on the Ecuadorean coast. It can become a real 24-hour party town during the high season (July-September) as well as at weekends and national holidays. The beach is none too clean at these times. The west end of Atacames is a little less noisy than the rest and, for those who appreciate peace and quiet, there are much more tranquil alternatives such as Punta Galera further south (see above). Northeast of Atacames are **Castelnuovo** and **Tonsupa**, two additional resorts with a variety of hotels and clubs behind walls and chain-link fences.

Ins and outs

Orientation and safety Most hotels are on a peninsula between the Río Atacames and the ocean. The main park, most services and the bus stops are to the south of the river.

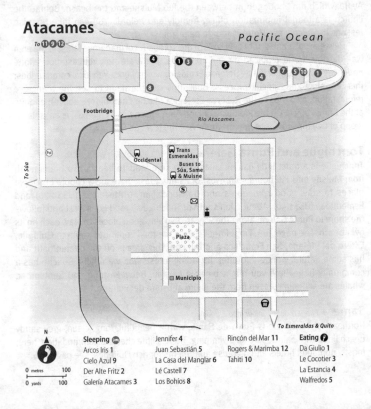

Atacames

Pacific Ocean

Río Atacames

Footbridge

Occidental

Trans Esmeraldas
Buses to Súa, Same & Muisne

Plaza

Municipio

To Súa

To Esmeraldas & Quito

N
0 metres 100
0 yards 100

Sleeping
Arcos Iris **1**
Cielo Azul **9**
Der Alte Fritz **2**
Galería Atacames **3**

Jennifer **4**
Juan Sebastián **5**
La Casa del Manglar **6**
Lé Castell **7**
Los Bohíos **8**

Rincón del Mar **11**
Rogers & Marimba **12**
Tahiti **10**

Eating
Da Giulio **1**
Le Cocotier **3**
La Estancia **4**
Walfredos **5**

Many **assaults** on campers and beach strollers have been reported in recent years. People walking along the beach from Atacames to Súa have been mugged at all hours; never take valuables. Note also that the sea can be very dangerous; there is a powerful undertow and many people have drowned.

The sale of **black coral jewellery** has led to the destruction of much of the offshore reef. Consider the environmental implications before buying.

Sights and trips

The **Museo del Mar** ① *at the east end of the Malecón, daily 1000-2200, US$1,* is an aquarium with an interesting collection of fish, gastropods and other sea creatures. Tours for **fishing** or **whale watching** can be organized from Atacames in season (June-September), see **Hotel Der Alte Fritz** page 367, or ask around.

Esmeraldas → *Phone code 06   Colour map 2, grid A2   Population 95,000*

Esmeraldas is the capital of the province. The city itself has little to recommend it. It is hot, sticky, not too safe and suffers from water shortages. The beaches to the north, though, are quieter and cleaner than those around Atacames and good for swimming. A paved road runs from Esmeraldas north to Borbón and San Lorenzo, with a paved link up to Ibarra in the Northern Highlands. **Ministerio de Turismo** ① *Cañizares entre Bolívar y Sucre, T06-2711370. Mon-Fri 0830-1300, 1400-1700.*

Sights

The area is rich in culture. **La Tolita**, one of the earliest cultures in Ecuador, developed in this region, and the most important archaeological site is at La Tolita Island to the north. This culture's ceramic legacy can be seen at the **Museo del Banco Central** ① *Bolívar y Piedrahita.*

North of Esmeraldas

Rio Verde → *Phone code 06*

There are good beaches for swimming north of Esmeraldas. The polluted water of the Río Esmeraldas reaches no further than **Camarones**, 20 km north of the city, where there are simple places to stay and eat and you can arrange to go out with the fishermen. **Río Verde**, at the outflow of the river of the same name, which was the setting for Moritz Thompson's books on Peace Corps life, *Living Poor* and *Farm on the River of Emeralds*, is a good place to spend a few relaxing days. It's two hours north of Esmeraldas. The beach gets little use and the water temperature is pleasant all year round.

Las Peñas → *Phone code 06*

Beyond Río Verde is **Rocafuerte**, a hot town with no hotels, but recommended as having the best seafood in the province. About 25 km further east, and just 2 km from the paved coastal highway, is **Las Peñas**, once a sleepy seaside village with a nice wide beach. The completion of a paved highway from Ibarra has made Las Peñas the closest beach to any highland capital (only four hours by bus), and it is undergoing rapid haphazard development with generally unattractive results. Ibarreños pack the place on weekends and holidays; it is more tranquil at other times.

La Tola → *Phone code 06   Colour map 2, grid A3   Rural population 4,300*

At the outflow of the Río Cayapas, 122 km north of Esmeraldas (8 km from Las Peñas) is **La Tola**, a hot town, dusty in the dry season, muddy in the wet, the access point for Limones and La Tolita (see below). Here the shoreline changes from the sandy beaches of the south to mangrove swamp in the north. The wildlife is varied and spectacular, especially the birds. East of town is **El Majagual** forest with the tallest mangrove tree in the world (63.7 m): there is a walkway, good birdwatching and many mosquitoes, take repellent. In this area, **Action for Mangrove Reforestation** (ACTMANG), a Japanese NGO, is working with the community of **Olmedo**, just northwest of La Tola, on environmental protection projects. The **Women's Union of Olmedo** runs an ecotourism project; they have accommodation, cheap meals and tours in the area.

To the northeast of La Tola and on an island on the northern shore of the Río Cayapas is **La Tolita**, a small, poor village, where the culture of the same name thrived between 300 BC and AD 700. Many remains have been found here; several burial mounds are still to be explored and looters continue to take out artefacts to sell. Inmense quantities of gold were stolen and the streets are paved with broken pre-Columbian pot shards and lithics. A small site museum was also looted, so replicas have replaced some valuable pieces. Archaeologic studies continue, now at a site further inland. **Note** La Tola in not a pleasant place to stay, women especially may be harassed.

Limones → *Phone code 06 Colour map 2, grid A3 Population 5,300*

Officially called **Valdez**, but generally known as Limones, the town is the focus of traffic downriver from much of northern Esmeraldas Province, where bananas from the Río Santiago are sent to Esmeraldas for export. The Cayapa Indians live up the Río Cayapas and can sometimes be seen in Limones, especially during the crowded weekend market, but they are more frequently seen at Borbón. Limones has two good shops selling the very attractive Cayapa basketry. It is also 'the mosquito and rat capital of Ecuador', a title disputed by Borbón, see below.

There has been a great deal of migration from neighbouring Colombia to the Limones, Borbón and San Lorenzo areas. Smuggling, including drugs, is big business and there are occasional searches by the authorities.

Borbón → *Phone code 06 Colour map 2, grid A3 Rural population 6,200*

On the Río Cayapas, upriver from La Tola and about 110 km along the coastal road from Esmeraldas, is Borbón, a lively, dirty, busy and somewhat dangerous place, with the highest rate of malaria in the country. It is a centre of the timber industry that is destroying the last rainforests of the Ecuadorean coast. Ask for Papá Roncón, the King of Marimba, who, for a beer or two, will put on a one-man show. Chachi handicrafts are sold in town and at the road junction outside town. The local *fiestas* with marimba music and other Afro-Ecuadorean traditions are held the first week of September.

Upriver from Borbón are Cayapa Indian villages and Afro-Ecuadorean communities. On the Río Cayapas, above its confluence with the Río Onzole, is **Santa María**, 2¼ hrs by launch from Borbón (US$5), and nearby the **Chocó Lodge**, see page 368. **Zapallo Grande**, further upriver, is a friendly village with many gardens, where the American missionary Dr Meisenheimer has established a hospital, pharmacy, church and school. There is a ceremonial centre downriver from town, interesting during holidays. There is also an expensive shop. You will see the Cayapa Indians passing in their canoes and in their open longhouses on the shore.

San Miguel, the access point to **Reserva Ecológica Cotacachi-Cayapas**, has a church, a shop (but supplies are cheaper in Borbón) and a few houses beautifully situated on a hill at the confluence of the San Miguel and Cayapas rivers. Borbón to San Miguel, US$10 per person, five hours, none too comfortable but an interesting jungle trip. Trips from San Miguel into the Reserva cost US$100 for a group with a guide. One guide in this area is Don Cristóbal. You can sleep in the basic rangers' hut, take mosquito nets (no running water, no electricity, shared dormitory, cooking facilities, rats), or camp alongside, but beware of chiggers in the grass.

Borbón to San Lorenzo

From Borbón, the coastal road follows the Río Cayapas south, then crosses it and goes east to cross the Río Santiago. Just off the road on the south bank of the Río Santiago is the village of **Maldonado**. This is the access to the **Humedal de Yalare**, a wetland rich in birdlife, located to the north of the river, along the highway (more information on this site from the **Care** office in Borbón). A secondary road goes east of Maldonado, following the south bank of Río Santiago to **Selva Alegre** (with a couple basic *residenciales*). This is the access to **Reserva Playa de Oro**, on the north bank of the Santiago, another good place for birdwatching. The reserve can also be reached by boat from Borbón, but this is much more expensive.

From the Río Santiago the coastal road goes northeast through Yalare, crosses the railway line and, near the town of **Calderón,** meets the Ibarra-San Lorenzo road. The two roads run together northwest towards San Lorenzo for a few kilometres before the coastal road turns north to the town of **Mataje** on the eponymous river, which is the border with Colombia. The road from Ibarra continues to San Lorenzo.

San Lorenzo → *Phone code 06 Colour map 2, grid A4 Population 15,000*

The hot, humid town of San Lorenzo stands on the Bahía del Pailón, which is characterized by a maze of canals. The town was once notable as the disembarkation point of the spectacular train journey from Ibarra, but this has been replaced by a paved road and regular bus service. Fewer travellers visit San Lorenzo these days but it can still be interesting. There's a very different feel to the place owing to a large number of Colombian immigrants, and the people are open and friendly. This is a good place to hear *marimba* music, see the wonderfully sensual dances and learn more about Afro-Ecuadorean culture. There is a local festival in August and groups practise throughout the year, Thursday-Saturday; one is on C Eloy Alfaro, another near the train workshops, ask around. There are also opportunities for trips to the rainforest, mangroves, wetlands and beaches; see excursions below.

Ins and outs

Orientation and safety When arriving in San Lorenzo, you may be hassled by children wanting a tip to show you to a hotel or restaurant. During the rainy season, insect repellent is a must, also make sure your hotel has a good mosquito net. **Note** San Lorenzo is close to the Colombian border. Enquire about public safety before venturing outside town.

Excursions

San Lorenzo is in the Chocó bio-geographic region (see Vegetation and Wildlife, page 475). There are a number of nature reserves, including the **Reserva Ecológica Cayapas-Mataje**, which protects some of the islands in the estuary northwest of town; the lowland section of the **Reserva Ecológica Cotacachi-Cayapas**, inland and upriver along the Río Cayapas (see Borbón above); **Reserva Playa de Oro**, upriver along the Río Santiago (see Borbón above); **Bosque Protector La Chiquita**, north of the junction of the Mataje and Ibarra roads; **Bosque Humedal del Yalare**, a wetland on the road to Esmeraldas (see Borbón above); and **El Majagual** (see La Tola above). There are also some reserves which are home to the last indigenous groups of the Ecuadorean coast, the Awa and the Cayapas or Chachi. Launches can be hired for excurret to San Lorenzo Transport, below

To visit the **Reserva Playa de Oro** ① *enquire with Victor Grueso, Barrio Kennedy near the hospital, T06-2780257 (after 1900), US$40-50 per person per day*. The truly adventurous can take a trip further upriver from Playa de Oro into unspoiled rainforest, where you can see howler and spider monkeys and maybe even jaguar. Mauro Caicedo is the local contact in Playa de Oro. Arrangements can also be made in Cotacachi or Ibarra.

At the seaward end of the bay are several **beaches** which can be reached by canoe. There are no hotels or restaurants, but you can usually arrange for a meal or to stay with a family or in the community hall. On weekends canoes go to the beaches around 0700-0800 and 1400-1500. The cost is about US$3 for the one to two hour ride. **San Pedro** is one hour from San Lorenzo, **Palma Real** is 1¾ hours away towards the border, and there are others. Note that this area is close to the Colombian frontier and it may not be safe. Enquire locally before going.

Frontier with Colombia

The Río Mataje is the border with Colombia. From San Lorenzo, Colombia can be reached by a combination of boat and land transport, arriving eventually at the Colombian port of **Tumaco** (see Transport page 371). Inland, a paved road runs to the Ecuadorean village of **Mataje**, where it ends. There are no immigration facilities at either of the above locations. Given the poor public safety situation and the armed conflict in Colombia, travel in this area is not recommended.

 Sleeping

Mompiche *p360*
A Casablanca, near Mompiche, T02-2252077 (Quito), www.ccasablanca.com Includes breakfast, fan, spacious cabins, expensive restaurant and bar by the beach. Advance booking required, see **Club Casablanca** in Atacames, below.
B-C Iruna, east along the beach, access only at low tide or by launch, T09-9472458. A lovely secluded hideaway, nice gardens, Spanish-run.
C-D Gabeal, 300 m east of town, T09-9969654 . Bamboo construction with nice ocean views, balconies, small rooms. Good restaurant, the owner can arrange visits to his private forest reserve, good for birdwatching.
Simpler places include **Delfín Azul**, cabins, and **Chao Pescao**, in town, popular with surfers.

Muisne *p361*
D-E Playa Paraíso, turn left as you face the sea, then 200 m, T06-2480192. Shared bath, cold water, mosquito nets, basic but clean rooms and cabins, friendly and good value.
E Marango, at the beach, 40 m to the left, T06-2480301, www.marango.org Shared bath, cooking facilities, Spanish lessons US$5 per hour. German-Ecuadorian run.
There are a couple of other basic places to stay.

Tonchigüe and Punta Galera *p361*
A Cumilinche Club, 11 km west of Tonchigüe and 5 km east of Punta Galera, T06-2733258. Expensive restaurant by the beach, comfortable cabins for 4-6 persons, hammocks, popular with family groups.
C-D Playa Escondida, 10 km west of Tonchigüe and 6 km east of Punta Galera, T06-2733106, www.intergate.ca /playaescondida A charming beach hideaway, set in 100 ha stretching back to dry tropical forest and run by Canadian Judith Barett on an ecologically sound basis. Volunteers are welcome for reforestation. Excellent but pricey restaurant, rooms cheaper with shared bath, cold water, accommodation is in nice rustic cabins overlooking a lovely little bay, camping possible. Good swimming and walking along the beach at low tide. The place is completely isolated and wonderfully relaxing. Recommended.

Same *p361*
Booking is advisable at holiday times and weekends. Discounts may be negotiated in low season.
LL Club Casablanca, T02-2252077 (Quito), www.ccasablanca.com A self-contained luxury holiday resort with all facilities, restaurant, pool, also runs a hotel in Mompiche. Advance booking and payment are required through their Quito office.

A El Acantilado, on a hill by the sea, 5 min south of Same, T06-2733466, T02-2453606 (Quito). Pool, rooms and cabins for up to 8 people (minimum 4, no singles or doubles), whale-watching tours in season.

A El Rampiral, at south end of the beach, T06-2733299, T02-2264134 (Quito), rampiral@andinanet.net Restaurant, fan, pool, fridge, parking, comfortable seaside cabins for 4-5, popular with Ecuadorean families, reservations required, may close out of season.

B Cabañas Isla del Sol, at south end of beach, T06-2733470. Restaurant, fan, pool, kitchenette, comfortable cabins.

B-C La Terraza, on the beach, T06-2733320. Good restaurant and pizzeria, fan, nice rooms and cabins for 3-4 with hammocks and large terrace, the newer ones are clean and spacious. Spanish-Italian run.

C Seaflower, on the beach, T06-2733369. Excellent expensive restaurant, fan, mosquito net, simple rooms, German-Chilean run, English spoken.

Súa *p362*

D Buganvillas, ½ block from the Malecón, T06-2731008. Very nice, room 10 has the best views.

D Chagra Ramos, on the beach, T06-2731006. Good restaurant, fan, nice views, friendly, good value but noisy disco in season.

D El Shamán, across from the police station, T06-2731486. Fan, rooms with balconies, Spanish owner, new in 2004.

D Los Jardines, 150 m from the beach, T06-2731181. Cold water, fan, pool, parking, very nice and good value.

E Súa, on the beach. Café-restaurant, fan, 4 rooms, reasonably comfortable.

Atacames *p362, map p362*

There are well over 100 hotels in Atacames, of which we list but a few. A foul smell sometimes emanates from the Río Atacames and can affect all hotels on the river side of the peninsula.

AL Juan Sebastián, towards the east end of the beach, T06-2731049, hjsebastian@hotmail.com Buffet breakfast, restaurant, a/c, pool and spa, fridge, parking, luxurious, popular with wealthy Quiteños.

A Arco Iris, at east end of beach, T06-2731069, F2731437. A/c, pool and jacuzzi, fridge, charming place, very clean, tropical garden, English spoken. Recommended.

A La Marimba, T06-2731321. Includes breakfast, restaurant, a/c, pool, parking, quiet and comfortable, nice gardens.

A Lé Castell, T06-2731476, F2731442. Includes breakfast, restaurant, pool, parking, modern and comfortable.

B Cielo Azul, on the beach near the stadium, T06-2731813, www.hotelcieloazul.com Fan, pool, fridge, new in 2004.

B Marbella, on the beach, T06-2731129. Fan and pool, friendly clean and nice.

B-C Tahiti, T06-2731078. Good restaurant, a/c, cheaper in cabins with fan, pool, parking, mosquito nets provided.

B-D Rogers, west end of the beach, T06-2731041, F2731599. Restaurant and bar, constant water supply, a/c, cheaper with fan, pool, nice and reasonably quiet, good value. Recommended.

C Der Alte Fritz, on the Malecón, T06-2731610, www.deraltefritz-ecuador.com Good breakfast, restaurant serving German and international food, German and English spoken, discounts for longer stays, owner organizes whale-watching and fishing trips.

C Rincón del Mar, on the beach, T06-2760360. Cosy quiet place with lots of palm trees, good location. English, French and German spoken.

D Galería Atacames, on the Malecón, T06-2731149. Restaurant, fan, simple.

D Los Bohíos, 1 block from the beach by the footbridge, T06-2731089. Pool, simple bungalows, good value. Recommended.

E Jennifer, ½ block from the beach on a perpendicular street, T06-2731055, jennifer@andinanet.net Private bath, some cabins have cooking facilities, parking.

E La Casa del Manglar, 150 m from the beach beside the footbridge, T06-2731464. Cheaper with shared bath and without fan, small dark rooms.

Esmeraldas *p363, map p368*

B Apart Hotel Esmeraldas, Libertad 407 y Ramón Tello, T06-2728700, aparthotelesmeraldas@andinanet.net Includes breakfast, good restaurant, casino, a/c, fridge, parking, excellent quality.

Northern Pacific Lowlands Esmeraldas Province Listings

D El Cisne, 10 de Agosto y Olmedo, T06-2723411. Cold water, a/c, parking, friendly and good.

D Galeón, Piedrahita 330 y Olmedo, T06-2723820. Cold water, a/c, cheaper with fan, adequate.

D Zulema 2, Malecón y Rocafuerte, T06-2726757. Cold water, fan, parking, large rooms, modern.

E Diana, Cañizares y Sucre, T06-2724519. Private bath, cold water, fan, small rooms.

Río Verde *p363*

C Hostería Pura Vida, on a stretch of deserted beach just south of Palestina, which is just south of Río Verde, T06-2744203. Excellent restaurant and bar with a wide range of fruit juices, a/c, pool, parking, cabins with balcony and hammocks, also some simpler rooms. All rooms have mosquito nets and are very clean. Recommended: beautiful and peaceful.

D Cabañas Manabitas, in town, 100 m from the beach, T06-2744112. Cabins with thatched roof.

E Hostal Río Verde, in town, 50 m from the beach, T06-2744274. Private bath, fan, adequate rooms.

There are a couple of other *residenciales*.

Las Peñas *p363*

D Cumbres Andinas, at the beach, T06-2786065. Restaurant, rooms with fan. There are various other places to stay and new ones are being built.

La Tola *p363*

D Casa del Manglar, in Olmedo, a 20-min walk or short boat ride from town. The best option in the area. Meals available, shared bath, clean, quiet and pleasant, balcony with hammocks. Organizes tours to El Majual and other spots.

Limones *p364*

D Mauricio Real, by the dock, T06-2789219. Cheaper with shared bath, cold water, fan, basic. There are several other very basic places, but San Lorenzo has much better choices (see below).

Borbón *p364*

A San Miguel Eco Project, in the San Miguel area, upriver from Borbón, Quito office: JL Mera N24-203 y Calama, T02-2528769, www.ecosanmiguel.org   Rustic cabins by the river, price includes 3 meals, transport and guiding. Advance booking advised.

B Chocó Lodge, a few minutes past the village of Santa María, 2¼ hours upriver from

Esmeraldas

To **5** (4 blocks)

Rocafuerte

Av Eloy Alfaro
Av Colón
Av Olmedo
Av Sucre
Bolívar

Aerotaxi
Trans Esmeraldas
Costeñita

10 de Agosto

Parque Central

9 de Octubre

Occidental

TAME

Piedrahita

Museo del Banco Central

Coop del Pacífico

Cañizares

Río Esmeraldas

Isla Piedad

Malecón Maldon

N

0 metres 50
0 yards 50

Sleeping
Apart Hotel Esmeraldas **5**
Diana **1**

El Cisne **2**
Galeón **3**
Zulema 2 **4**

Eating
Chifa Asiático **1**
Las Redes **2**

Borbón, T02-2507245 (Quito). Includes full board, run by the Chachi community of El Encanto, tours and packages available. Part of a tourism project sponsored by **Fundeal**, a Quito-based NGO. Contact well in advance.
D Castillo, near Trans Esmeraldas bus office, T06-2786613. Cold water, fan, parking.
E-F Tolita Pampa de Oro, T06-2786260. Cheaper with shared bath and without fan, mosquito nets, cold water, picturesque setting by the water, clean, helpful, popular.

There are several other basic places to stay, both in town and in the villages upriver.

San Lorenzo *p365*
D Continental, C Imbabura y Ayora, T06-2780125, F2780127. A/c, cheaper with fan, parking, mosquito nets, family-run.
D-E Pampa de Oro, C 26 de Agosto y Tácito Ortiz, T06-2780214. Cold water, cheaper with fan, mosquito net, adequate.
D-E Puerto Azul, C 26 de Agosto near the train station, T06-2780220. A/c, cheaper with fan, adequate.
D-E San Carlos, C Imbabura near the train station, T06-2780240, F2780284. Cheaper with shared bath, cold water, fan, mosquito nets, friendly.

There are several other basic places to stay, make sure your room has a good mosquito net.

🍴 Eating

Mompiche *p360*
There are several good local *comedores* serving fish.

Muisne *p361*
Encocado de cangrejo, crab in coconut sauce, is a local speciality.
🍴🍴 **Las Palmeiras**, near the beach. Good seafood, try their *camarones a la plancha*.
🍴 **El Tiburón**, good quality and value.

Same *p361*
In season there are many *comedores* serving fish along the beach.

Súa *p362*
🍴🍴 **El Caracol**, good seafood, friendly. There are several other simple places to eat at the beach.

Atacames *p362, map p362*
The beach is packed with restaurants and bars, too numerous to list. Most offer seafood at similar prices: cheap set meals and mid-range à la carte. The best and cheapest *ceviche* is found at the stands at the west end of the beach and at the market, but avoid *concha*.
🍴🍴🍴🍴 **La Estancia**, on the Malecón. Very good food, recommended.
🍴🍴🍴 **Da Giulio**, on the Malecón. Spanish and Italian cuisine, good pasta.
🍴🍴🍴 **Marco's**, good steak and fish, popular.
🍴🍴🍴-🍴🍴 **Le Cocotier**, on the Malecón. Very good pizza.
🍴🍴 **El Tiburón**, on the beach. Good seafood.
🍴🍴 **Walfredos**, by the river. Clean and popular.

Esmeraldas *p363, map p368*
🍴🍴🍴 **Chifa Asiatico**, Cañizares y Bolívar. A/c, excellent Chinese and seafood.
🍴🍴🍴-🍴🍴 **La Marimba Internacional**, Libertad y Lavallén. Recommended.
🍴 **Las Redes**, Main Plaza. Set meals and à la carte, friendly.

Las Peñas *p363*
Comedores are set up along the beach selling fish and seafood.

Borbón *p364*
There are many *comedores*, serving fish and other regional dishes. The *panadería* across from the church is good for breakfast.

San Lorenzo *p365*
🍴🍴 **La Conchita**, 10 de Agosto. Excellent fish, recommended. Various other *comedores*.

🍸 Bars and clubs

Atacames *p362, map p362*
There are more little bars at the beach than you can count, **Nagibas Oasis** has been recommended as lively.
Scala, on the Malecón, disco with varied music, admission US$2.

Esmeraldas *p363, map p368*
El Portón, Colón y Piedrahita, peña and disco.
El Guadal de Ña Mencha, 6 de Diciembre y Quito, peña upstairs, marimba at weekends.

Northern Pacific Lowlands Esmeraldas Province Listings

⊙ Shopping

Esmeraldas *p363, map p368*
There is a Cayapa **basket market** across
from the post office, behind the vegetables.
Also 3 doors down, **Tolita** artefacts and
basketry. The **market** near the bus station
is good for buying mosquito nets.
Más por Menos supermarket has a good
selection of imported goods.

⊛ Festivals and events

Borbón *p364*
Sep The local **fiestas** with marimba music
and other Afro-Ecuadorean traditions are
held the first week of Sep.

San Lorenzo *p365*
Aug 6-10 Local Afro-Ecuadorian festival,
marimbas and dancing.

⊝ Transport

For main inter-city routes see the bus
timetable p52.

Mompiche *p360*
Bus to **Esmeraldas**, 3 a day, US$3.50, 3½ hrs.

Muisne *p361*
All buses go from El Relleno, across the
Río Muisne. To **Esmeraldas**, every 30 mins,
US$2.5, 2½ hrs. To **Quito**, 2 direct buses,
both at night. For **Pedernales**, take a bus to
El Salto, US$0.50, 30 mins, on the Esmeraldas
road, from where there are buses going south
to **Chamanga**, US$1.50, 1½ hrs, where you
change for Pedernales, US$1.60, 1½ hrs. At
0600 there is a direct bus Muisne-Chamanga.

Tonchigüe and Punta Galera *p361*
You can take a *ranchera* or bus from
Esmeraldas for Punta Galera, 5 a day, US$2,
2 hrs. A taxi from Atacames costs US$12 and
a pick-up from Tonchigüe US$5.

Same *p361*
To **Atacames**, 15 mins, US$0.35. If coming
into Same, make sure the bus drops you
there and not at **Club Casablanca**. To
Muisne, US$0.60, 30 min.

Atacames *p362, map p362*
A tricycle rickshaw ride costs US$0.50-$1.00.
To **Esmeraldas**, bus every 15 mins, US$0.80,
40 mins. To **Guayaquil**, US$8, 8 hrs. To
Quito, 3 daily, US$8, 6½ hrs.

Esmeraldas *p363, map p368*
Air
General Rivadeneira Airport is near the
town of **Tachina**, on the east shore of the Río
Esmeraldas. A taxi to the city centre (30 km)
costs around US$6. Buses to the *Terminal
Terrestre* from the road outside the airport
pass about every 30 mins. Daily flights
except Wed and Sat to **Quito** with **TAME**
(office at Bolívar y 9 de Octubre,
T06-2726863), 30 mins, US$40 one way.
Check in early as planes may leave 30 mins
before scheduled time. Buses to La Tola,
Borbón, San Lorenzo or Ibarra pass near the
airport so it is not necessary to go into town
if northbound.

Boat
The paved road to **San Lorenzo** and the
Colombian border runs slightly inland. To
reach small villages allong the coast, you can
take a bus to **La Tola** (see above) from where
there are launches to points north.

Bus
To **Quito** and **Guayaquil** there is *servicio
directo* or *ejecutivo*, a better choice as they
are fancier buses, faster, and don't stop on
the side of the road to take passengers.
　　La Costeñita (Malecón y 10 de Agosto) to
La Tola 7 daily, US$3, 3 hrs. To **Borbón**,
frequent service, US$3, 3 hrs. To **San
Lorenzo**, 8 daily, US$4, 4 hrs. To **Muisne**,
every 30 mins, US$2, 2 hrs. To **Súa**, **Same**
and **Atacames**, every 15 mins from
0630-2030, to Atacames US$0.80, 1 hr.

La Tola *p363*
There are buses to **Esmeraldas**, 7 daily,
US$3, 3 hrs. Launches to **Limones** connect
with buses to/from **Esmeraldas**, US$3, 1 hr.

Limones *p364*
There are launches to **La Tola** (see above)
and **San Lorenzo**, 1 hr, US$3. You can also
hire a launch to **Borbón**, a fascinating trip
through mangrove islands, passing hunting
pelicans, approximately US$10 per hr.

Borbón *p364*

To **Esmeraldas**, frequent bus service, US$3, 3 hrs. To **San Lorenzo**, US$1.20, 1 hr. Four motor launches a day run to different communities upriver, leaving 1030-1200. Check how far each one is going as only the first one to leave goes as far as **San Miguel**.

San Lorenzo *p365*
Boat

Two companies that offer boat services are Coopseturi, C Imbabura, T/F06-2780161; and Costeñita, on the same street. The following routes are all subject to change or cancellation, always enquire in advance. To **Limones**, 3 daily, US$3, 2 hrs. To **La Tola**, US$6, 4 hrs. To **Palma Real**, for beaches, 2 daily, US$3, 3 hrs. To **Tumaco** (Colombia), combination boat and land transport, US$15, 3 hrs. Note public safety warnings for this area. You can also hire boats to any destination you please. Price varies according to the size of vessel (4-40 passenger boats are available) and distance covered, US$20-$50 per hr, negotiable.

Bus

Buses leave from the train station or environs. To **Esmeraldas** via **Borbón**, 8 daily, US$4, 3 hrs. To **Ibarra**, 10 daily, US$4, 4 hrs.

Train

The spectacular rail journey up to Ibarra is no more. However, the train still runs once a day to **Cachaví**, serving inland communities that are not on the road; US$1-2 return.

❶ Directory

Muisne *p361*
Banks There are no banks, ask for Marco Velasco's store near the dock, he may change travellers' cheques.

Atacames *p362, map p362*
Banks Banco del Pichincha, 1 block from the plaza. Hotel Der Alte Fritz, changes TCs and Euros. **Internet** US$2.50 per hr. **Laundry** Zum Tucan, 1 block east of the bridge, on the south side , US$1 per kg.

Esmeraldas *p363, map p368*
Banks Banco de Guayaquil, Bolívar y Rocafuerte. Banco del Pichincha, Bolívar y 9 de Octubre.

Western Lowlands

Between the foothills of the Andes and the coast lie the western lowlands, a vast expanse of flat or rolling country, devoted to agriculture. This warm and lush land produces Ecuador's number one agricultural export product, the banana. Other crops include African palm for oil extraction, cocoa, rice, palm hearts and tropical fruits. The region has a few nature reserves protecting remnants of tropical rainforest and wetlands. It is a good area for rafting, taking a dip in one of its many rivers, and observing butterflies or tropical birds. ⇥ *For Sleeping, Eating and other listings, see pages 374-376.*

Ins and outs

This area is laced by roads joining the highlands and coast. Santo Domingo de los Colorados is a major transport hub, and the bus service is good throughout the region.

Quito to Santo Domingo

From **Alóag,** about one hour's drive south of Quito on the Panamericana, a paved toll road goes west to the lowlands. This is the most important link between Quito and Guayaquil and one of the busiest highways in the country. After the pass, it follows the valley of the **Río Pilatón**, and continues past **Tandapi** (rural population 3,100, the official name Manuel Cornejo Astorga is seldom used), 45 km from Alóag. There are a couple basic hotels and many roadside restaurants here. Then comes **Alluriquín** (phone code: 02, rural population: 16,000), in a subtropical valley with several *hosterías*. Various secondary roads branch off before (east of) Alluriquín. From La Palma, an old cobbled road goes to Quito via Chiriboga. From Unión del Toachi, a road follows the Río Toachi south towards Las Pampas and Sigchos (page 212), along this route is **Reserva Otonga** (page 152). Just east of Alluriquín a road goes north to La Florida and San Miguel de los Bancos (page 155).

The drive from Alóag is scenic, sit on the right for the best views going down, but on the left side look for El Poder Brutal, a devil's face complete with horns and fangs, carved into the rock 2½ km west of Tandapi. This road is very busy. It gets a lot of heavy truck traffic and it can be dangerous owing to careless drivers passing on the many curves, especially when foggy and at night. A good paved alternate route from Quito to Santo Domingo goes via Calacalí, San Miguel de los Bancos and La Independencia (see page 150); this sees a lot less traffic. There is also the much smaller road through Chiriboga mentioned above.

The main road to Santo Domingo passes near some forest remnants with many birds, flowers and butterflies. Between Alluriquín and Santo Domingo, is the 100-ha **Tinalandia Reserve**, a great introduction to the world of tropical birds, where more than 360 species have been seen. Many colourful birds are easier to see here than at most other places. There is an unused golf course overlooking the Toachi valley and many trails in the woods behind. The reserve is open to Tinalandia lodge guests; US$10 for day-visitors. For further information, see page374.

Santo Domingo de los Colorados

→ *Phone code 02 Colour map 2, grid C3 Population 200,000 Altitude:500 m*
Santo Domingo de los Colorados, usually refered to as simply 'Santo Domingo', is an important commercial centre 129 km from Quito. The city became Ecuador's main transport hub in the mid 1960s when the road from Quito through Alóag was completed. Since that time it has experienced very rapid growth and many immigrants from Colombia have settled here.

The name *de los Colorados* is a reference to the native Tsáchila men. The Tsáchila nation are known locally as the *Indios Colorados* because of their custom of coating their hair with red vegetable dye, although they do not approve of this name. There are less than 2,000 Tsáchilas left, living in eight communities off the roads leading from Santo Domingo to Quevedo, Chone and Quinindé. Their lands make up a reserve of some 8,000 ha. Today the Tsáchila only wear their native dress on special occasions and they can no longer be seen in traditional garb in the city. At **Complejo Turístico Huapilú**, off the road to Quevedo, there is a **Tsáchila museum** and cultural presentations are performed for tourists. Visits can be arranged with Santo Domingo tour operators, US$22 per person.

Ins and outs
Orientation and safety Santo Domingo is a very important commercial centre for the surrounding palm oil- and banana-producing areas. The city is noisy, streets are prone to flooding after heavy rains, and it has little to offer the tourist except for access to nature reserves nearby. Sunday is market day and therefore many shops in town are only open from Tuesday to Sunday. **Note** Santo Domingo is not safe at night. Take care at all times in the market areas, the walkway along 3 de Julio and in peripheral neighbourhoods.

Excursions

There are several options for rafting, horse riding, fishing and bird/butterfly watching excursions in the Santo Domingo area. With an all-terrain vehicle, the road to Las Pampas, and the old road to Quito via Chiriboga (see Quito to Santo Domingo above), offer access to forested areas. Secondary roads going to San Miguel de los Bancos from Santo Domingo and Alluriquín, as well as the Valle Hermoso area (see Santo Domingo to Esmeraldas below) are also interesting. Tours can be arranged through local tour operators, see page 376. See also Western slopes of Pichincha, page 150, for details of other nature reserves in this area.

Santo Domingo to Esmeraldas

A busy paved highway connects Santo Domingo de los Colorados with Esmeraldas, 185 km to the northwest (see page 363). Some 26 km from Santo Domingo a secondary road branches off northeast to San Miguel de los Bancos (see page 155). Along this road in 2 km you reach the pleasant town of **Valle Hermoso** (phone code 02, rural population 8,400), surrounded by scenic country on the shores of the Río Blanco, with a nice place to stay.

Along the main road to Esmeraldas, 14 km northwest of the turn-off to Valle Hermoso, is the entrance to the private **La Perla Forest Reserve**, rich in birdlife and a nice place for a walk (US$3 entry, T02-2725344). Just north of the reserve and 40 km from Santo Domingo is **La Concordia** (phone code 02, population 34,000), a commercial town sprawling along the sides of the highway. Five kilometres north of La Concordia is the small town of **La Independencia** with a few fruit stalls, and just north of it the junction with the road from San Miguel de Los Bancos, Calacalí and Quito. Along the latter road are a number of reserves and lodges, see page 150.

Quinindé (phone code 06, population 23,000), the official name of which is **Rosa Zárate**, the second largest city in the province of Esmeraldas, is 40 km north of La Independencia. The road deteriorates north of Quinindé.

Near Quinindé is the **Bilsa Reserve and Biological Station**, owned by the Jatun Sacha Foundation. It protects 3,000 ha of very unusual lowland and foothill forest at an altitude of 300-750 m. The forest here contains many bird species virtually impossible to see elsewhere, including the Long-Wattled Umbrellabird and Banded Ground-Cuckoo. From town take a truck to La Y de la Laguna; from there hike three hours to the reserve. Accessibility depends on weather conditions and is easiest July to August; at other times a much longer hike may be required. Accommodation in our C range. Contact **Jatun Sacha Foundation** for visits or volunteer opportunities (see page 84).

To the west of Quinindé is the **Cordillera de Conandé**, a foothills area with forest and several waterfalls. It is accessed throught the villages of Las Golondrinas and Cristóbal Colón. The **Asociación Cristiana de Jóvenes** has a lodge there, T02-3703020 (Quito) and guides are available in Cristóbal Colón, T09-9821049.

Santo Domingo to the Province of Manabí

Another paved road from Santo Domingo to the coast runs west to **El Carmen** (phone code 05, population 33,000), a supply centre with basic accommodation. From El Carmen a paved road goes to **Pedernales** on the coast (see page 353). Continuing southwest of El Carmen is **Chone** (see page 352) where the road to the coast divides, either to **Bahía de Caráquez** (see page 350), or to **Portoviejo** and **Manta** (see page 347).

Santo Domingo to Guayaquil

South from Santo Domingo another highway goes southwest to Quevedo, 1½ hours by bus. At Km 47 (Km 54 from Quevedo) is the **Río Palenque scientific station**, set in one of the last remaining islands of western lowland forest, at an altitude of 200 m. It is a very rich birding area, with 370 species. It has, however, begun to lose some species because of its isolation from other forests. Here is **Río Palenque** ① *accommodation in our A range, US$5 for a day visit; reservations required from Fundación Wong, Guayaquil, T04-2208680 (ext 1431), on site T09-9745790, www.fundacionwong.com*, a lodge with capacity for 20 and with a restaurant.

Quevedo (phone code 05, population 120,000) is set in fertile rice and banana lands and often flooded in the rainy season. It has an important Chinese community. Quevedo is a hot, noisy, crowded and unsafe city which has grown exceptionally rapidly over the last 25 years. Quevedo is connected with Guayaquil by two paved highways: one runs through Balzar and Daule; the other passes through the city of **Babahoyo** (phone code 05, colour map 4, grid B4, population 77,000), capital of the province of Los Ríos. Located in the heart of a rice producing area and surrounded by rivers, it is also prone to flooding. From Babahoyo a scenic road goes to Guaranda in the highlands (see page 224).

Quevedo to Latacunga

The old highway which runs from Quevedo up to Latacunga in the highlands carries very little traffic. It is extremely twisty in parts but it is one of the most beautiful of the routes connecting the highlands with the coast.

La Maná (phone code 03, population 17,300), 39 km from Quevedo, is a pleasant town in a subtropical setting. Between La Maná and Zumbahua, along the **Quilotoa circuit** (see page 211) are the pretty little towns of **El Tingo** (two restaurants and basic lodging) and **Pilaló** (two restaurants and petrol stations). The road is paved from Quevedo to Pilaló and has poor gravel from there to Zumbahua. This is a great downhill bike route from the highlands to the coast.

● Sleeping

Santo Domingo de los Colorados *p372*
There are many hotels along Av 29 de Mayo, which is a busy noisy street, so ask for a room away from the road. Several of the cheaper establishments cater for short-stay customers.
LL Tinalandia, 16 km from Santo Domingo on the way to Alluriquín, on the south side of the road, poorly signposted, look for a large rock painted white, T09-9467741, T02-2449028 (Quito), www.tinalandia.com Includes full board, nice chalets in a cloud forest reserve, excellent meals, golf course, spring-fed pool. Good birdwatching, entry to reserve US$10 for non-residents.
A Grand Hotel Santo Domingo,
Río Toachi y Galápagos, T02-2767947, www.grandhotelsd.com Includes breakfast, restaurant, a/c, pool and spa, parking, modern 3-storey hotel, comfortable rooms.

A Zaracay, Av Quito 1639, 1½ km from the centre, T02-2750316, F2754535. Includes breakfast, restaurant, gardens and swimming pool, parking, casino, noisy disco, good rooms and service. Advance booking advised, especially on weekends.
B Hotel del Toachi, Av Quito Km 1, just west of Zaracay, T/F03-2754688. Pool, parking, spacious rooms.
B Tropical Inn, Av Quito Km 1, just west of Zaracay, T03-2761771, F2761775. Pool, fridge, parking, modern.
D Aracelly, Vía a Quevedo esquina Galápagos, T03-2750334, F2754144. Restaurant, electric shower, parking, large rooms. Also run **Complejo Campestre Santa Rosa**, out of town.
D Diana Real, 29 de Mayo y Loja, T02-2751380, F2754091. Restaurant serves good set meals, there's hot water only at

night, but rooms are comfortable and spacious with fan and fridge.

D Jennifer, 29 de Mayo y Latacunga, T02-2750577. Restaurant, parking, rooms away from the street are quieter, good value.

D Puerta del Sol, 29 de Mayo y Cuenca, T/F02-2750370. Small upscale restaurant, fan, nice rooms, good value.

E Sheraton, on Av Abraham Calazacón opposite the bus terminal, T02-2751988. Private bath, cold water, parking, simple, modern and good value.

Santo Domingo to Esmeraldas *p373*

AL La Cascada, 600 m from the plaza in Valle Hermosa, on the road to Los Bancos, T02-2773193, F2773194. In a 50-ha reserve by a 15-m waterfall, includes breakfast, restaurant, pool and spa, comfortable rooms, horse riding, bike rentals, kayaking, rafting.

B Atos, at southeast end of La Concordia, T02-2725445, www.hotelatos.com Nice restaurant, a/c, fridge, comfortable and very good.

D Sanz, on main street in Quinindé, T06-2736522. Cold water, fan, parking, clean but very noisy.

D Turista, Km 1 Vía a Santo Domingo, Quinindé, 8 blocks south of town, T06-2736784. Fan, parking, on main road but quieter than central hotels.

D-E Los Pinos, opposite the plaza in La Concordia. Cheaper with shared bath, cold water, fan.

Santo Domingo to the Province of Manabí *p373*

There are several basic hotels in **El Carmen** on the noisy main street, and some quieter ones behind the central plaza.

E Puerta de Oro, 4 de Diciembre y Eloy Alfaro, El Carmen, T05-2660274. Cheaper with shared bath, hot water, fan, clean and good.

E San Miguel, next to the church in El Carmen, T05-2660189. Private bath, hot water, fan, adequate.

Santo Domingo to Guayaquil *p374*

All hotels in Quevedo are noisy.

A Olímpico, Bolívar y 19a near stadium, Quevedo, T05-2750455. Restaurant, a/c, huge pool (open to the public for US$2), best hotel and restaurant in town.

B Quevedo, Av 7 de Octubre y C 12, T05-2751875. Good restaurant, a/c and fridge, parking, modern rooms.

C Hotel Cachari, Bolívar 120 y Gen Barona, Babahoyo, T05-2734443, F2731317. Restaurant, a/c, adequate.

C-D Emperador, Gen Barona, Babahoyo, T05-2730535. Includes breakfast, restaurant serves set lunch, a/c, cheaper with fan and cold water, adequate.

D Rancho San Vinicio, 1 km from the centre of Quevedo on the road to La Maná, T05-2753674. A/c, cheaper with fan, pool, quiet rooms.

Quevedo to Latacunga *p374*

C Carlos Patricio, 1 km from La Maná, on the road to Parroquia El Carmen (taxi from town US$1.50), T03-2688002. Electric shower, fan, pool and water park.

C-D Las Pirámides, 2½ km west from La Maná on the way to Quevedo, T03-2688003. Restaurant, a/c, cheaper with fan, pool, accommodation in cabins and pyramids, friendly. Also several basic hotels in town.

● Eating

Santo Domingo de los Colorados *p372*

There are several restaurants on Av Abraham Calazacón across from the bus terminal, also *marisquerías* on Av 29 de Mayo, and chicken places in the Cinco Esquinas area, where Avs Quito and 29 de Mayo meet. Along the roads leading out of town are *paradores* serving meals, where long distance buses stop.

♥♥♥ Parrilladas Che Luis, on the road to Quito. One of the best grills in town.

♥♥♥-♥♥ D'Marco, Circunvalación y Pasaje Zamora. Good steaks and international food.

♥♥♥-♥♥ El Conchal Cavelita, at the corner of C Latacunga. Good *ceviches*.

♥♥♥-♥♥ La Cocina de Consuelo, Av Quito y Chimbo. Very good à la carte dishes and 4-course set meals.

● *For an explanation of the Sleeping and Eating price codes used in this guide, see the*
● *inside front cover. Other relevant information is provided in Essentials, pages 58-64.*

Santo Domingo to Esmeraldas *p373*

♔ **Jean**, 3 blocks south of Quinindé, on the main road. Excellent steaks and seafood, huge portions, good salads, probably the best restaurant for miles around.

Santo Domingo to Guayaquil *p374*

There are several *chifas* in Quevedo, most on Av 7 de Octubre.

♔ **Chifa Sin Log**, 10 de Agosto y Sucre, Babahoyo. Chinese.

♔ **Münich**, Eloy Alfaro y 10 de Agosto, Babahoyo. Local and international food.

⊕ Bars and clubs

Santo Domingo de los Colorados
p372

Faces, Guayaquil, modern music, popular. **Fiber**, Cocaniguas at 5 Esquinas, varied music, mixed crowd.

Note Discos in peripheral neighbourhoods are not safe.

▲ Activities and tours

Santo Domingo de los Colorados *p372*
Tour operators

Turismo Zaracay, 29 de Mayo y Cocaniguas, T02-2750546, zaratur@andinanet.net Runs tours to the Tsáchila commune, rafting, fishing trips, bird/butterfly watching tours.

⊖ Transport

For main inter-city routes see the bus timetable p52.

Santo Domingo de los Colorados
p372

This is a very important transportation centre and you can get buses going everywhere in the country. The *Terminal Terrestre* is on Av Abraham Calazacón, at the north end of town, along the city's bypass. Long-distance buses don't enter the city. A taxi downtown from the bus terminal costs US$1.

To **Quito**, there are two main routes, via Alóag, 3 hrs and via San Miguel de los Bancos, 5 hrs, both scenic. To **Pedernales**, US$4, 3 hrs.

Santo Domingo to Esmeraldas *p373*

To **Valle Hermoso** From the terminal in Santo Domingo, take any bus bound for La Concordia or Quinindé, get off at the turn-off (US$0.50) from where there are taxis to town (US$1.50). From the centre of Santo Domingo, by the Monumento al Colorado, you can get a bus that goes right through Valle Hermoso on its way to San Miguel de los Bancos, but these take longer. There are buses from **Quinindé** to **Santo Domingo**, US$1.50, 1½ hrs, and to **Esmeraldas**, US$1.50, 1½ hrs.

Santo Domingo to Guayaquil *p374*

The *Terminal Terrestre* in **Quevedo** is along a city bypass (*variante*), near the road to Santo Domingo. There are buses from here to **Quito**, US$5, 5 hrs; to **Santo Domingo**, US$2, 2 hrs; to **Latacunga**, via La Maná and Zumbahua, US$4, 5 hrs; to **Guayaquil**, via Babahoyo, US$3, 3½ hrs, and to **Manta**, US$6, 4½ hrs.

From **Babahoyo** there are buses to **Santo Domingo**, US$4, 4 hrs, and **Guayaquil**, US$1, 1 hrs.

Santo Domingo to the Province of Manabí *p373*

From **El Carmen** there are buses to **Santo Domingo**, US$0.80, 40 mins; **Pedernales**, US$3.20, 2½ hrs; **Bahía de Caráquez**, US$4.20, 4 hrs, and **Manta**, US$5, 5½ hrs.

Quevedo to Latacunga *p374*

From **La Maná** there are buses to **Quevedo**, US$0.80, 1 hr; to **Zumbahua**, US$2, 2 hrs; to **Latacunga**, US$3.20, 4 hrs.

⊕ Directory

Santo Domingo de los Colorados *p372*
Banks Banco de Guayaquil, Av Quito y Calazacón. Produbanco, Av Quito 1246 y Chorrera de Napa. **Internet** Many in the centre, US$0.50-0.80 per hour. **Post office** Av de los Tsáchilas y Río Baba, 0800-1830.

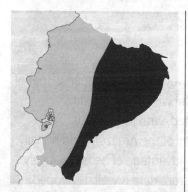

Introduction

East of the Andes the hills fall away to the vast green carpet of Amazonia. Some of this beautiful wilderness remains unspoiled and sparsely populated, with indigenous settlements along the tributaries of the Amazon. Additionally, the Ecuadorean jungle has the advantage of being relatively accessible and tourist infrastructure here is well developed.

Most tourists love the exotic feeling of El Oriente, and El Oriente needs tourists. Large tracts of jungle are under threat; colonists are clearing many areas for agriculture, while others are laid waste by petroleum exploration or gold mining. The region's irreplaceable biodiversity and unique traditional ways of life can only be protected if sustainable ecotourism provides a viable economic alternative.

The eastern foothills of the Andes, where the jungle begins, offer the easiest access and a good introduction to the rainforest for those with limited time or money. Further east lie the remaining large tracts of primary rainforest, teeming with life, which can be visited from several excellent (and generally expensive) jungle lodges. Southern Oriente is as yet less developed, for tourism as well as other activities. Precisely for this reason, it offers unique opportunities and demands extraordinary respect.

★ Don't miss...

1 **Ecotourism in the forest** Keep in harmony with the wilds of Ecuador with a visit to Oriente's jungle lodges and reserves, page 380.

2 **San Rafael Falls** See these stunning falls northeast of Baeza, page 385.

3 **Whitewater rafting** Take the plunge for an adrenaline surge from Tena, page 387.

4 **Misahuallí** See the 'near oriente' from this small port, page 388.

5 **Southern Oriente** Explore this undeveloped area from Macas or Zamora, page 405.

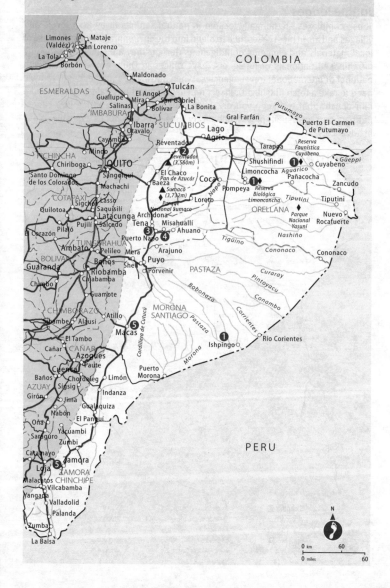

Oriente Jungle

Ecotourism in the Oriente

The Northern Oriente offers an extensive variety of ecotourism services and programmes, which can be divided into three basic types: lodges, guided tours, and indigenous ecotourism. A fourth option would be independent jungle travel without a guide, but this is not advisable for reasons given below. The Southern Oriente, comprising the provinces of Morona-Santiago and Zamora-Chinchipe, is less developed and lacks the same level of tourist infrastructure, but nonetheless offers a few very interesting and worthwhile opportunities.

Jungle lodges

These complexes are normally located in natural settings away from towns and villages and are in most cases built to blend into the environment through the use of local materials and elements of indigenous design. They are generally owned by urban-based nationals or foreigners, have offices in Quito and often deal with national or international travel agencies. When staying at a jungle lodge, you will need to take a torch (flashlight), insect repellent, protection against the sun and a rain poncho that will keep you dry when walking and when sitting in a canoe. Rubber boots are usually provided, but very large sizes may not be available so ask in advance.

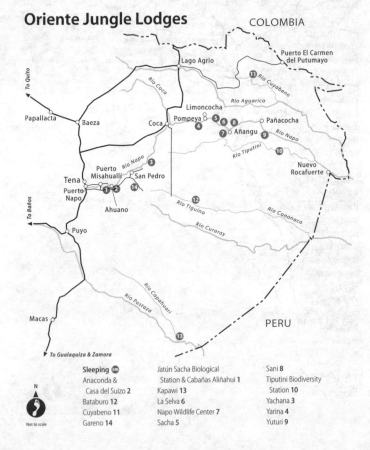

Oriente Jungle Lodges

Sleeping		
Anaconda &	Jatún Sacha Biological	Sani **8**
Casa del Suizo **2**	Station & Cabañas Aliñahui **1**	Tiputini Biodiversity
Bataburo **12**	Kapawi **13**	Station **10**
Cuyabeno **11**	La Selva **6**	Yachana **3**
Gareno **14**	Napo Wildlife Center **7**	Yarina **3**
	Sacha **5**	Yuturi **9**

N

Not to scale

Experiencing the jungle in this way usually involves the purchase of an all-inclusive package in Quito or abroad, quick and convenient transport to the lodge, a comfortable stay at the lodge and a leisurely programme of activities suited to special interests. Getting to the lodge may involve a long canoe ride, with a longer return journey upstream to the airport, perhaps with a pre-dawn start. Standards of services are generally high and most lodges claim a high degree of environmental awareness, have made arrangements with neighbouring indigenous communities and rely on well-qualified personnel. Their contribution to local employment and the local economy varies.

Guided tours

Guided tours of varying length are offered by tour operators, river cruise companies and independent guides. These should, in principle, be licensed by the Ministerio de Turismo. Tour companies and guides are mainly concentrated in Quito, Baños, Puyo, Tena, Misahuallí, Coca and Lago Agrio – and to a lesser extent in Macas and Zamora – where travellers tend to congregate to form or join groups and arrange a jungle tour, usually of between one and seven days. In these towns there is always a sufficient number of guides offering a range of tours to suit most needs, but there may be a shortage of tourists for group travel outside the months of July and August.

Since the cost of a tour largely depends on group size, the more budget-conscious travellers may find that in the off-season it will take several days to assemble a reasonably sized group. In order to avoid such delays, it may be easier to form a group in Quito or Baños, before heading for the Oriente. At the same time, the lack of tourists in the off-season can give you more bargaining power in negotiating a price.

When shopping around for a guided tour ensure that the guide or agency specifies the details of the programme, the services to be provided and whether park fees and payments to indigenous communities are involved. Be especially wary of cheaper tour agencies and independent guides, some are excellent but we have also received negative reports. Try to get a personal recommendation from a previous customer. Serious breaches of contract can be reported to the Ministerio de Turismo, but you should be reasonable about minor details. Most guided tours involve sleeping in simple cabañas or camping shelters (open-sided raised platforms) which the guides own or rent. On trips to more remote areas, camping in tents or sleeping under plastic sheets is common.

Indigenous ecotourism

A number of indigenous communities and families offer ecotourism programmes in their territories. These are either community-controlled and operated, or organized as joint ventures between the indigenous community or family and a non-indigenous partner. These programmes usually involve guides who are licensed as *guías natívos* with the right to guide within their communities. Accommodation is typically in simple native shelters of varying quality. Local food may be quite good, but keep an eye on hygiene. A growing number of independent indigenous guides are working out of Puyo, Tena, Macas, Coca and Misahuallí, offering tours to their home communities. You should be prepared to be more self-sufficient on such a trip than on a visit to a jungle lodge or a tour with a high-end operator. Bring rubber boots, a light sleeping bag, rain jacket, trousers (not only shorts), binoculars, torch (flashlight), insect repellent, sunscreen and hat, water-purifying tablets, and a first aid kit. Wrap everything in several layers of plastic bags to keep it dry.

Tours without a guide

Though it may seem attractive from a financial point of view, this is not recommended for several reasons. Some native groups prohibit the entry of outsiders to their territory, navigation in the jungle is difficult, and there are a variety of dangerous animals. Additionally, public safety is a concern north of the Río Napo, especially along the Colombian border. For your own safety as well as to be a responsible tourist, the Oriente is not a place to wander off on your own.

Choosing a rainforest

A tropical rainforest is one of the most exciting things to see in Ecuador, but it isn't easy to find a good one. The key is to have realistic expectations and choose accordingly. Think carefully about your interests. If you simply want to relax in nature and see some interesting plants, insects, small birds and mammals, you have many choices, including some that are quite economical and/or easily accessible. If you want to experience something of the cultures of rainforest people, you must go farther. If you want the full experience, with large mammals and birds, you will have to go farther still and spend more, because large creatures have been hunted or driven out around settled areas.

A visit to a rainforest is not like a visit to the Galápagos. The diversity of life in a good rainforest far exceeds that of the Galapagos, but creatures don't sit around and let themselves be seen. Even in the best forests, your experiences will be unpredictable – none of this 'today is Wednesday, time to see sea lions'. A rainforest trip is a real adventure; the only guarantee is that the surprises will be genuine, and hence all the more unforgettable.

There are things that can increase the odds of really special surprises. One of the most important is the presence of a canopy tower. Even the most colourful rainforest birds are mere specks up in the branches against a glaring sky, unless you are above them looking down. Towers add an important dimension to bird and mammal watching. A good guide is another necessity. Avoid guides (and lodges) that emphasize medicinal plants over everything else. This usually means that there isn't anything else around to show. If you are interested in exploring indigenous cultures, give preference to a guide from the same ethnic group as the village you will visit.

If you want to see real wilderness, with big birds and mammals, you generally can't go to any lodges you can drive to (an exception at the moment is **Gareno Lodge**). Expect to travel at least a couple of hours in a motorized canoe. Don't stay near villages even if they are in the middle of nowhere. In remote villages people hunt a lot, and animals will be scarce. Indigenous villages are no different in this regard; most indigenous groups (except for a very few, such as certain Cofán villages that now specialize in eco-tourism) are ruthlessly efficient hunters.

The newest and least well established lodges offer the best values. An economic alternative to a lodge is a canoe camping trip on a remote river like the Cononaco. These trips are also a good way to experience real jungle cultures. Another economic alternative to the fancy jungle lodges are the community-based lodges run by local people. An added advantage of these lodges is that your money goes straight to the community, providing an economic incentive for conservation.

Responsible jungle tourism

Some guides or their boatmen will try to hunt meat for your dinner – don't let them, and report such practices to other tourists and to guidebooks. Don't buy anything made with animal or bird parts. Avoid making a pest of yourself in indigenous villages; don't take photographs or videos without permission, and don't insist. Many native people believe that photographs can steal one's soul. In short, try to minimize your impact on the forest and its people. Also remember when choosing a guide that the cheapest is not the best. What happens is that guides undercut each other and offer services that are unsafe or harm local communities and the environment. Do not encourage this practice.

Orellana's River

The legends of the Incas fuelled the greed and ambition of the Spanish invaders, dreaming of untold riches buried deep in the Amazon jungle. The most famous and enduring of these was the legend of El Dorado, which inspired a spate of ill-fated expeditions deep into this mysterious and inhospitable world.

Francisco Pizarro, conqueror of the Incas, had appointed his younger brother, Gonzalo, as governor of Quito. Lured by tales of fresh lands to be conquered to the east, and riches in cinnamon and gold, an expedition under the command of Gonzalo Pizarro left Quito at the end of February 1541. It was made up of 220 Spanish soldiers, 4,000 Indian slaves, 150 horses and 900 dogs, as well as a great many llamas and other livestock. They headed across the Andes not far from Papallacta and down through the cloud forest until they reached a place they called Zumaco. Here Pizarro was joined by Francisco de Orellana, founder of Guayaquil, accompanied by 23 more conquistadores who had left Quito a few weeks after the main expedition.

After proceeding to the shores of the Río Coca, the Spaniards began to run out of food and built a small ship, the *San Pedro*. Rumours that they would find food once they reached the Río Napo led Pizarro to dispatch Orellana and his men to look for this river and bring back provisions. Orellana and his party sailed down river in the *San Pedro* but found nothing for many days, and claimed they could not return against the current. Pizarro, for his part, was convinced that he had been betrayed and abandoned by Orellana.

On February 12, 1542, Orellana reached the confluence of the Napo and the Amazon – so called by him because he said he had been attacked by the legendary women warriors of the same name. Another name for the mighty new river, but one which never caught on, was *El Río de Orellana*.

On August 26, 1542, 559 days after he had left Guayaquil, Orellana and his men arrived at the mouth of the Amazon, having become the first Europeans to cross the breadth of South America and follow the world's greatest river from the Andes to the Atlantic. Totally lost, they then followed the coastline north and managed to reach the port of Cubagua in Venezuela. In the meantime, Gonzalo Pizarro had suffered enormous losses and limped back to Quito at about the same time, with only 80 starving survivors.

Orellana returned to Spain and, with great difficulty, organized a second expedition which sailed up the Amazon in 1544 only to meet with disaster. Three of his four vessels were shipwrecked and many of the survivors, including Orellana himself, died of fever.

Dominican friar Gaspar de Carvajal, who accompanied Orellana on his first voyage, penned a 31-page chronicle of this odyssey. Carvajal's manuscript survives to this day and the story has been re-told countless times. Orellana is a national hero in Ecuador and his journey is a pillar of the country's assertion that it "is, was, and will be" an Amazonian nation. Some 200 years later, a less famous but no less valiant Ecuadorean named Isabela Godin travelled from Riobamba to the mouth of the Amazon under even harsher conditions than Orellana.

See books, page 482, for further reading on the historic voyages and legendary tales of both Orellana and Isabela Godin.

Ins and outs

Getting there
There are scheduled commercial flights from Quito to Lago Agrio, Coca and Macas. From Quito, Macas and Shell, light aircraft can also be chartered to any jungle village with a landing strip. Much of western Oriente is also accessible by roads which wind their way down from the highlands. Baños to Puyo and Loja to Zamora are fully paved, and Quito to Tena is in reasonable shape. The remainder are mostly narrow and tortuous, subject to landslides in the rainy season. Nonetheless, all have regular if rough bus service. Most of these roads can also be attempted in an ordinary car with good ground clearance, but a four-wheel-drive is an asset. Deeper into the rainforest, motorized canoes provide the only alternative to air travel.

Public safety
There are frequent military checkpoints in the Oriente, so always have your passport handy. Oriente is also affected by ongoing armed conflict in neighbouring Colombia.

‡ Do not venture along the Colombian border, and enquire before visiting remote areas north of the Río Napo.

Caution is particularly required throughout the province of Succumbíos. Always enquire about public safety before visiting remote sites north of the Río Napo, and avoid all areas immediately adjacent to the Colombian border. At the same time, it is worth remembering that the Ecuadorean Amazon has traditionally been safe and tranquil, and the very few incidents which have taken place mostly involved foreign oil workers rather than tourists.

Health
A yellow fever vaccination is required. Anti-malaria tablets are recommended and be sure to take an effective insect repellent. A mosquito net may be helpful if you are travelling independently.

Foothills

The eastern foothills of the Andes are the western boundary of Oriente. Here, where the jungle meets the mountains, are Tena and Puyo, capitals of the provinces of Napo and Pastaza, respectively. Much of the surrounding countryside has been turned into pastureland and primary rainforest is scarce, but this area is nonetheless of interest to visitors. There is convenient road access from highland tourist centres such as Quito and Baños, and enough forest fragments remain to offer an introduction for those tight on time or money. Among the region's many attractions: Baeza is the gateway to Cascada San Rafael, Ecuador's largest waterfall; whitewater rafting and ethnotourism flourish around Tena; Misahuallí provides access to the upper Río Napo; and Puyo is surrounded by several small private nature reserves. ▸▸ For Sleeping, Eating and other listings, see pages 389-395.

Quito to Lago Agrio

Quito to Baeza
The most northerly route into the Oriente is from Tulcán to Lago Agrio via La Bonita. This new road was completed in 2003 but the area is close to the Colombian border and suffers from serious public safety problems. Next to the south, much safer and more frequently travelled, is the road from Quito to Baeza. It crosses the Eastern

Cordillera at the pass of Guamaní (usually called La Virgen), just north of the volcano **Antisana** (5,705 m), and then descends via the small village of **Papallacta** to the old mission settlement of **Baeza**. The road is paved and in very good condition until 5 km before Papallacta, with plans to eventually pave all the way from Quito to Tena. The trip between the pass and Baeza has beautiful views of the heavily glaciated slopes of **Antisana** (clouds permitting), high waterfalls, *páramo* and a lake contained by an old lava flow.

This is a colonist dairy-farming region with little indigenous presence, surrounded by the **Cayambe-Coca**, **Antisana** and **Sumaco-Galeras Nature Reserves**. The mountain landscape and high rainfall have created many spectacular waterfalls, pristine rivers and dense vegetation. Because of the climate, *ceja de montaña* (cloud forest), orchids and bromeliads abound. The numerous hiking trails make this ideal territory for trekking, and for fishing enthusiasts, the lakes and rivers have trout. For interesting hiking, fishing, great thermal baths, and accommodation in this area see page 147.

Baeza → *Phone code 06 Colour map 3, grid B1 Population 1,200 Altitude 1,800m*

This is a small town in the beautiful setting of the Quijos pass. The town is about 1 km from the main junction of the Lago Agrio and Tena roads. You need to get off the Lago Agrio bus at the police checkpoint and walk up the hill, but the Tena bus goes through the town. The town of Baeza is divided in two: **Baeza Colonial** (Old Baeza) and **Andalucía** (New Baeza). The old settlement, however, is dying as people have moved to the new town, 1 km down the road towards Tena, where the post office and Andinatel are located. Regular buses to Tena can be caught outside the **Hostal San Rafael**; two hours. Buses to Quito stop at the bus stop just below the **Hotel Jumandí** in the old town. There are many hiking trails in this region which generally can be done without a guide. A recommended source for maps and route descriptions is *The Ecotourist's Guide to the Ecuadorian Amazon*, by Rolf Wesche, which is available in Quito, or in the **Hostal San Rafael**.

Baeza to Lago Agrio ↠ *see also Lago Agrio, page 396*

At Baeza the road divides. One branch heads northeast to Lago Agrio, following the Río Quijos past the villages of **Borja**, a few kilometres from Baeza, and **El Chaco** (cabins on the edge of town and excellent food at the restaurant on the road) to the slopes of **Volcán Reventador**. At the village of Reventador there are a couple of basic places to eat, and a decent new *hostal*.

Volcán Reventador (3,560 m) is an active volcano which lies on the edge of the **Reserva Ecológica Cayambe-Coca**, poking up from the Oriente rainforest. A sudden eruption in 2002 produced pyroclastic flows and a 20-km high cloud which covered Quito in ash. There have been smaller eruptions since and at the close of this edition (Spring 2005) the area was not safe for climbing or trekking. Those who are determined to visit should consult the **National Geophysics Institute** ⓘ *www.igepn.edu.ec*, and also make detailed local enquiries before approaching the volcano.

The road to Lago Agrio winds along the north side of the Río Quijos, past the **San Rafael Falls**. To get to them take a Quito-Baeza-Lago Agrio bus. About two to three hours past Baeza (500 m before the bridge crossing the Río Reventador), look for a covered bus stop and a disused construction camp.

It's an easy 1½-hour round trip through cloud forest to the thundering cascade. At the ridge overlooking the falls is a small cross commemorating the death of a Canadian photographer who got too close to the edge. A steep and slippery trail leads down to the bottom of the falls but enquire locally before attempting it. Birds can be spotted along the trail, including Cock-of-the-Rock, and there are swimming holes and waterfalls near the *hostería*, making this a worthwhile stopover on the way to or from Coca (page 398) or Lago Agrio (page 396).

‡ *The falls are an impressive 145 m tall, believed to be the highest in Ecuador.*

Oriente Jungle Foothills

Baeza to Tena

The other branch of the road from Baeza heads south to Tena, with a branch off this road going to Coca via Loreto (see below). The route from Baeza to Tena passes near several important lodges, reserves and national parks. See listings, page 390, for details of places that offer accommodation. **Yanayacu** is a biological station in this area, run by Harold Greeney, intended as a base for students studying the cloud forest. Contact Harold at yanayacu@hotmail.com

About 20 minutes towards Tena from Cosanga is the **Guacamayos Ridge**, part of the Reserva Ecológica Antisana. There is a good stone path at the antennae (just before the shrine on the right side of the road), which enters one of the wettest and most interesting cloud forests in the area. Many rare birds and plants are found here, including several orchids found nowhere else in the world. On a clear day there is a view of the vast Oriente spread out below. The **Guacamayos trail** is described in *Trekking in Ecuador* (see page 482).

Much of the Baeza-Tena road southeast of the Guacamayos antennae is flanked by very good forest, making this stretch ideal for birdwatching. Further south is the Hollín-Loreto road which branches off the Baeza-Tena road near Narupa and goes on to Coca. The upper half of this road is famous for exciting and colourful birds, butterflies and plants. Even such rare birds as military macaws can sometimes be seen from there. It is worth going at least as far as the beautiful gorge of the Río Hollín but a car is necessary, as buses are scarce.

Archidona → *Phone code 06 Colour map 3, grid C1 Population 4,200 Altitude 500m*

Archidona, 65 km from Baeza, was founded in 1560 at the same time as Tena, 10 km further south. Once an important mission and trading centre, Archidona is now something of a backwater, but with several pleasant rural hotels and reserves nearby. The small painted church is striking and is said to be a replica of one in Italy (possibly in Siena).

Around Archidona

The road leaving Archidona's plaza to the east goes to the village of **San Pablo**, and beyond to the Río Hollín. Along this road, 7 km from Archidona, is the **Reserva Ecológica Monteverde** ① *Day visits cost US$2 and they can arrange pick up from Archidona for an extra charge. Reservations are necessary, contact Residencial Regina (see Archidona Sleeping, page 393) or Quito T02-2891041*, a 25-ha reserve with primary and secondary forest, and medicinal plants. There are walking trails, river bathing, fishing, cultural presentations for groups, and five cabins with bath and cold water (C per person with full board, minimum 10 people).

Along the same road, 15 km from Archidona, is **Reserva El Para**, an 80-ha forest reserve with many rare birds. It is owned by **Orchid Paradise** (see Archidona Sleeping, page 393), who run tours to the reserve and other attractions, US$5 per person.

Tours can be arranged to the **Izu Mangallpa Urcu (IMU) Foundation** ① *Contact Elias Mamallacta in Archidona, T06-2889553, www.izu-mangallpa-urcu. freehomepage.com*, 3 km east of Archidona off a side turning down the road to San Pablo, set up by the Mamallacta family to protect territory on Galeras mountain. They charge US$35 per day for accommodation (private rooms, mosquito nets) and guiding, minimum two people. It is tough going but the forest is wonderful.

Just outside Archidona, to the south, a small turning leads to the river. About 200 m along there is a large rock with many **petroglyphs** carved on its surface. There are quite a few others within a 30-km radius of Archidona, but most are very difficult to find. These pre-Columbian petroglyphs are unique to this area. The symbols are no longer understood by the local Quichua people.

Some 75 km south of Baeza, and 10 km south of Archidona, is Tena, the capital of Napo Province. Once one of the important early colonial missionary and trading posts of the Amazon, it is now a relaxed and friendly town on a hill above the confluence of the Ríos Tena and Pano. In recent years, it has become an important centre for whitewater rafting and ethnotourism.

Ins and outs The road from the north passes the airstrip and market and heads through the town centre as Avenida 15 de Noviembre on its way to the bus station, nearly 1 km south of the river. Tena is quite spread out. There is a pedestrian bridge and a vehicle bridge which link the two halves of the town. **Tourist Information Offices** ①
García Moreno between Calderón and JL Mera, near the river, T06-2886536, Mon-Fri 0800-1230, 1330-1700, several jurisdictions all under one roof.

Excursions from Tena

The **Jumnadí caves** ① *T06-2889185, daily 0900-1700, US$2,* are located 15 km north of Tena, 5 km north of Archidona. The main cave has electric lights (take a torch anyway), and a recreation complex with pools and waterslides has been built at the entrance. It gets crowded at weekends.

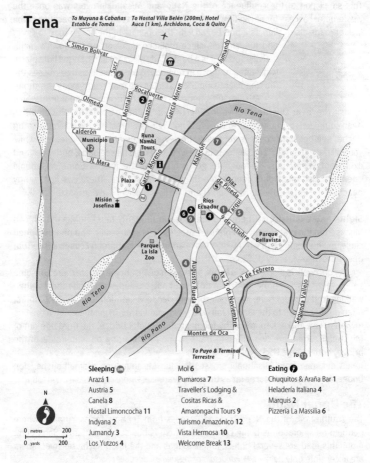

Tena

To Muyuna & Cabañas
Establo de Tomás
To Hostal Villa Belén (200m), Hotel
Auca (1 km), Archidona, Coca & Quito

Oriente Jungle Foothills

Sleeping ⬤	Mol 6	Eating ⬤
Arazá 1	Pumarosa 7	Chuquitos & Araña Bar 1
Austria 5	Traveller's Lodging &	Heladería Italiana 4
Canela 8	Cositas Ricas &	Marquis 2
Hostal Limoncocha 11	Amarongachi Tours 9	Pizzería La Massilia 6
Indyana 2	Turismo Amazónico 12	
Jumandy 3	Vista Hermosa 10	
Los Yutzos 4	Welcome Break 13	

Comunidad Capirona ⓘ *Contact the Red Indígena de las Comunidades del Alto Napo para la Convivencia Intercultural y El Ecoturismo (Ricancie), 15 de Noviembre 722, T/F06-2887072, http://ricancie.nativeweb.org*, is one hour by bus, then three hours on foot from Tena. Visits can be arranged here or to nine other communities in the area. This is part of a highly regarded project which combines eco/ethnotourism and community development. There are also opportunities for volunteers. Various other excursions can be arranged through local hotels and tour operators, see page 394.

Tena to Misahuallí

From Tena the main highway runs south towards Puyo (curiously, only the northbound lane is paved). **Puerto Napo** is a small town a few kilometres south of Tena, with a suspension bridge across the Río Napo. On the north bank a road runs east to Misahuallí, about 17 km downstream. From Puerto Napo you can catch a local bus from Tena to Misahuallí. If you are travelling north from Puyo to Misahuallí, you can avoid going into Tena by getting off the bus here.

Misahuallí → *Phone code 06 Colour map 3, grid C2 Population 4,400 Altitude 400m*

This small port at the confluence of the Napo and Misahuallí rivers was once the westernmost access for navigation on the Río Napo and very important because of the lack of roads. Its decline as a port began with the opening of the Loreto road to Coca, and tourism has since replaced transport as the town's major activity. Today, it is a particularly pleasant and tranquil little place, well suited to those in no hurry. A suspension bridge crosses the Río Napo at Misahuallí and joins the road south along the shore.

> ❢ A local curiosity is the troop of mischievous capuchin monkeys who live in the park.

Misahuallí is perhaps the best place in Ecuador from which to visit **the 'near Oriente'**, but your expectations should be realistic. The area has been colonized for many years and there is no virgin rainforest nearby (except at Jatun Sacha, see below). Access is very easy, however, prices are reasonable, and while you will not encounter large animals in the wild, you can still see birds, butterflies and exuberant vegetation – enough to get a taste for the jungle. Some Misahuallí operators also offer tours deeper into the jungle, past Coca. There is a fine, sandy beach on the Río Misahuallí, but don't camp on it as the river can rise unexpectedly.

Sights and excursions There is a **mariposario** (butterfly farm) in Misahuallí, two blocks from the plaza. Several colourful species can be observed and photographed close up. Interesting and worthwhile. Make arrangements through **Ecoselva** (see Tour operators below), entry US$1.50.

A good walk is along the **Río Latas**, 7 km west of Misahuallí, where there are some small waterfalls. For protection from both mud and snakes, wear rubber boots when walking in the forest here. You walk through dense vegetation for about 1½ hours, often muddy, to get to the largest fall where you can bathe. To get there catch the bus towards Tena and ask to get off by the river at the metal bridge, the third one out of Misahuallí. There are two different trails to the falls starting on either side of the bridge, both charge US$1.50.

A dirt road from Misahuallí crosses the Río Misahuallí on a small suspension bridge, and continues east as far as **Union Bolivarense**, where caves have been found.

The Upper Napo

The south shore of the Napo has road access from Tena as far as Yuralpa, where petroleum exploration is being carried out. There is bus service as far as San Pedro. Along this road are several hotels, jungle lodges and the Jatun Sacha reserve; others are accessible only by river. ▶▶ *For details of the jungle lodges, see page 391.*

About 8 km downriver from Misahuallí, reached by road or river, is the **Jatun Sacha Biological Station** ① *Quito office: Fundación Jatun Sacha, Pasaje Eugenio de Santillán N34-248 y Maurian, T02-432246, F453583, www.jatunsacha.org*, ('big forest' in Quichua), a reserve set aside for environmental education, field research, community extension and ecotourism. The biological station and the adjacent Aliñahui project together conserve 1,300 ha of tropical wet forest. So far, 507 birds, 2,500 plants and 765 butterfly species have been identified at Jatun Sacha. They offer excursions with good views and walking on a well-developed trail system.

Puyo → *Phone code 03   Colour map 5, grid A2   Population 25,000   Altitude 950m*

The capital of the province of Pastaza is the largest urban centre in the whole of Oriente. It feels more like a small lowland city anywhere, rather than a typical jungle town. Visits can nonetheless be made to nearby forest reserves and tours deeper into the jungle can also be arranged from Puyo. Sangay and Altar volcanoes can occasionally be seen from town.

Ins and outs Puyo is the junction for road travel into the northern and southern Oriente, and for traffic heading to or from Ambato via Baños. The road from Macas enters from the southeast, the road to Tena leaves to the north. **Ministerio de Turismo** ① *Francisco de Orellana y 24 de Mayo, Mon-Fri 0830-1700.* **Consejo Provincial** ① *Orellana 145 y 27 de Febrero, ground floor.*

Sights
The **Museo Etno-Arqueológico** ① *Atahualpa y 9 de Octubre, 3rd floor*, has displays of the traditional dwellings of various cultures of the province of Pastaza.

Omaere ① *daily 0800-1700, US$3, www.omaere.net*, is a 15.6-ha ethnobotanical reserve located 2 km north of Puyo on the road to Tena. It has three trails with a variety of plants, an orchidarium and traditional native homes.

There are other small private reserves of varying quality in the Puyo area and visits are arranged by local tour operators (see page 394). You cannot, however, expect to see large tracts of undisturbed primary jungle here nor many wild animals. Sites include: **Criadero de Vida Silvestre Fátima** ① *9 km north on the road to Tena, which attempts to 'rehabilitate' captive jungle animals, entry US$2*; **Jadín Botánico La Orquideas** ① *3 km south on the road to Macas, with orchids and other tropical plants, entry US$5*; **Fundación Ecológica Hola Vida** ① *27 km from Puyo near Porvenir, which offers rustic accommodation in the forest, and a 30-minute canoe trip.*

Puyo to Baños
The road from Puyo to Baños is fully paved and a spectacular journey with superb views of the Pastaza valley and a plethora of waterfalls. **Shell** is 13 km west of Puyo, 50 km from Baños (1 hr). It has an army base and an airfield, watch out for aircraft crossing the road! The town is linear, sprawled along the main road. For the journey from Shell west to Baños, see page 234.

◉ Sleeping

Baeza *p385*
D Casa Bambú, in the new town. Cheaper with shared bath, adequate.
D Mesón de Baeza, on the plaza in the old town. Popular with kayakers, shared bath, electric shower.

E San Rafael, in the new town, T06-2320114. Private bath, hot water, parking, spacious rooms, friendly owner. Recommended.
E-F El Nogal de Jumandí, in old town. Breakfast available, hot showers extra, basic, lots of character, lots of holes in the walls.

E-F **Samay**, in the new town. Shared bath, electric shower, basic.

Baeza to Tena *p386*

LL **Cabañas San Isidro**, near Cosanga, approximately 30 minutes south of Baeza, T02-2547403 (Quito), www.ecuador explorer.com/sanisidro This is a 1,200-ha private reserve with rich bird life, comfortable accommodation and warm hospitality. Includes 3 excellent meals, there is a small easily accessible Cock-of-the Rock lek on the reserve, and feeders make the local hummingbirds easy to see. Reservations required. Recommended.

C **The Magic Roundabout**, 12 km south of Baeza, T09-9345264, www.themagicroundabout.org Rooms in cabins or cheaper beds in dorm, includes good breakfast and supper, shared bath, horse riding, friendly, British- Ecuadorean run, "the only English pub for miles".

Archidona *p386*

A **Hakuna Matata**, Vía Chaupi Shungu Km 3.9, off the road between Tena and Archidona, T06-2889167 (answering machine and fax), www.hakunamat.com Comfortable cabins in a lovely setting by the Río Inchillaqui. Includes all meals, walks, river bathing and horse riding. Very good food, friendly Belgian hosts, pleasant atmosphere. Warmly recommended.

B **Orchid Paradise**, 2 km north of town, T06-2889232. Cabins in nice secondary forest with lots of birds. Includes breakfast, other meals available, owner organizes various tours in the area.

D **Palmar del Río**, Av Napo y Transverasl 13, several blocks south of the plaza, T06-2889274. Restaurant, cold water, parking.

D **Regina**, Rocafuerte 446, 1 block north of the plaza, T06-2889144. Cold water, ample parking, modern, pleasant and friendly.

Tena *p387, map p387*

The water supply in some of the cheaper hotels is poor.

B **Los Yutzos**, Augusto Rueda 190 y 15 de Noviembre, T06-2886458, www.geocities.com/losyutzos Comfortable rooms and beautiful grounds overlooking the Río Pano, quiet and family-run. Includes breakfast, a/c, cheaper with fan, parking, clean and simple annexe next door is cheaper. Recommended.

C **Establo de Tomás**, in Muyuna village, 5 km from Tena on the road to San Antonio, T09-8778709, paorivade@hotmail.com Cabins in a pleasant setting with river bathing nearby. Meals available on request, solar hot water, parking, nice but can get busy on weekends.

C **Pumarosa**, on Malecón near vehicle bridge, T/F06-2886320. A/c, parking, nice grounds and adequate rooms.

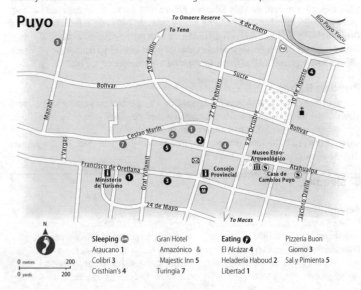

Puyo

Sleeping
Araucano 1
Colibrí 3
Cristhian's 4
Gran Hotel
Amazónico &
Majestic Inn 5
Turingia 7

Eating
El Alcázar 4
Heladería Haboud 2
Libertad 1
Pizzería Buon
Giorno 3
Sal y Pimienta 5

Oriente Jungle Foothills Listings

C-D **Arazá**, 9 de Octubre y Tarqui.
A/c, parking, pricier rooms are comfortable,
others are small but good value.
C-D **Mol**, Sucre 432 y Simon Bolívar, T06-
2886215. Restaurant, a/c, cheaper with fan,
laundry, cooking facilities, parking, spacious.
D **Austria**, Tarqui y Diaz de Pineda,
T06-2887205. Electric shower, fan, ample
parking, spacious rooms, quiet, friendly and
good value. Recommended.
D **Canela**, Amazonas y Abdón Calderón,
T06-2886081. Fan, parking, modern,
clean and nice.
D **Indiyana**, Bolívar 349 entre Amazonas y
García Moreno, T06-2886334. Restaurant
for breakfast only, parking, very nice and
friendly, organizes tours.
D **Traveler's Lodging**, 15 de Noviembre 438,
T06-2888204, amarongachitours@yahoo.com
Restaurant and tour agency, fan, some rooms
have fridge, several different kinds of rooms,
better ones are on second floor.
D **Villa Belén**, on Baeza Rd (Av Jumandy)
just north of town, T06-2886228, F2888091.
Fan, laundry and cooking facilities, parking,
excellent rooms, quiet. Recommended.
D **Vista Hermosa**, 15 de Noviembre 622,
T06-2886521. Restaurant, a/c, cheaper
with fan, parking, nice rooftop terrace
with views over river, friendly.
D-E **Limoncocha**, Sangay 533, Sector
Corazón de Jesús, on a hillside 4 blocks
from the bus station, ask for directions,
T06-2887583, limoncocha@andinanet.net
Concrete house with terrace and hammocks.
Cafeteria, cheaper with shared bath, hot
water, fan, internet, laundry and cooking
facilities, parking, German-Ecuadorean run,
enthusiastic owners organize tours, pleasant
atmosphere. Out of the way in a humble
neighbourhood, sometimes noisy but nice
views and good value.
D-E **Turismo Amazónico**, Amazonas y Abdón
Calderón, T06-2886508. Cheaper with shared
bath, cold water, fan, some rooms have fridge,
older basic place but good value.
E **A Welcome Break**, Augusto Rueda 331 y
12 de Febrero, T06-2886301. **Veronica's
Place** restaurant, shared bath, hot water,
cooking facilities, parking, good value, basic.
F **Jumandy**, Amazonas y Abdón Calderón,
T06-2886419. Very basic but clean and
friendly. Shared bath, cold water, run by the
Cerda family who also arrange tours.

Misahuallí *p388*

LL **Jardín Alemán**, on the banks of the
Río Misahuallí, several ks from town,
access is along a road north before
you reach Misahuallí, T06-2890139,
www.eljardinaleman.com Includes 3 meals
and river tour, small pool, comfortable
rooms, pleasant garden setting.
A **Misahuallí Jungle Hotel**,
across the river from town, T03-2890063,
www.misahuallijungle.com Includes
breakfast, restaurant, electric shower, fan,
pool, cabins for up to 6, nice setting.
C **France Amazonia**, on road from Tena
across from high school. Includes very good
breakfast, parking, small rooms (not for tall
people), French-run, helpful.
D **El Albergue Español**, on Arteaga,
T06-2890127, www.albergueespanol.com
Screened rooms with balconies overlooking
the river, nice place but not the friendliest.
Upscale restaurant, fan, arranges tours to
Hotel Jaguar jungle lodge, 1½ hrs
downstream on the Río Napo.
D **La Posada**, Napo opposite the plaza,
T06-2890113. Restaurant, simple, offers tours.
D **Marena Inn**, Arteaga y Santander,
T06-2890002, F2890085. Fan, fridge,
parking, nice and comfortable.
D-E **Centro de Recreación Ecológica**,
on Santander at entrance to town,
T06-2890062. Fan, simple but adequate.
E **El Paisano**, Rivadeneyra y Tandalia,
T06-2890027. Restaurant, private bath,
hot water, simple rooms, friendly owner,
pleasant atmosphere and good value.
E **La Casa Eduardo**, 200 m from bus stop,
ask around. Cooking facilities, terrace,
pleasant, owner Eduardo is a guide.
E **Shaw**, Santander on Plaza, T06-2890019,
ecoselva@yahoo.es Café downstairs, private
bath, hot water, simple clean rooms, operate
their own tours, English spoken, friendly and
knowledgeable. Good value. Recommended.
E-F **Sacha**, by river beach, T06-2890065.
Cheaper with shared bath, cold water,
very basic but nice location.

Upper Napo *p388*
Jungle lodges

LL **Yachana Lodge**, Quito T02-2523777,
www.yachana.com. Based in the indigenous
village of Mondaña, 2 hrs downstream from
Misahuallí. All proceeds from the lodge go

Oriente Jungle Foothills Listings

towards supporting community development projects. The lodge is comfortable, has 10 double rooms and family cabins and solar power. Highly recommended packages include river transport, all meals, lodging and guides; US$336 per person for 4 days (3 nights).

L Cabañas Aliñahui, lodging for Jatun Sacha Biological station. Quito office: Fundación Jatun Sacha, Pasaje Eugenio de Santillán N34-248 y Maurian, T06-432246, www.jatunsacha.org. Eight cabins with 2 bedrooms and bath, lush tropical garden, rainforest and nature trails. Includes 3 delicious meals in the dining hall. Profits contribute to conservation of the area's rainforest.

L Casa del Suizo, Quito office at Julio Zaldumbide 375 y Toledo, T02-2566090, www.casadelsuizo.com. Opposite **Anaconda**, on the north bank at Ahuano is Swiss-Ecuadorean-owned, price includes all meals and tour, buffet meals only which cater for vegetarians, every room has a private bath, 24-hr electricity, pool, trips arranged. Recommended for their hospitality.

L Gareno Lodge, south of the Río Napo, along an oil company road from San Pedro. Contact Michael Saur, T02-2344350, or Roeland Van Lede, T02-2249225 (both in Quito), www.guaponi.com. A new lodge surrounded by good forest in Huarorani territory. Occasional sightings of nesting Harpy Eagles have been reported here. Five-days/4-nights cost US$240 per person, plus a US$25 contribution to the Huaorani community. Includes accommodation, meals, and native guiding in Spanish. Can arrange transport from Tena.

A Anaconda, on Anaconda Island in the Río Napo, about 1 hr down river by canoe from Misahuallí. Quito office: Foch 635 y Reina Victoria, 1st floor, T/F02-2224913, anacondaec@andinanet.net Ten bungalows of bamboo and thatch, with space for about 48 guests, no electric lights, but flush toilets and cold showers. The meals are good. Canoe and hiking trips arranged, guides only speak Spanish.

A Cotococha Amazon Lodge, Av Amazonas N24-03 y Wilson, Ed CJ, Piso 2, Quito, T02-2234336, www.cotococha.com Jungle lodge with various packages including and excluding transport, on the shores of the Napo river, offering jungle treks, rafting, tubing, community visits, canoeing, cascade visits and more.

Puyo *p389, map p390*

A Flor de Canela, Paseo Turístico, Barrio Obrero, T03-2885265, F2886083. Includes breakfast, restaurant and bar, pool (US$1.50 for non-residents), comfortable cabins, pleasant location but a bit out of the way.

A-B Finca El Pingual, C Tungurahua, Barrio Obrero, T03-2886137. Modern cabins on large grounds with sports fields. Includes breakfast, restaurant, large pool (US$1.50 for non residents), popular with Ecuadorean families, gets busy on weekends and holidays.

A-B Hostería Safari, outside town at km 5 on the road to Tena, T03-2885465, www.hosteriasafari.com Includes breakfast, restaurant, pool, parking, ample grounds, peaceful and out of the way.

B Turingia, Ceslao Marín 294, T03-2885180, www.hosteriaturingia.com Restaurant, fan, small pool, parking, comfortable , nice garden.

C **Gran Hotel Amazónico**, Ceslao Marín y Atahualpa, T03-2883094, F2884753. Includes breakfast, restaurant, fan, parking, small rooms.

D **Colibrí**, C Manabí entre Bolívar y Galápagos, T03-2883054, cascadayanarumi@yahoo.es Parking, away from centre, modern, friendly, good value. Recommended.

D **Cristhian's**, Atahualpa entre 9 de Octubre y 27 de Febrero, T03-2883081, F2885874. Includes breakfast, fan, fridge, large modern carpeted rooms, but could be cleaner.

D **Libertad**, Francisco de Orellana opposite the Coliseo Municipal, T03-2883282. Restaurant, electric shower, parking, basic but clean and good value.

D **Majestic Inn**, Ceslao Marín y Vaillamil, T03-2885417, F2885238. Fan, clean and simple rooms.

D-E **Araucano**, Ceslao Marín 576, T03-2885686, F2883834. Includes breakfast, restaurant, fan, different types of rooms at various prices, ranging from simple to basic.

Puyo to Baños *p389*
The following are all in Shell.

D **Germany**, down a side street, ½ block from the main rd, T03-2795134. Simple cabins in a nice setting, restaurant, family-run and friendly.

D **Los Copales**, West of Shell towards Baños, T03-2795290. Restaurant, parking, comfortable cabins in a quiet setting. Friendly.

D **Wakany**, Abelardo Quiñónez y Zulay, T03-2795158. Parking, clean and modern, larger rooms are in back.

D-E **Esmeraldita**, on main road, T03-2795133. Restaurant, cheaper with shared bath, simple but clean and adequate.

E-F **Azuay**, on main rd, T03-2795574. Restaurant, cheaper with shared bath, simple but adequate.

● Eating

Baeza *p385*
¶¶ **Gina**, In the old town. Best, friendly and popular, serves great trout.
¶ **El Viejo**, Next to Hostal San Rafael. Decent set meals.

Archidona *p386*
There are not many places to eat but **Restaurant Los Pinos**, near **Res Regina**, is reportedly good.

Tena *p387, map p387*
¶¶¶¶ **The Marquis**, Amazonas 251 y Rocafuerte, T06-2886513. Upscale grill.
¶¶¶ **Chuquitos**, García Moreno by Plaza, T06-2887630. Good food, à la carte only, seating on a balcony overlooking the river. Pleasant atmosphere and nice views. Popular and recommended.
¶¶¶ **Pizzería La Massilia**, Malecón y 9 de Octubre, by the river, open from 1700 onwards. Really nice pizza.
¶¶ **Cositas Ricas**, 15 de Noviembre, next to Hostal Traveler's Lodging. Tasty set meals, vegetarian available, good fruit juices.

There are also various *chifas* and cheap *comedores* in town.

Ice cream parlours
Heladería Italiana, 9 de Octubre y Tarqui, daily 0930-2130. Excellent ice cream made fresh on the premises.

Misahuallí *p388*
¶¶ **Peco's Café**, on the plaza. Tacos are their speciality.
¶ **Doña Gloria**, Arteaga y Rivadeneyra by corner of plaza, daily 0730-2030. Very good set meals.
¶ **Ecocafé**, Hotel Shaw, on the plaza. Good breakfast, à la carte dishes and cappuccino.
¶ **La Posada**, on the plaza. Varied à la carte, nice porch setting, good food, slow service.
¶ **Nico**, on the plaza. Set meals.

Puyo *p389, map p390*
¶¶¶ **El Alcázar**, 10 de Agosto 936 y Sucre, T03-2885330, Mon-Sat 0900-2300, Sun 0900-1600. Very good restaurant with an unexpectedly Spanish-European flavour in the Ecuadorean Amazon. Good value set meals and varied à la carte. Recommended.
¶¶¶ **El Jardín**, on the Paseo Turístico in Barrio Obrero, T03-2886101, Tue-Sun 1200-2200. Pleasant setting and atmosphere, international food, meat and pasta are specialities.

Oriente Jungle Foothills Listings

● *For an explanation of the price codes used in this guide, see inside the front cover. Other*
● *relevant information can be found in Essentials, pages 58-64.*

¶¶¶ **La Carihuela**, Mons Alberto Zambrano, near the bus station, T03-2883919, Tue-Sun 0900-1600, 1800-2100. Upmarket for Puyo, good set meals and à la carte.

¶¶¶-¶¶ **Pizzería Buon Giorno**, Orellana entre Villamil y 27 de Febrero, Mon-Sat 1200-2300. Good pizza, lasagne and salads, pleasant atmosphere, very popular and recommended.

¶ **La Posada de Gurmiek**, Ceslao Marín y 27 de Febrero, daily 0730-2200. Nice place, good value set lunch.

¶ **Panadería Susanita**, Ceslao Marín y Villamil. Bakery, also serves breakfast and set lunch.

¶ **Sal y Pimienta**, Atahualpa y 27 de Febrero, daily 0700-2300. Grilled meats and good value set lunch, popular.

Ice cream parlours
Heladería Haboud, 27 de Febrero y Atahualpa. Good.

Puyo to Baños *p389*
There are several cheap and simple *comedores* on the main road in Shell.

⊙ Bars and clubs

Tena *p387, map p387*
Araña Bar, García Moreno by the plaza and near the riverfront, open from 1700. Nice.
Choza Bar, Malecón margen izquierda, daily 1400-0200. Choza by the river.
Gallera, at Hotel Pumarosa. Large disco open Sat and Sun.

Puyo *p389, map p390*
At Barrio Obrero, along the river on the road north to Tena, there are several bars and discos in a pleasant setting.

⊙ Shopping

Puyo *p389, map p390*
Amazonía Touring, Atahualpa y 9 de Octubre, good selection of local crafts.

▲ Activities and tours

Tena *p387, map p387*
Most Tena hotels and tour operators offer cultural and jungle tours as well as rafting and kayaking. Be mindful of safety standards for the latter activities. We have received a serious complaint

about guide René Shiguango, working with 'Sachaursay'.
Amarongachi Tours at Hostal Traveler's Lodging, see Sleeping, above.
Ecoindiana, at Hostal Indiana, see Sleeping, above.
Limoncocha, at Hostal Limoncocha, see Sleeping, above. German spoken.
Ríos Ecuador / Yacu Amu, 15 de Noviembre y 9 de Octubre, on the Malecón between the bridges, T06-2886346, www.riosecuador.com Highly recommended whitewater rafting and kayak trips and a 4-day kayak school. See also Rafting, p78.
Runa Ñambi, JL Mera 628 y Abdón Calderón, T06-2886318, runanambi@yahoo.com

Misahuallí *p388*
There are guides available to take parties into the jungle for trips of 1-10 days, all involving canoeing and varying amounts of hiking. The going rate is US$25-$40 per person per day, depending on the season, size of group and length of trip. This should include food and rubber boots, which are absolutely essential. Quality varies, so try to get a personal recommendation from travellers who have just returned from a trip. Tours can be arranged by most hotels as well as the following:
Ecoselva, Santander on the plaza, T06-2890019, ecoselva@yahoo.es Recommended guide Pepe Tapia speaks English and has a biology background. Trips last from 1-6 days. Well organized and reliable.
Quindi Tours, at Hotel La Posada, see Sleeping, above.

Puyo *p389, map p390*
All of the following offer jungle tours of varying lengths. Prices range from US$25 to US$50 per person per day.
Amazonía Touring, Atahualpa y 9 de Octubre, T/F03-2883064.
Coka Tours, 27 de Febrero y Atahualpa, T03-2886108, cokatours@andinanet.net
Daayme Expeditions, 27 de Febrero y Atahualpa, T03-2883782, daaymexpeditions@hotmail.com
Entsa Tours, T09-8016642. Mentor Marino is helpful and knowledgeable.

Nave de Santos, at the Terminal Terrestre, T03-2883262, F2883267.

Papangu Tours, 27 de Febrero y Sucre, T03-2887684, papangu@andinanet.net Operated by the **Organización de Pueblos Indigenas de Pastaza** (OPIP).

◎ Transport

For main inter-city routes see the bus timetable p1.

Tena *p387, map p387*
To **Archidona**, every 20 mins, US$0.25, 15 mins. To **Misahuallí**, hourly, US$1, 45 mins. Buses leave from the local bus station not the long distance terminal.

Misahuallí *p388*
Bus
Local buses run from the plaza. To **Tena**, every 45 mins 0745-1800, US$1, 45 min. Make long distance connections in Tena, or get off at Puerto Napo to catch southbound buses although you may not get a seat. To **Quito**, 1 direct bus a day at 0830, US$6, 6 hrs.

Canoes
With the increase in roads, river traffic has dwindled along the upper Napo and scheduled passenger service from Misahuallí has been discontinued. Motorized canoes for 8-10 passengers can nonetheless be chartered for the journey to Coca (5-7 hrs, US$200) or other destinations.

Puyo *p389, map p390*
The terminal terrestre is on the outskirts of town, on the Shell and Baños road in the southwest, a 10-15 min walk from the centre or take a taxi (US$1).

Puyo to Baños *p389*
Military flights from **Shell** are generally not open to foreigners, but light aircraft can be chartered by the hour. Companies include: **Aerotaxis Ecuatorianos S.A. (ATESA)**, T03-2795877, Quito T02-3301181; **SAEREO**, Quito T02-3301152 ext 223, www.saereo.com, and **Transportes Aereos Orientales** (TAO), T03-2795146, Quito T02-2446779.

---

❶ Directory

Baeza to Tena *p386*
Tena
Banks Travellers' cheques can be difficult to change in Tena. In a pinch, try **Hostal Limoncocha**. Banco del Pichincha, Amazonas y JL Mera. **Banco del Austro**, 15 de Noviembre y Diaz de Pineda.
Laundry Lavafacil, 15 de Noviembre 1125, near bus station.

Puyo *p389, map p390*
Banks Casa de Cambios Puyo, Atahualpa y 9 de Octubre, T/F03-2883064. 3% commission for Amex US$ TCs. Helpful, friendly and recommended. **Banco del Austro**, Atahualpa entre 10 de Agosto y Dávila.

Downriver

The heart of Ecuador's remaining primary rainforest lies in the east of Oriente, in the provinces of Sucumbíos and Orellana (capitals Lago Agrio and Coca) as well as eastern Pastaza. Here there are two vast national parks, Cuyabeno and Yasuní, as well as the Huaorani Reserve, both with many excellent lodges for an unforgettable immersion into life in the rivers, canopy and understorey. Although not cheap, this is Ecuadorean jungle tourism at its best. Despite all the lip-service paid to conservation and ecotourism here, the eastern jungle is also under severe threat from petroleum development and colonization. It is hoped that sustainable tourism can help tip the economic balance in favour of conserving the rainforest and its people. Those who wish to contribute to the effort, as well as those who want to see how the experiment will work, had better come and visit soon. ▸▸ *For Sleeping, Eating and other listings, see pages 400-405.*

⁑ The high price of petroleum

Lago Agrio and Coca are the main towns serving the petroleum industry operating in the Ecuadorean Oriente. The oil companies and their subcontractors have come from various parts of the world, the USA, Canada, France, Brazil and Argentina among others, and they are in effect the new *conquistadores*. Large and powerful, they have turned the Ecuadorean Amazon into a place where barrels of oil mean more than biodiversity or human rights. Neither drawn-out international litigation by indigenous communities nor protests by environmental groups have been able to halt their relentless advance.

Hundreds of thousands of barrels of oil flow out of the jungle every day through two pipelines that snake over the Andes and down to the coast for export. In their wake, feeder pipes criss-cross the devastated terrain and toxic waste sumps contaminate watersheds. If this were not bad enough, a February 2005 scandal revealed that some oil spills were deliberate, encouraged by lucrative clean-up contracts and juicy compensation payments. The natural habitat around Lago Agrio was the first to be decimated, followed by that along the Vía Auca, an oil company road running south from Coca into Huaorani territory. The same tragic history is currently being repeated in primary forest south of

the Río Napo, between Coca and Misahuallí.

Yet all the direct damage caused by the petroleum industry pales in comparison to that inflicted by the colonists who inevitably follow in its wake. The oil companies build access roads to their wells, and these become corridors of deforestation as settlers take out timber and introduce cattle and crops. Their agricultural practices are unsuited to the poor or non-existent soils of the rainforest. The result is desert-like areas where only useless grasses cover the land. And the way of life of the native lowland Quichua, Cofán, Siona, Secoya and Huaorani people has been permanently altered.

These issues are not unique to Ecuador but since the country's slice of the Amazon is among the smallest and biologically richest in South America, the prospect of catastrophe is more imminent. The high international price of petroleum in recent years has led to a flurry of new exploration, actively encouraged by the Quito government even within national parks and reserves. But whatever the future price of a barrel of crude in London or New York, the price paid by the Ecuadorean Amazon has already been too high.

See *Amazon Crude*, and other works by Judith Kimerling; *Savages*, by Joe Kane; and *Confessions of an Economic Hit Man*, by John Perkins (Books, page 481).

Lago Agrio and around

→ *Phone code 06 Colour map 3, grid B3 Population 34,000*

Despite its importance for tourists as the access for Cuyabeno Wildlife Reserve, Lago Agrio is first and foremost an old oil town and is the capital of the province of Sucumbíos. It is also has close commercial ties with neighbouring Colombia. Lago Agrio has grown in recent years and the infrastructure is adequate, but it remains very much on the frontier.

The town's official name is Nueva Loja, owing to the fact that the majority of the first colonizers were from the southern province of Loja. The name Lago Agrio comes from *Sour Lake*, the US headquarters of Texaco, the first oil company to exploit the crude reserves beneath Ecuador's rainforest. Avenida Quito is the main street where many hotels and restaurants are located, but there are no street signs. Information is provided by the **Camara de Turismo de Sucumbíos** ① *Av Quito y Pasaje Gonzanamá, T06-2832502.*

Safety

Lago Agrio is among the places in Ecuador that has been most severely affected by the armed conflict in neighbouring Colombia. Enquire about public safety before travelling here and enquire again in Lago Agrio before visiting outlying regions of the province of Sucumbíos. Due to the risk of bus hold-ups, do not travel to Lago Agrio overnight. The streets of Lago Agrio are not safe after 2000.

As a result of the violence in the neighbouring department of Putumayo (Colombia), Lago Agrio and surroundings have seen a large influx of Colombian refugees. Broad spectrum herbicides are sprayed from aircraft to destroy coca plantations across the border, under the auspices of the US-sponsored 'Plan Colombia'. Local agriculture, wildlife, and the health of the population of Sucumbíos are being affected.

> ❖ *On no account venture into areas directly along the Colombian border.*

Reserva Faunística Cuyabeno

This large tract of pristine rainforest, covering 602,000 ha, is located about 100 km east of Lago Agrio. The extensive jungle area is along the Río Cuyabeno, which eventually drains into the Aguarico. In the reserve are many lagoons and a great variety of wildlife, including river dolphins, tapirs, capybaras, five species of caiman, ocelots, 15 species of monkey and over 500 species of birds.

Cuyabeno ① *Reserve entrance fee US$20*, is among the best places in Ecuador to see jungle animals and the reserve is very popular with visitors. Despite the area's proximity to the Colombian border and precarious public safety situation (see Lago Agrio safety, above), there have been relatively few incidents involving tourists. A tour group was robbed by heavily-armed men in November 2003, but no one was hurt and no further incidents were reported to the close of this edition (Spring 2005).

Access to Cuyabeno is either by road from Lago Agrio, or by river along the Río Aguarico. Within the reserve, transport is mainly by canoe. In order to see as many animals as possible and minimally impact their habitat, seek out a small tour group

Lago Agrio

To Terminal Terrestre
To Colombia
9 de Octubre
Progreso
Vilcabamba
24 de Mayo
Narváez
Guayaquil
TAME
Orellana
La Ronda
Plaza
Av Colombia
18 de Noviembre
To Gran Hotel de Lago
Eloy Alfaro
12 de febrero
Añasco
Manabí
Pasaje Gonzanama
To Airport (5 km)
Av Quito
To Market & Busses to Coca

N
0 metres 100
0 yards 100

Sleeping 🛏
Arazá 1
D'Mario & Gran
  Colombia 4
El Cofán 5

La Cascada &
Cafetería
Jaqueline 10
Lago Imperial 8
Machala 2 9

Casa Blanca,
Americano &
Un Pedacito de
Colombia
Restaurant 12

Eating 🍴
Machala 1

(eight people or less) which scrupulously adheres to responsible tourism practices. Most Cuyabeno tours are booked through agencies in Quito or other popular tourist destinations. ▸▸ *For further details, see Activities and tours, page 404.*

Coca and around → *Phone code 06   Colour map 3, grid B3   Population 19,000*

Officially named Puerto Francisco de Orellana, Coca is a hot, bustling and sprawling oil town located at the junction of the Ríos Payamino and Napo, just upstream from the confluence of the Coca and Napo. It is the capital of the province of Orellana, and a small monument at the foot of Calle Napo commemorates the passage of Francisco de Orellana through the area in 1542, on his way to discover the Amazon (see box, Orellana's River, page 383). A bridge crosses the Río Napo at Coca, the start of the Vía Auca leading to oilfields and Huaorany territory to the south.

The view over the water is nice, and the riverfront can be a pleasant place to spend time around sunset. As a tourist centre, however, Coca offers few attractions other than being closer to undisturbed primary rainforest than the larger jungle towns further west. Coca is also the starting point for the adventurous river journey down the Río Napo to Peru and Brazil (see Coca to Iquitos, page 400).

Hotel and restaurant provision is adequate and there are plenty of bars and discos, usually filled with oil workers. Electricity and water supply are erratic, better hotels have reserve tanks and generators. Ironically, the petroleum production capital of Ecuador also suffers from occasional gasoline shortages. Although further from the Colombian border and generally safer and more tranquil than Lago Agrio, Coca nonetheless calls for common sense precautions.

Coca

N

0 metres   50
0 yards   50

Sleeping
Amazonas 1
Coca 2
Cotopaxi 3
El Auca 4
Florida 5
Lojanita 6
Oasis 7
San Fermin 8

Eating
Dragón Dorado 1
El Portón 2
Media Noche 3
Ocaso 4
Pappa John's 5
Parrilladas Argentinas 6

⁞ The Huaorani people

South of Coca is the homeland of the Huaorani, a forest people who traditionally lived a simple, nomadic life in the jungle as hunters and subsistence farmers. They refer to anyone living outside their communities as *cohuode*, meaning either "those that cut everything to pieces" or "people from other places/not living in the territory". Until recently, they lived in complete isolation. There are presently 18 Huaorani communities spread over a large area reaching south into Pastaza province.

Since the 1970s, the Huaorani have been greatly affected by the activities of the petroleum industry and have also suffered at the hands of an uncontrolled tourist trade. Both have dramatically changed their culture and disturbed their traditional village life. The Huaorani have responded to the tourist invasion by imposing tolls for the use of their rivers and entrance fees to their communities as well as demanding gifts. This latter practice has been encouraged by oil companies who have used it to their advantage when bargaining with Huaorani communities. In addition to oil companies and tourism, further pressures are placed on the Huaorani by illegal loggers in their territory.

Randy Smith, author of *Crisis Under the Canopy*, who has worked with the indigenous peoples of Ecuador on the development of ecotourism projects, states that tourism has taken a major toll in the deculturation process of the Huaorani as the guides offer gifts or cash for the use of their lands or services. He continues that the tourist dollar offers the Huaorani a chance to join the cash economy. The Huaorani visit the various centres outside their territory for food, staples and clothes and therefore require money to sustain this new way of life that many of them have chosen.

For some time, **ONHAE** (the Huaorani indigenous organization) opposed tourism, but revised its position in 1992, allowing a number of ONHAE-approved guides to operate in their territory. As the Huaorani have become more integrated into the money economy, a number of communities have shown greater interest in getting involved in ecotourism and are now aware of the amount of money that outside guides receive for taking tourists through their land. They would like to have more control over the tourism that comes through their area and derive more benefits from it. If you wish to visit the Huaorani then, for your own safety as well as for the sake of their critically endangered culture, do so only with an ONHAE-approved guide. See *Savages*, by Joe Kane, in addition to the work of Randy Smith (Books, page 481).

Oriente Jungle   Downriver

Jungle lodges and floating hotels

Offering one of the best ways to experience the jungle first hand, the jungle lodges and floating hotels accessed from Coca are some of Ecuador's finest. It is hoped that sustainable tourism can help tip the economic balance in favour of conserving the rainforest and its people, despite the heavy threat from petroleum and commercial logging in the area.▸▸ *For full details of lodges and hotels, including wildlife-spotting opportunities and packages, see page 402 and map page 380.*

Coca to Iquitos (Peru)

This is becoming a popular journey and offers a good insight into life on the Río Napo. It is still rough and adventurous, however, requiring plenty of time and patience. There has been talk for several years of tourist boats being introduced along this route, but none was in operation at the close of this edition (February 2005). Those interested should ask around Quito agencies.

At present, a thrice-weekly motorized canoe service from Coca goes to Nuevo Rocafuerte on the Peruvian Border, stopping en route at **Pompeya**, **Pañacocha** and other communities. See Coca river transport, page 404. **Nuevo Rocafuerte** has one basic hotel with a dormitory, and equally basic options for eating. There is an Ecuadorean immigration office for exit stamps and boats can be hired for the two-hour trip downriver to the Peruvian border town of **Pantoja**, US$60 per boat, try to share the ride. Peruvian entry stamps are given in Pantoja and, although there is no hotel, you can arrange to stay with a family for a small charge. In addition to immigration, you may have to register with the navy on either side of the border so have your passport at hand.

The difficult part of the journey begins in Pantoja, as departure dates of boats to Iquitos are irregular and you could be faced with a very long wait. In late 2004, four *lanchas* – the Peruvian term for riverboats – were operating between Iquitos and Pantoja: the the *Victor* and the *Camila* (same owner, Iquitos T+51-65-242082) as well as the *Jeisawell* and the *Siempre Adelante* (same owner, Iquitos T+51-65-266159, mob T51-65-9613049). These boats only come upriver as far as Pantoja when they have sufficient cargo, so several weeks can go by without any boat calling on the town. Try calling Iquitos in advance, to enquire when the next boat will sail from Pantoja. This information is not available in Coca.

All the *lanchas* are small and basic, conditions onboard can get crowded and unsanitary. They have no berths, only deck space to hang your hammock. The five to seven day trip from Pantoja all the way to Iquitos costs US$30 including very basic food, but there are several ways you can shorten the arduous journey. You can try to sail with the *lancha* only as far as Santa Clotilde, about half way to Iquitos, which has basic places to sleep and eat. From Santa Clotilde there are usually *rápidos* (speedboats) to Mazán (5 hrs, US$24), but check before you get off the *lancha*. From Mazán, which can also be reached by *lancha*, you cross by road to Indiana and then take another speedboat to Iquitos (US$3). If you are lucky, you could travel from Coca to Iquitos in four to five days, but you should be prepared for two to three weeks or more.

Take a hammock, cup, bowl, cutlery, extra food and snacks, drinking water or a way to purify it, insect repellent, toilet paper, soap, towel, etc. Cash dollars and *soles* in small notes are indispensable, but *soles* cannot be purchased in Coca. Maps and details of river travel further downstream through Peru to Brazil are found in *Footprint Peru* and the *South American Handbook*.

● Sleeping

Lago Agrio and around *p396, map p397*
AL-A Arazá, Quito 610 y Narváez, T06-2830223, arazahot@uio.satnet.net Quiet location away from centre. Includes breakfast, restaurant, a/c, pool (US$5 for non-residents), fridge, parking, comfortable, clean and nice. Best in town. Recommended.

B El Cofán, 12 de Febrero 2-12 y Av Quito, T06-2830526, F2832409. Includes breakfast, restaurant, a/c, fridge, parking, well cared-for.
B Gran Hostal de Lago, Km 1½ Vía Quito, T06-2832415. Includes breakfast, restaurant, a/c, pool, internet, parking, cabins, nice gardens, quiet. Recommended.

B-C **La Cascada**, Quito y Amazonas, T06-2830124, aliarcos@yahoo.com A/c, cheaper with fan and cold water, some rooms have fridge, a variety of different rooms, they are small but nice.

C **D'Mario**, Quito 171, T06-2830172, F2830456. Restaurant serves good set meals and pizza in the evening, cheaper with cold water, a/c, small pool, some rooms have fridge, good clean place, helpful owner. Recommended.

C **Gran Colombia**, Quito y Pasaje Gonzanamá, T06-2831032, F2831031. Good restaurant, a/c, cheaper with fan and cold water, centrally located, many different types of rooms, modern and adequate.

D **Lago Imperial**, Colombia y Quito, T06-2830453. Cold water, a/c, cheaper with fan, central location, good value.

D **Machala 2**, Colombia entre Quito y Añazco, T06-2830673. Good restaurant, cold water, fan, parking, friendly.

E **Americano**, Quito 118 y Colombia, T06-2830555. Private bath, cold water, fan, small rooms but good value.

E **Casa Blanca**, Quito y Colombia, T06-2830181. Private bath, hot water, fan, nice bright rooms, good value.

There are many other places to stay, mostly cheap and basic.

Reserva Faunística Cuyabeno *p397*

Cuyabeno Lodge, Neotropic Turis, Av Amazonas N24-03 y Wilson, Quito, T02-2521212, www.neotropicturis.com Pioneer eco-lodge in the Laguna Grande with independent cabins and private bathrooms, solar energy, naturalist guides.

Coca and around *p398, maps p380 and p398*

A-C **El Auca**, Napo entre Rocafuerte y García Moreno, T06-2880600, www.interactive.net.ec/hotel-auca Restaurant, disco on weekends, a/c, cheaper with fan, parking, a variety of different rooms and mini-suites. Comfortable, garden with hammocks, manager speaks English. Popular and centrally located but can get noisy.

B **La Misión**, by riverfront 100 m downriver from the bridge, T06-2880260, F2880263. Restaurant and disco a/c and fridge, cheaper with fan, pool and water-slide, internet, parking, upscale for where it is, nice location by the river, English spoken, arranges tours.

B **Puerto Orellana**, Av Alejandro Labaka, at the entrance to town from Lago Agrio, T06-2880129, jesseniabrito@andinanet.net Electric shower, a/c, parking, out of the way, modern and very nice. Popular, best book in advance.

B-C **Amazonas**, 12 de Febrero y Espejo, T06-2880444. Relaxed setting by the river, away from centre, restaurant, a/c, cheaper with fan, parking, quiet, friendly and good.

C-D **Payamino**, Rocafuerte y Quito, T06-2880097. Cold water, a/c, cheaper with fan, simple but modern.

C-D **San Fermín**, Bolívar Y Quito, T06-2880802. A/c, cheaper with fan and cold water, parking, very nice, modern and comfortable, good value.

D **Coca**, Inés Arango entre Cuenca y Rocafuerte, T06-2881841. Cold water, fan, parking, modern.

D-E **Florida**, Alejandro Labaka y Rocafuerte, on main road to the airport, T06-2880177. Cheaper with shared bath, cold water, fan, basic.

Cuyabeno Lodge

Ecolodge in the Cuyabeno National Park

- Naturalist Bilingual and Natives Guides
- Richest wildlife in the Amazon
- Located in the Laguna Grande
- Pioneer Lodge in the Cuyabeno Reserve
- Operation with minimum impact to the environment
- Independent cabins with private bathrooms.
- Solar energy

Neotropic Turis. Avda. Amazonas N24-03 y Wilson, Quito
Tel: (00 593) (2) 2521212 Fax: (00 593) (2) 2554902
Mobile: (00 593) (9) 9803395 (24 hrs.)
Email: info@neotropicturis.com www.neotropicturis.com

D-E Oasis, between the bridge and La Misión, T06-2880206. Electric shower, fan, parking, quiet, simple but adequate.

Jungle lodges and floating hotels

Note that all Napo area lodges count travel days as part of their package, which means that often a '3-day tour' spends only 1 day actually in the forest. Also, keep in mind that the return trip must start before dawn if it is to connect to that day's Coca-Quito flight; if it starts later it will be necessary to spend the night in Coca.

Most lodges have fixed departure days from Coca (eg Mon and Fri) and it is very expensive to get a special departure on another day. Ask the lodges for up-to-date departure day information before planning your trip. Bookings can usually be made on the internet and through most Quito agencies. The prices given below include accommodation, 3 meals and guiding, but do not include transport to Coca or national park fees. They are all subject to change.

Except for **Kapawi**, which is nowhere near Coca but also operates through Coca airport, the following lodges, sites and riverboats are listed in order of their distance downriver from Coca, the closest first.

Yarina, is the closest lodge to Coca, about 1 hr downstream along the Río Napo, Quito office: Amazonas N24-240 y Colón, T/F02-2504037, www.yuturilodge.com. It has accommodation in thatched roof cabins and a 40-ft canopy tower. Four days (3 nights) cost US$200. Itineraries can combine visits here and to **Yuturi**, see below.
Sacha, Julio Zaldumbide 397 y Valladolid, Quito, T02-2566090, www.sachalodge.com, is an upmarket lodge 2½ hrs downstream from Coca. Cabins are very comfortable, with private bath and hot water, and meals are excellent. The bird list is outstanding; the local bird expert, Oscar Tapuy (T06-2881486) can be requested in advance by birders. Guides are generally knowledgeable. Boardwalks through swamp habitats allow access to some species that are difficult to see at other lodges, and nearby river islands provide another distinct habitat. Also have a butterfly farm and a canopy tower. Several species of monkey are commonly seen. Five-days/4-nights cost US$750 per person.

La Selva, is also an upmarket lodge, 2½ hrs downstream from Coca and close to Sacha, Quito office: San Salvador E7-85 y Martín Carrión, T02-2550995, www.laselvajunglelodge.com. It is professionally run and situated on a picturesque lake surrounded by excellent forest, especially on the far side of Mandicocha. Bird and animal life is exceptionally diverse. Many species of monkey are seen regularly. A total of 580 bird species can be found here, one of the highest totals in the world for a single elevation site, and some of the local guides (eg José) are very good at finding them. There is a biological station on the grounds (the **Neotropical Field Biology Institute**) as well as a butterfly farm. Cabins have private bath and hot water. Meals are excellent. Usually the guides are biologists, and in general the guiding is of very high quality. A new canopy tower was completed in 2004. Five-days/4-nights cost US$756 per person.
Napo Wildlife Center, operated by and for the local Añangu community, across the Río Napo from La Selva, 2½ hrs downstream from Coca. Five days/4 nights costs US$795 per person. Quito office T02-2897316, www.ecoecuador.org This area of hilly forest is rather different from the low flat forest of some other sites, and the diversity is slightly higher. There are big caimans and good mammals, including giant otters, and the birding is excellent. The local guide, Giovanny Rivadeneyra, is one of the most knowledgeable birders in the Oriente.
Sani, is another lodge near La Selva, Quito office: Roca 736 y Amazonas, Pasaje Chantilly, T02-2558881, www.sanilodge.com. All proceeds go to the Sani Isla community, who run the lodge with the help of outside experts. It is located on a remote lagoon which has 4-5 m long black caiman. This area is rich in wildlife and birds, including many species such as the scarlet macaw which have disappeared from most other Napo area lodges. There is good accommodation and a canopy tower. An effort has been made to make the lodge accessible to people who have difficulty walking; the lodge can be reached by canoe (total 4 hrs from Coca) without a walk. Five-days/4-nights cost US$493 per person, which is very good value.

Pañacocha, is a village located halfway between Coca and Nuevo Rocafuerte, nearby is the magnificent lagoon of Pañacocha on the Río Panayacu. This has been declared a protected forest region. Several agencies and guides run tours from Coca. Basic local accommodation is available.

Yuturi, is 5 hrs downstream from Coca, Quito office: Amazonas N24-240 y Colón, T/F02-2504037, www.yuturilodge.com. Birdwatching is excellent, and there are some species (eg black-necked red cotinga) that are difficult to find at other lodges. There is a wide variety of habitats here, and wildlife is good. The guides are usually local people accompanied by translators. Five-days/4-nights cost US$350 per person. Itineraries can combine visits here and to Yarina, see above.

Tiputini Biodiversity Station, on the Río Tiputini, is far from any settlement and has experienced very little hunting, not even by native people. The result is the best site in Ecuador for observing the full range of Amazonian wildlife and birds. Facilities are extremely well designed and merge into the forest; the canopy tower and canopy walkway are exceptional. Food is good. It is a scientific station, not a tourist facility, and potential visitors must form or join an educational group and receive approval in advance; services are orientated towards scientists. Spider monkeys, curassows, large macaws, large raptors and other threatened wildlife are more common and more confident here than at most other sites, and this is the best place in Ecuador for jaguar (but you still have to be lucky to see one). If you would like to join an educational workshop contact Carol Walton, USA T1-512-2630830, http://tiputini.usfq.edu.ec

Bataburo, Quito office: Kempery Tours, Ramirez Dávalos 117 y Amazonas, Oficina 101, T02-2505599, www.kempery.com A lodge in Huaorani territory near Parque Nacional Yasuní, on the Río Tiguino, a 3-6 hr canoe ride from the end of the Vía Auca out of Coca. Some cabins have private baths and there are shared shower facilities. Guides are mostly local people. The birds here have been little studied but macaws and other large species are present. The mammal population also appears to be quite good. Five-days/4-nights cost US$230 per person.

Manatee floating hotel, this luxury 30 passenger vessel sails on the Río Napo between Coca and Pompeya, Quito office: Advantage Travel, El Telégafo E10-63 y Juan de Alcántara, T02-2462871, www.advantagecuador.com Five-days/4-nights cost US$485 per person.

Kapawi, is a top-of-the-line jungle lodge located on the Río Capahuari near its confluence with the Pastaza, in the heart of Achuar territory not far from the Peruvian border. Operated by Canodros, Guayaquil T04-2285711, www.kapawi.com, or book through agencies in Quito or abroad. It is accessible only by small aircraft and motor canoe, visitors are usually flown in through Coca. The lodge was built in partnership with the Achuar indigenous organization OINAE and is due to be turned over to them in 2011. Kapawi is built according to the Achuar concept of architecture, using typical materials, and emphasizes environmentally friendly methods such as solar energy, biodegradable soaps and rubbish recycling. It is in a zone rich in biodiversity, with many opportunities for seeing the forest and its inhabitants. Five-days/4-nights cost US$835 per person, plus US$200 for transport to and from Quito. The location, indigenous participation, quality of service, cabin accommodation, and food have all been highly recommended.

Eating

Lago Agrio and around p396, map p397
There are decent mid-range restaurants at the better hotels. Those at D'Marios and Machala are recommended. There are also a great many very cheap and basic comedores, all along Av Quito between Manabí and Colombia.
† Cafetería Jaqueline, Quito y Amazonas, bakery serving breakfast and snacks.
† Un Pedacito de Colombia, Quito y Colombia, bakery with set lunch and typical Colombian baked goods like buñuelos.

Coca and around p398, map p398
††† El Portón, Bolívar y Quito. Grill.
††† Parrilladas Argentinas, Cuenca e Inés Arango. Argentine-style grill.
†††-†† Pizza Choza, Rocafuerte y Napo, daily 1700-2200. Good pizza, English spoken.

¶¶ **Las Ensaladas**, Rocafuerte y Quito.
Fruit salads and snacks.
¶¶ **Media Noche**, Napo, in front of **Hotel El
Auca**, open 1800-0000. Chicken dishes.
¶¶-¶ **Ocaso**, Eloy Alfaro between Napo and
Amazonas. Good value set meals and à la carte.
There are other cheap *comedores* in town.

🍷 Bars and clubs

Coca and around *p398, map p398*
Pappa Dan's, Napo y Chimborazo by the
river, open from around 1600 hrs, pleasant
location. There are many others in town.

▲ Activities and tours

Reserva Faunística Cuyabeno *p397*
The following Quito operators all run tours
to the reserve.
Neotropic Turis, T02-2521212,
www.neotropicturis.com Operates the
Cuyabeno Lodge, cabins with private or
shared baths, US$295 per person for 4
days/3 nights, including all meals and
bilingual guides, but excluding transport to
and from Lago Agrio and the park entry fee.
Ecuador Verde Pais, T02-2220614,
www.cabanasjamu.com Operates **Jamu
Lodge**, 4 days/3 nights cost US$180 per
person plus transport and park fees, starting
in the village of Cuyabeno.
   All of the following also offer tours
in the reserve: **Dracaena**, T02-2546590,
dracaena@andinanet.net, recommended;
Green Planet, T02-2520570, greenpla
@interactive.net.ec; and **Kapok Expeditions**,
T02-2556348, www.kapokexpeditions.com

Coca and around *p398, map p398*
A common misconception is that it is easy
to find a cheap jungle tour in Coca. In fact,
the majority of tours out of Coca are booked
through agencies in Quito (see Jungle lodges,
above, and Quito tour operators p134) and
other tourist centres. There are not many tour
operators left in Coca itself. Prices here start
at around US$40 per person per day.

Tour operators
River Dolphin Expeditions, Ramiro Viteri,
no storefront, contact T09-4603087
rde4amazon@yahoo.com or through **Hotel
El Auca**.

Wymper Torres, no storefront, contact
T06-2880336, ronoboa@latinmail.com He
specializes in the Río Shiripuno and
Pañacocha areas, Spanish only.

🚌 Transport

For main inter-city routes, see the bus
timetable, p52.

Lago Agrio and around *p396, map p397*
Air
The airport is 5 km southeast of the centre.
TAME and **Icaro** fly to **Quito**, daily except
Sun, US$60 one way. It's best to book 1-2
days in advance, and reconfirm often. If there
is no space available to **Lago Agrio** then you
can fly to **Coca** instead, from where it is only
2 hrs by bus on a good road.

Bus
The *Terminal Terrestre* is located in the north
of town, but buses for Coca leave from the
market area on Orellana, 3 blocks south of
Av Quito. There are 2 routes from Lago Agrio
to **Quito**, both with bus service. Although
slower, the southern route through Coca
and Loreto may be somewhat safer from
hold-ups than the northern one through El
Dorado de Cascales and Lumbaqui. Do not
travel to or from Lago Agrio overnight.

Coca and around *p398, map p398*
Air
The airport is in the north of town. To/from
Quito, 3-4 flights daily Mon-Sat, only 1 on
Sun, with **TAME** and **Icaro** Mon-Sat US$60
one way; reserve as far in advance as
possible and always reconfirm. Flights in and
out of Coca are heavily booked, oil workers
may have priority. **Icaro** office is in **Hotel La
Misión**, T06-2880546. **TAME** office is at Napo
y Rocafuerte, T/F06-2881078, Mon-Fri
0800-1200, 1300-1700.

Bus
Long distance buses depart from company
offices in town (see map); local destinations,
including **Lago Agrio**, are served from the
terminal a little to the north.

River
Down the Río Napo to **Nuevo Rocafuerte**
on the Peruvian border, motorized canoes

depart Mon, Tue and Thu before 0800, 10-12 hrs, US$15 (cheaper on Tue); take water, hat, sunscreen, etc. Stops on route at **Pompeya** and **Pañacocha**. Contact **Cooperativa de Transporte Fluvial Orellana**, T06-2880087.

There is no regular boat service from Coca upriver to **Misahuallí**. For a price, however, the willing traveller can hire a canoe with owner and outboard motor to take them anywhere along the Napo; ask around at dock and Capitanía.

ⓘ Directory

Lago Agrio and around *p396, map p397*
Banks There are no reliable ATMs in Lago Agrio and travellers' cheques are very difficult to use or exchange, try **Hotel Americano** if you are stuck. Credit cards are only accepted at the best hotels. Colombian *pesos* are exchanged in shops and on the street, ask around.

Coca and around *p398, map p398*
Banks Banco de Pichincha, Bolívar y 9 de Octubre. **Cambiaria Ramírez**, Napo y García Moreno, T06-2881229, Mon-Sat 0800-2000, sometimes changes travellers' cheques for 4% commission. Does not change Peruvian *soles*. **Internet** Prices around US$2 per hr. **Useful addresses** Immigration, Rocafuerte y Napo, Edificio Amazonas, 3er piso, 0730-1230, 1500-1800. For those travelling to or from Peru passports are normally stamped at Nuevo Rocafuerte, not Coca, but you can confirm details here before sailing.

Southern Oriente

Stretching south of the Río Pastaza, the southern Oriente is made up of the provinces of Morona-Santiago and Zamora-Chinchipe. This is a less developed region and, although tourism is only just getting started, it has a great deal to offer. The area has maintained its natural and cultural integrity in part because of the traditionally determined – at times hostile – attitude of the Shuar and Achuar people who live here, and also due to the relatively little petroleum development to date, although mining poses a hazard. The signing of a peace treaty in 1998 between Ecuador and Peru over their disputed border has also helped to introduce tourism to the region. There is a great deal to explore here, but all visitors to virgin territory should remember that they have an especially important obligation to be responsible tourists in this region (see page 46). ▸▸ For Sleeping, Eating and other listings, see pages 409-412.

Puyo to Macas

The first leg of the Puyo-Macas bus journey goes for three hours as far as the Río Pastaza, where there is an impressive and hair-raising suspension bridge suitable only for small cars. Bus passengers disembark and walk across, there are small vehicles to shuttle heavy luggage. Construction began on a new bridge in 2004 but this may take several years. On the opposite shore, another bus takes you the rest of the way (2½ hrs) to Macas, some of this road is paved. The jungle here has become pastures and secondary forest.

Macas → *Phone code 07 Colour map 5, grid B1 Population 14,000 Altitude 1,000 m*

Capital of Morona-Santiago province, situated high above the broad Río Upano valley, Macas is a pleasant tranquil town, established by missionaries in 1563. The immense snow-capped Sangay volcano can be seen on rare clear mornings from the plaza, creating an amazing backdrop to the tropical jungle surrounding the town. Puffs of smoke may sometimes be seen and, even more infrequently, a red glow at night from the crater of this still very active volcano – an unforgettable sight!

Ins and outs

Macas is small enough to walk around. Hotels are dotted around a bit but easy to get to; the airport runway is right alongside town. The climate is not too hot and the nights are even cool. **Camara de Turismo** ① *Bolívar 7-37 y Soasti, Mon-Fri 0730-1230.*

Sights

The modern **cathedral**, completed in 1992, with beautiful stained-glass windows, houses the much venerated image of La Purísima de Macas. It overlooks a neat central plaza. Five blocks north of the cathedral, along Don Bosco, is the shady **Parque Recreational** which affords great views of the Upano Valley. It has a small orchid collection. The **Museo de la Casa de la Cultura Ecuatoriana** ① *10 de Agosto y Soasti, 3rd floor, Mon-Fri 0800-1230, 1400-1730, free*, has a small collection of local artefacts.

Excursions

Complejo Hombre Jaguar is an archaeological site of the Upano and Tayos cultures, 1200-300 BC. It is north of town near Santa Rosa and Guapú; US$12 by taxi from Macas to Guapú norte, then a one-hour walk. Day tours can be arranged with **Winia Sunka**, US$30 including transport, guide and lunch, see Macas Tour Operators page 411.

Parque Nacional Sangay. The lowland area of the park has interesting walking with many rivers and waterfalls, and can be reached by taking a bus to the little village of 9 de Octubre (no services), daily at 0700 and 1600, US$1.50, 1½ hours. Local residents may be able to guide you from there to Sardinayacu and other natural attractions. Take all gear and provisions or arrange a tour from Macas. 9 de Octubre is also the start of a controversial new road which runs from **Macas to Atillo and Riobamba** in the central highlands near Riobamba, cutting through the middle of the national park (see page 248). The road has been 'almost completed' for many years

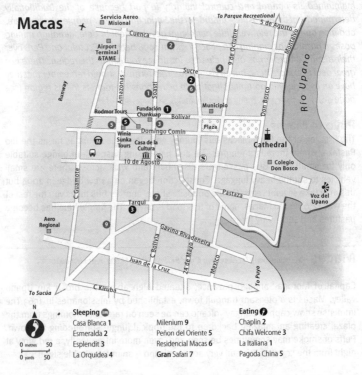

Macas

To Parque Recreational

Servicio Aereo Misional · Cuenca · Airport Terminal & TAME · Amazonas · Runway · Rodmor Tours · Fundación Chankuap · Soasti · Sucre · 9 de Octubre · 5 de Agosto · Montalvo · Don Bosco · Río Upano · Municipio · Bolívar · Plaza · Domingo Comín · Winia Sunka Tours · Casa de la Cultura · 10 de Agosto · Cathedral · Colegio Don Bosco · C Guamote · Pastaza · Tarqui · Voz del Upano · Aero Regional · Gavino Rivadeneira · C Bolívar · 24 de Mayo · Mexico · Juan de la Cruz · C Kiruba · To Puyo

To Sucúa

N

0 metres 50
0 yards 50

Sleeping 🛏
Casa Blanca 1
Esmeralda 2
Esplendit 3
La Orquídea 4
Milenium 9
Peñon del Oriente 5
Residencial Macas 6
Gran Safari 7

Eating 🍴
Chaplin 2
Chifa Welcome 3
La Italiana 1
Pagoda China 5

Sucúa and south → *Phone code 07 Colour map, grid B1 Population 6,300*

Located 23 km south of Macas, Sucúa was of particular interest as the centre of a branch of the ex-head-hunting Shuar (Jívaro) Indians. You can contact the **Federacíon Shuar** at Domingo Comín 17-38, T/F07-2740108, for information about visiting traditional villages, but the federation is officious and generally uninterested in tourists. It is better to go through a tour agency in Macas, see page 411.

Nearby is the Río Upano, a 1½-hour walk, with plenty of Morpho butterflies. Also close by is the Río Tutanangoza, a 15-minute walk, with rapids and good swimming, but be careful of the current after rain.

Logroño

From Sucúa the road becomes rougher and narrower, and heads south for 23 km to the quiet little town of **Logroño**, with a large shady plaza. An extensive network of limestone caves is found 2 km from town, a 30-minute walk. They are on the property of Sr. Mario Crespo, who lives one block south of the park, T07-2702520. He is friendly and helpful and can organize visits to the cave, entry US$2, there is a locked gate. The best months to visit are during dry season, December-January, but the caves are subject to flash flooding throughout the year. Spelunking equipment is required for more extensive exploration. Rustic camping is possible by the shores of the Río Upano, not far from the cave mouth.

Méndez and around

Located 29 km further south, (Santiago de) **Méndez** is a nice town with a pleasant round plaza and modern church. Méndez is a crossroads. From here a road climbs west through **Guarumales** and **Paute** to **Cuenca**. Another, described as the worst in all of Ecuador, heads east through **Patuca**, with a military checkpoint (have passport at hand), to **Santiago** and **San José de Morona**, near the Peruvian border. There is basic accommodation and meals in Santiago. This is untouristed country and there is scope for exploration. See Macas transport (page 412) for details of bus service and Macas Activities and tours (page 411) for river travel to Peru along the Río Morona. Note however that this is not an official border crossing, you will be turned back unless special arrangements have been made in advance.

Limón and around

Limón, official name General Leónidas Plaza Gutiérrez, is 35 km south of Méndez, a mission town founded in 1935, and now a busy, friendly place surrounded by high jungle. Buses, all from Calle Quito, go to Cuenca, Macas and Gualaquiza.

Around 11 km south of Limón, a rough road branches west at the **Plan de Milagro** police checkpoint and climbs to **Cuenca** (132 km) via **Gualaceo**. From Limón this road rises steeply with many breathtaking turns and the vegetation changes frequently, partly through cloud forest and then, at 4,000 m, through the *páramo*, before dropping very fast down to the valley of Gualaceo. This is one of the best roads in Ecuador for birdwatching but there is nowhere to stay along the way. See Macas Transport for details of bus service (page 412).

Gualaquiza → *Phone code 07 Colour map 6, grid B5 Population 6,500*

Continuing south from Plan de Milagro the road passes **Indanza** (6 km, very basic *residencial* and *comedor*), before reaching **Gualaquiza** in a further 45 km. Gualaquiza is a pleasant pioneer settlement with an imposing church on a hilltop overlooking town. There are lovely waterfalls, rivers (good for tubing), caves, and undeveloped archaeological sites in the area. The **Chorrera de Guabi** is a beautiful cascade but access is difficult, best take a guide. The **El Remanso ruins** near **El Aguacate village** are of interest on the road to Sigsig. Information is provided by the **Oficina Municipal de Turismo** ① *on the plaza, T07-2780109.* Also try Antonio Quezada at the **Hotel Wakis/Aroma Café** ① *T07-2780138.*

Gualaquiza is also the end of the **Jima (Gima) to La Florída trek**, see page 278. Tourist infrastructure and information are both lacking outside Gualaquiza itself, so you should be reasonably self-sufficient and prepared to do a lot of asking around.

At Gualaquiza a very rough and narrow road forks northwest to climb steeply to **Cuenca** via **Sigsig**. Gualaquiza is therefore a crossroads for travel north to Macas, south to Zamora and Loja, and up to Cuenca. ▶ *For details of bus services, see Gualaquiza transport, page 412.*

Gualaquiza to Zamora

It is 35 km south from Gualaquiza to **El Pangui**, a linear roadside town with two simple hotels and interesting orchid nurseries nearby, see **Ecuagénera** page 277. Around 20 km further south is **Yantzaza**, a dusty supply town for nearby ranching and mining, with basic accommodation and *comedores*. **Zumbi** is 8 km south of Yantzaza, where a bridge crosses the Río Zamora and a road leads east to **Paquisha** on the upper Río Nangaritza and beyond to the **Cordillera del Condór** – the formerly disputed border with Peru. Tourism is beginning to develop in the **Alto Nangaritza**; Cabañas Yankuám ① *2½ hrs east of the turn-off at Zumbi, contact Zamora T07-2605739,* have been built here.

South of Zumbi along the road to Zamora, the broad valley of the Río Zamora becomes progressively narrower, with forested mountains and lovely views on either side. There is a turn-off at **La Saquea**, 10 km south of Zumbi, northwest to **Yacuambi**, a curious little place which is the terminus of the trek from **Saraguro** (see page 286). Yacuambi has basic services, and *aguardiente* (cane liquor) is produced and liberally consumed here. From La Saquea, the main road continues south for another 25 km to Zamora.

Zamora → *Phone code 07 Colour map 6, grid B4 Population 10,500 Altitude 950 m*

The southernmost city in Oriente and capital of the province of Zamora-Chinchipe, Zamora is an old mission settlement at the confluence of the Ríos Zamora and Bombuscara. It is most easily reached on a paved road from Loja with frequent bus service, and is also connected to Oriente towns further north. Zamora is hilly and services are a bit spread out, which makes for pleasant walking up and down the narrow streets. It has traditionally been far off the beaten path, but worthwhile attractions are gradually opening it up to tourism. Mining is an important part of the province's economy and also a threat to its natural environment. **Oficina Municipal de Turismo** ① *3rd floor of the Palacio Municipal, Diego de Vaca y 24 de Mayo, main plaza, T07-2605996.*

Sights

Refugio Ecológoco Tzanka ① *José Luis Tamayo y Jorge Mosquera, US$2, T07-2605692,* has a small zoo and an interesting collection of plants including some rare specimens (not for sale). There is also a simple furnished apartment for rent here. The owners, Mario and Alva González, are very friendly and enthusiastic.

Orquideario Pafinia ① *Av del Ejercito Km 2 via a Yantzaza, T07-2605911, call ahead to arrange a visit,* has an extensive orchid collection. The owner, Sr. Melecio Jiménez, speaks English.

Zamora's most important attraction is the easy access it provides to the subtropical part of **Podocarpus National Park**, via the **Bombuscara** entrance ① *Park entry fee US$10; pick-up from the Terminal Terrestre to park entrance, US$4 each way. Take the road east out of Zamora and turn right when you reach the Río Bombuscara. Do not cross the river; take the road that follows the river upstream. The road ends in 6 km at a car park, where the trail begins. There are basic facilities at the visitors' centre where you can arrange to stay, but you must bring your own food, sleeping bag, mosquito protection (important in the rainy season), etc.* The entrance trail along the Bombuscara river is very pleasant and full of subtropical birds hard to find elsewhere in Ecuador (such as coppery-chested jacamar, white-breasted parakeet, several rare fruiteaters, and many more). About 30 minutes' walk takes you to the visitors' centre and more trails, including a river trail and a 30-minute loop trail. It is highly recommended for nature lovers, especially those who might have difficulty walking on steep trails. The trail to the visitors' centre is virtually flat, unlike almost all other trails at this elevation in Ecuador.

Half-way from Zamora to the park entrance is **Copalinga**, an 80-ha private reserve with nice forest, good trails (some very steep) and excellent birdwatching. There are comfortable cabins on the site and meals are available if arranged in advance, see Zamora Seeping for details (page 410). They also offer volunteer opportunities.

● Sleeping

Macas *p405, map p406*

AL Cabañas Ecológicas Yuquipa, on the Río Yuquipa, 1½ hrs walk from Km 12 on the road to Puyo, enquire in advance at Panadería Pancesa, Soasti y 10 de Agosto, T07-2700071. Package includes room, 3 meals, guide and transport.

B-C Manzana Real, at southern entrance to town, T07-2700191. More expensive rooms incude breakfast, restaurant, pool, parking, suite available. Upscale for where it is but some rooms are small.

C Cabañas del Valle, Vía a Sucúa km 1.5, T07-2700302. Includes breakfast, electric shower, parking, small modern cabins on pleasant grounds. Friendly owner can organize tours but he is not easy to reach, best book in advance.

C-D Casa Blanca, Soasti 14-29 y Sucre, T07-2700195, F2701584. Includes breakfast, clean, modern and comfortable, very friendly and helpful. Often full, best book in advance. Recommended.

D California, 29 de Mayo at south end of town, T/F07-2701237. Cheaper with shared bath, electric shower, some rooms have fan, parking, modern and adequate.

D Esmeralda, Cuenca 6-12 y Soasti, T07-2700130. Family-run, clean and friendly but some rooms are a bit small.

D Gran Safari, Soasti y Tarqui, T07-2700113.

Modern new building, cheaper rooms in older annexe.

D La Orquídea, 9 de Octubre 13-05 y Sucre, T07-2700970. Cheaper with cold water.

D Milenium, Amazonas y Tarqui, T07-2700805. Cheaper with shared bath, small modern rooms, bottled water and coffee on tap on small terrace, good value and friendly.

D Peñón del Oriente, Domingo Comín 8-37 y Amazonas, near market and bus terminal, T07-2700124, F2700450. In multi-storey building, noisy, rooms vary but overall a bit run down.

D-E Esplendit, Soasti 15-18 y Domingo Comin, T07-2700120. Parking, new section is nice and comfortable, older rooms are cheap and basic with shared bath and cold water.

E Residencial Macas, 24 de Mayo 14-35 y Sucre, T07-2700254. Above **Chaplin** restaurant, cheaper with shared bath, cold water, old wooden building, simple but clean and good value.

Sucúa *p407*

C Arutam, Vía a Macas Km 1, north of town, T07-2740851. Restaurant, pool and spa, modern and comfortable, very nice.

D Don Guimo, Domingo Comín y Kiruba, T07-2740483. Cheaper with shared bath, parking, modern and comfortable.

E Karina, on the southwest corner of the plaza, T07-2740153. Cheaper with shared bath, hot water, clean and bright.

Logroño *p407*

D-E Brisas del Upano, on the plaza, T07-2702267. One room with private bath, cold water, friendly and adequate.

Méndez and around *p407*

D Interoceanico, C Quito on the plaza, T07-2760245, F2760082. Parking, very clean and modern, good value. Best in town.
D-E Los Ceibos, C Cuenca 1 block west of the plaza, T07-2760133. Cheaper with shared bath, clean and modern, small rooms.
E Los Sauces, C Cuenca 1 block west of the plaza, T07-2760165. Cheaper with shared bath, hot water, small rooms but adequate.

Limón and around *p407*

D-E Residencial Dianita, C Quito, T07-2770122. Cheaper with shared bath, cold water, basic.
E Dream House, C Quito. Friendly, adequate.
E Residencial Limón, C Quito, T/F07-2770114. Shared bath, cold water, basic clean and friendly, front rooms noisy.

Gualaquiza *p407*

D Internacional, C Cuenca y García Moreno, T07-2780637, F2780781. Restaurant, cheaper with cold water, most rooms have fan, modern and best in town.
E Guadalupe, Gonzalo Pesántez 8-16 y García Moreno, T07-2780113. Cheaper with shared bath, cold water, indoor parking, simple but clean and friendly, popular, good value.
E Wakis, Orellana 08-52 y Domingo Comín, T07-2780138. **Aroma Café** downstairs, cheaper with shared bath, cold water, small rooms, enthusiastic owner Antonio Quezada speaks English and organizes tours.
F Amazonas, Domingo Comín 08-65 y Gonzalo Pesantes, on main plaza, T07-2780715. Shared bath, cold water, basic.

Gualaquiza to Zamora *p408*

E Yanku, on main plaza in Yantzaza, T07-2301183. Private bath, cold water, fan, simple but best in town.
E-F Hotel El Pangui, Across the street from the bus station in El Pangui, T07-2310240.

Cheaper with shared bath, cold water, parking, adequate.

Zamora *p408*

B-D Copalinga, Km 3 on the road to the Bombuscara entrance of Podocarpus national park, T07-2605043 or T09-3477013, jacamar@impsat.net.ec Comfortable wooden cabins in a lovely setting with balconies overlooking the forest, meals available if arranged in advance. Some cabins have private bath, excellent birdwatching, English and French spoken, Belgian-run, friendly and helpful. Recommended.
C Hostería El Arenal, Km 12½ on the road to Yantzaza, T07-2606763. Modern hotel, out of town in a pleasant setting, restaurant, pool, fridge, parking, horse riding available. Popular with local families, busy on weekends and holidays.
D Betania, Francisco de Orellana entre Diego de Vaca y Amazonas, T07-2607030, hotelbetaniaz@hotmail.com Includes breakfast, parking, clean and modern.
D Gimyfa, Diego de Vaca y Pío Jaramillo, T07-2605024. Carpeted rooms, a bit bare but clean and good value.
D Orillas del Zamora, Diego de Vaca y Alonso de Mercadillo, T07-2605754. Modern, clean, comfortable and good value. Recommended.
D-E Chonta Dorada, Pío Jaramillo y Diego de Vaca, T07-2606384. Electric shower, clean and adequate.
F Seyma, 24 de Mayo y Amazonas, T07-2605583. Shared bath, cold water, basic.
   There are several cheap and basic places to stay on C Tarqui.

● Eating

Macas *p405, map p406*

¶¶¶ **Pagoda China**, Amazonas y Domingo Comín, daily 1130-2230. Very good Chinese food, generous portions, authentic decor, popular and recommended.
¶¶¶-¶¶ **La Italiana**, Bolívar 6-07 y Soasti, daily 1000-0000. Pizza and pasta.
¶ **Chaplin**, 24 de Mayo 14-55 y Sucre, daily 0700-2130. Good set meals, popular.
¶ **Chifa Welcome**, Tarqui entre Soasti y Amazonas. Very cheap set lunch.
   Several small *comedores* along Domingo Comín serve local specialities such as

aymapacos, spiced chicken or palm hearts wrapped in *bijao* leaves and roasted over the coals. They are tasty but keep an eye on cleanliness.

Sucúa *p407*
Gyna, Domingo Comín, ½ block south of the park. Set meals and à la carte.
La Orquidea, 8 de Diciembre y Domingo Comín. Good set meals.

South of Sucúa *p407*
There are a couple of cheap *comedores* around the plaza in **Logroño** and several simple places to eat along C Cuenca in **Méndez**. There are several basic *chifas* in **Limón** aswell as the **El Viajero** restaurant at bus the terminal.

Gualaquiza *p407*
Cabaña Los Helechos, 12 de Febrero y Gonzalo Pesántez, near bus station. Set meals.
Copacabana, 12 de Febrero y Gonzalo Pesántez, near bus station. Set meals, pleasant location on a 2nd-floor balcony.

Zamora *p408*
King Burguer, Diego de Vaca y José Luis Tamayo, by the plaza, one of the few places open Sun. Chicken and burgers.
Don Pepe, Sevilla de Oro y Pío Jaramillo, opposite the Hospital, daily 0600-2100. Good set meals and à la carte.

There are also several cheap *comedores* near the market and bus station, but again, keep an eye on cleanliness.

Bakeries
Spiga Pan, 24 de Mayo, ½ block downhill from the plaza. Great bakery with a variety of hot bread, cream cakes and fresh fruit yoghurt. This is actually the best place to eat in this decidedly un-gastronomic town! Recommended.

Bars and clubs

Macas *p405, map p406*
Cachorros, 24 de Mayo y Bolívar, starting 2100 daily except Sun. Varied music, pleasant atmosphere.

Gualaquiza *p407*
Aroma Café, at Hotel Wakis, nice and low key.

Shopping

Macas *p405, map p406*
Shops are well stocked with most supplies but prices are a little higher because of the remote location.
Fundación Chankuap, Soasti y Bolívar, T07-2701176, www.chankuap.com This cooperative sells a nice variety of locally produced crafts and food products.

Activities and tours

Macas *p405, map p406*
Tour opportunies include rafting on the **Río Upano**, visits to lowland portions of **Parque Nacional Sangay**, to local native communities as well as deeper into the jungles of the **Cordillera de Cutucú** and beyond to the **Peruvian border**. An interesting new route being opened up is along the Río Morona to the **Marañón** and **Reserva Nacional Pacaya-Samiria** in Peru, ending in Iquitos. This requires preparations well in advance, contact **Winia Sunka** in Macas (see below) or **Neotropic Turis** in Quito (p136).

Tour operators
Rodmor Tours, Domingo Comín 7-35 y Soasti, T07-2701328, tours run by Taylor Rodríguez.
Winia Sunka, Domingo Comín y Amazonas, the kiosk in front of **Chifa Pagoda China**, T/F07-2700088, pablovguias@hotmail.com Owner Pablo Velín is an experienced and recommended guide.

Zamora *p408*
Discovery Zamora, T07-2606207. Vinici Macanchi rents kayaks and organizes rafting trips on the Ríos Zamora and Bombuscara, US$40 per person per day.
Wellington Valdivieso is a naturalist guide who can organize tours to the Alto Nangaritza. Contact him well in advance, T07-2605132 (office hours), manacus_manacus@yahoo.es

⊖ Transport

For main inter-city routes, see the bus timetable, p52.

Macas *p405, map p406*
Air
The small modern airport is within walking distance, at Cuenca y Amazonas. Flights to /from **Quito** with TAME, Tue and Thu, US$60. TAME office is at the airport, T/F07-2701162. **Servicio Aereo Misional**, at the airport, T/F07-2700142, serves small communities in the jungle. No scheduled routes and they are normally not permitted to carry tourists, but can charter aircraft for special projects and emergencies. **Servicio Aereo Regional**, C Tarqui by the runway, T07-2702433, charters light aircraft by the hr.

Bus
All buses leave from the small *Terminal Terrestre* near the market. There are 2 different routes to **Cuenca**, one through Méndez and Paute, 8-9 hrs; the other through Limón and Gualceo, 10 hrs. Both cost US$8.50, and are rough and subject to landslides after heavy rain. No direct buses to **Loja** or **Zamora**, you must change in Gualaquiza, US$8, 9 hrs.

Two buses a day to **San José de Morona** via Santiago along the 'worst road in Ecuador', US$8.50, 10-12 hrs. To **Sucúa**, every 30 mins, US$0.80, 1 hr.

Gualaquiza *p407*
There is a small but surprisingly busy Terminal Terrestre, Gonzalo Pesántez y 12 de Febrero, at the south end of town. 8 buses a day to **Zamora**, US$3.50, 5 hrs; and **Loja** US$6, 7 hrs. To **Macas**, at 1800 and 1900, US$8, 9 hrs. There are 2 routes to **Cuenca**: one via Plan de Milagro and Gualaceo, daily at 2130 with **Turismo Oriental**, US$7, 8 hrs; and another on the shorter but rougher road via Sigsig, 0300 and 0900 daily with **Express Sigsig** or **Cenepa**, US$6.35, 6 hrs. There are *rancheras* serving outlying communities and pickups can be hired for excursions, eg US$25 to El Agucate.

Zamora *p408*
To **Gualaquiza**, US$3.50, 5 hrs, where you can change buses for **Macas**, see above.

❶ Directory

Macas *p405, map p406*
Banks Nowhere to change TCs. Banco del Austro, 24 de Mayo y 10 de Agosto. Banco del Pichincha, Soasti y 10 de Agosto. **Internet** US$1 per hr. **Laundry** Serviclin, 24 de Mayo y Juan de Salinas, at south end of town, US$3 a dozen, wash and dry. **Post office** 9 de Octubre y Domingo Comín, next to the park.

Gualaquiza *p407*
Internet Small place 1 block south of bus terminal, US$1/hr.

Zamora *p408*
Banks Bring cash. There are no ATMs, and nowhere to get cash advances or change TCs. **Internet** 1 or 2 small cybercafés, US$1/hr.

Galápagos Islands

⁑ Footprint features

Introduction

A trip to the Galápagos is a unique and unforgettable experience. As Charles Darwin put it: "The Natural History of this archipelago is very remarkable: it seems to be a little world within itself". The islands are world-renowned for their fearless wildlife but no amount of hype can prepare the visitor for such a close encounter with nature. Here, you can snorkel with penguins and sea lions, watch giant 200 kg tortoises lumbering through cactus forest and enjoy the courtship display of the blue-footed booby and frigate bird, all in startling close-up.

A visit to the islands doesn't come cheap. The return flight from Quito and national park fee add up to almost US$500; plus a bare minimum of US$70 per person per day for sailing on the most basic boat, which, at this price, are in high demand and not easy to find. Top-end luxury cruises cost up to US$4,000 for eight days. Land-based and independent travel on the populated islands are both viable alternatives, but there is at present simply no way to enjoy Galápagos on a shoestring. The once-in-a-lifetime Galápagos experience is well worth saving for, however, and at the same time, these high prices are one way of keeping the number of visitors within reasonable levels, thereby limiting the impact on the islands and their wildlife.

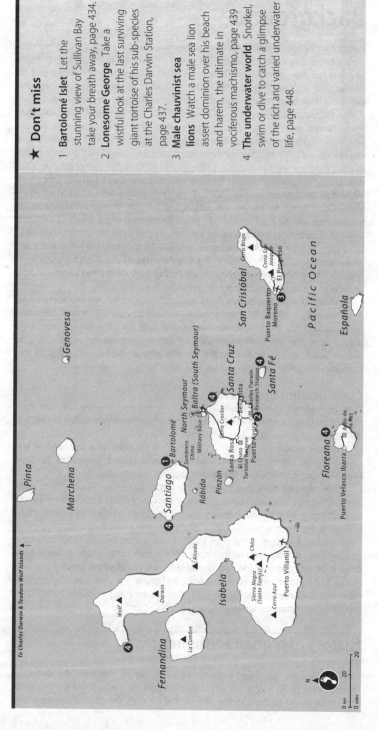

★ **Don't miss**

1 **Bartolomé Islet** Let the stunning view of Sullivan Bay take your breath away, page 434.

2 **Lonesome George** Take a wistful look at the last surviving giant tortoise of his sub-species at the Charles Darwin Station, page 437.

3 **Male chauvinist sea lions** Watch a male sea lion assert dominion over his beach and harem, the ultimate in vociferous machismo, page 439.

4 **The underwater world** Snorkel, swim or dive to catch a glimpse of the rich and varied underwater life, page 448.

Galápagos Islands

Background

Lying on the Equator, 970 km west of the Ecuadorean coast, the Galápagos consist of six main islands: San Cristóbal, Santa Cruz, Isabela, Floreana, Santiago and Fernandina (the last two are uninhabited). There are also 12 smaller islands – Baltra and the uninhabited islands of Santa Fe, Pinzón, Española, Rábida, Daphne, Seymour, Genovesa, Marchena, Pinta, Darwin and Wolf – as well as over 40 small islets.

The Galápagos have never been connected with the continent. Gradually, over many hundreds of thousands of years, animals and plants from over the sea somehow migrated there and as time went by they adapted themselves to Galápagos conditions and came to differ more and more from their continental ancestors. Thus many of them are unique: a quarter of the species of shore fish, half of the plants and almost all the reptiles are found nowhere else. In many cases different forms have evolved on the different islands. Charles Darwin recognized this speciation within the archipelago when he visited the Galápagos on the Beagle in 1835 and his observations played a substantial part in his formulation of the theory of evolution. Since no large land mammals reached the islands (until they were recently introduced by man), reptiles were dominant just as they had been all over the world in the very distant past. Another of the extraordinary features of the islands is the tameness of the animals. The islands were uninhabited when they were discovered in 1535 and the animals still have little instinctive fear of man.

Only the four populated islands (San Cristóbal, Santa Cruz, Isabela and Floreana) can be visited independently. All the other islands can only be visited on cruises. Galápagos has been called the greatest wildlife show on earth but it is worth keeping in mind that it is not a theme park. The Islands have a unique natural history, as well as a controversial human history, and understanding the interplay between the two will help place your experience in context. ▶▶ For Sleeping, Eating and other listings, see pages 442-451.

Classification of species

Plant and animal species in the Galápagos are grouped into the following three categories. These are terms which you will hear often during your visit to the islands. ▶▶ For further details, refer to the colour wildlife section, pages 9-16.

Endemic species are those which occur only in the Galápagos and nowhere else on the planet. Examples are the **Marine** and **Land Iguana, Galápagos Fur Seal, Flightless Cormorant** and the **'Daisy tree'** (*Scalesia pedunculata*).

Native species make their homes in the Galápagos as well as other parts of the world. Examples include all three species of **boobies, Frigate birds** and the various types of **mangroves**. Although not unique to the islands, these native species have been an integral part of the Galápagos ecosystems for a very long time.

Introduced species on the other hand are very recent arrivals, brought by man, and inevitably the cause of much damage. They include **cattle, goats, donkeys, pigs, dogs, cats, rats** and over 500 species of plants such as **elephant grass** (for grazing cattle), and fruit trees such as the **raspberry** and **guava**. The unchecked expansion of these introduced species has upset the natural balance and seriously threatens the unique endemic species for which Galápagos is so famous.

History of human settlement

The islands were discovered accidentally by Tomás de Berlanga, the Bishop of Panama, in 1535. He was on his way to Peru when his ship was becalmed and swept 800 km off course by the currents. Like most of the early arrivals, Bishop Tomás and

✷ The Galápagos Affair

One of the more bizarre and notorious periods of human life on the islands began in 1929 with the arrival of German doctor and philosopher, Friedrich Ritter, and his mistress, Dore Strauch. Three years later, the Wittmer family also decided to settle on the island, and Floreana soon became so fashionable that luxury yachts used to call in. One of these visitors was Baroness von Wagner de Bosquet, an Austrian woman who settled on the island with her two lovers and grandiose plans to build a hotel for millionaires. (Such inflated ambitions were eventually realized in 2002 with the opening of the *Royal Palm* hotel on Santa Cruz Island, see Puerto Ayora Sleeping, p442.)

Soon after landing in 1932, the Baroness proclaimed herself Empress of Floreana, which was not to the liking of Dr Ritter or the Wittmer family, and tensions rose. There followed several years of mysterious and unsavoury goings-on, during which everyone either died or disappeared, except Dore Strauch and the Wittmer family. The longest survivor of this still unexplained drama was Margret Wittmer, who lived at Black Beach on Floreana until her death in 2000, at age 95. Her account of life there, entitled *Floreana, Poste Restante*, was published in 1961 and became a bestseller, but she took the story of what really happened on the island in the 1930s with her to the grave. See *The Galápagos Affair*, by John Treherne, under Books, page 482.

his crew arrived thirsty and disappointed at the dryness of the place. He did not even give the islands a name, although he did dub the giant tortoises 'Galápagos'.

The islands first appeared on a map in 1574, as 'Islands of Galápagos', which has remained in common use ever since. The individual islands, though, have had several names, both Spanish and English. The latter names come from a visit in 1680 by English buccaneers who, with the blessing of the English king, attacked Spanish ships carrying gold and relieved them of their heavy load. The pirates used the Galápagos as a hide-out, in particular a spot North of James Bay on Santiago island, still known as Buccaneers' Cove. The pirates were the first to visit many of the islands and they named them after English kings and aristocracy or famous captains of the day.

The Spanish called the islands *Las Encantadas*, 'enchanted' or 'bewitched', owing to the fact that for much of the year they are surrounded by mists giving the impression that they appear and disappear as if by magic. Also, the tides and currents were so confusing that they thought the islands were floating and not real islands.

Between 1780 and 1860, the waters around the Galápagos became a favourite place for British and American whaling ships. At the beginning of the whaling era, in 1793, a British naval captain erected a barrel on Floreana island to facilitate communication between boats and the land. It is still in Post Office bay to this day.

The first island to be inhabited was Floreana, in 1807, by a lone Irishman named Patrick Watkins, who grew vegetables to trade for rum with passing ships. After two years he commandeered a lifeboat and a handful of sailors but later arrived in Guayaquil without his companions, who were never seen again. After his departure the Galápagos were again uninhabited for 25 years, but the bizarre episode set the tone for many more unusual colonists and nefarious events. Their story is told in *The Curse of the Tortoise*, by Octavio Latorre; see Books page 481.

In 1832 Ecuadorean General José Villamil founded a colony on Floreana, mainly composed of convicts and political prisoners, who traded meat and vegetables with whalers. The same year, following the creation of the young republic, Colonel Ignacio

Hernández took official possession of the archipelago for Ecuador. Spanish names were given to the islands, in addition to the existing English ones, and both remain in use. From 1880 to 1904 Manuel J. Cobos ran a large sugar cane plantation and cattle ranch on San Cristóbal, notorious for mistreatment of its workers who eventually mutinied and killed him. The cruelty of prison colonies and slave farms like Cobos' cast a dark shadow over human presence in the archipelago. There followed Norwegian fishermen and German philosophers, among others, many of whom met with some strange and tragic fate. Among the earliest colonists to endure were the Wittmer family on Floreana and the Angermeyers on Santa Cruz, whose story is beautifully told in *My Father's Island*, by Johanna Angermeyer; see Books page 481.

Current population

Human settlement on the Galápagos is currently limited to about 3% of the islands' land area of 7,882 sq km, but nevertheless, the resident population of the islands has grown very rapidly in recent years. The latest census (2001) counted almost 19,000 people but this does not include a floating population (people 'temporarily' living on the islands, sometimes for many years) of 3,000 or more. The population is concentrated in eight settlements. Two are on San Cristóbal (Chatham), at Puerto Baquerizo Moreno and a small village inland called El Progreso. San Cristóbal has a population of 5,600, and Puerto Baquerizo Moreno is the administrative capital of the province of Galápagos and Ecuador's second naval base. There are three settlements on Santa Cruz (Indefatigable) – Puerto Ayora, the largest town and the main tourist centre, Bellavista and Santa Rosa, two small farming communities inland. Santa Cruz is the most populated island, with 11,400 inhabitants. On Floreana, the longest inhabited island, there are 88 souls, most of which are at Black Beach and on Isabela (Albemarle), the largest island, there is a thriving community of 1,600 mostly at Puerto Villamil and a agricultural zone inland at Tomás de Berlanga. Residents of the Islands, now into their third and fourth generation, call themselves *colonos*, *Galapagueños* or *carapachudos*. The latter literally means 'those with a shell', a tongue-in-cheek reference to the giant tortoises.

Evolution and conservation

Galápagos has unique marine and terrestrial environments. This is due to the continuing volcanic formation of the islands in the west of the archipelago and its location at the nexus of several major marine currents, among other factors. Their interaction has created laboratory-type conditions where only certain species have been allowed access. Others have been excluded, and the resulting ecology has evolved in a unique direction, with many of the ecological niches being filled from some unexpected angles. A highly evolved sunflower, for instance, has in some areas taken over the niche left vacant by the absence of trees.

There are some formidable barriers here which prevent many species from travelling within the islands, hence a very high level of endemism. For example, not only have the tortoises evolved differently from those in the rest of the world, but each of the five main volcanoes on Isabela has evolved its own subspecies of giant tortoise. This natural experiment has been under threat ever since the arrival of the first whaling ships and even more so since the first permanent human settlement. New species were introduced and spread very rapidly and the unique endemic species are at risk. More recently still, quarantine programmes have been implemented by the authorities in an attempt to prevent the introduction of even more species. There have also been campaigns to eradicate some of the introduced species on some islands, but this is inevitably a very slow, expensive and difficult process. ►► *For details and photographs of Galápagos wildlife, see pages 9-16.*

⁞ Charles Darwin and the Galápagos

Without doubt, the most famous visitor to the islands is Charles Darwin. His short stay in the archipelago proved hugely significant for science and for the study of evolution.

In September 1835, Darwin sailed into Galápagos waters on board the HMS *Beagle*, captained by the aristocratic Robert FitzRoy whose job was to chart lesser-known parts of the world. FitzRoy had wanted on board a companion of his own social status and a naturalist, to study the strange new animals and plants they would find en route. He chose Charles Darwin to fill both roles.

Darwin was only 22 years old when he set sail from England in 1831 and it would be five years before he saw home again. They were to sail around the world, but most of the voyage was devoted to surveying the shores of South America, giving Darwin the chance to explore a great deal of the continent. The visit to the Galápagos had been planned as a short stop on the return journey, by which time Darwin had become an experienced observer. It was indeed a stroke of luck that he had been picked for this unique cruise.

During the five weeks that the *Beagle* spent in the Galápagos Darwin went ashore to collect plants, rocks, insects and birds. The unusual life forms and their adaptations to the harsh surroundings made a deep impression on him and eventually inspired his revolutionary theory on the evolution of species. The Galápagos provided a kind of model of the world in miniature. Darwin realized that these recently created volcanoes were young in comparison with the age of the Earth, and that life on the islands showed special adaptations. Yet the plants and animals also showed similarities to those from the South American mainland, where he guessed they had originally come from.

Darwin concluded that the life on the islands had probably arrived there by chance drifting, swimming or flying from the mainland and had not been created on the spot. Once the plants and animals had arrived, they evolved into forms better suited to the strange environment in which they found themselves. Darwin also noted that the animals were extremely tame, because of the lack of predatory mammals. The islands' isolation also meant that the giant tortoises did not face competition from agile mammals and could survive.

On his return to England, Darwin in effect spent the rest of his life publishing the findings of his voyage and developing the ideas it inspired. It was, however, only when another scientist, named Alfred Russell Wallace, arrived at a similar conclusion to his own that he dared to publish a paper on his theory of evolution.

Then followed his all-embracing *The Origin of Species* by means of natural selection, in 1859. It was to cause a major storm of controversy and to earn Charles Darwin recognition as the man who "provided a foundation for the entire structure of modern biology".

The human effect

The most devastating of the newly introduced species are human beings, both visitors and settlers. To a large degree, the two groups are connected, one supporting the other economically, but there is also a sizeable proportion, over half of the islands' permanent residents, who make an income independent of tourism from working the land or at sea.

While no great wealth has accumulated to those who farm, fortunes are being made by exporters and fishermen in a series of particularly destructive fisheries: black coral, lobster, shark fin, sea cucumber and most recently sea horse. Sharks were caught by setting gill nets across a bay. These nets took a wide range of marine animals and birds as a by-catch, including pelicans, boobies, seals, turtles and dolphins. As none have any commercial value, they were dumped. Each successive fishery is encouraged by foreign demand involving large amounts of money and fishermen have become an especially powerful and at times aggressive lobby group. In late 2004, for example, when their demands for increased quotas and new fishing techniques were not immediately met, some fishermen slaughtered giant tortoises in reprisal.

It is, however, farmers who are responsible for the largest number of introduced species. Recent introductions (since the formation of the National Park) include elephant grass to provide pastures, the ani to eat parasites living on cattle (although in the Galápagos it prefers baby finches when it can get them) and walnut trees planted on Isabela.

Neither are tourists nor the industry which they support blameless. In 2001 a small tanker which supplied fuel for tour boats and locals ran aground in the entrance to Puerto Baquerizo Moreno harbour. Thanks to favourable currents most of the resulting oil spill was carried out to sea and relatively little damage was inflicted on any of the Galápagos Islands or their animals. It was, however, a very close call and stringent regulatory measures are required if such accidents are to be prevented in the future.

The number of visitors to the islands is, in principle, controlled by the authorities to protect the environment. Limits were increased from 25,000 in 1981, reached 50,000 by 1997 and had exceeded 100,000 by 2004. At the close of this edition (Feb 2005) there were a total of 84 permits for tourist boats, ranging in capacity from 8 to 110 passengers, as well as growing land-based tourism; but no new permits are supposed to be issued in the near future. Even by international standards, tourism in Galápagos is well organized and regulated; by Latin American standards or those of mainland Ecuador, it seems remarkably so. Yet Galápagos is not inherently immune to the short-sighted and unsustainable development practices that have caused so much destruction elsewhere in Ecuador and Latin America. The islands cannot sustain further uncontrolled growth in tourism or population. Exceptional foresight, vigilance and altruism are required by all parties if Galápagos is to remain intact for the next generation of visitors.

The authorities

At least five different authorities have a say in running Galápagos – the islands and surrounding marine reserve. These include: 1) **Instituto Nacional Galápagos** (INGALA), under control of the president of Ecuador, which was once responsible for most of the islands' infrastructure and today decides who is entitled to the status of *'colono'* (colonist, or Galápagos resident); 2) the **National Park Service**, under the authority of the Ministerio del Ambiente, which regulates tourism and manages the 97% of the archipelago which is parkland; 3) the **Charles Darwin Research Station**, part of an international non-profit organization devoted to supporting scientific research and channelling international funds for conservation; 4) the **Ecuadorean Navy**, which patrols the waters of the archipelago and attempts to enforce regulations regarding both tourism and fishing; 5) local **elected authorities** including municipalities and the provincial council, which – in principle – advocate the interests of all the islands' residents. All of the above must work together but since they represent different sets of interests, this is seldom an easy task.

Visiting Galápagos

Most visitors to the Islands book all-inclusive cruises or land-based tours and do not need to make any additional arrangements. Their only challenge is selecting a boat or agency; for advice about how to do so see Touring, page 424. Also refer to Unpopulated islands visitor sites, page 434, for information about the sites visited on these tours.

Some travellers may wish to extend their stay on the Islands, either before or after their tour, and a very few others are interested in independent travel on the populated islands, the only places where such travel is permitted. For these travellers, local information is given in Ins and outs (below) and under each populated island, see pages 436-441.

Ins and outs

Getting there

Air There are two airports which receive flights from mainland Ecuador, but no international flights to Galápagos. The most frequently used airport is at **Baltra** (South Seymour), across a narrow strait from Santa Cruz, the other at **Puerto Baquerizo Moreno**, on San Cristóbal. The two islands are 96 km apart and on most days there are local flights in light aircraft between them, as well as to Puerto Villamil on Isabela island. There is also boat service between Puerto Ayora, Puerto Baquerizo Moreno, Puerto Villamil and occasionally Floreana island. See Getting around, below.

All flights to Galápagos originate in Quito. **TAME** has two flights daily to Baltra and operates Monday, Wednesday and Saturday to San Cristóbal. **AeroGal** flies daily to Baltra, and Monday, Thursday, Saturday and Sunday to San Cristóbal. These schedules are subject to change. The return fare in high season (1 November-30 April and 15 June-14 September) is US$390 from Quito, US$345 from Guayaquil. The low season fare costs US$334 from Quito, and US$300 from Guayaquil. The same prices apply regardless of whether you fly to San Cristóbal or Baltra; you can arrive at one and return from the other. You can also depart from Quito and return to Guayaquil or vice versa. The ticket is valid for 21 days from the date of departure. Independent travellers should always reconfirm their bookings, especially in high season.

The prices indicated above are subject to change without notice. Discount fares for Ecuadorean nationals and residents of Galápagos are not available to foreigners and these rules are strictly enforced. On both **TAME** and **AeroGal**, a 15% discount off the high season fare applies to students with an ISIC card.

Baltra Two buses meet flights from the mainland at Baltra: one runs to the port or muelle (10 minutes, no charge) where the cruise boats wait; the other goes to Canal de Itabaca, the narrow channel which separates Baltra from Santa Cruz. It is 15 minutes to the Canal, free, then you cross on a small ferry for US$0.75, another bus waits on the Santa Cruz side to take you to Puerto Ayora in 45 minutes, US$1.80. If you arrive at Baltra on one of the local inter-island flights (see below) then you have to wait until the next flight from the mainland for bus service, or you might be able to hire a taxi (US$15). For the return trip to the airport, buses leave from opposite the two companies offices near the pier (see map, page 443) to meet flights at Baltra (enquire locally for current schedules).

Puerto Baquerizo Moreno This pleasant little airport is within walking distance of town, but those on prearranged tours will be met by transport. Pick-up trucks can be hired if you are on your own and have lots of gear (US$1).

Sea The small and decrepit **cargo vessels** which sail from Guayaquil to Galápagos are not permitted to carry passengers and the rules are strictly enforced.

Yachts may occasionally take on passengers (usually for a daily fee) for the one to two week sail from Panama to Galápagos or the marathon 3000 nautical mile (minimum 30 days) crossing from Galápagos to the Marquesas. You can ask around the docks or look for notices posted in cybercafés and other spots frequented by travellers. This involves placing a great deal of trust in the boat owner since there is no way to change your mind once at sea. Negative experiences have been reported by some travellers, especially lone women.

Entry tax Every foreign visitor to Galápagos must pay a National Park Tax of US$100 on arrival, cash only. Be sure to have your passport to hand. Do not lose your park tax receipt; boat captains need to record it. A 50% reduction on the national park fee is available to children under 12, but only those foreigners who are enrolled in an Ecuadorean university are entitled to the reduced fee for students.

Getting around
Air Emetebe Avionetas ① *offices in Puerto Baquerizo Moreno, Puerto Ayora and Puerto Villamil are given in the corresponding sections below. In Guayaquil T04-2292492, emetebe@ecua.net.ec*, offers inter-island flights in two light twin-engine aircraft (a five-seater and a nine-seater). Two daily flights operate between Puerto Baquerizo Moreno (San Cristóbal), Baltra and Puerto Villamil (Isabela), on most days, but this may vary depending on passenger demand. Baggage allowance is 30 lbs, strictly enforced. Fares range from US$80-90 one way, including taxes.

Sea INGALA ① *San Cristóbal, T05-2520133*, operate a boat twice a week between Puerto Ayora and Puerto Baquerizo Moreno and once a month between Puerto Ayora and Floreana. The **Municipio de Isabela** ① *contact Galaven in Puerto Ayora, T05-2526359*, run the *Estrella de Mar III* twice a week between Puerto Ayora and Puerto Villamil; US$46.

Fibras (fibreglass launches with outboard motors) operate irregularly between all ports, US$25-30 per person (negotiable) one way if there are enough passengers, or you can charter a *fibra* for yourself. Ask around the docks and at the Capitanía de Puerto. Safety standards are not enforced for *fibras* as they are for other craft. Make sure there are enough life vests onboard, take your own drinking water, and try to avoid single-engine boats. You must be flexible in your itinerary and allow plenty of time if you wish to travel between islands in this way.

Special permits Those planning to carry out scientific research, commercial or documentary filming and any other special activities which are not part of usual tourism may require permits. It is best to enquire and make all arrangements well in advance. A useful contact is Roslyn Cameron at the **Charles Darwin Research Station** ① *Puerto Ayora, Santa Cruz, T05-2526146 (ext 120), cdrs@fcdarwin.org.ec, www.darwinfoundation.org* For the **National Park Service** in Puerto Ayora contact the **Departamento de Comunicación** ① *T05-2526511 (ext 130), png@spng.org.ec*

Touring in Galápagos

There are two main ways to travel around the islands: a cruise (also called 'tour navegable'), where you sleep on the boat, or slightly less expensive land-based tours where you sleep ashore at night and travel during the day. On a cruise you travel at night, arriving at a new visitor site each day, with more time ashore. On a land-based

tour you spend less time ashore, cover less ground and cannot visit the more distant islands. A third option is independent travel on the populated islands. Although neither cheap nor a substitute for either of the above, it can be done and allows those with plenty of time to explore a small part of the archipelago at their leisure. All tours begin with a morning flight from the mainland on the first day and end on the last day with a midday flight back to the mainland. Prices are somewhat cheaper in the low season and you will have more options available.

Cruises

It is not possible to generalize about exactly what you will find on the boat in which you cruise around the Galápagos Islands. The standard of facilities varies from one craft to another and you basically get what you pay for in terms of comfort, service and food. Once on shore at the visitor sites, no matter what price you have paid, each visitor is shown the same things because of the strict park rules on limited access. Note however that smaller and cheaper boats may not visit as many or as distant sites. On the other hand, larger vessels may not be allowed to take passengers to some of the more fragile landings such as Daphne Major.

The less expensive boats are normally smaller and less powerful so you see less and spend more time travelling; also the guiding may be only in Spanish. The more expensive boats will probably have air conditioning, hot water and private baths. All boats have to conform to certain minimum safety standards and have VHF radio; more expensive boats are better equipped. A water maker can be a great asset. Note that boats with over 18 passengers take quite a time to disembark and re-embark people, while the smaller boats have a more lively motion, which is important if you are prone to seasickness. Note also that there may be limitations for vegetarians on the cheaper boats, enquire in advance.

Each day starts early and schedules are usually full. If you are sailing overnight, your boat will probably have reached its destination before breakfast. After eating, you disembark for a morning on the island. The usual time for snorkelling is between the morning excursion and lunch. The midday meal is taken on board because no food is allowed on the islands. If the island requires two visits (for example Genovesa/Tower, or Española/Hood), you will return to shore after lunch, otherwise part of the afternoon may be taken up with a sea voyage. After the day's activities, there is time to clean up, have a drink and relax before the briefing for the next day and supper.

Itineraries are controlled by the National Park to distribute tourism evenly throughout the islands. Boats are expected to be on certain islands on certain days. They can cut landings, but have to get special permission to add to a planned itinerary. All boats must re-provision and this is done in Puerto Ayora once a week. On

Galápagos Islands Visiting Galápagos

the day the boats are in port the passengers visit the Darwin Station and either the highlands or lava tubes or Tortuga Bay. Boats do not put into port just to take off or put on passengers, however some boats do take advantage of the day they are in Puerto Ayora anyway, to change some or all of their passengers.

Price categories

The least expensive boats (economy class) cost about US$70-100 per person per day; they are usually small and slow. For around US$100-150 per day (tourist and tourist superior class) you will be on a faster small boat which can travel more quickly between visitor sites, leaving more time to spend ashore. US$150-200 per day (first class) is the price of the majority of better boats. Over US$200 per day is entering the luxury bracket, with far more comfortable and spacious cabins, as well as a superior level of service and cuisine. No boat may sail without a park-trained guide.

Note however, that the above classification is somewhat arbitrary and involves considerable overlap. An excellent Galápagos experience can be had on even the cheapest boats if you are willing to rough it a little. Almost all visitors are thoroughly satisfied, but there is the occasional complaint. Remember that all boats look good in brochures and websites, and nothing is more valuable than a personal recommendation by a recent passenger if you can find one. **Note** We have received repeated complaints about the vessel *Free Enterprise*.

Booking a cruise

You can book a Galápagos cruise in several different ways: 1) over the the internet; 2) from either a travel agency or directly though a Galápagos wholesaler in your home country; 3) from one of the very many agencies found throughout Ecuador, especially in Quito but also in Guayaquil; or 4) from agencies in Puerto Ayora but not Puerto Baquerizo Moreno. The trade-off is always between time and money: booking from home is most efficient and expensive, Puerto Ayora cheapest and most time-consuming, while Quito and Guayaquil are intermediate. Prices for a given category of boat do not vary all that much, however, and it is not possible to obtain discounts or make last-minute arrangements in high season. Those who attempt to do so in July, August or over Christmas/New Year often spend several very frustrating weeks in Puerto Ayora without ever sailing the islands. The following section lists recommended agencies and operators abroad and in Puerto Ayora. Agencies in Quito and Guayaquil are listed on pages 134 and 318, respectively.

> **!** The islands get very busy in July and August, when it is impossible to make last-minute cruise arrangements.

UK agents

Select Latin America (incorporating Galapagos Adventure Tours), 79 Maltings Pl, 169 Tower Bridge Rd, London SE1 3LJ, T020-74071478, www.selectlatinamerica.com David Horwell arranges quality tailor-made holidays and small group tours to Ecuador and the Galápagos Islands.
Galapagos Classic Cruises, 6 Keyes Rd, London NW2 3XA, T020-8933 0613, F8452 5248, www.galapagoscruises.co.uk Specialists in tailor-made cruises and diving holidays to the islands with additional land tours to Ecuador and Peru on request.
Penelope Kellie, Steeple Cottage

Easton, Winchester, T01962-779317, F779458, www.quasarnautica.com, pkellie@yachtors.u-net.com She is the UK agent for **Quasar Nautica** (see Quito Tour operators, p134) and comes recommended.

North American agents

Galapagos Holidays, 14 Prince Arthur Av, Suite 109, Toronto, Ontario M5R 1A9, T416-4139090, T1-800-6612512, www.galapagosholidays.com
Galápagos Network, 5805 Blue Lagoon Dr, Suite 160, Miami, FL 33126, T305-2626264, T800-6337972 (toll free), F305-2629609, www.ecoventura.com

Inca Floats, Bill Robertson, 1311 63rd St,
Emeryville, CA 94608, T510- 4201550
F4200947, www.inca1.com
International Expeditions,
One Environs Park, Helena, Alabama, 35080,
T205-4281700, T1-800-6334734 (toll free),
www.internationalexpeditions.com
Quasar Nautica (see also Quito Tour
operators, p134), 7855 N.W. 12th St, Suite
221, Miami, FL 33126, T1-800-884-2105,
T1-800-247-2925, T305-599-9008,
www.quasarexpeditions.com
Sol International, 13780 S. W., 56 St,
Suite 107, Miami, FL 33175, T561-8260173,
T1-800-7655657 (toll free), F305-3829284,
www.solintl.com
Tambo Tours, 20919 Coral Bridge La,
Suite 225-A, Spring, TX 77388, USA,
T001-281 5289448, www.2GOPERU.com
Long-established adventure and tour
specialist with offices in Peru and USA.
Customized trips to the Amazon and

archaeological sites of Peru and Ecuador. **429**
Daily departures for groups and individuals.
Wilderness Travel, 801 Allston Way,
Berkeley, CA 94710, T1-800-3682704,
www.wildernesstravel.com

Quito and Guayaquil agents

Shopping around the many agencies
in Quito is a good way of securing a
value-for-money cruise, if you have the
time. It is worth asking if the vessel has
one to three spaces to fill on a cruise; you
can try to get them at a discount. There
are of course a great many other agencies
throughout Ecuador which sell Galápagos
tours, the key is to shop around carefully
and not let yourself be rushed into a
decision. See Tour operators in Quito, p134,
and Guayaquil, p318, for further details.

¦ Galápagos Tips

Responsible tourism
→ Never touch any of the animals, birds or plants.
→ Do not transfer sand, seeds or soil from one island to another.
→ Do not leave litter anywhere – it is highly undesirable in a National Park and is a safety and health hazard for wildlife.
→ Do not take food on to the islands.

Making the most of your trip
→ Always bring some US$ cash, no other currencies are accepted. There is only one bank and ATM system on Galápagos, which may not work with all cards.
→ Daytime clothing should be lightweight and even on luxury cruises should be casual and comfortable. At night, particularly at sea and at higher altitudes, warm clothing is required.
→ Note that boots and shoes soon wear out on the lava terrain.
→ A remedy for seasickness is recommended.
→ A good supply of sun block and skin cream to prevent windburn and chapped lips is essential, as are a hat and sunglasses.
→ You should be prepared for dry and wet landings. The latter involves wading ashore.
→ Take plenty of memory cards or film with you. The animals are so tame that you will use far more than you expected. A telephoto lens is not essential, but bring it if you have one. Take filters suitable for strong sunlight.
→ An underwater camera is also an excellent idea.
→ Snorkelling equipment is particularly useful as much of the sea-life is only visible underwater. Few of the cheaper boats provide equipment and those that do may not have good snorkelling gear. If in doubt, bring your own, rent in Puerto Ayora, or buy it in Quito. It may be possible to sell it afterwards either on the islands or back in Quito.
→ A recommended map is *The Galápagos Islands*, 1:500,000 map by Kevin Healey and Hilary Bradt (Bradt Publications, 1985).
→ Also recommended is the *Galápagos Pocket Guide* (and map) by Nelson Gómez, available in most Quito bookshops.
→ On most cruises a ship's crew and guides are usually tipped separately. The amount is a very personal matter; you may be guided by suggestions made onboard or in the agency's brochures, but the key factors should always be the quality of service received and your own resources.
→ Legitimate complaints may be made to any or all of the following: the Ministerio de Turismo, Capturgal or the Capitanía de Puerto all in Puerto Ayora; see addresses below.

Puerto Ayora agents

In the low season, if you wish to wait until you reach the islands, Puerto Ayora is the only practical place for arranging a cruise; this cannot be done in Puerto Baquerizo Moreno. In Puerto Ayora you may find slightly better prices than the mainland, especially off-season at the last minute, but bear in mind that you could be faced with a long wait. In the high season (July, August, and mid-December to mid-January) there is no space available on a last-minute basis and you must book your cruise before arriving in Galápagos.

To arrange last-minute tours, a recommended contact is the **Moonrise** travel agency. There are also several other agencies in town, see Puerto Ayora Tour operators, page 449. Especially for cheaper boats, try to get a personal recommendation from someone who has recently taken a tour and check carefully about what is and is not included (for example drinking water, snorkelling equipment and so on).

Galápagos tourist vessels

The following table lists various categories of tourist vessels operating in Galápagos with their respective descriptions, capacities and websites. The list is not exhaustive and lack of inclusion does not necessarily imply poor quality. All sailers also have motors, and many frequently operate under engine power.

The categories and prices shown are approximate and subject to change. The names, owners, operators, agents or websites of boats may likewise change. Remember also that captains, crews and guides regularly change on all boats. These factors, as well as the sea, weather and your fellow passengers will all influence the quality of your experience.

Name	Description	Capacity	Website
Luxury and first class	**(over US$150 per person per day)**		
Galápagos Legend	cruise ship	110	www.kleintours.com
Galápagos Explorer II	cruise ship	100	www.canodros.com
Xpedition	cruise ship	98	various
Santa Cruz	cruise ship	90	www.galapagosvoyage.com
Polaris	cruise ship	80	www.expeditions.com
Eclipse	cruise ship	48	www.unigalapagos.com
Islander	cruise ship	47	www.expeditions.com
Isabela II	cruise ship	40	www.galapagosvoyage.com
Evolution	cruise ship	32	www.quasarnautica.com
Coral I	motor yacht	26	www.kleintours.com
Coral II	motor yacht	20	www.kleintours.com
Eric	motor yacht	20	www.ecoventura.com
Flamingo I	motor yacht	20	www.ecoventura.com
Galápagos Adventure	motor yacht	20	various
Letty	motor yacht	20	www.ecoventura.com
Archipel Eco	motor catamaran	18	www.galacruises.com
Lammar Law	2-masted trimaran	18	www.quasarnautica.com
Alta	3-masted ketch	16	www.quasarnautica.com
Amigo I	motor yacht	16	various
Beluga	motor yacht	16	www.enchantedexpeditions.com
Cachalote	2-masted schooner	16	www.enchantedexpeditions.com
Cruz Del Sur	motor yacht	16	www.galasam.com
Edén	motor yacht	16	www.galapagostours.net
Estrella de Mar	motor yacht	16	www.galasam.com
Galápagos Adventure II	motor yacht	16	various
Heritage	4-masted sailer	16	various
Integrity	motor yacht	16	www.inca1.com
Liberty	motor yacht	16	www.galasam.com
Millenium	motor catamaran	16	www.galasam.com

Parranda	motor yacht	16	www.quasarnautica.com
Reina Silvia	motor yacht	16	www.reinasilvia.com
Sagitta	3-mast sailing ship	16	www.angermeyercruises.com
The Beagle	2-mast schooner	16	angermeyercruises.com
Tip Top III	motor yacht	16	www.rwittmer.com
Samba	motor yacht	14	www.angermeyercruises.com
Diamante	2-mast sailer	12	www.angermeyercruises.com
Mistral II	motor yacht	12	www.quasarnautica.com
Nemo	1-mast catamaran	12	www.galapagos-tours.com
Panchita II	motor yacht	10	various
Sea Cloud	2-mast sailer	8	www.angermeyercruises.com

Tourist superior and tourist class   (US$100-150 per person per day)

Aida Maria	motor yacht	16	www.galapagostours.net
Angelique	2-mast sailer	16	www.galapagos-angelique.com
Angelito I	motor yacht	16	www.enchanted expeditions.com
Daphne	motor yacht	16	various
Darwin Explorer	motor yacht	16	www.unigalapagos.com
Floreana	motor yacht	16	various
Gaby I	motor vessel	16	various
Guantanamera	motor yacht	16	various
Lobo de Mar III	motor yacht	16	www.unigalapagos.com
Pelikano	motor yacht	16	www.galapagos-tours.com
Rumba	motor yacht	16	www.galapagostours.net
Sea Man	motor yacht	16	www.galacruises.com
Sulidae	2-mast ketch	16	www.hotelsilberstein.com
Tip Top II	motor yacht	16	www.rwittmer.com
Antartida	motor vessel	10	www.galasam.com
Golondrina I	motor vessel	10	various
Nortada	motor yacht	10	various
Ahmara	1-mast catamaran	8	various
Merak	1-mast sailer	8	various

Economy class   (under US$100 per person per day)

Darwin	motor vessel	16	various
Flamingo	motor vessel	12	various
Sarah Dayuma	motor vessel	12	www.galapagos-angelique.com
Yolita	motor vessel	12	various
Cormorant	motor vessel	10	various
Poseidon	motor vessel	10	various

Live-aboard diving cruises

Deep Blue	motor yacht	16	various
Sky Dancer	motor yacht	16	www.ecoventura.com
Jesús del Gran Poder	motor yacht	14	various
Encantada	2-mast schooner	12	www.scubagalapagos.com

The islands → *Colour map 1*

The Galápagos have been declared a World Heritage Site by UNESCO and 97% of the land area and 100% of the surrounding ocean are now part of the Galápagos National Park and Marine Reserve. Within the park there are some 60 visitor sites, each with defined trails, so the impact of visitors to this fragile environment is minimized. These sites can only be visited with a National Park guide as part of a cruise or tour.

Each of the visitor sites has been carefully chosen to show the different flora and fauna and, due to the high level of endemism, nearly every trail has flora and fauna that can be seen nowhere else in the world. The itineraries of tourist boats are strictly regulated in order to avoid crowding at the visitor sites and some sites are periodically closed by the park authorities in order to allow them to recover from the impact of tourism. Certain sites are only open to smaller boats and, additionally, limited to a maximum number of visits per month.

The 3% of Galápagos which is not National Park is made up of towns and agricultural zones on four populated islands: Santa Cruz, San Cristóbal, Isabela and Floreana. The populated parts of these islands are the only ones which may be visited independently, but there are also large restricted areas of National Park land on these populated islands. ▸▸ *For Sleeping, Eating and other listings on these islands, see pages 442-451.*

Unpopulated islands visitor sites

Baltra
Once a US Airforce base, Baltra is now a small military base for Ecuador and also the main airport into the islands. The island is quite arid and that, along with the rubble left by the USAF, gives it the appearance of a junk yard. Also known as South Seymour, this is the island most affected by human habitation. **Mosquera** is a small sandy bank just north of Baltra, home to a large colony of sea lions.

Bartolomé
Bartolomé is a small island located in Sullivan Bay off the eastern shore of Santiago. It is probably the most easily recognized, the most visited and most photographed, of all the islands in the Galápagos with its distinctive **Pinnacle Rock**. The trail leads steeply up to the summit, taking 30-40 minutes, from where there are panoramic views. At the second visitor site on the island there is a lovely beach from which you can snorkel or swim and see the penguins.

Daphne Major
West of Baltra, Daphne island has very rich birdlife, in particular the nesting boobies. Because of the possible problems of erosion, only small boats may land here and are limited to one visit each month.

Española
This is the southernmost island of the Galápagos and, following a successful programme to remove all the feral species, is now the most pristine of the islands with many migrant, resident and endemic seabirds. **Gardner Bay**, on the northeastern coast, is a beautiful white sand beach with excellent swimming and snorkelling. **Punta Suárez**, on the western tip of the island, has a trail through a rookery. As well as a wide range of seabirds (including blue-footed and masked boobies) there is a great selection of wildlife including sea lions and the largest and most colourful marine iguanas of the Galápagos plus the original home of the waved albatrosses.

66 99 Plaza Sur is the home of the Men's Club, a rather sad-looking colony of bachelor sea lions who are too old to mate and who get together to console each other...

Fernandina

Fernadina is the youngest of the islands, at about 700,000 years old, and also the most volcanically active, with eruptions every few years. The visitor site of **Punta Espinosa** is on the northeast coast of Fernandina. The trail goes up through a sandy nesting site for huge colonies of marine iguanas. The nests appear as small hollows in the sand. You can also see flightless cormorants drying their atrophied wings in the sun and go snorkelling in the bay.

Genovesa

Located at the northeast part of the archipelago, this is an outpost for many sea birds. It is an eight to ten hour all-night sail from Puerto Ayora. Like Fernandina, Genovesa is best visited on longer cruises or ships with larger range.

One of the most famous sites is **Prince Phillip's Steps**, an amazing walk through a seabird rookery that is full of life. You will see tropic birds, all three boobies, frigates, petrels, swallow-tailed and lava gulls, and many others. There is also good snorkelling at the foot of the steps, with lots of marine iguanas. The entrance to **Darwin Bay**, on the eastern side of the island, is very narrow and shallow and the anchorage in the lagoon is surrounded by mangroves, home to a large breeding colony of frigates and other seabirds.

Plaza Sur

One of the closest islands to Puerto Ayora is Plaza Sur. It's an example of a geological uplift and the southern part of the island has formed cliffs with spectacular views. It has a combination of both dry and coastal vegetation zones. Walking along the sea cliffs is a pleasant experience as the swallowtail gull, shearwaters and red billed tropic birds nest here. This is the home of the Men's Club, a rather sad-looking colony of bachelor sea lions who are too old to mate and who get together to console each other. There are also lots of blue-footed boobies and a large population of land iguanas on the island.

Rábida

This island is just to the south of Santiago. The trail leads to a salt water lagoon, occasionally home to flamingos. There is an area of mangroves near the lagoon where brown pelicans nest. This island is said to have the most diversified volcanic rocks of all the islands. You can snorkel and swim from the beach.

Santa Fe

This island is located on the southeastern part of Galápagos, between Santa Cruz and San Cristóbal, and was formed by volcanic uplift. The lagoon is home to a large colony of sea lions who are happy to join you for a swim. From the beach the trail goes inland, through a semi-arid landscape of cactus. This little island has its own sub-species of land iguana.

Santiago

This large island, also known as James, is to the east of Isla Isabela. It has a volcanic landscape full of cliffs and pinnacles, and is home to several species of marine birds. This island has a large population of goats, one of the four species of animals introduced in the early 1800s.

James Bay is on the western side of the island, where there is a wet landing on the dark sands of **Puerto Egas**. The trail leads to the remains of an unsuccessful salt mining operation. Fur seals are seen nearby. **Espumilla Beach** is another famous visitor site. After landing on a large beach, walk through a mangrove forest that leads to a lake usually inhabited by flamingos, pintail ducks and stilts. There are nesting and feeding sites for flamingos. Sea turtles dig their nests at the edge of the mangroves. **Buccaneer Cove**, on the northwest part of the island, was a haven for pirates during the 1600s and 1700s. **Sullivan Bay** is on the eastern coast of Santiago, opposite Bartolomé Island. The visitor trail leads across an impressive lunar landscape of lava fields formed in eruptions in 1890.

Seymour Norte

Just north of Baltra, Seymour Norte is home to sea lions, marine iguanas, swallow-tailed gulls, magnificent frigate birds and blue-footed boobies. The tourist trail leads through mangroves in one of the main nesting sites for blue-footed boobies and frigates in this part of the archipelago.

Sombrero Chino

This is just off the southeastern tip of Santiago, and its name refers to its shape. It is most noted for the volcanic landscape including sharp outcroppings, cracked lava formations, lava tubes and volcanic rubble. This site is only available to yachts of less than 12 passengers capacity.

Santa Cruz

This is the main inhabited island. Most of the 11,400 inhabitants live in and around **Puerto Ayora**, but there are farming settlements inland at **Bellavista** and **Santa Rosa**. Puerto Ayora is the economic centre of the Galápagos and every cruise visits it for one day anchoring at Academy Bay. There is free time to do some shopping, make phone calls and so on, but the main visit is to the **Charles Darwin Research Station.**

Tours can be arranged in Puerto Ayora and some cruise itineraries include a guided visit to the interior of the island. The highlands and settlement area of Santa Cruz are worth seeing for the contrast of the vegetation with the arid coastal zones.

Puerto Ayora → *Phone code 05 Colour map 1 Population 9,600*

Puerto Ayora, on the south shore of Isla Santa Cruz, is the largest town of Galápagos and the main tourist centre. It is a busy prosperous place, offering a wide range of hotels and restaurants. Most tourist services, including agencies for last-minute cruise bookings, are concentrated along the attractive Malecón Charles Darwin which also has many souvenir shops.

The 'real town' fills the streets back from the sea and some prices are a little lower here. Although cheap accommodation and simple meals can still be found in Puerto Ayora, the cost of most goods throughout Galápagos is up to double that on the Ecuadorean mainland. Puerto Ayora is safe and relaxed. If you are travelling independently and choose to arrange a cruise from here instead of the mainland, then it is a pleasant place to stay for a few days and a good base for several worthwhile excursions. Most streets have special bicycle lanes called *ciclovías*, running in both directions.

T05-2526174, mturgal@ec-gov.net, Mon-Fri 0800-1200, 1400-1700, has general
information and maps for all of Galápagos. The **Dirección Municipal de Turismo** ① *on
the same premises, T05-2526613,* has information about Puerto Ayora and Santa Cruz
Island. **CAPTURGAL** ① *Av Charles Darwin y Charles Binford, T05-2526206,
www.galapagostour.org Mon-Fri 0730-1200, 1400-1730*, the Galápagos Chamber of
Tourism, English spoken.

Charles Darwin Research Station

① *Academy Bay, a 20-min walk from the dock at Puerto Ayora, offices Mon-Fri
0700-1600, visitor areas 0600-1800 daily.*

In 1959, the centenary of the publication of Darwin's Origin of Species, the
Government of Ecuador and the International Charles Darwin Foundation
established, with the support of UNESCO, the Charles Darwin Research Station. A visit
to the station is a good introduction to the islands as it provides a lot of information.
Collections of several of the rare sub-species of giant tortoise are maintained on the
station as breeding nuclei, though, sadly, no mating partner has yet been found for
Lonesome George, the sole remaining member of the Isla Pinta sub-species. There is
also a tortoise-rearing area where the young can be seen.

There are some areas of interest at and near the grounds of the Darwin Station. A
small rocky beach is halfway between the interpretation centre and the entrance and
is popular with local families at weekends. Past the interpretation centre on the
paved road, and to the right of the Tomas Fischer Science building, a trail leads to a
rocky beach where marine iguanas and crabs can be observed. Following a small trail
between the gift shop at the entrance and the **Hotel Galápagos,** you can see the stone
house built by the Norwegian pioneer Sigurd Graffer in 1933.

Around Puerto Ayora

One of the most beautiful beaches in the Galápagos Islands is at **Tortuga Bay,** 45
minutes' easy walk (2.5 km each way) west from Puerto Ayora on an excellent cobbled
path through cactus forest. Start at the west end of Calle Charles Binford; further on
there is a gate where you must register, open 0600-1800 daily. Take sun screen,
drinking water, and beware of the very strong undertow. Camping is not permitted
anywhere. Do not leave your valuables unattended at the beach. Also, do not walk on
the dunes above the beach, which are a marine tortoise nesting area. Ten minutes'
walk to the west end of Tortuga Bay brings you to a trail to a lovely mangrove-fringed
lagoon, five minutes beyond. The water here is calmer and warmer, and there is nice
shade under the mangroves.

Las Grietas is a beautiful gorge with a pool at the bottom which is splendid for
bathing. Take a water taxi from the port to the dock at Punta Estrada (5 mins,
US$0.50). It is a five-minute walk from here to the Finch Bay hotel. Skirt around the left
side of the hotel and continue on the public path to the large lagoon behind it. Skirt
the lagoon on its left side and then follow a clear path; it is 15 minutes further over
rough lava boulders to Las Grietas – and well worth the trip.

Santa Cruz excursions and visitor sites

Tour operators in Puerto Ayora (see page 449) run excursions to the highland sites for
about US$20-30 per person, depending on the number of sites visited and the size of
the group. These may include visits to ranches such as Rancho Mariposa (enquire at
Moonrise Travel).

Bay excursions in glass-bottomed boats visit sites near Puerto Ayora such as **Isla
Caamaño, Punta Estrada, Las Grietas, Franklin Bay** and **Playa de los Perros**. It
involves some walking and you are likely to see sea lions, birds, marine iguanas and
marine life including sharks. Snorkelling can be part of the tour. Full-day tours

(0900-1600) are around US$25 per person and can be arranged through tour agencies, see page 449. Reservations are strongly recommended in the high season. Discounts may be available in low season.

The highest point on Santa Cruz Island is **Cerro Crocker** at 864 m. You can hike here and to two other nearby 'peaks' called **Media Luna** and **Puntudo**. The trail starts at Bellavista (7 km from Puerto Ayora) where a rough trail map is painted as a mural on the wall of the school! The round trip from Bellavista takes six to eight hours. A permit and guide are not required, but a guide may be helpful. Always take food, water and a compass or GPS.

There are a number of other sites worth visiting in the interior, including **Los Gemelos**, a pair of twin sinkholes, formed by a collapse of the ground above a fault. The sinkholes straddle the road to Baltra, beyond Santa Rosa. You can take a *camioneta* all the way, otherwise take a bus to Santa Rosa (see below), then walk. It's a good place to see the Galápagos hawk and barn owl.

There are several **lava tubes** (natural tunnels) on the island. Some are at **El Mirador**, 3 km from Puerto Ayora on the road to Bellavista. Barn owls can be seen here. Two more lava tubes are 1 km from Bellavista. They are on private land, it costs US$1.50 to enter the tunnels (bring a torch) and it takes about 30 minutes to walk through the tunnels. Tours to the lava tubes can be arranged in Puerto Ayora.

Another worthwhile trip is to the **El Chato Tortoise Reserve**, where giant tortoises can be seen in the wild during the dry season. The trail starts at Santa Rosa, 22 km from Puerto Ayora. Past the school in Santa Rosa, a **Parque Nacional Galápagos** sign warns that tourists have been lost along the trail. Turn left here and follow a badly overgrown path south between two barbed wire fences with pastures on either side. After 3 km you reach a wooden plaque erected in memory of an Israeli tourist who was lost and died in 1991, and a better trail running east-west. Turn right and follow the trail west for 20 minutes to a sign, "Entrada Al Chato". There are many trails in the reserve itself and it is easy to get lost; take food, water and a compass or GPS. There is also access along a side-road off the road from Santa Rosa to Salasaca. The round trip on foot takes a full day, or horses can sometimes be hired at Santa Rosa. Best take a guide if you have no hiking experience, tours can also be arranged in Puerto Ayora.

Near the reserve is the **Butterfly Ranch** (**Hacienda Mariposa**) ① *beyond Bellavista on the road to Santa Rosa (the bus passes the turn-off), US$3, including a cup of hierba luisa tea, or juice*, where you can see giant tortoises in the pastures, but only in the dry season. In the wet season the tortoises are breeding down in the arid zone. Vermillion flycatchers can be seen here also.

Other visitor sites on Santa Cruz include **Caleta Tortuga Negra**, on the northern part of the island (restricted to small groups). Here you can drift by dinghy through the mangrove swamps which are home to marine turtles, white-tipped sharks, spotted eagle rays and yellow cow-nosed rays. Nearby is **Las Bachas**, a swimming beach, also on the north shore. **Conway Bay** is a rarely visited visitor site on the northwest coast, inhabited by a large colony of sea lions. **Whaler Bay** is the site of one of the oldest whaling camps on Santa Cruz. It was to here and the other similar camps that the giant tortoises were brought before being loaded on board the whalers. **Cerro Dragón** is located on the north shore of Santa Cruz, where land iguanas may be seen as well as the occasional flamingo.

San Cristóbal

San Cristóbal is the easternmost island of Galápagos and one of the oldest. The principal town is **Puerto Baquerizo Moreno** which is the capital of the province of Galápagos. Always take food, plenty of water, and a compass or GPS when hiking on your own on San Cristóbal. There are many criss-crossing animal trails and it is easy to

get lost. Also watch out for the large-spined opuntia cactus and the poisonwood tree
(manzanillo), which is a relative of poison ivy and can cause severe skin reactions.

Puerto Baquerizo Moreno → *Phone code 05 Population 4,900*

Puerto Baquerizo Moreno is a pleasant tranquil place which sees its share of tourism,
but far less than Puerto Ayora. There are good beaches nearby, an interesting
National Park visitors' centre and worthwhile excursions to the highlands. In town,
the **cathedral** ① *Av Northía, 2 blocks up from the post office, 0900-1200, 1600-1800*,
has interesting mixed-media relief pictures on the walls and altar.

Information CAPTURGAL ① *Malecón Charles Darwin y Española, T05-2520592,
www.galapagostour.org Mon-Fri 0730-1200, 1400-1700*, the Galápagos Chamber of
Tourism, has general information and a book exchange. The **municipal tourist office**
① *by the muelle turístico, T05-2521166, www.sancristobalgalapagos.com, Mon-Fri
0730-1230, 1400-1700*, has local information.

Around Puerto Baquerizo Moreno

To the north of town, opposite Playa Mann, is the Galápagos National Park visitors'
centre or **Centro de Interpretación** ① *daily 0700-1800, free, T05-2520138 (ext 102)*. It
has an excellent display of the natural and human history of the islands. Highly
recommended.

A good trail goes from the Centro de Interpretación to the northeast through scrub
forest to **Cerro Tijeretas**, a hill overlooking town and the ocean, 30 minutes away
(take water). Along the way are good examples of the arid zone vegetation. Side trails
branch off to some lookouts on cliffs over the sea. Frigate birds nest in this area and
can be observed gliding about, there are also sea lions on the beaches below. To go
back, if you take the trail which follows the coast, you will end up at **Playa Punta
Carola,** a popular surfing beach, too rough for swimming. Closer to town is the small
Playa Mann (follow Avenida Northía to the north), more suited for swimming and in
town is **Playa de Oro**, where some hotels are located. Right in the centre of town,
along the sand by the tidal pool, sea lions can be seen, be careful with the male who
'owns' the beach. Further afield to the northeast, and reached by boat (15 mins) is
Puerto Ochoa, another beach popular with locals.

To the south of town, 20 minutes' walk past the airport, is **La Lobería,** a rocky bay
with shore birds, sea lions and marine iguanas. You can continue along the cliff to see
tortoises and rays, but do not leave the trail.

San Cristóbal excursions and visitor sites

From **El Progreso**, 6 km inland from Puerto Baquerizo Moreno, it's a 2½ hour walk to
El Junco lake, the largest body of fresh water in Galápagos. You can also hire a
pick-up truck to El Progreso (see Transport, page), continuing to the beaches at
Puerto Chino on the other side of the island past **La Galapaguera** – a man-made
tortoise area. At El Junco there is a path to walk around the lake in 20 minutes. The
views are lovely in clear weather but it is cool and wet in the *garúa* season, so take
adequate clothing.

Various small roads fan out from El Progreso and make for pleasant walking. An
interesting trail runs down from El Progreso via **Cerro Mundo** to **Puerto Ochoa,** near
Isla Lobos on the west coast. It is some four hours down and eight back up, so you
must arrange for a boat to pick you up at the beach or take all provisions (including
water) and camping gear. Note that it is easy to get lost, see below.

It's a three-hour hike from the visitor site at **Caleta Tortuga**, on the northwest
shore of the island, to **La Galapaguera Natural** where you can see tortoises in the wild.
Isla Lobos is an islet with a large sea lion colony and nesting site for sea birds
northeast of Puerto Baquerizo Moreno. It is also a dive site.

Kicker Rock (León Dormido), the basalt remains of a crater, is not strictly speaking a visitor site, but the rock is split by a narrow channel and is navigable to the smaller yachts. It is home to a large colony of many seabirds, including masked and blue-footed boobies, nesting in the cliffs rising vertically from the channel. This is also a diving site.

Punta Pitt, in the far northeast of the island, is a tuff formation which serves as a nesting site for many sea birds, including all three boobies. Up the coast is **Cerro Brujo** beach with sea lions, birds and crabs, though not in any abundance.

Isabela

The largest of the Galápagos Islands, Isabela is slowly developing for tourism. If you have a few days to spare and are looking for tranquillity, this is the place to visit. Isabela fits most people's image of a South Pacific island: coconut palms, azure ocean, white sand beaches, rocky inlets, mangroves, and a wonderfully laid-back feeling. There is a reasonable selection of accommodation, many little restaurants and a couple of bars. It is just the place for some to pursue hard-core relaxation while the more energetic can choose from several interesting excursions. Most residents live in Puerto Villamil on the south coast, the main settlement, founded in 1897 as the centre of a lime producing operation. It is today inhabited by some 1,600 people, many of whom are fishermen. There is no town as such in the highlands, just a cluster of farms in the area known as Santo Tomás.

Puerto Villamil → *Phone code 05 Population 1,400*

Information is available from the **Municipal Tourist Office** ① *at the pier at the foot of C Las Fragatas, T05-2529191, Mon-Fri 0730-1200, 1330-1700*. There are several lovely beaches right by town, but mind the strong undertow and enquire locally about the best spots for swimming. It is a 2½ hour walk west to **Muro de las Lágrimas**, a gruesome place built by convict labour under hideous conditions. It gets very hot, so start early and take plenty of water. Along the same road 30 minutes from town is the **Centro de Crianza**, a man-made breeding centre for giant tortoises surrounded by lagoons with flamingos and other birds, and pleasant walking trails.

In the opposite direction, 30 minutes east toward the *embarcadero* (fishing pier) is **Concha Perla Lagoon**, with a nice access trail through mangroves and a little dock from which you can go swimming with sea lions and other creatures. Fishermen can take you to **Las Grietas,** a set of small isletas in the harbour where *tintoreras* (white-tipped reef sharks) may be seen in the still crystalline water; there may also be penguins. About US$10 per boat, negotiate in advance.

Isabela excursions and visitor sites

Tours can be arranged to visit **Sierra Negra Volcano,** which has the largest basaltic caldera in the world, 7½ x 12 km. It is 18 km (1 hr) by pick-up truck to a spot called El Cura, where you switch to horses for the beautiful 1½ hour ride to the crater rim at 980 m. It is a further 1½ hour walk along bare brittle lava rock to **Volcan Chico**, with several fumaroles and more stunning views. The round trip takes a full day but there are only two buses a day along the road, no water, and it is easy to get lost; so going on your own is not advised. Tours can be arranged by most hotels, or contact **Antonio Gil** ① *Hotel San Vicente, T05-2529140; about US$20 per person, minimum 4 people*.

A visit to **Punta Moreno**, on the southwest part of Isabela, starts with a dinghy ride along the beautiful rocky shores where penguins and shore birds are usually

● *Five of the six volcanoes on Isabela are active and each have (or had) their own separate* ● *sub-species of giant tortoise.*

Elizabeth Bay, on the west coast, is home to a small colony of penguins living on a series of small rocky islets and visited by dinghy.

Urbina Bay, at the base of Alcedo Volcano on the west coast, was the site of a major uplift in 1954, when the land rose up about 5 m. This event was associated with an eruption of Alcedo volcano. The coastline rose as far as 1 km out to the sea and exposed giant coral heads. The uplift was so sudden that lobster and fish were stranded on what is now the shore.

Tagus Cove, located on the west coast across the narrow channel from Fernandina island, is an anchorage that has been used by visiting ships going back to the 1800s, and the ships' names can still be seen painted on the cliffs. A trail leads inland from Tagus Cove past **Laguna Darwin**, a large saltwater lake, and then further uphill to a ridge with lovely views. **Punta Tortuga**, on the north of Tagus Cove on the west coast of Isabela, is a bathing beach surrounded by mangroves. **Punta Albermarle**, on the northern part of Isabela, was used as a radar base by the US during the Second World War.

Floreana

This is the longest inhabited of the islands and the site of the mysterious 'Galápagos Affair' in the 1930s (see box, page 417). Most of its inhabitants live in Puerto Velasco Ibarra, by Black Beach. Among those born on the island are a former director of the National Park, a boat owner, several naturalist guides and captains.

Puerto Velasco Ibarra → *Phone code 05 Population 88*

The original settlers came to Floreana to get away from the rest of world. Even today, unless you come with one of the few cruise boats which land at Black Beach for a few hours, or make special advance arrangements, it is difficult to get to Floreana and even more difficult to leave. Staying with the Wittmers is delightful, the pace of life is gentle and the locally produced food is very good, but you will not be entertained. Margret Wittmer died in 2000 at age 95, however you can meet her daughter Floreanita, and granddaughter Erica. They are congenial hosts. The Cruz family, also descendants of early settlers, can organize local excursions by land and sea.

> 🔋 *There is electricity for a few hours each day, telephones and one small shop with very basic supplies, but you should be as self-sufficient as possible.*

Floreana excursions and visitor sites

A vehicle road runs 8 km up into the highlands, where the climate is fresh and comfortable. Sometimes there is a bus, but the round trip makes a good hike with interesting birdwatching. Some 200 species of ants have also been described here. Visit the natural spring (water supply for the island) at **Asilo de la Paz**, and the nearby cave where Patrick Watkins, the first inhabitant of Galápagos lived from 1807 to 1809. There are also shorter walks along the coast but be careful wandering off on your own as people have become lost and died of thirst.

Devil's Crown, a dramatic snorkelling site to the north of Punta Cormorant, is an almost completely submerged volcano. Erosion has transformed the cone into a series of jagged peaks with the resulting look of a crown. There is usually a wide selection of fish, sharks and turtles easily visible in about 6 m of water.

Punta Cormorant is on the northern part of Floreana. The landing is on a beach of green sand coloured by olivine crystals, volcanic-derived silicates of magnesium and iron. The trail leads to a lake normally inhabited by flamingos and other shore birds and continues to a beach of fine white sand particles known as Flour Beach, an important nesting site for turtles.

Post Office Bay is west of Punta Cormorant. The Post Office barrel was placed and used in the late 18th century by English whaling vessels and later by the American whalers. It is the custom for visitors to place unstamped letters and cards in the barrel, and deliver, free of charge, any addressed to their own destinations. There is a short walk to look at the remains of a Norwegian commercial fish drying and canning operation that was started in 1926 and abandoned after a couple of years. A lava tube that extends to the sea is also visited.

◉ Sleeping

Santa Cruz *p436*
Puerto Ayora *map p443*
LL Finch Bay Hotel, On a small bay south of Puerto Ayora, accessible only by boat, T05-2526297, www.finchbayhotel.com A top-of-the-line luxury hotel on a beautiful beach. Includes breakfast, restaurant, pool, fine restaurant and bar, good service, comfortable rooms. Used as a base for high-end sleep-ashore Galápagos tours, book through Metropolitan Touring in Quito.
LL Royal Palm, highlands of Santa Cruz, T05-2527409, www.millenniumhotels.com Includes breakfast, spa, villas and suites with all luxuries, private lounge at airport, part of Millennium International chain.
LL-L Red Mangrove Inn, Darwin y las Fragatas, on the way to the research station, T05-2527011, www.redmangrove.com A beautiful hotel with loads of character. Includes breakfast, restaurant, jacuzzi, deck bar and lovely dining room. Very tasteful rooms all overlooking the water, ample bathrooms. Owner Polo Navaro offers day tours and diving. Warmly recommended.
L Silberstein, Darwin y Piqueros, T/F05-2526277, www.hotelsilberstein.com Modern and very comfortable, with lovely grounds and a small pool, restaurant and bar, some rooms with a/c, others with fan, spacious rooms and common areas, very nice. Recommended.
AL Fernandina, 12 de Noviembre y Los Piqueros, T05-2526499, F2526122. Pleasant but a little out of the way. Includes breakfast, restaurant, a/c, pool (open weekends to non guests), rooms are a bit small.
AL Las Ninfas, Los Colonos y Berlanga, T05-2526127, galaven@pa.ga.pro.ec Modern and comfortable but bathrooms are small. Includes breakfast, good restaurant, a/c, large terrace and pool, fridge, full range of services, has its own boat for day trips, helpful with arrangements.

AL-C Lobo de Mar, 12 de Febrero y Darwin, T05-2526188, www.lobodemar.com.ec Modern building with balconies and rooftop terrace, great views over the harbour. Includes breakfast, a/c, cheaper with fan, small pool, the new section is modern and comfortable, older rooms are simpler but good value. Friendly and attentive service. Recommended.
A-B Palmeras, Berlanga y Naveda, T05-2526139, F2526373. Includes breakfast, restaurant, a/c, cheaper with fan, pool, their better rooms are modern and comfortable.
A-B Sol y Mar, Darwin y Binford, T05-2526281, F2527015. Right in town but with an exceptionally pleasant location. Offers a variety of rooms all with fan, each one is a little different. Lovely terrace on the water, attentive owners. Renovations planned in 2005. Recommended.
B-C Castro, Los Colonos y Malecón, T05-2526113, F2526508. Modern and pleasant. Restaurant, a/c, cheaper with fan, owner Miguel Castro arranges day tours on his own motor launch, he is an authority on wildlife.
B-C Estrella de Mar, by the water on a lane off 12 de Febrero, T05-2526427, F2526080. Includes breakfast, fan, spacious rooms (more expensive with sea view), communal sitting area.
B-C Fiesta, Brito y Las Ninfas, T/F05-2526440, www.islasdefuego.com Quiet out of the way location next to Laguna Las Ninfas, a 5-min walk inland from the seafront. A/c, cheaper with fan, pleasant garden, pool, patio, hammocks, ping pong and billiards. Rooms are simple compared to the grounds.
D España, Berlanga y Naveda, T05-2526101. Cold water, fan, spacious rooms, small sitting area with hammocks, good value. Recommended.

D Flamingo, Berlanga y Naveda, T/F05-2526556. Cold water, courtyard, basic but ok.
D Lirio del Mar, Naveda y Berlanga, T05-2526212. Electric shower, laundry facilities, terrace, adequate.

D Los Amigos, Darwin y 12 de Febrero, T05-2526265. Small place with a couple of 4-bed rooms, shared bath, cold water, laundry facilities, basic but friendly and good value.

Puerto Ayora

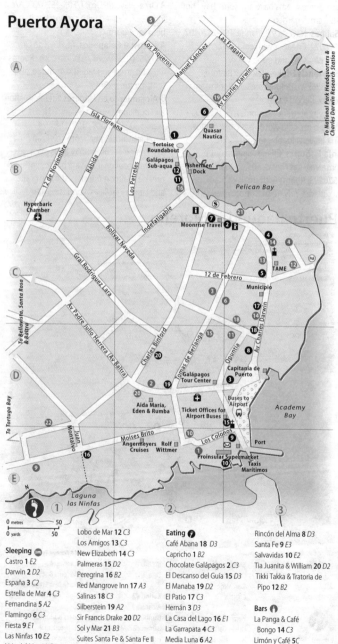

Sleeping
Castro 1 *E2*
Darwin 2 *D2*
España 3 *C2*
Estrella de Mar 4 *C3*
Fernandina 5 *A2*
Flamingo 6 *C3*
Fiesta 9 *E1*
Las Ninfas 10 *E2*
Lirio del Mar 11 *D3*
Lobo de Mar 12 *C3*
Los Amigos 13 *C3*
New Elizabeth 14 *C3*
Palmeras 15 *D2*
Peregrina 16 *B2*
Red Mangrove Inn 17 *A3*
Salinas 18 *C3*
Silberstein 19 *A2*
Sir Francis Drake 20 *D2*
Sol y Mar 21 *B3*
Suites Santa Fe & Santa Fe II
  Yacht Office 22 *D1*

Eating
Café Abana 18 *D3*
Capricho 1 *B2*
Chocolate Galápagos 2 *C3*
El Descanso del Guía 15 *D3*
El Manaba 19 *D2*
El Patio 17 *C3*
Hernán 3 *D3*
La Casa del Lago 16 *E1*
La Garrapata 4 *C3*
Media Luna 6 *A2*
New Island 7 *B2*

Rincón del Alma 8 *D3*
Santa Fe 9 *E3*
Salvavidas 10 *E2*
Tia Juanita & William 20 *D2*
Tikki Takka & Tratoria de
  Pipo 12 *B2*

Bars
La Panga & Café
  Bongo 14 *C3*
Limón y Café 5 *C*

D New Elizabeth, Darwin y Berlanga, T05-2526178. Fan, simple but adequate, helpful owner.

D Peregrina, Darwin e Indefatigable, T05-2526323. A small, simple family-run place. Some rooms have a/c, some have hot water, small garden.

D Salinas, Naveda y Berlanga, T05-2526107, F2526072. Cheaper with cold water, fan, clean, pleasant and good value.

D Sir Francis Drake, Herrera y Binford, T05-2526221. Cold water, fan, front rooms noisy but good value.

E Darwin, Herrera y Binford, T05-2526193. Private bath, cold water, basic but friendy, don't leave valuables in your room.

Santa Fe Suites, Charles Binford entre Juan Montalvo y Las Ninfas, T05-2526419, F2526593. Rooms with small kitchenettes in a quiet area, private bath, hot water, fan,

pool, convenient for long stays. Also operate motor yacht *Santa Fe II*.

San Cristóbal *p438*
Puerto Baquerizo Moreno *map p444*
A Orca, Playa de Oro, T/F05-2520233. A/c, fridge, often filled with groups, has its own boat for cruises.

A-B Hostal Galápagos, At Playa de Oro, T05-2520157, www.galahost.com Rooms are a bit small and faded, a/c, fridge, also rents by the month.

B Alojamiento en Hogares, for information and bookings contact Berenice Norris, T05-2520258, mobile T09-4148924, berenicenorris@gmail.com This is an association of community B&Bs offering accommodation in private homes. Includes breakfast, airport transfers, the use of kitchen and laundry facilities. Long stays also available.

Galápagos Islands The islands Listings

Puerto Baquerizo Moreno

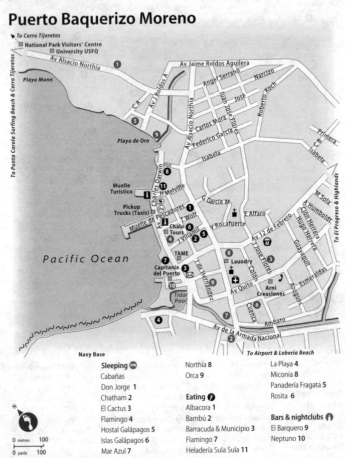

Sleeping 🛏
Cabañas
Don Jorge **1**
Chatham **2**
El Cactus **3**
Flamingo **4**
Hostal Galápagos **5**
Islas Galápagos **6**
Mar Azul **7**
Northía **8**
Orca **9**

Eating 🍴
Albacora **1**
Bambú **2**
Barracuda & Municipio **3**
Flamingo **7**
Heladería Sula Sula **11**
La Playa **4**
Miconia **8**
Panadería Fragata **5**
Rosita **6**

Bars & nightclubs 🍸
El Barquero **9**
Neptuno **10**

0 metres 100
0 yards 100

B Northía, Northía y 12 de Febrero, T/F05-2520041. A/c, pleasant but pricey.
B-C Chatham, Northía y Av de la Armada Nacional, on the road to the airport, T05-2520137. Patio with hammocks, some rooms with a/c and fridge, cheaper with fan, adequate.
C Islas Galápagos, Esmeraldas y Colón, T05-2520203, F2520162. Electric shower, a/c, a bit run down but adequate.
C Mar Azul, Northía y Esmeraldas, T05-2520139, F2520384. A/c, cheaper with fan, clean and pleasant, nice gardens, friendly and good value. Recommended.
D Cabañas Don Jorge, above Playa Mann, T05-2520208. Fan, simple cabins in a quiet setting overlooking the ocean, shared kitchen, very friendly proprietor.
D Los Cactus, Juan José Flores y Av Quito, Near Pacifictel, T05-2520078. Away from the centre, simple and family-run.
D San Francisco, Malecón Charles Darwin y Villamil, T05-2520304. Cold water, fan, rooms in front are nicer, simple but clean and good value.

Isabela *p440*
Puerto Villamil
AL La Casa de Marita, at east end of beach, T05-2529238, www.galapagosisabela.com Definitely upscale, even chic, for its location. Includes breakfast, other meals on request, a/c and fridge, right on the beach, very comfortable, each room is a bit different and some have balconies. A hidden gem. Recommended.
B-C Ballena Azul and Isabela del Mar, Conocarpus y Opuntia, T05-2529030, www.hosteriaisabela.com.ec An older wooden building next to modern cabins, both are very nice. Solar hot water, fan, large balcony, pleasant common area and dining room. Swiss-run, friendly and helpful. Recommended.
B-C Cormorant Beach House, Antonio Gil y Los Flamencos, T05-2529192, albemarle20@hotmail.com Nice location on the beach. A/c, cheaper with fan, fridge and use of cooking facilities, modern and comfortable, small terrace with hammock, very pleasant.
D San Vicente, Cormoranes y Pinzón Artesano, T05-2529140. Cold water, fan, fridge and use of cooking facilities, meals on

request, good value and popular. There are a couple of other basic places to stay in town.

Floreana *p441*
Puerto Velasco Ibarra
L Pensión Wittmer, right on Black Beach, T05-2529506. Includes 3 delicious meals, fan (when there is electricity), simple and comfortable, a very special place.

⊙ Eating

Santa Cruz *p436*
Puerto Ayora *map p443*
¶¶¶¶ Angermeyer Point, Across the bay, take a water-taxi from the port, T05-2526452, Tue-Sat 1900-2200, Sun brunch 1100-1600. Former home of Galápagos pioneer and artist Carl Angermeyer, with his works on display. Gorgeous setting over the water (take insect repellent). Excellent, innovative and varied menu, attentive service. Highly recommended.
¶¶¶ La Garrapata, Charles Darwin between 12 de Febrero and Tomás de Berlanga, closed Sun. Good food, attractive setting and good music, juice bar and sandwiches during the day, choice of 2 set meals at lunch, and à la carte at night.
¶¶¶ Café Habana, Charles Darwin & Bolívar Naveda, 0900-0130 daily. Restaurant and bar with music at night, economical set lunch, varied à la carte menu.
¶¶¶ Hernán, Av Baltra y Opuntia, T05-2526573, 0730-2230 daily. Restaurant and bar, menu caters to international tastes, includes pizza, burgers, cappuccino.
¶¶¶ New Island, Charles Darwin y Charles Binford, Mon-Sat 0900-2100. Breakfast, fruit juices, seafood, *ceviches*.
¶¶¶ Trattoria de Pippo, Charles Darwin entre Indefatigable y Isla Floreana, 2nd location called **El Patio** at Charles Darwin entre Naveda y 12 de Febrero, 1700-2200 daily. Italian and seafood, pleasant atmosphere, attentive owner.
¶¶¶-¶¶ Media Luna, Charles Darwin y Los Piqueros, 1500-2200, closed Tue. Good pizza and pasta, also sandwiches, great brownies.
¶¶ Capricho, Charles Darwin y Isla Floreana by the tortoise roundabout, daily 0630-2200, Mon to 1700. Good vegetarian food, salads and juices, breakfast.

Chocolate Galápagos, Charles Darwin entre Tomas de Berlanga y Charles Binford. Good breakfasts, soups, burgers and snacks.

Salvavidas, On the waterfront overlooking the activity at the pier. Good set lunch, breakfast and seafood. Good value and recommended.

El Descanso del Guía, Charles Darwin y Los Colonos, near bus company offices, no sign. Good value set meals, popular with locals.

El Manaba, Padre J Herrera y Tomás de Berlanga. Clean place, good set meals.

Kiosks. Along Charles Binford, between Padre J Herrera and General Rodríguez Lara are many kiosks selling traditional food, including good seafood at economical prices; Tía Juanita cooks well, as does William with Esmeraldeño specialities. All the kiosks have simple outdoor seating and a lively pleasant atmosphere, popular with locals and busy at night.

Cafés and bakeries

La Casa del Lago, Moisés Brito y Juan Montavo, in Barrio Las Ninfas, a quiet area away from the main drag, evenings only. Drinks and snacks, live music, cultured atmosphere.

Limón y Café, Charles Darwin y 12 de Febrero, evenings only. Good snacks and drinks, lots of music, pool table, popular.

Santa Fe, Charles Darwin y Los Colonos. Bar and grill, serving drinks, sandwiches and snacks, pleasant location, pool table.

Tikki Takka, Charles Binford y Charles Darwin, Mon-Sat 0800-2000. For breakfast and snacks, excellent bread flown in from Cyrano bakery in Quito, plus pastries.

San Cristóbal *p438*
Puerto Baquerizo Moreno *map p444*

La Playa, Av de la Armada Nacional, by the navy base. Varied menu, nice location, popular.

Miconia, Darwin e Isabela. Varied menu, meat, fish, pizza, Italian, recommended.

Rosita, Ignacio de Hernández y General Villamil. Set meals and varied à la carte, old-time yachtie hangout.

Albacora, Av Northía y Española. Good set meals.

Barracuda, Charles Darwin y 12 de Febrero. Tasty grilled meat, fish, and menestras.

Pizzería Bambú, Ignacio de Hernández y General Villamil. Pizza as well as other dishes, good.

Near El Progreso in the highlands, **La Quinta de Christi** does barbecues on weekends. A couple of simple food kiosks in El Progreso serve Ecuadorean specialities like *fritada* on Sundays.

Cafés and bakeries

Cabaña El Grande, Villamil y Darwin. Fruit juices are the speciality, also burgers and snacks. Popular.

Heldería Sula Sula, Charles Darwin y Herman Melville. Ice cream and snacks, nice terrace.

Panadería Fragata, Northía y Rocafuerte. Excellent bread and pastries, good selection, recommended.

Patagonia, Charles Darwin y Teodoro Wolf. Drinks and snacks.

Isabela *p440*
Puerto Villamil

El Encanto de la Pepa, Conocarpus y Pinzón Artesano. Lots of character, good food, attractive setting, friendly and pleasant.

La Choza, Antonio Gil y Las Fragatas. Order your pizza an hr in advance, the dough is made fresh.

Caballito de Mar, Los Cactos y Las Escalecias. Good set meals.

La Ruta, on the beach between 16 de Marzo and Las Fragatas. Good quality and value set meals.

Caracol, kiosk on C Conocarpus, next to police station. Simple set meals.

There are a couple of other simple places to eat around town.

Bars and clubs

Santa Cruz *p436*
Puerto Ayora *map p443*

Bar Bongo, Av Charles Darwin y Berlanga. **La Panga**, upstairs at the same location. Both are popular.

Also see **Café Habana** under eating and **La Casa del Lago** under cafés.

San Cristóbal *p438*
Puerto Baquerizo Moreno *map p444*

El Barquero, Hernández y Manuel J Cobos. Bar and *peña*. Open daily.

Neptuno, Charles Darwin y Herman Melville. Disco with young crowd, Tue-Sat 2030-0300. There are a couple of other bars along Av de la Armada Nacional towards the waterfront.

Isabela *p440*
Puerto Villamil
Beto's Beach Bar, Antonio Gil y Los Flamencos. Pleasant location, irregular hours, very relaxed.

O Shopping

Most items can generally can be purchased on the islands, but cost up to twice as much as the mainland. Do not buy crafts made of black coral as it is an endangered species.

Santa Cruz *p436*
Puerto Ayora *map p443*
Proinsular, opposite the pier, is the largest and best stocked supermarket.
The small **mercado municipal** is on Padre J Herrera, beyond the telephone office, on the way out of town to Santa Rosa.
There is a wide variety of T-shirt and souvenir shops along the length of Av Charles Darwin, all touristy and expensive.

San Cristóbal *p438*
Puerto Baquerizo Moreno *map p444*
There are a few souvenir shops along the Malecón selling T-shirts and crafts.
Paintings with Galápagos motifs can be bought from the following artists:
Arni Creaciones, Av Quito y Juan José Flores, T05-2520507. Run by artist Humberto Muñoz, very nice work, recommended.
Fabo Galería de Arte, Malecón Charles Darwin, opposite the whale statue. Paintings by the owner Fabián, silk screened T-shirts. He also directs the **Mar de Lava** theatre group which has periodic presentations at the Centro de Interpretación.
A good little supermarket is **Dos Hermanos**, Quito y Juan José Flores; a small **produce market** is located a block away at Juan José Flores y 12 de Febrero.

Isabela *p440*
Puerto Villamil
Isabela is the end of the Galápagos supply line and some items may not be available. Fresh fruits and vegetables are mostly limited to those which grow locally, but shops are reasonably well stocked with tins and other staples.

▲ Activities and tours

Santa Cruz *p436*
Puerto Ayora *map p443*
Cycling
Mountain bikes can be hired from travel agencies in town and the **Hotel Darwin**, US$8-16 per day; or at the **Red Mangrove Inn**, US$5 per hr. **Galápagos Tour Center**, T05-2526245, runs cycling tours in the highlands, US$16 per day.

Diving
There are several diving agencies in Puerto Ayora offering courses, equipment rental, dives within Academy Bay (2 dives for about US$90), dives to other central islands (2 dives, US$140), daily tours for 1 week in the central islands and several-day live-aboard tours. For a general description of diving on Galápagos see p448.
Note that safety standards vary and we therefore list only the most consistently recommended agencies. You are responsible for choosing a reliable operator and confirming that they (or you) carry adequate insurance. The hyperbaric chamber in Puerto Ayora charges US$850 per hour, see Hospitals under Directory, below.
Galápagos Sub-Aqua, Av Charles Darwin by Pelican Bay, T05-2526633, www.galapagos-sub-aqua.com (Quito: Pinto 439 y Amazonas, office 101, T02-2565294). Open 0800-1230, 1430-1830. Instructor Fernando Zambrano offers full certificate courses up to divemaster level (PADI or NAUI). Repeatedly recommended.
Scuba Iguana, www.scubaiguana.com, is a long-time reliable and recommended dive operator who was changing premises and telephones at the close of this edition. See the website for up-to-date information.

Horse riding
For horse riding at highland ranches, enquire with **Moonrise Travel**, below.

Kayaking and windsurfing
Equipment rental and tours available from the **Red Mangrove Inn**, US$10 per hr.

Galápagos Islands The islands Listings

Scuba diving

The Galápagos Islands are among the most desirable scuba diving destinations. At first look you might wonder why, with cold water, strong currents, difficult conditions and limited visibility (15 m or less). So what is the attraction?

Marine life
There are animals here in such profusion and variety that you won't find in any other place, and so close up that you won't mind the low visibility. Not just reef fish and schooling fish and pelagic fish, also sea lions, turtles, whalesharks, schools of hammerheads, flocks of several species of rays, diving birds, whales and dolphins; an exuberant diversity including many unique endemic species. You could be with a Galápagos marine iguana, the world's only lizard that dives and feeds in the sea, or perhaps meet a glittering man-size sailfish. Make no mistake, this is no tame theme park: Galápagos is adventure diving where any moment could surprise you.

Dive options
There are basically two options for diving in the Galápagos: live-aboard cruises and hotel-based day trips. Live-aboard operations usually expect the divers to bring their own equipment, and supply only lead and tanks. The day-trip dive operators supply everything. Day-trip diving is mostly offered by boats operating out of Puerto Ayora on Santa Cruz, and two operators in Puerto Baquerizo Moreno on San Cristobal (but service is not always available here).

Live-aboard cruises usually are reserved many months in advance. This is the only way to travel all around the archipelago, combining shore visits to the National Park and up to three dives per day and occasional night dives, on an itinerary of a week or more.

Day-trip diving is more economical and spontaneous, often arranged at the dive shop the evening before. The distances between islands limit the range of the day-trip boats to the central islands. Nevertheless, day boats can offer reliable service and superb dive locations including Gordon Rocks, world-famous for schooling hammerheads. The day-trip dive boats do not take passengers ashore at the more frequently visited marked trail sites, but can offer special trips to isolated landings for travellers who want a less structured experience of this teeming ecology.

A third option is a combination of the two. Through your agent or by email, make prior arrangements to combine the day-trip dive services with one of the non-diving live-aboard cruise yachts. Before or after the live-aboard cruise, visitors based at a hotel can make day-trip dives. Another way is a rendezvous of cruise yacht and dive boat at some other island.

See Puerto Ayora, p436, and Puerto Baquerizo Moreno, p439, for details of companies offering day trips, live-aboard diving tours or equipment hire.

General advice
Visitors should be aware of some of the special conditions in Galápagos. The National Park includes practically

Snorkelling
Masks, snorkels and fins can be rented from tour agencies agencies and dive shops, about US$5 per day or US$30 per week, deposit required. The closest place to snorkel is by the beaches near the Darwin Station.

Surfing
There is surfing at Tortuga Bay (see Excursions, above) and at other more distant beaches accessed by boat. Note that there is better surfing at Punta Carola near Puerto Baquerizo Moreno on San Cristóbal.

all of the land and the surrounding waters. The National Park prohibits collecting samples or souvenirs, spear-fishing, touching animals, or other environmental disruptions. Guides apply the National Park rules, and they can stop your participation if you do not cooperate. The experienced dive guides can help visitors have the most spectacular opportunities to enjoy the wildlife. Nonetheless, diving requires self reliance and divers are encouraged to refresh their skills and have equipment serviced before the trip. Though the day-trip operators can offer introductory dives and complete certification training, this is not a place where a complete novice should come for a diving vacation. On many dives you could meet any combination of current, surge, cold water, poor visibility, deep bottom and big animals.

Like many exotic dive destinations, medical care is limited. There is a hyperbaric chamber in Puerto Ayora, the cost is US$850/hr so you or your dive operator must carry adequate insurance. To avoid the risk of decompression sickness, divers are advised to stay an extra day on the islands after their last dive before flying to the mainland, especially Quito at 2,840 m above sea level.

Dive sites
Santa Fe This site offers wall dives, rock reefs, shallow caves, fantastic scenery and usually has clear calm water. You can dive with sea lions, schooling fish, pelagic fish, moray eels, rays and Galápagos sharks. Like everywhere in Galápagos, you can expect the unexpected.

Seymour Norte You can see sea lions, reef fish, hammerhead sharks, giant manta rays and white tip reef sharks. Occasionally whalesharks, humpback whale and porpoises.

Floreana Island The dive sites are offshore islets, each with its own character and scenery. *Devil's Crown* is a fractured ring of spiked lava around coral reefs. *Champion* is a little crater with a nesting colony of boobies, sea lion beaches and underwater rocky shelves of coral and reef fish. *Enderby* is an eroded tuff cone where you often meet large pelagics; rays, turtles, tunas and sharks. *Gardner* has a huge natural arch like a cathedral's flying buttress. These and other islets offer diving with reef fish, schooling fish, sea lions, invertebrates, rays, moray eels, white tip reef sharks, turtles, big fish including amberjack, red snapper, and grouper. Sometimes you can see giant mantas, hammerheads, Galápagos sharks, whales, seahorses, and the bizarre red-lipped batfish.

Gordon Rocks Just north of the Plazas are two large rocks that are that remains of the rim of a long extinct volcano. One the inner side of the collapsed caldera rim the seabed is a mass of rocks jumbled over each other while on the outer wall the sea drops away into thousands of feet of water. Currents here are exceptional strong here and the local name for the dive site is *La Lavadora*, The Dishwasher. Here you can see schools of hammerheads, amberjacks and pompano, eagle rays, golden cowrays, whitetips and green turtles.

Galápagos Tour Center rents surfboards for US$15 per day.

Tour operators
Touts sometimes approach tourists at the airport or in the street, claiming to represent well-known agencies and offering cheap tours. As elsewhere, their services are generally not recommended.
Galaptour, Rodríguez Lara y Genovesa, T05-526088, F527021. Last-minute cruise bookings.

Galápagos Tour Center, Padre J Herrera, opposite the hospital, T05-2526245, F2527081. Bicycle rentals and tours, surfboards, snorkelling gear, motorcycle rentals. Run by Victor Vaca who also arranges last-minute tours. They work with several different boats including the *Free Enterprise*; we have received repeated negative reports about the latter.

Moonrise Travel Agency, Av Charles Darwin entre Charles Binford y Tomás de Berlanga, opposite **Banco del Pacífico**, T05-2526348, sdivine@pa.ga.pro.ec Last-minute cruise bookings, day-tours to different islands, bay tours, highland tours, airline reservations. Knowledgeable, helpful and reliable. Highly recommended.

San Cristóbal *p438*
Puerto Baquerizo Moreno *map p444*
Cycling
Mountain bikes can be hired from several agencies in town.

Diving
There are several dive sites around San Cristóbal, most popular being Kicker Rock, Roca Ballena and Punta Pitt (at the northeastern side). Gonzalo Quiroga of **Chalo Tours** is a divemaster offering tours to these sites, however he is not always available. **Amparito y Angel**, who run a new diving agency at Teodoro Wolf y Darwin, are reported more dynamic. The nearest hyperbaric chamber is in Puerto Ayora.

Surfing
There is good surfing in San Cristóbal, the best season is Dec-Mar. **Punta Carola** near town is the closest surfing beach, popular among locals; there are several others. There is a championship during the local *fiestas*, the 2nd week of Feb.

Tour operators
Chalo Tours, Malecón Charles Darwin y Villamil, T05-2520953. Bay tours to Kicker Rock and Isla de los Lobos, boat tours to the north end of the island, highland tours to El Junco and Puerto Chino beach, occasional diving tours, bike rentals, snorkelling gear, surfboards, book exchange.

Isabela *p440*
Puerto Villamil
For horse riding and visits to the Sierra Negra Volcano, see p440.

⊖ Transport

See also Getting there, p422, and Getting around, p424, for buses to and from the airports, and transport between islands.

Santa Cruz *p436*
Santa Rosa and Bellavista From the bus stop in front of the Tropidurus store, Padre Herrera corner Jaime Roldos in Puerto Ayora, 3 daily buses leave for **Bellavista** ($0.25, 10 mins) and **Santa Rosa** (US$0.50, 20 mins). Or take a taxi or pick-up from anywhere in Puerto Ayora, US$2-3.

Puerto Ayora *map p443*
Pick-ups may be hired for transport throughout town and up to the highlands, US$2-3, agree on the fare in advance. Water taxis (*taxis marítimos*) from the pier to anchored boats, Punta Estrada and nearby beaches, US$1.

Airline offices
Aerogal, Padre J Herrera y 10 Mayo, T05-2521118, Mon-Fri 0800-1200, 1300-1700, Sat 0900-1300. Baltra airport counter, T050-2520405, daily 0800-1300. **Emetebe**, Av Charles Darwin opposite the port, 3rd floor, T05-2526177. **TAME**, Av Charles Darwin north of 12 de Febrero, T05-2526165, Mon-Fri 0700-1200, 1300-1800, Sat 0900-1200.

San Cristóbal *p438*
El Progreso 5 buses a day from Puerto Baquerizo Moreno, 15 mins, US$0.20, You can also hire a pick-up truck to El **Progreso**, US$2, US$15 to **El Junco**, US$40 to **Puerto Chino**, from main town. See p439. Prices are return and include waiting, the road through the highlands was under construction and in poor shape in early 2005.

Airline offices
Aerogal, at the airport, T05-2521118. **Emetebe**, at the airport, T05-2520615. **TAME**, Charles Darwin y 12 de Febrero, T05-2521351. Airport counter T05-2521089.

Isabela *p440*
Airline offices
Emetebe, Antonio Gil y Las Fragatas, T05-2529155, Mon-Fri 0730-1300, 1500-1730, Sat 0730-1300.

ℹ Directory

Santa Cruz *p436*
Puerto Ayora *map p443*
Banks Banco del Pacífico, Av Charles Darwin y Charles Binford, T05-2526282, F2526364, Mon-Fri 0800-1530, Sat 0930-1230. US$5 commission per transaction to change TCs, maximum US$500 a day. ATM works with Mastercard only, cash advances from tellers on some Visa and Mastercards. **Heladería Pingüino**, across the street from the bank, may change TCs outside business hours, 5% commission.
Embassies and consulates British Consul, David Balfour, c/o Etica, Barrio Estrada, T05-2526159. **Hospital** The local hospital on Padre J Herrera provides first aid and basic care. For anything more serious, locals usually fly to the mainland. **Hyperbaric Chamber**, 12 de Noviembre y Rodríguez Lara, T05-2526911, sss@puertoayora.com, www.sssnetwork.com Also has a private medical clinic. Hyperbaric treatment costs US$850/hr, unless you or your dive operator are covered by insurance. **Internet** There are several cybercafés throughout town, US$1.50-$3/hr. **Laundry** Lavagal, by the football stadium, machine wash and dry US$1.50 per kilo, good and reliable. **Post** By the port, it often runs out of stamps, never leave money and letters. Best take your postcards home with you. **Useful addresses** Immigration, at the police

station on 12 de Febrero. They are usually able to extend tourist visas up to 90 days, but always check well before your time expires. DHL courier and Western Union, accross the street from Hotel Silberstein.

San Cristóbal *p438*
Puerto Baquerizo Moreno *map p444*
Banks Banco del Pacífico, Charles Darwin entre Española y Melville. Same services as in Puerto Ayora. Open Mon-Fri 0800-1530, Sat 1000-1200. **Book exchanges** At Capturgal tourist information office and Chalo Tours. **Doctor** Dr David Basantes, Av Northía opposite Hotel Mar Azul, T05-2520126, is a helpful general practitioner. **Hospital** The local hospital at Av Northía y Quito offers only basic care. **Internet** Several cybercafés in town, US$1.50-$3/hr. **Laundry** Lavandería Limpio y Seco, Av Northía y 12 de Febrero. Wash and dry for US$2. Open daily 0900-2100. **Pharmacy** Farmacia San Cristóbal, Villamil y Hernández, is the best stocked pharmacy in town. **Post office** Charles Darwin y 12 de Febrero. **Useful addresses** Immigration at Police Station, Charles Darwin y Española, T/F05-2520129. Galápagos Radio Sociedad can assist visiting amateur radio operators, contact Guido Rosillo (HC8GR), T05-2520414.

Isabela *p440*
Puerto Villamil
Banks There are no banks on Isabela, no ATMs, and nowhere to use credit cards or change TCs. You must bring US$ cash. If you are stuck, ask at Hotel Marita.
Internet There are 1 or 2 slow and expensive cybercafés in town.

451

Galápagos Islands The islands Listings

Background

History and politics

Earliest civilizations

The oldest archaeological artefacts that have been uncovered in Ecuador date back to approximately 10000 BC. They include obsidian spear tips and belong to a pre-ceramic period during which the region's inhabitants are thought to have been nomadic hunters, fishers and gatherers. A subsequent formative period (4000-500 BC) saw the development of pottery, presumably alongside agriculture and fixed settlements. One of these settlements, known as **Valdivia**, existed along the coast of Ecuador and remains of buildings and earthenware figures have been found dating from 3500-1500 BC (see box, page 337).

Between 500 BC and AD 500, many different cultures evolved in all the geographic regions of what is today Ecuador. Among these were the Bahía, Guangalá, Jambelí and Duale-Tejar of the coast; Narrío, Tuncahuán and Panzaleo in the highlands; and Upano, Cosanga and Yasuní in Oriente. The period AD 500-1480 was an era of integration, during which dominant or amalgamated groups emerged. These included, from north to south in the Sierra, the Imbayas, Shyris, Quitus, Puruhaes and Cañaris; and the Caras, Manteños and Huancavilcas along the coast.

This rich and varied mosaic of ancient cultures is today considered the bedrock of Ecuador's national identity. It was confronted, in the mid-15th century, with the relentless northward expansion of the most powerful pre-Hispanic empire on the continent: the Incas.

The Inca Empire

The Inca kingdom already existed in southern Peru from the 11th century. It was not until the mid-15th century, however, that they began to expand their empire northwards. **Pachacuti Yupanqui** became ruler of the Incas in 1428 and, along with his son **Túpac Yupanqui,** led the conquest of the Andean highlands north into present-day Ecuador. The Cañaris resisted for a few years but were defeated around 1470. Their northern counterparts fought on for several more decades, defeating various Inca armies.

Huayna Capac, Túpac Yupanqui's son, was born in **Tomebamba** (present-day Cuenca), which became one of the most important centres of the Inca Empire. Quito was finally captured in 1492 (a rather significant year) and became the base from which the Incas extended their territory even further north. A great road was built between Cusco and Quito, but the empire was eventually divided; it was ruled after the death of Huayna Capac by his two sons, Huáscar at Cusco and Atahualpa at Quito.

Conquest and colonial rule

Civil war broke out between the two halves of the empire, and in 1532 **Atahualpa** secured victory over Huáscar and established his capital in Cajamarca, in northern Peru. In the same year, Pizarro's main Peruvian expedition set out from Tumbes, on the Peru-Ecuador border, finally reaching Cajamarca. There, Pizarro captured the Inca leader and put him to death in 1533. This effectively ended Inca resistance and their empire collapsed.

Pizarro claimed the northern kingdom of Quito, and his lieutenants Sebastián de Benalcázar and Diego de Almagro took the city in 1534. Pizarro founded Lima in 1535 as capital of the whole region, and four years later replaced Benalcázar at Quito with Gonzalo, his brother. Gonzalo Pizarro later set out on the exploration of the Oriente. He moved down the Napo River, and sent Francisco de Orellana ahead to prospect. Orellana did not return. He drifted down the river finally to reach the mouth of the Amazon, thus becoming the first white man to cross the continent in this way; an event which is still considered significant in the history of Ecuador (see box, page 383).

⁞ Ecuador fact file

Population: 12.9 million
Urban population: 62%
Population density:
50.3 inhabitants per sq km
Population growth rate:
1.8% per year

Infant mortality: 25 per 1,000
live births
Life expectancy: 70.5 years
GNI per capita: US$3,460
Minimum wage: US$0.97 an hour
Literacy: 92%

Quito became a *real audiencia* under the Viceroyalty of Peru. For the next 280 years Ecuador reluctantly accepted the new ways brought by the conqueror. Gonzalo Pizarro had already introduced pigs and cattle; wheat was now added. The Indians were Christianized, and colonial laws, customs and ideas introduced. The marriage of the arts of Spain to those of the Incas led to a remarkable efflorescence of painting, sculpting and building at Quito, one of the very few positive effects of conquest, which otherwise effectively enslave the native people. In the 18th century, the production and export of cocoa began and black slave labour was brought in to work cocoa and sugar plantations near the coast.

Independence and after

Ecuadorean independence came about in several stages beginning in 1809, but was not completed until royalist forces were defeated by Antonio José de Sucre in the Battle of Pichincha in 1822. For the next eight years Ecuador was a province of Gran Colombia under the leadership of Simón Bolívar. As Gran Colombia collapsed in 1830, Ecuador at last became a fully independent nation.

Following independence, Ecuadorean politics was dominated by various élites. They were sometimes divided along regional lines (Quito and the highlands versus Guayaquil and the coast) and frequently fought among each other. Rule by rival oligarchies under the cloak of constitutional democracy or military dictatorship, has endured to the present day.

There have been a great many presidents of Ecuador, but two stand out. **Gabriel García Moreno** (president 1860-65 and 1869-75) was an arch-conservative, renowned for his cruel dictatorship and attempts to force Catholicism on the population; he denied citizenship to non-Catholics. He was eventually hacked to death by machete at the entrance of the presidential palace. **Eloy Alfaro** (1895-1901 and 1906-11), was precisely the opposite; a liberal who sought to bring Ecuador into the modern world based on revenues from the cocoa boom. He introduced secular education, civil marriage and divorce, confiscated church lands and abolished capital punishment. Assassinated by his opponents, Alfaro's body was dragged through the streets of Quito before being publicly burned. Garcia Moreno and Alfaro had more in common than their gruesome fate, both were *caudillos* (strong-men) who ruled by force of arms, as well as charisma and oratory. *Caudillismo* is an enduring feature of Ecuadorean public life.

Ecuadorean politics has also kept time with the country's fragile economy, with greater stability during occasional periods of prosperity and chaos during the more frequent lean years. The Great Depression exemplified the latter. Between 1931 and 1948 there were 21 governments, none of which succeeded in completing its term of office. "There were ministers who lasted hours, presidents who lasted for days, and dictators who lasted for weeks." (G Abad, *El proceso de lucha por el poder en el Ecuador*, Mexico 1970.) Political stability was restored after the growth of coastal banana plantations created a fresh source of national revenue. The country's next larger-than-life president was **José María Velasco Ibarra**, who was elected four times in the 1950s and 60s, but ousted each time by a military coup.

Background History & politics

Like most other South American countries Ecuador experienced several periods of military rule during the 1960s and 70s, but it did not suffer the widespread human rights abuses which took places in some other nations. Since 1979, Ecuador has enjoyed its longest period of civilian constitutional government since independence.

Return to democracy

In 1978 a young and charismatic **Jaime Roldós** was elected president, but died three years later in a still-mysterious plane crash. His vice-president **Oswaldo Hurtado** of the **Democracia Popular** (DP) party took office until 1984 elections, which brought **León Febres Cordero** of the right-wing **Partido Social Cristiano** (PSC) to power. Febres Cordero's presidency was marked by violence, confrontation and repression, but he was subsequently elected to two consecutive terms as mayor of Guayaquil, then to Congress. Although in failing health, he retains considerable influence in all circles of power.

Rodrigo Borja of the centre-left **Izquierda Democrática** (ID) won the 1988 election. His government was benign, but weak and ineffective. 1992 elections were won by **Sixto Durán Ballén** of the centre-right **Partido de Unidad Republicana** in coalition with **Alberto Dahik** of the **Partido Conservador** (who became vice-president). A major corruption scandal culminated with Vice-President Dahik fleeing the country in 1996 at the controls of his private aircraft. He became the first of many contemporary national figures to seek asylum and self-imposed exile, until a controversial Supreme Court ruling allowed them to return en masse in 2005.

Social unrest and dollarization

By the end of Durán Ballén's government, disenchantment with the political establishment as a whole was so great that a flamboyant populist named **Abdalá Bucaram** of the **Partido Roldosista Ecuatoriano** (PRE) was swept to power in 1996. Bucaram's erratic government lasted barely six months and by February 1997 all manner of scandal had implicated his entire government and family. A national strike and mass demonstrations were followed by a congressional vote to remove the President from office on the grounds of 'mental incapacity' and replace him with Fabián Alarcón, until then president of congress. Bucaram fled to Panama from where he remained closely involved with Ecuadorean politics by remote control, until his triumphal return again upset the political apple-cart in April 2005.

A constituent assembly was convened during the Alarcón interim government and drew up the country's 18th constitution. It was in many ways a noble and progressive document but contributed little or nothing to solving the country's problems.

Jamil Mahuad of the DP, was narrowly elected president in 1998, amid border tensions with Peru. He immediately diffused this explosive situation and in less than three months had signed a definitive peace treaty, putting an end to decades – even centuries – of conflict (see Peru below). This early success was Mahuad's last, as a series of bank failures, many fraudulent and perpetrated by bankers who had helped finance the president's election campaign, sent the country into an economic and political tailspin. In 1999 Mahuad decreed an austerity package including a freeze on bank accounts. Even such a drastic measure did not prevent additional banks from collapsing, and the economy embarked on a process of hyperinflation, previously unknown in Ecuador.

By the end of 1999 the country's social, political and economic situation was completely out of control and Mahuad decreed the adoption of the US dollar as the national currency in a desperate bid for monetary stability. Less than a month later, on 21 January 2000, he was forced out of office by Ecuador's indigenous people led by the **Confederación de Nacionalidades Indígenas del Ecuador** (CONAIE) and disgruntled members of the armed forces. This was the first overt military coup in South America in more than two decades, but it lasted barely three hours before a combination of local intrigue and international pressure handed power to vice-president **Gustavo Noboa**. Mahuad soon joined the ranks of other Ecuadorean politicians in exile. Significantly, all the foregoing years of social unrest were never accompanied by serious bloodshed.

The 21st century

Noboa, a political outsider and academic, stepped into Mahuad's shoes with remarkable aplomb. With assistance from the US and the International Monetary Fund (IMF), his government managed to flesh out and implement the dollarization scheme. This achieved a measure of economic stability but significantly increased the cost of living, imposing further hardship on the majority of the population. Social unrest diminished, however, mainly out of weariness, as Ecuadoreans resigned themselves to sit out another interim administration.

In 2002 **Colonel Lucio Gutiérrez**, leader of the 2000 coup, was elected president by a comfortable majority. He had run on a populist platform in alliance with the indigenous movement and labour unions, but began to change his stripes soon after taking office. The first two years of his government were marked by constantly shifting coalitions with political parties of all persuasions which, along with high petroleum revenues, managed to keep the lacklustre administration in power. In late 2004, the dismissal of all the chief justices of the supreme court using unconstitutional legislation – and tear-gas – drew local and international criticism. It was a thinly veiled ploy to facilitate the return of exiled ex-president Abdalá Bucaram, the most recent ally to prop up the foundering Gutiérrez régime.

In Quito, there was a groundswell of popular opposition and a local radio station began to organize singularly peaceful and well-attended protests against the President. When he countered these with heavy-handed police repression, Gutiérrez was swept from office by mass demonstrations in the capital on 20 April 2005. His overthrow was legitimized by a congressional vote and ratified by the armed forces, who withdrew their troops guarding the presidential palace. Gutiérrez sought political asylum in Brazil and was replaced by his vice-president Alfredo Palacio.

Gutiérrez was the third Ecuadorean president to be deposed in eight years but, in keeping with historical precedent, the previous overthrows had resulted in no substantive change. Unusually, his ousting took place at a time of relative prosperity, reflecting the depth of popular frustration with political cronyism and corruption. As this edition went to press, the new government awaited international recognition. Such recognition is not assured, since President Palacio has been perceived as contrary to the interests of the USA (see page 458) and because the Ecuadorean example worries other unpopular South American régimes. The next presidential elections are due in October 2006, but might be moved forward under international pressure.

Ecuador's neighbours

Peru

After the dissolution of Gran Colombia in 1830 (largely present-day Venezuela, Colombia and Ecuador), repeated attempts to determine the extent of Ecuador's eastern jungle territory failed. While Ecuador claimed that its territory has been reduced from that of the old Real Audiencia de Quito by gradual Colombian and especially Peruvian infiltration, Peru insisted that its Amazonian territory was established in law and in fact before the foundation of Ecuador as an independent state.

The dispute reached an acute phase in 1941 when war broke out between the two countries. The war ended with military defeat for Ecuador and the signing of the Rio de Janeiro Protocol of 1942 which allotted most of the disputed territory to Peru. Since 1960 Ecuador denounced the Protocol as unjust (because it was imposed by force of arms) and as technically flawed (because it refers to certain non-existent geographic features). According to Peru, the Protocol adequately demarcated the entire boundary.

Sporadic border skirmishes continued throughout subsequent decades. In January 1995 these escalated into an undeclared war over control of the headwaters of the Río Cenepa. Argentina, Brazil, Chile and the USA (guarantors of the Rio de Janeiro Protocol) intervened diplomatically and a ceasefire took effect. Negotiations followed and a definitive peace treaty was signed on 26 October 1998, finally ending the seemingly interminable dispute.

Under the terms of the agreement, Ecuador gained access to two Peruvian ports on the Amazon, Ecuador's navigation rights on the river were confirmed and, in the area of the most recent conflict, it was given a symbolic square kilometre of Peruvian territory as private property. Relations have improved rapidly between the two former adversaries, new border crossings have opened and new international bus routes have been established. Adventurous travellers can now sail from the Ecuadorean Amazon to Peru (and Brazil), and tour operators offer an increasing number of interesting packages involving both countries. Drawn by the US dollar economy, a growing number of Peruvians are coming to work in Ecuador.

Colombia

Ecuador and Colombia have traditionally enjoyed excellent relations. Their bigger, more progressive, neighbour to the north was for many decades regarded as a role model by some Ecuadoreans. With escalating crime and violence in Colombia, however, that admiration has gradually turned to fear. At the same time, commercial ties remain very strong.

Colombia's long-standing internal armed conflict continues to escalate, fuelled in part by the hard-line Uribe administration in Bogotá and by ongoing US support for the Colombian military. Hundreds of thousands of Colombians live in Ecuador, either as refugees or as ordinary migrants, and are unfairly blamed for the rising crime rate throughout this country. They have on occasion been singled out for strict measures by the Ecuadorean authorities.

The northern border provinces of Ecuador, however, can rightfully claim to have been adversely affected by the conflict next door. Esmeraldas, Carchi, and especially Sucumbíos receive the highest number of Colombian refugees. Small armed groups from Colombia have occasionally entered Ecuadorean territory and carried out kidnappings or confronted the local armed forces. Drug producers and drug runners have likewise begun to operate in Ecuador, as an alternative to Colombia. Broad spectrum herbicides sprayed from aircraft near the border, to eradicate coca plantations in Colombia, have affected agriculture, wildlife and the health of people in Sucumbíos.

To date, the Ecuadorean government has always maintained an officially neutral policy, stressing that the Colombian armed conflict is internal to that country. It is becoming increasingly evident, however, that such a policy alone cannot shield Ecuador from the consequences of strife along its northern frontier. This point was brought home in 2004 by the arrest of a top Colombian *guerrilla* leader in Quito, in an operation apparently directed by US and Colombian intelligence services.

United States

Although not a geographic neighbour, the United States is certainly Ecuador's 'big brother'. The US is by far Ecuador's most important trading partner, it has a very important say in Ecuador's economy both directly and through multilateral institutions such as the International Monetary Fund (IMF), and it can exert unusually powerful leverage since the dollarization of the Ecuadorean economy. The implementation of a Free Trade Agreement, under negotiation in 2005, would give the US even greater economic influence over Ecuador.

US influence is not only economic. Going back as far as the Second World War, when a US airforce base was built on the Galápagos Islands to guard the Panama Canal, there has at times been a small but locally significant US military presence here. In 1999 the Ecuadorean government hastily approved a 10-year accord authorizing the use of a base at Manta by the US air force, ostensibly for drug surveillance flights. It has been a bone of contention ever since, with many Ecuadoreans opposed to the foreign military presence and concerned about possible retaliation by Colombian insurgents.

The USA has also been known to bring its influence to bear on Ecuadorean politics. At times of national uncertainty or deadlock, a visit to the presidential palace by the US ambassador has on occasion proven to be a decisive event. The overall complex relationship – economic and political – is examined from a global perspective in *Confessions of an Economic Hit Man*, by John Perkins, see Books page 481.

With large numbers of Ecuadorean migrants going legally and otherwise to the USA (see *Los Migrantes*, below), and American businessmen, retirees and tourists coming to Ecuador, there has also been cultural projection from the north. This is most noticeable in large urban centres, but exists to a lesser degree throughout the country.

Government

There are 22 provinces, including the Galápagos Islands. Provinces are divided into *cantones* which are subdivided into *parroquias* for administration.

Under the 1998 constitution, all citizens over the age of 18 are both entitled and required to vote. The president and vice-president are elected for a four-year term and may be re-elected. The president appoints cabinet ministers and provincial governors. The parliament, or Congress (*Congreso Nacional*), has 100 members who are elected for a four-year term at the same time as the president.

Modern Ecuador

Despite its troubled history and frequent economic woes, Ecuador is a land of outstanding opportunities. This is the case not only because of the country's extraordinary diversity in a very small area, but also because of the resilience and adaptability of its people. From the Inca invasion in the 1400s to Colombian insurgency in the 21st century, Ecuadoreans have had a knack for getting by despite adversity. They gleaned new manual skills from the *encomienda* (forced labour) system of early colonial times no less than they are acquiring new cosmopolitan competence from today's mass migrations to Europe and North America. At present, the country faces many important challenges and perceives the need to overhaul its infrastructure and institutions. This is indeed asking a lot, but it is also worth remembering that for the past 600 years or more, the common people of Ecuador have gone about their daily lives without paying much heed to national infrastructure or institutions.

Population → *Instituto Nacional de Estadística y Censos (INEC), www.inec.gov.ec*
The 2001 census counted 12.2 million Ecuadoreans, an 18% increase since 1990. Estimates for 2005 population are close to 13 million. Population pressure is strong on Ecuador's most elemental resources – land and water – and an important threat to the

country's outstanding biodiversity. Migration and a slowly declining birth rate have eased this pressure only slightly in recent years and the country's future depends, more than anything else, on achieving a sustainable balance between its population and renewable resources. This is true worldwide of course, but all the more so in Ecuador because of its small geographic size. Family planning programmes exist but are not widely accepted, and such efforts must contend with the great power and influence of the Roman Catholic Church.

Poverty

As in other Andean countries with large indigenous populations, wealth is distributed along ethnic lines, with indigenous people and blacks suffering the greatest poverty. (An exception which proves this rule is the economic dominance of native people in Otavalo, see page 168.) At the same time there is a tiny – mostly white – élite, who are spectrally wealthy. Government statistics released in 2004 suggests that 42% of urban Ecuadoreans live in poverty and almost 8% are indigent, but estimates almost double when the rural population is also taken into account. Many of those who are fortunate enough to be formally employed (the minority) must survive on a monthly take-home pay of barely US$150. The basic cost of living for an Ecuadorean family is estimated at US$420 per month, the minimum subsistence level is US$280 per month. As well as poverty, some Ecuadorean women also suffer domestic violence from drunken husbands, but in this macho culture such abuse often goes unreported and may even be tolerated, although attitudes have gradually begun to change.

In an attempt to escape rural poverty, many people have moved from the coast and the highlands to the towns and cities, particularly Guayaquil and Quito, where they are usually even worse off. In the countryside those with even a tiny plot of land or a fishing net can usually manage to eat, whereas in the city one must either earn or steal money in order to survive. This can be seen by the increase in crime as well as the many people trying to scrape together an honest living as *ambulantes*: by selling various goods or offering services on the streets of the major cities. Rather worryingly, a high percentage are young children.

Migration

The most recent economic crises forced many Ecuadoreans to seek even more distant opportunities, in North America and Europe, especially Spain. Collectively known as *Los Migrantes*, they account for over 5% of the country's population, who left Ecuador during the past decade. So many Ecuadoreans wanted to leave that passports at times became scarce and, once they managed to get one, people queued for days outside the Spanish embassy in Quito in hopes of obtaining a visa. Families were often split up as one spouse migrated in search of work, while the other remained behind with the children, and tearful farewells were an everyday sight at Quito and Guayaquil airports. Illegal emigrants faced much greater hardship; they paid US$10,000 or more to a *coyote* who offered to smuggle them overland through Central America, or in small vessels by sea, to the USA. Since few people have this sort of cash, the migrants usually signed over the family home or farm to *chulqueros* (loan sharks) who work together with the *coyotes*. Some were defrauded of their property without ever reaching the 'promised land' while others perished en route. Once in Spain, Italy, Germany, the USA or Canada, many of the illegal migrants were mistreated and underpaid, but there was sufficient demand for cheap labour in these countries that Ecuadoreans continue to emigrate. Some, especially those who eventually legalized their status, did well economically and began to send funds back to their relatives in Ecuador. In 2004 this income (locally known as *remesas*) added up to US$1,181 mn, Ecuador's second source of foreign revenue surpassed only by petroleum exports. Socially as well as economically, the mass migration of Ecuadoreans abroad has been the defining national phenomenon of the past decade.

Health

The gulf between rich and poor in Ecuador is exacerbated by the two-tier healthcare system. This division works on two levels – rural and urban and state and private. Two thirds of doctors and hospitals are concentrated in Quito and Guayaquil, and private hospitals thrive at the expense of a badly under-funded and crumbling state health service.

Despite this, things have improved in recent decades. Infant mortality has decreased to 25 per 1,000 live births (INEC 2004) and life expectancy has increased to an average of 70.5 years, according to the **Pan American Health Organization** (PAHO, www.paho.org) in 2002. The main causes of death are no longer those associated with a typical developing country but those of the developed world: cancer, heart and lung disease. A large number of people are also killed in traffic accidents. Although abortion is illegal, it is commonly carried out in unsanitary conditions and many admissions to gynaecological departments are related to the termination of pregnancies.

Education → *UNESCO, www.unesco.org*

Children are entitled to nine years of compulsory education by law, but in practice this is not always the case. In rural areas most complete elementary school, but not all go on to secondary education. This is mainly because the rural population is greatly dispersed and the cost of travelling such large distances is prohibitive. Other factors are that many families cannot afford the costs of uniforms and materials and schools lack teaching resources.

Illiteracy is no longer the problem it was a generation or two ago. The literacy rate is almost 92% (UNESCO 2004, INEC 2002), and bilingual (Spanish and Quichua) education is available in some highland Indian communities. Overall standards for public education are extremely variable, however, with a handful of highly regarded state schools in Quito and provincial capitals, while more remote classrooms and teachers can be severely deficient. Funds are always scarce and education, especially much needed investment in teacher training, has not been a priority for recent governments.

Corruption

In 2005 **Transparency International** (TI, www.transparency.org), published a *Global Corruption Report* (www.globalcorruptionreport.org) which stated that "Mexico and Ecuador stand apart from the other [seven Latin American] countries [surveyed] as being far more subject to corruption..." This unenviable distinction is felt at various levels. Obviously, vast quantities of public resources can end up in the pockets of senior officials, but the real impact of widespread corruption is far more subtle and pervasive. Most minor official business, anything from the registration of a motor vehicle to the repair of a broken phone line, can be an agonizingly slow and complicated process. If, however, you have 'connections' or can pay for the services of a 'facilitator' then all is expedited. The Ecuadorean judicial system has likewise come in for its share of criticism, with political favouritism and other corrupt practices being blamed for both the extended detention of the innocent as well as the prompt release of criminals.

All this is not to say that most Ecuadoreans are dishonest people. Quite the contrary, they have strong sense of reciprocity, of always giving something in return for a favour received. Ironically perhaps, this attitude encourages rather than precludes the giving and receiving of favours in the situations described above.

Economy

In the 1970s, Ecuador underwent a transformation from an essentially agricultural economy to a predominantly petroleum economy. Substantial oil output began in 1972, from when economic growth has largely followed the fortunes of the international oil market and the country as a whole – economically, politically and socially – has been extremely vulnerable to these fluctuations.

Farming and fishing

The contribution of agriculture and fishing to GDP has dwindled since the start of petroleum exports, but many jobs are still in farming, and agro-exports still generate important foreign earnings. Ecuador is the world's largest exporter of bananas, generating revenues of US$1,022 mn in 2004. Efforts have been made to expand markets following the introduction of EU import restrictions, to introduce a variety of banana resistant to black sigatoka disease, and to reduce costs and increase efficiency; all with limited success. In 2004 Ecuador faced continued international criticism over the use of child labour on some banana plantations. Coffee is the most extensive of Ecuador's cash crops, accounting for over 20% of total agricultural land, but it is very low yielding. Cocoa yields have also fallen and a programme for better maintenance and replacement of old trees is under way. Several non-traditional crops are expanding rapidly, especially roses and other cut flowers in the Sierra within reach of Quito airport; also mangoes, strawberries, palm hearts, asparagus and other fruits and vegetables, many of which are processed before export.

The fishing industry is a major export earner, from the offshore catch of tuna as well as from shrimp farming along the coast. Shrimp farms offer employment in underdeveloped areas where other jobs are scarce, but their development is controversial and a large portion of Ecuador's mangroves has been destroyed. Most of the forest around Bahía and Muisne is gone and that which remains is threatened. In the Gulf of Guayaquil, the shrimp have suffered from high mortality in recent years, because of pollution from agrochemicals used intensively by banana growers. Since 1999, the shrimp industry as a whole has been hard hit by an epidemic disease known as *mancha blanca* (white spot) which caused mortality rates up to 100% on some farms.

Oil production

Although Ecuador's share of total world oil production is small (about 1%), foreign exchange earnings from oil exports are crucial. Since 1990, annual government revenue from petroleum exports has exceeded US$1,000 mn, and in 2004 it topped US$3,300 mn (35% of total revenues), based on production of 500,000 barrels per day. The main producing area is in the northern Oriente, and two trans-Andean pipelines carry the oil to Esmeraldas on the coast, where it is refined and/or exported. Over the years, millions of hectares of Amazon forest have been opened to exploration, totally disregarding Indian reserves and national parks. The oil industry has had a considerable adverse affect on the Oriente's unique biodiversity as well as on indigenous communities, who have seen their lands polluted and deforested, and their way of life irreparably altered (see page 396).

Tourism

Tourism is a very important sector of the Ecuadorean economy, and the country's third or fourth most important source of foreign revenue. Ecuador has received over 600,000 visitors a year since 2000, and the Ministerio de Turismo set 900,000 as

The Galápagos islands remain a particularly important destination for visitors from Europe and North America, but there is an increasing trend toward eco- and ethno-tourism in both the Highlands and Oriente jungle. At the same time, tourism remains highly focused on certain well-known centres in Ecuador, with the economies of places like Galápagos, Otavalo, Baños and Vilcabamba very heavily dependent on foreign visitors.

Mining

Mining is not an important sector nationwide, but the discovery of about 700 tonnes of gold reserves around Nambija (Zamora Chinchipe) in the southeast created intense interest in the late 1980s, and over 12,000 independent miners rushed to prospect there. Over nine tonnes of gold are produced a year by prospectors along the Andean slopes, polluting the waters with cyanide and mercury. Legislation has been designed to encourage investors in large projects with better technology which would, in principle, be less harmful and could be more strictly controlled.

Hydropower

Despite the abundance of oil, over two-thirds of electricity generation comes from hydropower. Hydroelectric projects on the Paute, Pastaza and Coca rivers could raise capacity from 2,300 MW to 12,000 MW. However, in the mid-1990s drought revealed the dangers of overdependence on hydro and power shortages were widespread. Several thermal plants subsequently came into operation and the government eased restrictions on diesel imports. Privatization, especially in the electric energy sector, has long been resisted by the labour movement. Recent governments have none-the-less managed to break up the nationwide public electric company (INECEL) into a number of smaller regional operators.

Recent trends → *Banco Central del Ecuador (BCE), www.bce.fin.ec*

In 1999 the government of Ecuador defaulted on all its debts, national and foreign. The *sucre* – which had been the nation's currency for the previous 116 years – reached 25,000 to US$1 and President Mahuad announced the adoption of the US dollar as the national currency in a desperate bid for monetary stability. He was deposed shortly thereafter and the government of his successor, Gustavo Noboa, was left to implement the dollarization scheme. The following year saw 100% real annual inflation (mostly at the outset as prices adjusted to the new US dollar economy), which hit hard at the already battered Ecuadorean population. In 2001 inflation was 25% and by 2004 it was down to approximately 2%, according to government statistics.

Based on indicators like the above and a 2004 balance-of-trade surplus of US$260 mn, Ecuador's economy looked good from the outside in early 2005, even drawing praise from the International Monetary Fund (IMF). Many observers, however, felt the optimism was temporary and due only to the high world price of petroleum rather than any sustainable economic achievements within Ecuador. In the meantime, the gap continued to widen for the Ecuadorean bread-winner. In 2003, 2.4 minimum wages were required to cover the basic cost of living for an average family; by 2005 this figure had risen to 2.8.

Culture

People

About half of Ecuador's 12 million people are *mestizo*, descendants of Indians and Spaniards. *Cholo* is another (mildly derogatory) term for this group, infrequently used in Ecuador. Rural coastal dwellers are referred to as *montubios*. Roughly a quarter of all Ecuadoreans today belong to one of 14 different indigenous peoples.

Andean peoples

The largest indigenous group are the **Andean Quichuas**, who number around three million. The common language, Quichua, has deep roots and is closely related to the Quechua spoken in parts of Peru and Bolivia (see page 30). Though they speak a common language, indigenous dress differs from region to region. In the north, **Otavaleño** women are very distinctive with their blue skirts and embroidered blouses, while in the south the **Saraguros** traditionally wear black. A very important part of indigenous dress is the hat, which also varies from region to region.

Rainforest peoples

The largest native groups in the Oriente are the **Quichuas**, in the north, and the **Shuar**, in the south. They number about 70,000 each. The Amazonian Quichuas speak a different dialect than their highland counterparts, and their way of life is markedly distinct. Other Amazonian peoples of Ecuador include the **Achuar** (3,000 people) and **Huaorani** (2,000) as well as the **Cofán**, **Secoya**, **Shiwiar**, **Siona** and **Zápara**, all of whom have less than 1,000 members and are clearly in danger of disappearing.

Those jungle peoples who maintain a traditional lifestyle, hunt and practise a form of itinerant farming which requires large areas of land, in order to allow the jungle to recover. Their way of life is under threat and many Amazonian Indian communities are fighting for land rights in the face of oil exploration and colonization from the highlands.

There are also small groups of Indians on the coastal plain. In Esmeraldas and Carchi provinces live around 1,000 **Awas**; nearer the coast and a little further south live around 4,000 **Chachis** and 250 **Eperas**; in the lowlands of Pichincha around Santo Domingo are some 2,000 **Tsáchilas**, also known as *Colorados*. These coastal Indians are also under threat from colonization.

Native organizations

Despite the many pressures they have faced throughout history and still today, the various indigenous groups of the Sierra, the coast and the Amazon rainforest have managed, to some degree, to survive and preserve their cultural identity. The interests of these different groups vary widely. Whereas in the Sierra and on the coast the main issues are obtaining infrastructure for native communities and access to water for irrigation, in the Amazon it is resistance to colonization and the ever-encroaching oil and mining industries. The single biggest threat to the Amazonian rainforest is the oil industry and its irresponsible methods.

Today, Ecuador's native people are among the best organized and politically savvy of any in Latin-America. They have grouped themselves into various regional bodies as well as some other entities set up along religious lines (ie Catholic or Protestant). The national body which brings together many, but not all, of these regional organizations is the **Confederación de Nacionalidades Indígenas del Ecuador** (CONAIE). In addition to their political activities, these groups work with foreign NGOs and at times with the government, to foster native interests.

CONAIE in particular has played a key role in national political events, such as the overthrow of former president Jamil Mahuad. The organization's leadership has at times been criticized for pursuing its own political agenda rather than lobbying for the most immediate needs of its rank and file communities. The matter is controversial. Whatever the case, there can be little doubt that the *Indígenas* of Ecuador have made their voices heard in recent years and will certainly continue to do so in the future. In 2003 **Nina Pacari** became the first indigenous (and female) foreign minister of Ecuador. **Auki Tituaña**, the mayor of Cotacachi, is another indigenous leader who has achieved prominence and may have potential as a future presidential candidate.

Afro-Ecuadoreans

Ecuador's black population is estimated at about 500,000. They live mostly in the coastal province of Esmeraldas and in neighbouring Imbabura, and are descended from slaves who were brought from Africa in the 18th century to work on coastal plantations. Although the slave trade was abolished in 1821, slavery itself continued until 1852. Even then, freedom was not guaranteed until the system of debt tenancy was ended in 1881, and slaves could at last leave the plantations. However, the social status of Ecuador's blacks remains low and most of them still work on banana plantations or in other types of agriculture. Furthermore, they suffer from poor education and the racism endemic in all levels of society.

Racism in Ecuador is not solely aimed at black people, but Indians in general. Its roots run deep and some whites and *mestizos* still view Indians as second-class citizens, but attitudes are changing.

Background Culture

Indigenous cultures

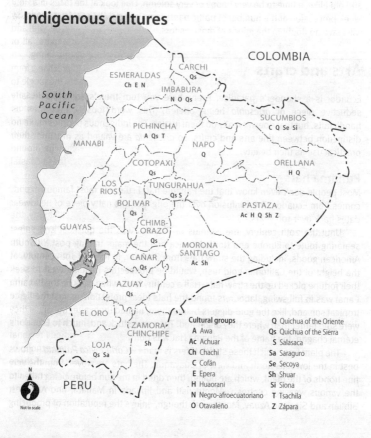

Cultural groups		
A Awa	Q Quichua of the Oriente	
Ac Achuar	Qs Quichua of the Sierra	
Ch Chachi	S Salasaca	
C Cofán	Sa Saraguro	
E Epera	Se Secoya	
H Huaorani	Sh Shuar	
N Negro-afroecuatoriano	Si Siona	
O Otavaleño	T Tsachila	
	Z Zápara	

Religion

According to official statistics, over 90% of the population belongs to the Roman Catholic faith and the church remains a formidable force in society. In recent decades a variety of Evangelical Protestant groups from the US, Seventh-Day Adventists, Mormons and Jehovah's Witnesses, have increased their influence. Freedom of worship is guaranteed by the Ecuadorean constitution.

Just as many of the great colonial churches of Ecuador are built over Inca and pre-Inca temples, the nation's impressive edifice of Roman Catholic faith rests firmly on pre-Christian foundations. The syncretism (mixing) of Catholic and earlier beliefs can be seen in many traditions and practices. *Fanesca* is a traditional soup eaten during Holy week, made with salt fish and many different grains. The Catholic component is the lack of meat, which was not consumed during Lent, while the many grains came from native traditions to celebrate the beginning of the harvest at this time of year. The original native *fanesca* might have been made with *cuy*.

Further examples of syncretism are found among the traditions for *Día de los Difúntos* (Day of the Dead, 2 November). *Colada morada*, a sweet drink made from various fruits and purple corn is prepared, as are *guaguas de pan* (bread dolls). In a few places, native families may build a special altar in their homes or take their departed relatives' favourite food and drink to the cemetery.

In this way, the beliefs of Ecuadoreans have evolved over the centuries but they have not diminished in intensity. A *fiesta* remains a very important occasion for young and old alike, a time to be very happy or very solemn. One look at the faces in a Holy Week procession or the number of participants in a *Pase del Niño* Christmas parade will leave no doubt in the minds of most visitors.

Arts and crafts

Ecuador is a shopper's paradise. Everywhere you turn there's some particularly seductive piece of *artesanía* being offered. This word loosely translates as handicrafts, but that doesn't really do them justice. The indigenous peoples make no distinction between fine arts and crafts, so *artesanía* are valued as much for their practical use as their beauty.

Panama hats

Most people don't even know that the Panama hat, Ecuador's most famous export, comes from Ecuador. The confusion over the origin of this natty piece of headwear dates back over 100 years.

Until the 20th century, the Isthmus of Panama was the quickest and safest seafaring route to Europe and North America and the major trading post for South American goods, including the straw hats from Ecuador. In the mid 19th century, at the height of the California gold rush, would-be prospectors heading west to seek their fortune picked up the straw hats. Half a century later, when work on the Panama Canal was in full swing, labourers found the hats ideal protection against the fierce tropical sun and, like the gold-diggers before them, named them after the place they were sold rather than where they originated. The name stuck and, much to Ecuador's eternal chagrin, the name of the Panama Hat was born.

The plant from which these stylish titfers is made – *Carludovica Palmata* – grows best in the low hills north and west of Guayaquil. The hats are woven from the very fine fronds of the plant, which are boiled, then dried in the sun before being taken to the various weaving centres – Montecristi and Jipijapa in Manabí, and Azogues, Biblián and Sigsíg in Azuay. Montecristi, though, enjoys the reputation of producing the best *superfinos*. These are Panama hats of the highest quality, requiring up to three months' work. They are tightly woven, using the thinnest, lightest straw. When turned upside down they should hold water as surely as a glass, and when rolled up, should be able to pass through a wedding ring.

From the weaver, the hat passes to a middleman, who then sells it on to the factory. The loose ends are trimmed, the hat is bleached and the brim ironed into shape and then softened with a mallet. The hat is then rolled into a cone and wrapped in paper in a balsawood box ready for exporting. The main export centre, and site of most of the factories, is Cuenca, where countless shops also sell the *sombreros de paja toquilla*, as they are known locally, direct to tourists.

Weavers of Otavalo

During Inca times, textiles held pride of place, and things are no different today. Throughout the highlands, beautiful woven textiles are still produced, often using techniques unchanged for centuries. One of the main weaving centres is Otavalo, which is a nucleus of trade for more than 75 scattered Otavaleño communities, and home of the famous handicrafts market which attracts tourists in their thousands.

The history of weaving in Otavalo goes back to the time of conquest when the Spanish instead exploited the country's human resources through the feudal system of *encomiendas* (see page 454). A textile workshop (*obraje*) was soon established in Otavalo using forced indigenous labour. *Obrajes* were also set up elsewhere in the region, for example in Peguche and Cotacachi, using technology exported from Europe: the spinning wheel and treadle loom. These are still in use today.

Though the *encomiendas* were eventually abolished, they were replaced by the equally infamous *huasipungo* system, which rendered the indigenous people virtual serfs on the large *haciendas* that were created. Many of these estates continued to operate weaving workshops, producing cloth in huge quantities for commercial purposes.

The textile industry as it is known today was started in 1917 when weaving techniques and styles from Scotland were introduced to the native workers on the Hacienda Cusín. These proved successful in the national market and soon spread to other families and villages in the surrounding area. The development of the industry received a further boost with the ending of the *huasipungo* system in 1964. The *indígenas* were granted title to their plots of land, allowing them to weave at home.

Today, weaving in Otavalo is almost exclusively for the tourist and export trades by which it is quite naturally influenced. Alongside traditional local motifs, are found many designs from as far afield as Argentina and Guatemala. The Otavaleños are not only renowned for their skilled weaving, but also for their considerable success as traders. They travel extensively, to Colombia, Venezuela, North America and as far afield as Europe, in search of new markets for their products. As these begin to saturate, Otavaleños are now beginning to peddle their wares in Asia.

Woodcarving

During the colonial era, uses of woodcarving were extended to provide the church with carved pieces to adorn the interiors of its many fine edifices. Wealthy families also commissioned work such as benches and chairs, mirrors and huge *barqueños* (chests) to decorate their salons.

In the 16th and 17th centuries woodcarvers from Spain settled north of Quito, where San Antonio de Ibarra has become the largest and most important woodcarving centre in South America. Initially the *mudéjar*, or Spanish-Moorish styles, were imported to the New World, but as the workshops of San Antonio spread north to Colombia and south to Chile and Argentina, they evolved their own styles. Today, everyone in San Antonio is involved with woodcarving and almost every shop sells carved wooden figures, or will make items to order.

Background Culture

Plant fibre is used not only for weaving but is also sewn into fabric for bags and other articles. *Mochilas* (bags) are used throughout the continent as everyday holdalls.

In Cotopaxi province, *shigras*, bags made from sisal, were originally used to store dry foodstuffs around the home. It is said that very finely woven ones were even used to carry water from the wells, the fibres swelling when wet to make the bags impermeable. These bags almost died out with the arrival of plastic containers, until Western demands ensured that the art survived. *Shigras* can be found at the market in Salcedo (early in the morning) and are also re-sold at tourist shops throughout the country.

Like the small backstrap looms and drop spindles of the Andes, the bags are portable and can be sewn while women are herding animals in the fields. Today, women's production is often organized by suppliers who provide dyed fibres for sewing and later buy the bags to sell. A large, blunt needle is used to sew the strong fibres and the finished article is likely to last a lot longer than the user.

Bread figures

The inhabitants of the town of Calderón, northeast of Quito, know how to make dough. The main street is lined with shops selling the vibrantly-coloured figures made of flour and water which have become hugely popular in recent years.

The origins of this practice are traced back to the small dolls made of bread for the annual celebrations of All Soul's Day. The original edible figures, made in wooden moulds in the village bakery, were decorated with a simple cross over the chest in red, green and black, and were placed in cemeteries as offerings to the hungry souls of the dead. Gradually, different types of figures appeared and people started giving them as gifts for children and friends. Special pieces are still made for All Soul's Day, such as donkeys and men and women in traditional costume.

Primitivist paintings

In the province of Cotopaxi, near Zumbahua and the Quilotoa crater, a regional craft has developed specifically in response to tourist demand. It is the production of 'primitivist' paintings on leather, now carried out by many of the area's residents, depicting typical rural or village scenes and even current events. Following the volcanic eruptions of 1999, these began to figure prominently in the Tigua paintings – named after the town where the work originated. The paintings vary in price and quality and are now also widely available in Quito, Otavalo and other tourist destinations.

Music and dance

Culturally, ethnically and geographically, Ecuador is very much two countries – the Andean highlands with their centre at Quito and the northern Pacific lowlands behind Guayaquil. In spite of this, the music is relatively homogeneous and it is the Andean music that would be regarded as 'typically Ecuadorean'.

The principal highland rhythms are the Sanjuanito, Cachullapi, Albaza, Yumbo and Danzante, danced by Indian and *mestizo* alike. These may be played by brass bands, guitar trios or groups of wind instruments, but it is the *rondador*, a small panpipe, that provides the classic Ecuadorean sound, although of late the Peruvian *quena* has been making heavy inroads via pan-Andean groups and has become a threat to the local instrument.

The coastal region has its own song form, the *Amorfino*, but the most genuinely 'national' song and dance genres, both of European origin, are the *Pasillo* (shared with Colombia) in waltz time and the *Pasacalle*, similar to the Spanish Pasodoble.

Music of the highland Indian communities is, as elsewhere in the region, related to religious feasts and ceremonies and geared to wind instruments such as the *rondador*, the *pinkullo* and *pifano* flutes and the long *guarumo* horn with its mournful note. The guitar is also usually present and brass bands with well worn instruments can be found in even the smallest villages. Among the best-known recorded musical groups are **Los Embajadores** (whose 'Tormentos' is superb); the duo **Benítez-Valencia** for guitar-accompanied vocal harmony; **Ñanda-Mañachi** and the **Conjunto Peguche** (both from Otavalo) for highland Indian music, and **Jatari** and **Huayanay** for Pan-Andean music.

There is one totally different cultural area, that of the black inhabitants of the Province of Esmeraldas and the highland valley of the Río Chota in Imbabura. The former is a southern extension of the Colombian Pacific coast negro culture, centred round the marimba, a huge wooden xylophone. The musical genres are also shared with black Colombians, including the Bunde, Bambuco, Caderona, Torbellino and Currulao dances and this music is some of the most African sounding in the whole of South America. The Chota Valley is an inverted oasis of desert in the Andes and here the black people dance the Bomba. It is also home to the unique Bandas Mochas, whose primitive instruments include leaves that are doubled over and blown through.

Literature

Much Ecuadorean literature has reflected political issues such as the rivalry between Liberals and Conservatives and between *costa* and *sierra*, and the position of the Indian and the marginalized in society, and many of the country's writers have adopted a strongly political line. Among the earliest were Francisco Eugenio de Santa Cruz y Espejo, who led a rebellion against Spain in 1795, José Joaquín de Olmedo, Federico González Suárez (archbishop of Quito) and Juan Montalvo.

The 19th century

José Joaquín de Olmedo (born Guayaquil 1780, died 1847) was a disciple of Espejo and was heavily involved first in the independence movement and then the formative years of the young republic. In 1825 he published *La Victoria de Junín, Canto a Bolívar*, a heroic poem glorifying the Liberator. His second famous poem was the *Canto al General Flores, Al Vencedor de Miñarica* (Juan José Flores was the Venezuelan appointed by Bolívar to govern Ecuador). He also wrote political works.

Juan Montalvo (1832-1889) was an essayist who was influenced by French Romantics such as Victor Hugo and Lamartine, also by Lord Byron and by Cervantes. One of his main objectives as a writer was to attack what he saw as the failings of Ecuador's rulers, but his position as a liberal, in opposition to conservatism such as García Moreno's, encompassed a passionate opposition to all injustice. His *Capítulos que se le olvidaron a Cervantes* (1895) was an attempt to imitate the creator of Don Quijote, translating him into an Ecuadorean setting.

Montalvo's contemporary and enemy, **Juan León Mera** (born Ambato 1832, died 1894), did write a book about the Indian, *Cumandá* (1979). But this dealt not so much with the humiliated Sierra Indians as the unsubjugated Amazonian Indians, '*los errantes y salvajes hijos de las selvas*' (the wandering and savage sons of the jungles), a book which created much debate.

The 20th century

In 1904, **Luis A Martínez** (1869-1909) published *A la costa*, which attempts to present two very different sides of the country (the coast and the highlands) and the different customs and problems in each. *Plata y bronce* (1927) and *La embrujada* (1923), both by **Fernando Chávez**, portray the gulf between the white and the indigenous Indian communities.

For the next 15 to 20 years, novelists in Ecuador produced a realist literature which was heavily influenced by French writers like Zola and Maupassant, Russians like Gorki and the North Americans Sinclair Lewis, Dos Passos, John Steinbeck and Ernest Hemingway. This was realism at the expense of beauty. The novelists in this period wrote politically committed stories about marginalized people in crude language and stripped-down prose.

The 1960s ushered in the so-called boom, with writers such as **Gabriel García Márquez, Mario Vargas Llosa, Carlos Fuentes** and **Julio Cortázar** gaining international recognition for the Latin American novel. At the same time, the Ecuadorean poet, essayist and novelist, **Jorge Enrique Adoum** (born 1923), wrote *Entre Marx y una mujer desnuda* (1976). This extraordinary novel is a dense investigation of itself, of novel-writing, of Marxism and politics, sex, love and Ecuador, loosely based around the story of the writer and his friends in a writing group, their loves and theorizing. Adoum has also written *Ciudad sin angel* (1995), plays (eg *El sol bajo las patas de los caballos* – 1972) and several collections of poetry, which is also intense and inventive (eg *No son todos los que están, 1949-79*).

20th-century poetry

The major figure, perhaps of all Ecuadorean poetry, was **Jorge Carrera Andrade** (1903-78). Son of a liberal lawyer, Carrera Andrade was involved in socialist politics in the 1920s before going to Europe. In the 1930s and 1940s, Carrera Andrade moved beyond the socialist realist, revolutionary stance of his contemporaries and of his own earlier views, seeking instead to explore universal themes. His first goal was to write beautiful poetry. He published many volumes, including the haiku-like *Microgramas*; see *Registro del mundo: antología poética* (1922-39), *El alba llama a la puerta* (1965-66), *Misterios naturales* and others. See also *Selected Poems*, translated by H R Hayes, Albany, New York, 1972, and *Winds of Exile* by Peter R Beardsell, Oxford, 1977.

Many schools and workshops continue to promote poetry in Ecuador, notably the **Centro Internacional de Estudios Poéticos del Ecuador** (CIEPE), which has published collections like *Poemas de luz y ternura* (Quito 1993).

Fine art and sculpture

16th and 17th centuries

Colonial Quito was a flourishing centre of artistic production, exporting works to many other regions of Spanish South America. The origins of this trade date back to the year of the Spanish foundation of Quito, 1534, when the Franciscans established a college to train Indians in European arts and crafts. Two Flemish friars, Jodoco Ricke and Pedro Gosseal, are credited with teaching a generation of Indians how to paint the pictures and carve the sculptures and altarpieces that were so urgently needed by the many newly founded churches and monasteries in the region. As well as the initial Flemish bias of the first Franciscans, stylistic influences on the Quito school came from Spain, particularly from the strong Andalucian sculptural tradition.

Colonial painting was as much influenced by Italy as by Spain. An important early figure in this was the Quito-born *mestizo* Pedro Bedón (1556-1621). Educated in Lima where he probably had contact with the Italian painter Bernardo Bitti, Bedón returned home to combine the duties of Dominican priest with work as a painter. He is best-known for his illuminated manuscripts.

Indigenous influence is not immediately apparent in painting or sculpture despite the fact that so much of it was produced by Indians. The features of Christ, the Virgin and saints are European, but in sculpture the proportions of the bodies are

often distinctly Andean: broad-chested and short-legged. In both painting and
sculpture the taste – so characteristic of colonial art in the Andes – for patterns in gold
applied over the surface of garments may perhaps be related to the high value
accorded to textiles in pre-conquest times.

18th century

Representations of the Virgin are very common, especially that of the Virgin
Immaculate, patron of the Franciscans and of the city of Quito. This curious local version
of the Immaculate Conception represents the Virgin standing on a serpent and crescent
moon as tradition dictates, but unconventionally supplied with a pair of wings.

In the later 18th century the sculptor Manuel Chili, known to his contemporaries
as *Caspicara* 'the pockmarked', continued the tradition of polychrome images with
powerful emotional appeal ranging from the dead Christ to sweet-faced Virgins and
chubby infant Christs. Outside Quito the best-known sculptor was Gaspar Sangurima
of Cuenca who was still producing vividly realistic polychrome crucifixions in the early
19th century.

Painting in the later 18th century is dominated by the much lighter, brighter
palette of Manuel Samaniego (died 1824), author of a treatise on painting which
includes instructions on the correct human proportions and Christian iconography,
as well as details of technical procedures and recipes for paint.

Independence and after

As elsewhere in Latin America, the struggle for Independence created a demand for
subjects of local and national significance and portraits of local heroes. **Antonio
Salas** (1795-1860) became the unofficial portrait painter of the Independence
movement. His paintings of heroes, military leaders and notable churchmen can be
seen in Quito's Museo Jijón y Caamaño. Antonio's son, Rafael Salas (1828-1906), was
among those to make the Ecuadorean landscape a subject of nationalist pride, as in
his famous bird's-eye view of Quito sheltering below its distinctive family of mountain
peaks (private collection).

Rafael Salas and other promising young artists of the later 19th century studied
in Europe, returning to develop a style of portraiture which brings together both the
European rediscovery of 17th-century Dutch and Spanish art and Ecuador's own
conservative artistic tradition. They also brought back from their travels a new
appreciation of the customs and costumes of their own country. The best-known
exponent of this new range of subject matter was **Joaquín Pinto** (1842-1906).
Although he did not travel to Europe and received little formal training, his
affectionate, often humorous paintings and sketches present an unrivalled
panorama of Ecuadorean landscape and peoples.

The 20th century

Pinto's documentation of the plight of the Indian, particularly the urban Indian,
presaged the 20th-century indigenist tendency in painting whose exponents include
Camilo Egas (1899-1962), **Eduardo Kingman** (1913-97) and most famously **Oswaldo
Guayasamin** (1919-99). Their brand of social realism, while influenced by the Mexican
muralists, has a peculiarly bitter hopelessness of its own. Guayasamin's home also
includes a museum which is well worth a visit and Kingman's work can be seen at the
Posada de las Artes Kingman.

The civic authorities in Ecuador, particularly during the middle years of the 20th
century, have been energetic in peopling their public spaces with monuments to
commemorate local and national heroes and events. Inevitably such sculpture is
representational and often conservative in style, but within these constraints there
are powerful examples in most major town plazas and public buildings are
generously adorned with sculptural friezes, such as in the work of **Jaime Andrade**

(1913-89) on the **Central University** and **Social Security buildings** in Quito. **Estuardo Maldonado** (born 1930) works in an abstract mode using coloured stainless steel to create dramatic works for public and private spaces.

In recent years there have been lots of interesting artistic experiments which can be appreciated in museums and especially the galleries of the **Casa de Cultura** across the country. **Cuenca** hosts an important Biennial and Ecuador is unusual among the smaller Latin American countries for its lively international art scene.

Land and environment

Ecuador, named for its position on the equator, is the smallest country of South America (256,370 sq km) after Uruguay and the Guianas. It is bounded by Colombia in the north, by Peru to the east and south, and by the Pacific Ocean to the west. Its population of 12.2 million (in Nov 2001) is also small, but is larger than Bolivia and Paraguay as well as Uruguay and the Guianas. It has the highest population density of any of the South American republics, at 50.3 inhabitants per sq km.

The border had been a source of conflict with its neighbours, and Ecuador lost a significant part of its former territory towards the Amazon to Peru in 1941-42 (see Ecuador's neighbours, page 457).

The Galápagos Islands were annexed by Ecuador in 1832. They lie in the Pacific, 970 km west of the mainland, on the equator, and consist of six principal islands and numerous smaller islands and rocks totalling about 8,000 sq km and scattered over 60,000 sq km of ocean. They are the most significant island group in the eastern Pacific Ocean.

Geology

Geologically, Ecuador is the creation of the Andean mountain-building process, caused in turn by the South American Plate moving west, meeting the Nasca plate which is moving east and sinking beneath the continent. This process began in the late Cretaceous Period around 80 million years ago and has continued to the present day. Before this, and until as late as perhaps 25 million years ago, the Amazon basin tilted west and the river drained into the Pacific through what is now southern Ecuador.

The Andes between Peru and Colombia are at their narrowest (apart from their extremities in Venezuela and southern Chile), ranging from 100-200 km in width. Nevertheless, they are comparatively high with one point, Chimborazo, over 6,000 m and several others not much lower. Unlike Peru to the south, most of the peaks in Ecuador are volcanoes, and Cotopaxi is one of the highest active volcanoes in the world, at 5,897 m. The 55 volcanic craters that dot the landscape of the northern highlands suggest a fractured and unstable area beneath the surface. A dramatic example of volcanic activity was an eruption of Cotopaxi in 1877 which was followed by a pyroclastic flow or *nuée ardente* (literally, a burning cloud) which flowed down the side of the volcano engulfing many settlements. Snow and ice at the summit melted to create another volcanic phenomenon called a *lahar*, or mud flow, which reached Esmeraldas (150 km away) in 18 hours! The most recently volcanic episodes began in 1999, with the eruptions of Guagua Pichincha and Tungurahua.

The eastern third of the country is part of the Amazon basin filled with sedimentary deposits from the mountains to the west. The coastlands rise up to 1,000 m and are mainly remnants of Tertiary basalts, similar to the base rocks of the Amazon basin on the other side of the Andes.

The Galápagos are not structurally connected to the mainland and, so far as is known, were never part of the South American Plate. They lie near the boundary between the Nasca Plate and the Cocos Plate to the north. A line of weakness, evidenced by a ridge of undersea lava flows, stretches southwest from the coast of Panama. This meets another undersea ridge running along the equator from Ecuador but separated from the continental shelf by a deep trench. At this conjuncture appear the Galápagos. Volcanic activity here has been particularly intense and the islands are the peaks of structures that rise over 7,000 m from the deepest parts of the adjacent ocean floor. The oldest islands are San Cristóbal and Española in the east of the archipelago: three to 3.5 million years old. The youngest ones, Fernandina and Isabela, lie to the west, and are between 700,000 and 800,000 years old. In geological terms, therefore, the Galápagos islands have only recently appeared from the ocean and volcanic activity continues on at least five of them.

The Andes

The Andes form the backbone of the country. In Colombia to the north, three distinct ranges come together near Pasto, with three volcanoes overlooking the border near Tulcán. Although it is essentially one range through Ecuador, there is a trough of between 1,800 m and 3,000 m above sea level running south for over 400 km with volcanoes, many active on either side. The snowline is at about 5,000 m, and with 10 peaks over that height, this makes for a dramatic landscape.

Overlooking Quito to the west is **Pichincha**, which was climbed by Charles-Marie de La Condamine in 1742, and, in 1802, by Alexander Von Humboldt. Humboldt climbed many other Ecuadorean volcanoes, including Chimborazo. Although he did not make it to the summit, he reached over 6,000 m, the first recorded climb to this height. He christened the road through the central Andes the 'Avenue of the Volcanoes'.

Further south, near Riobamba, is **Volcán Sangay**, 5,230 m, which today is the most continuously active of Ecuador's volcanoes. There are fewer volcanoes towards the Peruvian border and the scenery is less dramatic. The mountains rarely exceed 4,000 m and the passes are as low as 2,200 m. Although active volcanoes are concentrated in the northern half of the country, there are many places where there are sulphur baths or hot springs and the whole Andean area is seismically active with severe earthquakes from time to time.

The central trough is crossed by several transversal ranges called *nudos*, made up of extruded volcanic material, creating separate basins or *hoyas*. South of Quito, the basins are lower, the climate hotter and drier with semi-desert stretches. The lack of surface water is aggravated by large quantities of volcanic dust which is easily eroded by wind and water and can produce dry 'badland' topography. Landslides in this unstable and precipitous terrain are common. A serious example was in the Paute valley near Cuenca in 1993 when a hillside which had been intensively cultivated gave way in unusually heavy rains. An earth dam was formed which later collapsed, causing further damage downstream.

The coast

West of the Andes, there are 100-200 km of lowlands with some hilly ground up to 1,000 m. The greater part is drained by the Daule, Vinces and Babahoyo rivers that run north to south to form the Guayas, the largest river on the Pacific coast of South America, which meets the sea at Guayaquil. There are several shorter rivers in the north including the Esmeraldas, whose headwaters include the Río Machángara which unfortunately is the open sewer of Quito. Another system reaches the ocean at La Tola. All of these rivers have created fertile lowlands which are used for banana, cacao and rice production, and there are good cattle lands in the Guayas basin. This is one of the best agricultural areas of South America.

Mangrove swamps thrived on coastal mudflats in tropical rainforest zones and were typical of parts of Esmeraldas, Manabí and Guayas provinces. These are now having to compete with shrimp fisheries, an important export product. Attempts are being made to restrict the destruction of mangroves in the Guayas estuary. South of Guayaquil, the mangroves disappear, and by the border with Peru, it is semi-arid.

Amazonia

The eastern foothills of the Andes are mainly older granite (Mesozoic) rocks, more typical of Brazil than the Pacific coast countries. As with most of the western Amazon basin, it has a heavy rainfall coming in from the east and much is covered with tropical forest along a dozen or so significant tributaries of the Amazon. Partly as a result of the territory being opened up by oil field exploitation, land is being cleared for crops at a high rate. However, certain areas are being developed for ecotourism and it remains to be seen if this will help to arrest the destruction of the environment.

With good water flow and easy gradients, many of the rivers of this region are navigable at least to small craft. The Napo in particular is a significant communications route to Iquitos in Peru and the Brazilian Amazon beyond. Following the end of the border conflict with Peru in 1998, an international navigation route has been opened downstream from Coca.

Climate

In spite of its small size, the range of tropical climates in Ecuador is large. The meeting of the north-flowing Humboldt current with the warm Pacific equatorial water takes place normally off Ecuador, giving the contrast between high rainfall to the north and desert conditions further south in Peru. Changes in the balance between these huge bodies of water, known as the *El Niño* phenomenon, can lead to heavy rains and flooding in various parts of the country. This anomaly affects the region and the world in an irregular five to 10 year cycle, see www.elnino.noaa.gov.

Coast

The climate along the Pacific coast is a transition area between the heavy tropical rainfall of Colombia and the deserts of Peru. The rainfall is progressively less south of Guayaquil. This change of climate is due to the offshore Humboldt current which flows north along the South American Pacific coast from Chile to Ecuador. This relatively cold water inhibits rain-producing clouds from 27° south northwards, but just south of the equator, the current is turned west and the climate is dramatically changed.

Andes and Oriente

Inland, the size of the Andean peaks and volcanoes create many different microclimates, from the permanent snows over 5,000 m to the semi-desert hollows in the central trough. Most of the basins and the adjoining slopes have a moderate climate, though at altitude daily temperature fluctuations can be considerable. In the north, the basins are higher and temperatures are warm by day and cool at night. It rains mostly between October and May; Quito has an average of 1,300 mm per year. Near the border with Peru, the mountain climate can be very pleasant. Vilcabamba in Loja province is reputed to have a most favourable climate for a long and healthy life. In the Oriente the climate is indistinguishable from the hot, very humid lands of the western Amazon basin. There is heavy rainfall all year round, particularly May to December.

Although lying on the equator, there is considerable variation in the weather of the Galápagos Islands. The islands are affected by the cool water from the southeast Pacific which turns west near the equator. Surface water temperatures can fall to 20°C in July-September, causing low cloud and cool air conditions. Temperatures are highest from January to May and brief tropical downpours occur frequently at this time.

Wildlife and vegetation → *For the Galápagos islands, see p416*

No country in the world has as much biological diversity in as little space as Ecuador. The geologically-recent uplift of the Andes has caused this diversity by dividing the country into two parts, west and east, and by creating a complex topography that fosters the evolution of new species. It is an exciting thing to experience this diversity first hand, and Ecuador's extensive road system makes it easy. Our brief survey of this diversity, from west to east, gives an idea of the enormous range of Ecuador's life forms.

Northwestern lowlands
The westernmost part of mainland Ecuador is a broad rolling plain covered in the north by some of the wettest rainforest in the world. (There are some low coastal mountains but they do not reach significant elevations.) The biological centre of this region is the Chocó forest of neighbouring Colombia, so Ecuador's northwest shares many species with that area. Among the so-called Chocó endemics that reach Ecuador are some very fancy birds like the **Long-wattled Umbrellabird**, **Banded Ground-Cuckoo** and **Scarlet-breasted Dacnis**. Many other birds, mammals and plants of this region are found all along the wet Pacific lowlands from northwest Ecuador to Central America. Visitors familiar with Central American wildlife will feel at home here amongst the **Mantled Howler Monkeys**, **Chestnut-mandibled Toucans** and **Red-capped Manakins**. Unfortunately this forest is severely endangered by commercial logging, cattle ranching and farming, and good examples of it are now hard to find.

Southwestern lowlands
The cold Humboldt ocean current creates a completely different environment in the southwestern lowlands. Here the forest is deciduous (driest in July and August), and the southernmost parts of this area are desert-like. The birds and plants of this region are very different from those of the wet northwest; they belong to the Tumbesian bioregion and many are restricted to this small corner of Ecuador and adjacent northwest Peru. Some of the Tumbesian endemic birds are the recently discovered **El Oro Parakeet**, **Rufous-headed Chachalaca** and **Elegant Crescent-chest**. This is a densely populated region, however, and many of the species endemic to it are threatened with extinction.

Western slopes
Rising suddenly from these flat lowlands are the western Andes, very steep and irregular. Here the constant mists keep the forest wet all the way from north to south. In southern Ecuador it is therefore possible to go from desert to cloud forest in the space of a few hundred metres of elevation. This cloud forest is thick, tall and dark, and every branch is loaded with bromeliads, orchids and mosses. Orchids reach their maximum diversity in Ecuadorean cloud forests, and many spectacular varieties are found in the west, especially the weird Draculas. Many of the birds in these mountains are restricted to western Ecuador and western Colombia, including spectacular species like the gaudy **Plate-billed Mountain-Toucan**. At higher elevations there are more similarities with the eastern slope of the Andes. Among the highlights of these forests are the mixed foraging flocks of colourful tanagers, with exotic names like **Glistening-green**, **Beryl-spangled** and **Flame-faced Tanagers**. Mammals are scarce; lower elevations

have **capuchin**, **spider** and **howler monkeys**, while high elevations have the elusive **Spectacled Bear**. Insects too diminish as elevation increases and their role as flower pollinators is taken over by myriads of hummingbirds, including the **Violet-tailed Sylph**, **Velvet-purple Coronet** and **Gorgeted Sunangel**, to name but a few.

National parks & reserves

Background | Land & evironment

Western páramo

The cloud forest becomes low and stunted above about 3,300 m, and at higher elevations the forest is replaced by the grassland environment called *páramo*. Here, in contrast to the lower forests, the plants are largely from familiar temperate-zone families like the daisy and blueberry. They take on increasingly bizarre forms as the altitude increases, and the species of the highest elevations look like cushions of moss. Mammals are scarce but include **Spectacled Bear**, which feed on the terrestrial bromeliads called Puyas or achupallas (which look a lot like pineapple plants); and **rabbits**, which can be so numerous that they make broad trails in the vegetation. Preying on the rabbits are a form of **Great Horned Owl** and the **Andean Fox**. The birds and insects of these elevations are mostly drab, and many of the families represented here have their origins in North America or temperate southern South America. Forming islands of high forest in the *páramos* are the Polylepis trees, in the rose family; their distinctive flaky reddish bark is the favorite foraging substrate for the **Giant Conebill**.

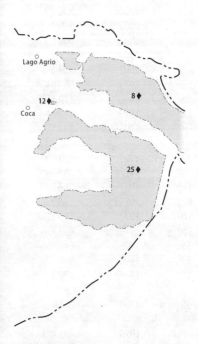

COLOMBIA

Lago Agrio

Coca

12◆

8◆

25◆

Inter-Andean basins

Between the western and eastern Andes lies the Inter-Andean Basin, really a series of basins formed by various river valleys. This region is in the rain shadows of both the western and eastern Andes, so it is relatively dry all year. Much of the original vegetation was destroyed centuries ago, replaced with grasses and more recently with introduced pine and eucalyptus trees. Only on high mountains like Chimborazo or Cotopaxi do relatively undisturbed habitats remain. Here a desolate zone of volcanic ash and bare rock marks the upper end of the *páramo*. There is little vegetation beyond, apart from the colonization of lichens, which grow well even up to 5,000 m.

Eastern páramo

To the east of the Inter-Andean Basins are the high eastern *páramos*, very much like the western ones but wetter. Here **Mountain Tapirs** are the largest animal, but they, like all big chunks of meat in Ecuador, survive only in remote regions. **Spectacled Bears** are here too, along with **White-tailed Deer** and its

Galápagos

Pinta
(Abingdon)

Marchena
(Bindloe)

Santiago (San
Salvador/James)

Santa Cruz
(Indefatigable)

Fernandina
(Narborough)

San Cristóbal
(Chatham)

Isabela

11◆

Floreana
(Charles, Santa Maria)

To Ecuador coast
(1,000 km)

N

Not to scale

National Parks Table

The entry fees given in the table are those officially given by the Ministerio del Ambiente in 2005. They are subject to change without notice.
Further details of each park are given in the travelling text.

Map	Name	Fee (US$)	Year created	Size (ha)
Coast				
26	Arenillas	-	2001	17,082
3	Cayapas-Mataje	$5	1995	51,300
32	El Lago	-	2002	2,283
28	El Salado	-	2002	5,217
30	Isla Corazón	-	2002	700
22	Isla Santa Clara	-	1999	5
31	La Chiquita	-	2002	809
15	Machalilla	$20	1979	56,184
16	Mache-Chindul	$5	1996	119,172
17	Manglares-Churute	$10	1979	49,894
29	Río Muisne	-	2003	3,173
Highlands				
1	Antisana	$5	1993	120,000
2	Cajas	$10	1977	28,808
5	Chimborazo	$10	1987	58,530
7	Cotopaxi	$10	1975	33,396
9	El Angel	$10	1992	15,715
10	El Boliche	$10	1979	400
14	Ilinizas	$5	1996	149,900
19	Pasochoa	$7	1996	500
21	Pululahua	$5	1966	3,383
Highlands to coast				
6	Cotacachi-Cayapas	$5	1968	204,420
Highlands to Oriente				
4	Cayambe-Coca	$10	1970	403,103
13	Llanganates	$5	1996	219,707
20	Podocarpus	$10	1982	146,280
23	Sangay	$10	1975	517,765
Oriente				
27	Cofán Bermeo	-	2002	55,451
8	Cuyabeno	$20	1979	603,380
18	El Cóndor	-	1999	2,440
12	Limoncocha	$5	1985	4,613
24	Sumaco	$5	1994	205,249
25	Yasuní	$10	1979	982,000
Galápagos				
11	Galápagos	$100	1936	693,700
	Marine Reserve	-	1996	14,110,000

Those fees not shown have not yet been established.
In the more remote areas there may not be anyone to collect fees.

Habitats/features	Access	Page
dry forest, restricted access	Arenillas	-
mangrove	San Lorenzo	365
recreation area	Guayaquil	312
mangrove	Guayaquil	-
mangrove, nesting frigate birds	Bahía de Caráquez	351
island	Puerto Bolívar	326
jungle	San Lorenzo	365
beach, dry forest, Isla de la Plata	Puerto López	340
dry forest	Esmeraldas	361
mangrove, dry forest	Guayaquil	313
mangrove	Muisne	361
glacier, páramo	Quito	146
páramo	Cuenca	278
glacier, páramo, vicuñas	Riobamba	247
glacier, páramo	Machachi, Latacunga	203
páramo, frailejones	El Angel	192
planted pine forest, recreation area	Quito	147
glacier, páramo	Machachi	202
páramo, cloud forest, recreation area	Quito	146
agricultural, extinct volcanic crater	Quito	145
páramo to jungle	Cotacachi, Borbón	173
glacier to jungle	Cayambe, Papallacta	163
páramo, cloud forest	Píllaro, Baños	220
páramo to jungle	Loja, Zamora	287
glacier to jungle, active volcanoes	Baños, Riobamba, Macas	248
jungle	Lago Agrio	396
jungle	Lago Agrio	397
jungle, international park		-
jungle	Coca	398
jungle	Loreto	385
jungle	Coca	395
island	Quito, Guayaquil	413
ocean	Quito, Guayaquil	413

Background Land & evironment

faithful predator the **Mountain Lion**. A miniature deer, the **pudu**, also lives here but is rarely seen. **Andean Condors**, one of the largest flying birds in the world, can be seen soaring majestically overhead. Condors are scavengers and clean up the larger animals after they die.

Eastern slopes

The eastern slope of the Andes is clothed in cloud forest like the western slope, but this cloud forest is much less seasonal, and has a higher diversity. Many west slope species of plants and birds have east slope sister species; the Plate-billed Mountain-Toucan, for example, is here replaced by the **Black-billed Mountain-Toucan**. The lower elevations have some Amazonian species like **Woolly Monkey**, and there are a few birds that have no western or Amazonian counterparts, like the strange **White-capped Tanager**. Plant diversity is very high here; orchids are especially diverse, even more so than in the west. The eastern cloud forests are much less damaged by man than the western ones, and there are still large wildernesses that are virtually unknown biologically.

Eastern lowlands

The eastern Amazonian lowland rainforest is the most diverse habitat in Ecuador for birds and mammals, with up to 14 primate species and 550 bird species at a single site. This is as diverse as life gets on this planet. Here is the home of the biggest snake in the world, the semiaquatic **Anaconda**, and various species of alligator-like caimans. The birds are very impressive, like the multicoloured **macaws**, the monkey-eating **Harpy Eagle**, the comical **Hoatzin** and the elusive **Nocturnal Curassow**. Mammals include five species of cats, three anteaters, a couple of sloths, two dolphins and an endless variety of bats – bats that troll for fish, bats that suck nectar, bats that catch sleeping birds by smelling them, bats that eat fruit, bats that catch insects, and even vampire bats that really drink blood. The variety of fish is even greater than the variety of birds and bats, and include piranhas, stingrays, giant catfish and electric eels. There are fewer epiphytes here than in cloud forests, but many more species of trees: 1 ha can have over 300 species of trees! Insect life reflects the diversity of plants; for example, there can be over 700 species of butterflies at a single site, including several species of huge shining **blue Morphos**. If one wants to see spectacular birds and animals and has only one opportunity to visit one mainland region of Ecuador, then this should be it. But you must choose the site carefully if you really want to see these things, see Choosing a rainforest, page 382.

National parks and reserves → *map page 476*

Ecuador has an outstanding array of protected natural areas, national parks and reserves. These cover all of the country's regions and include many unique tracts of wilderness. But the term 'protected' may not mean what it does in other parts of the world; native communities, settlements, *haciendas*, and even oil drilling camps can be found in the heart of some Ecuadorean national parks. Park boundaries are seldom clearly defined, and less often respected. What park facilities exist, along with most park rangers, are concentrated at the access points to a very few frequently visited areas. Elsewhere, infrastructure ranges from very basic to nonexistent.

Ministerio del Ambiente ① *Quito, in the Ministerio de Agricultura y Ganadería building, 8th floor, Amazonas y Eloy Alfaro, T02-2506337*. They can provide some limited tourist information but it is best to contact the office in the city nearest the park you wish to visit, for example the Cuenca office for Cajas, Loja for Podocarpus and so on. ↠ *For further details, see pages 478-479.*

Books

Contemporary

Perkins, John, *Confessions of an Economic Hit Man* (Berrett-Koehler, 2004). A recent book which has attracted attention in Ecuador and the USA .

Travelogues

Barrera Valverde, Alfonso, *El País de Manuelito*, (Editorial El Conejo, Quito, 1981). A different sort of travelogue, presented through the eyes of an orphaned Ecuadorean child.

Condamine, Charles-Marie de la, *Diario del viaje al Ecuador* (Ediguias, Quito, 1745, N Gómez ed (1994).

Darwin, Charles, *Voyage of the Beagle* (see Galápagos below for details).

Izaca, Jorge, *Huasipungo* (London, 1962).

Lara, Dario, Viajeros Franceses al Ecuador en el Siglo XIX (1972) *Casa de la Cultura Ecuatoriana, Quito*, (1972) and *Gabriel Lafond de Lurcy: Viajero y testigo de la historia ecuatoriana* (Banco Central del Ecuador, Quito,1988).

Michaux, Henri, *Ecuador* (OUP, 1929, 1952).

Miller, Tom, *The Panama Hat Trail* (Abacus,1986).

Thomsen, Moritz, *Living Poor, Eland*; also *The Saddest Pleasure* and *Farm on the River of Emeralds*.

Whymper, Edward, *Travels Amongst the Great Andes of the Equator* (Gibbs M Smith, Salt Lake City, 1891; 1987)

Coffee-table books

There are a great many gorgeous photo collections of Ecuador. Among the most original and beautiful are:

Anhalzer, Jorge and Guevara Nogales, Marcelo, *Ecuador as Seen from Space* (Imprenta Mariscal, Quito, 2003).

Oxford, Pete and Bish, Reneé, *Ecuador* (Imprenta Mariscal, Quito, 2004).

Birdwatching

Canaday, C and Jost, L, *Common Birds of Amazonian Ecuador: a guide for the wide-eyed ecotourist* (Ediciones Libri-Mundi, Quito, 1997). A nice beginner's guide with some excellent illustrations.

Hilty, S, *Birds of Tropical America: A Watcher's Guide to Behavior*, (Breeding and Diversity Chapters Publishing, Shelburne, VT, USA). An excellent book on the natural history of tropical birds.

Hility, S and Brown, W, *A Guide to the Birds of Colombia* (Princeton University Press, USA, 1986). Also very good, but missing some southern species.

Ridgely, R and Greenfield, P, *Birds of Ecuador* (Cornell University Press, Ithaca, NY, 2001). The definitive guide.

Williams, R, Best, B and Heijnen, T, *A Guide to Birdwatching in Ecuador and the Galápagos* (Biosphere Publications, UK). Has much detailed site information.

John V Moore's tapes and CDs of Ecuadorean birds are highly recommended and are available at **Libri Mundi** in Quito.

Climbing

Brain, Y, *Ecuador: A Climbing Guide* (The Mountaineers, Seattle, 2000). The most up-to-date reference and covers routes on all the 'big 10' plus 10 additional mountains.

Cruz, M, *Montañas del Ecuador* (Dinediciones, Quito, 1993). A beautiful coffee-table book packed full of colour photographs, taken by Ecuador's leading guide of the last 20 years. In Spanish.

Cruz, M, *Die Schneeberge Ecuador*. In German, excellent.

Koerner, M, *The Fool's Climbing Guide to Ecuador and Peru* (Buzzard Mountaineering, 1976). Concise and funny more than practical due to its age, but a very enjoyable read.

Landazuri, F, *Cotopaxi: Mountain of Light* (Campo Abierto, 1994). A thorough history of the mountain in Spanish and English.

Landazuri, F, Rojas, I and Serrano, M, *Montañas del Sol* (Campo Abierto, Quito, 1994) . A good climbing guidebook but it lacks top diagrams and public transport information. In Spanish.

Rachowiecki and Thurber, *Climbing and Hiking in Ecuador* (see below under Trekking). Offers a number of treks and sub-5,000 m peaks suitable for acclimatizing as well as general descriptions of routes on the 'big 10'.

Schmudlach, G, *Bergfürer Ecuador* (Panico Alpinverlag, 2001). Excellent climbing book, in German.

Whymper, E, *Travels Amongst the Great Andes of the Equator* (details above). An absolute classic, one of the best books written about climbing anything anywhere. Mountaineering journals include: *Campo Abierto* (not produced by the travel agency of the same name), an annual magazine on expeditions, access to mountains etc, US$1. *Montaña*, annual magazine of the Colegio San Gabriel mountaineering club, US$1.50.

Trekking

Kunstaetter, R and D, *Trekking in Ecuador* (The Mountaineers, Seattle, 2002). The most up-to-date reference, covering 29 treks throughout Ecuador, mostly new routes; see www.trekkinginecuador.com

Rachoweicki, R and Thurber, M, *Climbing and Hiking in Ecuador* (Bradt, 5th ed 2004). New edition of an older comprehensive hiking guide.

Culture and exploration

Kane, J, *Savages* (Vintage Books, New York, 1996).

Kimerling, J, *Amazon Crude* (Natural Resource Defense Council, 1991).

Latorre, O, *La Expedición a la Canela y el Descubrimiento del Amazonas* (1995). Detailed and interesting account of Orellana's voyage from an Ecuadorean perspective, see also box, p383.

Smith, A, *The Lost Lady of the Amazon* (Carroll & Graf, 2003). Beautifully told story of Isabela Godin, see box, p383.

Smith, A, *Explorers of the Amazon* (University of Chicago Press, 1990). Good brief account of Orellana's voyage. See also box, p383.

Smith, R, *Crisis Under the Canopy: Tourism and other problems facing the present day Huaorani* (Ediciones Abya-Yala, Quito).

Galápagos Islands

Many of these books are available at **Libri Mundi** and other bookshops in Quito, see p129.

General

Angermeyer, J, *My Father's Island* (Anthony Nelson, 1998). The story of another Galápagos pioneer family, beautifully told.

Darwin, C, *Journal of the Voyage of HMS Beagle*, (first published in 1845). Penguin Books (UK) have published Darwin's account of the Galápagos in their Penguin 60s Classics series.

Latorre, O, *The Curse of the Tortoise* (Quito, 2001). Includes many other strange and tragic tales.

Melville, H, *The Encantadas [1854]*, published in *Billy Bud, Sailor and Other Stories* (Penguin, 1971).

Treherne, J, *The Galápagos Affair* (Jonathan Cape, 1983). Describes the bizarre events on Floreana in the 1930s.

Wittmer, M, *Floreana* (Michael Joseph, 1961). Autobiography of Margret Wittmer.

Field guides

Castro, I and Phillips, A, *A Guide to the Birds of the Galápagos Islands* (Christopher Helm, 1996).

Constant, P, *The Galápagos Islands* (Odyssey, 2000).

De Roy, T, *Galapagos: Islands Born of Fire* (Swan Hill Press, 2001). A highly acclaimed collection of photos and essays about the islands and the need to conserve them.

Horwell, D, *Galápagos: the Enchanted Isles* (Dryad Press, 1988). Available through **Select Latin America**, the author's UK tour agency.

Hickman, J, *The Enchanted Isles: The Galápagos Discovered* (Anthony Nelson, 1985).

Humann, P, *Reef Fish Identification* (Libri Mundi, 1993).

Jackson, M H, *Galápagos: A Natural History Guide* (University of Calgary Press, 1985). Considered the Bible by all guides and the staff at the Charles Darwin Research Station.

Merlen, G, *A Field Guide to the Fishes of Galápagos* (Libri Mundi, 1988) .

Schofield, E, *Plants of the Galápagos Islands* (Universe Books, New York, 1984) .

White, A and Epler, B, with photographs by **Gilbert, C**, *Galápagos Guide*. Published in several languages.

483

Footnotes

Basic Spanish for travellers

Learning Spanish is a useful part of the preparation for a trip to Spain and no volumes of dictionaries, phrase books or word lists will provide the same enjoyment as being able to communicate directly with the people of the country you are visiting. It is a good idea to make an effort to grasp the basics before you go. As you travel you will pick up more of the language and the more you know, the more you will benefit from your stay.

General pronunciation

For travelling purposes, everyone in Andalucía speaks Spanish, known either as *castellano* or *español*, and it's a huge help to know some. The local accent, *andaluz*, is characterized by dropping consonants left, right and centre, thus *dos tapas* tends to be pronounced *dotapa*. Unlike in the rest of Spain, the letters 'C' and 'Z' in words such as *cerveza* aren't pronounced /th/ (although in Cádiz province, perversely, they tend to pronounce 'S' with that sound).

Vowels

a	as in English *cat*
e	as in English *best*
i	as the *ee* in English *feet*
o	as in English *shop*
u	as the *oo* in English *food*
ai	as the *i* in English *ride*
ei	as *ey* in English *they*
oi	as *oy* in English *toy*

Consonants

Most consonants can be pronounced more or less as they are in English. The exceptions are:

	before *e* or *i* is the same as *j*
h	is always silent (except in *ch* as in *chair*)
j	as the *ch* in Scottish *loch*
ll	as the *y* in *yellow*
ñ	as the *ni* in English *onion*
rr	trilled much more than in English
x	depending on its location, pronounced *x, s, sh* or *j*

Spanish words and phrases

Greetings, courtesies

hello	*hola*
good morning	*buenos días*
good afternoon/evening/night	*buenas tardes/noches*
goodbye	*adiós/chao*
pleased to meet you	*mucho gusto*
see you later	*hasta luego*
how are you?	*¿cómo está?¿cómo estás?*
I'm fine, thanks	*estoy muy bien, gracias*
I'm called...	*me llamo...*
what is your name?	*¿cómo se llama? ¿cómo te llamas?*
yes/no	*sí/no*
please	*por favor*
thank you (very much)	*(muchas) gracias*
I speak Spanish	*hablo español*
I don't speak Spanish	*no hablo español*
do you speak English?	*¿habla inglés?*
I don't understand	*no entiendo/no comprendo*
please speak slowly	*hable despacio por favor*
I am very sorry	*lo siento mucho/disculpe*
what do you want?	*¿qué quiere? ¿qué quieres?*
I want	*quiero*
I don't want it	*no lo quiero*
leave me alone	*déjeme en paz/no me moleste*
good/bad	*bueno/malo*

Basic questions and requests

have you got a room for two people?	*¿tiene una habitación para dos personas?*
how do I get to_?	*¿cómo llego a_?*
how much does it cost?	*¿cuánto cuesta? ¿cuánto es?*
I'd like to make a long-distance phone call	*quisiera hacer una llamada de larga distancia*
is service included?	*¿está incluido el servicio?*
is tax included?	*¿están incluidos los impuestos?*
when does the bus leave (arrive)?	*¿a qué hora sale (llega) el autobús?*
when?	*¿cuándo?*
where is_?	*¿dónde está_?*
where can I buy tickets?	*¿dónde puedo comprar boletos?*
where is the nearest petrol station?	*¿dónde está la gasolinera más cercana?*
why?	*¿por qué?*

Basic words and phrases

bank	*el banco*
bathroom/toilet	*el baño*
to be	*ser, estar*
bill	*la factura/la cuenta*
cash	*el efectivo*
cheap	*barato/a*
credit card	*la tarjeta de crédito*
exchange house	*la casa de cambio*
exchange rate	*el tipo de cambio*
expensive	*caro/a*
to go	*ir*
to have	*tener, haber*
market	*el mercado*
note/coin	*el billete/la moneda*
police (policeman)	*la policía (el policía)*
post office	*el correo*
public telephone	*el teléfono público*
shop	*la tienda*
supermarket	*el supermercado*
there is/are	*hay*
there isn't/aren't	*no hay*
ticket office	*la taquilla*
travellers' cheques	*los cheques de viajero/los travelers*

Getting around

aeroplane	*el avión*
airport	*el aeropuerto*
arrival/departure	*la llegada/salida*
avenue	*la avenida*
block	*la cuadra*
border	*la frontera*
bus station	*la terminal de autobuses/camiones*
bus	*el bus/el autobús/el camión*
collective/fixed-route taxi	*el colectivo*
corner	*la esquina*
customs	*la aduana*
first/second class	*la primera/segunda clase*
left/right	*izquierda/derecha*
ticket	*el boleto*
empty/full	*vacío/lleno*
highway, main road	*la carretera*
immigration	*la inmigración*
insurance	*el seguro*
insured person	*el asegurado/la asegurada*

to insure yourself against	*asegurarse contra*
luggage	*el equipaje*
motorway, freeway	*el autopista/la carretera*
north, south, west, east	*el norte, el sur, el oeste (occidente), el este (oriente)*
oil	*el aceite*
to park	*estacionarse*
passport	*el pasaporte*
petrol/gasoline	*la gasolina*
puncture	*el pinchazo/la ponchadura*
street	*la calle*
that way	*por allí/por allá*
this way	*por aquí/por acá*
tourist card/visa	*la tarjeta de turista/visa*
tyre	*la llanta*
unleaded	*sin plomo*
waiting room	*la sala de espera*
to walk	*caminar/andar*

Accommodation

air conditioning	*el aire acondicionado*
all-inclusive	*todo incluido*
bathroom, private	*el baño privado*
bed, double/single	*la cama matrimonial/sencilla*
blankets	*las cobijas/mantas*
to clean	*limpiar*
dining room	*el comedor*
guesthouse	*la casa de huéspedes*
hotel	*el hotel*
noisy	*ruidoso*
pillows	*las almohadas*
power cut	*el apagón/corte*
restaurant	*el restaurante*
room/bedroom	*el cuarto/la habitación*
sheets	*las sábanas*
shower	*la ducha/regadera*
soap	*el jabón*
toilet	*el sanitario/excusado*
toilet paper	*el papel higiénico*
towels, clean/dirty	*las toallas limpias/sucias*
water, hot/cold	*el agua caliente/fría*

Health

aspirin	*la aspirina*
blood	*la sangre*
chemist	*la farmacia*
condoms	*los preservativos, los condones*
contact lenses	*los lentes de contacto*
contraceptives	*los anticonceptivos*
contraceptive pill	*la píldora anticonceptiva*
diarrhoea	*la diarrea*
doctor	*el médico*
fever/sweat	*la fiebre/el sudor*
pain	*el dolor*
head	*la cabeza*
period/sanitary towels	*la regla/las toallas femininas*
stomach	*el estómago*
altitude sickness	*el soroche*

Family

family	*la familia*
brother/sister	*el hermano/la hermana*
daughter/son	*la hija/el hijo*
father/mother	*el padre/la madre*
husband/wife	*el esposo (marido)/la esposa*
boyfriend/girlfriend	*el novio/la novia*
friend	*el amigo/la amiga*
married	*casado/a*
single/unmarried	*soltero/a*

Months, days and time

January	*enero*
February	*febrero*
March	*marzo*
April	*abril*
May	*mayo*
June	*junio*
July	*julio*
August	*agosto*
September	*septiembre*
October	*octubre*
November	*noviembre*
December	*diciembre*
Monday	*lunes*
Tuesday	*martes*
Wednesday	*miércoles*
Thursday	*jueves*
Friday	*viernes*
Saturday	*sábado*
Sunday	*domingo*
at one o'clock	*a la una*
at half past two	*a las dos y media*
at a quarter to three	*a cuarto para las tres/a las tres menos quince*
it's one o'clock	*es la una*
it's seven o'clock	*son las siete*
it's six twenty	*son las seis y veinte*
it's five to nine	*son cinco para las nueve/las nueve menos cinco*
in ten minutes	*en diez minutos*
five hours	*cinco horas*
does it take long?	*¿tarda mucho?*

Numbers

one	*uno/una*
two	*dos*
three	*tres*
four	*cuatro*
five	*cinco*
six	*seis*
seven	*siete*
eight	*ocho*
nine	*nueve*
ten	*diez*
eleven	*once*
twelve	*doce*
thirteen	*trece*
fourteen	*catorce*

fifteen	*quince*
sixteen	*dieciséis*
seventeen	*diecisiete*
eighteen	*dieciocho*
nineteen	*diecinueve*
twenty	*veinte*
twenty-one	*veintiuno*
thirty	*treinta*
forty	*cuarenta*
fifty	*cincuenta*
sixty	*sesenta*
seventy	*setenta*
eighty	*ochenta*
ninety	*noventa*
hundred	*cien/ciento*
thousand	*mil*

Food

avocado	*el aguacate*
baked	*al horno*
bakery	*la panadería*
banana	*el plátano*
beans	*los frijoles/las habichuelas*
beef	*la carne de res*
beef steak or pork fillet	*el bistec*
boiled rice	*el arroz blanco*
bread	*el pan*
breakfast	*el desayuno*
butter	*la mantequilla*
cake	*el pastel*
chewing gum	*el chicle*
chicken	*el pollo*
chilli pepper or green pepper	*el ají/el chile/el pimiento*
clear soup, stock	*el caldo*
cooked	*cocido*
dining room	*el comedor*
egg	*el huevo*
fish	*el pescado*
fork	*el tenedor*
fried	*frito*
garlic	*el ajo*
goat	*el chivo*
grapefruit	*la toronja/el pomelo*
grill	*la parrilla*
guava	*la guayaba*
ham	*el jamón*
hamburger	*la hamburguesa*
hot, spicy	*picante*
ice cream	*el helado*
jam	*la mermelada*
knife	*el cuchillo*
lime	*el limón*
lobster	*la langosta*
lunch	*el almuerzo/la comida*
meal	*la comida*
meat	*la carne*
minced meat	*el picadillo*
onion	*la cebolla*
orange	*la naranja*

pepper	*el pimiento*
pasty, turnover	*la empanada/el pastelito*
pork	*el cerdo*
potato	*la papa*
prawns	*los camarones*
raw	*crudo*
restaurant	*el restaurante*
salad	*la ensalada*
salt	*la sal*
sandwich	*el bocadillo*
sauce	*la salsa*
sausage	*la longaniza/el chorizo*
scrambled eggs	*los huevos revueltos*
seafood	*los mariscos*
soup	*la sopa*
spoon	*la cuchara*
squash	*la calabaza*
squid	*los calamares*
supper	*la cena*
sweet	*dulce*
to eat	*comer*
toasted	*tostado*
turkey	*el pavo*
vegetables	*los legumbres/vegetales*
without meat	*sin carne*
yam	*el camote*

Drink

beer	*la cerveza*
boiled	*hervido/a*
bottled	*en botella*
camomile tea	*té de manzanilla*
canned	*en lata*
coffee	*el café*
coffee, white	*el café con leche*
cold	*frío*
cup	*la taza*
drink	*la bebida*
drunk	*borracho/a*
firewater	*el aguardiente*
fruit milkshake	*el batido/licuado*
glass	*el vaso*
hot	*caliente*
ice/without ice	*el hielo/sin hielo*
juice	*el jugo*
lemonade	*la limonada*
milk	*la leche*
mint	*la menta/la hierbabuena*
rum	*el ron*
soft drink	*el refresco*
sugar	*el azúcar*
tea	*el té*
to drink	*beber/tomar*
water	*el agua*
water, carbonated	*el agua mineral con gas*
water, still mineral	*el agua mineral sin gas*
wine, red	*el vino tinto*
wine, white	*el vino blanco*

Index

Footnotes Index

Map index

Advertisers' index

Credits

Footprint credits
Editor: Laura Dixon
Deputy editor: Sophie Blacksell
Editorial assistant: Angus Dawson
Map editor: Sarah Sorensen
Picture editor: Kevin Feeney

Publisher: Patrick Dawson
Editorial: Alan Murphy, Sarah Thorowgood,
Claire Boobbyer, Felicity Laughton,
Nicola Jones
Cartography: Robert Lunn, Claire Benison,
Kevin Feeney, Angus Dawson, Thom Wickes,
Esther Monzón García
Series development: Rachel Fielding
Design: Mytton Williams and
Rosemary Dawson (brand)
Advertising: Debbie Wylde
Finance and administration:
Sharon Hughes, Elizabeth Taylor,
Lindsay Dytham

Photography credits
Front cover: Petr Svarc
(view of Chimborazo)
Back cover: Danny Aeberhard for South
American Pictures (blue-footed booby)
Inside colour section: Jamie Marshall,
Nature pl, Powerstock, South American
Pictures

Print
Manufactured in Italy by LegoPrint
Pulp from sustainable forests

Footprint feedback
We try as hard as we can to make each
Footprint guide as up to date as possible
but, of course, things always change.
If you want to let us know about your
experiences – good, bad or ugly – then don't
delay, go to www.footprintbooks.com
and send in your comments.
   Hotel and restaurant price codes
should only be taken as a guide to
the prices and facilities offered by the
establishment. It is at the discretion of
the owners to vary them from time to time.

Publishing information
Footprint Ecuador & Galápagos
5th edition
© Footprint Handbooks Ltd
May 2005

ISBN 1 904 777 38 4
CIP DATA: A catalogue record for this book is
available from the British Library

® Footprint Handbooks and the Footprint
mark are a registered trademark of
Footprint Handbooks Ltd

Published by Footprint
6 Riverside Court
Lower Bristol Road
Bath BA2 3DZ, UK
T +44 (0)1225 469141
F +44 (0)1225 469461
discover@footprintbooks.com
www.footprintbooks.com

Distributed in the USA by
Publishers Group West

Every effort has been made to ensure that
the facts in this guidebook are accurate.
However, travellers should still obtain
advice about travel and visa requirements
before travelling. The authors and publishers
cannot accept responsibility for any loss,
injury or inconvenience however caused.

Acknowledgements

The authors warmly thank their team of correspondents: **Guido** and **Jeaneth Abad** (Cuenca), language teachers *con buena cuchara*; **Jean Brown** (Quito), partner in Safari Tours and unrivaled expert in all things Ecuadorean; **Lou Jost** (Baños), botanist, ornithologist and aspiring house builder; **Grace Naranjo** (Quito), the authors' very own panic button; **Michael Resch** (Baños), veteran traveller, *hacendado* and president of the LBC; **William Reyes** and **Popkje van der Ploeg** (Riobamba), owners of Julio Verne Travel; **Peter Schramm** (Vilcabamba), devoted hotelier serving the longest breakfast in Ecuador; **Gabriela (Kotty) Rodríguez** (Manta), tourism student and local night-life expert; and **Delia María Torres** (Guayaquil), a proud *costeña* with her heart in the sierra.

The authors gratefully acknowledge the auspices of the **Ecuadorean Ministerio de Turismo**. We also thank the following individuals, all of whom provided valuable assistance: **Dennis and Laura Barniak, Alberto Dorfzaun, Diego Falconí, Miguel Falk, Nelson Gómez, Minard (Pete) Hall, Harry Jonitz, Craig Kolthoff, Michel Leseigneur, Joanna May, Nicola Mears, Patricia Mothes, Jack Nelson, Steve Nomchong, Luis Reyes, Dr. John Rosenberg, Guido and Chelita Rosillo, Piet Sabbe, Betti Sachs, Pattie Serrano, Pepe and Margarita Tapia, Marco Toscano, Wellington Valdiviezo, Pablo Velín.** The following specialists wrote or reviewed the corresponding sections: **Mark Eckstein**, resposible tourism; **Paul Heggarty**, Quichua language.

The current edition is built on the hard work of several generations of Footprint travel writers and editors, among them **John Brooks**, **Ben Box** and **Alan Murphy**. Special gratitude goes to Ben and Alan for their ongoing friendship and collaboration. We thank the entire Footprint editorial and production team, in particular **Laura Dixon, Sophie Blacksell** and **Sarah Sorensen**.

By far our most important vote of thanks, however, goes to you: the readers and travellers who help make this book a living, evolving, thing. The following readers contributed their experiences and insights to the current edition: Caroline Alberti, Inbal Amitay, Pablo Andrade, Marc Andrévöll, Sarah Anthony, Lauren Armistead, Martina Arpagaus, Stephan Arsand, Peter & Tricia Ashwood, Aria Avdal, Jonathan M Barnett, Ian Bickerstaff, Clint & Carly Blackbourn, Adi Borovich, Marieke Bosman, Carl Boyer, Ian Brodrick, Nick & Hazel Buller, Sarah Buzi, Renato Caderas, Marshall Carter-Tripp, Jonathan Cassidy, Melissa Caughey, Cindy Chin, Kasper Claes, Mike Cotgreave, Martin Couell, Sebastien Crespo, Richard Cuff, Jennifer Dahnke, Guy Danhieux, Sue Dean, Patrick Debouck, Sonali Deheragoda, Kathryn Elmer, Nina Elter, Julie E Esca, Barbara Etter, Fernando Gaviria, Stefan Giger, Steven Goldie, Sandra Gomez, Diane B Goodpasture, Joris Gresnigt, Thomas Gribsholt, Bill Grimes, Susana Guerrero, Simone Häfelfinger, Arne Hannibal, Staley & Meg Heatly, Carsten Hendricks, Jeroen Hes, Silvia Hodel, Timo Hogenhout, Friederike Holland, Martina Hunkeler, John Hurley, Rachel Jackson, Jacklyn F Johnson, Peter Jost, Jeremy Kanga, Jack Kaplan, Jane Keogh, Cheryl Kororowotny, Ingrid Korpershoek, Brad Krupsaw, Pirmin Kurzmeyer, Sara Lang, Danica Larson, Pascal Le Colletter, Chris & Simon Leary, Carola Lotz, Daniel Mack, John Magen, Doris Manser, Michael A Mcclure, Ellen Mette Finsveen, Bryan Miles, Wim Muys, Henrik Nilsson, Christopher Obetz, Patrick Oconnell, Dominik Ott, Andrew Por, Simon Pyne, Joanna Reason, Mary Reed, Rebecca Rice, Patrick Riedijk, Reidun Riisehagen, Santiago Rivera, Cornelia & Marcel Rueeesch, Eran Salant, Michaela Schau, Martin Schwarz, Esther Segers, Dave Shirt, Caius Simmons, Glenn Simpson, Jason Smith, Maria Soledad Riquetti, Barbara Stewart, Christian Suarez, Graham Thrower, Jon Magne Torset, Mark Unger, Jon Unoson, Jaap van den Burg, Wouter van der Heijde, Wendy van Driel, J van Heijst, Monika Vetsch, Maria Viteri, Rose Waldron, Mark Wanless, Nathan Ward, Helen Watson, Peter Wegener, Manuel Weiss, Sean Welton, David Wilamowski, Slaney Wright, Carmen Wuethrich, Gabby Zegers, and Deborah Zierten.

Map symbols

Administration

□ Capital city
○ Other city/town
International border
Regional border
Disputed border

Roads and travel

—— Main road (National highway)
—— Unpaved or *ripio* (gravel) road
---- 4WD track
······ Footpath
⊦■ Railway with station
✈ Airport
🚌 Bus station
Ⓜ Metro station
---- Cable car
+++++ Funicular
⛴ Ferry

Water features

River, canal
Lake, ocean
Seasonal marshland
Beach, sand bank
Waterfall

Topographical features

Contours (approx)
Mountain
Volcano
Mountain pass
Escarpment
Gorge
Glacier
Salt flat
Rocks

Cities and towns

Main through route
Main street
Minor street
Pedestrianized street

Tunnel

)⊏ ⊐(Tunnel
→ One way street
||||||| Steps
⇌ Bridge
Fortified wall
Park, garden, stadium
🛏 Sleeping
🍴 Eating
🍸 Bars & clubs
🎭 Entertainment
cp Casa particular
▨ Building
▪ Sight
✝✝ Cathedral, church
卍 Chinese temple
Hindu temple
Meru
Mosque
Stupa
✡ Synagogue
🛈 Tourist office
🏛 Museum
✉ Post office
Police
Ⓢ Bank
@ Internet
♪ Telephone
Market
Hospital
🅿 Parking
Petrol
Golf
[A] Detail map
◁A Related map

Other symbols

∴ Archaeological site
♦ National park, wildlife reserve
✿ Viewing point
Λ Campsite
⌂ Refuge, lodge
Castle
Diving
Deciduous/coniferous/palm trees
⇧ Hide
Vineyard
△ Distillery
Shipwreck
✕ Historic battlefield

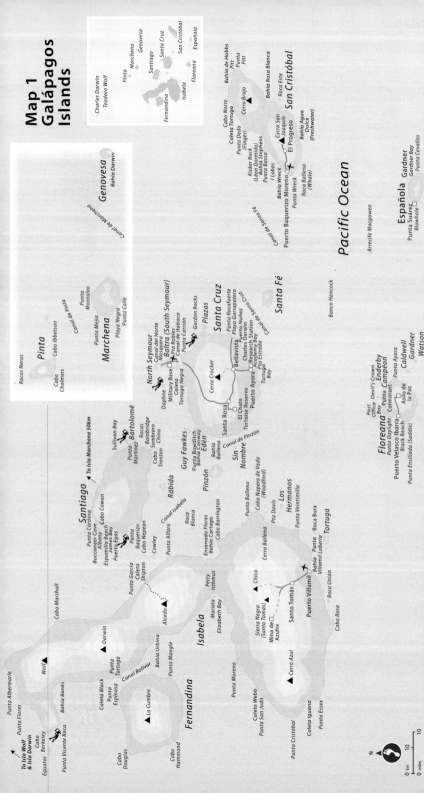

Map 1
Galápagos Islands

Map 2

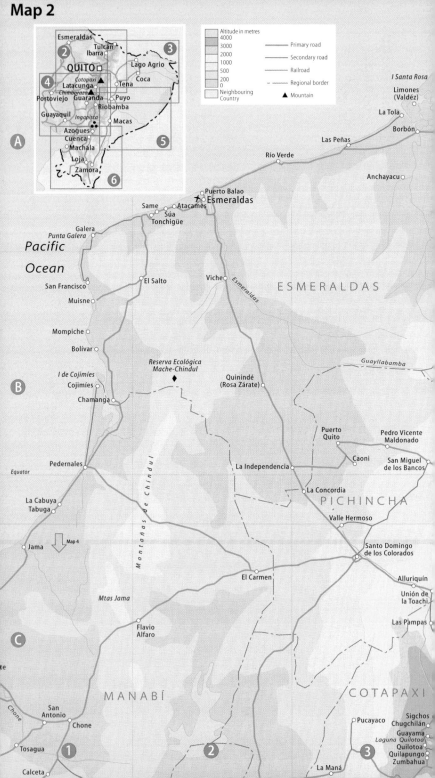

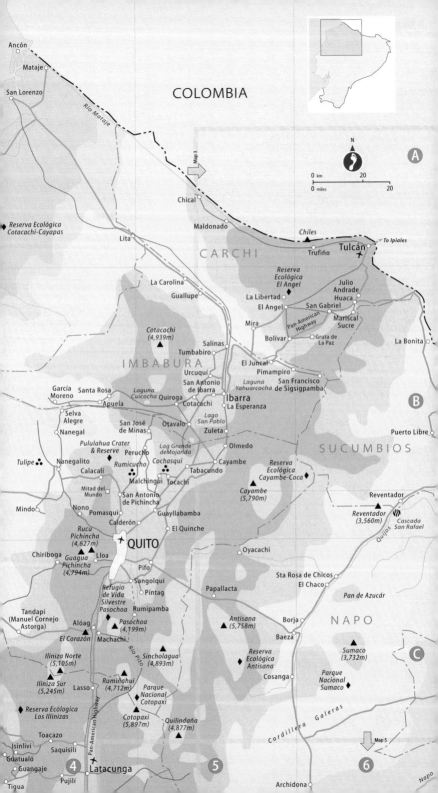

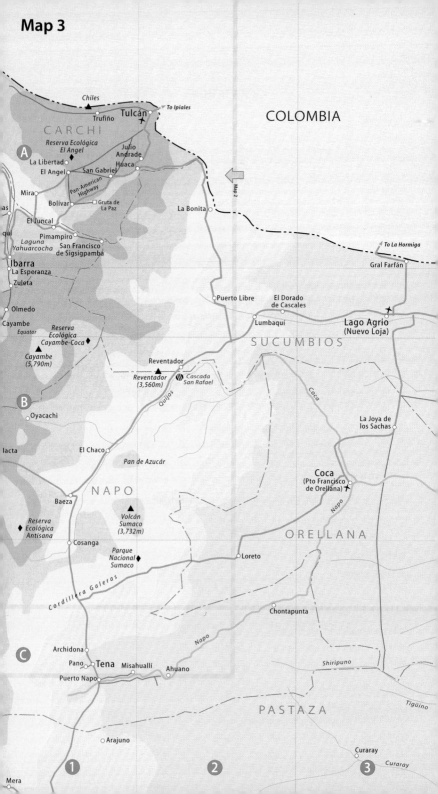

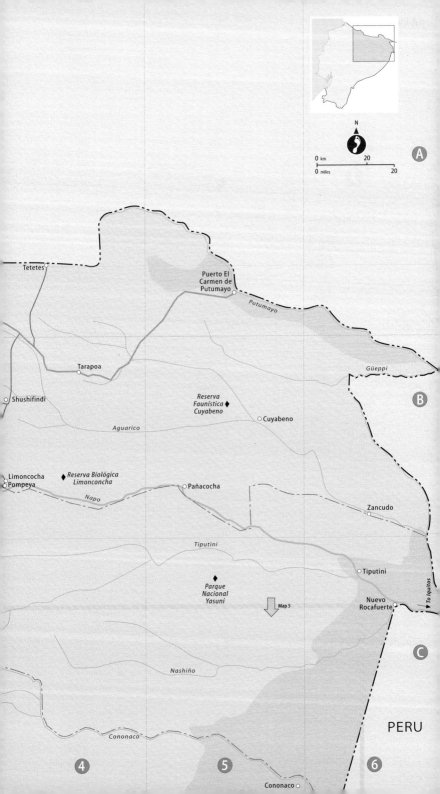

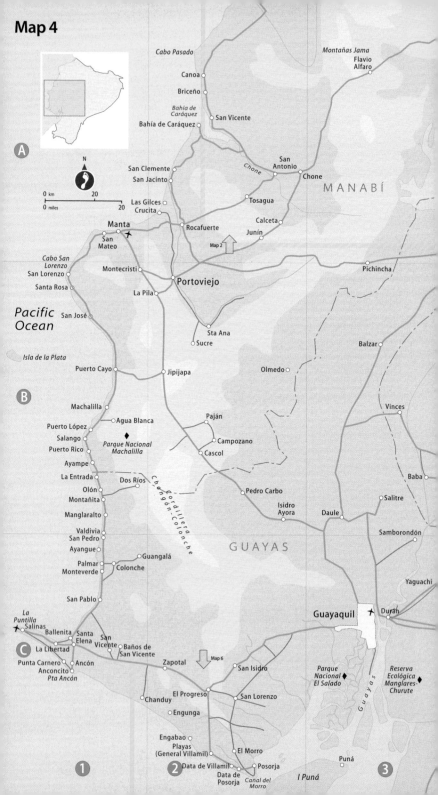

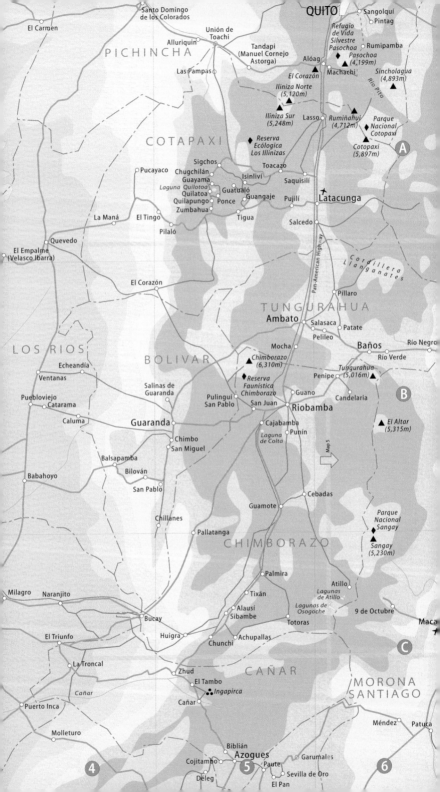

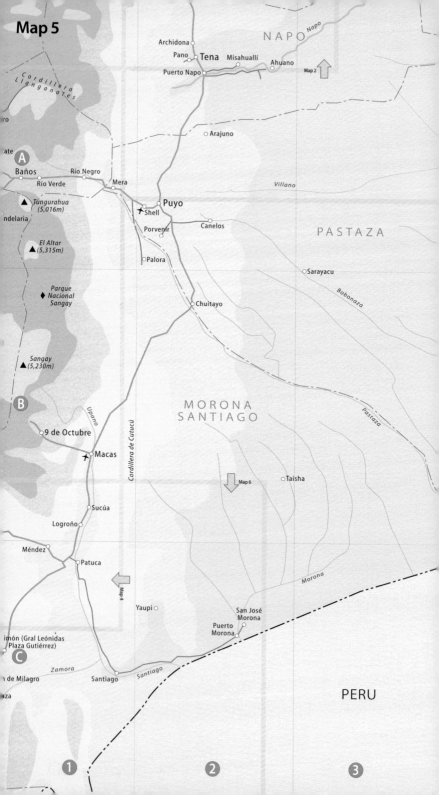

Map 5

NAPO

Napo

Archidona
Pano
Tena
Misahuallí
Ahuano
Puerto Napo

Map 2

Cordillera
Llanganates

Arajuno

A
Baños
Río Negro
Río Verde
Mera

Villano

PASTAZA

Tungurahua
(5,016m)

Shell
Puyo

Candelaria

Porvenir
Canelos

El Altar
(5,315m)

Palora

Sarayacu

Bobonaza

Parque
Nacional
Sangay

Chuitayo

Sangay
(5,230m)

MORONA
SANTIAGO

Pastaza

B

Upano

9 de Octubre

Macas

Cordillera de Cutucú

Map 6
Taisha

Sucúa

Logroño

Méndez

Patuca

Map 4

Morona

Yaupi

San José
Morona
Puerto
Morona

...imón (Gral Leónidas
Plaza Gutiérrez)

C

Zamora

Santiago

Santiago

PERU

...n de Milagro

...aza

1   2   3

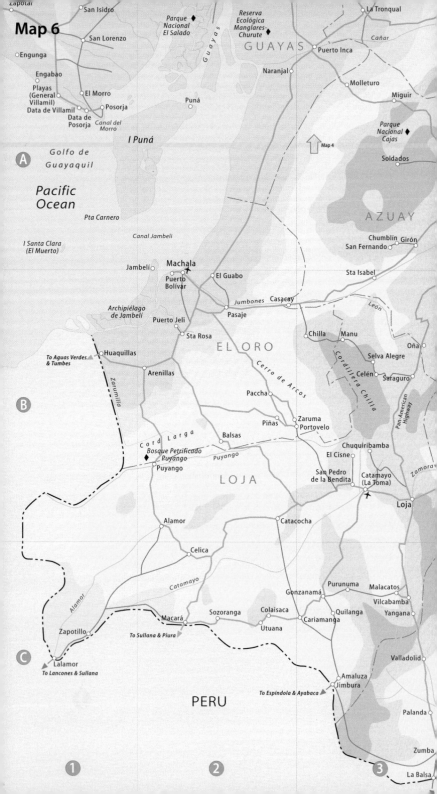